Chile

ID0946754

Ben Box with Chris Wallace
& Anna Maria Espsäter

Chileans say that, when God had almost completed the act of creation, there was a little of everything left, so He threw it all down in a narrow strip of land and called it Chile. The national pride is justifiable, for this is a fantastically diverse country. With an almost comical geographical shape and virtually every climate imaginable, this beautiful, memorable sliver of the world is a place of extremes and contradictions.

Few countries have quite such a split geographical personality. Here, you can often glimpse the snows of the high Andes from the Pacific Ocean, ski in the mountains in the morning and be drinking pisco sours on the beach come sundown. To the south, the country is hemmed in by thick temperate rainforest, fast-flowing rivers, icefields and glaciers, while to the north is the memorable Atacama Desert, with its endless space and pristine skies, where some places have not seen a raindrop for centuries. The desert's geoglyphs bear testament to the ingenuity of some of prehistoric America's most complex civilizations, while an intermingling of the old world with the new has produced some of the most enduring aspects of Chilean culture, such as the legend of the Inca princess La Tirana, which spawned the country's biggest religious fiesta.

THIS PAGE Isluga, Atacama desert
PREVIOUS PAGE Torres del Paine

PERU

Arica

Parque Nacional Lauca **5**

BOLIVIA

Iquique
La Tirana

Calama

San Pedro de Atacama

Antofagasta

Parque Nacional Llullaillaco **4**

3 Taltal

Parque Nacional Pan de Azúcar

El Salvador

Chañaral

Copiapó

← *To Easter Island*

Vallenar

La Serena

Parque Nacional Fray Jorge Ovalle

Pacific Ocean

Illapel

ARGENTINA

2 Valparaíso

Parque Nacional La Compana

SANTIAGO **1**

Rancagua

6 San Fernando

Curicó

Talca

Parque Nacional Siete Tazas

Cauquenes

Parral

Concepción

Chillán

Los Angeles

Parque Nacional Conguillio

Temuco

Pucón

Valdivia **7**

Lago Llanquihue

Bariloche

Puerto Montt

Parque Nacional Alerce Andino

Chiloé

10 *Parque Pumalin*

8

Futaleufú

9

Parque Nacional Queulat

Coyhaique

Lago General Carrera

Laguna San Rafael

Atlantic Ocean

Puerto Yungay

Villa O'Higgins

Parque Nacional Los Glaciares

Parque Nacional Torres del Paine **11**

Puerto Natales

Punta Arenas

Tierra del Fuego

Isla Navarino

N

8 km
8 miles

Easter Island

Tahai

Ahu Tongariki

Vinapu

12

N

200 km
200 miles

Rapa Nui

Don't miss...

See colour maps at end of book

Making fresh tracks through the Portillo backcountry

Itineraries for Chile

Chile is hemmed in by the Pacific Ocean, the Atacama Desert and the Andes. When combined with the country's shape, these geographical barriers rule out circular routes within the country – the choice therefore comes down to whether to go north or south.

THE NORTH
One week
First, fly from Santiago to La Serena to spend perhaps three days exploring the area around the city. Pick two attractions, choosing from the Elqui Valley and the public observatory, the Parque Nacional Fray Jorge, the penguins, dolphins and sea lions at Isla Damas, the cave paintings at the Valle del Encanto or the Limarí

Valley. Fly on to Calama and the oasis of San Pedro de Atacama and spend three days visiting the geysers, altiplano lakes, the salt flat and the Valley of the Moon, before flying back to Santiago.

Two weeks
Head to Valparaíso before catching a bus north to La Serena, the journey providing a good introduction to the beauties of the mountains of the semi-desert. Continue to Chañaral to see the awe-inspiring Parque Nacional Pan de Azúcar, before moving on directly to San Pedro to continue with the one-week itinerary. Take an overnight

TRAVEL TIP
If you have less than three weeks to ex-plore, it makes sense to focus on either the north or the south of the country.

Volcán Parinacota and Lago Chungará, Lauca National Park

the stunning Parque Nacional Lauca and the world's highest lake, Chungará, before flying back to the capital.

One month

A month allows you to visit some fascinating additional destinations in the north of the country. Spend two or three days exploring the hinterland around Illapel, Salamanca and Combarbalá, for example, which is spectacularly rugged country and full of minerals and ancient rock art. Heading north from Chañaral, break your journey at the attractive coast town of Taltal and then visit Chuquicamata, the largest open-cast copper mine on earth. With two extra days at San Pedro, tour the beautiful altiplano villages, before travelling to Arica. Take a four-day altiplano tour, visiting Lauca, Surire and Isluga parks and ending in Iquique where you can relax on the beach for a couple of days, jump off a cliff on a tandem paraglide over the city, or visit the nearby thermal baths at Pica.

Quirky Valparaíso

Church of San Francisco, Chiloé

THE SOUND
One week
Fly from Santiago to Puerto Montt, allowing two to three days to visit either the beautiful island of Chiloé or the southern Lake District. In Chiloé, visit the penguins at Puñihuil, the town of Ancud and many of the island's Jesuit churches. Visiting Chiloé in 1835, Charles Darwin found that the rolling hills reminded him of England. It has changed little since, and, with its rich mythology and close-knit agricultural communities, it still evokes a bygone age. Just north of Puerto Montt is the Lake District. Use the German-founded town of Puerto Varas as a base to visit the area around Lago Llanquihue, where the Osorno volcano provides a spectacular backdrop to the lake. The impressive Petrohué waterfalls are an hour to the east. Fly to Puerto Natales and spend four days visiting the mountains and eerie blue glaciers of Torres del Paine, one of the world's greatest national parks, before flying back to Santiago.

Two weeks
After arriving in Santiago, visit the port of Valparaíso before heading south by bus and spending a few days in the Central Valley, the heart of Chile. Explore the high mountains around Vilches, or the Parque Nacional Siete Tazas. Wine buffs can sample some of Chile's best wines, while beach-lovers might prefer surfing at Pichilemu. Move on to the famous

TRAVEL TIP
You could combine elements from the two-week itineraries to create a month-long trip that takes in the best of north and south.

forests and hills around Lago Villarrica, perhaps climbing the volcano nearby, doing a day trek in the araucaria forests of Huerquehue or Cañi, braving a day of whitewater rafting or relaxing in natural thermal springs, before flying from Puerto Montt to Puerto Natales to visit Torres del Paine (as in the one-week itinerary).

One month

Spend a further two or three days on Chiloé, visiting the Parque Nacional Chiloé and Castro. Catch a boat to Chaitén and spend the next eight or nine days exploring the fabulous region of the Carretera Austral. See giant alerce forests in the Parque Pumalín, experience some of the world's best whitewater rafting around Futaleufú and hike around Cerro Castillo, before (if money is no object) making for Puerto Chacabuco and taking a cruise to the Laguna San Rafael glacier. Fly down to Punta Arenas and visit the nearby penguin colonies or splash out on a whale-watching trip before heading on to Torres del Paine, adding the wilds of Tierra del Fuego or the Glaciares National Park in Argentina.

Lago Grey, Torres del Paine

Windswept landscape, Puyehue National Park

Preparing Chilean wine the old-fashioned way

King penguin, sub-Antarctic islands

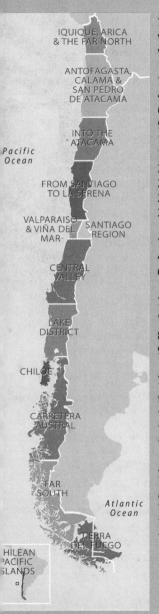

IQUIQUE, ARICA
& THE FAR NORTH

ANTOFAGASTA,
CALAMA &
SAN PEDRO
DE ATACAMA

INTO THE
ATACAMA

Pacific
Ocean

FROM SANTIAGO
TO LA SERENA

VALPARAISO
& VIÑA DEL   SANTIAGO
MAR   REGION

CENTRAL
VALLEY

LAKE
DISTRICT

CHILOE

CARRETERA
AUSTRAL

FAR
SOUTH   Atlantic
                          Ocean

TIERRA
DEL FUEGO

CHILEAN
PACIFIC
ISLANDS

Contents

Contents

Essentials

Planning your trip

Where to go in Chile

The north is generally drier. Much of it is desert except for an occasional oasis and the verdant Altiplano, and there are often large distances between places of interest. Unlike the south, it is pleasant to visit during the colder months of the year (May to September). Highlights include the peaceful Elqui Valley, whose green vine-laden floor contrasts with the stark metallic colours of its mineral-stained mountains where the Milky Way traces a path through a night sky filled with a billion stars. Further north is the oasis of San Pedro de Atacama, surrounded by archaeological sites and awesome natural phenomena. At the northern tip of Chile the desert rises up to meet the lush green of the Altiplano, home to a dozen volcanoes and a wide variety of wildlife.

The Central Valley is the heart of the country and is where most Chileans live. Santiago has a couple of world-class museums and is a good base for many of the country's best ski resorts, while Valparaíso, the so-called Pearl of the Pacific, is a multi-coloured amphitheatre of a city with an artistic, bohemian atmosphere unlike anywhere else in Chile. Beach lovers can head to the nearby resort of Viña del Mar or to any number of quiet fishing villages. A word of warning, though: the water is very cold! Stretching from Santiago to the south are Chile's prime wine valleys. Many wineries offer tours and an increasing number are home to some of Chile's more innovative restaurants.

Southern Chile is filled with lush green forests rising up from fractured fjords, fast-flowing rivers and waterfalls, pristine lakes and smoking snow-capped volcanoes overlooked by the majestic mountain range to the east. In the Lake District adventure tourism is easy, with numerous agencies offering a dozen day-long activities in the nearby lakes, rivers, forests and mountains with all the creature comforts of Pucón or Puerto Varas awaiting you in the evening. For a taste of the real Patgonia, head south to the Carretera Austral. The Parque Pumalín is an incredible conservation project with a diverse ecosystem and excellent trails to explore.

Towards the Argentine border, Futaleufú has the best whitewater rafting in the southern hemisphere, while further south, the azure waters of Lago General Carrera turn an even more unbelievable blue as they flow into the broad Río Baker that winds westwards, splitting Patagonia's two enormous ice fields before reaching the sea at Tortel, a village where houses are connected by wooden walkways. South of the ice fields is Torres del Paine, whose glaciers and granite towers are the jewel in the crown of Chilean Patagonia.

Best time to visit Chile

When planning your trip you should take into account the time of year. High season is during the summer (especially January and February), although the Altiplano (the high plain of the Andes east of the Atacama) can have heavy rain. Many destinations are busy with Chilean and Argentine tourists at this time, especially in the far south, and bus fares and hotel prices are up to 50% higher. The north has another high season in July and August, but these are winter months in the south, meaning that many services here are closed and transport links are reduced. Probably the ideal seasons for a visit are spring (October to December) and

Packing for Chile

Travelling light is recommended. Your specific list will depend largely on what kind of travelling you plan to do. Cotton clothes are versatile and suitable for most situations although if travelling extensively in Chile you need to be prepared for anything from desert heat to mountain snow. You'll need waterproof clothing (essential for the south at any time of year), very warm clothes for the northern highlands and the far south, light clothing for the summer, plus a sun hat. If planning to hike, bring a pair of strong shoes/boots (outside Santiago sizes over 10½/44 are very hard to find). A sarong is useful as it can be used as a skirt, curtain, bedsheet or a towel.

Other useful items include an inflatable travel pillow for neck support, a small first aid kit and handbook, earplugs and airline-type eye mask to help you sleep in noisy and poorly curtained hotel rooms, a sheet sleeping bag and pillowcase, a universal plug, a Swiss Army knife, an alarm clock or watch and a torch or headlamp. Remember not to throw away spent batteries containing mercury or cadmium; take them home to be disposed of, or recycled properly.

It's a good idea to travel with wipes (such as Wet Ones) and toilet paper; cheap hotels and restaurants do not supply it.

autumn (March to April) when many facilities in the south are open, but are less crowded, and temperatures in the northern and central regions are lower.

It is also worth planning your trip to coincide with certain festivals (see page 22), but book transport and accommodation well in advance. The period around the national Independence festivals on 18 September is especially busy wherever you are.

What to do in Chile

Chile might well have been designed for adventure tourism. In a country where you can often see the Andes from the coast, you are never more than a few hours' drive away from mountains.

Canopy tours

This activity has become all the rage in Chile and can be found near most tourist destinations in the centre and south. It consists of whizzing down zip-lines through native forests. Runs are of different lengths and range from easy, child-friendly lines to vertigo-inducing descents from 60 m up. Check your equipment carefully.

Climbing

There are various types of climbing available in Chile, including rock climbing, mountain climbing, ice climbing, volcano climbing and canyoning. There are hundreds of volcanoes to climb, ranging from the high-altitude Parinacota in the far north to the chain of much lower cones in the Lake District and along the Carretera Austral. The southern bank of the Río Petrohué in the Lake District has many fantastic canyons for climbing. Nearby, rope ladders have been fixed in the canyon of the Río León, 30 mins by boat from Petrohué on the southern shore of Lago Todos los Santos.

ENAM (Escuela Nacional de Montaña de Santiago), www.enamchile.cl, website in Spanish only, runs rock- and ice-climbing courses. It also administers the *Carnet de La Federación de Chile*, a card which is often required to climb mountains especially where CONAF control access. To climb many mountains in border areas, permission must be obtained from the **Dirección de Fronteras y Límites**, T02-827 5900, www.difrol.cl. Apply well in advance.

Horse riding

There is more of an equine culture south of Santiago than further north, but some of the best riding country is to the north and east of the capital. Horse treks are organized in Santiago, in Ritoque near Valparaíso, in the Elqui and Hurtado valleys, in the Lake District and on Chiloé, and in numerous remote areas of the south. One of the best places for hiring and riding horses is along the west coast of the island of Chiloé.

Mountain biking

Mountain biking is a popular activity, particularly on descents from the Andes and from refugios on volcanoes such as Antillanca and Osorno. Touring the length of the Carretera Austral by mountain bike is a great way of seeing this part of the country.

Skiing

Chile's major international ski resorts lie in the Andes near Santiago, but skiing is possible from Santiago to Punta Arenas. Skiing elsewhere is mostly on the volcanoes to the south of Santiago. The larger resorts in the south are Termas de Chillán, Villarrica/Pucón and Antillanca.

Watersports

Watersports, such as diving and surfing, are best in northern Chile, except for at Pichilemu, a resort 3 hrs to the southwest of Santiago, which is famous for surfing. Over a dozen rivers between Santiago and Tierra del Fuego are excellent for whitewater rafting. The main ones are the Maipo, the Trancura, Fuy, Bueno, Rahue and Petrohué, the Yelcho, Futaleufú, Corcovado, Palena and Baker and the Serrana and Tyndall. The most attractive waters for sea kayaking are around the islands off eastern Chiloé or around Hornopirén in the fjords of the sheltered Gulf of Ancud.

Getting to Chile

Air

Long-haul flights generally allow two pieces of 23 kg, but this varies according to carrier and route. Check with your airline before you fly; if you are over the limit you are likely to be charged extra. If you cannot avoid being over the limit, arrive early. Weight limits for internal flights are usually 23 kg for economy class, but can be as low as 10 kg on smaller aircraft in Patagonia.

From Europe

Flights from the UK take 18 to 20 hours, including a change of plane. It is impossible to fly directly to Santiago from London, so connections have to be made on one of the following routes: **Aerolíneas Argentinas** ① *www.aerolineas.com.ar*, via Madrid/ Rome and/or Buenos Aires; **Air France** ① *www.airfrance.com*, via Paris; **British Airways** ① *www.ba.com*, connecting through **LAN** in Buenos Aires; **Iberia** ① *www.iberia.com*, via Madrid or Barcelona; **LAN** ① *www.lan.com*, via Madrid or through TAM in Sao Paulo;

Earthquakes

It is impossible to spend much time in Chile without becoming aware of the fragility of the land beneath your feet. Earth tremors and violent quakes are a part of everyday life. The most severe earthquakes in recent decades occurred in 1960, causing devastation to the Lake District around Valdivia (see box, page 300), and in 2010, which affected the O'Higgins, Maule and Biobío regions. A subsequent tsunami destroyed many coastal communities.

Quite apart from the terror of the earthquakes, tremors are commonplace. These are most often felt at night, owing to the fact that everything is otherwise still. If sleeping, your first feeling may be that someone is gently shaking your bed.

There is no way of telling at the beginning of a tremor whether it will develop into a full-scale earthquake. If you are unfortunate enough to experience an earthquake, do not panic. Rushing outside into the street leaves you vulnerable to falling masonry; the safest place to hide is beneath the lintel of a doorway.

Lufthansa ① *www.lufthansa.com*, via Frankfurt or Munich and São Paulo; **TAM** ① *www.tam.com*.br, via Madrid and São Paulo, or with one of the American carriers via New York, Atlanta or Miami.

From North America

American Airlines ① *www.aa.com*, and **LAN fly** direct from Miami (nine hours), New York and Dallas Fort Worth to Santiago. **LAN** also has flights to Santiago from Los Angeles (connecting in Lima), while **Delta** ① *www.delta.com*, has a service from Atlanta. Additional flights from Los Angeles, Miami and New York to Santiago are operated by **Copa** ① *www.copaair.com*, via Panama City, and **Taca** ① *www.taca.com*, via any one or more of **San Salvador** ① *San José, Bogotá and Lima*.

From Canada, **Air Canada** ① *www.aircanada.com*, has the only direct flights from Toronto, connecting from all other major cities. **LAN** offers connections with sister airlines from Vancouver to Los Angeles and thence to Santiago, or from Toronto to New York or Miami and on to Santiago. Both **American** and **Delta** also have services via the US.

From Australia, New Zealand and South Africa

LAN flies from Auckland, New Zealand and from Japan via Los Angeles and Lima. LAN also flies between Sydney and Santiago, direct or via Auckland. From South Africa it is possible to connect to Santiago through Buenos Aires, Rio de Janeiro or São Paulo on **South African Airways** from Johannesburg.

From other Latin American countries

There are about 13 flights a day to Santiago from Buenos Aires (Argentina), operated by **LAN**, **Aerolíneas Argentinas**, **Sky** and **others**. There are also flights by **LAN** from Bariloche (via Buenos Aires), Córdoba and Mendoza, and summer flights from Ushuaia (also via Buenos Aires). LAN has services from Montevideo (Uruguay). **TAM** connects with Asunción (Paraguay). Flights from Rio de Janeiro (Brazil) are run by **LAN** and **Gol**. There are also services from São Paulo by **LAN**, **TAM** and **Gol**. Flights from La Paz and Santa Cruz (Bolivia) are offered by LAN. There are many flights from Lima (Peru) by **LAN**, **Avianca and Sky**. From Ecuador, **LAN flies** nonstop from Guayaquil or Quito. **Avianca** and **LAN** also fly from Bogotá (Colombia) and Caracas (Venezuela), and Avianca flies from Havana (Cuba); Mexico City and Cancún are served by **LAN**.

To other Chilean destinations

There are flights to Arica and Iquique from La Paz and Santa Cruz with **LAN**. LAN flies to Santiago from Stanley on the Falkland Islands (Malvinas) via Punta Arenas. **DAP** flies between Punta Arenas and Ushuaia.

Prices and discounts

The very busy seasons are 7 December to 15 January (until the end of February for flights within South America) and 10 July to 10 September. If you intend travelling during those times, book as far ahead as possible. From February to May and September to November special offers may be available. Fares vary according to airline and the time of year. Most airlines offer discounted fares on scheduled flights and these fares are offered through specialist agencies, but always check the reservation with the airline concerned to make sure the flight still exists.

Student (or under 26) fares: Student tickets are not always the cheapest though they are often very flexible. Some airlines are flexible on the age limit, others are strict.

Round-the-world fares: Many airlines now offer code-sharing round-the-world fares. Some cheaper ones tend to miss out South America, but Santiago often features on routes between Sydney and Lima or Rio de Janeiro, costing in the region of US$3000 plus taxes.

Open-jaw fares: These are for people intending to travel a linear route, arriving at and departing from different airports. Open jaws are available as student, yearly or excursion fares. Many require a change of plane at an intermediate point, and a stopover may be permitted, or even obligatory, depending on schedules. Simply because a flight stops at a given airport does not mean you can break your journey there; the airline must have traffic rights to pick up or set down passengers between points A and B before it will be permitted. This is where dealing with a specialized agency (such as **Journey Latin America**) will really pay dividends. On multi-stop itineraries, specialist agencies can often save clients hundreds of pounds.

Airport information

Aeropuerto Arturo Merino Benítez ⓘ *26 km northwest of Santiago at Pudahuel, help desk T02-690 1798, www.aeropuertosantiago.cl*, handles both international and domestic flights, and is the only airport in Chile with intercontinental connections. It is a modern, safe and efficient terminal. Domestic and international flights leave from different sections of the same terminal. Procedures at customs (*aduana*) are quick and efficient. Facilities include ATMs accepting both Visa and MasterCard, fast food outlets, a **Sernatur** tourist information office, which offers an accommodation booking service, a *casa de cambio* (poor rates) and several car hire offices. Left luggage is expensive (open 0600-2300). Outside customs there are kiosks for minibus and taxi companies serving Santiago, as well as car hire companies; you are likely to be approached by people offering taxi and bus services as you emerge from the customs area. ▸▸ *See Arriving in Santiago, page 41.*

Check-in time for international flights is at least two hours before departure, one hour for domestic flights. Most airlines expect you to check in online. If a flight does not involve e-tickets or online check-in, you should reconfirm bookings in advance. Airport **departure tax** is US$30 for international flights, US$11.80 for flights under 500 km; US$4.65-11.80 for domestic flights, as well as occasional fuel surcharges, all of which

Main border crossings

To Argentina

There are good road connections between Chile and Argentina, but note that any of the passes across the Andes to Argentina can be blocked by snow from April onwards (including the main Mendoza crossing, where travellers are occasionally stranded at the border posts). Travelling to or from Argentina anywhere north of Mendoza is likely to be an adventure you will not forget in a hurry. Crossings include: Cristo Redentor tunnel, see page 72; Paso Agua Negra, see page 130; Paso San Francisco, see page 148; three crossings at San Pedro, see page 189; Puerto Montt, see page 327. There are also several crossing points in the Lake District, see page 266.

To Bolivia

Ollagüe, see page 175; San Pedro, see page 190; Chungará and Visviri, see page 216.

To Peru

Chacalluta, see page 211.

should be included in the price of the ticket. In theory, there are **entry taxes** (officially called **reciprocity charges**) to be paid in US dollars at all international borders, for nationals of Albania (US$30), Australia (US$117), Canada (US$132) and Mexico (US$23); in practice, however, this tax is only charged at airports and is valid for the lifetime of the passport. These fees vary according to how much is charged to Chilean citizens for tourist visas to these countries. Since Chile joined the US Visa Waiver Program in 2014, US citizens no longer have to pay a reciprocity fee.

Sea

Around 50 cruise ships, operated by the major cruise lines, visit Chile every summer. Enquiries regarding sea passages to Chile should be made through agencies in your own country. In the UK, try **Cargo Ship Voyages Ltd** ⓘ *10 Westway, Cowes, Isle of Wight, PO31 8QP, T01983-303314, www.cargoshipvoyages.com*; **Strand Voyages** ⓘ *Unit 605 The Chandlery, 50 Westminster Bridge Rd, London SE1 7QY, T0207-953 7607, www.strandtravelltd.co.uk;* or **The Cruise People** ⓘ *88 York St, London W1H 1DP, T020-7723 2450 (reservations T0800-526313).* In the USA contact **Travltips Cruise and Freighter Travel Association** ⓘ *25-37 Francis Lewis Blvd, Flushing, NY 11358, T800-872 8584, www.travltips.com.*

Transport in Chile

Internal transport is usually straightforward. Most of Chile is linked by one road, the paved **Pan-American Highway** (or *Panamericana*), marked on maps as Ruta 5, which runs from the Peruvian border south to Puerto Montt and the island of Chiloé. However, some of the most popular destinations in Chile lie to the south of Puerto Montt, and travelling to this part of the country requires careful planning. Though much of this area can be reached by the **Carretera Austral**, a gravel road marked on maps as Ruta 7, bus services here are far less reliable than elsewhere in the country. Furthermore, the Carretera Austral is punctuated by three ferry crossings, with a further crossing at Villa O'Higgins for those on the direct overland route to the far south (summer only). Alternatives are to travel by sea and air from Puerto Montt. Ferries provide vital links in this region: notably from Chiloé to both Puerto Montt and Chaitén for the Carretera Austral; from Puerto Montt to Puerto Chacabuco (for Coyhaique); and from Puerto Montt to Puerto Natales in the far south.

Air

LAN flies between Santiago and major cities under the banner **Lan Express**. There other main domestic airline is **Sky** ① *T+562-2352 5600, www.skyairline.cl*. To the north and Concepción flights are offered by **PAL** ① *www.palair.cl*. Details of useful flights are given throughout the guide.

Check with airlines for student and other discounts. Note that with some fares it may be cheaper to fly long distance than take a *salón cama* bus, and that flight times may be changed without warning; always double check the time of your flight when reconfirming. You should book several months in advance for flights to Easter Island in January and February.

LATAM (LAN/TAM) sells a **South America Airpass** (www.latamairpass.com), which can be used on all LAN and TAM routes throughout South America, available to anyone who has purchased an international ticket with LAN/TAM, Iberia, or a One World Alliance and certain other airlines (eg United). This is only recommended if you are planning on doing several long-distance flights; domestic air taxes are payable in addition for each flight. The airpass must be purchased outside South America (except Brazil). It is valid for 12 months, and must include at least three single flights and a maximum of 16. Reservations should be made in advance; flight dates and routes can be altered with a charge of US$100 for each change. A refund with a surcharge of US$100 can be obtained prior to travel.

Rail

In the north, only the line from Arica to Tacna (Peru) carries passengers, but it was not operating in 2014. There are plans to revive the Arica–La Paz line. The main passenger service south from Santiago runs to Chillán; this journey is more relaxed than travelling by road along the *Panamericana* and it is faster than the bus. Services further south have been suspended but may reopen. There are also suburban passenger trains around Santiago and inland from both Concepción and Valparaíso, as well as the scenic line from Talca along the valley of the Río Maule to Constitución (see page 242), and a tourist steam train inland from Valdivia on Sundays in summer.

Trains in Chile are moderately priced, and snacks are available on the main Chillán line. For further information on all domestic lines, visit www.efe.cl.

Road

Chile has 77,570 km of roads, of which about 24% are paved. Many other roads are described as *ripio*, meaning the surface is unmade gravel and/or stones; speed limits on these roads are usually lower. The region round the capital and the Central Valley has the best road connections. The main road is the Pan-American Highway (Ruta 5; see also page 9), which is dual carriageway from La Serena to Puerto Montt. This is a toll road;

the charge includes towing to the next city and free ambulance in case of an accident. Good toll motorways also link Santiago with Valparaíso and Viña del Mar, and Chillán with Concepción. A coastal route running the length of Chile is also being paved.

Bus

Bus services in Chile are frequent and, on the whole, good. Buses tend to be punctual, arriving and leaving on time. Apart from at holiday times, there is little problem getting a seat on a long-distance bus and there is no need to reserve far in advance out of season. Services are categorized as *salón-cama* (25 seats), *semi-cama* (34 seats) and *salón-ejecutivo* or *clásico* (44 seats), all with reclining seats. There are also *prémium* services with seats that fully recline into flat beds. *Premium* and *salón-cama* services run between main cities and stops are infrequent; **Tur Bus** ① *www.turbus.cl*, and **Pullman Bus** ① *www. pullman.cl*, have nationwide coverage and are among the best companies.

With lots of competition between bus companies, lower fares are sometimes on offer, particularly just before departure and out of season. Prices are highest between December and March, and during the Independence celebrations in September. Students with ISIC cards may get discounts, except in high season; discounts are also often available for return journeys. Most bus companies will carry bicycles, but may ask for payment.

The best way of sending luggage around Chile is by *Encomienda*: your package is taken by bus from terminal to terminal and stored for up to one month at the destination (**Tur Bus** can deliver to a specified address). This means you can *Encomienda* bags when you don't need them, and pick them up when you do, which is great if you only need camping or cold weather gear for, say, Torres del Paine.

Car

Documents Always carry your passport and driving licence. Foreigners must have an international driving licence. Car drivers require the original registration document of their vehicle. Motorcyclists require the bike registration document and are also advised to carry an international *carnet de passages*. Bringing a private vehicle into Chile is a frustrating, time-consuming affair. Dozens of documents and a good deal of patience are required. The best advice is to find a good customs agent and let them do all the groundwork.

Insurance It is very expensive and increasingly difficult to insure against accident, damage or theft. If the car/motorbike is stolen or written off you will be required to pay very high import duty on its value. Get the legal minimum cover, which is not expensive, as soon as you can, because if you should be involved in an accident and are uninsured, your vehicle could be confiscated. If anyone is hurt, do not pick them up (you may become liable). Seek assistance from the nearest police station or hospital if you are able to do so.

Car hire Car hire is an increasingly popular way of travelling around Chile, although it reduces your contact with Chileans. Rates quoted should include insurance and 19% VAT, but always check first. The legal age for renting a car is 22. A small car with unlimited mileage costs about US$50 a day around Santiago, a pickup much more, but shop around for a deal, as there is plenty of competition. In the Lake District prices are about 50% higher, while in Patagonia they can be double. If intending to leave the country in a hired car, you must obtain an authorization from the hire company otherwise you will be turned back at the frontier. If you plan to leave more than once you will need to photocopy the authorization.

Information and maps Members of foreign motoring organizations may join the **Automóvil Club de Chile** ⓘ *Av Andrés Bello 1863, Santiago, T600-450 6000, www. automovilclub.cl,* and obtain discounts and roadside assistance. Road maps are available at the Santiago headquarters or from other regional offices. Several individual maps provide greater detail than the Club's road atlas. Good maps are available from many Copec filling stations, which mark police posts; make sure you are not speeding when you pass them, as *carabineros* are strict about speed limits. ▸▸ *For details of other maps, see page 544.*

Fuel Petrol (Bencina) costs about US$1.50-1.60 per litre, but becomes more expensive the further north and further south you go. Petrol is unleaded, 93, 95 or 97 octane. Diesel fuel (confusingly known as Petróleo) is widely available, US$1.25 a litre. Larger service stations accept credit cards, but check before filling up; the standard of facilities is generally good. When driving in the south (on the Carretera Austral particularly) and in the northern desert and Altiplano always top up your fuel tank and carry spare fuel in a steel container. Car hire companies may not have fuel cans and they are not obtainable from service stations, although some supermarkets may stock them.

Safety and security Chile is much safer than most South American countries and you need do no more to protect your vehicle than you would at home. Remove all belongings and detach the radio panel when a car is unattended. Be sure to note down key numbers and carry spares of the most important ones (but don't keep all spare keys inside the vehicle). Wheels should be secured by locking nuts. Driving at night is not recommended; be especially careful on major roads into and out of cities in the early evening because people tend to cross the highway without warning. Watch out for cyclists without lights at night in rural areas.

Cycling

At first glance a bicycle may not appear to be the most obvious vehicle for a major journey, but given ample time and reasonable energy it is certainly one of the best. A mountain bike can be ridden, carried by almost every form of transport from a plane to a canoe, and lifted across your shoulders over short distances. Cyclists can be the envy of travellers using more orthodox transport, since they can travel at their own pace, explore more remote regions and meet people who are less commonly in contact with tourists. Bring a tool-kit and as many spare parts as you can. Try not to leave a fully laden bike on its own, and always secure your bike with a lock.

Useful tips Wind, not hills, is the enemy of the cyclist. Try to make the best use of the times of day when there is little; mornings tend to be best but there is no steadfast rule. Take care to avoid dehydration. In northern Chile, where supplies of water are scarce between towns, be sure to carry an ample supply. Give your bicycle a thorough daily check for loose parts, and to see that they all run smoothly. A good chain should last 3000 km or more but keep it as clean as possible and oil it lightly from time to time. Most towns have some kind of bike shop, but it is best to do your own repairs and adjustments whenever possible. Most cyclists agree that the main danger comes from other traffic. A rearview mirror has been frequently recommended to forewarn you of vehicles which are too close behind. Make yourself conspicuous by wearing bright clothing. Wearing a helmet is a legal requirement. Several good handbooks on long-distance cycle touring are available in larger bookshops. In the UK there is also the **Cyclist's Touring Club** (CTC)

① *Parklands, Railton Rd, Guildford, Surrey, GU2 9JX, T01483-237 051, www.ctc.org.uk*, for touring and technical information.

Hitchhiking

Hitchhiking in Chile is relatively easy and safe, and when a lift does come along it is often in the shape of an exhilarating open-air ride in the back of a pickup truck. However, in some regions – especially in the south – traffic is sparse, and roads in places like Tierra del Fuego rarely see more than two or three vehicles per day. Drivers will sometimes make hand signals if they are only going a short distance beyond; this is not a rude gesture.

Taxis and colectivos

Taxis usually have meters and can be engaged either in the street or by phoning, though they tend to be more expensive when booked from a hotel. A minimum fare is shown on a large sticker in the windscreen, with increments (usually per 200 m or 60 seconds) below. A surcharge (typically around 50%) is applied after 2100 and on Sunday. Agree beforehand on fares for long journeys out of city centres or for special excursions; also compare prices among several drivers for this sort of trip. There is no need to give a tip unless some extra service is performed. Bear in mind that taxi drivers may not know street locations away from city centres.

Colectivos (collective taxis) operate on fixed routes (identified by numbers and destinations) and are a good way of getting around cities. They are usually flagged down on the street corner, although in some cities such as Puerto Montt there are signs. The fixed charges are normally advertised in the front windscreen and increase at night and weekends. It is best to use small denominations when paying, as the driver takes the money and offers change while driving along. Yellow *colectivos* also operate on some inter-urban routes, leaving from a set point when full. They are usually faster than buses but not as comfortable.

Sea

In the south of Chile, maritime transport is very important. Vital routes are, from north to south: Puerto Montt to Chiloé (many daily); Puerto Montt to Chaitén (several weekly) and Puerto Chacabuco (weekly); Puerto Montt to Puerto Natales (weekly); Castro or Quellón to Chaitén (several weekly in summer, fewer in winter); Quellón to Puerto Chacabuco (once weekly); Punta Arenas to Porvenir (six times weekly); and Punta Arenas to Puerto Williams (twice monthly). Details of all routes and booking information are given under the relevant chapters. Note that routes and timetables change frequently.

Maps

A good map of Santiago is the *Plano de Santiago* published annually by **Publiguías**. Maps of Santiago are also available at kiosks and bookshops in the capital. Maps of the major tourist and trekking areas are published by **Matasi** and are sold locally at newspaper kiosks and good bookshops. However, they do contain the odd error which can be rather serious if you are stuck in a remote area. Order good trekking maps for central Chile from www.trekkingchile.com.

Geophysical and topographical maps are available from **Instituto Geográfico Militar**
① *Dieciocho 369, T02-2410 9363, www.igm.cl, Mon-Thu 0830-1300, 1400-1700, Fri 0830-*

1300, 1400-1600. The **Instituto Geográfico** has published a *Guía Caminera* with roads and city plans (not 100% accurate). It is only available at IGM offices, although the **Biblioteca Nacional** in Santiago has an excellent collection of IGM maps, sections of which can be photocopied. **Copec** service stations sell guidebooks with good general maps (see page 544).

Stanfords ① *12-14 Long Acre, Covent Garden, London WC2E 9LP, T020-7836 1321, www. stanfords.co.uk*, is the world's largest map and travel bookshop. It also has a branch at 29 Corn Street, Bristol BS1.

Where to stay in Chile

Chile is still relatively behind the times with accommodation, so the swisher hotels are often part of uninspiring international chains, while the 'historic' hotels are often run down. Characterful B&Bs and boutique hotels are, however, becoming more common. In most parts of Chile accommodation is plentiful and finding a room to suit your budget should be easy. During the summer holiday months of January and February, at Easter and around the Independence Day holidays in mid-September rooms can be more scarce, especially in upmarket hotels in the more popular holiday venues of the south. In larger cities, the cheapest and often worst hotels tend to be around bus terminals. If you arrive late and are just passing through, they may be OK, but better quality accommodation is often to be found near the main plaza.

Types of accommodation
The term **hotel** implies an expensive establishment in the south (but not necessarily in the north). Top-class hotels are available in Santiago and major cities, but elsewhere choice is more limited. **Hosterías** tend to be in rural areas and may have many of the facilities of a hotel, while the terms **hostal**, **residencial** and **hospedaje** usually refer to a small family-run establishment with limited facilities and services. A **motel**, especially if it is situated on the outskirts of a city, is likely to rent rooms by the hour. In the south, many families offer bed and breakfast, which may be advertised by a sign in the window. People here often meet buses to offer rooms, but the quality is variable.

Backpackers should see www.backpackerschile.com, which lists good standard hostels charging around US$15-25 per person.

Prices
Accommodation is more expensive in Santiago than elsewhere, although prices also tend to be higher in Patagonia, as well as in some northern cities such as Antofagasta. In tourist areas, prices rise in the high season (January-February, plus during any local festivity), but off season you can often bargain, though you will usually have to stay for two or more days to be successful; ask politely for a discount (*descuento*). Single travellers get a better deal in Chile compared to some other Latin American countries. In the south, *hospedajes* charge per person (although you may have to share your room), while in the north, single rooms are about 60-70% the price of a double.

Value Added Tax (known as **IVA**) at 19% is charged on hotel bills and should be included in any price quoted in pesos. The government waives VAT for bills paid in dollars or euros rather than pesos in authorized hotels. However, they will often have such a poor dollar exchange rate that you can end up paying more in dollars than in pesos.

Price codes

Where to stay

$$$$	over US$150	$$	US$30-65
$$$	US$66-150	$	under US$30

Unless otherwise stated, prices are for two people sharing a room in high season, excluding taxes.

Restaurants

$$$	over US$12	$$ US$6-12	$ under US$6

Prices refer to the cost of a main course or set menu for one person, excluding drinks and service charge.

Ask for prices in both currencies and see which is cheaper. Find out in advance what is included in the price.

Rooms and facilities

Most *hospedajes* offer breakfast, which usually consists of tea or instant coffee with bread and jam; but in the north fewer hotels offer breakfast. An increasing number of cheaper places have kitchen facilities for guests but check them out first. Many hotels offer parking, though in large cities this may be a few blocks away. Motorcycle parking is widely available.

Reception areas can be misleading; try and see the room before booking. If you're shown a room without a window, ask if there is a room with a window (*con ventana*). In large cities the choice may be between an inside windowless room and a room with a window over a noisy street. Many mid-range places have rooms with private bathroom (*con baño privado*) and without (*con baño compartido*), so ask if there is anything cheaper.

Many hotels, restaurants and bars have inadequate water supplies. With few exceptions, toilet paper should not be flushed down the pan, but placed in the receptacle provided. This applies even in expensive hotels. Remember to carry toilet paper with you, as cheaper establishments as well as restaurants, bars, etc, frequently do not supply it.

Camping

Camping is not always cheap at official sites. A common practice is to charge US$18 or more for up to five people, with no reductions for fewer than five; however, if a site is not full, owners will often give a pitch to a single person for US$8-10. A few hostels allow camping in their garden and offer very good value rates per person. Cheap gas stoves can be bought in camping shops in Santiago and popular trekking areas, and green replaceable cylinders are available throughout the country. Campsites are very busy in January and February.

Wild camping is easy and safe in remote areas of the far south and in the *cordillera* north of Santiago. However, in much of central and central southern Chile the land is fenced off and it is often necessary to ask permission to camp. In Mapuche and Aymará communities it is both courteous and advisable to make for the primary school or some other focal point of a village to meet prominent members of the community first. Wild camping in the north is difficult due to the absence of water. In the Lake District and Chiloé between mid-December and mid-January huge horseflies (*tábanos*) can be a real problem when camping, hiking and fishing: do not wear dark clothing.

Albergues (youth hostels)

Albergues spring up in summer all over the south of Chile. These are usually schools earning extra money by renting out floor space. They are very cheap (rarely more than US$7 per person) and are excellent places to meet young Chileans. Do not go to them if you want a good night's sleep, though; guitars often play on into the small hours. There is no need for a Hostelling International (HI) card to stay in *albergues*, but there is rarely much in the way of security either.

HI youth hostels throughout Chile cost about US$12-24 per person. The HI card (US$22) is usually readily accepted. In practice, HI hostels in Chile, while generally decent, are not necessarily better than any other hostel. You can often find other better value places.

Food and drink in Chile

Food

Chile's cuisine is varied and often delicious. The Mediterranean climate of the central regions is perfect for growing a wide variety of fruit and vegetables; avocados are especially good. The semi-tropical climate of northern Chile supplies mangoes, papayas, *lúcumas* and *chirimoyas* (custard apples). In the central valley, grapes, melons and watermelons abound. The lush grasslands of the south are ideal for dairy and beef farming as well as for growing grain crops, apples, cherries and plums, while in Patagonia, sheep roam the plains and rhubarb grows wild.

Although Chilean cuisine has mainly Spanish roots, it has also been influenced by immigrant populations. The pastry-making skills of Germans have produced '*onces Alemanas*', a kind of high tea with *Küchen. Pan de Pascua*, a traditional Christmas fruit loaf, is also from Germany.

The main meals are breakfast (*desayuno*), lunch (*almuerzo*) and dinner (*cena*). Lunch is eaten any time from 1300 to 1530, and dinner between 2000 and 2230. Breakfast usually consists of bread, butter and jam, served with coffee (usually instant) or tea. *Las onces* (elevenses) is the name given to a snack usually including tea, bread and cheese. Lunch is the main meal of the day, and many restaurants serve a cheaper fixed-price meal; when this is a single dish it's called *la colación*, whereas if there's more than one course it's called *el menú*. In more expensive places, this may not be listed on the menu.

Seafood Perhaps the most outstanding type of food is seafood. The best seafood and fish is on the coast, but there are also good fish restaurants in Santiago, and fine seafood can be found at the Mercado Central. The excellent fish restaurants between Playa Ancha and Concón, near Valparaíso, are especially popular with Santiaguinos. Almost every port on the Chilean coast has a small market or a row of seafood restaurants where excellent seafood can be eaten very cheaply; in smaller harbours, it is often possible to eat with the fishermen. Most of these seafood restaurants receive their supplies of fish and shellfish from local fishing boats that land their catch every morning in the harbour. Watching the unloading at a port such as Talcahuano can be fascinating. If you have the courage to bargain you may be able to pick up some delicious, fresh fish from the boats or from the stalls along the harbour; whole crates of shellfish go for the equivalent of a few dollars.

In the north, great seafood can be had at Caleta Hornos, north of La Serena, and at Huasco. In the centre and south the best seafood is found at Concón, Valparaíso,

Constitución, Talcahuano, Angelmó (Puerto Montt) and on Chiloé, where you should try the famous *curanto*, a stew of shellfish, pork, chicken and other ingredients. Beware of eating seafood that you have bought unofficially in the far south because of the poisonous *marea roja* (toxic algae blooms).

The most popular fish are *merluza* (hake), *congrio* (kingclip or ling), *corvina* (bass), *reineta* (a type of bream), *lenguado* (sole), *albacora* (swordfish) and *salmón*. *Congrio* is very popular, and particularly delicious served as *caldillo de congrio*, a soup containing a large *congrio* steak. *Ceviche*, raw fish marinated in lemon juice, is usually made with *corvina*.

There is an almost bewildering array of shellfish. Look out for *choritos*, *cholgas* and *choros maltón* (all varieties of mussel), *ostiones* (queen scallops), *ostras* (oysters) and *erizos* (sea urchins). Prawns are known as *camarones*, but these are often imported from Ecuador and can be tasteless and expensive. Chile's most characteristic products are the delicious *erizos*, *machas*, *picorocos* and *locos*, which are only found in these seas. *Machas a la parmesana* are a kind of razor clam prepared in their shells with a parmesan cheese sauce, grilled and served as a starter. *Picorocos* (giant barnacles), which are normally boiled or steamed in white wine, are grotesque to look at but have a very intense taste: it may be very disconcerting to be presented with a plate containing a rock with feathery fins but it is well worth taking up the challenge of eating it, although only the white fleshy part is edible. *Locos*, a kind of abalone, are the most popular Chilean mollusc, but because of overexploitation its fishing is frequently banned. The main crustaceans are *jaiba* (purple crab), *langosta* (lobster) and *centolla*, an exquisite king crab from the south.

Packages of dried seaweed, particularly *cochayuyo* (which looks like a leathery thong), are sold along coastal roads. Both *cochayuyo* and *luche* are made into a cheap, nutritious stew with vegetables, and eaten with potatoes or rice, although these dishes are rarely available in restaurants.

Other specialities Savoury Chilean dishes tend to be creative. Specialities include *humitas* (mashed sweetcorn mixed with butter and spices and baked in sweetcorn leaves), *pastel de papas* (meat pie covered with mashed potatoes) and, the most common everyday dish, *cazuela*. This is a nutritious stew made with pumpkin, potato, coriander and rice, and maybe onions and green peppers, and is either *de ave* (chicken) or *de vacuno* (beef). In central and southern Chile stews with beans (*porotos*) are common. A typical dish from Valparaíso is the *chorillana*; chips covered with sliced steak, fried onions and scrambled eggs. *Pastel de choclo* is a casserole of chicken, minced beef and onions with olives, topped with polenta, baked in an earthenware bowl. *Prieta* is a blood sausage stuffed with cabbage leaves. *Bife* or *lomo a lo pobre* (a poor man's steak) is a steak topped by two fried eggs, chips and onions. A *paila* can take many forms (a *paila* is a serving dish), but the most common are made of eggs or seafood. In the north, *paila de huevos* (scrambled eggs with *hallulla*, a kind of bread) is common for breakfast. A *paila marina* is a delicious shellfish stew.

Chileans tend to have a very sweet tooth, and their **desserts** can be full of *manjar* (caramelized condensed milk).

Snacks Among the many snacks sold in Chile, the most famous are *empanadas*, pastry turnovers made *de pino* (with meat, onions, egg and an olive), *queso* (cheese) or *mariscos* (shellfish). The quality of *empanadas* varies: many are full of onions rather than meat; by the coast the *empanadas de mariscos* are tasty and usually better value.

Wine tasting in Chile

Although there are a few areas of vine cultivation further north, the main wine-producing region in Chile is the Central Valley, which offers ample scope for visits to vineyards and wine tasting, whether independently, or on a tour on one of several *rutas del vino* (wine routes). The following all accept visitors, although a day's notice is usually required:

Elqui Valley page 121
Falernia, Ruta 41, Km 46, Vicuña, T051-241 2260, www.falernia.com.
Cavas del Valle, Ruta R-485, Km 14.5, Montegrande, T09-6842 5592, www.cavasdelvalle.cl.

Limarí Valley page 116
Casa Tamaya, Camino Quebrada Seca, Ovalle, T053-686014, www.tamaya.cl.
Tabalí, T02-477 5535, www.tabali.cl.

Aconcagua Valley page 71
Errázuriz, Nueva Tajamar 481, No 503, Santiago, T02-339 9100, www.errazuriz.com.
San Esteban, Av La Florida 2074, San Esteban, T034-481477, www.vse.cl.
Von Siebenthal, O'Higgins s/n, Panquehue, San Felipe, T09-9459 6173, www.vinavonsiebenthal.com.

Casablanca Valley page 94
Among the newest of Chile's wine valleys, Casablanca has a series of microclimates. To the west the coastal mist and cool sea breezes regulate temperatures to produce crisp, citric Sauvignon Blancs, while further inland, in Alto Casablanca, they are more rounded with less pronounced acidity. In this part of the valley, Pinot Noir and even corpulent Merlots are made. As a non-traditional valley, many of the wineries have extravagant, modern designs and house expensive, often innovative restaurants. Tour operators in Valparaíso and Santiago offer tours, but independent access to most vineyards is easy, the majority being directly off the main highway linking the two cities.
Casas Del Bosque, Hijuelas 2, Ex Fundo Santa Rosa, Casablanca, T02-2480 6940, www.casasdelbosque.cl.
Indómita, Ruta 68, Km 72, T032-215 3900, www.indomita.cl.
Matetic, Fundo Rosario, Lagunillas, T02-2232 3134, www.mateticvineyards.com.
Veramonte, Ruta 68, Km 64, T032-232 9999, www.veramonte.cl.
Viña Mar, Ruta 68, Km 72, T032-275 4300, www.vinamar.cl.
William Cole, Camino Tapihue, Km 4.5, Casablanca, T032-215 7777, www.williamcolevineyards.cl.

San Antonio Valley page 101
Casa Marín, Camino Lo Abarca Km 4, San Antonio, T02-2334 2986, www.casamarin.cl.

Maipo Valley page 68
The traditional home to Chile's top Cabernet Sauvignons and easily accessed from Santiago, the Maipo Valley is reasonably well set up for tourism. There are two main wine-producing zones, to the southeast of the capital around Pirque, where the influence of the Andes is strongly felt, and further down the valley around Isla de Maipo, which is much warmer and ideal for producing full-bodied Cabernet Sauvignon and Carmenère. Day tours are available from Santiago.

Cachapoal Valley
This valley, to the south of Rancagua, produces a wide variety of wine, especially lively Cabernet Sauvignon, fruity Merlot and excellent Carmenère. There are also small plantations of Viognier and Cabernet Franc. There is no organized wine route as such,

but independent visits can be made to several wineries.

Altair, Totihue, Requinoa, T02-2477 5598, www.altairwines.com.
Anakena, Camino a Pimpinela, Requínoa, T02-2433 8600, www.anakenawines.cl.
Gracia, Camino Totihue, Requínoa, T02-2240 7600, www.gracia.cl.

Colchagua Valley page 232

Based around San Fernando and Santa Cruz, Colchagua is one of the great success stories of modern Chilean wine, with the Apalta region producing some world-beating Cabernet Sauvignons, while some of Chile's best Carmenère and Syrah is also produced in the valley. Santa Cruz is home to Chile's oldest and best-organized wine route (www.rutadelvino.cl), with tours of three or six hours from around US$40-200 per person. Independent visits can also be made.

Bisquertt, Fundo Lihueimo, Santa Cruz, T02-2756 2500, www.bisquertt.cl.
Casa Lapostolle, Ruta I-50 Camino San Fernando at Pichilemu Km 36, Santa Cruz, T072-295 3300, www.lapostolle.com.
Casa Silva, Hijuela Norte, San Fernando, T072-271 6519, www.casasilva.cl.
Estampa, Ruta 90 Km 45, Palmilla, Santa Cruz, T02-2202 7000, www.estampa.com.
Los Vascos, Camino Pumanque Km 5, Peralillo, T072-350 900, www.vinalosvascos.com.
Montes, Finca de Apalta, Santa Cruz, T072-281 7815 Ext 108, 101, www.monteswines.com.
Montgras, Camino Isla Yaquíl, T072-282 2845, www.montgras.cl.
Siegel, Fundo San Elias s/n, Palmilla, T072-282 3836, www.siegelvinos.com.
Viña Santa Cruz, Camino Lolol Km 25, Santa Cruz, T072-235 4920, www.vinasantacruz.cl.
Viu Manent, Carretera del vino, Km 37, T02-237 90020, www.viumanent.cl.

Curicó Valley page 237

This valley is where the Chilean wine revolution began in 1980 with the arrival of the Spanish winemaker Miguel Torres. It now produces fruity reds in the lower valley and good-quality Sauvignon Blancs in the cooler foothills of the Andes. The valley has a wine route (www.rutadelvino curico.cl) with circuits ranging from half-day tours to a two-day tour with meals.

Alta Cima, Panamericana Km 202, T075-247 1034, www.altacima.cl.
Miguel Torres, Panamericana Km 195, T075-256 4100, www.migueltorres.cl.
Millamán, Peteroa, Curicó, T075-245 1038, www.millaman.com.
San Pedro, Panamericana, Km 205, T02-247 75300, www.sanpedro.cl.

Maule Valley page 240

The Maule Valley, traditionally the home of the insipid Pais grape, has now been replanted with noble varieties, and produces decent well-balanced reds. The wine route's offices are in the Villa Cultural Huilquilemu, a well-preserved 19th-century hacienda, www.chile wineroute.cl. They offer tours and can also help arrange independent visits. Although this valley does not produce world-beating wines, the vineyards tend to be more intimate than in other valleys. A pleasant day can be had hiring a bicycle and pedalling your way at your own pace from winery to winery.

Balduzzi, Balmaceda 1189, San Javier, T073-232 2138, www.balduzziwines.com.
Casa Donoso, Camino Palmira Km 3.5, Talca, T071-234 1400, www.casadonoso.com.
Gillmore, Camino Constitición Km 20, San Javier, T073-197 5539, www.gillmore.cl.

Itata Valley page 247

Viña Chillán, Km 7 Tres Esquinas, T042-197 1573, www.vinachillan.com.

Chilean sandwiches tend to be fairly substantial: the *churrasco* is a minute steak in a bun and can be ordered with any variety of fillings. *Chacareros* contain thinly sliced steak and salad; *barros lucos* have steak and grilled cheese; and *barros jarpas* have grilled cheese and ham.

Completos are the cheapest and most popular snacks: German influenced, these are hot dogs served with plenty of extras, including mustard, sauerkraut, tomatoes, mayonnaise and *ají* (hot sauce). An *Italiano* is a *completo* with avocado and without the sauerkraut. Avocado is very popular at family *onces*, mashed up and served on bread. Bread comes in pairs of fluffy rolls (*marraquetas*) or as a crisper slim roll (*hallullas*).

Drink

Coffee and tea While Argentine cafés have excellent coffee, if you ask for coffee in many places in Chile you will get a cup of boiling water and a tin of instant coffee, even in quite high-class restaurants. There are espresso bars in major cities; elsewhere specify *café-café, espresso*. A *cortado* is an expresso with hot frothed milk served in a glass. Tea is usually served with hot water only. If you order *café*, or *té, con leche'*, it will come with all milk; to have just a little milk ask for your tea or coffee *'con un poco de leche'*. After a meal, instead of coffee, try an *agüita*, a herbal infusion.

Wine The international reputation of Chilean wine continues to grow. Chilean reds tend to be full bodied with lots of tannins and high alcohol content. Production centres around the great Bordeaux grapes, Cabernet Sauvignon, Merlot and Chilean wine's latest claim to fame, the lost Carmenère grape, wiped out in France over a century ago and rediscovered in Chile a decade ago. Pinot Noir is also now being successfully produced. Chilean whites are also getting better every year. Sauvignon Blancs from Casablanca and San Antonio tend to be crisp and fruity and are excellent when drunk young, while the Chardonnays have been winning awards for years. The very best wines can sell for upwards of US$50 a bottle, while a good reserve wine might set you back around US$10. Anything over US$3 should be perfectly drinkable, and even cheaper wine sold in tetrapacks (US$2.50 a litre) can sometimes be surprisingly good. Anything cheaper than this should be avoided. ▸▸ *For more on wine, see page 540.*

Beer The emergence in recent years of several small independent breweries means that Chilean beer is no longer as bland as it used to be. Chile's best-selling beer is the rather insipid *Cristal*. *Escudo* is slightly more full bodied, while *Royal Guard* has a more flowery flavour. *Austral* brewed in Patagonia is good, but mediocre elsewhere. *Báltica* is good, strong and cheap. *Heineken* and *Brahma* are also worth trying, but *Dorada* is best left for the drunks. *Kunstmann* is the best of the nationwide beers. *Malta*, a dark beer, is recommended for those wanting a British-type beer; however, there are different breweries, and the *Malta* north of Temuco is more bitter than that to the south. Of the regional beers, *Cerveza del Puerto* and Mestiza (both from Valparaíso), Guayacán (Valle de Elqui), *Kross* (Curacaví), *Los Colonos* (Llanquihue) and *Imperial* (Punta Arenas) are all recommended. European beers are increasingly available. Beer is sold in returnable and disposable bottles and in cans. Draught lager is generically known as *Schop*. Bars in the capital are currently giving much greater prominence to beers than to wine.

Pisco and other spirits The most famous spirit is *pisco*, made with grapes, usually drunk with lemon or lime juice as pisco sour. *Pisco* is also often mixed with Coca Cola or Sprite.

Pisco is graded in strength from 30-46°; surprisingly, the stronger versions are much more pleasant and easy to drink, as they have generally had more time to mature in the barrel. Recommended brands of *pisco* are *Alto del Carmen* and *Bauzá*; avoid the ironically named *Pisco Control*, especially at 30°C. Local rum and brandy are very cheap and tend to lead to poisonous hangovers. *Manzanilla* is a local liqueur, made from *licor de oro* (like Galliano). Two delicious drinks are *vaina*, a mixture of brandy, egg and sugar, and *cola de mono*, a mixture of *aguardiente*, coffee, milk and vanilla served very cold at Christmas. There are many seasonal fruit liqueurs which are delicious; *eguindado*, made from cherries, is particularly recommended. *Chicha* is any form of alcoholic drink made from fruit; *chicha cocida* is three-day-old fermented grape juice boiled to reduce its volume and then bottled with a tablespoonful of honey, while *chicha fresca* is fresh fermented grape juice. Cider (*chicha de manzana*) is popular in the south.

Other drinks Drinks made with fruit, such as cheap and freshly squeezed juices, are not as common as in other Latin American countries. Note that a *jugo natural* is fresh fruit liquidized with water and sugar added. If you want a 100% pure fresh juice you should ask for a *vitamina*. *Mote con huesillo*, made from wheat hominy and dried peaches, is very refreshing in summer.

Restaurants
Fashionable Chilean society has seen something of a gastronomic boom over the last few years. An increasing number of boutique restaurants have been opening in Santiago (and to a lesser extent in other major cities). Typically, with upper-class Chile's insecurity with its own identity they almost all shun Chilean food in favour of the flavour of the month, whether it's sushi or 'ethnic fusion'. Increasingly there are new restaurants that use uniquely Chilean ingredients, or fuse them with international styles, and these are worth looking out for. The older established elegant restaurants rarely offer traditional Chilean food either and stick to Mediterranean fare.

If you are travelling in small villages off the beaten track, it is usually possible to find someone who will cook for you; ask around. In cheaper eateries a *colación* usually costs around US$3 or less. The most inexpensive restaurants in urban areas tend to be by transport terminals and markets or, in coastal areas, by the port. Most towns also have *casinos de bomberos* (firemen's canteens), which serve good, cheap food. Fire stations are not paid for by the state, and firemen are all voluntary, so these canteens are a fundraiser.

Although there are **vegetarian restaurants** in major cities, vegetarians will find that their choice of food is severely restricted, especially in smaller towns and away from tourist areas. Vegetarians should explain which foods they cannot eat rather than saying '*Soy vegetariano*' (I'm a vegetarian) or '*No como carne*' ('I don't eat meat'), as carne means only red meat, not all meat. Bread known as *hallulas* is often made with lard (*manteca*); ask first.

Entertainment in Chile

Bars and clubs

Santiago and other university towns as well as major tourist resorts have a thriving nightlife. In resorts, bars may get busy at around 2000 or 2100, whereas in big cities things rarely gets going before midnight. Bohemian nightlife in Santiago centres around Barrio Bellavista, below Cerro San Cristóbal, where you can listen to anything from 1980s pop to salsa, jazz or the latest in Latin and European music, and the streets are crowded until after 0500. Valparaíso has become a centre for the electronic music scene and in summer there are several events. Most towns and villages of any size will have a club open at weekends and at least one bar, although invariably this will be populated by no more than two old drunks sharing a tetrapack of cheap wine. There is quite a severe alcoholism problem, especially on Chiloé and in the far south.

Cinema

With the expansion of mall culture in Chile, most of the larger cities have multiplex cinemas. Prices are usually cheaper on weekday afternoons and student discounts are common. Santiago has a thriving arts cinema scene and there are several repertory cinemas in the capital. Outside the capital there is an arts cinema in Viña, and in Valparaíso there are a number of film clubs with several screenings a week. Many universities throughout the country also show films. In summer there are important film festivals in Santiago, Valparaíso, Viña del Mar and Valdivia.

Performing arts

Rock and pop concerts are common, especially in summer. Chileans are very musical and if you go to a party in someone's house don't be surprised if someone starts playing guitar. Classical concerts are less prevalent, with Santiago naturally being the focus. In the provinces there are a few good chamber orchestras, and in summer there is a good classical festival in Frutillar as well as a series of concerts in Viña del Mar.

Santiago is the hub of Chile's theatre culture. There are dozens of small theatres showing both classic and contemporary works, as well as occasional performances by national and international dance troupes.

Festivals in Chile

Festivals

Festivals are held in all of Chile's towns, rotating from week to week (see throughout the main text for details).
20 Jan Fiesta de la Piedra Santa. Mapuche festival of the Holy Stone in the Lake District.

1st Sun in Feb Fiesta de la Candelaria. One of northern Chile's most important religious festivals, see page 151.
Mid-Feb Festival de la Canción. Viña del Mar hosts the dreaded (and often dreadful) international music festival, see page 105.

End Mar-Apr Campeonato Nacional de Rodeo. National rodeo competition in Rancagua, see page 234.

29 Jun Fiesta de San Pedro. Processions, dancing and lots of fish eating in all coastal towns and villages in celebration of the patron saint of fishermen.

16 Jul La Tirana. This festival near Iquique, celebrating the Virgin del Carmen, is an exhilarating combination of indigenous and Catholic folklore, attended by people from all over Chile and from neighbouring Bolivia and Peru, see box, page 201.

16-22 Sep La Pampilla. The week-long independence celebrations in Coquimbo are the biggest in the country, see page 134.

8 Dec Fiesta de la Virgen de Lo Vásquez. The main Santiago–Valparaíso highway is closed as 80,000 faithful make the pilgrimage on foot (and sometimes even on hands and knees) to the church at Lo Vásquez.

8 Dec Día de la Virgen. Pilgrimage to Quinchao, off Chiloé; see page 356.

23-27 Dec Fiesta Grande. Vast pilgrimage to Andacollo, see page 120.

Late Dec Carnavales Culturales. 3 days of dance, music, theatre and street performance in Valparaíso leading up to the New Year celebrations.

Public holidays

1 Jan New Year's Day
2 days in Mar/Apr Easter
1 May Labour Day
21 May Navy Day/Glorias Navales
29 Jun San Pedro y San Pablo
16 Jul Virgen del Carmen
15 Aug Assumption
1st Mon in Sep Day of National Unity
18/19 Sep Independence
12 Oct Columbus Day/Día de la Raza
31 Oct and 1 Nov All Saints' Day/
Día Nacional de las Iglesias
Evangélicas y Protestantes
8 Dec Immaculate Conception
25 Dec Christmas Day

Shopping in Chile

There is an excellent variety of handicrafts including woodwork, pottery, copperware, leatherwork and indigenous woven goods including rugs and ponchos. However, many of the goods sold in main handicraft markets are from elsewhere in South America, in some cases with the country of origin labels cut off; if going on in South America, these goods are almost always cheaper in the northern Andean countries. Among the most interesting handicrafts is jewellery made with the semi-precious lapis lazuli stone. There are also less well-known stones unique to Chile (such as the *combarbalita*, found around Combarbalá, near Illapel), and many fine jewels and knick-knacks (such as paperweights) made with stones such as onyx. Another good buy is traditional Chilean food or drink, such *pisco*, *ají chileno* or *manjar*.

Bargaining is rare in Chile, and is often seen as impolite. Asking for a *descuento* may be seen as implying that the goods you want to buy are defective. Instead you should ask for una atención, and you will often do well to knock more than 5% off the asking price.

Responsible travel in South America

Since the early 1990s there has been a phenomenal growth in tourism that promotes and supports the conservation of natural environments and is also fair and equitable to local communities. While the authenticity of some ecotourism operators' claims needs to be interpreted with care, there are a great many whose aims and credentials are laudable and we try to highlight these in the book.

Try to balance the negative aspects of travel with positives by following these guidelines:

Cut your emissions Plan an itinerary that minimizes carbon emissions whenever possible. This might involve travelling by train, hiring a bike or booking a walking or canoeing tour. See below for details of carbon offset programmes. Visit www.seat61.com for worldwide train travel.

Check the small print Choose travel operators that abide by a responsible travel policy (it will usually be posted on their website). Visit www.responsibletravel.com.

Keep it local Try to use public transport, stay in locally owned accommodation, eat in local restaurants, buy local produce and hire local guides.

Cut out waste Take biodegradable soap and shampoo and leave excess packaging, particularly plastics, at home.

Get in touch Find out if there are any local schools, charities or voluntary organizations that you could include in your itinerary. For a list of projects that could benefit from your support, see www.stuffyourrucksack.com.

Learn the lingo Practise some local words. Respect local customs and dress codes and always ask permission before photographing people. Once you get home, remember to honour any promises you've made to send photographs.

Avoid the crowds Consider travelling out of season to relieve pressure on popular destinations, or visit a lesser-known alternative.

Take only photos Resist the temptation to buy souvenirs made from animals or plants. For more information, refer to CITES, the Convention on International Trade in Endangered Species (www.cites.org) and the Coalition Against Wildlife Trafficking (www.cawtglobal.org).

Use water wisely Water is a precious commodity in many countries. Treating your own water avoids the need to buy bottled water. If you don't carry water treatment equipment, support places that encourage the reuse of plastic bottles.

Don't interfere Avoid disturbing wildlife, damaging habitats or interfering with animals' natural behaviour. Leave plants and shells where you find them.

Code green for hikers and campers

- Take biodegradable soap, shampoo and toilet paper, long-lasting lithium batteries and plastic bags for packing out all rubbish.
- Use a water filter instead of buying bottled water.
- Keep to trails. Don't take short cuts, especially at high altitude where plants may take years to recover.
- If possible, use an existing campsite.

- Before setting up camp, contact land-owners for area restrictions and permit requirements. Seek advice on sensitive areas. Always register with the appropriate authorities and advise friends or relatives of your itinerary and expected return date.
- Try to pitch your tent on non-vegetated areas, avoiding particularly sensitive habitats.
- Avoid disturbing wildlife or livestock, and avoid areas where access would cause unnecessary erosion.
- Avoid damaging historical, archaeological and palaeontological sites.
- Do not dig trenches around your tent unless flash flooding is a real threat.
- For cooking use a camp stove. If you need to build a fire, use only fallen timber. Allow the fire to burn down to a fine ash. Aim to leave no trace of your fire. Be sure to observe any fire-use restrictions in place.
- If alternatives are not available, dig latrines at least 50 m from water sources, trails and camp sites. Cover the hole with natural materials and either burn or pack out your toilet paper.
- Wash clothing and cooking items well away from water sources and scatter grey water so that it filters through soil. Use biodegradable, phosphate-free soap.
- Pack out all rubbish and unused food, plus litter left by others.

Code green for ecological welfare
- Do not hire any mule or horse that is lame or has open sores from badly fitting tack.
- Avoid handling, feeding or riding on marine life or aquatic mammals.

This Handbook does not support the keeping of marine mammals (eg dolphins) in captivity.
- Choose resorts and lodges that treat sewage and support protected areas.
- Help conserve underwater and riverine environments by taking part in local clean-ups, or in diving areas collecting data for Project AWARE (www.projectaware.org).
- Choose dive operators that use mooring buoys or drift diving techniques, rather than anchors.
- Never touch coral. Practice buoyancy control skills and tuck away trailing equipment.

Offsetting carbon emissions
Carbon offsetting schemes allow you to offset greenhouse gas emissions by donating to various projects, from tree planting to renewable energy schemes. Although some conservation groups are concerned that carbon offsetting is being used as a smokescreen to delay the urgent action needed to cut emissions and develop alternative energy solutions, it remains an important way of counterbalancing your carbon footprint.

For every tonne of CO_2 you generate through a fossil fuel-burning activity such as flying, you pay for an equivalent tonne to be removed elsewhere through a 'green' initiative. There are numerous online carbon footprint calculators (such as www.carbonfootprint.com). Alternatively, book with a travel operator that supports a carbon offset provider like TICOS (www.ticos.co.uk) or Reduce my Footprint (www.reducemyfootprint.travel).

Essentials A-Z

Accident and emergency

Air rescue T138; **Ambulance** (*ambulancia*) T131; **Fire brigade** (*bomberos*) T132, www.bomberos.cl; **Forest fires** (*incendios forestales*) T130; **Police** (*carabineros*) T133; **Police** detectives T134; **Sea rescue** T137. **Policía Internacional** head office E Ramírez 852, Santiago, T02-2737 1292, Mon-Fri 0900-1700, handle immigration and lost tourist cards.

Children

Chile is a good place for travelling with children as there are few health risks and children are very popular. Officials tend to be more amenable where children are concerned, and even thieves and pickpockets seem to have respect for families and may leave you alone.

However, given Chile's geography, a lot of time can be spent travelling. Train journeys are easier, as they allow more scope for moving about, but there are few of these in Chile. On all long-distance buses you pay for each seat; there are no half-fares, so it is cheaper, if less comfortable, to seat small children on your knee for shorter trips. On urban and local buses, small children generally travel free, but are not entitled to a seat if paying customers are standing. On sightseeing tours you should always bargain for a family rate; often children can go free. Airlines charge a third less for under 12s.

You will find that people will be very friendly to children in restaurants. As far as health is concerned, remember to be very careful about sunburn in the south, due to the lack of ozone.

In hotels, try to negotiate family rates. If charges are per person, always insist that 2 children will only occupy 1 bed. If rates are per bed, the same applies. You can often get a reduced rate at cheaper hotels.

Customs and duty free

The following may be brought into Chile duty free: 400 cigarettes or 50 cigars or 500 g of tobacco, plus 2500 cc of alcoholic drinks, and all articles for personal use, including vehicles, radios, cameras, personal computers and similar items. Chile's agricultural sector is free of many diseases, and so fruit, vegetables, meat, flowers and milk products may not be imported; these will be confiscated at all borders, where there are thorough searches. This applies even to those who have had to travel through Argentina in the far south to get from one part of Chile to another. There are also internal customs checks for all travellers going south from Región I. This is mainly to inspect for duty-free goods from Iquique but fruit, vegetables, meat, flowers and milk products may also be confiscated.

Disabled travellers

Chileans are usually very courteous, and disabled travellers will be helped and assisted where possible. The law requires that new public buildings provide disabled access and the more expensive hotels usually have dedicated facilities, although transport provision is a different matter. The línea 5 subway line in Santiago has no disabled access, but there are plans to make the entire system accessible by the second half of 2015. Although bus companies are helpful, and the Transantiago buses are supposed to be disabled-friendly, the majority do not have any dedicated services. Where possible, therefore, disabled travellers might be better off hiring their own transport, especially since reserved parking for the disabled is now reasonably common.

Useful websites

The Global Access – Disabled Travel Network website, www.globalaccessnews.com, is useful. Another informative site, with lots of advice on how to travel with specific disabilities, plus listings and links, belongs to the **Society for Accessible Travel and Hospitality**, www.sath.org.

Electricity

220 volts AC, 50 cycles. Sockets are 3 round pins in a line, and accept 2-pin plugs.

Embassies and consulates

For information on Chilean embassies and consulates abroad or foreign embassies and consulates in Chile, see embassy.goabroad.com.

Gay and lesbian travellers

In a macho culture, it is no surprise that there is quite a lot of homophobia in Chile, and gay and lesbian travellers should be aware that derogatory jokes about homosexuals (especially men) are widespread. Having said that, attitudes are beginning to loosen up, and there is a lively gay scene in most large cities. See http://santiago.gaycities.com and the sites of movements such as www.acciongay.cl, www.mums.cl (Movimiento por la Diversidad Sexual) and www.movilh.org (Movimiento de Integración y Liberación Homosexual).

Health

See your GP or travel clinic at least 6 weeks before departure for general advice on travel risks and vaccinations. Try phoning a specialist travel clinic if your own doctor is unfamiliar with health conditions in Chile.

Make sure you have sufficient medical travel insurance, get a dental check, know your own blood group and if you suffer a long-term condition such as diabetes or epilepsy, obtain a Medic Alert bracelet/necklace (www.medicalert.org.uk). If you wear glasses, take a copy of your prescription.

Vaccinations

Vaccinations for hepatitis A, tetanus, typhoid and, following the 2009 outbreak, influenza A (H1N1) are commonly recommended for Chile. Sometimes advised are vaccines for hepatitis B and rabies. The final decision, however, should be based on a consultation with your GP or travel clinic. You should also confirm your primary courses and boosters are up to date.

Health risks

The most common cause of travellers' diarrhoea is from eating contaminated food. Be wary of salads (what were they washed in, who handled them), re-heated foods or food that has been left out in the sun having been cooked earlier in the day. There is a simple adage that says wash it, peel it, boil it or forget it. It is also standard advice to be careful with water and ice. Ask yourself where the water came from. If you have any doubts then boil it or filter and treat it. Tap water in the major cities, especially in Santiago, should be safe to drink but it may be advisable to err on the side of caution and drink only bottled or boiled water. Avoid having ice in drinks unless you trust that it is from a reliable source. There are many filter/treatment devices now available on the market. Swimming in sea or river water that has been contaminated by sewage can also be a cause; ask locally if it is safe. Diarrhoea may be also caused by viruses, bacteria (such as E-coli), protozoal (such as giardia), salmonella and cholera. It may be accompanied by vomiting or by severe abdominal pain. Any kind of diarrhoea responds well to the replacement of water and salts. Sachets of rehydration salts can be bought in most chemists and can be dissolved in boiled water. If the symptoms persist, consult a doctor.

Travelling in high altitudes can bring on altitude sickness. On reaching heights above 3000 m, the heart may start pounding and the traveller may experience shortness of breath. Smokers and those with underlying heart or lung disease are often hardest hit. Take it easy for the first few days, rest and drink plenty of water – you will feel better soon. It is essential to get acclimatized before undertaking long treks or arduous activities.

Travellers should also be aware of hanta virus (carried by rodents and causing a flu-like illness which can be fatal); hypothermia; *marea roja* (FAN – Floraciones Algales Nocivas), caused by excessive toxins in seafood at certain times of year (see www.ispch.cl/marea-roja-0); sexually transmitted diseases; sunburn (a real risk in the far south due to depleted ozone); and ticks.

If you get sick

Contact your embassy or consulate for a list of doctors and dentists who speak your language, or at least some English. Doctors and health facilities in major cities are also listed in the Directory sections of this book. Good-quality healthcare is available in the larger centres of Chile but it can be expensive, especially hospitalization. Make sure you have adequate insurance (see below).

Useful websites

www.bgtha.org British Global Travel Health Association.
www.cdc.gov US government site that gives excellent advice on travel health and details of disease outbreaks.
www.fco.gov.uk British Foreign and Commonwealth Office travel site has useful information on each country, people, climate and a list of UK embassies/consulates.
www.fitfortravel.scot.nhs.uk A-Z of vaccine/health advice for each country.

www.nhs.uk/nhsengland/ Healthcareabroad/ UK Department of Health advice for travellers.
www.nathnac.org National Travel Health Network and Centre (NaTHNaC).

Insurance

It is vital to take out fully comprehensive travel insurance (including medical insurance). As well as full medical insurance (including evacuation by air ambulance and repatriation), it is important to check that you are covered for any special activities, as many policies exclude so-called dangerous sports (including, in some cases, trekking). Also, many cases there's a limit of cover per item, so, if you are taking something valuable and want it fully insured, you may need to pay extra.

If you do have the misfortune to be robbed (or even just to lose something), you need to make a report to the police and get a police certificate within 24 hrs in order to make a successful claim on your insurance. Be prepared for a bureaucratic nightmare. Police will either want you to make a *denuncia* (complaint) or a *constancia* (report). Beware of making a *denuncia* as you will be making a formal request to the police to follow up on the theft. As a consequence of this, if a case eventually comes to court you will be subpoenaed, and by failing to attend the trial you will be breaking the law and may well face serious problems should you visit Chile again. In most cases you should make a *constancia*. However, usually you will be presented with a stamped receipt which has no reference to the items you have reported stolen. The document you really require is called a *certificado*, and it should list all your missing goods. You may find that outside popular tourist areas the local police may not know what the *certificado* is, and you will need to explain your situation to a superior officer.

Internet

Internet cafés in tourist centres, cities and towns are everywhere. This means that prices tend to be competitive, ranging from US$0.60-1 per hr. Connection speeds may be slow in rural areas. Increasing numbers of hotels and hostels now offer Wi-Fi.

Language

→ For Spanish words and phrases, see page 546.
Although English is understood in many major hotels and tour agencies (especially in Santiago), you are strongly advised to learn some Spanish. Chilean pronunciation – very quick and lilting, with final syllables cut off – can present difficulties. Chileans have a wide range of idioms that even other Latin Americans find difficult to understand. How to Survive in the Chilean Jungle by John Brennan and Alvaro Taboada, lists Chilean colloquialisms and slang and is available in bookshops in larger cities. In some rural areas people speak indigenous languages – Mapudungun (the Mapuche language) in the south, Aymará in the north – but most usually also speak Spanish.

For Spanish language schools see the Directory sections of cities and towns in the text. **Contact Chile**, Rafael Cañas 174, Providencia, Santiago, T02-2264 1719, www. contactchile.cl, offers courses throughout the country and several hostels outside Santiago have Spanish schools attached.

Local customs

Politeness – even a little ceremoniousness – is much appreciated in Chile. Men should always remove any headgear and say 'permiso' when entering offices, and be prepared to shake hands; always say 'buenos días' (until midday) or 'buenas tardes' (in the afternoon and evening). You should be aware that the stereotype of the corrupt Latin American official does not apply in Chile, where most officials are scrupulously honest.

Clothing

Urban Chileans are very fashion conscious. You should dress reasonably smartly in the towns and cities as scruffiness will make things needlessly difficult. People dress smartly at bars and clubs in urban centres, with Santiago, Viña del Mar, La Serena and Iquique being particularly swish. Away from the cities, though, and in areas where there are many foreign tourists, people are less concerned about dress.

Media

Newspapers and magazines

Santiago daily papers are El Mercurio (centre-right, a heavyweight broadsheet), La Nación (the official state newspaper, liberal-left and worth buying on Sun), La Segunda (middle-market tabloid), La Tercera (more serious tabloid), La Cuarta (salacious and gossip-mongering) and Las Ultimas Noticias. Look out for The Clinic, a satirical weekly paper named after the hospital at which General Pinochet was arrested in 1998. International newspapers can sometimes be bought at kiosks on the Paseo Ahumada in Santiago.

Radio and TV

South America has more community radio stations than practically anywhere else in the world so a compact portable digital short-wave radio is recommended as a practical means to brush up on the language, sample popular culture and absorb some regional music. It's worth listening to news in English or Spanish via international broadcasters such as the **Voice of America** (6130 or 7370 KHz), **Monitor Radio International** (operated by Christian Science Monitor in Boston, Mass (15.30 or 9.755 MHz) and the Quito-based evangelical station, **HCJB**. Unfortunately the **BBC World Service** has stopped broadcasting to Chile, although it can be heard on the internet.

There are 6 domestic terrestrial TV channels. Soap operas (teleseries) and soccer constitute the most popular programmes.

Cable TV is widely available. Channels vary from region to region, but there are usually some channels in English, French, Italian and German.

Money

→ *US$1 = CL$578, £1 = CL$925, €1 = CL$730, AUS$1 = CL$508 (Oct 2014).*

Currency

The unit is the Chilean peso; its sign is $. Notes are for 1000, 2000, 5000, 10,000 and 20,000 pesos; coins come in denominations of 1, 5, 10, 50, 100 and 500 pesos. Inflation is low. Official exchange rates for many currencies are quoted in the press, and the best rates are to be had in Santiago. Travellers to rural areas should carry supplies of 1000- and 2000-peso notes; higher denominations are difficult to change. This is also good advice when travelling on local transport or when shopping in small stores early in the day.

ATMs and exchange

The easiest way to obtain cash in Chile is by using ATMs. These are situated at the major banks and often in other locations, especially in shopping malls, bus stations, at the larger supermarkets and at many petrol stations. You can choose to be guided through the transaction in English. ATMs operate under the sign **Redbanc**; Cirrus (MasterCard), Maestro and Plus (Visa) are accepted for daily transactions of up to 200,000 pesos chilenos per day. The exception is the **Banco Estado** whose **Redbanc** machines accept MasterCard but not Visa. A full list of **Redbanc** machines in Chile is listed by town at www.redbanc.cl. Note that ATMs in Chile charge 4000 pesos commission and 1800 pesos fees (US$10.50 in total) for each transaction, except in ATMs of BancoEstado or ServiEstado in Líder supermarkets. At BancoEstado ATMs, if you choose the Spanish option, you can opt not to have a receipt and save yourself a further US$2 in charges; in English you don't get this choice.

Most major currencies can be readily exchanged in tourist centres, but rates for the US dollar, and increasingly the euro, remain much better than for any other currency. US dollars and euros are widely accepted by banks, *casas de cambio* and some hotels, but rarely if ever by shops and other establishments. Foreign notes are often scrutinized carefully and rejected if torn or marked in any way. Before changing currency, check whether any commission is charged. If crossing to Argentina take some low-value US dollar bills.

Visa and MasterCard are readily accepted but American Express and Diners' Club are less useful. Credit card use does not usually incur a commission or higher charge in Chile. In shops, ID is usually required for credit cards; places accepting Visa and MasterCard usually display a **Redcompra** sticker in the window. In case of loss or theft of your card make sure that you carry the phone numbers to report this; make a photocopy of the numbers and keep them in a safe place. Some travellers have reported problems with their credit cards being frozen by their bank when a charge is incurred in a foreign country. To avoid this problem, notify your bank before departure that you are going to Chile (and other countries, where applicable). To avoid charges from your bank, top up your credit card account with sufficient cash before departure. If you need to make very expensive one-off purchases, you may want to specify that your daily spending limit should not be applied to the amount by which your account is in credit, although this will prove dangerous if your card is stolen.

Exchanging TCs is possible in most large cities, although the rate will be up to 5% lower than for cash. It is generally not advisable to change cash or TCs in banks as the rate is much worse than at *casas de cambio*.

Transferring money

Before leaving your home country, find out whether any Chilean bank is correspondent to your own bank. Then, when you need funds, arrange for your bank to transfer the money to the local bank (confirming by fax). Be sure to provide the exact details of the SWIFT code of the receiving bank. Funds can be received within 48 banking hours. This is useful for transferring large amounts. Otherwise, money can be sent within minutes (and with a very large commission) through **Western Union** (in Chile operated by **Chile Express**, www.chilexpress.cl); if collecting money in a city with more than one Western Union agent, you can go to any one of them to receive the money.

Cost of living and travelling

The minimum wage in Chile is approximately US$405 per month, while the wage for relatively senior office workers may be around US$1000-1350 per month. This is low considering the general cost of living in the country. The cost of accommodation or rent is higher (usually double) in Santiago than elsewhere, and within the capital, the eastern part, encompassing Vitacura, Las Condes and to a lesser extent Providencia, is much more expensive than the rest of the city.

You can usually find a basic lunch for around US$4-5. City bus fares are a little over US$1 in Santiago (using the Transantiago system), less in the provinces. Prices for food tend to rise in proportion to the distance from central Chile (being highest in Punta Arenas).

Chile is more expensive than much of South America and southern Chile is even more expensive from 15 Dec to 15 Mar. A budget of US$45 per person per day will allow for basic lodgings, food and overland transport (not taking into account flights, tours, car hire, etc). With a budget of US$700 a week, you will be able to stay in good hotels, eat in smart restaurants and not skimp on excursions.

Opening hours

Banks Mon-Fri 0900-1400.
Businesses Mon-Fri 0830-1230, 1400-1800.
Government offices Mon-Fri 1000-1230 (the public is admitted for a few hours only).
Shops (Santiago) Mon-Fri 1030-1930, Sat 0930-1330.

Police and the law

There are several types of police operating in Chile: *Carabineros* (green uniforms) handle all tasks except immigration; *Investigaciones* (in civilian dress) are the detectives; *Policía Internacional*, a division of the *Investigaciones*, handle immigration and customs.

If you get into trouble with the police, the worst thing that you can do is offer a bribe to get yourself out of trouble. Chilean police will assume any attempt to bribe them is both an insult and an admission of guilt. Legal penalties for most offences are fairly similar to what you might expect in a western European or North American country, although the possession of soft drugs, such as cannabis, is treated very seriously. If you get into trouble, first call your consulate, which should be able to put you in touch with an English-speaking lawyer.

Post

The Chilean postal system is usually efficient. Airmail takes around a week from both the UK and the US. Seamail takes 8-12 weeks from the UK. There is a daily airmail service to Europe. There is no overseas surface mail service from Chile. The poste restante service (*lista de correo*) only holds mail for 30 days, then returns it to sender. The *Lista de Correo* in the Central Post Office in Santiago is good and efficiently organized, but letters are kept separately for men and women so envelopes should be marked Señor or Señora/Señorita.

Safety

Chile is generally a safe country to visit. Police stations in rural areas very rarely have people in their one cell. Like all major cities, though, Santiago and Valparaíso do have crime problems. Avoid the *poblaciones* (shanty towns) of Santiago, especially if you are travelling alone or have only recently arrived. The following suggestions are particularly applicable in central Santiago, in some of the hills of Valparaíso and in Coquimbo, which has a reputation for theft.

Keep valuables out of sight. Cameras should be kept in bags when not in use, and expensive watches or jewellery should not be worn. It is best to leave any valuables you don't need in the hotel safe deposit when sightseeing locally. Always keep an inventory of what you have deposited. If you lose valuables, always report to the police and note details of the report for insurance purposes (see also Insurance above).

Keep all documents and money secure. When travelling with all your gear, hide your main cash supply in different places or under your clothes; you may wish to use extra pockets sewn inside shirts and trousers, pockets closed on the outside with a zip or safety pin, money belts (best worn under clothes, below the waist rather than around the neck), neck or leg pouches or elasticated support bandages for keeping money above the elbow or below the knee.

Try not to appear nervous as this is a clear sign to any thief that you are carrying valuables or that you are unsure where you're going. Look out for tricks, employed by thieves to distract your attention and separate you from your possessions. One common ruse is the mustard trick: the victim is sprayed with mustard, ketchup or some other substance, apparently accidentally, and an accomplice offers sympathy and helps to clean your jacket, removing your wallet at the same time.

Don't fight back. If you are attacked, remember your assailants may well be armed, so it is better to hand over your valuables rather than risk injury.

Student travellers

If you are planning to study in Chile for a long period it is essential to get a student visa in advance, by contacting a Chilean embassy or consulate (see page 27); you will be asked for proof of affiliation to a Chilean university. Note that students are not allowed to undertake paid employment in Chile.

If you are in full-time education you are entitled to an **International Student Identity Card (ISIC)**, distributed by student travel offices and travel agencies worldwide. The ISIC gives you discounts on transport, and access to a variety of other concessions and services. To find the location of your nearest ISIC office, look at www.isic.org. In Chile, student ID cards can be obtained from the ISIC offices, Hernando de Aguirre 201, of 602, Providencia, Santiago, T02-411 2000, www.isic.cl, and cost US$16.25 (photo and proof of status required). If travelling with a student card, it is always worth asking for discounts for museum entry and bus tickets, although all student ID cards must have a photograph.

Telephone

→ *International dialling code +56. International access code (IDD) 0.*

Ringing: a single ring (as in the US). Engaged: equal tones with equal pauses. *Centros de llamados* (phone centres) are abundant and are the easiest way to make a call. They have private booths where you can talk for as long as you like and pay afterwards, the price sometimes being displayed on a small screen in your booth. They often have internet and photocopying services too. For international calls it is cheaper to use a *Centro de llamados* or pre-paid phone scratch cards, available from *kioskos*. Alternatively, **Skype**, www.skype.com, is the cheapest way to keep in touch.

Mobile phones

International roaming is becoming more common, although buying a cheap local pay-as-you-go may be a cheaper option. Major airports and hotels often have rental desks, or can advise on local outlets. Mobile numbers are preceded by 09 if calling from a landline.

Time

GMT -4 hs; -3 hrs in summer. Clocks change from mid-Sep or Oct to early Mar.

Tipping

In restaurants 10% is a good tip, but you should only leave about 100 pesos (US$0.15) in bars and *fuentes de soda*. Taxi drivers are not tipped.

Tour operators

UK and Ireland
Cox & Kings Travel, T020-7873 5000, www.coxandkings.co.uk. Exclusive set tours all over the continent.
Exodus Travels, T0845-287 3647, www.exodus.co.uk. Experience in adventure travel around the world; good trips to all parts of Chile.
Journey Latin America, T020-8747 8315, www.journeylatinamerica.co.uk. Long-established company running escorted and bespoke tours throughout the region, and offering a wide range of flight options.
Last Frontiers, T01296-653000, www.lastfrontiers.co.uk. Tailor-made Latin American travel.
Pura Aventura, T01273-676 712, www.pura-aventura.com. Small Chilean specialist with a wide range of organized and tailor-made tours.
Scott Dunn, T020-3432 6904, www.scottdunn.com. Wide range of tailor-made packages throughout the region.

Select Latin America, T020-7407 1478, www.selectlatinamerica.co.uk. Specialist in tours to Latin America.
Steppes Latin America, T0843-636 8323, www.steppestravel.co.uk. Tailor-made holidays including Patagonia escorted tours, horse-riding trips and birdwatching.

North America
International Expeditions, T1-855 246 0412, www.internationalexpeditions.com. Travel company specializing in nature tours.
Ladatco Tours, T1-800 327 6162, www.ladatco.com. Specialist operator based in Miami, runs explorer tours themed around mysticism, wine, etc.
Mila Tours, T1-800-367 7378, www.milatours.com. Arranges a wide variety of tours from rafting to photography.
Mountain Travel Sobek, T1-888 831 7526, www.mtsobek.com. A specialist in Chile, offering a range of trekking tours.
Myths and Mountains, T1-800-670 6984, www.mythsandmountains.com. Cultural, wildlife and environmental trips.
South American Explorers Club, T1-607 277 0488, T1-800-2740568 (toll-free in USA), www.saexplorers.org. Gives good advice.
Wilderness Travel, T1-800-368 2794 (toll free), www.wildernesstravel.com. Organizes trips worldwide, including very good tours of Patagonia.

South America
CAT Argentina and Chile, Buenos Aires, www.cat-travel.com. With offices in several Latin American countries, this Dutch-owned company offers tailor-made trips.

Australia
Australian Andean Adventures, T61-29 953 4401, www.andeanadventures.com.au. Specialists in trekking in South America for Australians.
South America Travel Centre, T61-1300 784 794, www.satc.com.au. Good tailor-made trips to Chile.

Tourist information

The national secretariat of tourism, **Sernatur**, www.sernatur.cl, has offices throughout the country (addresses are given throughout this guide). Most of the larger tourist offices around the country are run by Sernatur and can provide town maps, leaflets and other useful information, otherwise contact the head office. **CONAF** (Corporación Nacional Forestal), Paseo Bulnes 285, Santiago, T02-2663 0125, www.conaf.cl, manages national parks throughout Chile. CONAF's staff are dedicated and knowledgeable, though their offices in the parks themselves are usually much more helpful than the regional head offices. CONAF also publishes a number of leaflets and has documents and maps about the national park system that can be consulted or photocopied in its Santiago office; but these are not very useful for walking. **CODEFF** (Comité Nacional Pro-Defensa de la Fauna y Flora), Ernesto Reyes 35, Providencia, Santiago, T02-2777 2534, www.codeff.cl, can also provide information on environmental questions. **Ancient Forest International**, Box 1850, Redway, CA 95560, T707-923 4475, USA, www.ancient forests.org, can be contacted regarding Chilean forests.

Visas and immigration

Regulations change frequently, so it is imperative to check visa requirements before you travel. At the time of writing, citizens of the UK, EU, USA, Canada, Australia, New Zealand and South Africa require only a passport, valid for at least 6 months, and a tourist card, which is handed out at major border crossings and at Chilean airports. This allows visitors to stay for 90 days and must be surrendered on departure from Chile. Other foreign nationals should consult with the Chilean

embassy in their home country about visa requirements. After 90 days the tourist card must either be renewed by leaving and re-entering the country at a land border or extended (US$100) at the Ministerio del Interior (Extranjería) in Santiago (www. extranjeria.gob.cl) or (preferably) at any local government office (Gobernación), where the procedure is slightly less time-consuming. Remember that it is your responsibility to ensure that your passport is stamped in and out when you cross borders. The absence of entry and exit stamps, or passports stamped with the wrong date of entry, can cause serious difficulties. It is essential that you keep the tourist card safe, since you must surrender it on departure. Onward travel tickets are officially required for entry but these are rarely asked for. On arrival you will be asked where you are staying in Chile; just give the name of any hotel. See Airport information (page 8) on reciprocal fees charged to some nationalities on arrival in Chile.

Chilean officials are very document-minded, but also often exceptionally hospitable and helpful. In remote areas, you should register your documents with the *carabineros* (police), not only as a matter of courtesy, but also because the local police are usually a mine of information about local conditions, and may be able to help you find accommodation and transport. If staying for a while, it is also worth registering at your embassy or consulate because if your passport is stolen, the process of replacing it is simplified and speeded up. Keeping photocopies or digital scans of essential documents is recommended; always carry a photocopy of your passport on your person as, legally, some form of identification must always be carried.

Weights and measures

The metric system is used.

Women travellers

Chile presents no special problem for women travellers. Most Chileans are courteous and helpful. The following useful tips have been supplied by women, although most apply to any single traveller.

When you set out, err on the side of caution. Unless actively avoiding foreigners like yourself, don't go too far from the beaten track; there is a very definite 'gringo trail' that you can join. This can be helpful when looking for safe accommodation, especially if arriving after dark. Remember that a taxi at night can be as dangerous as wandering around on your own, particularly in Santiago. At borders, dress as smartly as possible. Buses are much easier than trains for a person alone; on major routes seats are reserved and bags are locked in the hold.

Women may be subject to much unwanted attention. To help minimize this, you could wear a wedding ring and carry a photograph of your 'husband' and 'children'. If politeness fails, do not feel bad about showing offence and departing. When accepting a social invitation, make sure that someone knows the address and the time you left. Ask if you can bring a friend (even if you do not intend to do so). A good rule is always to act with confidence, as though you know where you are going, even if you do not. Someone who looks lost is more likely to attract unwanted attention. Finally, be aware that anywhere calling itself a 'nightclub' is in fact a brothel.

Working in Chile

It is not difficult to find short-term or temporary work as a foreigner in Chile. The most obvious opening is teaching English; even those without the appropriate TEFL qualification should be able to find this kind of work, especially in Santiago, but also in other cities such as Viña del Mar,

Concepción and La Serena. Teachers are expected to be well-dressed and to have the correct paperwork. Pay is often poor, especially if you do not have appropriate qualifications. The best paid work is private, one-to-one tuition, mainly found through word of mouth (although it may also be worth placing an advertisement in a newspaper such as *El Mercurio*). Prospective English language teachers should apply in mid-Feb/early Mar with a CV and photo. Those with appropriate skills and experience may also find work with foreign companies (especially in engineering or financial services sectors) with offices in Chile (usually in Santiago).

A work visa should be obtained as soon as you have found a contract (see below); beware that, without this, you will be liable to deportation and fines if discovered. We have received reports of unscrupulous language institutes employing teachers with 90-day tourist visas and then 'discovering', as this expires, that the teacher is not entitled to work, at which point unpaid wages may be withheld.

The main obstacle to finding work in Chile is the problem of obtaining and maintaining a working visa. All sorts of extraordinary pieces of paper may be asked for, and, at the very least, you will need proof of an employment offer before a visa is issued. Those planning to work may enter Chile on a tourist visa and then get a working visa on presentation of a contract.

Volunteering

There is considerable scope for volunteer work in Chile, both in inner cities and on environmental projects. The following organizations offer volunteering opportunities in Chile:

Earthwatch, Australia, T03-9016 7590, www. earthwatch.org. Organizes volunteer work on scientific and cultural projects around the world (also has offices in Oxford, UK).

Project Trust, UK, T01879-230444, www.projecttrust.org.uk. Volunteer work for foreigners.

Raleigh International, UK, T0207-7183 1270, www.raleighinternational.org. Volunteer projects for young people.

Voluntary Horizons, Chile, T56-2 2374 1236, www.voluntaryhorizons.com. Volunteer travel programmes in Chile and Argentina.

Contents

Santiago Region

At a glance

⊖ **Getting around** The efficient metro system is easier to use than the local bus network. Otherwise take taxis and provincial buses.
⟳ **Time required** 2 days to acclimatize. Chile's highlights lie elsewhere.
☁ **Weather** Warm days and cool nights. Dry season Oct-Apr.
✖ **When not to go** Jan can be on the hot side, while smog can be a problem in winter (Jun-Aug).

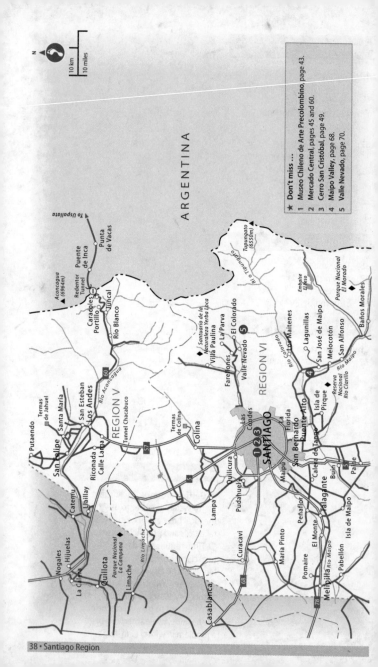

ARGENTINA

REGION V

REGION VI

SANTIAGO

To Uspallata

N

10 km
10 miles

Aconcagua (6964m)
Redentor Tunnel
Puente de Inca
Punta de Vacas
Caracoles
Portillo
Juncal
Río Blanco
Tupungato (6550m)
Río Tupungato
Río Colorado
Embalse El Yeso
Parque Nacional El Morado
Baños Morales
San Alfonso
Melocotón
San José de Maipo
Lagunillas
Los Maitenes
Reserva Nacional Río Clarillo
Río Maipo
Isla de Pirque
Santuario de la Naturaleza Yerba Loca
Villa Paulina
El Colorado
La Parva
Farellones
Valle Nevado
Las Condes
La Florida
Puente Alto
Calera de Tango
Buin
Paine
Isla de Maipo
Pabellón
Melipilla
Pomaire
El Monte
Talagante
Peñaflor
Maipú
María Pinto
Curacaví
Casablanca
Pudahuel
Lampa
Quilicura
Colina
Termas de Colina
Tunnel Chacabuco
Calle Larga
Rinconada
San Esteban
Los Andes
San Felipe
Santa María
Termas de Jahuel
Putaendo
Catemu
Llaillay
Nogales
Hijuelas
Quillota
La Cruz
Limache
Parque Nacional La Campana
Río Limáche
Río Aconcagua
San Bernardo

If you are flying into Chile, you will probably arrive in Santiago. No one can deny that the Chilean capital has an impressive setting, in a hollow surrounded by mountains, with peaks over 5000 m visible on clear days. They are most dramatic just after rainfall in winter, when the smog clears and the new snows glisten.

Santiago is a vibrant, progressive city. With its many parks, interesting museums, glittering high-rises and boutiques, it bursts with possibilities. As far as entertainment goes, there are popular scenes in everything from techno and progressive rock to Bohemian hang-outs and most of the bits in between. Certainly, those who spend an extended period of time in Santiago soon find plenty of things to do at night and at the weekends.

The region around the capital encompasses several of the country's highlights. The resorts on the coast are less than two hours away and also within easy reach are the best ski resorts in South America, which are great spots for weekend hikes in summer. Meanwhile, the area south of Santiago is perhaps the best wine-producing area in Chile. Autumn, when the grapes are being harvested, is a particularly good time to visit the vineyards.

Santiago

Situated in the Central Valley and with a population of six million, Santiago has grown to become the sixth largest city in South America, as well as the political, economic and cultural capital of Chile. The city is crossed from east to west by the long-suffering Río Mapocho, into which most of the city's sewage is dumped; however, the magnificent chain of the Andes provides a more appropriate natural landmark.

It is easy to see Santiago as just another Westernized Latin American city but, away from the centre and wealthier suburbs, the reality is more complicated. Street vendors are often newly arrived from rural areas, many living in appalling 'villas miserias' on the city's outskirts. (Pudahuel and La Pintana are both especially chastening barrios for those who claim that poverty does not exist in Chile.) Some barrios in the south of the city have a higher concentration of indigenous Mapuche people than the Mapuche heartlands of the south.

If you are just passing through, Santiago is unlikely to be the highlight of your trip to Chile – it can take a while to get a real feeling for the city's pulse. However, if you have the time, it does warrant a visit of a few days. On top of its setting and nightlife, there are excellent museums, and you will find that the contrast with the rest of the country is stark. Over a third of Chileans live in Gran Santiago, so, if you want to understand the country you are visiting, Santiago is a must.

Getting there

Air International and domestic flights arrive at the **Aeropuerto Merino Benítez** ⓘ *information T02-2690 1752, www.aeropuertosantiago.cl*, 26 km northwest of the city at Pudahuel, off Ruta 68, the motorway to Viña del Mar and Valparaíso. The terminal has most facilities, including Afex *cambio*, ATMs, tourist offices that will book accommodation and a fast-food plaza. Left luggage costs US$9 per bag per day.

Frequent bus services between the international and domestic terminals and the city centre are operated by two companies: **TurBus** ⓘ *T02-2822 7741, to/from Terminal Alameda (metro Universidad de Santiago, line 1), every 30 mins 0615-2400, US$4*; and **Centropuerto** ⓘ *T02-2601 9883, to/from metro Los Héroes, every 15 mins 0640-2330, US$3.50*. En route the buses stop at Pajaritos metro station (not 0645-0815), **Estación Central Terminal Santiago** and most other regular bus stops. From the airport you could take Tur-Bus to Pajaritos, US$3, and take the metro from there. Minibus services between the airport and hotels or other addresses in the city are operated by several companies with offices in the airport. These include **elfos** ⓘ *T02-2913 8800, www.transferdelfos.cl*, and **Transvip** ⓘ *T02-2677 3000, www.transvip.cl*. They charge US$10-12 for a shared vehicle or US$32-42 for exclusive use, depending on the zone; there's a 10% discount if you book your return to airport with same company. Otherwise, transfers to the airport should be booked a day ahead. Many hotels also run a transfer service. **Taxi** drivers offer rides to the city outside Arrivals, but the official taxi service, T02-2601 9880, is more reliable, if a little more expensive: US$30 to Pajaritos or **Quinta Normal**, US$34 to the centre, US$38 to **Providencia**, up to US$40 to Las Condes.

Bus and train The railway station, Estacíon Central, only serves the south of the country. It is on the Alameda (Avenida Libertador Bernardo O'Higgins), west of the centre, close to the four main bus terminals, which are served by frequent, good interurban buses to/from all parts of Chile. The station and the terminals are all convenient for the metro. There is a fifth bus terminal at Metro Pajarito, handy for connections to the airport (see above), Valparaíso and Viña del Mar. ▶▶ *For details of each terminal, see Transport, page 62.*

Getting around

The metro (www.metrosantiago.cl) has four lines: **Line 1** runs west–east between San Pablo and Los Dominicos, under the Alameda, linking the bus and train stations, the centre, Providencia and beyond; **Line 2** runs north–south from Vespucio Norte to La Cisterna; **Line 4** runs from Tobalaba on Line 1 south to Plaza de Puente Alto, with a branch (4a) from V Mackenna to La Cisterna; **Line 5** runs north, east and southeast from Plaza de Maipú via Baquedano to Vicente Valdés on Line 4. City buses are operated under the **Transantiago** ⓘ *www.transantiago.cl*, system, which is designed to reduce congestion and pollution, but has not entirely succeeded. The city is divided into 10 zones lettered A to J. Within each zone, buses (known as *micros*) are the same colour as that given to the zone (eg white for zone A: central Santiago). Zones are linked by trunk lines, run by white *micros* with a green stripe. The system integrates with the metro. Buses display the number and direction of the route within the system. Payment is by prepaid *Bip* card only. A card costs US$2.75, to which you add however much you want to pay in advance. They are most conveniently bought at metro stations. For a day or so

Moving mountains

While Santiago's smog is not too bad in spring, summer and autumn, those who arrive here during winter could be in for an unpleasant shock. It might not take more than half an hour for your throat to begin to itch and your eyes to water due to one of Santiago's biggest problems – pollution. When Pedro de Valdivia founded the city in 1541, between the coastal mountains and the Andes, it must have seemed like a perfect site; he could never have imagined that the city would one day engulf the whole valley, and that the mountains would become a serious problem.

The principal reason for Santiago's high levels of pollution is that it lies in a bowl, encircled by mountains, which means that the smog is trapped. This, combined with the centralization of Chilean industry in Santiago, the fact that many buses are not equipped with catalytic converters and the sheer volume of cars that choke the city's highways, conspires to create a problem that cannot easily be resolved. It is a serious issue: asthma rates are high and older people sometimes die during the winter *emergencias*, when the pollution gets particularly bad.

Over the years, all sorts of solutions have been proposed. A team of Japanese scientists once even suggested blowing up the part of the Andes nearest the city, so that the pollution could disperse more easily. Each weekday, cars that have number plates ending in one of two digits are prohibited from circulating. But, until the government finds a means of dispersing the population more widely throughout the country, the problem is likely to remain.

it's probably not worth investing in a *Bip* card (just use the metro), but for a few days it's good value. Long-term visitors can buy personalized cards, to prevent theft, etc. There are also *colectivos* (collective taxis) on fixed routes to the suburbs. Routes are displayed with route numbers. Fares vary, depending on the length of the journey, but are usually between US$1.50-2.50 (higher fares at night). Taxis are abundant, but Radio Taxis, called in advance, tend to be safer. ▸▸ *For further information, see Transport, page 62.*

Orientation

The centre of the old city lies between the Mapocho and the Avenida O'Higgins, which is usually known as the Alameda. This is the main east-west avenue through the city and is within easy reach of line 1 of the metro. From the Plaza Baquedano (usually called Plaza Italia), in the east of the city s central area, the Mapocho flows to the northwest and the Alameda runs to the southwest. From Plaza Italia the C Merced runs due west to the Plaza de Armas, the heart of the city, five blocks south of the Mapocho. An urban motorway runs the length of Santiago from east to west under the course of the Río Mapocho.

Tourist offices

Servicio Nacional de Turismo Sernatur ① *Av Providencia 1550, metro Manuel Montt, next to Providencia Municipal Library, T02-2731 8310, info@sernatur.cl, Mon-Fri 0900-1900, Sat 0900-1400, maps, brochures and posters. Good notice board. Information office also at the airport, daily 0900-2100, T02-2601 9320.* **Municipal Tourist Board** ① *north side of Plaza de Armas, T02-2713 6745, and at Cerro Santa Lucía, T02-2664 4206, www.ciudad.cl, Mon-Thu 1000-1800, Fri 1000-1700, offers free walking tours most days of the week. Almost all museums are closed on Monday and on 1 November.*

Security

Like all large cities, Santiago has problems of theft. Pickpockets and bag-snatchers, who are often well-dressed, operate especially on the metro and around the Plaza de Armas. Avoid the *poblaciones* (shanty towns), notably Pudahuel and parts of the north (such as Conchalí), especially if you are travelling alone or have only recently arrived.

Background

Santiago was founded by Pedro de Valdivia on 12 February 1541 on the site of a small indigenous settlement between the southern bank of the Río Mapocho and the Cerro Santa Lucía. During the colonial period, it was only one of several Spanish administrative and cultural centres; also important were Concepción to the south and La Serena in the north. Nevertheless, by 1647 there were 12 churches in the city but, of these, only San Francisco (1618) survived the earthquake of that year. A further earthquake destroyed most of the city in 1730.

Following Independence, the city became more important. In the 1870s, under the Intendente (regional governor) Benjamín Vicuña MacKenna, an urban plan was drafted, the Cerro Santa Lucía was converted from being a makeshift protestant cemetery into a public park and the first trams were introduced. As the city grew at the end of the 19th century, the Chilean elite, wealthy from mining and shipping, built their mansions west of the centre around Calle Dieciocho, Avenida España and República. One of these families was the Cousiños, who built the Palacio Cousiño and later donated this and what became the Parque O'Higgins to the city. Expansion east towards Providencia began in 1895. Until the 1930s, much of the city centre had colonial buildings in the style of Quito or Lima, but expansion and modernization meant that these were gradually replaced. In the latter part of the 20th century, like most Latin American capital cities, Santiago spread rapidly. Many older Santiaguinos who live in areas that are now relatively central tell how, when they first arrived in the city, their homes were right on the outskirts. In general, the more affluent moved east into new neighbourhoods in the foothills of the Andes, and poorer neighbourhoods were established to the west of the centre. This geographic division of wealth continues today.

Places in Santiago → For listings, see pages 53-66.

Santiago centre

Around the Plaza de Armas On the eastern and southern sides of the Plaza de Armas there are arcades with shops; on the northern side is the post office and the Municipalidad; and on the western side the Cathedral and the archbishop's palace. The **Cathedral**, much rebuilt, contains a recumbent statue in wood of San Francisco Javier; the chandelier which lit the first meetings of Congress after independence; and an interesting **museum** ① *0930-1230, 1530-1830, free*, of religious art and historical pieces. In the Palacio de la Real Audiencia is the **Museo Histórico Nacional** ① *T02-2T02-2411 7010, www.museonacionalhistorico.cl, Tue-Sun 1000-1800, US$1.15, free on Sun, signs in Spanish*, covering the period from the Conquest until 1925. The Plaza and the Casa Colorada (below) were being remodeled in 2014.

Just west of the Plaza is the **Museo Chileno de Arte Precolombino** ① *in the former Real Aduana, Bandera 361, T02-2928 1500, www.precolombino.cl, Tue-Sun 1000-1800, US$6.35, students and children free, displays in English, brochure US$17.75*. Its collection of objects from the pre-Columbian cultures of Central America and the Andean region is highly recommended for the quality of the objects and their presentation. At Calle Merced 864, is the **Casa Colorada** (1769), home of the Governor in colonial days and then of Mateo de Toro, first president of Chile. It is now the **Museo de Santiago** ① *T02-2T02-2633 0723, Tue-Sat 1000-1800, Sun and holidays, 1100-1400, US$1, students free, closed for renovation in 2014*. It covers the history of Santiago from the Conquest to modern times, with excellent displays and models, some signs in English, guided tours. Paseo Ahumada, a pedestrianized street lined with cafés runs south to the Alameda four blocks away, crossing Huérfanos.

1 Santiago orientation

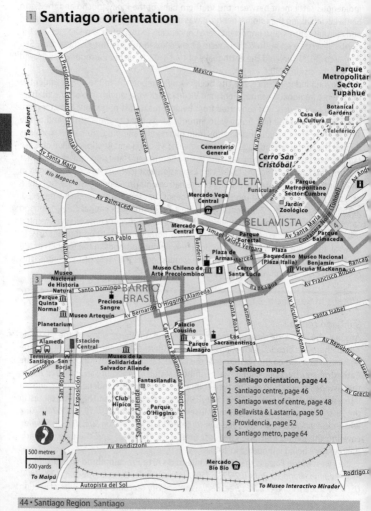

→ **Santiago maps**

North of the Plaza de Armas Four blocks north of the Plaza de Armas is the interesting **Mercado Central** ⓘ *21 de Mayo y San Pablo*, the best place in Santiago for seafood. The building faces the **Parque Venezuela**, on which is the Cal y Canto metro station and, at its western end, the **Centro Cultural Estación Mapocho** ⓘ *www.estacionmapocho.cl*, in the old Mapocho station. Immediately south of the Mapocho and east of the Mercado Central is the **Parque Forestal**, through which you can reach Plaza Italia. In the park, the **Museo Nacional de Bellas Artes** ⓘ *www.mnba.cl (Spanish only), Tue-Sun 1000-1850, US$1, students and seniors US$0.50, free Sun, café*, is in an extraordinary example of neoclassical architecture. It has a large display of Chilean and foreign painting and sculpture; contemporary art exhibitions are held several times a year. In the west wing is the **Museo de Arte Contemporáneo** ⓘ *www.mac.uchile.cl*.

Plaza Italia, Lastarria and around From the **Plaza Italia**, where there is a statue of Gen Baquedano and the Tomb of the Unknown Soldier, the Alameda runs through the heart of the city for over 3 km. It is 100 m wide and ornamented with gardens and statuary: the most notable are the equestrian statues of Generals O'Higgins and San Martín; the statue of the Chilean historian Benjamín Vicuña MacKenna who, as mayor of Santiago, beautified Cerro Santa Lucía (see below); and the great monument in honour of the battle of Concepción in 1879.

Between Plaza Italia, the Parque Forestal and the Alameda is the **Lastarria** neighbourhood (Universidad Católica Metro). Calle José Victorino Lastarria itself has a number of popular, smart restaurants, while the **Plaza Mulato Gil de Castro** ⓘ *C Lastarria 307*, has a mural by Roberto Matta and the **Museo Arqueológico de Santiago** and the **Museo de Artes Visuales** ⓘ *T02-2664 9337, www.mavi.cl, Tue-Sun 1030-1830, US$2 for both, free on Sun*. The former exhibits Chilean archaeology, anthropology and pre-Columbian art, and the latter, modern art.

West along the Alameda Heading west from here the Alameda skirts, on the right, **Cerro Santa Lucía**, and on the left, the Catholic University. **Cerro Santa Lucía** ⓘ *closes at 2100; visitors must sign* *a register at the entrance, giving their ID card number*, bounded by Calle Merced to the north, Alameda to the south, calles Santa Lucía and Subercaseaux, is a cone of rock rising steeply to a height of 70 m (reached by stairs and a lift from the Alameda). It can be climbed from the Caupolicán esplanade, on which stands a statue of that Mapuche leader, but the ascent from the northern side, with a statue of Diego de Almagro, is easier. There are striking views of the city from the top, where there is a fortress, the **Batería Hidalgo** (no public access). It is best to descend the eastern side, to see the small **Plaza Pedro Valdivia** with its waterfalls and **statue of Valdivia**. The area is not safe after dark.

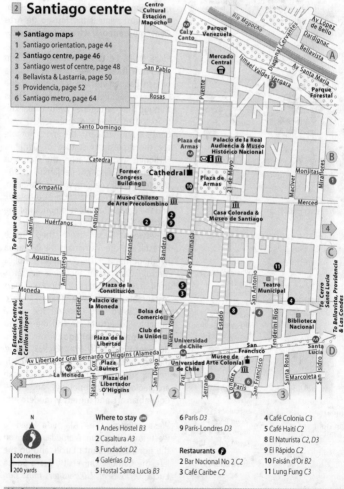

2 Santiago centre

➡ Santiago maps
1 Santiago orientation, page 44
2 Santiago centre, page 46
3 Santiago west of centre, page 48
4 Bellavista & Lastarria, page 50
5 Providencia, page 52
6 Santiago metro, page 64

Where to stay 🛏
1 Andes Hostel *B3*
2 Casaltura *A3*
3 Fundador *D2*
4 Galerías *D3*
5 Hostal Santa Lucía *B3*
6 París *D3*
9 París-Londres *D3*

Restaurants 🍴
2 Bar Nacional No 2 *C2*
3 Café Caribe *C2*
4 Café Colonia *C3*
5 Café Haití *C2*
8 El Naturista *C2, D3*
9 El Rápido *C2*
10 Faisán d'Or *B2*
11 Lung Fung *C3*

Beyond the hill the Alameda passes the neoclassical **Biblioteca Nacional** ⓘ *Av O'Higgins 651, Santa Lucía metro, www.bibliotecanacional.cl, Mon-Fri 0900-1900, Sat 0910-1400 (Jan-Feb, closed Sat), free,* good concerts, temporary exhibitions. Beyond, on the left, between calles San Francisco and Londres, is the oldest church in Santiago: the red-walled church and monastery of **San Francisco** (1618). Inside is the small statue of the Virgin that Valdivia carried on his saddlebow when he rode from Peru to Chile. The **Museo Colonial San Francisco** ⓘ *by Iglesia San Francisco, Londres 4, T02-2639 8737, http://museosanfrancisco.com, Mon-Fri 0930-1330, 1500-1800, Sat-Sun 1000-1400, US$2,* houses religious art, including 54 paintings of the life of St Francis; in the cloisters is a room containing poet Gabriela Mistral's Nobel medal. South of San Francisco is the **Barrio París-Londres**, built 1923-1929, now restored. Two blocks north of the Alameda is **Teatro Municipal** ⓘ *C Agustinas 794, T02-2463 8888, www.municipal.cl,* renovated in 2014, which has programmes of opera, ballet, concerts and other events.

A little further west along the Alameda, is the **Universidad de Chile**; the **Club de la Unión** (www.clubdelaunion.cl), a National Monument, is almost opposite. Nearby, on Calle Nueva York is the **Bolsa de Comercio**; the public may view the trading; passport required. One block further west is **Plaza de la Libertad.** North of the plaza, hemmed in by the skyscrapers of the Centro Cívico, the **Presidential Palace** is housed in the **Palacio de la Moneda** (1805) ⓘ *T02-2690 4000, visitas@presidencia.cl for reservations, Mon-Fri for guided tours of the palace, for access to courtyards Mon-Fri 1000-1800, ceremonial changing of the guard every other day, 1000,* containing historic relics, paintings and sculpture, and the elaborate '**Salón Rojo**' used for official receptions. Although the Moneda was damaged by air attacks during the military coup of 11 September 1973, it has been fully restored. The large new **Centro Cultural Palacio La Moneda** ⓘ *T02-2355 6500, www. ccplm.cl, Tue-Sun 0900-2100, exhibitions Tue-Sun 0900-1930, US$9 for foreigners, US$4.50 for foreign students,* houses temporary exhibitions as well as an arts cinema and an interesting gallery of Chilean handicrafts.

West of the centre
South of the Alameda Five blocks south of the Alameda is the **Palacio Cousiño** ⓘ *C Dieciocho 438, www.palaciocousino.cl, Metro Toesca, closed due to earthquake damage, but you can tour the grounds.* This large mansion in French rococo style has a superb Italian marble staircase and other opulent items. A little further west and four blocks south of the Alameda is the **Museo de la Solidaridad Salvador Allende** ⓘ *Av República 475, T02-2689 8761, www.mssa.cl, Tue-Sun 1000-1800, US$2, Sun free,* which houses a highly regarded collection of 20th-century works donated by Chilean and other artists (Picasso, Miró, Matta and many more) who sympathized with the Allende government, plus some personal items of the president himself. The contents were hidden during the Pinochet years.

Parque O'Higgins ⓘ *10 blocks south of Alameda; take Metro Line 2 to Parque O'Higgins station, bus from Parque Baquedano via Av MacKenna and Av Matta.* It has a small lake, tennis courts, swimming pool (open from 5 December), an open-air stage, a club, the racecourse of the **Club Hípico** and an amusement park, **Fantasilandia** ⓘ *www. fantasilandia.cl, daily in summer, winter weekends only 1200-1900, US$18, US$9 children and seniors, families US$22.55, unlimited rides.* There are also about 20 basic restaurants, craft shops, and two small museums: **Acuario Municipal** ⓘ *Local 9, T02-2556 5680, daily 1000-2000, small charge*; **Museo de Insectos y Caracoles** ⓘ *Local 12, daily 1000-2000, small charge,* with a collection of insects and shellfish.

Barrio Brasil to Parque Quinta Normal **Barrio Brasil**, with **Plaza Brasil** at its heart and the **Basílica del Salvador** two blocks from the plaza, is one of the earliest parts of the city. It has some fine old buildings, especially around Calle Concha y Toro, but now it's a more bohemian, studenty area with lots of places to stay as well as numerous bars, clubs, cafés and lively restaurants (Metro República). The next barrio west, Yungay, is in much the same vein, with many once elegant buildings, a leafy plaza and, today, a lot of street art. Visit the historic **Peluquería Francesa** ① *Compañía y Libertad, www.boulevardlavaud.cl*, which houses a barber's shop dating from 1868, a restaurant, deli and antiques.

The Alameda, meanwhile, continues west to the **Planetarium** ① *Alameda 3349, T02-2T02-2718 2900, www.planetariochile.cl, US$7*. Opposite it on the southern side is the railway station (**Estación Central** or **Alameda**). On Avenida Matucana, running north from here, is the popular Parque Quinta Normal (at Avenida D Portales; you can walk from Brasil through Yungay to the park). It was founded as a botanical garden in 1830

3 Santiago west of centre

➡ **Santiago maps**
1 Santiago orientation, page 44
2 Santiago centre, page 46
3 **Santiago west of centre, page 48**
4 Bellavista & Lastarria, page 50
5 Providencia, page 52
6 Santiago metro, page 64

Where to stay
2 Conde de Ansúrez
3 Happy House Hostel
4 Hostal de Sammy
6 La Casa Roja
7 La Princesa Insolente
8 Moai Hostel
9 Res Mery
10 Tur Hotel Express

Restaurants
1 Club Santiago
2 Confitería Torres
3 El Hoyo
4 Fuente Mardoqueo

and now contains several museums. **Museo Ferroviario** ⓘ *www.corpdicyt.cl, Tue-Fri 1000-1800, Sat and Sun 1000-1900, US$1.50,* contains the former presidential stagecoach and steam engines built between 1884 and 1953, including a rare Kitson-Meyer. **Museo Nacional de Historia Natural** ⓘ *www.mnhn.cl, Tue-Sat 1000-1730, Sun and holidays 1100-1730,* was founded in 1830 and is one of Latin America's oldest museums. Housed in a neoclassical building, it has exhibitions on zoology, botany, mineralogy, anthropology and ethnography. Near the park is **Museo Artequín** ⓘ *Av Portales 3530, T02-2681 8656, www.artequin.cl, Tue-Fri 0900-1700, Sat-Sun 1100-1800, closed Feb, US$1.50.* Housed in the Chilean pavilion built for the 1889 Paris International Exhibition, it contains prints of famous paintings and activities and explanations of the techniques of the great masters. The Quinta Normal metro station has an underground cultural centre with theatres and a free art cinema (part of the Metro Arte project), which shows independent films. Some 200 m from the station is the **Biblioteca de Santiago** (public library, www. bibliotecasantiago.cl), in front of which is **Centro Cultural Matucana 100** (www. m100.cl), with several exhibition halls and a theatre. Across Avenida Matucana from Quinta Normal metro station is the **Museo de la Memoria de los Derechos Humanos** ⓘ *Av Matucana 501, T02-2597 9600, www. museodelamemoria.cl, Tue-Sun 1000-2000, free, audio guide for non-Spanish speakers,* a huge block covered in oxidized copper mesh suspended above an open space. On three floors it concentrates on the events and aftermath of 11 September 1973, with videos, testimonies, documents and other items. It also has information on human rights struggles worldwide and temporary exhibits, a gift shop and café.

5 Las Vacas Gordas
6 Los Buenos Muchachos
7 Los Chinos Ricos
8 Majestic
9 Ostras Azócar

Bellavista and Cerro San Cristobal

The **Bellavista district**, on the north bank of the Mapocho from Plaza Italia at the foot of Cerro San Cristóbal, is one of the main eating and nightlife districts in the old city. On its streets are restaurants and cafés, theatres, galleries and craft shops (most selling lapis lazuli on C Bellavista itself). You can cross the Mapocho by bridges from Baquedano or Salvador metro stations, or by a pedestrian bridge between the two which is adorned with hundreds of lovers' eternity padlocks. **La Chascona** ⓘ *F Márquez de la Plata 0192, Bellavista, T02-2777 8741, www.fundacionneruda.org, Tue-Sun 1000-1800, US$7.50 with audio tour,* was the house that the poet Pablo Neruda built for Matilde Urrutia, with whom he lived from 1955. It was wrecked during the 1973 coup, but Matilde restored it and lived there till her death in 1985.

Northwest of Bellavista, in the *barrio* of Recoleta, is the **Cementerio General** ① *www. cementeriogeneral.cl, to get there take any Recoleta bus from C Miraflores.* This cemetery contains the mausoleums of most of the great figures in Chilean history and the arts, including Violeta Parra, Víctor Jara and Salvador Allende. There is also an impressive monument to the victims, known as '*desaparecidos*' (disappeared) of the 1973-1990 military government.

The sharp, conical hill of **San Cristóbal**, to the northeast of the city, forms the **Parque Metropolitano** ① *www.parquemet.cl, daily 0900-2100, the main entrance is at Plaza Caupolicán at the northern end of C Pío Nono in Bellavista,* from where a **funicular**

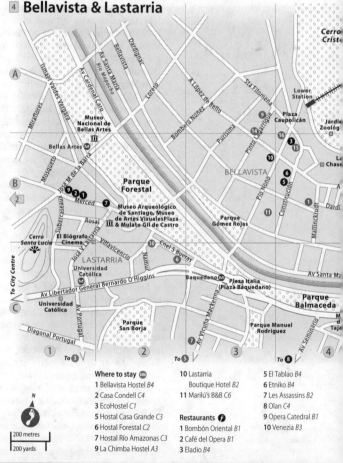

④ Bellavista & Lastarria

Where to stay
1 Bellavista Hostel *B4*
2 Casa Condell *C4*
3 EcoHostel *C1*
5 Hostal Casa Grande *C3*
6 Hostal Forestal *C2*
7 Hostal Río Amazonas *C3*
9 La Chimba Hostel *A3*
10 Lastarria
   Boutique Hotel *B2*
11 Marilú's B&B *C6*

Restaurants
1 Bombón Oriental *B1*
2 Café del Opera *B1*
3 Eladio *B4*
5 El Tablao *B4*
6 Etniko *B4*
7 Les Assassins *B2*
8 Olan *C4*
9 Opera Catedral *B1*
10 Venezia *B3*

ⓘ *daily 1000-1900, Mon 1300-1900, US$3.70 Mon-Fri, US$4.75 weekends return, US$2.75 and US$3.60 one way respectively; on the way up only you can get out at the zoo half way up, reductions for children,* runs to near the summit. Further east is an entrance from Pedro de Valdivia Norte, from where a teleférico used to run (no longer). Taxi-*colectivos* run to the summit and, in summer, to the swimming pools (see What to do, page 61); to get to Tupahue on foot from Pedro de Valdivia metro station is about 1 km. Vehicles have to pay to enter. It is the largest and most interesting of the city's parks. Souvenirs and snacks are sold at the top of the funicular. On the summit (300 m) stands a colossal statue of the Virgin, which is floodlit at night; beside it is the astronomical observatory of the Catholic University which can be visited on application to the observatory's director. Further east in the **Tupahue** sector there are terraces, gardens and paths; nearby is the **Casa de la Cultura Anahuac** which has art exhibitions and free concerts at midday on Sunday. There are two good swimming **pools** at Tupahue and Antilén. East of Tupahue are the **Botanical Gardens** ⓘ *daily 0900-1800, guided tours available*, with a collection of Chilean native plants.

Statue of
the Virgin

Upper Station
(Funicular)

**Parque
Metropolitano**

Sofía Concha

Arz Casanova

M Concha

Bellavista

To Providencia & Las

Andrés Bello

Av Providencia

Gral Salvo

Salvador

Av Eliodoro Yáñez

Av José
M Infante

To ⑪

⑤

& Ñuñoa

⑥

Bars & clubs 🎵
11 Patio Bellavista with
   Back Stage Life,
   La Casa en el Aire
   & many more *B4*
14 Jammin' Club *A3*
15 La Bodeguita de Julio *B4*
16 La Otra Puerta *B3*

East of the centre: Providencia and Las Condes

East of Plaza Italia, the main east–west axis of the city becomes **Avenida Providencia,** which heads out towards the residential areas in the eastern and upper areas of the city. Just beyond the centre it skirts **Parque Balmaceda** (Parque Gran Bretaña), perhaps the most beautiful in Santiago. The **Museo de los Tajamares** here ⓘ *Av Providencia 222, T02-2340 7329,* an exhibition of the 17th- and 18th-century walls and subsequent canalization developed to protect the city from flooding, was due to reopen in late 2014.

The neighbourhood of Providencia is a modern area of shops, offices, bars and restaurants around Pedro de Valdivia and Los Leones metro stations; it also contains the offices of **Sernatur**, the national tourist board. At Metro Tobalaba Avenida Providencia becomes **Avenida Apoquindo**. Here, in **El Bosque Norte**, there are lots more good, mid-range and expensive restaurants. Northeast of Providencia is the residential area of **Las Condes** and two worthwhile museums: **Museo Ralli** ⓘ *Sotomayor 4110, Vitacura, T02-2206 4224, www.museoralli.cl, Tue-Sun 1030-*

1700, Jan weekends only, closed Feb, free, has an excellent collection of works by modern European and Latin American artists, including Dali, Chagall, Bacon and Miró; **Museo de la Moda** ① *Vitacura 4562, Metro Escuela Militar, T02-2219 3623, www.museodelamoda.cl, Tue-Fri 1000-1800, Sat-Sun 1100-1900, US$7 including optional guided tour or audio tour, El Garage café Mon-Fri 1000-1800,* is South America's only fashion museum.

Other places of interest

Southeast of the centre, in La Florida district, is the excellent **Museo Interactivo Mirador** (**MIM**) ① *Punta Arenas 6711, Mirador Metro (Line 5), T02-2828 8000, www.mim.cl, Tue-Sun 0930-1830, US$7, concessions US$5,* a fun, interactive science and technology museum, perfect for a family outing. There is also an **aquarium** in the grounds.

A memorial to the troubled Pinochet era is in the southeastern suburb of Peñalolén, the **Parque por la Paz** ① *Av Arrieta 8401, http://villagrimaldi.cl; from Tobalaba Metro take any bus marked Peñalolén heading south down Tobalaba, get off at Tobalaba y José Arrieta and catch a bus, or walk 15-20 mins, up Arrieta towards the mountains.* It stands on the site of **Villa Grimaldi**, the most notorious torture centre. Audioguides are available in English

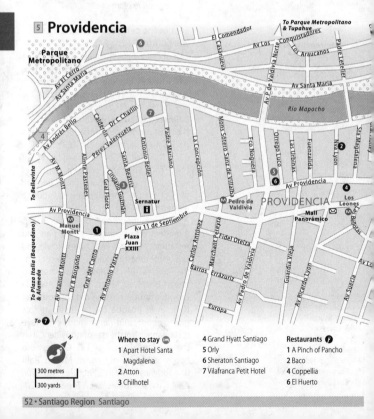

5 Providencia

Where to stay
1 Apart Hotel Santa Magdalena
2 Atton
3 Chilhotel
4 Grand Hyatt Santiago
5 Orly
6 Sheraton Santiago
7 Vilafranca Petit Hotel

Restaurants
1 A Pinch of Pancho
2 Baco
4 Coppellia
6 El Huerto

300 metres
300 yards

(leave passport at reception). The Irish missionary Sheila Cassidy documented the abuses that she underwent when imprisoned without trial in this place. The walls are daubed with human rights graffiti and the park makes for a moving and unusual introduction to the conflict that has eaten away at the heart of Chilean society for over 30 years.

The suburb of Maipú, 10 km southwest of Santiago, is a 45-minute bus ride from the Alameda, also reached from Plaza de Maipú metro station (Línea 5). Here, a monument marks the site of the Battle of the Maipú, 5 April 1818, which resulted in the final defeat of the Spanish royalist forces in mainland Chile. Nearby is the monolithic **National Votive Temple of Maipú** ① *Tue-Sun 1000-1830*. This is a fine example of modern architecture and stained glass (best viewed from the inside). It is located on the site of an earlier temple, built in 1818 on the orders of Bernardo O'Higgins to commemorate the battle. The walls of the old construction stand in the forecourt, having fallen into ruin due to successive earthquakes. Pope John Paul II gave a mass here on his visit to Chile in 1987. The **Museo del Carmen** ① *Tue-Fri 0930-1400, 1500-1700, http://museodelcarmen. blogspot.co.uk*, is part of the same building and contains carriages, furniture, clothing and other items from colonial times and later.

7 Oriental

Bars & clubs 🎧
8 Brannigan Pub

⊙ Santiago listings

For hotel and restaurant price codes and other relevant information, see pages 14-21.

⊜ Where to stay

Accommodation in Santiago is generally about 20% more expensive than elsewhere in the country. Check if breakfast is included in the price quoted. Most 3-, 4- and 5-star hotels do not charge the 19% tax to foreigners who pay in US$ cash. Hostels have double rooms with private or shared bath, **$$**, and dorms for US$13-18pp, **$**.

If you are staying for weeks or months rather than days, serviced apartments are available. Staying with a family is also an economical and interesting option. For private rentals, see the classified ads in *El Mercurio (www.impresa.elmercurio.com)* – where flats, homes and family *pensiones* are listed by district – or in www.elRastro.cl, or try the noticeboard at the tourist office. Rates for 2-bed furnished apartments in a reasonable neighbourhood start at around US$350 per month. A month's rent and a month's deposit are normally required. Some offer daily and weekly lets. Estate agents handle apartments.

Santiago centre *p43, maps p46 and p50*

$$$$-$$$ Fundador, Paseo Serrano 34, T02-2387 1200, www.hotelfundador.cl. Helpful, charming, stylish, good location, pool, spa, bar, restaurant.

$$$$-$$$ Galerías, San Antonio 65, T02-2470 7400, www.hotelgalerias.cl. Excellent, large rooms, generous breakfast, good location, welcoming.

$$$-$$ París-Londres, Londres 54, T02-2638 2215, www.londres.cl. 1920s mansion with original features in perfect location near San Francisco church, pleasant common rooms, laundry service, usually full, advance bookings in high season.

$$$-$ Andes Hostel, Monjitas 506, T02-2632 9990, www.andeshostel.com. In Bellas Artes neighbourhood, dorms, rooms or apartments, bar downstairs with pool table, barbecue nights on roof terrace, well run.

$$$-$ Casaltura, San Antonio 811, T02-2633 5076, www.casaltura.com. 'Boutique hostel', up a long wooden staircase in a renovated house, roof terrace, comfortable and convenient, private rooms and dorms, attentive staff.

$$ París, París 813, T02-2664 0921, carbott@latinmail.com. Great location, good meeting place, 3 standards of room, breakfast extra, Wi-Fi available in some parts. Phone in advance in summer.

Plaza Italia, Lastarria and around

$$$$ Lastarria Boutique Hotel, Cnel Santiago Bueras 188, T02-2840 3700, www.lastarriahotel.com. In a converted 1927 building, beautifully decorated, spacious rooms, with personalized service. Lounge for breakfast and light meals, cocktails and wines, garden, swimming pool.

$$$ Hostal Río Amazonas, Plaza Italia, Vicuña Mackenna 47, T02-2635 1631, www.hostalrioamazonas.cl. In a restored mansion, good value, helpful, lots of information, parking.

$$$-$$ Hostal Casa Grande, Vicuña MacKenna 90, T02-2222 7347, Baquedano metro, www.hostalcasagrande.cl.

Labyrinthine, old high-ceilinged building, colourful, pleasant patio garden, quiet.

$$ EcoHostel, Gral Jofré 349B, T02-2222 6833, www.ecohostel.cl. Popular with groups, comfortable beds, well run, smoking patio, tours arranged.

$$-$ Hostal Forestal, Cnel Santiago Bueras 120, T02-2638 1347, www.hostal forestal.cl. On a quiet side street near the Plaza Italia. Comfy lounge with big screen TV, barbecue area, pool table, information, English spoken.

West of the centre *p47, map p48*

$$$ Conde de Ansúrez, Av República 25, T02-2696 0807, República metro, www.ansurez.cl. Convenient for airport bus, central station and bus terminals, helpful, safe.

$$$ Tur Hotel Express, O'Higgins 3750, p 3, in the Turbus Terminal, T02-2685 0100, www.turbus.cl. Comfortable business standard. Useful if you need to take an early flight as buses leave for the airport from here. There is an Ibis hotel here, too.

$$ Residencial Mery, Pasaje República 36, off 0-100 block of República, T02-2699 4982, http://residencialmery.cl. Big green art deco building down an alley, most rooms without bath, all with single beds, quiet, breakfast extra.

$$-$ Happy House Hostel, Moneda 1829, Barrio Brasil, T02-2688 4849, www.happyhousehostel.cl. In a restored mansion with all mod-cons. One of the best hostels in the city, spacious kitchen and common areas, pool table, bar, spa, free tea and real coffee all day, book exchange, English and French spoken, lots of information.

$$-$ Hostal de Sammy, Toesca 2335, T02-2689 8772, www.hostaldesammy.com. Good-value US-run hostel with decent common areas, table tennis, pool table, big-screen TV with hundreds of films. Good info, helpful.

$$-$ La Casa Roja, Agustinas 2113, Barrio Brasil, T02-2696 4241, www.lacasaroja.cl. Huge, renovated mansion, dorms and private rooms, no breakfast, pool party on

Sat, guests can be chef for the night, live music, 2 bars, cricket net, lots of activities and tours, Spanish classes, lively. Shares services with **La Princesa Insolente**, below.
$$-$ Moai Hostel, Toesca 2335, T02-2723 6499, www.moaiviajerohostel.cl. Airport transfer, book exchange, film library, Spanish classes arranged, gay-friendly, popular. 5 blocks from República metro.
$ La Princesa Insolente, Moneda 2350, T02-2671 6551, www.princesainsolente hostel.cl. Shared rooms and 1 private room (**$$$**), organic café, mountain bike rental, has apartments opposite, travel information. Also has hostels in Pichilemu and Pucón, surfing with www. deepconnection.cl. In same group as **La Casa Roja**, above.

Bellavista and Cerro San Cristóbal *p49, map p50*
$$-$ Bellavista Hostel, Dardignac 0184, T02-2899 7145, www.bellavista.hostel.com. European-style, sheets provided but make your own bed, good fun hostel in the heart of this lively area. Guests over 35 not allowed in dorms, only private rooms.
$ pp La Chimba Hostel, Ernesto Pinto Lagarrigue 262, Bellavista, T02-2899 7145, www.lachimba.hostel.com. Popular backpacker hostel with good facilities.

East of the centre *p51, maps p50 and p52*
$$-$ Casa Condell, Condell 114, T02-2209 2343, Salvador metro. Pleasant old house, central, quiet, nice roof-terrace, free local phone calls, English spoken, good but baths shared between rooms can be a problem.
$$ Marilú's Bed and Breakfast, Rafael Cañas 246, T02-2235 5302, www.bed andbreakfast.cl. Comfortable, quiet, convenient, some rooms with shared bath with 1 other room, good beds, English and French spoken, secure, very helpful and welcoming, lots of information.

Providencia and Las Condes
For longer-stay accommodation, contact **Apart Hotel Santa Magdalena**, Helvecia 240 L3, Las Condes, T02-2374 6875, www.santamagdalena.cl, which has well-serviced apartments.
$$$$ Grand Hyatt Santiago, Av Kennedy 4601, Las Condes, T02-2950 1234, http://santiago.grand.hyatt.com. Superb, beautifully decorated, large outdoor pool, gym, 3 restaurants.
$$$$ Sheraton Santiago, Santa María 1742, T02-2233 5000, www.sheraton.cl. One of the best, good restaurant, good buffet lunch, and all facilities.
$$$$-$$$ Atton, Alonso de Córdova 5199, Las Condes, T02-2422 7900, www.atton.cl.

Comfortable, very helpful, full disabled access. Has 2 other branches.

$$$ Orly, Pedro de Valdivia 027, Metro Pedro de Valdivia, T02-2231 8947, www.orlyhotel.com. Small, comfortable, convenient, **Cafetto** café attached with good value meals.

$$$ Vilafranca Petit Hotel, Pérez Valenzuela 1650, T02-2235 1413, www.vilafranca.cl. Manuel Montt metro. High end B&B, small but impeccable rooms, quiet, cosy, pleasant garden, English spoken.

$$$-$$ Chilhotel, Cirujano Guzmán 103, T02-2264 0643, metro Manuel Montt, www.chilhotel.cl. Small, comfortable, family-run, airport transfer.

🍴 Restaurants

For good seafood restaurants go to the **Mercado Central** (by Cal y Canto Metro, lunches only, including **Donde Augusto**, www.dondeaugusto.cl, **El Galeón**, www.elgaleon.cl, and others; www.mercadocentral.cl), or the **Vega Central** market on the opposite bank of the Mapocho, or Av Cumming and C Reyes in Barrio Brasil. It is difficult to eat cheaply in the evening apart from fast food, so if you're on a tight budget, make the lunchtime *almuerzo* your main meal.

Santiago centre *p43, maps p46 and p50*
$$$-$$ Majestic, Santo Domingo 1526, T02-2694 9400, in hotel of same name ($$$, www.hotelmajestic.cl). Excellent Indian restaurant, with a good range of vegetarian dishes.

$$$-$$ Opera Catedral, Jose Miguel de la Barra 407, Bellas Artes metro, T02-2664 3038, www.operacatedral.cl. Very good, if expensive, French restaurant on the ground floor. Upstairs is a minimalist pub-restaurant, usually packed at night, serving fusion food at reasonable prices.

$$ Faisán d'Or, Plaza de Armas. Good *pastel de choclo*, pleasant place to watch the world go by.

$$ Lung Fung, Agustinas 715 (downstairs). Delicious oriental food, the oldest Chinese restaurant in Santiago.

$ Bar Nacional No 2, Bandera 317. Popular, local specialities, big portions; also at Huérfanos 1151 (No 1).

$ Confitería Torres, Alameda 1570. Traditional bar/restaurant, good ambience, live music Fri-Sat.

$ El Naturista, Moneda 846 and Huérfanos 1046. Excellent vegetarian, "healthy portions", wide-ranging menu, as well as juices, beer and wine, closes 2100.

$ El Rápido, Bandera 347, next to Bar Nacional No 2. Specializes in *empanadas* and *completos*, good food, good fun.

Cafés
Café Caribe and **Café Haití**, both on Paseo Ahumada and elsewhere in centre and Providencia. Good coffee, institutions for the Santiago business community.

Café Colonia, MacIver 133 and 161. Splendid variety of cakes, pastries and pies, fashionable and pricey.

Café del Opera, Merced 391. For breakfasts, sandwiches, salads, ice creams and breads.

Plaza Italia, Lastarria and around *p45, map p50*
On C Lastarria are many smart eateries, several in the precinct at Lastarria 70: also **Sur Patagónico**, **Victorino**, **El Callejón de Mesías**, **El Observatorio** and **Zabo**. **El Biógrafo** cinema also has a café.

$$$ Les Assassins, Merced 297, T02-2638 4280. Good French cuisine in small, family-run bistro, with decent wine list; good-value set lunches.

$$$-$$ Los Adobes del Argomedo, Argomedo 411 y Lira, 10 blocks south of the Alameda, T02-2222 2104, www.losadobesde argomedo.cl. Long-established traditional restaurant. Good Chilean food, floor show (Mon-Sat) includes *cueca* dancing, salsa and folk.

$$-$ Bombón Oriental, Merced 333 and 355, Lastarria, T02-2639 1069. Serves Middle

Eastern food, Turkish coffee, arabic snacks and sweets.

West of the centre *p47, map p48*
$$$-$$ Las Vacas Gordas, Cienfuegos 280, Barrio Brasil, T02-2697 1066. Good-value grilled steaks, nice wine selection, very popular, book in advance.
$$ Club Santiago, Erasmo Escala 2120, www.clubsantiago.cl. Open 1230-0100, happy hour 1700-2200. Historic restaurant/bar in Concha y Toro district, lunches, snacks, cocktails.
$$ El Hoyo, San Vicente 375, T02-2689 0339. Closed Sun. Celebrated 100-yr-old *chichería* serving hearty Chilean fare.
$$ Fuente Mardoqueo, Libertad 551, www.fuentemardoqueo.cl. Daily 1200-2300. Simply sandwiches, with a limited choice of fillings, and beer, a wide range, popular.
$$ Los Buenos Muchachos, Cumming 1031, T02-2566 4660, www.losbuenos muchachos.cl. Cavernous hall seating over 400 serving plentiful traditional Chilean food, traditional Chilean dance shows at night. Very popular.
$$ Los Chinos Ricos, Brasil 373, www.loschinos ricos.cl. Good Chinese, popular with families on Sun lunchtime.
$$ Ostras Azócar, Gral Bulnes 37, www.ostrasazocar.cl. Good prices for oysters. Other seafood places in same street.

Bellavista and Cerro San Cristóbal *p49, map p50*
Bellavista is full of restaurants, cafés and bars too, particularly C Dardignac and Patio Bellavista, the block between Dardignac, Pío Nono, Bellavista and Constitución.
$$$-$$ Etniko, Constitición 172, Bellavista, T02-2732 0119, www.etniko.cl. Fusion restaurant with oriental influences and seafood, also tapas bar/*cevichería* and dance floor under transparent roof for night sky, live DJs at weekends.
$$ El Tablao, Constitución 110, T02-2737 8648. Traditional Spanish restaurant. The food is reasonable but the main

attraction is the live flamenco show on Fri-Sat nights.
$$ Eladio, Pío Nono 251. Good steaks, Argentine cuisine, excellent value, also has bingo.
$$ Venezia, Pío Nono, corner of López de Bello. Huge servings of traditional Chilean home-cooked fare (allegedly one of Neruda's favourite haunts), good value.
$$-$ Olan, Seminario 96A-B. Excellent value, tasty Peruvian food in unpretentious surroundings. Another branch at No 67, slightly higher prices.

Providencia *p51, map p52*
$$$-$$ A Pinch of Pancho, Gral del Canto 45, T02-2235 1700. Very good fish and seafood on a wide-ranging menu.
$$$-$$ Baco, Nueva de Lyon 113, T02-231 4444. Metro Los Leones. Sophisticated French restaurant, good food, extensive wine list with many quality wines available by the glass.
$$$-$$ Oriental, Manuel Montt 584. Excellent Chinese, one of the best in Santiago.
$$ El Huerto, Orrego Luco 054, **Providencia**, T02-2233 2690. Vegetarian. Open daily, varied menu, very good.

Cafés
For snacks and ice cream there are several good places on Av Providencia including **Coppellia**, No 2211, **Bravissimo**, No 1406. There are lots of cafés and some restaurants in the passageways at Metro Los Leones and in the streets nearby, including **Café di Roma**, **The Coffee Factory**, **Sebastián**, Fuenzalida 26, and **Salón de Té Tavelli**, drugstore precinct, Av Providencia 2124.

Las Condes *p51*
This area has many first-class restaurants, including grills, serving Chilean (often with music), French and Chinese cuisine. They tend to be more expensive than central restaurants. Many are located on El Bosque Norte, near Tobalaba metro stop.

$$$-$$ Miguel Torres, Isidora Goyenechea 2874, T02-2245 7332, http://restaurante migueltorres.cl. Tapas bar owned by the well-known Spanish winery.
$$$-$$ Puerto Marisko, Isidora Goyenechea 2918, T02-2233 2096, www. restaurantmariscos.cl. Renowned for seafood but also serves pasta and meat dishes, over 20 years of experience.

🎵 Bars and clubs

For all entertainments, nightclubs, cinemas, theatres, restaurants, concerts, **El Mercurio Online** website has all listings and a good search feature, www.emol.com. Listings in weekend newspapers, particularly *El Mercurio* and *La Tercera*. Also *Santiago What's On*. For an organized night out, contact **Santiago Pub Crawl**, T09-7165 9977, www.santiagopubcrawl.com, US$20, every Thu, Fri and Sat.

West of the centre *p47, map p48*
There are a number of bars and restaurants dotted around the Plaza Brasil and on Avs Brasil and Cumming, popular with Chilean students (Metro República).

Bellavista *p49, map p50*
Bellavista has a good selection of varied restaurants, bars and clubs (Metro Baquedano).
Back Stage Life, Patio Bellavista. Good-quality live jazz and blues.
Jammin' Club, Antonia López de Bello 49. Reggae.
La Bodeguita de Julio, Constitución 256. Cuban staff and Cuban cocktails, excellent live music and dancing possible, very popular, free entry before 2300, very good value.
La Casa en el Aire, Patio Bellavista. Pleasant atmosphere, live music.
La Otra Puerta, Pío Nono 348. Lively salsoteca with live music.

East of the centre *p51, maps p50 and p52*
The 1st couple of blocks of Román Díaz (between metros Salvador and Manuel Montt) have a collection of bars and eateries, eg **Kleine Kneipe**, No 21, also in Ñuñoa, www.kleinekneipe.cl, and **Santo Remedio**, No 152. In Providencia, Av Suecia and Av Gral Holley are popular and largely pedestrianized. From Av Providencia, Condell leads to the middle class suburb of Ñuñoa, 18 blocks, passing various small bars and restaurants on the way, eg at junctions with Rancagua and Santa Isabel, or take metro to Irarrázaval. Plaza Ñuñoa itself has a number of good bars. There are also many smart places in Las Condes.
Brannigan Pub, Suecia 35, T02-2232 7869. Good beer, live jazz, lively.
Golden Bell Inn, Hernando de Aguirre 27. Popular with expats.
Ilé Habana, Bucaré just off Suecia. Bar with salsa music, often live, and a good dance floor.

🎭 Entertainment

Santiago *p40, maps p44, p46, p48, p50 and p52*
Cinemas
There's a good guide to cinema in the free newspaper *publimetro*, given out at metro stations on weekday mornings. 'Ciné Arte' (quality foreign films) is popular. Many multiplex cinemas across the city show mainstream releases, nearly always in the original English with subtitles. Seats cost US$4-7 with reductions on Mon, Tue and Wed (elsewhere in the country the day varies). Some cinemas offer discounts to students and over 60s (proof required).

Theatres
Teatro Municipal, Agustinas y San Antonio, www.municipal.cl. Stages international opera, concerts by the Orquesta Filarmónica de Santiago, and the Ballet de Santiago, throughout the year. The full range of events

and ticket prices is given on the website. Some cheap seats are often sold on the day of concerts. Free classical concerts are sometimes given in **San Francisco** church in summer. Arrive early for a seat.
Teatro Municipal de Nuñoa, Av Irarrázaval 1564, T02-2277 7903, www.ccn.cl. Dance, art exhibitions, cinema, children's theatre.
Teatro Universidad de Chile, Plaza Baquedano, T02-2978 2480, www. ceacuchile.com, is the home of the Orquesta y Coro Sinfónica de Chile and the Ballet Nacional de Chile. There are a great number of theatres which stage plays in Spanish, either in the original language or translations.

⊛ Festivals

Santiago *p40, maps p44, p46, p48, p50 and p52*
Religious festivals and ceremonies continue throughout **Holy Week**, when a priest washes the feet of 12 men. The image of the **Virgen del Carmen** (patron of the Armed Forces) is carried through the streets by cadets on **16 Jul**. On **Independence Day**, **18 Sep**, many families get together or celebrate in *fondas* (small temporary constructions made of wood and straw where people eat traditional dishes, drink *chicha* and dance *cueca*). During **Nov** there is a **free art fair** in the Parque Forestal on the banks of the Río Mapocho, lasting a fortnight.

⊙ Shopping

Santiago *p40, maps p44, p46, p48, p50 and p52*
Bookshops
Book prices are high compared with neighbouring countries and Europe. There are several bookshops in and around the Drugstore precinct off Av Providencia 2124 between La Urbinas and Fuen zalida, including **Feria Chilena del Libro**, www. feriachilenadellibro.cl, with many other

branches, good for travel books and maps.
LOM Ediciones, Concha y Toro 23, www. lom.cl, large stock from its own publishing house (literature, history, sociology, art, politics), also bar and reading room with recent Chilean papers and magazines.

Camping and outdoor equipment
There are a number of 'hunting' shops on Bulnes 1-2 blocks south of the Alameda, with a basic range of outdoor equipment.
Andes Gear, Helvecia 210, Las Condes, T02-2245 7076, www.andesgear.cl. Good range of quality clothes and equipment. Imported camping goods from **Club Andino** and **Federación de Andinismo** (see page 60).
La Cumbre, Av Apoquindo 5220, T02-2220 9907, www.lacumbreonline.cl. Mon-Fri 1100-2000, Sat 1100-1600. Dutch-run, very helpful, good climbing and trekking equipment.
Lippi, http://lippioutdoor.com. With several branches. Chile's premier outdoor equipment maker. Excellent-quality clothes, boots, tents, etc.
Mountain Service, Paseo Las Palmas 2209, Local 016, T02-2234 3439, Providencia. English spoken, tents, stoves, clothing, equipment rental.
Parafernalia, Huérfanos 1973 y Brasil, also in Drugstore precinct, Providencia, http://parafernaliaoutdoor.cl. New and second-hand gear.
Peregrin, del Arzobispo 0607, Bellavista, T02-2735 1587, see Facebook. Salvador metro. Decent-quality locally made outdoor clothes.
Tatoo Adventure Gear, Av Los Leones 81, Providencia, and MallSport, Las Condes 13451, www.tatoo.ws, has all the best brands of outdoor gear.

Crafts
For good-quality crafts go to Pomaire· (see page 67), where items from all over Chile are for sale at competitive prices. The gemstone, lapis lazuli, can be found

in a few expensive shops in Bellavista but is cheaper in the arcades on the south side of the Plaza de Armas. Other craft stalls can be found in an alleyway 1 block south of Av O'Higgins between A Prat and Serrano; on the 600 to 800 blocks of Santo Domingo and at Pío Nono y Av Santa María in Bellavista.

Centro Artesanal Santa Lucía, Santa Lucía metro, south exit. Generic *artesanía*. Lapis lazuli can be bought here cheaply. Also has a wide variety of woollen goods, jewellery, etc.

Centro Artesanal Los Domínicos, Apoquindo 9805, Las Condes, www.cultural lascondes.cl. Metro Los Domínicos. The best upmarket craft fair in Chile. A good range of modern and traditional Chilean crafts from ceramics to textiles, a pleasant central piazza, places where the artisans can be seen working on wood, silver, glass and so on, cafés, toilets, information.

Markets

Mercado Central, between Puente y 21 de Mayo by the Río Mapocho (Cal y Canto Metro) is excellent for fish and seafood. There is a cheaper market, the **Vega Central**, on the opposite bank of the river. The **Bío Bío** flea market on C Bío Bío, Metro Franklin (follow crowds), on Sat and Sun morning is huge; everything under the sun, lots of it having fallen off the back of a lorry.

Wine

El Mundo del Vino, Isidora Goyenechea 3000, T02-2584 1173, www.elmundodel vino.cl. For all types of Chilean wines, good selection across the price range; also in the Alto Las Condes, Parque Arauco and Costanera Center malls.

Vinopolis, El Bosque Norte 038 and Pedro de Valdivia 036. Mon-Fri 0900-2300, Sat 1000-2300, Sun 1000-2200. Also at airport. Sells all types of Chilean wines, good selection across all the prices.

⚙ What to do

Santiago *p40, maps p44, p46, p48, p50 and p52*

Cricket

There is a burgeoning cricket league based around Santiago, see www.cricketchile.cl for more information. **La Casa Roja** hostel, see above, has a cricket net on its premises.

Cycling

For parts and repairs go to C San Diego, south of the Alameda. The 800 and 900 blocks have scores of bike shops with spare parts, new models and repairs.

Football

Colo Colo play at the **Estadio Monumental** (reached by any bus to Puente Alto; tickets from Av Monumental 5300, Macul, T02-2294 7300), **Universidad de Chile**, play at Estadio Nacional, Av Grecia 2001, Ñuñoa, Ñuble metro, line 5 (tickets from Av General Miranda 2094, Ñuñoa), and **Universidad Católica** play at San Carlos de Apoquindo, reached by bus from Metro Escuela Militar, tickets from Andrés Bello 2782, Providencia, T02-2231 2777.

Skiing and climbing

Club Alemán Andino, El Arrayán 2735, T02-2232 4338, www.dav.cl. Tue and Fri, 1800-2000, May-Jun.

Club Andino de Chile, Av Lib O'Higgins 108, clubandino@ski lagunillas.cl. Ski club (open 1900-2100 on Mon and Fri).

Federación de Andinismo de Chile, Almte Simpson 77, T02-2222 0888, www.feach.cl. Daily (frequently closed Jan/Feb), has the addresses of all the mountaineering clubs in the country and runs a mountaineering school.

Skitotal, Apoquindo 4900, of 40-46, T02-2246 0156, www.skitotal.cl, for 1-day excursions and good value ski hire. Equipment hire is much cheaper in Santiago than in ski resorts. For ski resorts in the Santiago area see below.

Soccer nation

Football arrived in Chile towards the end of the 19th century, courtesy of the British. The role of British workers – most of whom were employed in the construction of the railway system – is reflected in the names of several of the leading teams, notably Santiago Wanderers (who are based in Valparaíso), Everton (based in Viña) and Rangers (based in Talca). The game's popularity grew rapidly; by the 1940s most large towns boasted their own team and stadium. In 1962, Chile's importance as a soccer nation was recognized internationally when it hosted the World Cup and the national side finished third. The quarter final between Chile and Italy became known as the 'Battle of Santiago', one of the most vicious games in the sport's history (Chile won 2-1).

Although Chilean football may not enjoy the worldwide recognition given to Argentina and Brazil, Chileans follow 'the beautiful game' with as much passion as their illustrious neighbours. Indeed, in the 2014 Fifa World Cup in Brazil, it took a penalty shoot-out for Brazil to defeat the Chilean squad in the first knock-out stage following a 1-1 draw after extra time.

The local season is currently split into two tournaments, the *apertura* running in the second half of the year and the *clausura* in the first half of the following year (the format changes every so often; see www.futbolchileno. com). Most of the support (and money) goes to the big three clubs, all based in Santiago: Universidad de Chile (known as 'La U'), Colo-Colo and Universidad Católica (which tends to be favoured by the well-off). The greatest rivalry is between La U and Colo-Colo (who are also known as Los Indios, as their strip carries an image of the great Mapuche leader after whom they were named). The most fervent supporters of the former are known as *los de abajo* (the underdogs), while those of the latter are called *la garra blanca* (the white claw).

A visit to a match, especially either an international game or a *clásico* (local derby), is an unforgettable experience. Watching football is still very much a family affair and the supporters dance, sing and wave their team colours beneath a non-stop rain of confetti, fireworks and coloured smoke. Cheap tickets cost around US$12.50 (you must present identification along with your ticket when you arrive at the ground).

Swimming

In Parque Metropolitano, Cerro San Cristóbal: **Antilén**, summer Wed-Mon 1000-1900, US$11, fine views, and **Tupahue**, large pool with cafés, Tue-Sun 1000-1900, entry US$9 but worth it (check if they are open in winter, one usually is). In **Parque O'Higgins**, T02-2556 9612, 1330-1830 summer only, US$4. Olympic pool in **Parque Araucano** (near Parque Arauco Shopping Centre, Metro Escuela Militar), Nov-Mar Tue-Sat 0900-1900.

Tour operators

A number of agencies offer walking tours of the city and others day trips from Santiago. Typical excursions are to the Wine Valleys, US$42-90 (by bike if you wish), Isla Negra (Pablo Neruda's seaside villa) US$72, visits to nearby haciendas and adventure tours such as whitewater rafting, rock climbing or trekking in the Cajón del Maipo, southeast of the city. Many agencies advertise in the **Sernatur** tourist office (see above).

Adventure tours **Altue**, Coyancura 2270, Of 801, Providencia, T02-2333 1390, www.altue.com. For wilderness trips including tour of Patagonia.

Azimut 360, Gral Salvo 159, Providencia, T02-2235 3085, www.azimut360.com. Adventure and ecotourism including mountaineering.

Cascada Expediciones, Don Carlos 3227C, Las Condes, T02-2923 5950, www.cascada. travel. Activity tours in remote areas.

Chile Excepción, T02-2951 5476, www.chile-excepcion.com. French/ Argentine agency offering tailor-made, upper end tours, fly-drives, themed trips and other services.

Chile Off Track, T02-2979 0251, 9133 4083, www.chileofftrack.com. Customized and tailor-made tours around Santiago and in Patagonia, 6 languages spoken, features include horse riding, mountain excursions, wine tours, visits to hot springs.

Santiago Adventures, T02-2244 2750, www.santiagoadventures.com. US-run, offering adventure day tours, wine tours, city tours, skiing and Patagonia.

Travel Art, Europa 2081, T02-2378 3494, http://chile-reise.com. Biking, hiking and multi-active tours throughout Chile. German-run.

City tours **La Bicicleta Verde**, Loreto 6 esq Santa María, T02-2570 9338, www. labicicletaverde.com. Sightseeing tours around the capital and of vineyards by bike. Also rents bicycles.

Spicy Chile, www.spicychile.cl. 3 walking tours of the city, Mon-Sat, pay by tip, good reputation.

Tours4Tips, T02-2737 5649, www. tours4tips.com. 2 daily walking tours, pay by tip, also in Valparaíso, popular.

Turismo Reportaje, Candelaria Goyenechea 3983, dpto 503, Vitacura, T09-6551 2429, www.turismoreportaje.com. City walking tours with emphasis on history, pay by tip.

Turistik, T02-2820 1000, www.turistik.cl. Hop-on, hop-off bus tours of the city,

US$47, also offers tours outside the city and tour, dinner and show.

⊖ Transport

Santiago *p40, maps p44, p46, p48, p50, p52 and p64*

Air
International and domestic flights leave from **Arturo Merino Benítez Airport** at Pudahuel, 26 km northwest of Santiago. For terminal and onward transport information, see Arriving in Santiago, page 41. For flight information, see Essentials, pages 6 and 10.

Bus
Long distance There are frequent, and good, interurban buses to all parts of Chile. Take a look at the buses before buying the tickets (there are big differences in quality among bus companies); ask about the on-board services, many companies offer drinks for sale, or free, and luxury buses have meals, videos, headphones. Reclining seats are standard and there are also *salón cama* sleeper buses. Fares are given in the text. On Fri evening, when night departures are getting ready to go, the terminals can be chaotic. There are 5 bus terminals:

1) Terminal Alameda, which has a modern extension called Mall Parque Estación with good left luggage (US$3.40 per day), ATMs and internet, O'Higgins 3712, Metro Universidad de Santiago, T02-2776 2424. All **Pullman-Bus** and **Tur-Bus** services go from here, they serve almost every destination in Chile, good quality but prices a little higher than others. **Tur-Bus** also has booking offices at Universidad de Chile and Tobalaba metro stations, at Cal y Canto, at Av Apoquindo 6421, T02-2212 6435, and in the Parque Arauco and Alto Las Condes malls for those beginning their journeys in Las Condes.

2) Terminal Santiago, O'Higgins 3878, 1 block west of Terminal Alameda, T02-2376 1750, www.terminaldebusessantiago.cl,

Metro Universidad de Santiago. Services to all parts of southern Chile, including the only service to **Punta Arenas** (48 hrs). Also international departures. Has a Redbanc ATM.

3) **Terminal San Borja**, O'Higgins y San Borja, 1 block west of Estación Central, 3 blocks east of Terminal Alameda, Metro Estación Central (entrance is, inconveniently, via a busy shopping centre, Mall Arauco Estación), T02-2776 0645. Mainly departures to the Central Valley area, but also to **northern Chile**. Booking offices and departures organized according to destination.

4) **Terminal Los Héroes**, on Tucapel Jiménez, just north of the Alameda, Metro Los Héroes, T02-2420 0099. A smaller terminal with booking offices of 8 companies, to the north, the south and Lake District and some international services (Lima, Asunción, Montevideo, Buenos Aires, Bariloche, Mendoza).

5) **Metro Pajaritos** (Metro Línea 1), to **Valparaíso**, **Viña del Mar** and places on the central coast; airport shuttle buses call here. It can be more convenient to take a bus from here than from the central terminals. Some long-distance buses call at **Las Torres de Tajamar**, Providencia 1108, which is more convenient if you are planning to stay in Providencia. Check if student rates are available (even for non-students), or reductions for travelling same day as purchase of ticket; it is worth bargaining over prices, especially shortly before departure and out of summer season.

International buses Most services leave from **Terminal Santiago**, though there are also departures from **Terminal Los Héroes**. There are frequent bus and minibus services from **Terminal Santiago** through the Cristo Redentor tunnel to **Mendoza** in Argentina, 6-7 hrs, US$34-44, many companies, departures around 0800, 1200 and 1600, touts approach you in Terminal Santiago. Minibuses have shorter

waiting time at customs. Many of these services continue to **Buenos Aires**, 24 hrs, and many companies in Terminal Santiago have connections to other Argentine cities. For destinations like **Bariloche** or **Neuquén**, it is better make connections in Temuco or Osorno. To **Lima**, **Ormeño** (Terminal Santiago), Tue and Fri 0900, 51 hrs. It is cheaper to take a bus to Arica, a *colectivo* to Tacna, then bus to Lima.

Car hire

Prices vary a lot so shop around first. Tax of 19% is charged, usually included in price quoted. If possible book a car in advance. Information boards full of flyers from companies at airport and tourist office. A credit card is usually asked for when renting a vehicle. Many companies will not hire a car to holders of a driver's licence from a left-hand drive country unless they have an international licence.

Remember that in the capital driving is restricted according to licence plate numbers; look for notices in the street and newspapers. Main international agencies and others are available at the airport (see Essentials for web addresses). **Automóvil Club de Chile**, www.automovilclub.cl, car rental from head office, discount for members and members of associated motoring organizations. **Alameda**, Av Bernardo O'Higgins 4332, T02-2779 0609, www.alamedarentacar.cl, San Alberto Hurtado metro, line 1, also in the airport, good value. **Rosselot**, call centre T02-2314 0366, www.rosselot.cl. Reputable Chilean firm with national coverage. **Verschae**, T600 5000 700, www2.verschae.com. Good value, branches throughout country.

Ferry and cruise operators

Navimag, Naviera Magallanes SA, Av El Bosque Norte 0440, p 11, Las Condes, T02-2442 3120, www.navimag.com. For services from **Puerto Montt** to **Puerto Chacabuco**, **Puerto Natales** and **Laguna San Rafael**. **M/n Skorpios**, Augusto Leguía Norte 118,

Las Condes, T02-2477 1900, www.skorpios.cl.
For luxury cruise out of **Puerto Montt** to
Laguna San Rafael and adventure trips
from Puerto Natales to Puerto Edén and
the Campo Hielo del Sur.

Metro

See www.metrosantiago.cl. The trains are
modern, fast, quiet, and very full at peak
times. The first train is at 0600 (Mon-Sat),
0800 (Sun and holidays), the last about
2300 (2330 on Fri-Sat, 2230 on Sun). Fares
vary according to time of journey; there are
3 charging periods, according to demand:
the peak rate is US$1.25, the general

rate US$1.15 and there is a cheaper rate
at unsociable hours, US$1. The simplest
solution is to buy a **tarjeta Bip** (see Local
buses, above), the charge card from which
the appropriate fare is deducted.

Taxi

Taxis (black with yellow roofs) are abundant
and fairly cheap: minimum charge of
US$0.35, plus US$0.20 per 200 m. In every
type of taxi always double check the
fare (see www.taximetro.cl). Drivers are
permitted to charge more at night, but in
the daytime check that the meter is set
to day rates. At bus terminals, drivers will

6 Santiago metro

→ **Santiago maps**
1 Santiago orientation, page 44
2 Santiago centre, page 46
3 Santiago west of centre, page 48
4 Bellavista & Lastarria, page 50
5 Providencia, page 52
6 Santiago metro, page 64

Line 1
Line 2
Line 4
Line 4a
Line 5
🚌 Bus terminal
🚆 Train station

Not to scale

charge more – best to walk a block and flag down a cruising taxi. Avoid taxis with more than one person in them especially at night. Various Radio Taxi services operate (eg **Radio Taxis Andes Pacífico**, T02-2912 6000, www.andespacifico.cl); rates are above those of city taxis but they should be more reliable.

Train
Trenes Metropolitanos, T600-585 5000, www.tmsa.cl, has details of services. All trains leave from **Estación Central (Alameda)** at O'Higgins 3322. **TerraSur** south to **Chillán** with 10 intermediate stops; **Metrotren** suburban route to **San Fernando**; **Expreso Maule** to **Talca**; **Buscarril** links **Talca**, **Maule**, **Pencahue** and **Constitución**. **Expreso del Recuerdo** is a tourist train to **San Antonio**, T02-2585 5991, www.tren.cl or www.efe.cl, 4 standards of coach, runs on special occasions only.
Booking offices Alameda O'Higgins 3170, daily 0650-2310; Universidad de Chile metro, loc 10, Mon-Fri 0900-2000, Sat 0900-1400 and others. Left luggage office at Estación Central, open till 2300. Schedules change with the seasons, so check timetables in advance. Summer services are booked up a week in advance.

⦿ Directory

Santiago *p40, maps p44, p46, p48, p50 and p52*
Banks Open 0900-1400, closed on Sat. Exchange rates are published in *El Mercurio* and *La Nación*. For Cirrus/MasterCard and Visa ATMs just look for the Redbanc sign, most commonly in banks, pharmacies or Copec petrol stations. *casas de cambio* (exchange houses) in the centre are mainly situated on Paseo Ahumada and Huérfanos (metro Universidad de Chile or Plaza de Armas). In Providencia several on Av Pedro de Valdivia. Some *casas de cambio* in the centre open Sat morning (but check first). Avoid street money

changers (particularly common on Ahumada, Bandera, Moneda and Agustinas): they pull any number of tricks, or will usually ask you to accompany them to somewhere obscure. The passing of forged notes and muggings are reported.
Embassies and consulates For all foreign embassies and consulates in Santiago de Chile, see http://embassy.goabroad.com. **Hospitals** Emergency hospital at Marcoleta 377, T02-2633 2051 (emergency), T02-2354 3266 (general enquiries). **Hospital del Salvador**, Av Salvador 334 or J M Infante 551, T02-2274 0093 emergency, T02-2340 4000 general, Mon-Thu 0800-1300 and 1330-1645, Fri 0800-1300 and 1330-1545 (has **Vacunatoria Internacional** at Salvador 467, 4 blocks south of Salvador metro). Also **Vacunatoria Internacional**, Hospital Luis Calvo, MacKenna, Antonio Varas 360. **Clínica Alemana**, Av Manquehue 1410, p 2, Vitacura, T02-2210 1301, pacienteinternacional@alemana.cl. **Clínica Central**, San Isidro 231-243, Santa Lucía metro, T02-2463 1400, open 24 hrs, German spoken. **Emergency pharmacy**, Portugal 155, Universidad Católica metro, T02-2631 3005. Consult www.farmaciasahumada.cl for other emergency pharmacies. **Note** If you need to get to a hospital, it is better to take a taxi than wait for an ambulance.
Language schools Bellavista, C del Arzobispado 0605, Providencia, T02-2732 3443, www.escuelabellavista.cl. Group and individual classes, lodging with families, free activities. **Escuela de Idiomas Violeta Parra**, Triana 853, Providencia, T02-2236 4241, www.tandemsantiago.cl. Courses aimed at budget travellers, information programme on social issues, arranges accommodation and visits to local organizations and national parks.
Natalislang Language Centre, Arturo Bürhle 047, Metro Baquedano, Providencia, T02-2222 8685, www.natalislang.com. Also has a branch in Valparaíso: Plaza Justicia 45, of 602, T032-225 4849. Many

¿Huevón, Señor?

If you spend any time in Chile, it is almost impossible not to come across *huevón*. This versatile word is used by all classes of Chilean society to describe a person. Literally meaning 'big egg', it is by turns an expression of endearment ('mate', 'buddy') and a slang expression of disgust ('idiot', 'fool'), and is used equally often in both senses. In some conversations, virtually every other word may seem to be *huevón*.

Legend has it that an expatriate living in Santiago a few years ago made the mistake of ordering a sandwich with *huevón* rather than *huevo* (egg). The waiter was so overcome that he had to finish his shift early. The hilarity with which mistakes of this sort are greeted can work to the visitor's advantage, however: tell any Chilean acquaintance that you have been to the shop to buy *huevón* and your friendship will be secured for life.

The use of *huevón* is symptomatic of the distinctiveness of Chilean Spanish, which has an unusually wide range of idioms and slang not used elsewhere in Latin America.

If you are serious about getting to grips with Chilean Spanish, several webpages give an introduction to Chilean colloquialisms, for instance: http://aricachile.wordpress.com/article/chilean-slang-made-easy-lyuza29o3r5u-8/ and www.thisischile.cl/2011/05/chilean-slang-from-a-to-z/?lang=en

private teachers, including **Lucía Araya Arévalo**, T02-2749 0706 (home), 2731 8325 (office), lusara5@hotmail.com. Speaks German and English. **Carolina Carvajal**, Av El Bosque Sur 151, dpto Q, Las Condes, T02-2734 7646, ccarvajal@interactiva.cl. Exchange library, internet access. **Patricio Ríos**, Tobalaba 7505, La Reina, T02-2226 6926. Speaks English. **Useful addresses**

Immigration To extend tourist visa, or any enquiries regarding legal status, go to **Departamento de Extranjería**, San Antonio 580, p 3, T600-486 3000, Mon-Fri 0900-1600, www.extranjeria.gob.cl. Expect long queues. Note that this can also be done at any provincial *extranjería* office. **Policia Internacional**: For lost tourist cards, see Accident and emergency, page 26.

Around Santiago

This region can be divided into three: to the east are the peaks of the Andes; to the west is the coastal range; and between is the Central Valley. On the eastern edge of the Central Valley lies Santiago, its more affluent suburbs spreading east into the foothills of the Andes. Some of the highest peaks in the range lie in this region: just over the border in Argentina, Aconcagua is the highest mountain in the world outside Asia, rising to 6964 m. There is a mantle of snow on all the high mountains, while the lower slopes are covered with forests. Between the forest and the snowline there are pastures; during the summer, cattle are driven up there to graze. In this area you can ski in winter, hike in summer and soothe your limbs in thermal springs year round. The less energetic may opt for a vineyard tour, sampling en route.

Pomaire
A small town 65 km west of Santiago, Pomaire is in a charming setting surrounded by high grassy hills dotted with algarrobo bushes. The town is famous for its clayware; the main street is full of shops selling dark clay pots and kitchenware, as well as diverse *artesanía* from all over Chile including fine basketwork from the Central Valley and some lovely items made from the *combarbalita* stone from the north. There are probably few better places in Chile in which to buy general souvenirs and presents (although bargaining is not really entered into); pottery can be bought and the artists can be observed at work, before visitors retire to any one of numerous restaurants serving traditional dishes such as *humitas*, giant *empanadas* and *pastel de choclo*.

Reserva Nacional Río Clarillo
① *Reached by paved road via Av Vicuña Mackenna to Puente Alto, where it continues as Av Concha y Toro, turn right at the T-junction where the road leads to El Principal after 2 km. Open all year. US$5.30.*
This reserve covers 10,185 ha and is situated 45 km southeast of Santiago in the *precordillera* at between 850 m and 3000 m. It offers excellent views of the higher mountains and of the surprisingly green pastures of the foothills. The information centre is at the entrance, 2 km southeast of El Principal. There are guided trails and wildlife, including the endangered Chilean iguana, salamanders and the rare bird, torcaza. The reserve is also the only remaining home to *sclerophyllous* (hard leaved) trees in central Chile. In summer it is very hot and horse flies are a nuisance. There are no places to stay and camping is forbidden. If you are in the city for a while it is a good place to get away from the bustle for a day.

Santuario de la Naturaleza Yerba Loca

ⓘ *Park administration office, Villa Paulina, 4 km north of Route G21, 25 km northeast of Santiago, T09-5628 4381, www.yerbaloca.cl, Sep-Apr, US$4.50.*

Reached via a *ripio* side road off the paved Route G21, 25 km northeast of Santiago towards Farellones, this park covers 39,000 ha of the valley of the Río Yerba Loca, ranging in altitude between 900 and 5500 m. It was founded in 1973. From the park administration office a four-hour walk leads north to **Casa de Piedra Carvajal**, which offers fine views. Further north are two hanging glaciers, **La Paloma** and **El Altar**. You may spot eagles and condors in the park. Native tree species include the mountain olive. Maps and information available from CONAF. There is no accommodation here.

Maipo Valley vineyards → *For listings, see pages 73-76.*

The Maipo Valley is considered by many experts to be the best wine-producing area in Chile. Several vineyards in the area can be visited and this makes a good excuse to get away from the smog. The following is a small selection of the better tours or wineries that are easily accessible:

Aquitania ⓘ *Av Consistoral 5090, Peñalolen, T02-2791 4500, www.aquitania.cl, bus D17 or taxi from metro Quilín.* Small vineyard making high-end wines, offering interesting tours in Spanish and English, with good tastings and fine views. Call in advance. Recommended.

Cousiño-Macul ⓘ *Av Quilín 7100, on the eastern outskirts of the city, T02-2351 4100, www.cousinomacul.cl, US$16, metro Quilín.* Tours in Spanish and poor English, Monday to Friday. Call in advance if you wish to visit. Guides tend to be rather disinterested.

Concha y Toro ⓘ *Virginia Subercaseaux 210, Pirque, near Puente Alto, 25 km south of Santiago, T02-2476 5000, www.conchaytoro.cl, US$16, metro to Las Mercedes, then taxi or colectivo.* Short tours (three a day in Spanish, four daily in English). Reserve two days in advance and enquire about the specific time of tours in your language of choice. Professional but very commercial. Has been described as the McDonalds of wine tours.

De Martino ⓘ *Manuel Rodríguez 229, Isla de Maipo, 40 km southwest of Santiago, T02-2819 2959, www.demartino.cl.* Quality tours in this high-end winery with a reputation for producing excellent carmenère. Book in advance. Lunch available for large groups.

Undurraga ⓘ *Santa Ana, 34 km southwest of Santiago, T02-2372 2900, wwwundurraga.cl, US$14.20.* Allows entry to vistors who have made a prior reservation. Three tours daily.

Viña Santa Rita ⓘ *Padre Hurtado 0695, Alto Jahuel, Buin, 45 km south of Santiago on the Camino a Padre Hurtado, T02-2362 2590, www.santarita.cl, US$17.75.* Good tours in English and Spanish; reserve in advance. The vineyard has a good restaurant and a private museum.

Cajón del Maipo → *For listings, see pages 73-76.*

This rugged and green valley southeast of Santiago provides an easy escape from the smog and bustle of Santiago. The valley is lined by precipitous mountains and the snows of the high Andes can easily be seen. There are many interesting and beautiful side tracks, such as that to Lagunillas (see page 71) or Los Maitenes, but the upper reaches of the valley around El Volcán and Baños Morales are amazingly deserted.

The road into the valley runs east from Puente Alto via Las Vizcachas, where the most important motor racing circuit in Chile is located, past **Centros Vacacionales** with a variety of activities and through many villages to the main town of **San José de Maipo**. Its historic centre has a walking route to visit the old station, the church and other sites.

There are places to eat, banks and other services; tourist office in the Municipalidad on the Plaza. The mountain town of **Melocotón** is 6 km south of San José de Maipo and 11 km from San José is **San Alfonso**. Near here is the Cascada de Animas waterfall (entry through a lodge and vacation centre, 1-1½ hours walk to falls, entry US$9-18 depending on season). Next is San Gabriel (11 km) with a few places selling drinks and snacks and, 2km further, the bridge over the Río Yeso, a scruffy picnic spot with two eating places in dramatic scenery. The road then divides. One branch forks northeast along a very poor road (4WD essential) via Embalse El Yeso to **Termas del Plomo**, Km 33, thermal baths with no infrastructure, but stunning scenery. The other branch continues and climbs the valley of the Río Volcán. At **El Volcán** (1400 m), 21 km from San Alfonso, there are astounding views, but little else. It is possible to cross the river and camp in the wild on the far side, surrounded by giant rock walls and with a real sense of isolation: If visiting this area or continuing further up the mountain, be prepared for military checks: passport and car registration numbers may be taken. From El Volcán the poor road runs 14 km east to Lo Valdés, a good base for mountain excursions. Nearby are warm natural baths at **Baños Morales** ① *open from Oct, US$4*. This is a wonderful area to come and get away from it all and it is possible to spend days here exploring the paths that lead high into the mountains. (This is the old southerly horse trail linking Santiago and Mendoza, with a path still leading over into Argentina.) Some 12 km further east up the mountain is **Baños Colina** ① *US$14.50*, (not to be confused with Termas de Colina, see page 71) with hot thermal springs and horses for hire. This area is popular at weekends and holiday times, but is otherwise deserted. There are no shops so take food. Try the local goat's cheese if you can; it may be sold by the roadside or at farmhouses.

Situated north of Baños Morales, **Parque Nacional El Morado** ①*T02-8901 9775, mn.elmorado@yahoo.es, or www.conaf.cl, Oct-Apr, US$3.65, administration near the entrance, check with Conaf which parts of the park are open,* covers an area of 3000 ha including the peaks of **El Morado** (5060 m), **El Mirador del Morado** (4320 m) and **El Morado glacier**. It is in an exceptionally secluded and beautiful place with wonderful views, well worth making the effort to reach. There is a good day hike from the park entrance to the glacier and back. Lakeside camping is possible near the glacier.

Cajón del Maipo

There are six main ski resorts near Santiago, four of them around the mountain village of Farellones. All have modern lift systems, international ski schools, rental shops, lodges, mountain restaurants and first-aid facilities. The season runs from June to September/October, weather permitting, although some resorts have equipment for making artificial snow. Many professional skiers from the northern hemisphere come here to keep in practice during the northern summer. Altitude sickness can be a problem, especially at Valle Nevado and Portillo, so avoid over-exertion on the first day or two.

Farellones
ⓘ *32 km east of Santiago, see below under El Colorado for passes.*
The first ski resort built in Chile, Farellones is situated on the slopes of Cerro Colorado at 2470 m and is reached by road from the capital in an hour. From the resort there are incredible views for 30 km across 10 Andean peaks. It is a service centre for the three other resorts and provides affordable accommodation and several large restaurants. It also has a good beginners' area and is connected by lift to El Colorado, www.elcolorado.cl. Perhaps the most popular resort for residents of Santiago, it is busy at weekends.

El Colorado
ⓘ *8 km from Farellones, www.elcolorado.cl, daily lift ticket including Farellones ski lifts, US$75 in high season (weekends, holidays and 7 Jul-8 Aug), US$60 in low season (Mon-Fri, except 7 Jul-8 Aug). You have to buy a rechargeable card for US$8.65 first, onto which you can load day passes, extensions to La Parva or Valle Nevado and other packages.*
Further up Cerro Colorado along a circuitous road, El Colorado has a large but expensive ski lodge at the base, which offers all facilities, and a mountain restaurant higher up. There are 16 lifts in total, giving access to a large intermediate ski area with some steeper slopes. La Cornisa and Cono Este are two of the few bump runs in Chile. This is a good centre for learning to ski.

La Parva
ⓘ*www.laparva.cl, daily lift ticket US$71 high season, US$51.50, low season.*
Situated nearby at 2816 m, La Parva is the upper-class Santiago weekend resort with 30 pistes and 14 lifts. Accommodation is in a chalet village and there are some good bars in high season. Although the runs vary, providing good intermediate to advanced skiing, skiers face a double fall-line so it is not suitable for beginners. Connections with Valle Nevado are good. Equipment rental is from US$60.35. In summer, this is a good walking area, with a trail that leads to the base of Cerro El Plomo, which can be climbed.

Valle Nevado
ⓘ *16 km from Farellones, T02-2477 7000, www.vallenevado.com, daily lift ticket US$76.35, high season, US$67.45, low season.*
Valle Nevado was the site of the 1993 Pan-American winter games and offers the most modern ski facilities in Chile. It has been described as a deluxe hotel complex high up in the mountains. Although not to everyone's taste, it is highly regarded and efficient. There are 40 km of slopes accessed by 41 lifts. The runs are well prepared and are suitable for intermediate skiers and beginners. There's also a ski school and excellent heli-skiing.

Portillo

ⓘ *145 km north of Santiago, www.skiportillo.cl, daily lift ticket US$70, except in bad weather it is reached by any bus from Santiago, Valparaíso or Los Andes to Mendoza; you may have to hitch back.*

Situated at 2855 m, Portillo lies 62 km east of Los Andes, near the customs post on the route to Argentina, and is one of Chile's best-known resorts. The 23 pistes (including one of the fastest in the world) are varied and well prepared, equipped with snow machines and connected by 12 lifts, two of which open up the off-piste areas. This is an excellent family resort, with a very highly regarded ski school, and there are some gentle slopes for beginners near the hotel. The major skiing events are in August and September. Discount packages that include food can be arranged at the beginning and out of season; equipment hire costs US$40.

Nearby, at an altitude of 2835 m, is the **Laguna del Inca**, 5.5 km long, 1.5 km wide and surrounded on three sides by accessible mountain slopes. This lake, frozen over in winter, has no outlet and its depth is not known. From **Tío Bob's** there are magnificent views of the lake and condors may be spotted from the terrace. There are boats for fishing; but beware, the afternoon winds often make the homeward pull three or four times as long as the outward pull. Mules can be hired for stupendous expeditions to the glacier at the head of the valley or to the Cerro Juncal.

Lagunillas

ⓘ *67 km southeast of Santiago, www.skilagunillas.cl, daily lift ticket US$44.50 high season, US$26.65 low season.*

Lagunillas lies in the Cajón del Maipo (see page 68), 17 km east of San José de Maipo, along a beautiful *ripio* road clinging to the edge of a chasm with stunning views of the far reaches of the Andes. It is more basic than the other ski centres in the region, with less infrastructure, but the skiing is good. It is owned by the **Club Andino de Chile**, and is the only not-for-profit ski centre in the country. There are 13 pistes and four ski lifts. Being lower than the other resorts, its season is shorter but it is also cheaper.

From Santiago to Argentina → *For listings, see pages 73-76. Argentine phone code: +54.*

The route across the Andes via Los Andes and the Redentor tunnel is one of the major crossings into Argentina. Route 57 runs north of Santiago through the rich Aconcagua Valley, known as the Valle de Chile. The road forks at the Santuario de Santa Teresa, the west branch going to San Felipe, east to Los Andes and Mendoza. Before travelling, you should always check on weather and road conditions beyond Los Andes. It is difficult to hitchhike over the border, and Spanish is essential; try getting a ride on trucks leaving from the Aduana building in Los Andes.

Termas de Colina

Based at **Hotel Termas de Colina** at 915 m, 43 km north of Santiago (see page 74), this is an attractive, popular spa in the mountains. The temperature of the water is on the cool side (25°C) but it is supposedly good for rheumatism and nervous disorders. There is a large swimming pool, plus individual baths that can be filled with the thermal water, and a sauna. There are some pleasant short walks in the area. The springs are in a military-controlled area, so do not take photos or even show your camera when passing the military base.

Border crossing: Chile–Argentina

Cristo Redentor tunnel

Traffic crosses the border through the 4-km Cristo Redentor tunnel, open September-May 24 hours, June-August 0800-2000 (Chilean time), toll US$3. Note that this pass is closed after heavy snowfall, when travellers are occasionally trapped at the customs complex on either side of the border.

Just beyond Argentine customs and immigration is Puente del Inca, a sports resort named after the natural bridge that crosses the Río Mendoza. The bridge, apparently formed by sulphur-bearing hot springs, is 19 m high, 27 m wide and has a span of 21 m. At the resort are Hostería Puente del Inca as well as camping, transport to Mendoza and information and access for climbing Aconcagua (6964 m), the highest mountain peak on earth outside Asia.

Some 17 km further east is Punta de Vacas, from where there is a good view of Tupungato (6550 m). The only town of any size between the border and Mendoza is Uspallata, from where two roads lead to Mendoza: the paved, southern branch of Route 7, via Potrerillos; and the mostly paved, northern branch via Villavicencio.

The Chilean border post of Los Libertadores is at Portillo, 2 km from the tunnel. Bus and car passengers are dealt with separately. Bicycles must be taken through on a pick-up. There may be long delays during searches for fruit, meat and vegetables, which may not be imported into Chile. A casa de cambio is in the customs building in Portillo.

San Felipe and around

The capital of Aconcagua Province, 96 km north of Santiago, San Felipe is an agricultural and mining centre with an agreeable climate. Part of the Inca Highway has been discovered in the city; previously, no traces had been found south of La Serena. **Curimón**, 3 km southeast of San Felipe, is the site of the Convento de Santa Rosa de Viterbo (1727), which has a small museum attached. A paved road (13 km) runs north from San Felipe to the old town of **Putaendo**; in its church there is an 18th-century baroque statue of Christ. Situated high in the *cordillera*, **Termas de Jahuel** lies 18 km by road northeast of San Felipe; see Where to stay. The mountain scenery includes a distant view of Aconcagua.

Los Andes

Some 16 km southeast of San Felipe and 77 km north of Santiago, Los Andes is situated in a wealthy agricultural, fruit-farming and wine-producing area, but is also the site of a large car-assembly plant. It is a good place for escaping from Santiago and a convenient base for skiing at nearby Portillo, see page 71. There are monuments to José de San Martín and Bernardo O'Higgins in the Plaza de Armas and a monument to the Clark brothers, who built the Transandine Railway to Mendoza (now disused, although there are tentative plans to re-establish it). There are good views from El Cerro de la Virgen, reached in an hour via a trail from the municipal picnic ground on Independencia.

The road to the border: Los Libertadores

The road to Argentina follows the Aconcagua Valley for 34 km until it reaches the village of **Río Blanco** (1370 m), where the ríos Blanco and Juncal meet to form the Río Aconcagua. There is a fish hatchery with a small botanical garden at the entrance to the Andina copper mine. East of Río Blanco the road climbs until Juncal where it zigzags steeply through 29 hairpin bends at the top of which is the ski resort of Portillo (see page 71). This is the location of the Chilean border post. If entering Chile, there may be long delays during searches for fruit, meat and vegetables, which may not be imported.

Above the tunnel is the old pass, used before the tunnel was built, and above this again, at 3854 m, is the statue of **El Cristo Redentor** (Christ the Redeemer), which was erected jointly by Chile and Argentina in 1904 to commemorate King Edward VII's decision in the boundary dispute of 1902. It is completely dwarfed by the landscape. The old road over the pass is in a very poor state, especially on the Chilean side, and is liable to be blocked by snow even in summer. When weather conditions permit, the statue can be reached on foot from **Las Cuevas**, a modern settlement on the Argentine side (4½ hours up, two down).

◉ Around Santiago listings

For hotel and restaurant price codes and other relevant information, see pages 14-21.

◉ Where to stay

Cajón del Maipo *p68, map p69*
$$$$-$$$ Hostería Millahue, El Melocotón, T02-2861 2020, www.hosteriamillahue.com. Accommodation in *cabañas* including full board. There is also a games room and an outdoor heated swimming pool.
$$$-$$ Cabañas Corre Caminos, Estero Morales 57402, Baños Morales, T02-9269 2283, www.loscorrecaminos.cl. Cabins sleeping 2-5 people, open all year. Food available, activities including horse riding.
$$$ Hostería Los Ciervos, Camino al Volcán 31411, San Alfonso, T02-2861 1581. With breakfast, full board also available, good.
$$ pp Refugio Lo Valdés, 14 km east of El Volcán, Lo Valdés, T02-9230 5930, refugiolovaldes@dav.cl. Stone-built chalet accommodation or dorm. Good restaurant. Lots of trekking and climbing information, part of **Club Alemán Andino**.
$$ Residencial España, Av Argentina 711, San Alfonso, T02-2861 1543. Clean, comfortable, with restaurant.
$$ Residencial Los Chicos Malos, Baños Morales, T02-2624 5412, T09-9323 6424, www.banosmorales.cl. Comfortable, fresh bread, good meals. There are also *cabañas*, horse riding, open in winter for hot drinks.

Camping
Comunidad Cascada de las Animas, 500 m off the main road, San Alfonso, T02-2861 4019, www.cascadadelasanimas.cl. US$14 per site (up to 6 people). Also cabins with hot water, cooking equipment, etc, sauna and horse riding. There are a dozen or so other campsites throughout the valley.

Farellones *p70*
$$$$ Lodge Andes, Camino La Capilla 662, www.lodgeandes.cl. Shared rooms with shared bathrooms or private double rooms, rate includes half board. English spoken. Good value.
$$$$ Posada de Farellones, T02-2201 3704, www.skifarellones.com. Cosy and warm, Swiss style, transport service to slopes, decent restaurant. Price for half board. Also **Farellones**, www.hotelfarellones.cl, and **La Cornisa**, www.lacornisa.cl.
$$ pp Refugio Universidad de Chile, Los Cóndores 879, T02-2321 1595, www.uchile.cl. Shared rooms half board. Standard *refugio*, often fills up with university students at weekends.

El Colorado *p70*
Apartments are available for daily or weekly rental in El Colorado.
$$$$ Colorado Apart Hotel, Av Apoquindo 6275, of 88, Las Condes, T02-2245 3401, www.skiandes.co.cl. Fully furnished apartments, half board. Also has cheaper cabins.

$$$$ Edificio Monteblanco, bookings from ChileanSki.com (www.chileanski.com/eng/el-colorado/monteblanco-building.htm). Apartments that can be rented by the day or week. Food and room service available at extra cost.

La Parva *p70*
$$$$ Condominio Nueva La Parva, reservations in Santiago, El Bosque Norte 0177, piso 2, T02-2339 8482, www.laparva.cl. Good hotel and restaurant. 3 other restaurants.

Valle Nevado *p70*
Apartment and reso rt hotel facilities (**$$$$**) in Valle Nevado, where the 5-star resort has boutique shops, gourmet dining, and backpacker facilities, www.vallenevado.com.

Portillo *p71*
$$$$-$$$ Hotel Portillo, Renato Sánchez 4270, Las Condes, T02-2263 0606, www.skiportillo.com. On the shore of Laguna del Inca. From lakeside suites with full board and fabulous views, to bunk rooms without bath. Self-service lunch, open all year, minibus to Santiago. Cinema, nightclub, pool, sauna and medical service.

Lagunillas *p71*
$$$ Refugio Club Andino, T07-600 8057, www.skilagunillas.cl. Cabins sleep 2-5, shared bathrooms, room only, B&B or full board.

Termas de Colina *p71*
$$$$ Hotel Termas de Colina, T02-2844 0990, hotel.colina@ejercito.cl (see www.guiature.cl) Modern, expensive thermal baths, a beautiful swimming pool. Formal restaurant. Facilities open to public, crowded at weekends.

San Felipe and around *p72*
$$$$ Termas de Jahuel, T02-2411 1720, www.jahuel.cl, northeast of San Felipe.

Luxury health resort with thermal pool, spa, and gym.

Los Andes *p72*
$$$$ Baños El Corazón, at San Esteban, 2 km north of Los Andes, T02-2236 3636, www.termaselcorazon.cl. Full board, with use of pool; also day passes for thermal baths, spa, meals and combinations. Take bus San Esteban/El Cariño.
$$$ Plaza, Rodriguez 368, T034-2240 2157. Good, expensive restaurant.
$$ Residencial Italiana, Rodríguez 76, T034-2423 544. Clean rooms without bath.

The road to the border *p72*
$$$ Hostería Guardia Vieja, 8 km east of Río Blanco. Expensive but untidy, campsite.
$$ Hostería Luna, 4 km west of Río Blanco, T034-2249 4186. Good value, clean, helpful, good food.

🍴 Restaurants

Cajón del Maipo *p68, map p69*
$$ El Rancho del Ché, on the road between Puente Alto and San José, El Canelo. Excellent Argentine meat dishes.
$$ La Petite France, on the road between Puente Alto and San José, nearer San José. Good French food, not cheap.
$$ Restaurant El Campito, Camino al Volcán 1841, San José. Very good.
$$ Restaurant La Isidora, on the plaza, San José. Smart, good, meat dishes.

Portillo *p71*
$$$-$$ Restaurant La Posada, opposite Hotel Portillo. Cheaper than the hotel, but open evenings and weekends only.

San Felipe and around *p72*
$$ La Piedra del Molino, in the Sector Almendral, 2 km east of San Felipe on the road to Santa María. Excellent traditional food.

⊖ Transport

Pomaire *p67*
Bus
From **Santiago** take the **Melipilla** bus from **Terminal San Borja**, every few mins, US$2.35-3 each way, 1 hr; alight at side road to Pomaire, 2-3 km from town, *colectivos* every 10-15 mins. It's easier to visit on a tour, often combined with Isla Negra, see page 101, or by car.

Reserva Nacional Río Clarillo *p67*
Bus from **Puente Alto** to **El Principal**, 1 hr.

Santuario de la Naturaleza
Yerba Loca *p68*
Colectivos with **Taxis Transarrayán Ltda** leave from Plaza San Enrique in Lo Barnechea. Take any bus for **Barnechea** from Alameda or Providencia in Santiago.

Maipo Valley *p68*
For **Undurraga**, take a Talagante bus from the Terminal San Borja to the entrance. For **Viña Santa Rita**, get a bus direct to Alto Jahuel from Terminal San Borja, T02-2776 0645. For **De Martino**, get a bus direct to Isla de Maipo from Terminal San Borja.

Cajón del Maipo *p68, map p69*
Take line 5 metro to Bellavista La Floridaza, change to Metrobus 72 to the Plaza in **San José de Maipo**, or take line 4 to Las Mercedes and take bus No 72, to San José, 40 mins, US$1.50, or a *colectivo* which can go as far as **San Gabriel**. *Colectivo* fares: Las Mercedes to San José US$2.35, to **San Alfonso** US$3, to San Gabriel, US$5. San José to San Alfonso US$1.10, to San Gabriel, US$3. San Alfonso-San Gabriel US$2.35. There is a bus every 30 mins from San José to San Alfonso, every hr to San Gabriel and at 1400 to El Volcán. In summer only 1 morning bus to **Baños Morales**, US$14.

Ski resorts *p70*
Bus
Centro de Ski El Colorado y Farellones buses leave from CC Omnium, Av Apoquindo 4900 (Escuela Militar Metro) in Santiago daily 0900-1100 with minimum of 6 passengers, return 1630-1730, essential to book in advance, T02-2363 0559, US$23.50 return. Note that the road to Farellones and El Colorado is one way 1 Jun-30 Sep: up 0800-1330; down 1530-2000. **Ski Total**, T02-2246 6881, www.skitotal.cl, and **Ski Van**, T02-2219 2672, www.skivan.cl, offer transport to ski resorts. Reserve in advance; also for hotel or airport pick-up and minibuses to Portillo. It is easy to hitch from the junction of Av Las Condes/El Camino Farellones (YPF petrol station in the middle), reached by a Barnechea bus. **Portillo** is easily reached by any bus from Los Héroes terminal, Santiago, or Los Andes to **Mendoza**. You may have to hitch back.

Termas de Colina *p71*
From Santiago take the **bus** from Av La Paz 302 (40 mins). From here a rough road leads through countryside 6 km; last return bus at 1900.

Los Andes *p72*
Los Héroes terminal has services to **Mendoza** (Argentina) with **Tas Choapa**, **Fenix Pullman Norte**, **Cata** and **Ahumada**. Any of these will drop passengers off at **Portillo**.

The road to the border *p72*
Saladillo buses hourly from Los Andes to **Río Blanco**; there are also services from Santiago, **Ahumada**, 1930 daily, direct, 2 hrs, US$6. For Transport into Argentina, see page 63.

🛈 Directory

San Felipe has similar facilities to Los Andes, but there is little infrastructure elsewhere.

Los Andes *p72*
Banks ATMs on the Plaza de Armas.
Cambio Inter, Rodriguez 390. Also *casa de cambio* in Portillo customs building and at **Ingeniero Roque Carranza**, 13 km from tunnel.

Contents

Valparaíso & Viña del Mar

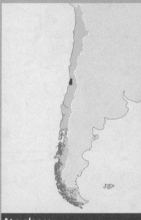

At a glance

⊖ **Getting around** Local buses and *colectivos* pass every few seconds and most other places of interest can be reached by provincial buses. Valparaíso is best explored on foot.

⟳ **Time required** 2 or 3 days in either Valparaíso or Viña. 1 day to visit a fishing village and another day or 2 to visit La Campana National Park.

☁ **Weather** Pleasantly warm and dry in summer. Winter is cool but not cold, with sunny days interspersed with cloud and rain.

✘ **When not to go** Viña del Mar and nearby beaches are unpleasantly crowded from New Year until mid-Feb.

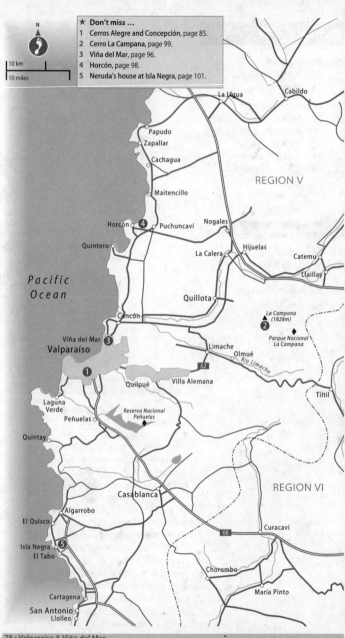

★ Don't miss ...
1 Cerros Alegre and Concepción, page 85.
2 Cerro La Campana, page 99.
3 Viña del Mar, page 96.
4 Horcón, page 98.
5 Neruda's house at Isla Negra, page 101.

N

10 km
10 miles

Cabildo

La Ligua

REGION V

Papudo

Zapallar

Cachagua

Maitencillo

Horcón ○ ④ Puchuncaví

Nogales

Quintero

La Calera

Hijuelas

Catemu

Llaillay

Pacific
Ocean

Quillota

La Campana
(1828m) ▲ ②

Concón

Parque Nacional
La Campana

Viña del Mar ③
Valparaíso

Limache

Olmué

①

62

Río Limache

Quilpué

Villa Alemana

Tiltil

Laguna
Verde

Reserva Nacional
Peñuelas

Peñuelas ○

Quintay ○

REGION VI

Casablanca

Algarrobo

El Quisco ○

68

Curacaví

Isla Negra ⑤
El Tabo

Chorombo

Cartagena

María Pinto

San Antonio ○
Llolleo

This was one of the first areas to be settled by the Spanish, the lands being assigned to prominent *conquistadores* during the 16th century. In the 19th century Valparaíso rose to become the most important port on the Pacific coast of South America, but there were few other large centres of population along this coastline until the 1880s, when the fashion for holidaying near the sea spread from southern Europe. The coastal strip west of Santiago is now one of the most popular destinations for regional tourists. The coastline enjoys a Mediterranean-style climate: the cold sea currents and coastal winds produce less extreme temperatures than in Santiago and the Central Valley; rainfall is moderate in winter and the summers are dry. Midway along the coast is Viña del Mar, one of the most famous resorts in South America, awash with Argentines and Chileans strutting their stuff in summer. Near Viña are other popular resorts, such as Reñaca and Concón, plus a host of more secluded spots, including Horcón to the north and Quintay to the south. While the beaches on this stretch of coast are attractive, the water is very cold and swimming is dangerous in many places because of a heavy undertow.

The place that makes this part of Chile really worth visiting is Valparaíso, the most beguiling city in the country, part of which has been declared a UNESCO World Heritage Site. Nearby is the lumpy summit of Cerro La Campana, a high hill between the coast and the Central Valley, which offers some of the best views in Chile and can be climbed in a day. South of Valparaíso, towards the mouth of the Río Maipo, are a number of other centres, including Algarrobo, perhaps the most affluent resort along this coast, and Isla Negra, a village famous as the home of Pablo Neruda, in which the Nobel laureate gathered together a collection of *objets d'art* from around the world.

Valparaíso

Sprawling over a crescent of 42 *cerros* (hills) that rear up from the sea 116 km west of Santiago, Valparaíso is a one-off. The main residential areas here are not divided into regimented blocks, as in all other Chilean cities; instead Valparaíso is really two cities: the flat, vaguely ordered area between the bus terminal and the port known as 'El Plan', and the chaotic, wasp-nest *cerros*, in which most porteños (people from Valparaíso) live. It is possible to spend weeks exploring the alleyways of the *cerros*, where packs of dogs lie sunning themselves, brightly painted houses pile on top of one another and half-forgotten passageways head up and down the hills, offering fantastic views of the Pacific, the city and – on a clear day – right over to the snow-capped *cordillera*. The Bohemian and slightly anarchic atmosphere of the *cerros* reflects the urban chaos of the city as a whole. Here you will find such unusual sights as a 'monument to the WC' (Calle Elias) and a graveyard from which all the corpses were shaken out during a severe earthquake. Valparaíso is all about contradictions – the fact that both Salvador Allende and Augusto Pinochet were born and raised here expresses this fact more eloquently than anything else – but the oppositions can also be seen in the juxtaposition of flat El Plan against the labyrinthine *cerros*; the sea against the views of Aconcagua; and the city's grandiose mansions mingling with some of Chile's worst slums. Given this it is no surprise that Valparaíso has attracted a steady stream of poets and artists throughout the last century.

Arriving in Valparaíso → *Colour map 3, B2. Population: 300,000.*

Getting there The long-distance bus terminal is on Pedro Montt 2800 block (one of the main streets running east from the Cathedral), at the corner of Rawson, opposite the Congreso Nacional, 1 block from Avenida Argentina, T032-293 9695; plenty of city buses run between the terminal and Plaza Sotomayor. There are inter-urban buses to Valparaíso from every major Chilean city (even including connections through to Punta Arenas), and it makes an interesting change to most travellers' itineraries to get a bus to Valparaíso instead of Santiago. Valparaíso also has international connections to Mendoza, Córdoba and Buenos Aires. Valparaíso can also be reached relatively easy by public transport from Santiago's airport at Pudahuel, 108 km away (see page 41): take a bus to Pajaritos, US$2.50, cross the platform and take a bus to Valparaíso, US$6-7.50. ➡ *See Transport, page 94.*

Getting around The lower city along the waterfront is called El Plan and is connected to the upper city in the 'cerros' by steep winding roads, flights of steps and *ascensores* or funicular railways as well as taxis, *colectivos* and certain bus routes. You should never have to wait more than 30 seconds to travel anywhere within El Plan (between Plaza Aduana and Avenida Argentina): buses along Pedro Montt are cheap but slow; Errázuriz buses are faster. Valparaíso is the only city in Chile still to have trolleybuses (see below). They ply the length of El Plan and cost the same as a local bus fare. Buses to Cerro Alegre and the top of Cerro Concepción leave from Calle Chacabuco, behind the bus terminal (No 607) or Avenida Argentina (No 514). Bus 612, popularly known as the 'O', links the hills of Valparaíso from Avenida Argentina all along the Avenida Alemania, down to the port and around the coast to Playa Ancha. Catching it is a sightseeing tour in itself. Taxis and *colectivos* usually wait around at the bottom of each *cerro*; otherwise, you can use the *ascensores* (funicular railways). If you are going to Viña or one of the nearby towns to the north, catch a *micro* from Errázuriz or Brasil; *colectivos* to Viña leave from the same place. The Metro train to Viña runs along the waterfront. Taxis from the bus terminal are metered and can be reasonable if there are three or four of you sharing. ➡ *See Transport, page 94.*

Security Robbery is an occasional problem in El Puerto and around the *ascensores* on Avenida Argentina. The upper outskirts of town, as well as Cerro Cordillera, while offering amazing views, are not the safest of places. The poorer and rougher districts tend to be those furthest from the centre. Also be aware that Calle Chacabuco (on which some hotels are located) is the pickup point for local rent boys. Keep your personal items secure, keep your camera in a bag or rucksack, only taking it out when you want to take a photo. Beware of the mustard trick (see page 32).

Tourist information Sernatur ① *in the Consejo Nacional de la Cultura y Las Artes, Prat y Sotomayor, T032-223 6264 , infovalparaiso@sernatur.cl, Mon-Sat 0900-1800.* The **Municipal office** ① *C Condell, opposite Ramírez, Mon-Fri 0830-1400, 1530-1745, www. ciudaddevalparaiso.cl,* is in the old **Municipalidad** building, with a kiosk in Casa La Sebastiana (see below). There are also two information offices in the bus terminal, but these are privately run on a commission basis and hence do not give impartial advice. There is also a university-run tourist office, **DUOC**, in Edificio Cousiño, Blanco 997.

Neruda on Valparaíso

"The hills of Valparaíso decided to dislodge their inhabitants, to let go of the houses on top, to let them dangle from cliffs that are red with clay, yellow with gold thimble flowers, and a fleeting green with wild vegetation. But houses and people clung to the heights, writhing, digging in, worrying, their hearts set on staying up there, hanging on, tooth and nail, to each cliff. The port is a tug-of-war between the sea and nature, untamed on the *cordilleras*. But it was man who won the battle little by little. The hills and the sea's abundance gave the city a pattern, making it uniform, not like a barracks, but with the variety of spring, its clashing colours, its resonant bustle. The houses became colours: a blend of amaranth and yellow, crimson and cobalt, green and purple."

Pablo Neruda, *Memoirs*, Penguin, 1978.

Background

Founded in 1542, Valparaíso became, in the colonial period, a small port used for trade with Peru. It was raided at least seven times during the colonial era by pirates and corsairs, including Drake. The city prospered from Independence more than any other Chilean town. It was used in the 19th century by commercial agents from Europe and the US as their trading base in the southern Pacific and became a major international banking centre as well as the key port for shipping between the northern Pacific and Cape Horn. Until the 1840s, the journey from the port to El Almendral (site of the congress and the old road to Santiago) took several hours and passed over wild hills but, as the city's wealth and importance grew, part of the original bay was filled in, creating the modern day El Plan. Fine buildings were erected here, including several banks, South America's first stock exchange and offices of *El Mercurio*, the world's oldest newspaper in the Spanish language, first printed in 1827 and still in publication. (The impressive *Mercurio* building, built in 1900, stands on the site of a famous pirates' cave.) Wealthy European merchants began to populate Cerro Concepción and Cerro Alegre in this period, building churches and fine mansions in every conceivable architectural style.

The city's decline was the result of two factors: the opening of the Panama Canal in 1914 and the breakdown in world trade during the depression in the 1930s. Further decline followed the development of a container port in San Antonio, the shift of banks to Santiago and the move of the middle classes to nearby Viña del Mar. Recently money has been pumped in through UNESCO, the Inter-American Development bank and to some extent tourism, and the city is slowly being restored to its former splendour.

Little of the city's colonial past survived the pirates, tempests, fires and earthquakes, but a remnant of the old colonial city can be found in the hollow known as El Puerto, grouped round the low-built stucco church of La Matriz. Very few wooden buildings predate the devastating earthquake of 1906, which was followed by a series of fires.

Places in Valparaíso → *For listings, see pages 89-95.*

The lower part of the city, El Plan, is the business centre, with fine office buildings on narrow streets that are strung along the edge of the bay and cluttered with buses. Above, covering the hills or *cerros* is a fantastic agglomeration of buildings in every conceivable shape that seem literally to tumble down the slopes. Part of the charm of the *cerros* is the lack of order. It is as if every individual bought a plot of land and built whatever they saw fit, resulting in a hotchpotch of size, style and colour. Spanish colonial mansions lie alongside adobe shacks and neoclassical monoliths.

Superb views over the bay are offered from most of the *cerros*, each of which provides its own unique vista and distinct atmosphere. It is enjoyable to spend an afternoon exploring the hills and, however lost you might feel, a few minutes' walk downhill will always lead you back to El Plan. The lower and upper cities are connected by steep winding roads, flights of steps and 15 *ascensores* (funicular railways) dating from the period 1883-1914.

For several years there have been problems keeping the *ascensores* running, and some operate irregularly for lack of funding for repairs and maintenance. In 2014 seven or eight were open, but the municipality was working on more. One of the best ways to see the lower city is on the historic **trolley bus**, which takes a circular route from the Congress to the port (US$0.50). Some of the cars, imported from Switzerland and the US, date from the 1930s. Another good viewpoint is from top of Ascensor Barón, near the bus terminal.

El Plan and El Puerto

The old heart of El Plan is the **Plaza Sotomayor**, dominated by the former **Intendencia** (Government House), now the seat of the admiralty. Be careful when crossing the plaza, which, although it appears pedestrianized, is in fact criss-crossed by busy roads. Opposite is a fine monument to the 'Heroes of the Battle of Iquique', which also serves as a mausoleum housing the bodies of all who fought in the battle. Visitors are occasionally allowed inside and on 21 May it is the focus of a massive procession of the armed forces through the city celebrating the anniversary of the battle. While excavating under Plaza Sotomayor in order to build a new underground car park, parts of Valparaíso's original **old quay** were uncovered; they can be visited in summer. Alternatively, they can be viewed from above ground through the glass ceiling, although the glass tends to mist up. Look out, too, for the bronze plaques on the ground illustrating the movement of the shoreline over the centuries.

Southeast of Plaza Sotomayor, calles Prat, Cochrane and Esmeralda run through the old banking and commercial centre to **Plaza Aníbal Pinto**, around which are some of the city's oldest bars and cafés. Above this part of El Plan are *cerros* Concepción and Alegre (see below). Heading in the other direction, one block away from Plaza Sotomayor is the port entrance (take a boat trip from here around the bay, recommended if sunny; see What to do, page 94) and the **railway station**, from which passenger services run on the newly modernized metropolitan line to Viña del Mar and Limache.

One block northwest of Plaza Sotomayor, on Calle Serrano, is the **Ascensor Cordillera** (closed 2014) and the **Escalera de la Muerte** (the Stairs of Death; just try climbing them to find out why). At the top, on Plazuela Eleuterio Ramírez, take Calle Merlet to the left and you will find the **Museo del Mar Almirante Cochrane** ⓘ *Merlet 195, Tue-Sun 1000-1800, free,* which hosts temporary art exhibitions in a small colonial house with excellent views over the bay (the New Year fireworks are filmed from here). Note that thieves and pickpockets are known to work in this area.

Back in El Plan, continue another block along Serrano into the heart of El Puerto to reach **Plaza Echaurren**, Valparaíso's oldest square, tree-lined and with a picturesque fountain. It was once the height of elegance but is now surrounded by cheap restaurants and frequented by a sizeable population of local drunks. Near Plaza Echaurren stands the church of **La Matriz**, built in 1842 on the site of the first church in the city and unusual for its sloping nave and stained-glass windows all depicting Valparaíso themes. Further northwest, along Bustamante, lies Plaza Aduana, named after the customs building, from where the **Ascensor Artillería** (closed 2014) takes you up to the Mirador 21 de Mayo and the imposing **Museo Naval y Marítimo** ① *www.museonaval.cl, Tue-Sun 1000-1730, US$1.30, good English signs*, in the old Naval Academy, which documents naval history 1810-1880, and includes exhibitions on Chile's two naval heroes: Lord Cochrane (see box, page 303) and Arturo Prat, as well as one of the phoenix capsules used to rescue the 33 trapped miners in 2010. Great views are to be had from the Paseo 21 de Mayo at the upper station of the *ascensor*.

Playa Ancha and around

To the west of **Cerro Artillería**, the Avenida **Gran Bretaña** winds its way to the municipal stadium on Cerro Playa Ancha, which seats 20,000 people and is home to the local football team Santiago Wanderers. The buildings on Avenida Gran Bretaña are a good example of the suburb's eccentric architecture. Past the stadium the road continues

1 Valparaíso

➡ Valparaíso maps
1 Valparaíso, page 84
2 Cerro Concepción, Cerro Alegre & El Puerto, page 86

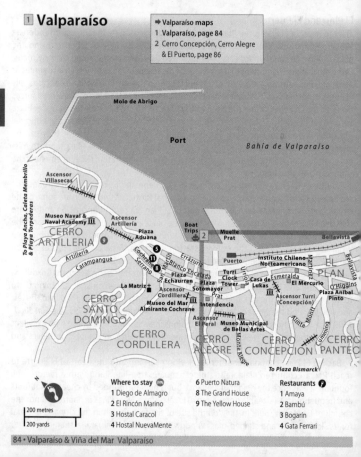

Where to stay
1 Diego de Almagro
2 El Rincón Marino
3 Hostal Caracol
4 Hostal NuevaMente
6 Puerto Natura
8 The Grand House
9 The Yellow House

Restaurants
1 Amaya
2 Bambú
3 Bogarín
4 Gata Ferrari

downhill to the foot of Cerro Playa Ancha at **Las Torpederas**, a small bathing beach. Just beyond the beach is a promontory topped by the **Faro de Punta Angeles** ① *30-40 mins' walk from Cerro Artillería, T09-8621 8728, T032-250 6100 or T032-220 8730, contacto@ farosdechile.com; visits to the lighthouse and attached museum by appointment*, which was the first lighthouse on the west coast of South America. There is a picturesque coastal road back to town, the Avenida Altamirano, passing **Caleta Membrillo**, which has a number of good seafood restaurants.

Around Cerros Alegre and Concepción
Above El Plan, **Cerro Alegre** and **Cerro Concepción** are the heart of the UNESCO-designated area and for many the undisputed symbols of the city. Both are filled with brightly painted mansions and high-ceilinged 19th-century houses, some falling down but many now being restored to their former glory and some being extended upwards, despite supposedly restrictive planning regulations, a contentious issue for many

5 Isabel a La Costeñita
6 J Cruz
7 La Otra Cocina
8 Los Porteños
9 Marco Polo
10 Natur-In
11 Porto Viejo
12 San Carlos

in the local community. Cerro Concepción is as posh as Valparaíso gets, while Cerro Alegre has a more artistic, bohemian feel: brightly coloured murals abound, most of the shops seem to double as art galleries and, during university term, students can be seen on practically every street corner sketching buildings or the panoramic views. The two hills are connected to El Plan by three *ascensores*, of which **Ascensor Concepción**, inaugurated on 1 December 1883, is the oldest in Valparaíso. A 2-km walk starts at the top of Ascensor Concepción, leading to Paseo Mirador Gervasoni and Calle Pupudo through a labyrinth of narrow streets and stairs. Three miradors offer views of the bay, over to Viña and beyond.

2 Cerro Concepción, Cerro Alegre & El Puerto

➡ **Valparaíso maps**
1 Valparaíso, page 84
2 Cerro Concepción, Cerro Alegre & El Puerto, page 86

Where to stay 🛏
1 Acontraluz *C2*
3 Casa Aventura *B2*
4 Casa Higueras
6 Catalejo House *B2*
8 Hostal Casa Verde Limón *B3*
9 La Bicyclette *B2*
10 La Nona *C2*
11 Luna Sonrisa & El Nidito *C2*
12 Manoir Atkinson *B2*
13 Pata Pata *B2*
14 Somerscales Boutique *C2*
15 Ultramar *B3*

Restaurants 🍴
1 Allegretto *B2*
2 Bar Inglés *A2*
3 Bote Salvavidas *A1*
4 Café con Letras *B2*
5 Café Vinilo *B2*
7 Color Café *B2*
9 Delicias Express *B1*
9 El Desayunador *B2*
25 E l Dominó *B3*
26 Fauna *B2*
27 La Cocó *C2*
10 La Colombina *B1*
11 La Concepción *B2*
12 La Rotonda *B1*
13 Le Filou de Montpellier *B2*
14 Malandrino *C2*
15 Mastodonte *A2*
16 Pan de Magia *C2*
17 Pasta e Vino *B2*
18 Pimentón *B3*
19 Turri *B2*
20 Zamba & Canuta *A2*

Bars & clubs 🍸
28 Cinzano *B3*
21 El Huevo *A3*
22 El Irlandés *A3*
23 La Piedra Feliz *A2*
24 La Playa *B1*

Museo Municipal de Bellas Artes ① *Paseo Yugoslavo 176, Cerro Alegre, T032-225 2332, Tue-Sun 1030-1900, US$3.65, concessions US$1; take Ascensor El Peral from Plaza de la Justicia, off Plaza Sotomayor*, is housed in Palacio Baburizza and has displays of Chilean landscapes and seascapes and some modern paintings. A visit is highly recommended and, if you are lucky, you may get to see the whole of this interesting rococo mansion; the games room, drawing room, shower and servants' quarters provide an insight into the contrasting lifestyles of *porteños* in the early part of the 20th century. Opposite, is the 1920s mansion, **Palacio Astoreca** ① *Montealegre 149, www.hotelpalacioastoreca.com*, which has been newly restored as a luxury hotel. Also worth a visit is the beautiful **Casa Mirador de Lukas** ① *Paseo Mirador Gervasoni 448, Cerro Concepción, T032-222 1344, www.lukas.cl, Tue-Sun 1100-1400 and 1445-1800, US$2.35*, dedicated to the work of Chile's most famous caricaturist. Lukas (real name Renzo Pecchenino) was originally from Italy but spent most of his life in Valparaíso. The museum holds a permanent exhibition of his work, which gives a humorous insight into the political and social history of Valparaíso and Chile. There are also temporary exhibitions and occasional films, as well as a café.

Avenida Alemania and the other cerros
Walking uphill along any of the main streets of Cerro Alegre will lead you to the Plazuela San Luis, from where **Avenida Alemania** runs southeast, following the contours of Valparaíso's hills. This is the only road that connects all the hills above Valparaíso and makes a pleasant walk, with ever-changing views, one of the best of which is to be had from **Plaza Bismark**. Calle Cumming heads back down to El Plan from Plaza Bismark passing the former prison (now a cultural centre housing temporary exhibitions and occasional concerts – worth a visit).

In this area are three cemeteries, all of which can be visited: **Cementerios I** and **II** are the city's two oldest Catholic cemeteries, while the third, **Cementerio de los Disidentes**, holds the graves of Protestant immigrants. Back on Avenida Alemania, meanwhile, a 20-minute walk will bring you to the former home of Pablo Neruda, **La Sebastiana** ① *Ferrari 692, off Av Alemania, Altura 6900, Cerro Florida, T032-225 6606, www.fundacionneruda.org, Tue-Sun 1010-1800 (Jan-Feb 1030-1850), US$7.50 including audio-guide, US$1.75 concessions; take bus 612 (O) from Av Argentina, US$0.65, or colectivo 38 or 39 from Plazuela Ecuador, US$0.65*. It now houses an art gallery as well as a collection of some of his objets d'art, showing his eccentric tastes to the full, and there is a small café in the garden, with fine views.

Cerro Bellavista and Plaza de la Victoria
From **La Sebastiana**, walk down **Cerro Bellavista** along Calle Ferrari and Calle Héctor Calvo to arrive at the **Museo al Cielo Abierto**. Opened in 1992, this open-air museum consists of large-scale murals painted on the outside walls of buildings in Cerro Bellavista by 17 of Chile's leading artists. Look out for the 6 m by 3 m mural by Chile's most famous contemporary artist, Roberto Matta, situated just before you reach the Ascensor Espíritu Santo (reopened in June 2014); it's a typical example of Matta's later work with sharp-toothed monsters hurtling through space. Here, as in Santiago, there is plenty of artistic activity, outside as well as indoors: people practising dance moves and circus skills, and the walls of many buildings are decorated with street art. For a study of this art form read *Street Art Chile* by Rod Palmer (8 Books); for tours of the best examples, contact **Valpo Street Art Tours** ① *T032-312 3014, www.valpostreetart.com*.

At the bottom of Cerro Bellavista is **Plaza de la Victoria** with the cathedral on its east side and the municipal library on Plaza Simón Bolívar just to the north. Plaza Victoria

A walk over the Cerros Alegre and Concepción

From the **Plaza Aníbal Pinto** walk up Calles Cumming and Elias and take the **Ascensor Reina Victoria** up to a viewing point. Walk along Paseo Dimalow to the end, then head down Urriola (opposite). After one block, turn right onto **Calle Templeman**. On the left are two alleyways: Pasaje Templeman has a couple of art workshops, while Pierre Loti has typical English-style houses. Further along Calle Templeman is the Anglican church of **San Pablo**, built in 1858. Follow the church round past the entrance on Pilcomayo and head down to the end of that street, where steps lead down to **Paseo Pastor Schmidt**, with views of the cemetery opposite. Carry on past the Lutheran church (1897) and along the revamped **Paseo Atkinson**, once home to merchants and ships' captains and with expansive views. At the end of the walkway, turn right onto Papudo. The next right leads to the **Paseo Gervasoni**, overlooking the port and the Turri clock tower, and home to the Lukas museum. Following the paseo round, take the steps down to the labyrinthine **Pasaje Galvez**, past restaurants, bars and art galleries.

Cross Calle Urriola, and head up **Pasaje Bavestrello**, ahead and to the right. At the top is an unusual building, four storeys high and 3 m wide. Turn right here onto the **Paseo Yugoslavo** and the **Palacio Baburizza**, with views of the Cochrane museum to the left and Playa Ancha beyond. Walk past the Ascensor Peral and follow the road up and round into **Pasaje Leighton**. The second road on the right is **Miramar**. Climb 100 m and turn left onto **Lautaro Rosas**, an avenue lined with fine houses and mansions. After two blocks the road crosses the stair-lined **Calle Templeman**, boasting one of Valparaíso's classic views.

If you still have any energy left you can climb three blocks to the **Plazuela San Luis** and begin exploring other hills along the Avenida Alemania.

is the official centre of Valparaíso and commemorates Chile's victory in the War of the Pacific; the statues and fountain were looted from Peru during the war.

One block west, on Calle Condell in the 19th-century Palacio Lyon is the **Museo de Historia Natural** ① *Condell 1546, T032-225 4840, www.mhnv.cl, Tue-Sat 1000-1800, Sun 1000-1400, open later in summer, free*, which has been redesigned with a library and café. Next door is the **Galería de Arte Municipal** ① *Condell 1550, T032-222 0062, Mon-Sat 1000-1900, free*.

Plaza O'Higgins and further east

East of Plaza de la Victoria, Pedro Montt leads to the Parque Italia and **Plaza O'Higgins**. The latter is dominated by the imposing **Congreso Nacional**, a monolithic arch in neo-fascist style, thoroughly out of keeping with the rest of the city. Opposite is the bus terminal, while four blocks north on Errázuriz is the Barón train station and the **Muelle Barón**, the new terminal for cruise ships. A walk to the end of this pier, past kite-flying children, gives a different view of Valparaíso, clearly showing the amphitheatre-like form of the city. Just off the pier is a small colony of sea-lions, while at the pier's base, kayaks and sailing boats can be hired and lessons are available (www.puertodeportivo.cl). A new coastal walkway has recently been built running northeast from here past several small beaches as far as **Caleta Portales**, a small fishing harbour with several seafood restaurants that lies almost at the border between Valparaíso and Viña del Mar.

To the east of the Congress building, Avenida Argentina runs south past four *ascensores* including **Ascensor Polanco** (entrance from Calle Simpson, off Avenida Argentina a few blocks southeast of the bus terminal). This is the most unusual *ascensor* in the city as it is in two sections: walk along a 160-m horizontal tunnel through the rock, then take a vertical lift to the summit on which there is a mirador. Note that the lower entrance is in an area that is unsafe: do not go alone and do not take valuables. Beyond Polanco the road branches left towards Santiago or continues straight on to Cerro O'Higgins, where there are several mansions built by the British in the 19th century. Nearby is the **Mirador O'Higgins**, from which the Supreme Director, Bernardo O'Higgins, saw the arrival of Cochrane's liberating squadron and proclaimed "On those four craft depends the destiny of America".

◉ Valparaíso listings

For hotel and restaurant price codes and other relevant information, see pages 14-21.

◉ Where to stay

El Plan and El Puerto *p83, map p84*
$$ The Yellow House, Capitán Muñoz Gamero 91, Cerro Artillería, T032-233 9435, www.theyellowhouse.cl. Tucked away on a cobbled side street. Australian/Chilean-run, rooms and an apartment, some with great views, good showers, non-smoking.

Cerros Alegre and Concepción
p85, map p86
Cerros Alegre, Concepción and, to a lesser extent, Bellavista have many *hostales*, more than we can list. For a selection, see http://hhyr.cl.
$$$$ Acontraluz, San Enrique 473, Cerro Alegre, T032-211 1320, www. hotelacontraluz.cl. Probably the best of the boutique hotels here. Rooms facing the sea have balconies with tremendous views. Bright, Victorian house with attention to detail and no expense spared. English, French, Russian spoken, most hospitable, 24-hr café, solar power, recycling, no TV.
$$$$ Casa Higueras, Higuera 133, Cerro Alegre, T032-249 7900, www.hotelcasa higueras.cl. Small, elegant hotel on 5 levels, variety of rooms, good views, fine restaurant, spa, sauna, pool and gardens.

$$$$ Manoir Atkinson, Paseo Atkinson 165, T032-327 5425, www.hotelatkinson.cl. A boutique hotel, 7 comfortable rooms, terraces with views of the city and bay, English and French spoken, meals, tours arranged.
$$$$ Palacio Astoreca, Montealegre 149, Cerro Alegre, T032-327 7700, www.hotel palacioastoreca.com. Boutique hotel in a 1920s mansion, rates between US$266 and US$570 for a double room including tax.
$$$$-$$$ Somerscales Boutique, San Enrique 446, Cerro Alegre, T032-233 1006, www.hotelsomerscales.cl. Spacious rooms in former home of English painter, period furniture. Basic English spoken, top-floor rooms lovely views.
$$$-$$ La Nona, Galos 660, Cerro Alegre, T032-249 5706, www.bblanona.com. Comfortable, welcoming B&B, some rooms with bath, plenty of information and activities, English spoken.
$$ Hostal Casa Verde Limón, Subida Cumming, Plaza El Descanso 196, Cerro Cárcel, T032-212 1699, www.casaverde limon.com. Double, single rooms, dorm and loft, shared bath, breakfast extra, laundry, good budget choice.
$$ La Bicyclette, Almte Montt 213, Cerro Alegre, T032-222 2215, www. bicyclette.cl. Basic, bright rooms, shared bath, book exchange, lovely patio, French-run, rents bicycles.

$$ Luna Sonrisa, Templeman 833, Cerro Alegre, T032-273 4117, www.lunasonrisa.cl. Room for 16 guests in doubles, singles or dorm with shared or en suite bath, owned by the previous author of this guidebook. Bright, comfortable, lots of information, excellent breakfast including wholemeal bread and real coffee, tours arranged, English and French spoken, helpful. Also **El Nidito**, www.elnidito.cl, one classically elegant apartment with 3 en suite bedrooms, large living/dining room with upright piano and spacious balcony, parking. Also 1 smaller apartment, sleeps 2-4.

$$-$ Casa Aventura, Pasaje Gálvez 11, off C Urriola, Cerro Concepción, T032-275 5963, www.casaventura.cl. One of Valparaíso's longest established backpackers' hostels, with rooms and dorms in a traditional house, German and English spoken, tours, helpful, deservedly popular, informative.

$$-$ Pata Pata, Templeman 657, T032-317 3153, www.patapatahostel.com. Family-run, doubles and big dorms (**$**), shared facilities, lots of movies, good choice.

Avenida Alemania and the other cerros p87, map p84

$$$ The Grand House, Federico Varela 25, Cerro La Cruz, T032-221 2376, www.thegrandhouse.cl. Charming house, almost Victorian decor, excellent breakfast, "a true gem".

$$$ Puerto Natura, Héctor Calvo 850, Cerro Bellavista, T032-222 4405, www.puertonatura.cl. Large grounds with fruit trees and small pool, café, excellent views. There is also a holistic centre with sauna, massages, reiki, reflexology and meditation.

$$$ Ultramar, Pérez 173, Cerro Cárcel, T032-221 0000, www.hotelultramar.cl. Italianate building (1907), modern design, buffet breakfast, café, attentive staff. Rooms are spacious with great views but may get stuffy in summer.

$$ Catalejo House, Bernardo Vero 870, Cerro San Juan de Dios, T032-225 9150, www.catalejohouse.com. Rooms with shared bath, good view, good reports.

Cerro Bellavista and Plaza de la Victoria *p87, map p84*
$$$ Diego de Almagro, Molina 76, T032-213 3600, www.dahoteles.com. Comfortable 4-star business standard hotel. Superior rooms look out over the bay.
$$ Hostal Caracol, Héctor Calvo 371, Cerro Bellavista, T032-239 5817, www.hostalcaracol.cl. Rooms or dorm. Pleasant patio and barbecue area, heating. English spoken. A good choice. Offers discounts at **Confieso** restaurant, Rudolph 254, T032-328 4116, just down the hill.

Plaza O'Higgins and around
p88, map p84
$$-$ El Rincón Marino, San Ignacio 454, T032-222 5815, www.rinconmarino.cl. Uninspiring location, but good-value *hostal*.
$$-$ Hostal NuevaMente, Pocuro 1088, T032-317 0184, hostalnuevamente. valparaiso on Facebook. Beautiful old hostel with big, light rooms, about 15 mins' walk from centre. Run by a helpful young couple, good local information, some English spoken, movies, tours, bike hire.

⊘ Restaurants

El Plan and El Puerto *p83, map p86*
$$$ Zamba & Canuta, Blanco 1065, T032-221 6013. Elegant, modern cuisine, wide range of dishes. Excellent views across the bay, also holds events.
$$$-$$ Bote Salvavidas, by Muelle Prat. Elegant fish restaurant overlooking the port.
$$ Bar Inglés, Cochrane 851 (entrance also on Blanco Encalada), T032-221 4625. Historic bar dating from the early 1900s, a chart shows the ships due in port. Good food and drink.
$$ Isabel a La Costeñita, Blanco 86. Good seafood, with incredibly kitsch decor.

$$ Los Porteños, Cochrane 102. A seafood favourite, terse service but good food.
$$ Porto Viejo, Cochrane y Valdivia. Good-value set lunch fish dishes, good service.
$ Mastodonte, Esmeralda 1139. No nonsense, very good value, traditional food in incredibly kitsch surroundings. Excellent service and cheap locally brewed draft beer.
La Rotonda, Prat 701. One of Valparaíso's more traditional cafés, good coffee and breakfast.

Playa Ancha and around *p84*
At Caleta Membrillo, 2 km northwest of Plaza Sotomayor (take any Playa Ancha bus), there are several good fish restaurants including **Club Social de Pescadores**, Altamirano 1480, and **El Membrillo**.

Cerros Alegre and Concepción
p85, map p86
These *cerros* have a great many places to eat, again more than we can list; wander around to see what takes your fancy.
$$$ La Concepción, Papudo 541, Cerro Concepción, T032-249 8192. Creative food, beautifully presented and well served, magnificent views.
$$$-$$ Café Vinilo, Almte Montt 448, T032-223 0665. Inventive lunchtime menus with gourmet interpretations of traditional Chilean dishes. Also a lively bar at night.
$$$-$$ Fauna, Dimalow 166, T032-212 1408. Varied menu, mostly seafood and fish, Chilean, desserts, large wine list, eat inside or on terrace. Also has a hotel, www.faunahotel.cl.
$$$-$$ La Colombina, Paseo Yugoeslavo 15, Cerro Alegre, T032-223 6254. The most traditional of the area's restaurants. Good food, wide range of wines, fine views, especially from the top floor.
$$$-$$ Le Filou de Montpellier, Almte Montt 382, T032-222 4663. French-run, set lunch menu deservedly popular, also open weekday evenings.
$$$-$$ Pasta e Vino, Templeman 352, Cerro Concepción, T032-249 6187.

Wonderfully inventive, tasty pasta dishes, haughty service. Advance booking essential, closed Mon.

$$$-$$ Turri, Templeman 147, Cerro Concepción, T032-225 9198. Reasonable food, good range of fish dishes, wonderful views, a bit of a tourist trap.

$$ Allegretto, Pilcomayo 529, Cerro Concepción, closed Mon-Fri 1530-2000, Sat and Sun 1630-2000. Lively British owned pizzería, exotic but very tasty toppings, can get busy.

$$ Malandrino, Almirante Montt 532, Cerro Alegre. Wed-Thu 1900-2300, Fri 1300-1600, 1900-2400, Sat 1300-1600, 2000-2400, Sun 1300-1700. Traditional pizzas baked in a clay oven using mostly organic ingredients. Cosy atmosphere. Popular with locals as well as tourists.

$ El Dominó, Cumming 67. Traditional, serves *empanadas*, *chorillanas*, *calagas de pescado* (fish nuggets), open till 0500.

Cafés and snack bars

Café con Letras, Almte Montt 316, Cerro Concepción (also on Plaza Sotomayor). Intimate café serving good coffee and snacks, soup in winter, lots of reading material.

Color Café, Papudo 526, Cerro Concepción. Cosy arty café serving tea and real coffee, fresh juice, good cakes, snacks and all-day breakfasts, regular live music, art exhibits, local art and craft for sale. Upstairs is **La Valija Hostel** (unrelated), good reports.

Delicias Express, Urriola, near Prat. A whole range of fried empanadas, good for a quick snack.

El Desayunador, Almte Montt 399, Cerro Alegre T032-275 5735. Breakfast bar open early. Wide range of teas, real coffee, cakes, also vegetarian lunches.

La Cocó, Monte Alegre 546, Cerro Alegre. A good selection of sandwiches, including vegetarian, tapas, desserts, teas, coffees and drinks. Live *cueca* music on Thu 2200.

Pan de Magia, Almte Montt 738 y Templeman, Cerro Alegre. Cakes, cookies,

fantastic empanadas and by far the best wholemeal bread in town, all take away.

Cerro Bellavista and Plaza Victoria *p87, map p84*

$$ Amaya, Rudolf 112, Cerro Bellavista, T032-249 3567. Fri-Sun. At the top of the *ascensor* Espíritu Santo. Peruvian food, mostly seafood-based, friendly service, good views from terrace.

$ Bambú, Independencia 1790, p 2, T032-223 4216. Closed Sun. Vegetarian lunches only.

$ J Cruz, Condell 1466, T032-221 1225. Valparaíso's most traditional restaurant/ museum, famous for its *chorillanas*, open all night, very popular, queues at lunchtime.

$ Pimentón, Ecuador 27. Home-cooked traditional Chilean dishes. Menu changes daily, good value.

$ San Carlos, Las Heras y Independencia. Traditional family-run restaurant with lots of character that hasn't changed in years. Lunch only. Good food guaranteed, always full of locals. Recommended.

Bogarín, Plaza Victoria 1670. Great juices, ice cream and snacks.

Gata Ferrari, Ferrari 103-A, Bellavista, T032-320 574. Little café and art gallery with sofas and comfy chairs, at the foot of the *subida* to Museo al Cielo Abierto.

Plaza O'Higgins and around *p88, map p84*

There are good cheap seafood lunches upstairs at Mercado Cardonal behind the bus terminal.

$$$-$$ Marco Polo, Pedro Montt 2199, www.marco-polo.cl. Traditional restaurant, *pastelería* and *salon de té*, since 1955, good value set lunches, plus mostly Italian dishes.

$$ La Otra Cocina, Yungay 2250, near Francia. Good seafood, cosy, good service.

$ Natur-In, Colón 2634, www.naturin.cl. Tasty home-made, mostly vegetarian food. Menu changes daily, excellent value, fills up quickly, lunch only.

🅾 Bars and clubs

El Plan and El Puerto *p83, map p86*
The area around El Puerto can be dangerous at night. There are many bars on Subida Ecuador, but be careful which ones you go into, as in some of them you risk being eaten alive (**El Muro**, for example, is rough and sordid). **El Coyote Quemado** is by far the best.

Cinzano, Plaza Aníbal Pinto 1182, T032-221 3043. Oldest bar in Valparaíso, also serves food. Flamboyant live music at weekends, noted for tango (no dancing by guests allowed).

El Huevo, Blanco 1386. One of Valparaíso's most popular nightspots with 3 levels of dancing and drinking.

El Irlandés, Blanco 1279. Mon-Sat from 1700 (1800 Thu, Sat). Decent and good fun Irish-run Irish bar with bitter on tap and a good selection of beer, live music at weekend.

La Piedra Feliz, Errázuriz 1054. Wed-Sat from 2000. Every type of music depending on the evening, large pub, live music area, and dance floor, clientele of all ages, entrance US$9.

La Playa, Serrano 567 through to Cochrane 558, near Plaza Sotomayor. Old English-style bar, live music, attracts a student crowd.

🅾 Entertainment

Valparaíso *p80, map p84*
It is worth checking out the 'Invite' supplement, inside the *Mercurio de Valparaíso*, www.mercuriovalpo.cl every Fri.

Cinema

Cinehoyts, Pedro Montt 2111, T600 5000 400. Mainstream movies, most from Hollywood.

Instituto Chileno-Norteamericano de Cultura (www.norteamericano.cl) also shows films, as do smaller film clubs. The 'Invite' supplement, inside the *Mercurio de Valparaíso* every Fri has details of these.

Galleries

In addition to the **Galería de Arte Municipal** and the **Museo Municipal de Bellas Artes**, occasional free exhibitions are held at the following galleries:

Cámara Lúcida, Subida Concepción 281, Cerro Concepción, www.camaralucida.cl. Photographic exhibitions and workshops.

Consejo de Cultura, Prat and Plaza Sotomayor, www.cultura.gob.cl/region/valparaiso/. Housed in the former post office building. Temporary exhibitions in the basement.

Cult-Art, Almte Montt y Galos, Cerro Alegre, www.cult-art.cl. Contemporary art by local artists.

Fundación Valparaíso, Héctor Calvo, Cerro Bellavista (between La Sebastiana and ascensor Espíritu Santo) www.fundacion valparaiso.com. Local contemporary art.

Instituto Chileno-Norteamericano, Esmeralda 1069. Temporary exhibitions of photos and paintings from all over Chile.

Sala El Farol, Blanco 1113, El Plan. Art gallery attached to the Universidad de Valparaíso with interesting temporary exhibitions.

Wenteche, Templeman 523, Cerro Concepción. Features work by Valparaíso artists.

✡ Festivals

Valparaíso *p80, map p84*
New Year Celebrated by a 3-day festival culminating in a superb 40-min firework display on the bay, which is best seen from the *cerros*. Over a million visitors and locals take supper and champagne to celebrate from vantage points around the bay. Accommodation can double or even triple in price at this time and needs to be booked well in advance.

🅾 Shopping

Valparaíso *p80, map p84*
Markets
Large **antiques market** on Plaza O'Higgins every Sun. Very good selection, especially old

shipping items. Along Av Argentina there is a huge, colourful **fruit and vegetable market on** Wed and Sat and a crowded **flea market** on Sun. Good locally made handicrafts on Cerro Alegre and Cerro Concepción.

☮ What to do

Valparaíso *p80, map p84*
Boat trips
Small boats make 45-min tours of the harbour from Muelle Prat, near Plaza Sotomayor, offering a pleasant view of the city, especially if it's sunny: US$7 pp plus tip for the commentator; wait for the boat to fill up. Boats run till 1930. There are also night trips at 2000. *Colectivo* boats run between Muelle Prat and Muelle Barón, US$5.50.

Cooking classes
Chilean Cuisine, T09-6621 4626, www. cookingclasseschile.cl. Fun introduction to Chilean food with English-speaking chef/ teacher, can include wine tour, wine tastings.

Skiing
Valposki, T032-273 4659, or T09-8428 3502, www.valposki.cl. Regular day-trips to El Colorado, Farellones and La Parva ski resorts.

Tours
Payment for these tours is by tip.
Free Tour, T09-9236 8789, www.freetour valparaiso.cl. 3-hr walking tour starting from Plaza Aníbal Pinto, daily 1000 and 1500.
La Porteña, valparaisopuertomagia@ gmail.com. Tours on foot or by bike.

Wine tours
Ask at the **Municipal Tourist Office** (see above) about wine tours to the Casablanca Valley (Fri 0930 from Plaza Sotomayor, US$27.50 for 2).
Wine Tours Valparaíso, T032-273 4659, or T09-8428 3502, www.wine tours valparaiso.cl. Small-group tours to the Casablanca Valley with an English-speaking guide.

⊖ Transport

Valparaíso *p80, map p84*
To reach the airport at Pudahuel, take a bus to Pajaritos, US$6-7.50, cross the platform and take a bus to the airport, US$2.50; alternatively, catch any Santiago bus and ask to be let off at the 'paradero de taxis' before the Cruce de Pudahuel; taxis wait here 0700-2000 and charge US$7.50 to the airport (about 7 mins' ride, compared with 1 hr if you go into Santiago). Only take a taxi with an official Airport Taxi sticker (pirates overcharge).

Ascensores
Municipal *ascensores* run daily 0700-2300 (US$0.20). Sometimes you pay on entrance, sometimes on exit.

Bus
Local US$0.50 within El Plan, US$0.65 to Cerros, US$0.90 to **Viña del Mar** from Av Errázuriz. Bus 612, known as the 'O', from Av Argentina near the bus terminal to Plaza Aduana gives fine panoramic views of the city and bay. Bus No 520 to **Laguna Verde** can be caught from Pedro Montt via Playa Ancha every 40 mins, 40 mins, US$1.20. A yellow *colectivo* from C 12 de Febrero behind the bus terminal in Valparaíso runs to **Quintay**; it won't go until it's full, but if you're in a hurry you can pay for the extra seats, 45 mins, US$2; otherwise, buses to Quintay leave from the corner of 12 de Febrero and Yungay.

Long distance To **Santiago**, 1¾ hrs, US$11-14.50, frequent (book return in advance on long weekends and public hols). Fares are much the same as from Santiago to places such as **Chillán**, 7 hrs, **Concepción**, 8 hrs, **Pucón**, 12 hrs, **Puerto Varas** and **Puerto Montt**, 14 hrs; to **La Serena**, 7 hrs, **Antofagasta**, 17 hrs, **San Pedro de Atacama**, 24 hrs. To **Mendoza (Argentina)** 5 companies, 8 hrs, early morning.

Taxi

More expensive than Santiago: a short run under 1 km costs US$2 and a journey across town about US$9-10. Taxi *colectivos*, slightly more expensive than buses, carry sign on roof indicating route, very convenient.

Train

Regular service on the modern **Metro Valparaíso** (Merval) line, T032-252 7633, www.metro-valparaiso.cl, between Valparaíso, **Viña del Mar**, **Quilpué** and **Limache**, with a bus service to **Olmué**; services every 10 mins. Travel cards cost US$2.50; fare depends on time of day and distance travelled, lowest fare about US$0.60, to **Viña del Mar** US$0-70-0.80.

ⓘ Directory

Valparaíso *p80*, *map p84*
Banks and currency exchange Banks open Mon-Fri 0900 to 1400. Many **Redbanc** ATMs on Prat, and one at the bus terminal. *Casas de cambio*: best exchange rates from **Marin Orrego**, 3rd floor of the stock exchange building, Prat y Urriola, only changes US$ and euro cash; for other currencies, there are several *casas de cambio* along Cochrane, Prat and Esmeralda.

Around Valparaiso

Viña del Mar and around → *For listings, see pages 102-106. Colour map 3,A/B2.*

Nine kilometres northeast of Valparaíso via the Avenida España, which runs along a narrow belt between the shore and precipitous cliffs, is Viña del Mar, one of South America's leading seaside resorts. Viña is also famous throughout Chile for its annual international music festival, during which the attention of the entire country is focused on the city; the festival used to bring in some top performers from all over Latin America, but this is no longer the case. In fact, neither the festival nor Viña itself are as wonderful as Chileans like to make out. This is the only place in Chile where road signs are in English as well as Spanish and much of the city feels like suburban North America. That said, with pleasant beaches and shady parks, Viña is a nice enough city to visit, especially if you have some pesos to burn, and makes an interesting contrast to nearby Valparaíso.

Arriving in Viña del Mar

Getting there and around There are inter-urban buses to Viña del Mar from many cities. The city also has daily connections through to Mendoza in Argentina. Viña del Mar can also be reached relatively easy by public transport from Santiago's airport. The bus station is two blocks east of Plaza Vergara at Avenida Valparaíso y Quilpué, T032-275 2000. Frequent *micros* link Viña and Valparaíso from Libertad or 1 Norte. *Colectivos* also serve these routes, as well as running to many of the city's outlying neighbourhoods and there are numerous buses along the coast. The Merval train runs along the waterfront. Taxis are plentiful and usually reasonably priced. ▸▸ *See Transport, page 106.*

Tourist information For **tourist information** in Viña del Mar contact **Sernatur** ① *8 Norte 580 y 2 Poniente, T032-297 5687, infovalparaiso@sernatur.cl.* The Municipal office is near Plaza Vergara on Arlegui, by Hotel O'Higgins. See also www.vinadelmarchile.cl and www.vinadelmar.cl.

Places in Viña del Mar

The older part of Viña del Mar is situated on the banks of a creek, the Marga Marga, which is crossed by bridges. Around Plaza Vergara and the smaller Plaza Sucre are the **Teatro Municipal** (1930) and the exclusive **Club de Viña**, built in 1910. It's a private club, but sometimes hosts public concerts and events. The municipally owned **Quinta Vergara**, formerly the residence of the shipping entrepreneur Francisco Alvarez, lies two blocks further south. The superb grounds include a double avenue of palm trees and encompass a children's playground and a large outdoor amphitheatre where the music festival takes place in February; it also hosts concerts and events throughout the year. See www.quintavergara.cl. Also here is the **Palacio Vergara** ① *T032-268 0618*, which houses the **Museo de Bellas Artes** and the **Academia de Bellas Artes**. It is in poor shape and was closed to the public in 2014). You can take a tour of the city in a horse-drawn carriage from the Plaza Vergara for around US$30 depending on the length of the trip.

Calle Libertad runs north from the plaza, lined with banks, offices and shops. At the junction with 4 Norte is the **Palacio Carrasco**, now a cultural centre housing temporary exhibitions. In the same grounds is the **Museo Fonck** ① *Calle 4 Norte 784,* *www.museofonck.cl, Mon-Fri 1000-1800, Sat and Sun 1000-1400, US$4*, an interesting archaeological museum, with objects from Easter Island and the Chilean mainland, including Mapuche silver. East of this is the **Palacio Rioja** ① *Quillota 214, T032-218 5722, closed for restoration in 2014*, built in 1906 by a prominent local family, but seriously damaged in the 2010 earthquake. Four blocks further east is the **Valparaíso Sporting Club** with a racecourse and playing fields, while to the north, in the hills is the **Estadio Sausalito**, home to Everton football club.

West of the plaza, on a headland overlooking the sea, is **Cerro Castillo**, the president's summer palace; its gardens can be visited. Below, on the coast, Castillo Wulff houses the **Museo de la Cultura del Mar** ① *T032-262 5427, Tue-Sat 1000-1300, 1430-1800, Sun 1000-1400*, which contains a collection devoted to the life and work of the novelist and maritime historian, Salvador Reyes. Just north, on the other side of the Marga Marga, is the **casino** ① *open all year, US$5*, completely rebuilt after a fire and set in beautiful gardens. North of this are the main beaches, Acapulco and Las Salinas (see below), while south of Cerro Castillo is another popular beach at **Caleta Abarca**.

Jardín Botánico Nacional ① *8 km southeast of the city, www.jardin-botanico.cl, daily 1000-1800 (till 1900 Sep-Apr), US$3.75, getting there: take bus No 203 from C Alvarez, or Av Errázuriz in Valparaíso, and get off at the Puente El Olivar, cross the bridge and walk 15 mins*. This was formerly the estate of the nitrate magnate Pascual Baburizza and is now administered by CONAF. Covering 405 ha, it contains over 3000 species from all over the world and is a good picnic spot. Within the gardens is a large collection of Chilean

Viña del Mar

Where to stay 🛏	Restaurants 🍴		
1 Agora	6 Hotel del Mar	3 Café Journal	9 La Flor de Chile
3 Cap Ducal	8 Offenbacher Hof	4 Cevasco	10 Las Delicias del Mar
		5 Ciboulette	11 Samoiedo
	Restaurants 🍴	6 Enjoy del Mar	13 Wok and Roll
	1 Alster	7 Fellini	
	2 Bogarín	8 Jerusalem	

cacti; it's very pretty, but unfortunately the different species are not labelled. There is also a canopy adventure tourism site with zip-lines linking trees within the park.

Resorts north of Viña del Mar → For listings, see pages 102-106.

North of Viña strung along the coast are several smaller settlements. Reñaca, now a suburb of Viña del Mar, is a well-to-do resort with extensive beaches, while further north, Maitencillo and Zapallar are fashionable seaside destinations, overflowing with tourists in summer. In between are the fishing towns of Concón, famous for its seafood, and Horcón, where horses are still used to tow the fishing boats onto land.

Reñaca and Cochoa

North of Viña del Mar the coast road runs past **Las Salinas**, a popular beach set between two towering crags. The suburb of **Reñaca** is a popular resort with access to excellent beaches, while to the north at **Cochoa**, there are giant sand dunes and a large sea lion colony 100 m offshore. This route affords lovely views over the sea, but there is also a much faster inland road between Reñaca and Concón.

Concón

Concón lies on the southern shore of a bay 18 km north of Viña del Mar at the mouth of the Río Aconcagua. The town claims to be the oldest settlement in Chile, having been founded by Pedro de Valdivia in 1541, prior to his arrival at what is now Santiago. Concón is famous for its restaurants and is known as the culinary capital of the V region. The area is very popular among Santiaguinos, who often come here for the weekend. A series of six beaches stretches along the bay between Caleta Higuerilla at the western end and La Boca at the eastern end. These beaches include **Playa Amarilla**, which is good for sunbathing; the very peaceful **Playa Higuerillas**, where there are lots of shells; **Playa Los Lilenes**, backed by sand dunes, and **Playa La Boca** itself, which is by far the largest of the six, and excellent for beach sports (horses andkayaks for hire). The helpful **tourist office** ① *annexed to the municipal museum, Maroto 1030, www.concon.cl*, can provide maps of the resort.

Quintero

Another 23 km north of Concón, Quintero is a dilapidated fishing town situated around a rocky peninsula with 16 small beaches, all of varying character and quality. The path running along the north side of the peninsula offers a good view of the sunset over the ocean from the Cueva del Pirata at its western end. Good fishing and windsurfing are available at **Playas Loncura** and **Ritoque** to the south of the town, while horses can be hired on **Playa Albatros**. Note that there are many touts and beggars in Quintero in the high season, when the atmosphere can become a little tense. On the opposite side of the bay is **Las Ventanas**, where a power station and copper processing plant rather spoil the outlook from the beach.

Horcón

Set back in a cove surrounded by cliffs, Horcón, also known locally as Horcones, is a pleasant small village, mainly of wooden houses. Although overcrowded in season, during the rest of the year it is a charming place, populated by fishermen and artists, with a tumbledown feel unlike the more well-to-do resorts to the north and south. Across the headland to the south of the village is **Playa Cau Cau**; scramble down a steep flight of log steps to reach the sandy, frequently deserted, tree-lined cove, sadly now dominated by a condominium development.

Maitencillo

Maitencillo, 19 km north of Las Ventanas, is an upmarket resort consisting mainly of chalets and frequented mainly by well-to-do Santiaguinos. There is a wonderful long beach here but the sea is notorious for its strong undercurrents. It is usually deserted off season.

Zapallar

A fashionable resort with a lovely beach, 33 km north of Las Ventanas, Zapallar is an expensive place to stay. The number of fine mansions along Avenida Zapallar are a clue to its luxurious heritage. At **Cachagua**, 3 km south, there are clear views of a colony of penguins on an offshore island from the northern end of the beach; take binoculars.

Papudo

Ten kilometres further north is the site of a naval battle in November 1865, in which the Chilean vessel *Esmeralda* captured the Spanish ship *Covadonga* during the War of Independence. Following the arrival of the railway Papudo rivalled Viña del Mar as a fashionable resort but it has declined a great deal since its heyday in the 1920s. Among the buildings surviving from that period is the **Casa Rawlings**, now the Casa de la Cultura. There are two fine beaches, which are empty except in high summer.

East of Valparaíso → *For listings, see pages 102-106.*

Towards Santiago

Reserva Nacional Peñuelas ① *US$4.50*, encompasses 9260 ha around the artificial Lago Peñuelas and is open to visitors for walking and fishing. The park, which is covered by pine and eucalyptus forest, is situated 30 km southeast of Valparaíso near the main road to Santiago (Route 68). Buses between the two cities pass the entrance where the park administration is located. Beyond the park, Route 68 passes the wine-producing Casablanca valley and through two tunnels (US$3 toll each).

Towards Argentina

The Troncal Sur highway runs through Viña del Mar, climbs out of the bay and passes south of **Quilpué**, Km 16, a dormitory town for Valparaíso and Viña, with an interesting municipal zoo. It crosses a range of hills and reaches the Aconcagua Valley at **Limache**, a sleepy market town, renowned for its alternative medicine and spiritual retreats, as well as its fruit and vegetable production. Limache is 40 km from Valparaíso on the Merval railway. In the town is the **Quinta Escondida** ① *Carrera 013, T09-8418 0531, www.quintaescondida.com*, a late 19th-century house with fruit orchards which offers B&B, self-catering, day visits, access to local sites and activities. This is the Chilean HQ for **South American Explorers** (www.saexplorers.org). On site is also Rosa Puga's healing centre. The Troncal Sur joins Route 60 just before **Quillota**, another fruit-growing centre, continuing to **La Calera**, Km 88, where it joins the Pan-American Highway; turn southeast and east for Llaillay, San Felipe, Los Andes and the Redentor tunnel to Mendoza (see page 72).

Parque Nacional La Campana

① *T033-244 1342, www.conaf.cl, daily 0900-1730 (until 1630 Fri), US$4.55 for foreigners*.
Situated north of Olmué (8 km east of Limache), the park covers 8000 ha and includes **Cerro La Campana** (1828 m), which Darwin climbed in 1835, and **Cerro El Roble** (2200 m). It is divided into three main sections, each with its own entrance: in the south

are **Sector Granizo** ① *paradero 45, 5 km east of Olmué*, from which the Cerro La Campana is climbed, and **Sector Cajón Grande** ① *paradero 41, reached by unpaved road off the Olmué–Granizo road*, while to the north is **Sector Ocoa** ① *reached by unpaved road (10 km) off the Pan-American Highway between Hijuelas and Llaillay*, which is where the main concentration of Chilean coconut palms (*kankán*) can be found. This native species is now found in natural woodlands in only two locations in Chile. The park can be crossed on foot (six hours) between Ocoa and Granizo or Cajón Grande along well-marked trails through the gamut of Chilean natural vegetation, from cactuses and palm trees to southern beech and lingue. A number of shorter trails lead from all three entrances.

A fair amount of agility is required to climb **Cerro La Campana**. Allow a whole day there and back from Olmué, although fit and experienced hikers could probably do it in around seven hours. There are three places where fresh water is available on the climb, but you should take your own food and drink. From the entrance at Granizo, a path leaves the road to the left just past the CONAF *guardería*, and climbs steeply through forest, fording a clear, rushing stream and providing increasingly fine views of the valley below until reaching an old mining area (two hours from the *guardería*). From here the path is well marked, but becomes more testing; after passing a plaque dedicated by the British community to Charles Darwin on the centenary of his visit, it climbs over loose rock to a pass to the northeast, before doubling back and rising over rocks (where scrambling and a little very basic climbing is required) to the summit. The wonderful views from the top of the Cerro la Campana take in a 300-km stretch of the Andes (including Aconcagua), as well as the rugged outline of the central cordillera losing itself in the haze to the north, the gentler scenes of the southern hills, and, when the haze is not too great, Valparaíso and the Pacific Ocean to the west. It is also possible to ascend La Campana from Quillota, but this route is more difficult and definitely requires a guide.

South of Valparaíso → *For listings, see pages 102-106.*

Laguna Verde, 12 km south of Valparaíso, is a picturesque bay with a huge beach that is peaceful and perfect for picnics, although the wind can get quite fierce in the afternoons and strong undercurrents make swimming dangerous.

Further south, **Quintay** is the least known of the villages on the *central littoral* and also one of the most picturesque. In its heyday, the village's **whaling station** ① *daily 0930-1800, US$1*, employed over 1000 workers, mostly from Chiloé, but now only the fishermen remain. Most people ignore the threatening sign warning you not to climb up to the lighthouse. If you take the risk, the view is worth the short climb to watch the sunset.

Quintay has two beaches, the larger of which is being overrun by a housing development. The other, **Playa Chica**, is accessed via an unsignposted route through a eucalyptus wood (entry by the *carabineros*). It is wild and deserted off season and is definitely worth the 20-minute walk.

Resorts south of Valparaíso → *For listings, see pages 102-106.*

This cluster of resorts stretches along the coast from the mouth of the Río Maipo north towards Valparaíso. The resorts here are not as upmarket as those north of Viña, but every summer tens of thousands of Chileans flock to them from the capital. Beaches range from classic wide white-sand affairs to secluded coves, and a wild, rocky zone around Isla Negra; off season, most are deserted.

Arriving south of Valparaíso

Road links between Valparaíso and the resorts to the south are poor, but there are two good routes from Santiago: one branch off the main Santiago–Valparaíso highway to Algarrobo and the other, Route 78, direct to San Antonio. Buses link the resorts in this area, but a hire car will allow you to explore more secluded coves.

San Antonio and around

Situated near the mouth of the Río Maipo, 112 km south of Valparaíso, San Antonio was at the epicentre of a large earthquake in 1985. Subsequently, the harbour was rebuilt and has now taken over from Valparaíso as the main container port for this part of the coast. It is the terminal for the export of copper brought by rail from the large mine at El Teniente, near Rancagua (see page 230) as well as being an important fishing port. Many restaurants buy their fish and seafood here and a visit to the docks just after the catch has been unloaded is an interesting experience. **Museo Municipal de Ciencias Naturales y Arqueología** ⓘ *Av Barros Luco, Mon-Fri 0900-1300, 1500-1900*, has displays on nature, pre-colonial culture and geology. There is also a botanical garden.

Nearby to the south are two resorts: **Llolleo**, 4 km, and 7 km further **Rocas de Santo Domingo**, the most attractive and exclusive resort in this area with 20 km of beaches and a golf course; even in high season it is not very crowded.

Cartagena → *For more information on Cartagena, see www.cartagena.cl.*

Eight kilometres north of San Antonio, Cartagena is the biggest resort on this part of the coast, but is a quieter place than San Antonio. It is filled with fish restaurants and ice cream shops and has lovely views sweeping north around the bay towards Isla Negra. In the early years of this century, it was a fashionable summer retreat for the wealthy of Santiago; a number of mansions survive, notably the **Castillo Foster** overlooking the bay. The centre lies around the **Plaza de Armas**, situated on top of the hill. To the south is the picturesque **Playa Chica**, overlooked by many of the older hotels and restaurants; to the north is **Playa Larga**. Between the two a promenade runs below the cliffs; high above hang old houses, some in disrepair but offering spectacular views. Cartagena is a very popular resort in summer but out of season it is a good centre for visiting nearby points of interest; there are many hotels and bus connections are good.

North of Cartagena

The road to Algarrobo runs north along the coast through several small resorts including **Las Cruces**, **El Tabo** and **El Quisco**, a small fishing port with two beautiful white-sand beaches (crowded during Chilean holidays).

Isla Negra

Four kilometres south of El Quisco in the village of Isla Negra is the beautifully restored **Museo-Casa Pablo Neruda** ⓘ *T035-246 1284, www.funcacionneruda.org, Jan-Feb Tue-Sun 1000-2000, rest of year Tue-Sun 1000-1800, US$7.25, students US$2.75, audio guides in several languages*. Bought by Neruda in 1939, this house overlooking the sea was the poet's writing retreat in his later years, and became the final resting place of Neruda and his last wife Mathilde. The house contains artefacts gathered from all over the world and the café specializes in Neruda s own recipes. The museum conveys a powerful sense of the poet and is well worth a visit. However, some Chileans feel that the **Fundación Pablo Neruda** should not be charging such high admission prices. For further information about Pablo Neruda, visit his Santiago house, La Chascona, page 49, and La Sebastiana in Valparaíso, page 87; see also box, page 525.

Algarrobo

Algarrobo is the largest resort north of Cartagena and the most chic, with large houses, a yacht club and a marina. Conveniently located for Santiago, it was the retreat of politicians in the 1960s. Today, it remains one of the most popular spots on the central coast: its shallow waters and sheltered bay ensure that sea temperatures here are much warmer than at most other resorts along the central Chilean coast, while good beaches are supplemented by activities such as fishing, surfing and sailing. From **Playa Canelo** there are good views of pelicans and boobies in a seabird colony on an offshore island. Boat tours circle round it in summer, departing from the jetty.

⊙ Around Valparaiso listings

For hotel and restaurant price codes and other relevant information, see pages 14-21.

⊜ Where to stay

Viña del Mar *p96, map p97*
There are lots of places to stay, mostly **$$$**, although many are in the business district and not convenient for the beaches. Out of season agencies rent furnished apartments. In season it's cheaper to stay in Valparaíso.
$$$$ Hotel Del Mar, San Martín 199, T032-600 700 6000, www.enjoy.cl/enjoy-vina-del-mar. Viña's top hotel, in spacious grounds above the casino, overlooking the bay. Gym, spa and several good restaurants.
$$$$-$$$ Cap Ducal, Marina 51, T032-262 6655, www.capducal.cl. Old mansion charm – a ship-shaped building literally overhanging the ocean, with an elegant restaurant, serving good seafood.
$$$ Agora, 5½ Poniente 253, T032-269 4669, www.hotelagora.cl. On a quiet side street, brightly coloured rooms, most with full-size bathtub, English spoken, helpful staff (on 4 floors but no lift).
$$$ Offenbacher Hof, Balmaceda 102, T032-262 1483, www.offenbacher-hof.cl. Large wooden house in a quiet residential street overlooking the city centre, peaceful, helpful.

Reñaca *p98*
Accommodation here is much cheaper out of season.
$$$$-$$$ Montecarlo, V MacKenna 136, T032-283 0397, www.hotelmontecarlo.cl. Comfortable if slightly dated style. Many rooms with sea view.
$$$$-$$$ Oceanic, Av Borgoño 12925, T032-283 0006, www.hoteloceanic.cl. Comfortable, spacious slightly dated rooms dramatically set on the ocean front. It is worth paying the extra for an ocean-facing room – for the views and also to escape the street noise. Good restaurant (mostly seafood).
$$$ Cabañas Don Francisco, Torreblanca 75, T032-283 4802, www.cabañasdonfrancisco dereñaca.cl. Helpful service, *cabañas* only available for week-long bookings.
$$$ Piero's, Av Segunda 89, T032-238 3737, www.pieroshotel.cl. Comfortable, with café, pool, some rooms with sea view.

Concón *p98*
$$$ Cabañas Los Romeros, Baldos 565 T032-903 937. Cabins for up to 3 people.
$$$ Cabañas Río Mar, T032-281 4644. Many other *cabañas* in this price range.

Camping
Mantagua, 3 km north, T032-215 5900, www.mantagua.cl. Well equipped but very expensive, also *cabañas*.

Quintero p98

There are lots of cheap *residenciales* here.
$$$ Nuevo Hotel Quintero, Lord
Cochrane 180, T032-293 0149. Hotel with
pool and large gardens on the seafront.
$$ Residencial Brazilian, 21 de Mayo
1336, T032-293 0590, anasatt@yahoo.com.
With breakfast, large windows but no view,
clean, well maintained, warm sea-water
baths for US$10.50.

Horcón p98

There are many *cabañas* around the village;
shop around for the best price, especially off
season. Rooms are also available in private
houses and, although there's no campsite,
camping is possible in people's gardens.
$$$ Cabañas Arancibia, T032-279 6169,
www.arancibiahostal.8m.com. Cabins with
or without bath, pleasant gardens, good
food, friendly. Recommended.
$$ El Ancla, Costanera 159, by the harbour,
T033-2791 6017, www.restaurantelancla.cl.
Pleasant *cabañas*, also serves good food in
its 2 restaurants.

Maitencillo p99

$$$$ Marbella Resort, 2 km south, T032-
279 5900, www.marbella.cl. 5-star resort,
conference centre, restaurants, golf course,
tennis courts, pools, and everything else
you would expect.
$$$ Cabañas La Mar, Av del Mar 524,
T032-277 1036, www.cabanaslamar.cl.
One of several options in this price range.

Zapallar p99

Accommodation is expensive especially
in the centre where it is sparse. There's
no campsite.
$$$$ Isla Seca, T033-2741224, www.
hotelislaseca.com. Small, with pool and
very expensive suites, good restaurant.
$$$ Residencial Villa Alicia, Moisés
Chacón 280, T033-741176. Good, and
one of the cheapest.

Papudo p99

There are several cheap *residenciales* on
Chorillos 100-150.
$$$ Carande, Chorrillos 89, T033-791105,
www.hotelcarande.cl. Best in town.
$$$ De Peppino, Concha 609, T033-
2791108. *Cabañas* for 4-6 people.

Parque Nacional La Campana p99

There are places to stay in all price
categories in Olmué for easy access to the
Granizo sector of the park. (See also Quinta
Escondida, Limache, above.)
$$$$ El Copihue, Diego Portales 2203,
Olmué, T033-244 1544, www.copihue.cl.
Small resort set in pleasant gardens, with
gym, games room, indoor and outdoor
pools. Half and full board available.
$$ La Alondra, Granizo 8459, Olmué,
T033-244 1163. Cheaper singles.
A reasonable budget choice.
$$ Sarmiento, Blanco Encalda 4689,
Olmué, T033-244 2838, Restoran Sarmiento
on Facebook. **$** singles. Cheap and cheerful,
also has a restaurant.

Camping

It is possible to camp in all sectors of
the park, with cold showers. In summer
reserve in advance, T033-244 1342.

South of Valparaíso p100

Camping is possible at Laguna Verde at
Camping Los Olivos, which has good
facilities and is well run and friendly.

San Antonio and around p101

$$$$-$$$ Rocas de Santo Domingo, La
Ronda 130, Santo Domingo, south of San
Antonio, T035-244 4356, www.hotelrocas.cl.
Clean, friendly, with restaurant, cable TV.
Good breakfast included in price. Also suites.

Cartagena p101

$$ Violeta, Condell 110, T035-245 0372.
With swimming pool, good views.
$ Residencial Carmona, Playa Chica, T035-245
0485. Small rooms, basic, clean, good value.

$ Residencial Paty's, Alacalde Cartagena 295, T035-245 0469. Nice spot, good value.

North of Cartagena p101
Accommodation is generally more expensive in El Quisco.
$$ Cabañas Pozo Azul, Capricornio 234, El Quisco, T09-733 5171, www.pozoazul.cl. Southeast of town, quiet.
$$ Gran Italia, Dubournais 413, El Quisco, T035-248 1631. Good beds and pool. Recommended.
$$ Residencial Julia, Aguirre 0210, El Quisco, T035-247 1546. Very clean, quiet, good value.

Isla Negra p101
$$ Casa Azul, Av Santa Luisa, T035-246 1154. With breakfast, kitchen and living room, English spoken, camping. Recommended.

🍴 Restaurants

Viña del Mar p96, map p97
Many good bars and restaurants on and around San Martín between 2 and 8 Norte; cuisine including Austrian, Mexican, Chinese and Italian. Cheap bars and restaurants around C Valparaíso and Von Schroeders. Not too safe at night.
$$$ Ciboulette, 1 Norte 191, T032-269 0084. Intimate Belgian-owned and run bistro serving traditional French cuisine. Good wine list.
$$$-$$ Enjoy del Mar, Av Perú s/n, T032-250 0785. Modern restaurant serving everything from gourmet dishes to barbecues and fast food, all on an open terrace on the seafront.
$$$-$$ Fellini, 3 Norte 88, T032-297 5742. Wide range of fresh pasta dishes in delicious sauces, good.
$$$-$$ Las Delicias del Mar, San Martín 459. Traditional Basque seafood restaurant.
$$ La Flor de Chile, 8 Norte 607 y 1 Poniente. T032-212 3480. Consistently good, typical Chilean food.

$$ Wok and Roll, 5 Norte 476. One of the better sushi restaurants in town. Free delivery service.
$$-$ Cevasco, Av Valparaíso 700, T032-271 4256. Freshly prepared Chilean fast food. Famous for its oversized hamburgers.
$ Café Journal, Agua Santa y Alvarez. Excellent-value set lunch.
$ Jerusalem, Quinta 259. Authentic middle-eastern fare, including falafel, shawarma and stuffed vine leaves.

Cafés
Alster, Valparaíso 225. Elegant but pricey.
Bogarín, in a mall on Valparaíso between Quinta and Etchevers. For juices and ice cream. Several other fast food places in the mall.
Samoiedo, Valparaíso 637. A large modern *confitería*, ice cream, coffee, popular.

Concón p98
Seafood is the name of the game here. Both Caleta Higuerilla and La Boca are renowned for their restaurants.
$$$ Among the most upmarket are located along Av Borgoño, 1 side fronting onto the road, the other onto the beach, including the following in Caleta Higuerilla: **Albatross**, No 21295; **Aquí Jaime**, No 21350; **Bellamar**, No 21550; **Don Chicho**, No 21410; and **Vista al Mar**, No 21270.
$$-$ Mid-range options include **La Picá de Emeterio**, and **Las Deliciosas**, both on Borgoño in La Boca, while cheaper eateries are to be found in Alto Higuerillas, where *picadas* have been converted by the fishermen into good-value restaurants: try **La Picá de Juan Segura**, Illapel 15; **La Picá El Horizonte**, San Pedro 120, and **La Picá Los Delfines**, San Pedro 130. Look out, too, for tasty seafood *empanadas* served in the resort's bars.

Quintero p98
There are several cheap seafood restaurants down by the harbour.

Horcón p98

Seafood lunches made from the catch of the day are sold at stalls on the seafront, where there also a number of restaurants.
$$ Nuevo Bahía. Good food, pleasant place.
$$ Santa Clara. Try the *chupe de mariscos* (cheesy shellfish soup) and *pastel de jaivas* (crabmeat cooked in cheese and breadcrumbs). Recommended.
$ Roty Schop. Acclaimed for its *empanadas*.

Maitencillo p99

$$$ Bar Rest La Canasta, Av del Mar 592. Mediterranean and Moroccan cuisine served in elegant surroundings; expensive but worth it.
$$ Bar Tsunami, Av del Mar 1366. Mid-range seafood.

Papudo p99

$$ La Maison des Fous, Blanco 151. Unusual bar-restaurant in lovely old house. Friendly staff, good food and atmospheric candle-lit piano bar with graffiti-covered pillars. There are several other seafood places in all price ranges.

South of Valparaíso p100

El Galeón restaurant in Laguna Verde serves good simple food. In Quintay try the local speciality *congrio arriero* (fish stew with chips on top!) at any of the reasonably priced restaurants on the harbour (**Miramar** is especially recommended for its huge portions, fresh fish and good service).

Bars and clubs

Viña del Mar p96, map p97
There are dozens of bars and clubs in the triangle formed by San Martín, 5 Poniente and 2 Norte. They tend to change name and style every other year.
Barlovento, 2 Norte y 5 Poniente, T032-297 7472. The designer bar in Viña, on 3 floors with a lovely roof terrace, serves tapas, wraps, etc, and good beer. Several other options between San Martín and Perú.

Reñaca p98

El Ciervo, Av Central y Segunda. Bar/café with live music in evenings. Recommended.

Papudo p99

Help, Glorias Navales 409. Disco with music from techno to salsa.
La Maison des Fous, see Restaurants, above.

Entertainment

Viña del Mar p96, map p97
Cinemas
Cine Arte, Plaza Vergara 42, www.cinearte.cl. Also a multiplex in the shopping mall on Libertad (see Shopping, below).

Galleries
Mar Pau, Valparaíso 595, local 18, www.marpau.com.
Palacio Carrasco, Libertad 250.
Sala de Arte Viña del Mar, Arlegui 683.

Festivals

Viña del Mar p96, map p97
Feb Festival Internacional de la Canción attracts an audience from all over Chile. Tickets are available from the Municipalidad and should be bought ahead of time; you should also reserve any accommodation well in advance.

Resorts north of Viña del Mar p98
29 Jun Since this area comprises coastal communities, it is no surprise that the **Fiesta de San Pedro** (the patron saint of fishermen) is an important event.

Shopping

Viña del Mar p96, map p97
The **market** is held on Wed and Sat at the intersection of Av Sporting and the river. There is a large **mall** on Libertad between 14 and 15 Norte, open till 2300.

La Vinoteca, San Martín 545 y 6 Norte, www.lavinoteca.cl. Stocks a good range of Chilean wine.

☉ What to do

Viña del Mar *p96, map p97*
Cycling
Bicitours, T09-4094 4506, www.bicitours.cl. 8 cycling tours based in Viña, from 2 to 5 hrs, city tours, to resorts, to Valparaíso, from US$12.75; also bicycle hire, US$9.25 per hr, US$33 per day.

Maitencillo *p99*
Paragliding
Parapente Aventura, Maitencillo, www.parapentemaitencillo.cl. Single tandem flight, US$88; classes, US$700.

Concon *p98*
Horse riding
Ritoque Expediciones, north of Concón, T09-9730 5212, www.ritoqueexpediciones.cl. Excellent day trips over a variety of terrain. Galloping encouraged. Full moon rides. Pick-up service from Valparaíso and Viña del Mar.

☉ Transport

Viña del Mar *p96, map p97*
Bus
To **Santiago**, US$11-14.50, 1¾ hrs, frequent, same companies as for Valparaíso from Pajaritos in Santiago, book in advance for travel on Sun afternoons. Long-distance prices and itineraries similar to Valparaíso.

Train
Services on the Metro Valparaíso line stop at Viña (see under Valparaíso).

Resorts north of Viña del Mar *p98*
Bus
From Valparaíso and Viña del Mar: to **Concón**, bus 601, US$1, frequent; to **Quintero** and **Horcón**, Sol del Pacífico,

every 30 mins, US$3, 2 hrs; to **Zapallar** and **Papudo**, Sol del Pacífico, 4 a day, US$6. All from Av Libertad in Viña, or Errázuriz in Valparaíso.

Parque Nacional La Campana *p99*
The entrances at **Granizo** (paradero 45) and **Cajón Grande** (paradero 41) are reached by local bus/*colectivo* from outside Limache train station. No public transport to **Ocoa**; Get a bus to La Calera and bargain with a taxi or *colectivo* driver. Expect to pay around US$30. Bus Santiago-Limache, **Pullman** from Alameda terminal, every 2 hrs, US$8, 2 hrs.

Resorts south of Valparaíso *p100*
Bus
Pullman Lago Peñuelas operates direct buses from Valparaíso to **San Antonio**, every 30 mins until 2000, 2 hrs, US$7. The coastal service from Valparaíso to **Algarrobo** and **Isla Negra**, every 30 mins, 1½ hrs, US$6, also continues to San Antonio. **Empresa de Buses San Antonio** and **Empresa Robles** run frequent services from Algarrobo to **San Antonio**, until 2000, 30 mins.

Pullman Bus runs services from Santiago to **San Antonio**, every 20 mins in summer, US$13. There are also frequent services from the capital with **Pullman Bus** (from Terminal Alameda) and other companies (from Terminal Sur) to **Isla Negra** and **Algarrobo**, US$12.50 (via Cartagena, US$12.50, and other resorts). Many tours go to Isla Negra, too.

☉ Directory

Viña del Mar *p96, map p97*
Banks Many Redbanc ATMs on Libertad and on Arlegui; also on C Valparaíso (but this is not a safe area at night). Many *casas de cambio* on Arlegui and Valparaíso; shop around for best rates and avoid changing money on the street, especially if alone.

Contents

From Santiago to La Serena

At a glance

⊖ **Getting around** Good bus services link the main cities and go up the Elqui Valley as far as Pisco. To explore the rugged interior a high-clearance vehicle should be hired.

⟲ **Time required** 3 to 5 days to see the sights around La Serena and the Elqui Valley; more if you want to head off the beaten track.

☁ **Weather** Moderate temperatures on the coast with morning fog not uncommon. Inland blue skies practically every day. The nights are cooler further up the valleys.

✖ **When not to go** Pleasant all year round, though if you want to star gaze, try to avoid the full moon.

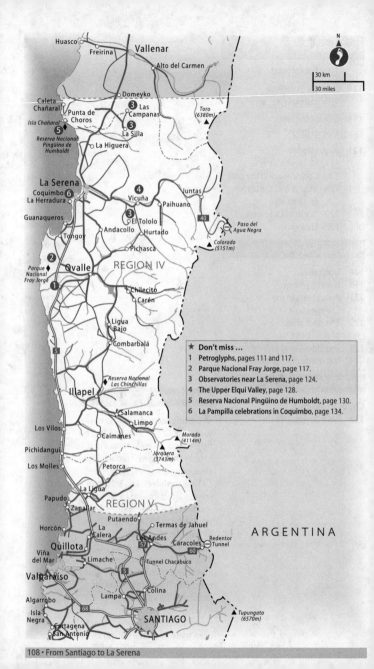

★ **Don't miss ...**

1 Petroglyphs, pages 111 and 117.

2 Parque Nacional Fray Jorge, page 117.

3 Observatories near La Serena, page 124.

4 The Upper Elqui Valley, page 128.

5 Reserva Nacional Pingüino de Humboldt, page 130.

6 La Pampilla celebrations in Coquimbo, page 134.

There is a common saying in Chile, "between Tongoy and Los Vilos". It is a way of saying "in the middle of nowhere". Most Chileans would have you believe that, a handful of coastal resorts aside (Tongoy and Los Vilos among them), the 500 km stretch between Santiago and La Serena is an uninteresting wasteland. Yet this could not be further from the truth. There are rich rewards for those prepared to rough it and take a few risks.

Inland you will find one of the world's highest concentrations of petroglyphs, spectacular mountainsides speckled different colours by rich mineral deposits, and desolate tracks winding through some of Chile's best high-mountain scenery. To the north is the resort of La Serena, a centre for visiting the *pisco* distilleries of the fertile Elqui Valley. This valley is one of the world's most important astronomical centres, with five observatories, including two built especially for visitors – it is also the focal point of Chile's New Age movement, and was the birthplace of Nobel laureate Gabriela Mistral. South of La Serena is the lively market city of Ovalle, an ideal centre for forays into the *cordillera* and for visiting the Parque Nacional Fray Jorge, a temperate rainforest that survives in this dry region due to the sea mists that hang almost constantly over its hills.

Mineral heaven

If you are at all interested in geology, you could spend months in this part of Chile and still not be satisfied. The mountains of the *cordillera* here are brimful of minerals that are easily visible to the naked eye. Near Combarbalá, the colours are white and red, showing that the *combarbalita* – a marble-type rock found nowhere else in the world – is nearby. In the high mountains inland from Ovalle is one of the world's two lapis lazuli mines; while at Andacollo, you may have your only chance in Chile to see small-scale gold mining in operation.

Miners in these areas often work independently and they are known as *pirquineros*. They process their findings in two types of small mills. The *trapiche* consists of two heavy vertical wheels in a container half filled with water. As the ore is ground between the wheels, the mineral sticks to mercury, which is spread on the sides of the container. The other type of mill, the *maray*, resembles a large mortar and pestle and is hand driven. Both the *trapiche* and the *maray* are rented by the miner, with the rent paid as a share of the ore.

Background

Stretching north from the Río Aconcagua to the Río Elqui, this area is a transitional zone between the fertile heartland and the northern deserts. Rainfall is rare and temperatures are relatively stable. North of the Aconcagua, the Andes and the coastal *cordillera* merge in a spectacular lattice of mountains and are crossed by river valleys separated by high ridges. The valleys of the Choapa, Limarí and Elqui rivers are green oases, where the land is intensively farmed and irrigated. Elsewhere, the vegetation is characteristic of semi-desert, except in those areas where frequent sea mists provide sufficient moisture to support temperate rainforest. The coastline is generally flat, with many beautiful coves, both rocky and sandy, and good surf.

Archaeological finds south of Los Vilos suggest a presence going back at least 10,000 years. The rise of the Molle culture happened around the same time as the rise of Christianity in Europe; sharing links with northern Argentina, the Molle people produced intricate ceramics and worked with copper. They were superseded by the Diaguitas, who crossed the Andes around AD 900 and settled throughout the area. The pre-Hispanic peoples left their mark in the form of petroglyphs (rock carvings).

Soon after the arrival of the Spanish and the foundation of Santiago, Pedro de Valdivia attempted to secure control over northern Chile by founding La Serena in 1544. The indigenous people here were less numerous than the Mapuche in the south and were soon subjugated and wiped out. Throughout the colonial period, La Serena dominated the rest of the region; although small, it was the only city in the north and its leading families had close ties to the main Spanish landowners in the other valleys. After Independence, the area became an important mining zone, producing large amounts of silver, copper and gold.

Mining is an ever more important industry in this area. El Romeral, north of La Serena, is one of the most important iron-ore deposits in the country. Many new copper mines are being opened up including a huge mine at Los Pelambres at the top of the Choapa valley. Quartz and the semi-precious stones lapis lazuli and combarbalita are also mined. Despite the dry climate, another regional industry is the distilling of *pisco* from grapes; by law, only grapes grown in the regions of Atacama and Coquimbo can be used to make *pisco*.

Choapa Province

The first stretch of the Pan-American Highway from Santiago heads inland through green valleys with rich blue clover and wild artichokes. North of La Ligua (known for its sweet white cookies as well as its woollen goods), it follows the coast, and the first intimations of the northern deserts appear. From Los Vilos, a paved road turns off the Pan-American Highway towards Illapel, climbing steeply up to a pass, from which there are staggering views of the Andes and the Choapa River.

Illapel is surrounded by barren hills, with good views of the cordillera to the east. While the town is not wildly interesting in itself, it is close to wonderful mountain country, best explored by the adventurous or those with their own transport. The Illapel region is largely ignored by travellers, yet it has some worthwhile attractions. This is the narrowest part of Chile between Arica and Aysén, and the Andes are never far away, with valleys carving right up towards the snowline. There are many examples of pre-Hispanic petroglyphs for those who take the trouble to find them.

Arriving in Choapa Province

Getting there and around There are direct buses to Los Vilos and Illapel from Santiago, Valparaíso and La Serena. There are regular bus services up and down the valley as far as Salamanca from where *colectivos* can be taken to the more remote upper valley. The towns are all small enough to explore on foot.

Los Vilos and the coast

Los Vilos is a small seaside resort 216 km north of Santiago. Set in a wide bay, it is a peaceful, windswept place, disturbed mainly by the noise of the kelp gulls and the waves, except in summer when it fills up with holidaymakers from Santiago. Halfway between the capital and La Serena, it is a good place to break the journey. Los Vilos was founded as a mineral port. Having suffered years of decline as a backwater fishing village, the local economy is being revitalized by the new port at the north tip of the bay serving the mine at Los Pelambres. There are several attractive *plazuelas* on the *costanera*, with stone benches among aloe and palm trees, from which you can watch the fishing boats bobbing in the sea; the water is cold for bathing. Also on the *costanera* is a small **municipal aquarium** ① *in theory open daily 0900-1300 and 1430-1700 but often closed off season*. Two blocks inland from here is the **Bodegón Cultural** ① *Elicura 135*, in a former port warehouse, now a gallery showing good-quality temporary exhibitions of artwork from the region and around Chile. Entrance is free but donations are welcome. The shop sells stoneware ceramics with diaguita motifs made by local craftswomen.

Offshore are two islands reached by frequent launches: **Isla de Los Huevos**, situated in the bay, and, 5 km south, **Isla de Los Lobos**, where there is a colony of seals. There is a **tourist office** ⓘ *Elicura 302, open summer only.*

Pichidangui, 26 km south, is a popular resort on a rocky peninsula, with a beautiful beach to the north. **Los Molles**, 10 km south of Pichidangui, is a fishing village where many wealthy residents of Santiago have their summer homes. Nearby are the **Puguén blow holes** and the **Piscina Los Molles**, a natural swimming pool.

Illapel

Nearly 480 km north of Santiago, Illapel is a poor town that depends on mining in the surrounding mountains for its survival. It is a small town and can easily be covered on foot. There is a small archaeological museum next to the library in the **Casa de la Cultura** ⓘ *Valdivieso y Constitución, just off the Plaza de Armas, free*, with a bizarre and disordered collection of arrowheads, jewellery, pottery, miners' boots and newspapers so dusty you almost choke. There is no tourist office (although you could try asking for information at the Municipalidad on the plaza, www.municipalidadillapel.cl), but there is a very helpful office run by **CONAF** ⓘ *Ignacio Silva 301, Mon-Sat 0830-1400.*

Salamanca and around

This small town lies 32 km southeast of Illapel along the Río Choapa. It is surrounded by the dusty foothills of the Andes and has a large shady plaza where craftspeople sometimes display their goods. Halfway along the road from Illapel is the **Los Cristales Pass**, from where there are views of distant snowy mountains. Salamanca

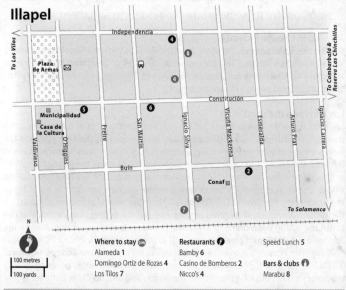

Illapel

To Los Vilos

Independencia ❹

❽

❹

Plaza de Armas ✉

Constitución

Municipalidad ❺

Casa de la Cultura ❻

Valdivieso | O'Higgins | Freire | San Martín | Ignacio Silva | Vicuña Mackenna | Esmeralda | Arturo Prat | Ignacio Carrera

To Combarbalá & Reserva Las Chinchillas

Buín

Conaf ▪ ❷

❶

❼

To Salamanca

N

100 metres
100 yards

Where to stay
Alameda **1**
Domingo Ortíz de Rozas **4**
Los Tilos **7**

Restaurants ❼
Bamby **6**
Casino de Bomberos **2**
Nicco's **4**

Speed Lunch **5**

Bars & clubs ❶
Marabu **8**

has lost some of its charm since it now doubles as a service town for the new mine at Los Pelambres.

Some 2 km north of Salamanca on the Illapel road is a turning for the small town of **Chalinga**, with a church dating from 1750 (ask at the nearby convent if entry is possible). A dusty road continues from Chalinga up into the Chalinga valley, passing plantations of *pisco* grapes, fruit orchards and irrigated vegetable patches before heading up into barren mountain scenery around **Zapallar**. There are many petroglyphs in the surrounding area – ask at the school for information and help in seeking them out.

North to Combarbalá

From Illapel, a paved road leads 15 km north to the **Reserva Nacional Las Chinchillas** ① *Tue-Sun 0900-1730, US$4.50*, passing impressive mountains speckled with cacti and minerals. The reserve covers 4229 ha and protects the last remaining colony of chinchillas in this region. The chinchillas and six related species can be viewed from behind two-way mirrors.

After Las Chinchillas, there is a fork in the road. To the left is a decent if sinuous road to Combarbalá via the village of **Los Pozos**. To the right the asphalt disappears and the mountainsides close in – red, purple and white with minerals, and covered with cacti. This poor road (high-clearance vehicle needed) climbs the **Cuesta El Espino** to a height of over 2000 m, from where there are unforgettable views of the multicoloured mountains and the white snows of the Andes. A much worse road – suitable for riders and cyclists only – branches off at the junction for Las Chinchillas and follows the old railway track on an even more remote and dramatic route to Combarbalá, via mining settlements at Farellón Sánchez and Matancillas. Eventually, it rejoins the main road below Cuesta El Espino and reaches the small town of Combarbalá, 73 km north of Illapel.

Combarbalá is set in a dusty bowl surrounded by mountains. The town is famous as the home of the *combarbalita*, a semi-precious stone that was declared the National Stone of Chile in 1993. *Combarbalita* is similar in appearance to marble and is found nowhere else in the world. There are lots of workshops on the north side of town, particularly on Calle Flores, where you can see the craftsmen at work and buy their goods. An astronomical observatory, the **Cruz del Sur** (www.observatoriocruzdelsur.cl), has been built near the town. For information, see www.combarbala.cl, the municipal website.

◉ Choapa Province listings

For hotel and restaurant price codes and other relevant information, see pages 14-21.

⊕ Where to stay

Los Vilos and the coast *p111*
$$$ American Motel, Km 224, T053-254 1163. Right on the highway and a convenient stopping place between Viña del Mar or Santiago and La Serena, good value.
$$$ Pichidangui, Francis Drake s/n, Pichidangui, T053-253 1115, www.hotel pichidangui.cl. Hotel with swimming pool

and restaurant. The town has various other hotels and *pensiones* at every price.
$$$-$$ Cabañas Mar y Sol, Av Los Vilos 20, T053-254 1705, cabanasmarysol.cl. Snug cabins with kitchenette. Great location, the lower cabins are practically on the beach while the upper cabins have a great view. Terrace with small pool and Wi-Fi area. Convenient for **TurBus** and **Pullman**.
$$$-$$ Lord Willow, Los Vilos1444, T053-254 8854, www.hotellordwillow.cl. Los Vilos's oldest hotel with a collection of old firearms and fossils, with bath, pleasant,

friendly, parking. Small but decent rooms, some with view across the road to the coast, others (quieter) to the good-sized swimming pool. Breakfast extra.

$$ Cabañas Los Delfines, Lautaro 048, Los Vilos, T09-9930 3900, www.losdelfines-lv.es.tl. Comfy spacious cabins that sleep 4. With kitchen and cable TV. Views across some wasteland to the Isla de los Huevos. Prices rise in high season.

$$-$ Bellavista, Rengo 020, Los Vilos, T053-254 1073. With breakfast, bath and TV in carpeted rooms, hot water, sea views. Pretty tatty but the singles are good value.

$ There are 2 cheap, central *residenciales* on Caupolicán in Los Vilos: **Turismo**, No 437, T053-254 2705, and **Residencial Punta de Chungo**, No 627, T053-254 1096.

Camping

Bahía Marina de Pichidangui, T053-253 1120, www.bahiamarina.cl. Sports facilities and *cabañas*.

Illapel *p112, map p112*

$$$ Domingo Ortíz de Rozas, Ignacio Silva 241, T053-252 2127, www.hotelortizderozas.cl. Spacious rooms with all mod cons at this attractive 3-star.

$$ Los Tilos, Ignacio Silva 45, T053-252 3335, hotellostiloss@hotmail.com. With bath, breakfast and TV, friendly, but small rooms. Laundry service and internet.

$$-$ Alameda, Ignacio Silva 20, T053-252 2378, www.alamedahotel.cl. With bath and TV, without breakfast, friendly, clean, nice patio with lemon and orange trees, cheap laundry service, recommended.

Salamanca and around *p112*

$$ My House, Infante 451, T053-255 2036, www.hotelmyhouse.cl. The nicest of Salamanca's hotels, good rooms, internet access in lobby, can arrange local tours.

$$-$ Residencial O'Higgins, O'Higgins 430. Some rooms with bath. Breakfast extra, friendly, clean, basic, patio.

Camping

There are several basic campsites in the Chalinga Valley, including one at Zapallar.

North to Combarbalá *p113*

$$$-$$ Yagnam, Valdivia 465, Combarbalá, T053-274 1329, www.hotelyagnam.cl. Clean hotel, friendly, room service, good value, recommended.

🍴 Restaurants

Los Vilos and the coast *p111*

Restaurants in Pichindangui tend to be pricey, although there is a food shop. There are countless places on the seafront in Los Vilos, either in Caleta San Pedro or, further around the coast towards the island, where there are several small eateries – watch out, touting for business here is intense!

$$ Alisio, Elicura 160, Los Vilos. Seafood and fish, good value, probably the best in town.

$$ Restaurant Turístico Costanera, Caleta San Pedro, Los Vilos. Good views over ocean, good meals and choice of wines, nice warm bread. Also serves a cheap menu.

$ El Rey de la Paila Marina Vileña, Caleta San Pedro, Los Vilos. Fish and seafood.

Cafés

Café Entrevientos, Caupolicán 298b, Los Vilos. Intimate café serving decent coffee and cakes.

Illapel *p112, map p112*

$$ Nicco's, Ignacio Silva 279. Good pizzas, fancy decor, vegetarian options.

$ Bamby 2.0 Restaurant, Ignacio Silva 392. Not great quality but very cheap.

$ Casino de Bomberos, Buín 590. Friendly, excellent value, good views of the town.

$ Speed Lunch, Constitución 160. Friendly, some vegetarian possibilities

Salamanca and around *p112*

Restaurants in Salamanca tend to be basic. There are cheap ice creams at a shop next to **ENTEL** on the plaza.

$ Restaurant Crillón, on the Plaza on Montepio. Friendly, excellent-value *almuerzos*.

🅞 Bars and clubs

Los Vilos and the coast *p111*
Several new bars open every year for the summer season.

Illapel *p112, map p112*
Pub Marabú, Ignacio Silva 254. US$4. Bar with free happy hour, salsa and merengue at the weekends.

🅭 Festivals

Salamanca and around *p112*
Feb/Mar Holy Week is a big event in Salamanca, with horse races at La Chilena and costumed processions through the town.

🅞 Transport

Los Vilos and the coast *p111*
Bus
Many north–south buses on the highway pass Los Vilos and Pichidangui. The main long-distance companies serving Los Vilos each have their own terminal: **Pullman Bus**, Caupolicán 1111; **TurBus**, Caupolicán 898, and **Expreso Norte**, Caupolicán 1159, each with at least 5 buses daily to **Santiago**, 3½ hrs, US$10, and **La Serena**, 4½ hrs, US$10.75, as well as frequent buses to **Illapel**, 1 hr, US$3, and **Salamanca**, US$4. **Intercomunal** have 5 buses daily to **Valparaíso**, leaving from Caupolicán 690 and there are 3 buses daily to **Combarbalá** from the same location. Buses between Los Vilos and **Pichidangui** leave every hour from Rengo at the junction with Caupolicán.

Illapel *p112, map p112*
Bus
The bus station is at San Martín, on the 200 block. **TurBus**, **Pullman Bus** and **Expreso Norte** all have services to **Santiago**, 4½ hrs,

US$13, and **La Serena**, 4½ hrs, US$10.75, via Los Vilos. **Intercomunal** has 4 buses daily to **Viña** and **Valparaíso**, US$10.75. Buses to rural destinations leave from Independencia y Ignacio Silva.

Salamanca and around *p112*
Bus
The long-distance bus company offices are on or around the plaza. There are rural buses most days from Salamanca to the mountain communities, as well as *colectivos* to Illapel (from the plaza) and further up the valley from Bulnes, 3 blocks east of the plaza. Buses to **Illapel** run in the daytime, continuing either north to **La Serena** or south to **Santiago**.

North to Combarbalá *p113*
Bus
There are buses linking Combarbalá with **La Serena** and **Ovalle**. Buses Combarbalá serve **Santiago**, **La Calera**, **La Ligua** and **Los Vilos**. There are also services to **Illapel** via **Reserva Nacional Las Chinchillas** although most of these are at night.

🅞 Directory

Los Vilos and the coast *p111*
Bank Banco Estado, Caupolicán y Guacolda, Los Vilos. MasterCard only. Also changes money. There is also an ATM that takes Visa in the **Supermercado Los Naranjos**, Caupolicán. **Post office** Lincoyán, Los Vilos.

Illapel *p112, map p112*
Banks Banco de Chile, Ignacio Silva 105. **Laundry** Alondra, Ignacio Silva 370, only one in town. **Medical services** Hospital: Independencia 512, T053-252 4227. **Post office** Plaza de Armas.

Salamanca *p112*
Banks Banco Estado, O'Higgins y Montepio, MasterCard only. There is a Visa ATM in the **Copec** petrol station on the corner of the plaza. **Post office** Bulnes 571.

Limarí Valley

The Limarí Valley contains much of the north of Chile in a microcosm: beaches at Tongoy, the mysteriously lush Parque Nacional Fray Jorge, a vibrant market town in Ovalle, countless examples of ancient rock art and wonderful mountain scenery. With remote tracks through the mountains and giant hillsides sprinkled with cacti and multicoloured minerals, it is a fine place to wander for a week or more.

Arriving in the Limarí Valley → *Colour map 2, C1.*
Getting there and around Ovalle is easily reached by regular buses: from La Serena and destinations as far as Arica in the north; and from Illapel, Valparaíso and Santiago in the south. Of Ovalle's various bus terminals, the **Terminal Media Luna** (by the rodeo ring on Ariztía Oriente, just south of the city centre) is the one used by long-distance buses. Numerous local buses and *colectivos* link Ovalle with outlying communities; most leave from one of the two terminals outside the Feria Modelo. ▸▸ *See Transport, page 120.*

Ovalle → *Colour map 2, C1.*
Situated inland in the valley of the Río Limarí – a fruit-growing and mining district – this lively town is a focal point for the numerous communities in the surrounding mountains and valleys. Edged by dusty hills, which are lined with vines for *pisco* grapes and orchards

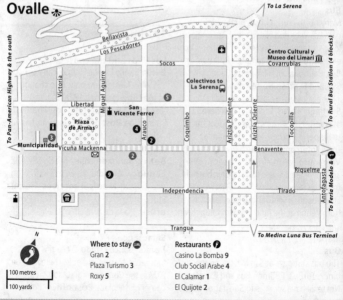

Ovalle

To La Serena
Bellavista
Los Pescadores
To Pan-American Highway & the south
Socos
Centro Cultural y Museo del Limarí
Covarrubias
To Rural Bus Station (4 blocks)
Victoria
Miguel Aguirre
Colectivos to La Serena
Libertad
San Vicente Ferrer
Plaza de Armas
Coquimbo
Ariztía Poniente
Ariztía Oriente
Tocopilla
Municipalidad
Arauco
Vicuña Mackenna
Benavente
Riquelme
Antofagasta
To Feria Modelo & 1
Independencia
Tirado
Trangue
To Medina Luna Bus Terminal

100 metres
100 yards

Where to stay 🛏
Gran 2
Plaza Turismo 3
Roxy 5

Restaurants 🍴
Casino La Bomba 9
Club Social Arabe 4
El Calamar 1
El Quijote 2

of avocado trees, it gets busy on market days, when local *campesinos* throng around the market area. That said, Ovalle remains a laid-back town with an almost rural feel to it. Although not a typical tourist destination it is an excellent window on the traditionally slow pace of life in the Norte Chico. It is famous for its *talabarterías* (saddleries) and for its products made of locally mined lapis lazuli, as well as *queso de cabra* (goat's cheese) and dried fruits (sold in the market). The central part of town can easily be covered on foot. **Museo del Limarí** ① *Covarrubias y Antofagasta, T053-243 3680, www.museolimari.cl, Tue-Fri 0900-1300, 1500-1900, Sat and Sun 1000-1300, US$1, Sun free,* is housed in the old railway station and has displays of petroglyphs and an excellent small collection of Diaguita ceramics and other artefacts. Information is in Spanish only. Annexed to the museum is a gallery with temporary art and crafts exhibitions. There is a semi-official **tourist information** centre in one of the kiosks selling *artesanía* on Aritzía. Failing that try the municipalidad just off the Plaza de Armas.

South of Ovalle

Embalse La Paloma, the largest reservoir in Chile, is 26 km southeast of town. On the northern shore is the small town of **Monte Patria**, with a *pisco* distillery that can be visited. From Monte Patria, a paved road leads to Chilecito and Carén, where there is the **Parque Ecológico La Gallardina** ① *T053-272 6009, www.parquelagallardina.cl US$3.65 (US$6.35 with use of pool)*, containing a beautiful collection of roses and other plants and flowers amid the dry mountains.

Monumento Nacional Valle del Encanto ① *about 22 km southwest of Ovalle, open all year 0800-1800, US$2*, is one of the most important archaeological sites in northern Chile. Artefacts from hunting peoples from over 2000 years ago have been found, but the most visible remains date from the Molle culture (AD 700). There are over 30 petroglyphs as well as great boulders, distributed in over sites. There are camping facilities at the site but no local bus services; instead, catch a southbound long-distance bus and ask to be dropped off, then it's a 5-km walk to the valley. You'll need to flag down a bus to return; alternatively, use a tour operator.

Termas de Socos ① *Pan-American Highway, 35 km southwest of Ovalle, www.termasocos.cl, US$9, bus US$2*, is a popular resort among Chileans. There are swimming pools and individual bath tubs fed by thermal springs, as well as a sauna, jacuzzi and water massage. It also boasts a reasonable hotel and a campsite.

Parque Nacional Fray Jorge

① *T09-9346 2706, parque.frayjorge@conaf.cl, Dec-Mar daily 0900-1730, last entry 1600, Apr-Nov Thu-Sun only, US$4.35. No public transport; take a tour from La Serena.*
Situated 90 km west of Ovalle and 110 km south of La Serena at the mouth of the Río Limarí, this UN World Biosphere Reserve covers 9959 ha and contains original temperate rainforests, which contrast with the otherwise barren surroundings. Receiving no more than 113 mm of rain a year, the forests survive because of the almost constant fog and mist covering the hills, the result of the discharge of the warm waters of the Río Limarí into the cold waters of the Pacific. The increasingly arid climate of this part of Chile has brought the habitat under threat and hence visits are closely controlled by **CONAF** ① *Regimiento Arica 901, Coquimbo, T051-224 4769, www.conaf.cl*. Scientific groups may obtain permission to visit otherwise inaccessible parts of the park from the Director of CONAF in La Serena. All visitors should take particular care to leave no trace of their presence behind them. The park is reached by a dirt road leading off the Pan-American

Highway. The entrance and administration are at Km 18, from where it is 10 km further to the summit of the coastal hills (known as the Altos de Talinay), which rise to 667 m. Waterproof clothing is essential.

Along the Río Limarí

From Ovalle, a road leads 77 km northeast, following the course of the Río Limarí to the village of Hurtado. The route passes the Recoleta Reservoir and then follows the valley, where fat horses graze on alfalfa, vines with *pisco* grapes are strung out across what flat land there is, and the glades are planted with orchards of orange and avocado trees.

The road is paved as far as Samo Alto; shortly after (about 42 km from Ovalle) is the turn-off (to San Pedro) for the **Monumento Natural Pichasca** ① *daily 0800-1800, US$4*. Some 47 km northeast of Ovalle at an altitude of 1350 m, this park contains petrified tree trunks and archaeological remains, including a vast cave with remnants of ancient roof paintings. Gigantic rock formations can be seen on the surrounding mountains. Encouraged by the local mayor, a bright green model of a dinosaur has been erected here. Sure to be a magnet for groups of local schoolchildren, the dinosaur is supposed to be the north's answer to the sloth in the Milodón Cave near Puerto Natales (see page 417), but as yet it is too early to claim that Jurassic Park has come to Pichasca. To reach the park, catch a daily bus from Ovalle to Hurtado and get off at the turn-off to San Pedro, about 42 km from the city; from here it is 3 km to the park and about 2 km more to sites of interest.

Beyond the village of **Pichasca** are several plantations, where rickety wooden suspension bridges cross to the far side of the Río Limarí. It is a further 32 km to Hurtado and the road continues winding along the side of the valley, with the Andes now easily visible at the head of the valley. At **Vado Morrillos**, 4 km before Hurtado, is the **Hacienda Los Andes** ① *T053-269 1822, www.haciendalosandes.com*, a centre for horse riding and trekking in the area, set in a very pretty location, with a 7-km nature trail. The hacienda is run by an experience, English-speaking German/Austrian team. Horse-riding tours from one to eight days are offered in the surrounding mountains; they also have an observatory. If coming by bus to the hacienda, ask the driver to let you off at the bridge at Vado Morrillos – the entrance to the hacienda is just before the bridge on the right.

The road continues on to **Hurtado**, a village set at 1300 m. Near Hurtado is the only petroglyph in Chile depicting the sun, hinting at possible links to the Incas, and it is also possible to climb the **Cerro Gigante** (2825 m) and visit the site of a Diaguita cemetery.

From Hurtado it is possible to continue north to Vicuña in the Elqui Valley (see page 127) only 46 km away. This is a stark, desolate but beautiful road, very poor in

Valley of the Limarí

La Serena
Vicuña
To Monte Grande & Pisco Elqui
Andacollo
Monumento Natural Pichasca
Hurtado
Río Limarí
Las Breas
Embalse La Recoleta
Pichasca
Path to Argentina
Pan-American Highway
Ovalle
Monte Patria
Termas de Socos
Valle del Encanto
Embalse La Paloma
Carén
To Combarbalá

N

20 km
20 miles

Where to stay 🛏
Hacienda Juntas **1**
Hacienda Los Andes **2**

Restaurants 🍴
Flor del Valle **1**

places; there is very little traffic and no public transport, but it may be possible to hire a pickup in Hurtado if you don't have a suitable vehicle of your own.

To Andacollo

The good road inland between Ovalle and La Serena makes an interesting contrast to Ruta 5, the Pan-American Highway, with a fine pass and occasional views of snow-capped Andes across cacti-covered plains and semi-desert mountain ranges. Some 66 km north of Ovalle, a winding side road runs 27 km southeast, to Andacollo.

Situated in a gorge, Andacollo has been a mining centre since before the arrival of the Spanish (see box, page 110). Ruins of mines and waste tips dot the area. Two mines, one copper and one gold, still operate and there are many independent mines and *trapiches*, small processing plants, which can be visited; the gold has, however, begun to run out and, in recent years, many miners have moved away. Andacollo, however, is more famous as one of the great pilgrimage sites in Chile. In the enormous **Basilica** (1893), 45 m high and with a capacity of 10,000, is a small, carved wooden statue of the Virgen del Rosario de Andacollo, brought from Peru in the 17th century and credited with miraculous powers. Nearby is the **Templo Antiguo**, smaller and dating from 1789. There is also a museum, **Museo de Andacollo** ① *www.santuariodeandacollo.cl, Mon-Fri 1000-1300, 1500-1900, Sat-Sun 1000-1900.* The tourist office on the Plaza de Armas can arrange tours to the Basilica and to mining operations.

◉ Limarí Valley listings

For hotel and restaurant price codes and other relevant information, see pages 14-21.

◐ Where to stay

Ovalle *p116, map p116*
$$$ PlazaTurismo, Victoria 295, T053-266 2500, www.plazaturismo.cl. Spacious rooms, some overlooking the plaza.
$$ Gran Hotel, Vicuña Mackenna 210 (entrance through Galería Yagnam), T053-262 1084. Decent rooms, good value and service.
$$ Roxy, Libertad 155, T053-262 0080. Big basic rooms, large colonial-style patio covered in vines in summer, a bit run down, but a good choice.

South of Ovalle *p117*
$$$ Hacienda Juntas, near Monte Patria, Km 38, T053-271 1290, www.hacienda juntas.cl. In 90 ha of vineyards, with pleasant gardens, spectacular views and pool. Restaurant open in high season.
$$$ Termas de Socos, Panamericana Norte Km 370, 35 km southwest of Ovalle,

T053-2198 2505, www.termasocos.cl. Reasonable hotel offering full board and access to thermal pools.

Camping
$ pp Camping y Piscina Los Pumas del Encanto, 10 mins' walk from Valle del Encanto, T053-262 3667, see Facebook. Nice place with lots of trees and plants, owner Adrián Tello is very knowledgeable.

Along the Río Limarí *p118, map p118*
$$$ Hacienda Los Andes, Vado Morillos, T053-269 1822, www.haciendalosandes.com. German/Austrian management at this highly regarded colonial-style hacienda, bed and breakfast, dinner also available, all meals use organic local produce, solar-powered hot water and heating, camping (US$8). See above for horse riding and other activities.

Parque Nacional Fray Jorge *p117*
1 *cabaña* (**$$$**) sleeping 5. Basic accommodation (**$$**) in an old hacienda and 2 campsites in the national park: 1 at

the administration centre, the other 3 km away at El Arrayancito.

To Andacollo p119
There are no hotels, but some *pensiones*. During the festival, private houses rent beds and some let you pay for a shower. Contact the tourist office for details.

🍴 Restaurants

Ovalle p116, map p116
$$ Club Social Arabe, Arauco 255. Spacious glass-domed premises, limited selection of Arab dishes.
$ Casino La Bomba, Aguirre 364. Run by fire brigade, good value *almuerzos*.
$ El Calamar, in the middle of the Feria Modelo. Good-value lunches. There are many more cheap eateries at the entrance to the market.
El Quijote, Arauco 294. Intimate old-timers' bar full of socialist posters and memorabilia.

Along the Río Limarí p118, map p118
$ Restaurant Flor del Valle, Pichasca. Cheap meals and basic accommodation.

🎭 Entertainment

Ovalle p116, map p116
Cine Cervantes, Centro Comercial G Corral. Cinema on the plaza.

🎉 Festivals

To Andacollo p119
23-27 Dec Fiesta Grande attracts 150,000 pilgrims from northern Chile (most important day 26 Dec). The ritual dances date from a pre-Spanish past. Transport is available from La Serena and Ovalle but 'purists' walk (torch and good

walking shoes essential). 2 villages are passed on the route, which starts on the paved highway, then goes along a railway track and lastly up a steep, dusty hill.
1st Sun of Oct Fiesta Chica.
A smaller festival.

🛍 Shopping

Ovalle p116, map p116
There are markets on Mon, Wed, Fri and Sat until 1600, and on Sun morning; the marketplace, **Feria Modelo**, is off Benavente, east of the town centre. Here you can find all kinds of fruit, vegetables, cheese, fish, dried fruit, herbs and spices as well as flowers and cheap clothes. There are many *talabarterías* nearby on Benavente.
For local *artesanía* including worked Combarbalita, lapis lazuli and Diaguita-style ceramic work, try the stalls in the middle of Ariztía or in the Feria Modelo.

🚌 Transport

Ovalle p116, map p116
Bus
Buses to **Santiago**, several, 6½ hrs, US$17-30; to **Valparaíso**, 6 hrs, US$17; to **Antofagasta**, 14 hrs; to **La Serena**, 1½ hrs, US$4.50. To **Hurtado**, Buses M&R, T053-269 1866, T09-9822 0320, has buses on Mon, Wed, Fri at 1200, 1230 and 1500, Sat 1400, Tue and Thu at 1615 and 1645, and Sun 1700 and 1730, US$4.

☎ Directory

Ovalle and around p116, map p116
Banks Many **Redbanc** ATMs on the Plaza de Armas, including **Banco de Chile**. **Internet** Several in and around the centre. **Post office** MacKenna on the Plaza de Armas.

Elqui Valley

A dramatic cleft in the heart of the mountains, the Elqui Valley is home to two of the north's most important cities, Coquimbo and La Serena. Inland, you will find star-filled nights lit up by shooting stars, *pisco* distilleries and villages in the mountains. The valley of the Río Elqui is one of the most attractive oases in this part of Chile. There are mines, orchards and vineyards set against imposing arid mountains. The contrast between the immense rock formations and the lush valley floor is overwhelming.

La Serena → For listings, see pages 130-135. Colour map 2, C1.

Situated nearly 500 km north of Santiago, La Serena is the capital of Región IV and is a pleasant if not particularly inspiring city. Built on a hillside 2 km inland from the Bahía de Coquimbo, the city is famous for its numerous churches, while the centre is made up of white buildings of neocolonial style. Beneath this façade, however, La Serena has a more ancient history and residents often claim to stumble across indigenous burial sites in their backyards. The city has rapidly become a major tourist centre, being popular for its long sandy beach and as a base for visiting nearby attractions. It is full of Chilean and Argentine holidaymakers in January and February, while the city's two universities ensure a vibrant atmosphere all year round.

Arriving in La Serena
Getting there and around La Serena is easily reached by countless buses from both north and south, provided by any one of more than 10 companies. The terminal is at El Santo y Amunátegui (about eight blocks south of the centre). Several flights daily from Santiago to Copiapó, Antofagasta and Iquique stop off at **Aeropuerto La Florida** ⓘ *5 km east of La Serena, T051-227 0236, www.aeropuertodelaserena.cl*. Microbuses and *colectivos* run between the airport and Avenida Francisco de Aguirre entre Balmaceda y Cienfuegos in the city centre, US$1.50. There are also taxis. La Serena and Coquimbo are linked by buses that pass down Avenida Francisco de Aguirre in La Serena before travelling along the Pan-American Highway. City buses cost US$0.75. Taxis are plentiful and cheap.

Tourist information The Edificio de Servicios Públicos houses **Sernatur** ⓘ *Matta 461 (next to post office), Plaza de Armas, T051-222 5199, infocoquimbo@sernatur.cl, Jan-Feb daily 0900-2000, Mar-Dec Mon-Fri 0900-1800, Sat 1000-1400*. There's also an information kiosk at the bus terminal (summer only). See also **www.laserena.cl**.

Background
La Serena was founded by Juan de Bohón, aide to Pedro de Valdivia, in 1544, destroyed by the Diaguita in 1546 and rebuilt by Francisco de Aguirre in 1549. The city was sacked by the English pirate Sharpe in 1680. In the colonial period, it was the main staging-post

on the route north to Peru; many of the religious orders built churches and convents here providing accommodation for their members. In the 19th century, the city grew prosperous from copper-mining; the neoclassical mansions of successful entrepreneurs from this period can still be seen. The characteristic neocolonial style of architecture in the centre, however, dates only from the 1950s, when the city was remodelled under the instructions of President González Videla, a lawyer, diplomat and Radical party politician, who was eager to leave his mark on his native city. González Videla ordered the drafting of an urban plan, under which Avenida Francisco de Aguirre was modernized and the Pedro de Valdivia gardens, west of the city, were built. All new buildings in the centre were constructed in Californian colonial style, although his regulation has since been modified, permitting the erection of some modern buildings.

Where to stay
1 Cabañas Bahía Drake
2 Camino de Luna
3 Del Cid
4 Hostal El Punto
5 Hostal Croata
7 Hostal El Hibisco
8 Hostal Family Home
9 Hostal Gladys

10 Hostal María Casa
11 Hostal Serena Centro
12 Hostal Villanueva
 de la Serena
13 La Serena Plaza
14 Londres
15 Res Suiza

Restaurants
1 Costa Inca
2 Daniela 2
3 Donde El Guatón
4 El Callejón
5 Govindas
6 La Mía Pizza
7 Porotos

Buccaneers of the Chilean coast

Sir Francis Drake was one of the first Europeans to commit piracy along the west coast of South America but his example was soon widely followed. By the second half of the 17th century, free-booting renegades – mostly English, French and Dutch – were roaming the South Seas preying on Spanish coastal towns and shipping in the hope of getting rich quick.

Basil Ringrose has a special place among these desperadoes because he left a fascinating first-hand account of his activities. Towards the end of 1679, he set out, under the command of a Captain Sharp, to take and plunder what Ringrose describes as the "vastly rich town of Arica". However, on finding the Spanish defence of Arica too strong to overcome, they had to continue south to nearby Hilo where they managed to land and occupy the sugar factory. The besieged Spaniards agreed to supply Ringrose and his comrades "four score of beeves" on the condition that they didn't burn the sugar factory to the ground. After several days of waiting for the "beeves" to arrive, the pirates began to smell a rat;

they decided to burn the factory down regardless and retreated to their ship. It was as well they did because they had no sooner re-embarked than they saw 300 Spanish horsemen advancing on their encampment. Ringrose was impressed by Hilo, describing it as "a valley very pleasant being all over set with figs, olives, oranges, lemons, and lime trees, and many other fruits agreeable to the palate". What Ringrose most remembered Hilo for, however, was its "good chocolate" of which they "had plundered some small quantity".

After the double disappointment of Arica and Hilo, the pirates continued south to the Bay of Coquimbo where they discovered the city of La Serena, "most excellent and delicate, and far beyond what we could expect in so remote a place". Ringrose was particularly impressed by the town's seven churches, which he and his companions hoped to loot. But, again, news of their activities preceded them and the Spaniards had already removed the churches' treasures. Instead they "found strawberries as big as walnuts and very delicious to the taste".

Places in La Serena

Around the attractive Plaza de Armas, most of the official buildings can be found, including the post office and the **Casa González Videla**, the great man's residence from 1927 to 1977, which now houses the **Museo Histórico Regional** ① *www.museo historicolaserena.cl, Mon-Fri 1000-1800, Sat 1000-1300, US$1.30 (ticket also valid for Museo Arqueológico)*, with several rooms dedicated to his life and the history of La Serena. Opposite is the **cathedral**, built in 1844 and featuring a carillon that plays every hour. There are 29 other churches, several of which have unusual towers. **Santo Domingo**, half a block southwest of the Plaza de Armas, built in 1755 with a clock tower dating from 1912, is fronted by a small garden with statues of sea-lions. Southeast of the plaza, on Balmaceda y de La Barra, is **San Francisco**, built between 1586 and 1627, which has a baroque façade and faces a small plaza with arcades. It is home to the **Museo De Arte Religiosa** ① *Mon-Sat 0900-1300, 1500-1800, Sun 1000-1400, US$1*, which includes the funeral mask of Gabriela Mistral.

San Augustín, northeast of the plaza at Cantournet y Rengifo, originally a Jesuit church, dates from 1755 but has been heavily modified. Opposite this church is

La Recova, the market, which includes a large display of handicrafts and, upstairs, several seafood restaurants. One block south is **Museo Arqueológico** ⓘ *Cordovez y Cienfuegos, T051-222 4492, www.museoarqueologicolaserena.cl, Tue-Fri 0930-1750, Sat 1000-1300, 1600-1900, US$1, free entry Sun 1000-1300*, which has an outstanding collection of indigenous Diaguita and Molle exhibits, especially of attractively decorated pottery, although they are poorly labelled. There are also some exhibits from Easter Island. Further from the centre, in the University of La Serena, is the **Museo Mineralógico Ignacio Domeyko** ⓘ *Benavente 980, Mon-Fri 0930-1230 in university term-time, US$0.50*, for those with a particular interest in geology.

One block west of the Plaza de Armas is the **Parque Pedro de Valdivia** ⓘ *daily 1000-2000, US$1.50*, with the Parque Japonés just south of it. Avenida Francisco de Aguirre, a pleasant boulevard lined with statues and known as the **Alameda**, runs from the centre to the coast, skirting the Parque Japonés and terminating at Faro Monumental, a neo-colonial mock-castle and lighthouse, now a pub. A string of beaches stretch from here all the way to **Coquimbo**, 11 km south, linked by the Avenida del Mar. Many apartment blocks, hotels, *cabañas* and restaurants have been built along this part of the bay. The sectors between 4 Esquinas and Peñuelas are probably the best bet for sunbathing or dipping a toe in the water.

Visiting the observatories

The clear skies and dry atmosphere of the valleys around La Serena have led to the area becoming one of the astronomical centres of the world (see box, opposite). There are five observatories, two (Mamalluca and del Pangue) built especially to receive visitors. Personal applications for visitor permits to the other three observatories must be made directly to the respective institutions. It is critical to reserve tours to these three in advance – up to three or four months ahead during holiday periods, although off season a few days' notice may be enough. Be aware that tours are subject to cancellation at short notice if there is inclement weather. Most tour operators in La Serena and Coquimbo arrange tours to Mamalluca. If you can arrange tickets directly with the observatory, taxi drivers will provide transport.

Some visitors to the three large observatories complain that they do not get as much of an insight as they had expected. Bear in mind that trained astronomers have to reserve years in advance to use the equipment and that a day tour will not be the beginning of your astronomical career – it will, though, give you a window onto the workings of some of the most important telescopes on earth.

El Tololo ⓘ *www.ctio.noao.edu, open to visitors by permit Sat 0900 and 1300, free. For permits write to: Casilla 603, La Serena, T051-220 5200, ctio@noao.edu. Pick your permit up from Colina Los Pinos, on a hill behind the new University before 1200 on the day before your visit; personal applications can also be made here for La Silla and Las Campanas.* Situated at 2200 m, 87 km southeast of La Serena in the Elqui Valley, 51 km south of Vicuña, this observatory belongs to Aura, an association of US and Chilean universities. It possesses one of the largest telescope in the southern hemisphere (diameter 4 m), six other telescopes and a radio telescope. This is the closest of the observatories to La Serena and the most accessible to visitors. During holiday periods you should apply for a visitor permit well in advance; at other times it is worth trying for a cancellation the day before. The administration will insist that you have private transport; you can hire a taxi, US$75, but you will require the registration number when you book, as well as your

The clear skies of northern Chile

With its large expanses of uninhabited desert and its dry, relatively thin atmosphere, northern Chile has become one of the great astronomical centres of the world. In the Elqui Valley alone, there are three large observatories, built by international organizations with important backing from Europe or the USA.

One, La Silla, is owned by European Southern Observatory (ESO), which is financed by the governments of some 10 European governments. The other two are El Tololo, which belongs to a consortium of US and Chilean universities, and Las Campanas, owned by the Carnegie Institute. Visitors are welcome at all these sites, but are not allowed to use the telescopes. For this experience, you should go to Mamalluca or El Pangue, two smaller observatories near the town of Vicuña built for the public. They offer night-time visits and provide an opportunity to view the southern skies from the vantage point of the Elqui Valley.

Astronomy in northern Chile is not confined to the Elqui Valley, however. In March 1999 ESO opened an observatory at Cerro Paranal, 120 km south of Antofagasta (see page 164). Known as the VLT ('very large telescope'), www. eso.org/public/teles-instr/vlt/, it consists of four 8-m telescopes that together are capable of picking out items on the moon as small as 1m long. When the lenses arrived at the port of Antofagasta, the city centre was closed down to allow them to be transported to their final destination. An even larger observatory is at Chajnantor, over 5000 m up in the Andes, www.astro.caltech.edu/chajnantor/. There are 64 12-m radio telescopes here, financed by ESO along with the governments of the USA and Japan.

passport. Motorcycles are, apparently, not permitted to use the access road. Visits last approximately two hours.

La Silla ① *www.ls.eso.org, register in advance and complete online visitor form for free tour Sep-Jun Sat 1330-1700.* Located at 2400 m, 156 km northeast of La Serena, this observatory has 14 telescopes. To reach La Silla, head north from La Serena for 120 km along the Pan-American Highway to the turn-off, then another 36 km.

Las Campanas ① *T051-220 7301, www.lco.cl, open with permission every Sat 1430-1730.* This observatory is at 2510 m, 162 km northeast of La Serena, 30 km north of La Silla. It belongs to the Carnegie Institute, has five telescopes and is altogether a smaller facility than the other two. To get to Las Campanas, follow the Pan-American Highway, take the turning for La Silla and then turn north after 14 km.

Mamalluca ① *Gabriela Mistral 260, Vicuña, T051-241 1352, www.munivicuna.cl, several night-time tours available, US$10 per person, guides in Spanish and English for groups of 5 or more, book in advance.* Situated at 1500 m, 6 km north of Vicuña, this municipally owned observatory was built specifically for the public; visitors here can actually look through a telescope at the night sky. The first telescope, diameter 30 cm, was donated by El Tololo. There is also a multimedia centre here, and tours are given by astronomy students in Spanish and English of variable fluency. Advance booking is strongly recommended in summer, when the tour groups may have up to 30 people.

Observatorio del Pangue ① *Bookings through agencies in La Serena as part of a tour or directly from San Martín 233, Vicuña, T051-241 2584, www.observatoriodelpangue.blogspot. com, 2 or 3 visits nightly, US$33.50 including transport*. This observatory is about 16 km south of Vicuña on the road to Hurtado. Focused exclusively at the visiting public, it limits groups to 12 people. Tours are informative and in good English and French as well as Spanish, and the telescopes are latest-generation and more powerful than those at Mamalluca.

Coquimbo and the coast → *For listings, see pages 130-135.*

Coquimbo

On the same bay as La Serena and only 84 km from Ovalle, Coquimbo was used during the colonial period as a port for La Serena, attracting attention from English pirates, including Francis Drake, who visited in 1578. Legends of buried treasure at Bahía la Herradura de Guayacán persist to this day. From these small beginnings, Coquimbo grew into a city in the 19th century, when it – and the separate centre of Guayacán – became important in the processing of copper. By 1854, there were two large copper foundries in Coquimbo and in 1858 the largest foundry in the world was built in La Herradura.

Coquimbo

Where to stay	Lig 2	Restaurants
Hostal Nomade 5		Sal y Pimienta del
Iberia 1		Capitán Denny 2

Today, the city depends on the port for its vitality and economic solvency. It has one of the best harbours on the coast and several major fish-processing plants. The city is strung along the north shore of a peninsula, with most of the commercial life centred on three streets that run between the port and the steep hillside on which are perched many of the poorer houses. The 19th-century mansions of the **Barrio Inglés** along Aldunate to the north of the Plaza de Armas have recently been restored and these are home to much of the city's nightlife. On the south shore of the peninsula lies the suburb of **La Herradura**, where there is an iron-ore loading port, a steel church designed by Eiffel, an English cemetery and a huge cross, the **Cruz del Tercer Milenio**, erected to mark the millennium. It is possible to climb the 83-m cross for a charge of US$2. In 1981, heavy rain uncovered 39 10th-century burials of humans and llamas, which had been sacrificed; the exhibits are on display in the **Museo del Sitio** ① *Plaza Gabriela Mistral, Jan and Feb only, Mon-Sat 0930-2030, Sun 0930-1400, free*. It doubles as a tourist information office. **The municipal office is at** ① *Las Heras 220, T051-231 3971*. In summer, it is possible to take **boat trips** ① *regular departures, US$5*, around the harbour and to Punta Lobos on the bay. Travellers should be aware that Coquimbo has a reputation for theft.

The coastal resorts

The coast around Coquimbo has some great beaches; the closest is at **La Herradura**, 2.5 km from Coquimbo, a slightly upmarket suburb that has the best beaches in the bay and numerous *cabañas* and restaurants. Also nearby is a resort complex called **Las Tacas**, with beach, swimming pool, tennis and apartments. Heading south, there are good swimming beaches at **Totoralillo**, 12 km beyond Coquimbo, and a 10-km beach east of **Guanaqueros**, a fishing village on the southern coast of a large bay, 37 km south of Coquimbo. **Tongoy**, 13 km further on is an old fishing port occupying the whole of a small peninsula. It is now a rapidly growing resort and well worth a visit, with two large beaches: the Playa Grande to the south (14 km long) and the Playa Socos to the north.

Vicuña and the Upper Elqui Valley → For listings, see pages 130-135.

Vicuña, the main town in the Elqui Valley, lies 66 km east of La Serena. The road is paved for another 37 km beyond, as far as Pisco Elqui. Most of the tiny towns here have just a single street. Many tour operators in La Serena offer day trips as far as Pisco Elqui, but you really need to stay overnight to experience the wonder of the upper valley. The valley is the centre of *pisco* production: of the nine distilleries in the valley, the largest is Capel in Vicuña. *Huancara*, a delicious fortified wine introduced by the Jesuits, is also produced in the valley. The Río Elqui has been dammed east of El Molle, 30 km east of La Serena. This has forced the relocation of five small towns in the valley and has also led to increased winds in the valley, according to locals.

Vicuña → Colour map 2, C2.

This small, friendly town was founded in 1821. On the west side of the plaza is the Municipalidad, built in 1826 and topped in 1905 by a medieval-style tower – the **Torre Bauer** – prefabricated in Germany and imported by the German-born mayor of the time. Inside the Municipalidad is a gallery of past local dignitaries as well as the **tourist office**. Also on the plaza is the **Iglesia Parroquial**, dating from 1860.

Museo Gabriela Mistral ① *Gabriela Mistral 759, www.portaldeelqui.cl/museo-gabriela-mistral, Mon-Fri 1000-1745, Sat 1030-1800, Sun 1000-1300, US$1.20, free on Mon Mar-Dec,* *students half price*, contains manuscripts, books, awards and many other details of the poet's life. Next door is the house where she was born. **Museo Entomológico** ① *C Chacabuco 334, daily 1030-2100 in summer; daily 1030-1330, 1530-1900 in winter, US$1.50*, has over 3000 insect species displayed. **Solar de los Madariaga** ① *Gabriela Mistral 683, www.solardelosmadariaga.cl, Jan, Feb and hols Wed-Mon 1000-1400, 1500-1900, Mar-Dec Wed-Mon 1100-1300, 1500-1800*, is a former residence containing artefacts belonging to a prominent local family. There are good views from Cerro La Virgen, north of town.

The **Capel Pisco distillery** ① *Camino a Peralillo, T051-255 4300, www.cooperativa capel.cl, guided tours (in Spanish) Dec-May Mon-Sat 1000-1800, free, no booking required*, lies 1.5 km east of Vicuña, to the right of the main road. There is a small museum dedicated to the history of *pisco* (entry US$1) and guided tours of the plant leave every 30 minutes. Tours in English are sometimes available but phone ahead to make sure. There are two observatories near Vicuña, **Mamalluca**, 6 km north and **El Pangue**, 16 km south (see above).

The upper valley

From Vicuña a *ripio* road (high-clearance vehicle necessary) runs south via **Hurtado** (Km 46), **Pichasca** (Km 85) and the **Monumento Natural Pichasca** to Ovalle (Km 120); see page 118. The main road through the Elqui Valley continues east another 18 km to **Rivadavia**, where the rivers Turbio and Claro meet. Here the road divides, the international road (Route 41) winds through the mountains on a good, partly paved road to the Argentine border at **Paso de Agua Negra** (4780 m; see box, page 130).

The other branch of the road runs through Paihuano to **Monte Grande**, where the schoolhouse in which Gabriela Mistral lived and was educated by her sister is now a **museum** ① *C Principal s/n, T051-241 5015, Tue-Sun 1000-1300, 1500-1800 (until 1900 in Jan and Feb), US$0.80*. The poet's tomb is situated at the edge of town, opposite the

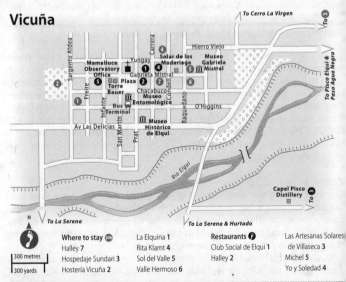

Vicuña

Where to stay 🛏
Halley **7**
Hospedaje Sundari **3**
Hostería Vicuña **2**

La Elquina **1**
Rita Klamt **4**
Sol del Valle **5**
Valle Hermoso **6**

Restaurants 🍴
Club Social de Elqui **1**
Halley **2**

Las Artesanas Solares de Villaseca **3**
Michel **5**
Yo y Soledad **4**

The Elqui Valley in the words of its poet

"It is a heroic slash in the mass of mountains, but so short as to be little more than a green-banked torrent, yet small as it is one comes to love it as perfect. It contains in perfection all that man could ask of a land in which to live: light, water, wine and fruit. And what fruit! The tongue which has tasted the juice of its peaches and the mouth which has eaten of its purple figs will never seek sweetness elsewhere.

The people of the Elqui take remarkable pride in their green soil. Whenever there is a hump, a ridge or bare patch without greenery, it is because it is naked rock. Wherever the Elquino has a little water and three inches of soil, however poor, he will cultivate something: peaches, vines or figs. That the leafy, polished vines climb only a little way up the mountainsides is because if they were planted higher, they would wither in the pitiless February sun."

Gabriela Mistral, quoted in Jan Reed, *The Wines of Chile* (Mitchell Beazley, 1994).

Artesanos de Cochiguaz *pisco* distillery, which is open to the public. Here the road forks, one branch leading to the **Cochiguaz Valley**. There is no public transport along this road, but there are several New Age settlements – it is said that the valley is an important energy centre – and a number of campsites. At night, there is no better place on earth to stargaze. When the moon is new, or below the horizon, the stars seem to be hanging in the air; spectacular shooting stars can be seen every couple of seconds, as can satellites crossing the night sky. Back on the main road, just south of Montegrande is the **Cavas del Valle** organic winery with free tastings and a salesroom.

Pisco Elqui, with a population of 500, is situated 2 km south of Monte Grande along the main road. It is an attractive village with the newly restored **Iglesia de Nuestra Señora Rosario** fronting onto a shady plaza. Here is the **Tres Erres** *pisco* distillery, which is open to the public and gives guided tours in Spanish for US$4; the vineyards themselves are now covered by nets to protect them from the winds caused by the new dam. Pisco Elqui is famous for its night skies and beautiful scenery and is also a New Age centre, where all sorts of alternative therapies and massages are available. Horses can be hired, for exploring the surrounding area. Ramón Luis, T051-245 1168, is a recommended guide. At the **Astropub** in the **Hotel Elqui** you can enjoy a few drinks while stargazing through telescopes. Some 4 km further up the valley at **Los Nichos** is a small *pisco* distillery open to the public for visits (closed lunchtime) and a store selling excellent dried fruit and other local products.

North of La Serena → *For listings, see pages 130-135.*

It is 218 km north from La Serena to Vallenar, through a sparsely populated district usually bypassed by travellers. Some 35 km north of La Serena is **Caleta Hornos**, an impoverished fishing village with several restaurants where excellent seafood is served. The *Panamericana* then climbs to an arid plateau; 21 km beyond Caleta Hornos is a turning eastwards to **La Higuera**, a small town that once thrived from the iron ore mine at **El Tofo** on the opposite side of the valley. This was once one of the largest iron ore mines in the world; the mine stacks can clearly be seen from the *Panamericana*, as can the eerie eucalyptus trees on top of the hill, kept alive by the coastal fog. Only the guardian of the mine lives here now, but it is worth driving up to El Tofo to see the ghost town and for the spectacular views down to the coast.

Border crossing: Chile–Argentina

Paso de Agua Negra

This high mountain pass is located 220 km east of La Serena on Route 41 at an altitude of 4780 m. The pass is open December to April but is closed by snow at other times. Route 41 is paved as far as Juntas, 84 km west of the border (88 km east of Vicuña) for Chilean immigration and customs (December-April daily 0700-1700). Beyond Juntas the road is good *ripio* across the pass, continuing into Argentina as RN150 to San Juán de Jachal in San Juan province. The Argentine immigration and customs post is located 47 km east of the pass. For further information, see www.pasodeaguanegra.org.

To Reserva Nacional Pingüino de Humboldt

Sixteen kilometres north of the turn-off for El Tofo, a road heads west from the *Panamericana*, signposted for **Punta de Choros**. This *ripio* road leads through a rugged dry river valley for 20 km before reaching the small village of **Los Choros Bajos**, where the main activity is growing olives; the groves of olive trees provide a beautiful green backdrop to the harshness of the desert. There is a restaurant serving basic meals, but it is better to continue a further 22 km towards the coast to **Punta de Choros**, the departure point for visiting the reserve. (East of the Panamericana here are two of the main observatories: La Silla and Las Campanas; see page 125.)

Reserva Nacional Pingüino de Humboldt consists of three islands: **Chañaral**, **Choros** and **Damas**. It was founded to preserve the coast's marine life, which includes many penguins, sea lions and dolphins, as well as wonderful birdlife. The combination of this and the coast's rugged isolation means that visits here will not be quickly forgotten. To visit the reserve, tours are available from La Serena and Vallenar or you can hire a boat with local fishermen (around US$80 for up to 10 people). Isla Damas is the only island at which it is possible to disembark (entrance to the island is US$4) and camping is allowed, but before visiting or camping on the island you must seek permission from **CONAF** in Punta de Choros, T09-544 3052. There is a toilet on Isla Damas but no drinking water.

From the turning to Punta de Choros, the *Panamericana* continues north, passing several small mining towns. At **Domeyko**, 165 km north of La Serena, a *ripio* road leads west to the coast towards the northern sector of the reserve, based around the small *caleta* at Chañaral.

● Elqui Valley listings

For hotel and restaurant price codes and other relevant information, see pages 14-21.

● Where to stay

La Serena *p121, map p122*

The tourist office in La Serena bus terminal is helpful. Do not be pressurized by touts at the bus station into choosing rooms. Similarly, do not be pressurized to buy tours in hotels: established agencies may give better service and deals.

$$$ Cabañas Bahía Drake, Av del Mar 1300, T051-222 3367, www.cabanasbahia drake.cl. Pleasant, fully equipped units for 2 to 6, on the seafront, with swimming pool.

$$$ Del Cid, O'Higgins 138, T051-221 2692, www.hoteldelcid.cl. Characterful, central, with smallish but spotless rooms around a courtyard. Parking available, English spoken.

$$$ La Serena Plaza, Francisco de Aguirre 0660, T051-222 5745, www.hotelserena plaza.cl. Upmarket hotel by the beach with spacious rooms, swimming pool, gym and restaurant.

$$$-$$ Hostal Villanueva de La Serena, Matta 269, T051-255 0268, www.hostal villanueva.cl. Large rooms sleeping up to 5, with private or shared bath in colonial house dating from 1800.

$$$-$$ Londres, Cordovez 550, T051-221 9066, www.hotellondres.cl. Simple, bright rooms with good beds, decent bathrooms.

$$ Hostal Croata, Cienfuegos 248, T051-222 4997, www.hostalcroata.cl. Small rooms, double or dorms, patio, hospitable.

$$ Hostal El Hibisco, Juan de Dios Peni 636, T051-221 1407, mauricioberrios2002@ yahoo.es. Delightful hosts, welcome drink, lots of information.

$$ Hostal El Punto, Andrés Bello 979, T051-222 8474, www.hostalelpunto.cl. Dorms and rooms with shared or private bath, tasteful, comfortable, good facilities, café, laundry, parking, book exchange, English and German spoken, tours to Elqui Valley.

$$ Hostal María Casa, Las Rojas 18, T051-222 9282, www.hostalmariacasa.cl. Very welcoming and helpful, near bus terminal, laundry facilities, garden, camping, book in advance, excellent value.

$$-$ Camino de Luna, Los Carrera 861, T08-889 8962, hostalcaminodeluna@ gmail.com. Nice rooms, some with bath. Bright patio. Owner from Valdivia keen to practise English.

$$-$ Hostal Family Home, Av Santo 1056, T051-221 2099, www.familyhome.cl. Private or shared bath, thin walls and slightly tatty, but it has a 24-hr reception and is close to the bus terminal so useful if you are arriving at night.

$$-$ Hostal Gladys, Gregorio Cordovez 247 (by the Plaza de Armas), T051-220 324. Shared bath, laundry service, helpful, Gladys works at tourist information in bus terminal (15 mins away).

$$-$ Hostal Serena Centro, Vicuña 431, T051-252 9581, www.hostalserenacentro.cl. New hostel with private rooms and dorms, family run, convenient location.

$$-$ Residencial Suiza, Cienfuegos 250, T051-221 6092, residencial.suiza@terra.cl. With breakfast, good beds, excellent value.

Coquimbo *p126, map p126*
Route 5 from La Serena to Coquimbo is lined with cheap accommodation; as is also Av del Mar, 500 m off the highway (buses run along Route 5, not Av del Mar). Generally accommodation is cheaper in Coquimbo than in La Serena.

$$$-$$ Lig, Aldunate 1577, T051-231 1171. Comfortable, friendly, with breakfast, near bus terminal.

$$ Hostal Nomade, Regimento Coquimbo 5, T051-231 5665. **$** per person in dorms. HI-affiliated. Kitchen and laundry facilities, internet, tours arranged, also camping. English spoken.

$$ Iberia, Lastra 400, T051-231 2141, www.hoteliberia.cl. Cheaper without bath. Friendly. Recommended.

The coastal resorts *p127*
$$$-$$ Cabañas Bahía Club, Guanaqueros, T051-239 5818. *Cabañas* for 3 people with kitchens, on the waterfront. Recommended. Camping also available.

$$ La Herradura, Av La Marina 200, La Herradura, T051-226 1647. Rooms with bath, restaurant attached.

Camping
Camping La Herradura, La Herradura, T051-226 3867, www.norterrenos.com/ camping/. Price for up to 5 people.

Camping Oasis, Guanaqueros, T051-239 5359, www.campingeloasis.cl. On the beach; price per site.

Vicuña *p127, map p128*
$$$ Hostería Vicuña, Sgto Aldea 101, T051-241 1301, www.hosteriavicuna.cl.

In spacious grounds, pool, tennis court, poor restaurant, parking. Has seen better days.

$$ Halley, Gabriela Mistral 542, T051-241 2070, turismohalley@yahoo.es. Pleasantly old-fashioned hotel with high-ceilinged rooms, colonial-style courtyard, and a pleasant pool.

$$ Hospedaje Sundari, C Principal 3, San Isidro (15 mins' walk from Vicuña), T051-241 2072. Delightful bungalows, with breakfast, spotless, bicycles, pool in lovely gardens, aloe and other herbal therapies.

$$ La Elquina, O' Higgins 65, T051-241 1317, anamorainostroza@terra.cl. Relaxed, quiet, lovely garden, private or shared bath.

$$ Rita Klamt, Condell 443, T051-241 9611, rita_klamt@yahoo.es. Impeccably kept B&B. Excellent breakfast, pleasant garden with pool, helpful, German and some English spoken.

$$ Sol del Valle, Gabriela Mistral 743, T051-241 1078, elquisoldelvalle@hotmail.com. Swimming pool, vineyard, restaurant.

$$ Valle Hermoso, Gabriela Mistral 706, T051-241 1206, nury_alvarez@hotmail.com. Comfortable, parking.

Camping

Camping y Piscina Las Tinajas, east end of Chacabuco. Swimming pool, restaurant.

The upper valley p128

Accommodation in the valley is much cheaper outside Jan and Feb. If you're heading for the Argentine border, there is basic, clean accommodation at **Huanta** (Guanta on many maps), Km 46 from Vicuña; ask for Guillermo Aliaga. Huanta is also the last chance to buy food.

$$$$-$$$ Los Misterios de Elqui, A Prat, Pisco Elqui, T051-245 1126, www.misteriosdeelqui.cl. Plush cabins, with swimming pool and restaurant.

$$$ Elqui Domos, Sector los Nichos s/n, Pisco Elqui, T09-7709 2879, www.elqui domos.cl. Accommodation in geodesic tent domes or observatory cabins with windows and roofs that open for a direct view of the night sky, English spoken.

$$$ El Tesoro del Elqui, Pisco Elqui, T051-245 1069, www.tesoro-elqui.cl. *Cabañas* for up to 4, shared room for up to 4 with shared bath (**$**), café, pool, pleasant gardens, German and English spoken.

$$$-$$ Los Dátiles, A Prat s/n, T09-9279 3264, www.losdatileselqui.cl/cabanas.htm. Self-catering cabins, pool and restaurant.

$$ Elqui, O'Higgins s/n by the plaza, Pisco Elqui, T051-245 1130. Hot shower, central, good restaurant and bar.

$$ Hostal Triskel, Callejón Baquedano, Pisco Elqui, T09-9419 8680, www.hostal triskel.cl. Single, double, twin, dorm rooms, attractive, bike rental, activities and tours arranged, therapies.

$$ Refugio La Isla, Sector La Isla, Pisco Elqui, T09-7476 9924, refugiolaisla@gmail. com. Idyllic retreat on a hillside overlooking the village. Simple, rustic, pool, meditation room. Access difficult without transport.

Camping

$ Campsite behind **Camping El Olivo** (which is closed). Excellent facilities, cold water, lots of trees by river, helpful owner, laundry facilities, very nice.

North of La Serena p129

$$ Cabañas Los Delfines, Pilpilen s/n, sitio 33, Punta de Choros, T09-9639 6678. Cabins for up to 6. There are other sleeping and eating options in the area.

🍴 Restaurants

La Serena *p121, map p122*
Most restaurants close off season on Sun. La Serena is generally more expensive than Coquimbo. The best place for seafood is the Sector de Pescadores (**$$**) at **Peñuelas**, on the coast halfway between La Serena and Coquimbo. Take any bus to Coquimbo and get out at the junction with Los Pescadores; walk 300 m to the coast.

$$$-$$ Donde El Guatón, Brasil 750. *Parrillada*, also good seafood, one of the better places in the town centre.
$$$-$$ Porotos, Av del Mar 900-B, Sector El Faro, T051-210937. Wide variety of well-presented dishes (fish, meat and pasta), decent portions and attentive service.
$$ Costa Inca, Av del Mar 2500, T051-212802. Good value and a range of delicious Peruvian dishes.
$$ La Mía Pizza, Av del Mar 2100, T051-212232. Italian, good-value pizzas and also fish dishes, good wine list.
$ Daniela 2, F de Aguirre 335. Good-quality Chilean home cooking.
$ Govindas, Lautaro 841, T051-224289. Mon-Fri lunchtime. Cheap vegetarian food served in a Hari Krishna yoga centre.
Diavoletto, Prat 565 and O'Higgins 531. Fast food and ice cream, popular. Other cafés on Prat 500 block and Balmaceda 400 block.

Coquimbo *p126, map p126*
According to the tourist office in La Serena, the best cheap seafood is to be had at the municipal market, Melgarejo, entre Bilbao y Borgoño. The casino has 3 supposedly top-class restaurants. For more inventive cuisine, try the Barrio Inglés.
$$$-$$ Sal y Pimienta del Capitán Denny, Varela 1301. One of the best in town, pleasant, old fashioned, mainly fish cooked in Chilean style.
$$ La Picada, Costanera. Excellent, good *pebre*. Near statue of O'Higgins.
$$-$ Centro Gastronómico El Suizo, Fritz Willy Linderman 2427, Guanaqueros. A collection of a dozen small restaurants all serving good-quality fresh seafood in abundant portions.
$ La Bahía, Av Playa Grande. Excellent, good value.

Vicuña *p127, map p128*
$$ Club Social de Elqui, Gabriela Mistral 435. Attractive patio, good value *almuerzo*, real coffee.

$$ Halley, Gabriela Mistral 404. Good meat, with local specialities, goat (huge portion) and rabbit.
$$ Las Artesanas Solares de Villaseca, 8 km east of Vicuña in Villaseca. Take a 'Peralillo-Diaguitas' *colectivo* from bus terminal, or go with a tour. 2 restaurants use pioneering techniques, cooking with solar ovens: **Delicias del Sol**, Chiloé 164, and **Donde Martita**, Magallanes 15.
$ Michel, Gabriela Mistral 180. Popular, good-value *almuerzo*.
$ Yo Y Soledad, Gabriela Mistral 364. Inexpensive, hearty Chilean food, good value.

The upper valley *p128*
$$$-$$ Miraflores, Camino a Horcón, Pisco Elqui. Off season, open weekends only. Excellent meat.
$$ Donde la Elke, O'Higgins y Rodríguez, Pisco Elqui. Well-prepared meat fish and pasta. Recommended.
$$ El Rincón Chileno, O'Higgins s/n, Pisco Elqui. Chilean country fare including roast goat.
$ Los Jugos, on the plaza, Pisco Elqui. Light snacks and fresh juices.

🍸 Bars and clubs

La Serena *p121, map p122*
Most clubs are on Av del Mar and in Peñuelas, but in town you could try the following:
El Callejón, O'Higgins 635. Lounge bar and patio, with a relaxed atmosphere, young crowd. Fills up with students at weekends.
El Nuevo Peregrino, Peni y Andrés Bello. Intimate bar with live music at weekends.

🎭 Entertainment

La Serena *p121, map p122*
There is a multiplex cinema complex in the **Mall Plaza** (see Shopping, below).
Centro Latino-Americano de Arte y Cultura, Balmaceda 824, T051-229344. Music and dance workshops, art gallery, handicraft workshops.

Nueva Acropolis, Peni 341, T051-249 9579. Lectures, discussions, free entry.

❂ Festivals

Coquimbo *p126, map p126*
14-21 Sep Coquimbo hosts **La Pampilla**, the biggest Independence Day celebrations in Chile. Between 200,000 and 300,000 people come from all over the country for the fiesta, which lasts for a week. Things get going on 14 Sep, and the partying does not stop until 21 Sep. It costs US$1.50 to gain access to the area where the main dancing tents are to be found, as well as much Chilean food and drink. You have to pay to enter the *peñas*, but there also free communal areas. Big bands such as **Illapu** and **La Ley** have played here, as well as *cumbia* bands from Argentina and Colombia.

⦿ Shopping

La Serena *p121, map p122*
For handicrafts try **Cema-Chile**, Los Carrera 562, or **La Recova** handicraft market on Cantournet and Cienfuegos, though many items sold here are imported.

Good supermarkets include **Santa Isabel**, Cienfuegos 500 block, and **Deca**, Balmaceda 1200 block. There is also a **Líder** by the Mall Plaza, on the *Panamericana*, next to the bus station (open from 1030). **Tintos y Blancos**, Prat 630, has a good selection of fine wines and good quality *piscos*. **Librería Inglesa**, Cordovez 309, on the plaza. T051-221 5699, www. libreriainglesa.cl, is an English-language bookshop, selling mostly school texts.

◔ What to do

La Serena *p121, map p122*
Responsible operators will not run tours to Mamalluca or Las Damas in bad weather. **Chile Safari**, Matta 367, T09-8769 7686, www.chilesafari.com. Biking, surfing.

Delfines, Matta 655, T051-222 3624, www. turismodelfines.com. Traditional and adventure tours, bike rental, birdwatching and full tourist service.
Elqui Total, Parcela 17, El Arrayán at Km 27 along the road from La Serena to Vicuña, T09-9219 7872, www.elquitotal.cl. Mountain biking, birdwatching, photography, trekking, astronomy tours, also equine tourism, www.mundocaballo.cl.
Elqui Valley Tours, Los Carrera 515, T051-221 4846, www.elquivalleytour.cl. Good for local tours, enthusiastic guides.
Jeep Tour La Serena, T09-9454 6000, www.jeeptour-laserena.cl. Private and small group tours (max 6 people) of the area led by Swiss guide Daniel Russ. Apart from the usual tours he also offers trips to the Paso Agua Negra and also a transfer service to San Juan in Argentina (summer only).
Talinay Adventure Expeditions, Prat 470, in the courtyard, T051-221 8658, www. talinaychile.com. Offers local tours, also trekking and climbing.

The upper valley *p128*
Elqui Enduro, Prat s/n, Pisco Elqui, T051-245 1069, www.elquienduro.com. Enduro motorbike tours.
Turismo Migrantes, O' Higgins s/n, Pisco Elqui, T051-245 1917, www.turismo migrantes.cl. Tours to the Cochihuaz and Alcohuaz valleys and the observatories.

⊖ Transport

La Serena *p121, map p122*
Air
There are flights to **Santiago** and **Copiapó**, with **LAN**.

Bus
Tur-Bus office, Balmaceda entre Prat y Cordovez, T051-221 7126. To **Santiago**, daily, a few companies, 7-8 hrs, US$18-33; to **Valparaíso**, 7 hrs. To **Caldera**, 6 hrs, US$14. To **Calama**, US$30-65, 16 hrs. To **Antofagasta**, 12-13 hrs, several companies,

US$28-43, and to **Iquique**, 17 hrs, US$35-69, and **Arica**, 20 hrs, US$43-55. To **Vicuña** and **Pisco Elqui**, see below. To **Coquimbo**, bus No 8 from Av Aguirre y Cienfuegos, US$1, every few mins.

Car hire
Daire, Balmaceda 3812, T051-222 6933. Good service. **Flota Verschae**, Av Balmaceda 3856, T051-224 1685. Good value. **La Florida,** at airport, T051-227 1947.

Taxi
Taxis charge US$0.75 plus US$0.25 every 200 m. *Colectivos* with fixed rates display their destination on the roof; those to **Coquimbo** depart from Aguirre y Balmaceda.

Coquimbo and the coast
p126, map p126
Bus
Terminal at Varela y Garriga. To **La Serena**, US$1, every few mins. There are also frequent buses and *colectivos* to **Guanaqueros** and **Tongoy**.

Vicuña *p127, map p128*
Bus
To **La Serena**, about 10 a day (more in summer), most by **Via Elqui/Megal Bus**, first 0800, last 1930, 1 hr, US$3, *colectivo* from bus terminal US$4. To **Pisco Elqui**, 10 a day with **Vía Elqui**, 1 hr, US$3.25. Buses from Pisco Elqui to **La Serena** go via **Vicuña**, US$3.25.

North of La Serena *p129*
Tours to the penguin reserve are readily available from La Serena; traffic on the road between Punta de Choros and the Pan-American Highway is relatively frequent, especially at weekends, so hitching is also possible.

Directory

La Serena *p121, map p122*
Banks ATMs are available at most banks and in the bus terminal. Several *casas de cambio*. If heading north note that La Serena is the last place to change TCs before Antofagasta.

Coquimbo and the coast
p126, map p126
Banks **Cambios Maya**, Portales 305. Also many **Redbancs** in the centre. **Medical services** Hospital: San Pablo, Videla s/n, T056-5133 6702. **Police** Carabineros, Varela 1545, T051-651 114.

Vicuña *p127, map p128*
Banks There is a Banco Estado and Banco Santander in Vicuña.

Contents

Footprint features

Border crossing

Into the Atacama

At a glance

⊖ **Getting around** As always there is good public transport between cities. To visit national parks you will have to hire a vehicle or take a tour.
⟳ **Time required** 2 or 3 days to take in the main sights, plus as much time as you want to relax on deserted beaches.
❀ **Weather** Warm on the coast. Inland hot days and cool nights.
✖ **When not to go** Access to Parque Nacional Tres Cruces is difficult in winter (May-Sep), while the Pan de Azucar tends to fill up with revelling students in Jan and Feb.

Llullaillaco
(6739m) ▲

Reserva
Nacional
Paposo ◆ 5

▲ Aguas
Blancas
(5780m)

Taltal

● Altamira

Parque Nacional
Pan de Azúcar ◆ 5

El Salvador

Salar de
Pedernales

▲ Colorado
(6080m)

Chañaral

Diego de
Almagro

Río Salado

Pacific
Ocean

● Potrerillos

La Olla ●

Piedra Parada
(5920m) ▲

Laguna
Escondido

Laguna
Wheelwright

Paso San
Francisco

● Inca de Oro

Laguna Verde

San
Francisco
(6020m) ▲

31

Salar de
Maricunga

Parque Nacional
Tres Cruces ◆ 4

Incahuasi
(6615m) ▲

Caldera
Bahía Inglesa

Laguna
Santa Rosa

Tres Cruces
(6749m) ▲

3 ▲ V Ojos del Salado
(6893m)

Desierto
de Atacama

● La Puerta

Puerto
Viejo

Copiapó

Laguna del
Negro
Francisco

● Chañarcillo

Río Copiapó

Totoral

Valle Hermoso

ARGENTINA

Carrizal
Bajo

Las Juntas

Parque Nacional
Llanos de Challe

REGION III

Huasco
Río Huasco

2

Freirina

Vallenar

Alto del Carmen

El Tránsito

Domeyko

San Félix

1

Las
Campanas

★ Don't miss ...

1 Tránsito Valley, page 142.
2 Flowering of the desert, page 143.
3 Ojos del Salado, page 147.
4 Parque Nacional Tres Cruces, page 148.
5 Pan de Azúcar, page 152.

● La Silla

● La Higuera

To La Serena

From La Serena, the shrubs and cacti of the semi-desert stretch north as far as the mining and agro-industrial centre of Copiapó. Beyond this city, the Atacama Desert begins. The main population centres are in the valleys of the rivers Huasco and Copiapó, and in the Salado Valley, where the most important economic activity is mining, especially inland at El Salvador.

Although much of this region appears lifeless and of limited interest to visitors, the area around Vallenar is famous for the flowering of the desert following the rare occasions when there is heavy rainfall; the upper reaches of the Huasco Valley are beautiful and tranquil, and make a good resting point en route to or from the Atacama, as does the beach resort of Bahía Inglesa, while the port of Huasco itself has excellent seafood. All along the coast of this region a variety of excellent inshore fish known as *pescado de roca* are caught. There are also three national parks: the Parque Nacional Pan de Azúcar, which protects a wide range of marine life; the Parque Nacional Llanos de Challe, which safeguards the habitat of one of the very rare flowers that bud with rainfall; and the Parque Nacional Tres Cruces, which covers extensive areas of salt flats northeast of Copiapó. East of the Parque Nacional Tres Cruces is the Paso San Francisco, a desolate yet spectacular border crossing into Argentina; near the pass are some of the highest peaks in the Andes, although most are best tackled from the Argentine side.

Background

Although small groups of Spanish settlers took over the fertile lands in the Huasco and Copiapó valleys in the 16th century, no towns were founded until late in the colonial period. Even the valleys were sparsely populated until the 19th century when the development of mining led to the creation of the ports of Caldera, Chañaral and Huasco and encouraged the building of railways. Mining remains a major economic activity: one of the largest copper mines is at El Salvador and over 50% of all Chilean iron ore is mined around Vallenar. Agriculture is limited to the valleys; the Copiapó Valley is an important producer of grapes, while the lower Huasco Valley is Chile's main olive-growing area. Fishing is centred on Caldera and, on a smaller scale, Chañaral and Huasco.

This part of the country can be divided into two: between the Río Elqui and the Río Copiapó the transitional semi-desert zone continues; north of the Copiapó the Atacama Desert begins and drivers should beware of high winds and blowing sand. The valleys of the rivers Huasco, Copiapó and Salado form oases in this barren landscape. On the coast, temperatures are moderated by the sea and mist is common in the mornings. Inland temperatures are higher by day and cooler by night; Vallenar and the upper valleys of the Copiapó and Huasco can be especially cold on winter evenings. Rainfall is sparse and occurs in winter only, with amounts decreasing as you go north.

East of Copiapó the Andes divide between the eastern range (Cordillera de Claudio Gay) and the western range (Cordillera de Domeyko); a basin collects the waters from the Andes. Here there are salt flats, the most extensive being the Salar de Pedernales. The eastern range has some of the highest peaks in Chile: Ojos del Salado (6893 m-6864 m, see box, page 147), Incahuasi (6615 m), Tres Cruces (6749 m) and San Francisco (6020 m).

Huasco Valley

This valley (known as the Jardín de Atacama) is an oasis of olive groves and vineyards. It is rugged and spectacular, reminiscent of the Cajón del Maipo near Santiago. At Alto del Carmen, 39 km east of Vallenar, the valley divides into the Carmen and Tránsito valleys. There are *pisco* distilleries at Alto del Carmen and San Félix, both of which have basic *residenciales*. A sweet wine known as *pajarete* is also produced. Today the Río Huasco is the last of the unpolluted rivers in the north. However, a huge goldmining project in the upper valley has been approved, to the displeasure of many locals.

Arriving in the Huasco Valley

The Huasco Valley's main town and transport hub is Vallenar, which is easily reached by regular buses from both north and south. **Tourist information** for the valley is available from the Municipalidad on the Plaza de Armas in Vallenar as well as the Municipalidades in Huasco and Alto del Carmen.

Vallenar → Colour map 2, B2. Phone code: 051. Population: 47,000.

Nearly 200 km north of La Serena is Vallenar, the chief town of the Huasco Valley. It was founded in 1789 as San Ambrosio de Ballenary to commemorate the birthplace in Ireland of Ambrosio O'Higgins. The town is centred on a pleasant Plaza de Armas, in which all the benches are made of Chile's purest marble, extracted from the Tránsito Valley. The plaza is dominated by the church, a kitsch monstrosity with its iron girder steeple and electric chimes on the hour. There is a summer-only information kiosk on the plaza. **Museo del Huasco** ⓘ *Sgto Aldea 742, Tue-Fri 1500-1800, free,* contains historic photos and artefacts from the valley. Opposite is the northernmost Chilean palm tree in the country.

West of Vallenar

Freirina, founded in 1752, was formerly the most important town in the valley, its prosperity based upon the nearby Capote goldmine and on later discoveries of copper. The pleasant main plaza with the Municipalidad (1870) and the Santa Rosa church (1869) is flanked by streets of multicoloured houses. There are scattered olive groves either side of town, and both olives and olive oil are sold from farmhouses and by the side of the road. It is easily reached by *colectivo*, 36 km west of Vallenar.

Situated at the mouth of the river, **Huasco** lies 56 km west of Vallenar. Those arriving from the desert north and heading down the valley will appreciate the change of scenery – poplars and olive groves with an occasional glimpse of the river below. Destroyed by an earthquake in 1922, Huasco is a modern town with a large beach that is popular in summer; a further expanse of deserted beach curves round to the north. There is a new coastal promenade with shaded benches looking out to sea and an esplanade for occasional concerts in summer. The port is interesting, as the fishermen unload their catches and hundreds of pelicans hover, waiting to snatch the fish that slip off the crates into the sea.

There is a thriving sea-lion colony on the small islands offshore, and fishermen may be willing to take people there for a small charge. However, the best reason to come to Huasco is undoubtedly the seafood. There is good tourist information in the Municipalidad.

Some 9 km east of Huasco, a road branches north at the settlement of Huasco Bajo, near which are the **Humedal de Huasco** wetlands, known for their variety of marine birdlife (there are over 100 species). Some 50 km further north (37 of them *ripio*) is the small *caleta* of **Carrizal Bajo**. Carrizal Bajo is the best place from which to visit the **Parque Nacional Llanos de Challe**, set up to preserve the habitat of the *garra de león* and other flowers during the rare occasions when the desert is in bloom. The park is also home to Copiapoa cacti and guanacos. A decent salt road follows the coastline north of Carrizal Bajo, passing a series of small *caletas* en route to Caldera, including the beautiful beach at Puerto Viejo.

East of Vallenar

East of Vallenar, a paved road leads 39 km to **Alto del Carmen**, the site of the distillery of one of the best *piscos* in Chile. The road clings to arid hillsides sprinkled with cacti and *maitén* bushes, passing the Santa Juana Reservoir, which was created following the damming of the Río Huasco in 1995 and has transformed agriculture in the area. The valley is filled with grapevines for *pisco* and with groves of pepper and eucalyptus trees.

At Alto del Carmen, the road forks: left for the **Tránsito Valley**, right for the **Carmen Valley**. The Tránsito Valley is wilder and extends further into the heart of the mountains, while the Carmen Valley is greener and more populous: both valleys are unlikely clefts in the rocky Andes and reward the traveller who is prepared to make the effort to get to know them. Some 21 km beyond Alto del Carmen along the Tránsito Valley is the *mina de*

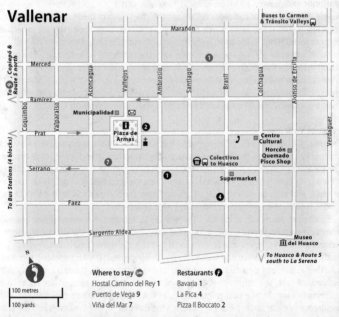

Vallenar

Buses to Carmen & Tránsito Valleys

To Copiapó & Route 5 north

To Bus Stations (4 blocks)

Marañon
Merced
Aconcagua
Vallejos
Ambrosio
Santiago
Brasil
Colchagua
Alonso de Ercilla
Ramírez
Coquimbo
Valparaíso
Municipalidad
Prat
Plaza de Armas
Serrano
Faez
Sargento Aldea
Verdaguer

Centro Cultural
Horcón Quemado Pisco Shop
Colectivos to Huasco
Supermarket

Museo del Huasco

To Huasco & Route 5 south to La Serena

N

100 metres
100 yards

Where to stay
Hostal Camino del Rey 1
Puerto de Vega 9
Viña del Mar 7

Restaurants
Bavaria 1
La Pica 4
Pizza Il Boccato 2

The flowering of the desert

The average annual rainfall in this region declines as you travel north: in Vallenar it is 65 mm, in Copiapó 20 mm. Most years, the semi-desert appears to support only bushes and cacti and these become sparser as you continue north. However, in years of heavier than usual winter rainfall, this semi-desert breaks into colour as dormant seeds and bulbs germinate to produce blankets of flowers, while insects that normally hide underground emerge to enjoy the foliage.

Although the *desierto florido* (flowering desert) used to occur every seven years or so, changing climatic conditions have led to an increase in the phenomenon.

The first traces of the *desierto florido* can be seen as far south as La Ligua and Los Molles, but from La Serena northwards,

the Pan-American Highway is fringed with expanses of different colours: there are great stretches of violet *pata de guanaco*, yellow *corona del fraile* and blue *suspiro del campo*. Not all of these species can be seen at the same time: as the brief spring unfolds, the colours change and new species push through to replace others.

The phenomenon is particularly worth seeing around Vallenar, where the colours are more varied as different species compete to celebrate this increasingly frequent coming of spring. The Pan-American Highway north of the city as far as Copiapó and the coastal road north of Huasco are both recommended for a prime view. For further information, contact Vallenar tourist office (see page 141).

---

mármol blanco, where Chile's finest marble is quarried. The peaceful village of **El Tránsito**, where there is basic accommodation and a cheap restaurant, is a further 10 km on. The village has a pleasant shady plaza, with snow-capped mountains as a backdrop in winter. The Carmen Valley stretches 25 km from Alto del Carmen to **San Félix**, the largest town in the valley, and the site of the distillery for Horcón Quemado *pisco*. A 39-km-long path connects the two valleys, from San Félix to the Quebrada de Pinte, 7 km south of El Tránsito, forming part of the Sendero de Chile. Allow two to three days for the trek. The tourist information office in Alto del Carmen's Municipalidad is helpful.

⊛ Huasco Valley listings

For hotel and restaurant price codes and other relevant information, see pages 14-21.

⊜ Where to stay

Vallenar *p141, map p142*
$$$ Puerto de Vega, Ramírez 201, T051-261 8534, www.puertodevega.cl. Probably the best in town, 12 individually decorated rooms, pleasant patio and pool.
$$ Hostal Camino del Rey, Merced 943, T051-261 3184. Good value, private or shared bath.
$ Viña del Mar, Serrano 611, T051-261 1478. Nice rooms, clean *comedor*, a good choice.

West of Vallenar *p141*
There is scant accommodation in Freirina. There are more options in Huasco.
$$$ Hostería Huasco, Carrera Pinto 110, Huasco, T051-253 1026, www.hosteriahuasco.cl. Parking, conference room, with TV and all mod cons.
$$$-$$ Cabañas Skitniza, Craig 833, Huasco, T051-253 1343, www.skitniza.cl. Parking available.
$$ Hostal San Fernando, Pedro de Valdivia 176, Huasco. Some rooms with bath. Parking, restaurant. The owner lived for several years in Norway.

Camping

Tres Playitas, 12 km north of Huasco along the coast towards Carrizal Bajo. Also in Huasco near the post office. Although there is no official campsite, camping is possible at Carrizal Bajo.

East of Vallenar *p142*

There is no accommodation in the **Tránsito Valley** but camping wild is easy.
$ Cabañas Camino al Oro, Serrano y Larraín, San Félix, T051-198 3173. Cabins. Price is per person.

⑦ Restaurants

Vallenar *p141, map p142*
There are cheap eating places along south end of Av Brasil.
$$ Bavaria, Serrano 802.
Chain restaurant, good.
$$ Pizza Il Boccato, Plaza O'Higgins y Prat.
Good coffee, good food, popular.
$ La Pica, Brasil y Faez. Good cheap meals, seafood, cocktails.

West of Vallenar *p141*

Aficionados of Chile's seafood should take a trip to Huasco for lunch; the journey takes only 45 mins from Vallenar. Simply prepared, perfectly fresh seafood is served at many cheap restaurants near Huasco's port.

⑧ Entertainment

Vallenar *p141, map p142*
It is worth checking out the **Centro Cultural Vallenar**, Vallenar y Colchagua, for cultural events, and occasional exhibitions and concerts.

⑨ Festivals

West of Vallenar *p141*

29 Jun Fiesta de San Pedro is celebrated by the fishing community in Huasco.

East of Vallenar *p142*

16 Jul Fiesta del Carmen, Alto del Carmen.
15 Aug Fiesta del Tránsito in Alto del Carmen with a rodeo, market. Famous for its ice creams made of snow.

○ Shopping

Vallenar *p141, map p142*
Local products are sold in Vallenar's market.
Horcón Quemado, Ercilla 660, Vallenar, T051-261 0985, sells some of Chile's finest *pisco*.

◑ What to do

Vallenar *p141, map p142*
If it rains (**Sep-Oct**), a tour of the desert in flower is offered by **Roberto Alegría**, T051-261 3865. Otherwise ask at the tourist kiosk in Vallenar (if it's open).

⊖ Transport

Vallenar *p141, map p142*
Bus
The main bus terminal is at Prat 137, a few blocks northwest of the city centre. Companies include: **Tur-Bus**, Prat 32, T051-611738, www.turbus.cl; **Pullman**, Serrano 551, T051-612461, www.pullman.cl, which has the most frequent buses going north; and **Tas Choapa**, www.taschoapa.cl. To **La Serena**, 2 hrs, US$6. To **Copiapó**, 2 hrs, US$6. To **Santiago**, 10 hrs, US$29-49.

① Directory

Vallenar *p141, map p142*
Banks Several on Prat, east of the plaza.
Laundry Lavexpress, Corona del Inca 164. **Medical services** Consulta Médico y Laboratorio Clínico, Pje Nicolás Naranjo 341, T051-261 6911.

Copiapó Valley

From Vallenar it is 148 km north to Copiapó, the largest city in the valley of the Río Copiapó, generally regarded as the southern limit of the Atacama Desert. This valley is a surprisingly green cleft of farms, vineyards and orchards in the desert, about 150 km long.

Arriving in the Copiapó Valley

Getting there and around The main centre is Copiapó, which is easily reached by regular buses from both north and south. The long-distance terminal is two blocks from centre on Chacabuco between Chañarcillo and Copayapu; the **TurBus** terminal is opposite at Chañarcillo 680, and Pullman is one block away at Colipí y Freire. **Desierto de Atacama Airport** is 45 km northwest of Copiapó and 15 km east of Caldera. There are several daily flights serving Copiapó from Santiago and La Serena, continuing on to El Salvador. For a transfer to the airport call **Buses Casther** ① *T052-221 8413, www.casther.cl*. There are many *colectivos* and public buses in Copiapó, which may be useful for those heading for some of the out-of-town sites, such as the Santuario de la Candelaria; the fare for buses is US$0.70. ▸▸ *See Transport, page 151.*

Tourist information The **Sernatur office** ① *on the north side of Plaza de Armas, Los Carrera 691, T052-221 2838, infoatacama@sernatur.cl, Mon-Fri 0830-1930, Sat 1030-1430, 1630-1930, Sun 1030-1430; out of season Mon-Fri 0830-1730 only*, is extremely helpful. English is spoken. In Copiapó there is also a **CONAF office** ① *Juan Martínez 55, T052-221 3404.*

Copiapó and around → *For listings, see pages 149-151. Colour map 2, B2.*

The capital of Región III Atacama, Copiapó, with a population of 127,000, is an important mining centre with a backdrop of arid hills to the north. In 2010 this region hit the international headlines, when 33 miners were successfully rescued from a collapsed mine, north of the city, after surviving 69 days underground. Founded in 1744, Copiapó became a prosperous town after the discovery in 1832 of the third largest silver deposits in South America at Chañarcillo. The wealth from Chañarcillo formed the basis of the fortunes of several famous Chilean families – most notably, the Cousiños – and helped finance the first railway line in the southern hemisphere, linking Copiapó to Caldera (1851). These days, Copiapó's economy still thrives on the large numbers of miners who descend on the city in order to seek distraction and spend their pay cheques.

Places in Copiapó

The neoclassical **cathedral**, on Plaza Prat, dating from 1851, was designed by William Rogers. Mass is held here every evening. The **Museo Mineralógico** ① *Colipí y Rodríguez, a block east of the plaza, Mon-Fri 1000-1300, 1530-1900, Sat 1000-1300, US$1*, is the most impressive museum of its type in Chile. It possesses a collection of weird, beautiful minerals from Chile and also from Asia, Europe and North America, plus a decent set of fossils. There is an unfortunate lack of narrative or explanation but a visit is highly recommended nonetheless; it is extraordinary how, although there are minerals from all over the world, the most colourful or striking are almost always Chilean.

Three blocks further north, at Infante near Yerbas Buenas, is the colonial Jesuit **Iglesia de Belén**, remodelled in 1856. Further west, at Atacama y Rancagua, you'll find the **Museo Regional del Atacama** ① *Mon 1400-1745, Tue-Fri 0900-1745, Sat 1000-1245, 1500-1745, Sun 1000-1245, US$1 (free Sun)*, containing collections on local history, especially from the 19th century up to the time of the War of the Pacific; it is also notable for its collection of artefacts from the Huentelauquén people, thought to have flourished 10,000 years ago. On the opposite corner of the same block, at Matta y O'Higgins, is the **Monument to Juan Godoy**, the muleteer, who, in 1832, discovered silver at Chañarcillo. Behind is the **Iglesia de San Francisco**, built in 1872 (the nearby convent is from 1662), which is a good example of a 19th-century construction using Pino Oregón and Guayaquil cane, popular materials of the day. The wealth of the 19th-century mining families is reflected in the **Villa Viña de Cristo**, built in Italian Renaissance style, three blocks northwest on Calle Freire, now part of the University of Atacama. A few blocks further on, the Norris Brothers steam locomotive and carriages used in the inaugural journey between Copiapó and Caldera in 1851 can be seen at the **Universidad de Atacama**; also at the university is an example of an old *trapiche* (see box, page 110). Nearby, in the old railway station on Calle Martínez, is the **Museo Ferroviario**, which has photos and artefacts from the railway age, but it opens only sporadically. In fact, the station mostly stands derelict, a sad indictment of how little importance is given to one of the pioneering railway lines in South America. Outside are two small 19th-century steam locomotives.

On the other side of the city, 3 km southeast of the centre, the **Santuario de la Candelaria** is the site of two churches, the older built in 1800, the other in 1922; inside the latter is the Virgen de la Candelaria, a stone image discovered whole in the Salar de Maricunga by the muleteer Mariano Caro in 1780. The Virgin is said to protect miners, hence her local importance, and is celebrated in the Fiesta de la Candelaria every February (see page 151).

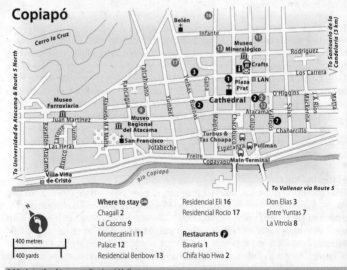

Copiapó

Where to stay 🛏️
Chagall **2**
La Casona **9**
Montecatini I **11**
Palace **12**
Residencial Benbow **13**

Residencial Eli **16**
Residencial Rocío **17**

Restaurants 🍴
Bavaria **1**
Chifa Hao Hwa **2**

Don Elias **3**
Entre Yuntas **7**
La Vitrola **8**

Climbing Ojos del Salado

Ojos del Salado is considered to be the third highest peak in the Americas and the highest active volcano in the world. Its true height is still under debate, with estimates ranging from 6864 m to 6893 m. A permit is required to climb it, available free from the Dirección de Fronteras y Límites, Bandera 52, piso 4, Santiago, T02-2671 4110, taking two or three days to issue. Permits can also be arranged at short notice from the Sernatur office in Copiapó.

The ascent is best attempted between January and March, though it's also possible in November and April. Note that in November, December and April this area can be hit by the *Invierno Boliviano*, a nasty weather pattern coming from the northeast; temperatures have been known to drop to -40°C with winds of 150 kph.

Access to the volcano is via a turn-off from the main Chile–Argentina road towards Paso San Francisco (see box, page 148) at Hostería Murray. Base camp for the climb is at the old Argentine frontier post (4500 m). There are two *refugios*: Refugio Atacama (four to six beds) at 5100 m and Refugio Tejos (better, 12 beds) at 5750 m. The spur to the former is not easy to find, but can be reached with a high-clearance 4WD vehicle. From Refugio Tejos it is 10 to 12 hours' climb to the summit. The climb is not very difficult (approximately Grade 3), except the last 50 m, which is moderate climbing on rock to the crater rim and summit. Take large quantities of water for the ascent. Guides and equipment can be hired in Copiapó.

Around Copiapó

The **Centro Metalúrgico Incaico** is a largely reconstructed Inca bronze foundry, the most complete example in existence, 90 km up the Copiapó Valley by paved road. Further up the valley at Km 98 is the 19th-century **Aquaducto de Amolana**, hidden 300 m off the main road. There is no accommodation in the nearby villages of Valle Hermoso or Las Juntas but there are *cabañas* at Los Loros, which was the site of a clinic for pulmonary diseases at the beginning of the 20th century, attended by the rich and unhealthy from Santiago.

South of Copiapó, about 59 km on the Pan-American Highway, is a signpost for the turning to the ghost town and former silver mine of **Chañarcillo**, along a very poor road. When Chañarcillo was at its peak, the town had a population of 7000; the mine was closed in 1875 but the tips have been reworked and this has destroyed many of the ruins. Now that the silver has gone, only a few goatherds live here among the ruins of dry stone walls. Note there are dozens of dangerously unmarked and unprotected mineshafts here, and if you have an accident, you are far from help.

East to Paso San Francisco → *For listings, see pages 149-151.*

The Argentine border can be crossed at **Paso San Francisco** (4726 m), which is situated just north of **Ojos del Salado** (see box, above). The pass can be reached by two poor *ripio* roads (high-clearance vehicle necessary) from Copiapó and by another *ripio* road that runs south and east from El Salvador. All these routes meet up near the northern sector of the **Parque Nacional Tres Cruces** (see below). The road from El Salvador meets the main *camino internacional* from Copiapó near the Salar de Maricunga, 96 km west of Paso San Francisco. The other two routes from Copiapó are branches off the *camino internacional*: the first forks off 10 km east of the Copiapó–Diego de Almagro road and continues

Border crossings: Chile–Argentina

Paso San Francisco

Although officially open all year, this pass at 4726 m is liable to closure after snow in winter. Always take spare fuel as there are no service stations between Copiapó and Fiambalá.

Chilean customs and immigration is near the Salar de Maricunga, 111 km west of the border, and is open daily 0900-1900 (in summer), 0830-1800 (in winter); US$2 is charged per vehicle crossing on Saturdays, Sundays and holidays. From here a *ripio* road continues along the southern shore of Laguna Verde, where there is a reasonable campsite and a police post, 22 km from the border. For information contact the Copiapó provincial government, T052-221 3131, and see www.pasosfronterizos.gov.cl/cf_sanfco.html.

On the Argentine side, a paved road continues to a police post at La Gruta, 24 km after the border, and on to **Argentine immigration and customs** at Fiambalá in Catamarca province, 210 km beyond the border, open daily 0700-1900 (see www.gendarmeria.gov.ar/pasos/chile/fichsanfran.html).

southeast through the Quebrada San Miguel to reach the Laguna del Negro Francisco in the southernmost sector of the Parque Nacional Tres Cruces, before turning north. This is a very poor road, where drivers can easily get lost. The second runs through the Quebrada de Paipote and then on through the northernmost sector of the park. Travellers taking either of these alternatives en route to Argentina should note that they will need to deviate north to pass through the Chilean immigration post at the Salar de Maricunga. Continuing east, the *ripio* road heads along the southern shore of Laguna Verde, where there are thermal springs and a reasonable campsite, en route to the border. (Turn off the road south of here to reach Hostería Murray for the ascent of Ojos del Salado; see box, page 147.) Before setting off it is advisable to speak to the *carabineros* in Copiapó as they will be able to give you information about the state of the various roads.

Parque Nacional Tres Cruces → *Colour map 2. B3.*

Extending over 59,082 ha, this park is in two sectors: the largest part, the northern sector, includes **Laguna Santa Rosa** and parts of the **Salar de Maricunga**, an expanse of salt flats covering 8300 ha at 3700 m; the southern sector covers the area around **Laguna del Negro Francisco**, a salt lake covering 3000 ha at 4200 m. The lakes are home to some 47 bird species, including all three species of flamingo found in Chile, as well as guanaco and vicuña. The park is stunningly beautiful and, owing to its isolation, rarely visited. The **park administration** ① *summer only daily 0830-1230, 1400-1800, US$7 (US$4.50 for Chileans)*, is located at a *refugio* southeast of Laguna del Negro Francisco.

Caldera and Bahía Inglesa → *For listings, see pages 149-151. Colour map 2, B2.*

Caldera, 73 km northwest of Copiapó, is a port and terminal for the loading of iron ore, with a population of 12,000. In the late 19th century, it was a major railway engineering centre and its train station was the southern hemisphere's first. The train station has been restored to its former glory and now houses a cultural centre and **tourist information office** ① *T052-231 6076, summer only*. The **Iglesia de San Vicente de Paul** (1862), on the poorly redesigned Plaza de Armas, was built by English carpenters working for the railway company. Caldera is home to the earliest non-denominational cemetery in Chile, where vestiges of a proud past can be glimpsed in the crumbling graves of European settlers.

Bahía Inglesa, 6 km south of Caldera and 6 km west of the Pan-American Highway, is popular with Chileans for its beautiful white sandy beaches and unpolluted, clear sea. Although the bay is now dominated by a scallop farm, this is not too noticeable from the beach. The water in this sheltered bay is warmer than around the neighbouring coast and it is safe to swim. Bahía Inglesa is rather expensive and can get crowded in January and February and at weekends, but off season makes a perfect, deserted retreat. It lies almost exactly half way between the capital and San Pedro and has two restaurants that are almost worth making a detour for, so it's a good place to break one's journey. It was originally known as Puerto del Inglés after the visit in 1687 of the English pirate, Edward Davis.

⊙ Copiapó Valley listings

For hotel and restaurant price codes and other relevant information, see pages 14-21.

⊜ Where to stay

Copiapó *p145, map p146*
$$$ Chagall, O'Higgins 760, T052-235 2900, www.chagall.cl. Executive hotel, central, some rooms with king-size beds and desk, modern fittings, spacious lounge and bar open to public.
$$ La Casona, O'Higgins 150, T052-221 7278, www.lacasonahotel.cl. More like a home than a hostel, desert colours, good beds, pleasant garden, restaurant, bar, English spoken.
$$ Montecatini, Infante 766, T052-221 1363, and at Atacama 374, T052- 221 1516, www. montecatini.cl. Helpful, best value in this price bracket. Rooms sleep 1-4, simple but OK for a night or 2 when passing through.
$$ Palace, Atacama 741, T052-221 2852. Comfortable, parking, central, nice patio. Good value.
$ Residencial Benbow, Rodríguez 541, T052-221 7634. Basic rooms, some with bath, but the best value of the many *residenciales* on this part of Rodríguez. Usually full of mine workers. Excellent value full-board deals.
$ Residencial Eli, Maipú 739, T052-221 9650. Singles cheaper. Simple rooms, good beds, decent choice.

$ Residencial Rocío, Yerbas Buenas 581, T052-221 5360. Singles cheaper. Some rooms with bath and cable TV, patio. Good budget option.

East to Paso San Francisco *p147*
There are 2 **CONAF** *refugios* (**$**) in the Parque Nacional Tres Cruces: 1 southeast of Laguna Santa Rosa, very basic; another southeast of Laguna del Negro Francisco, with bunk beds, heating, electric light and hot water. Price per person.

Caldera and Bahía Inglesa *p148*
Prices are for off season; in Jan/Feb they can rise by as much as 50%
$$$ Blanco Encalada, Copiapó y Pacífico, Bahía Inglesa, T052-231 5345, www.bahia inglesa.net. Comfortable, some rooms with balcony, roof terrace with great view, tours arranged. Cheap per person deals sometimes offered in low season, but prices rise to **$$$$** in high season (Sep-Mar).
$$$ El Coral, Av El Morro, Bahía Inglesa, T052-231 9160, www.coraldebahia.cl. Overlooking sea, good seafood, open all year. Also *cabañas*.
$$$ Hostería Puerta del Sol, Wheelwright 750, Caldera, T052-231 5205, www.hosteria puerta delsol.com. *Cabañas* with kitchen, all mod cons, laundry service, view over bay.
$$$ Los Jardines de Bahía Inglesa, Av Copiapó, Bahía Inglesa, T052-231 5359,

www.jardinesbahia.cl. *Cabañas*, open all year, good beds, swimming pool, games rooms, comfortable.

$$$ Portal del Inca, Carvallo 945, Caldera, T052-231 5648. Fully equipped 4-star *cabañas* with kitchen, English spoken, restaurant not bad, order breakfast on previous night.

$$$ Rocas de Bahía, El Morro 888, Bahía Inglesa, T052-231 6005, www.rocasde bahia.cl. 4-star hotel with all facilities, reasonable restaurant and swimming pool on the roof.

$$$-$$ Cabañas, Playa Paraíso, Av Costanera 6000, Bahía Inglesa, T09-9218 0050, www.cabanasparaiso.cl. On the shore about 6 km south of town. Cosy cabins with kitchenettes and barbecues. Idyllic location, almost like having your own private beach. No public transport, but the owners usually go into town once a day. Reiki and massages available. Recommended.

$$ Domo Chango Chile, Av El Morro 610, Bahía Inglesa, T052-231 6168. Comfortable accommodation in geodesic domes overlooking the bay. Restaurant and lots of activities offered, including surfing, bike rental and tours. English spoken. Recommended.

$ Residencial Millaray, main plaza, Cousiño 331, Caldera, T052-231 5528. Friendly, good value, basic. Price per person.

Camping

Camping Bahía Inglesa, Playa Las Machas, www.bahiaclub.com. Price per site. Also fully equipped *cabañas* for up to 6 persons.

🍴 Restaurants

Copiapó *p145, map p146*
$$ Bavaria, Chacabuco 487 (Plaza Prat) and on Los Carrera. Good variety, restaurant and café.
$$ Chifa Hao Hwa, Colipí 340 and Yerbas Buenas 334. Good Chinese, one of several in town.

$$ Entre Yuntas, Vallejos 226. Rustic but cosy, Peruvian/Chilean food, live music Fri and Sat.
$$-$ La Vitrola, Cosmocentro Plaza Real, p 2. Self-service lunch buffet, good range, reasonably priced, good views.
$ Benbow, Rodríguez 543. Good value *almuerzo*, extensive menu.
$ Don Elias, Los Carrera e Yerbas Buenas. Excellent seafood, popular.

Caldera and Bahía Inglesa *p148*
$$$-$$ Belvedere, Hotel Rocas de Bahía, Bahía Inglesa, www.rocasdebahia.cl. Reasonably elegant Italian/Chilean restaurant, with good service and views.
$$$-$$ El Plateao, El Morro 753 on the Costanera, Bahía Inglesa. Local specialities with Peruvian and oriental influences, mostly fish and shellfish, friendly service. Highly recommended, but watch out for the 10% tip automatically added to the bill.
$$ El Teatro, Gana 12, Caldera, T052-316768, www.cafeelteatro.com. Generally considered to be the best restaurant in Caldera.
$ Nuevo Miramar, Gana 090, Caldera. Good seafood at the pier.

🍸 Bars and clubs

Copiapó *p145, map p146*
Arte Pub, Maipú 641. Intimate bar with wooden interior and tables on 2 levels. Live music, karaoke. Also serves cheap healthy meals at lunchtime.
La Tabla, Los Carrera y Salas. Good pub, live music, very popular with locals.

Caldera and Bahía Inglesa *p148*
Bartholomeo, Wheelwright 747, Caldera. Lively bar with dancing at weekends.

🎭 Entertainment

Copiapó *p145, map p146*
Club de Ajedrez, Plaza Prat, www.ajedrez chileno.cl. Join the locals for a friendly game of chess on the south side of the plaza.

Sala de Cámara, M A Matta 292.
Cultural centre hosting exhibitions,
concerts, and seminars.

⊛ Festivals

Copiapó *p145, map p146*
1st Sun in Feb Fiesta de la Candelaria
begins, and lasts for 9 days. Up to 50,000
pilgrims and 3000 dancers congregate at
the Santuario de la Candelaria in Copiapó
(see page 146) from all over the north of
Chile for this important religious festival.

◉ Shopping

Copiapó *p145, map p146*
Sporting goods including basic camping
equipment are sold at **Albasini**, O'Higgins
420, www.albasini.cl. For handicrafts,
visit **Canto de Agua**, Atacama 240. This
workshop sells items crafted by local artists
out of fish skin, ostrich eggs, lapis lazuli and
other materials.

Caldera and Bahía Inglesa *p148*
Fresh seafood can be bought off the pier
in Caldera, while live scallops are available
from Inglesa's pier.

◑ What to do

Copiapó *p145, map p146*
A full list of guides, specializing in mountain
trekking and climbing, is available from
Sernatur in Copiapó (see page 145).
Aventurismo, Atacama 240, Copiapó,
T09-9599 2184, www.aventurismo.cl.
Mountaineering experts, concession
holders for Ojos del Salado, experienced in
trips to all of the higher peaks in the region.

East to Paso San Francisco *p147*
Azimut 360, Santiago, T02-235 1519, www.
azimut360.com. Based in the capital, this

French-run adventure and ecotourism
company offers mountaineering expeditions
to Ojos del Salado and Incahuasi.

Caldera and Bahía Inglesa *p148*
During the summer, many activities are
available in Bahía Inglesa including kite
surfing and boat tours.
Océano Aventura, Gabriela Mistral
57, Caldera, T09-9546 9848, www.
oceanoaventura.cl. Diving trips.

◒ Transport

Copiapó *p145, map p146*
Air
Flights to **Santiago**, **La Serena** and **El
Salvador** with **LAN**, Colipí 484, T052-221
3512 (and at the airport, T052-221 4360),
and **Sky**, Colipí 526, T052-221 4640.

Bus
To **Santiago** US$34.50-56, 12 hrs. To **La
Serena** US$11, 5 hrs. To **Antofagasta**, 7 hrs,
US$18-$48. To **Caldera**, US$2, 1 hr, cheapest
services are with **Buses Recabarren** and
Casther from the street 1 block west of the
main bus terminal.

Caldera and Bahía Inglesa *p148*
Bus
There are several bus services daily to
Santiago, and to **Antofagasta**, 7 hrs,
US$19, although to travel north it may
be better to take a bus to **Chañaral**,
then change.

ⓘ Directory

Copiapó and around *p145, map p146*
Banks Redbanc ATMs at central banks
and in Plaza Real shopping mall, including
Cambio Fides, office B123. **Bicycle
repairs** Biman, Los Carrera 998A,
T052-221 7391, excellent.

Salado Valley

The 93 km between Caldera and Chañaral are marked by vestiges of vegetation in the desert, but further north there is nothing but unremitting pampa until Antofagasta. The course of the Río Salado is almost permanently dry and the valley is less fertile and prosperous than the Copiapó or Huasco valleys to the south.

Arriving in the Salado Valley

Getting there and around There are two alternative routes from Copiapó to Chañaral: west on the Panamericana to Caldera and then north along the coast, 167 km; or the inland route, known as the Inca de Oro, via Diego de Almagro and then west to meet the *Panamericana* near Chañaral, 212 km. There are regular bus services to Chañaral along the Pan-American Highway from as far as Santiago to the south and Arica to the north. Copiapó airport is about 100 km south of Chañaral and there is another airport at El Salvador. There regular bus services between the main towns – Taltal, Chañaral and El Salvador. It is best to use rented transport or a tour to Pan de Azúcar or the Parque Nacional Tres Cruces.

Chañaral → *Colour map 2, B2. Population: 12,000.*

This is a small, sad town with wooden houses perched on the hillside. In its heyday, Chañaral was the processing centre for ore from the nearby copper mines of El Salado and Las Animas, but those mines have declined, and the town now ekes out a living processing the ores from other mines in the interior. Stone walkways climb up the desert hills behind the main street, Merino Jarpa, reaching platforms where you'll find several stone benches from which to watch the sea; behind the benches are religious murals daubed with the graffiti of impoverished, angry urban youth. There is a beautiful and often deserted white-sand beach just beyond the *Panamericana*, created by waste minerals from the old copper processing plant, stained green by its pollution and causing the bay to be entirely barren of marine life. To assuage their guilt, the copper company built a copper monument in the form of a lighthouse that dominates the bay, but in an ironic twist people started stealing the copper and now the monument can only be viewed through protective railings. Swimming is dangerous here.

Museo de Historia Natural ① *Buín 818, Mon-Fri 0900-1300 and 1500-1900, free*, has exhibits on the mineralogy, hydrobiology and entomology of the region; interesting for naturalists. There is a municipal **tourist information** kiosk on the *Panamericana*, south of town, open in summer, while to the north, a new coastal promenade is being built.

Parque Nacional Pan de Azúcar

① *CONAF office in Caleta Pan de Azúcar, daily 0830-1230, 1400-1800. Entry fee US$7 (US$4.35 for Chileans). There are heavy fines for driving in 'restricted areas' of the park. To get there, a taxi costs US$25 from Chañaral, or hitch a lift from fishermen at sunrise.*

This jewel of a national park north of Chañaral manages to combine four incredibly contrasting sets of geographical and ecological features in a stretch of land just 20 km from east to west. Offshore, the **Isla Pan de Azúcar** is home to Humboldt penguins and other sea birds, while fantastic white-sand beaches line the coast; they are popular at weekends and overcrowded in summer. A series of valleys run west to east. In pre-Colombian times they were inhabited by the Chango, a semi-nomadic coastal people. Occasionally archaeological artefacts such as pottery and arrowheads can be found. Dominating the park are coastal hills rising to 800 m, providing spectacular views. To the east the park extends into the desert. The park is inhabited by 103 species of bird as well as guanacos and foxes, and a sea lion colony can be observed by following the signs marked *loberías* from the park entrance. The *camanchaca* (coastal fog) ensures that the park has a unique set of flora that belies its desert location; after rain tall *alstroemerias* of many colours bloom in some of the gullies. The park is also one of the best places in Chile to see the flowering desert (see box, page 143), as well as extremely rare species of cactus.

There are three entrances to the park, all leading to the village of **Caleta Pan de Azúcar**: a good secondary road north from Chañaral, 28 km to Caleta Pan de Azúcar, or along two side roads from the Pan-American Highway, the closer being 45 km north of Chañaral. The **CONAF** office at Caleta has an exhibition room and cactarium. Basic maps are available, as well as entrance tickets to the park. It's a 2½-hour walk from the office to a mirador with extensive views over the southern section but, to experience the park fully, transport is needed. Although the penguins are sometimes visible from the mainland, for a closer look take a boat trip round Isla Pan de Azúcar from Caleta, from US$85 for 10 people.

El Salvador and around → *Colour map 2, A2.*

A road branches off the Pan-American Highway, 12 km east of Chañaral, heading inland along the Río Salado towards El Salvador. All along the valley people are extracting metal ore from the water with primitive settling tanks. Some 67 km from Chañaral on the El Salvador road is the smaller mining town of **Diego de Almagro**. About 12 km north of here, on a mining track through the desert, is the interesting **Pampa Austral** project, where Codelco, the state mining company, has used water resulting from the process of extracting copper from nearby mines to irrigate the desert, producing a 4-ha extension of plantations in the middle of the desert *pampa*.

Located 120 km east of Chañaral, just north of the valley of the Río Salado, **El Salvador** itself is a modern town, built near one of the biggest copper mines in Chile. A road heads southeast from here to the northern part of the Parque Nacional Tres Cruces and on to the border at Paso San Francisco (see page 148). East of El Salvador, meanwhile, 60 km by unpaved road is the **Salar de Pedernales**, salt flats 20 km in diameter and covering 30,000 ha at an altitude of 3350 m, where pink flamingos can be seen.

Taltal → *Colour map 2, A2.*

Situated 25 km off the Pan-American Highway and 146 km north of Chañaral, Taltal is the only town between Chañaral and Antofagasta, a distance of 420 km. Along Avenida Prat are several wooden buildings dating from the late 19th century when Taltal prospered as a railhead and mineral port of 20,000 people, exporting nitrates from 21 mines in the area. The town is now a fishing port with a mineral processing plant. There is a tourist information kiosk in the plaza in summer. Off season, ask at the municipalidad.

Although, like all towns in the north, Taltal has seen an increase in floating population caused by the mining boom, it still retains its relaxed laid-back air, with small fishing boats bobbing in the bay while pelicans preen themselves on the coastal wall. **Museo Augusto Capdeville** ① *Av Prat 5, free,* is a good local museum in the former *gobernación*, with rooms on prehistory, local history and the saltpetre industry, European immigration, and an exhibition on the Paranal observatory. The curator is very friendly. The surprisingly lush pleasant tree-lined plaza is laid out in the form of the Union Jack in honour of the historical importance of the British community in the town. Just north of town is the cemetery, where the European influence can clearly be seen. The impressive wooden church on the plaza burned down in 2007 and a new church was blessed and consecrated in June 2013. From the plaza walk up to the top of Torreblanca for views over the town and across the bay. A block from the plaza on the costanera is an odd-shaped bell tower, marking the site of the old pier, which used to sound whenever a ship was about to leave. Northeast of the plaza on Calle O'Higgins is an old steam engine with a pair of carriages behind which are the grounds of the former Taltal Railway Company.

There are excellent trekking opportunities around Taltal and deserted beaches line the coast both north and south, the best known of which is **Cifuncho**, some 40 km south. There's no accommodation here, but camping is easy. North along the coast by 72 km is the **Quebrada El Médano**, a gorge with ancient rock paintings along the upper valley walls.

⊙ Salado Valley listings

For hotel and restaurant price codes and other relevant information, see pages 14-21.

⊙ Where to stay

Chañaral *p152*
$$$ Hostería Chañaral, Müller 268, T052-248 0050. Dated and rather run-down, but spacious and attentive service, decent restaurant in beautiful dining room, pool room, parking.
$$$-$$ Portal Atacama, Merino Jarpa 1420, T052-248 9799, portalatacama@ hotmail.com. Decent standard, rooms with bath, TV. Also apartments, **$$$**, sleeping 6.
$$$-$$ Nuria, Almeyda 528, T052-248 0903. With bath and breakfast, parking, friendly, but a little basic and overpriced. Worth bargaining.
$$ Carmona, Almeyda 402, T052-248 0522. With bath and TV, friendly, decent value.
$$ Hotel Jiménez, Merino Jarpa 551, T052-248 0328, www.hoteljimenez.cl. Friendly, patio with lots of birds, clean rooms, modern bathrooms (some shared), good-value restaurant, convenient for **Pullman Bus**. Recommended.
$ La Marina, Merino Jarpa 562. Basic, many parakeets, no hot water.

Parque Nacional Pan de Azúcar *p152*
$$$-$$ There are a dozen or so *cabañas* in the park run by **Gran Atacama** in Copiapó (Mall Plaza Real, T052-221 9271, www.granatacama.cl). Reservations and advance payment are essential in high season. They are perfectly placed on a deserted beach behind the *caleta*, sleeping 2 or 6. Some fishermen in the *caleta* let out rooms; quite basic.

Camping
There are 3 campsites in the park: one in the Caleta, run by the fishermen, and **Camping El Piquero** and **El Soldado** run by Gran Atacama in Copiapó (see page 153).

El Salvador and around *p153*
$$$ Camino del Inca, El Tofo 330, El Salvador, T052-247 5223, htl_caminodelinca @hotmail.com. The upmarket choice.
$$-$ Hostería El Salvador, Potrerillos 003, El Salvador, T052-247 5749. Cheaper rooms here are without bath.

Taltal *p153*
Advance booking recommended as hotels are often full.

$$$-$$ Cabañas Caleta Hueso, Camino a Paposo, T055-261 2251, m.finger@entel chile.net. Good cabins 2 km from Taltal.

$$$-$$ Mi Tampi, O'Higgins 138, T055-261 3605. Best hotel in town, comfortable spacious rooms, good service, Wi-Fi. Advance booking essential. Recommended.

$$ Hostería Taltal, Esmeralda 671, T055-261 1173, www.taltalhosteria.galeon.com. On the seafront with great views and the sounds of waves to send you off to sleep. Passable restaurant, Wi-Fi zone, cheaper rooms without bath. Decent enough on the whole but doesn't do justice to its location.

$$-$ Hostal del Mar, Carrera 250, T055-261 3593. Clean basic rooms with cable TV and bathroom. Only the front 2 rooms have external windows. Breakfast extra.

$$-$ Residencial Paranal, O'Higgins 106. T055-261 3604, www.paranalresidencial. blogspot.com. Next door to Mi Tampi. Simple rooms with and without bath, parking, family-owned.

$ San Martín, Martínez 279, T055-261 1088. Without bath, good *almuerzo*.

Restaurants

Chañaral *p152*

There are also a couple of restaurants on the *Panamericana*, open 24 hrs.

$$ Capely, Merino Jarpa 1440, T052-480477. Simple, but slightly more upmarket than the rest. Serves good fish and usual Chilean fare. Set menu much cheaper than à la carte.

$ Rincón Porteño, Merino Jarpa 567, T052-480071. Good and inexpensive sandwiches, etc.

Parque Nacional Pan de Azúcar *p152*

Buy fish straight from the boats at around 1700 Tue-Sun and prepare it yourself. Take all other food with you.

Taltal *p153*

$$ Club Social Taltal, Torreblanca 162, just off the plaza. Good value *menú del día*

(à la carte much more expensive). The former club of the British community, with poker room, billiard table and ballroom.

$ Caverna, Martínez 247. Good seafood.

$ Las Brisas, Esmeralda y Moreno, by the *caleta*. Large servings, good and cheap. Recommended.

Festivals

Chañaral *p152*

15 Jul Fiesta de la Virgen del Carmen involves plenty of drumming and dancing around the plaza. The religious groups are dressed in elaborate costumes and vie with one another for the loudest band and the most complex dance; it's a moving manifestation of the faith of this impoverished but proud town.

26 Oct The town celebrates the anniversary of its founding with dancing and a parade.

Transport

Chañaral *p152*

Bus

There is no main terminal. The **Pullman Bus** terminal is at Los Baños y Costanera, **TurBus** is on Merino Jarpa, 600 block. To **Arica**, 15 hrs, US$41; to **Iquique**, 11 hrs, US$34; to **San Pedro**, 10 hrs, US$26; to **Antofagasta**, frequent, 5 hrs, US$16-33; to **Santiago**, 13 hrs, US$25-52; to **Copiapó**, 2 hrs, US$8.75; to **Taltal**, 3 daily, 2 hrs, US$8.75; *colectivos* to Copiapó depart from Merino Jarpa y Los Baños, try to leave early in the morning.

Towards El Salvador *p153*

LAN and **Sky** fly to/from **Santiago** via **Copiapó**. There are direct bus services daily to **Santiago**, **Copiapó** and **Chañaral**.

Taltal *p153*

Bus services to **Santiago**, 16 hrs, US$43.50; to **Antofagasta**, TurBus, 4 hrs, US$12; to **Chañaral**, 2 hrs, US$8.75. There are many more bus services from the Pan-American Highway.

Chañaral *p152*
Banks Poor rates for cash in **BCI** on the plaza. Nowhere to change TCs; **Redbanc** ATMs in the **TurBus** terminal and **ESSO**.

Taltal *p153*
Banks **Banco Estado** on the plaza.

Contents

Footprint features

Border crossings

Antofagasta, Calama & San Pedro de Atacama

At a glance

◒ **Getting around** Long distances between towns, but good bus services and regular tours. Some nearby destinations can be visited on mountain bike.

⟳ **Time required** 4 days to see the sights around San Pedro; 4 to visit the salt flats in Uyuni, 1 day for travelling.

☁ **Weather** Warm and often overcast (but never wet) on the coast. Inland hot days, cold nights and very dry, except for the occasional storm in winter.

⊗ **When not to go** High summer (Jan) can be unpleasantly hot inland. Occasional rain can cause havoc to dirt roads in the Altiplano in Feb-Mar and Jul.

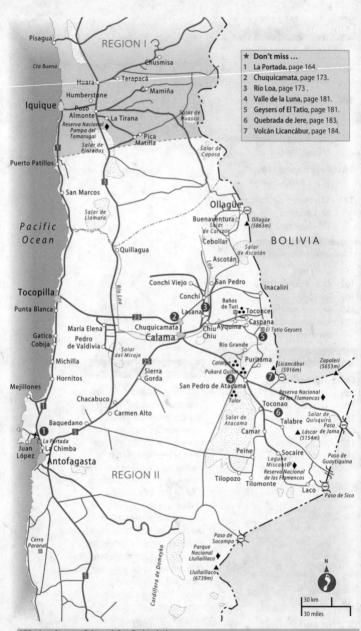

REGION I

Pisagua

Cta Buena

Chusmisa

Huara

Tarapacá

Humberstone

Mamiña

Iquique

Pozo Almonte

Salar de Huasco

Reserva Nacional Pampa del Tamarugal

La Tirana

Pica

Matilla

Salar de Pintados

Salar de Coposa

Puerto Patillos

Pacific Ocean

San Marcos

Salar de Llamara

Ollagüe

Salar de Carcote

Buenaventura

Ollagüe (5863m)

BOLIVIA

Cebollar

Salar de Ascotán

Quillagua

Ascotán

Tocopilla

Conchi Viejo

San Pedro

Inacaliri

Punta Blanca

Conchi

Baños de Turi

Gatico

Cobija

Lasana

Toconce

María Elena

Chuquicamata

Calama

Ayquina

Caspana

El Tatio Geysers

Pedro de Valdivia

Salar del Miraje

Chiu Chiu

Río Grande

Michilla

Sierra Gorda

Cataipe

Puritama

Mejillones

Chacabuco

Pukará Quitor

Licancábur (5916m)

Zapaleri (5653m)

San Pedro de Atacama

Hornitos

Carmen Alto

Tulor

Reserva Nacional de los Flamencos

Baquedano

Toconao

Salar de Quisquiro

Paso de Jama

La Portada

Juan López

La Chimba

Salar de Atacama

Talabre

Láscar de Jama (5154m)

Camar

Antofagasta

REGION II

Peine

Socaire

Paso de Guaytiquina

Laguna Miscanti

Reserva Nacional de los Flamencos

Tilopozo

Tilomonte

Laco

Paso de Sico

Paso de Socompa

Cerro Paranal

Parque Nacional Llullaillaco

Llullaillaco (6739m)

Cordillera de Domeyko

N

30 km

30 miles

This desolate region is one of the most striking in Chile. The Atacama Desert is punctuated by small oases in the all-encompassing yellowness; clefts of green such as the beautiful Quebrada de Jere, near Toconao, or the Alto Loa, from where the lifelessness of the surrounding desert seems somehow impossible.

The main cities are Antofagasta and Calama, both of which are service centres for the mining industry that dominates the region's economy. Most visitors, however, head straight to San Pedro de Atacama, an ancient centre of civilization in the region since well before the Spanish conquest, and the base for trips to spectacular desert landscapes such as the Valle de la Luna and the Salar de Atacama, as well as to the geysers of El Tatio and Altiplano lakes. San Pedro is home to one of the north's most important archaeological museums, and trips can also be made over the border into Bolivia to the Salar de Uyuni and to two beautiful lakes, Laguna Colorada and Laguna Verde.

Background

The Atacama Desert stretches 1255 km north from the Río Copiapó to the Chilean border with Peru. The Cordillera de la Costa, at its highest in this region (the highest peak is Cerro Vicuña; 3114 m), runs close to the coast, an inhospitable and spectacular cliff face rising sheer from the waters to a height of up to 900 m. Below this cliff is a ledge on which the city of Antofagasta and some smaller towns are situated. In the eastern branch of the Andes, several peaks rise to around 6000 m: Llullaillaco (6739 m), Socompa (6051 m), Licancábur (5916 m), Ollagüe (5863 m): The western branch of the Andes ends near Calama. In between these two ranges the Andean Depression includes several salt flats, including the Salar de Atacama and the smaller Salar de Ascotán.

Before the Spanish conquest, this part of Chile was populated both on the coast and inland. The Chango people fished in the Pacific out of boats made from the pelts of sea lions. They traded fish with the peoples of the interior, from whom they bought coca leaves and quinoa (the staple grain before the arrival of those from Europe); from around the first century AD, there is evidence of an extensive network of paths and trade routes crossing the desert, linking the coastal areas between Taltal and the estuary of the Río Loa with the Altiplano of Chile, Argentina and Bolivia. Until the arrival of the Incas in around 1450, the most important inland civilization was that of the Atacameños, based in the area around San Pedro de Atacama. The Atacameños are believed to have arrived around 9000 BC, and, over the course of the millennia, they managed to adapt to the harsh terrain in which they lived. After the arrival of the Incas, the Atacameños adapted their cultural rituals to suit their new masters.

The first Spanish expedition arrived in 1536, led by Diego de Almagro. Four years later, Pedro de Valdivia took San Pedro de Atacama and the fort at Quitor and, thereafter, the Spanish and the Atacameño peoples enacted the familiar and tragic pattern of subjugation and extinction. San Pedro was the colonial centre but, by the end of the colonial era, the Spanish had established urban settlements only here and in Chiu Chiu. At independence most of the region became part of Bolivia and several towns were established along the Pacific, notably Cobija (1825), Mejillones (1841), Tocopilla (1843) and Antofagasta (1872). After the war, when the territory passed to Chile, the increased exploitation of nitrates led to the construction of railways and ports and Antofagasta's growth into the north's most important city.

These days, mining is by far the most important economic activity. Fishing is also a major industry, with agriculture limited by the lack of water and poor soils to mainly tropical fruit production on the coast south of Antofagasta. Life in the area is artificial. Water has to be piped for hundreds of kilometres to the cities and the mining towns from the cordillera; all food and even all building materials have to be brought in from elsewhere.

As throughout northern Chile, there are major differences between the climate of the coast and that of the interior. Temperatures on the coast are fairly uniform and the weather is frequently humid and cloudy; *camanchaca*, a heavy sea mist caused by the cold water of the Humboldt current, is common in the morning and, in spite of the fact that this is one of the driest places in the world, it can seem that it is about to rain at any moment, with morning dew a common occurrence in summer. In the interior, the skies are clear day and night, leading to extremes of temperature; winter nights can often be cold as -10°C, and colder in the high Altiplano. Strong winds, lasting for up to a week, are common, especially, it is said, around the full moon, while between December and March there are sporadic but often violent storms of rain, snow and hail in the Altiplano, a phenomenon known as *invierno altiplánico* (highland winter) or *invierno boliviano* (Bolivian winter).

Antofagasta and around

On the edge of a bay, nearly 700 km south of Arica, Antofagasta is the largest city in northern Chile and the fourth largest in the country. It is not a terribly attractive place, perhaps only worth stopping at to break a long journey. That said, the combination of the tall mountains and the ocean is dramatic, and after a week in the desert interior it is pleasant to breathe the sea air while relaxing on one of the beaches south of town. Apart from the lack of rain, the climate is pleasant; the temperature varies from 16°C in June and July to 24°C in January and February, never falling below 10°C at night. The city's economy depends on the enormous mine at La Escondida in the interior, where 8000 people work, doing week-long shifts at the mine before spending a week in the city; the city's port also acts as the processing point for the copper from La Escondida and Chuquicamata. As well as being the capital of Región II, Antofagasta is also an important commercial centre and the home of two universities.

Arriving in Antofagasta → *Colour map 1, C1. Population 240,000.*
Getting there and around The bus terminal is at Aguirre Cerda 5750, on the northern edge of the city. Antofagasta is served by many regular buses from both north and south. All major companies serving the north stop here. Cerro Moreno Airport, 22 km north if the city is served by frequent flights to/from Santiago and north as far as Arica. A taxi to/from the airport costs US$30-40, but is cheaper if ordered from a hotel. For airport transfers, contact **Aerobus** ① *T055-226 2727, US$9-10*. Antofagasta is one of Chile's largest cities, and you may need to take *colectivos* or buses to get to more out-of-the-way places, particularly the discos and bars in the south and the university campuses. Avenida O'Higgins is also known as Avenida Brasil.

Tourist office ① *Prat 384, in the intendencia on Plaza Colón, T055-245 1818, infoantofagasta@sernatur.cl, Mon-Fri 0930-1730 (until 1930 in summer), Sat 1000-1400*, is very helpful. There is also a kiosk at the airport (open summer only). **CONAF** ① *Argentina 2510, T055-238 3320, antofaga@conaf.cl.*

Places in Antofagasta
In the main square, **Plaza Colón**, there is a clock tower donated by the British community in 1910. It is a miniature of Big Ben with a carillon that produces similar sounds. The pedestrianized calle Prat, which runs southeast from the plaza, is the main shopping street, full of crowds and busking musicians and performance artists. Two blocks north of

Archaeology of the Atacama

From early times, people settled along the northern coast of Chile, sustained by the food supply from the Pacific Ocean. From about 7600 BC, fisherfolk and foragers lived in large groups in permanent settlements, such as the Quebrada de Conchas, just to the north of Antofagasta. They fished with fibre nets, sometimes venturing inland to hunt for mammals.

About 2000 years later, the successors of these people, the 'Chinchorros', developed one of the most noted characteristics of Andean cultures: veneration for their ancestors. The role of the dead in the world of the living was vital to the earliest Andean people. As a link between the spiritual and the material world, the ancestor of each local kin group would protect his clan. The expression of these beliefs came in the form of veneration of the ancestors' bodies; sacrifices were made to them, funeral rites were repeated, and precious grave offerings were renewed. In the arid climate of the Atacama, the people observed how bodies were naturally preserved and the skilled practice of mummification was developed over a period of 3000 years, preserving the dead as sacred objects and spiritual protectors.

Another important cultural practice in northern Chile was the use of hallucinogens. Grave remains found in the region, dating from about AD 1000, include leather bags containing organic powder, wooden tablets and snuffer tubes. The tablets and snuffers were often decorated with supernatural figures, such as bird-headed angels, winged humans, star animals and other characters familiar in Altiplano cultures. Although the origins and function of taking hallucinogens is not known for certain, it is thought that the practice may have been brought down to the coast by traders from the highlands. There were also 'medicine men' who travelled throughout the central and south central Andes dispensing drugs and healing the sick. As in the Andes and Amazonia, it is possible that the drugs were taken as part of religious rituals and often for a combination of spiritual and physical healing.

Plaza Colón, near the old port, is the former **Aduana**, built as the Bolivian customs house in Mejillones and moved to its current site after the War of the Pacific. Inside is the **Museo Histórico Regional** ① *Balmaceda 2786, www.museudeantofagast.cl, Tue-Fri 0900-1700, Sat, Sun and hols 1100-1400, US$1, children half price,* which has fascinating displays on marine life, ecology, archaeology, anthropology and mining, as well as the nitrate era and a typically one-sided account of the War of the Pacific. The explanations are in Spanish only. Opposite are the former offices of the **Capitanía del Puerto** (harbourmaster) and the **Resguardo Marítimo** (coastguard).

East of the port are the buildings of the **Antofagasta and Bolivia Railway Company** (FCAB) dating from the 1890s and beautifully restored, but still in use and difficult to visit. These include the former railway station, company offices, workers' housing and the **Museo del Ferrocarril a Bolivia** ① *Bolívar 255, T055-220 6221, www.fcab.cl, free,* which has an interesting collection relating to the history of the Antofagasta–Bolivia railway. Just north of the port is the **Terminal de Pescadores**, where there are markets selling seafood, fruit and vegetables. Pelicans sit on the fish market roof and sea lions and sea turtles swim in the harbour; there are half-hour tours of the port available from **La Cabaña de Mario** ① *C Aníbal Pinto s/n, between the Museo Regional and the Terminal de Pescadores, 30 mins, US$5.*

The former main plaza of the **Oficina Vergara**, a nitrate town built in 1919 and dismantled in 1978, can be seen in the campus of the University of Antofagasta, 4 km south of the centre (take *colectivo* 114 or 333 from the town centre). Also on the university campus is the **Museo Geológico de la Universidad Católica del Norte** ① *Av Angamos 0610, inside the university campus, gchong@ucn.cl, Mon-Fri, 0930-1300, 1530-1800, free, colectivo 114 or 333 from town centre.* On a hill to the south of town (bus 103) are the imposing ruins of **Huanchaca**, a Bolivian silver refinery built after 1868 and closed in

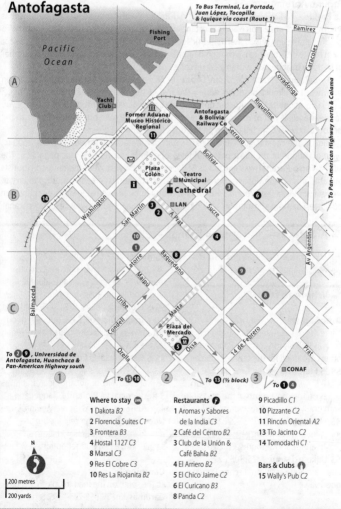

Antofagasta

To Bus Terminal, La Portada, Juan López, Tocopilla & Iquique via coast (Route 1)

Pacific Ocean

Fishing Port

Yacht Club

Former Aduana/ Museo Histórico Regional

Antofagasta & Bolivia Railway Co

Plaza Colón

Teatro Municipal
Cathedral

LAN

Plaza del Mercado

To ②⑨, Universidad de Antofagasta, Huanchaca & Pan-American Highway south

To ⑮⑩   To ⑬ (½ block)   To ①④

CONAF

To Pan-American Highway north & Calama

N

200 metres
200 yards

Where to stay 🛏
1 Dakota *B2*
2 Florencia Suites *C1*
3 Frontera *B3*
4 Hostal 1127 *C3*
8 Marsal *C3*
9 Res El Cobre *C3*
10 Res La Riojanita *B2*

Restaurants 🍴
1 Aromas y Sabores de la India *C3*
2 Café del Centro *B2*
3 Club de la Unión & Café Bahía *B2*
4 El Arriero *B2*
5 El Chico Jaime *C2*
6 El Curicano *B3*
8 Panda *C2*

9 Picadillo *C1*
10 Pizzante *C2*
11 Rincón Oriental *A2*
13 Tío Jacinto *C2*
14 Tomodachi *C1*

Bars & clubs 🍸
15 Wally's Pub *C2*

1903. From below, the ruins resemble a fortress. With the new casino and hotel opposite, the ruins are being cleaned up and a museum is planned.

There are two main beaches in town, the **Playa Paraíso** by the Líder supermarket just north of the centre or the nicer **Balneario municipal**, by the McDonald's about 2 km south of town (take bus 103). Alternatively stay on the 103 past the Balneario Municipal and get off at any quiet spot that takes your fancy. The coastal road has been redesigned with cycle paths north and south and is surprisingly pleasant.

Around Antofagasta

La Portada, 16 km north of the city, is a natural arch with fantastic rock formations that are the symbol of Region II and are often seen on postcards up and down the country. To get there take any bus to Mejillones or Juan López (see Transport, below), then walk for 2 km to the beach, which, although beautiful, is too dangerous for swimming. A number of bathing beaches are within easy reach.

A windsurfers' paradise, **Juan López**, is 38 km north of Antofagasta. Popular in summer, it is almost deserted during the rest of the year. The sea is alive with birds, especially at Caleta Constitución opposite Isla Santa María (fishermen there can take you to the island). If you have your own transport, follow the road out of Juan López to the beautiful cove at Conchilla. Keep on the track to the end at Bolsico.

High in the coastal *cordillera*, 132 km south of Antofagasta, is Cerro Paranal, 2600 m, location of one of the most powerful telescopes in the world (see box, page 125). The site at **Cerro Paranal** was chosen as 350 clear nights a year were guaranteed. Tourists are able to visit the observatory on the last two weekends of each month, January to November. Visits last around two hours and should be booked at least three months in advance. For more information, including an application form, see www.eso.org/paranal.

◉ Antofagasta and around listings

For hotel and restaurant price codes and other relevant information, see pages 14-21

● Where to stay

Antofagasta *p161, map p163*
There are several international chain hotels, such as Holiday Inn, Ibis and Radisson, and others designed for the business market.
$$$$ Florencia Suites, Croacia 0126, T055-279 8221, www.florenciasuites.cl. Luxury suites on the coast south of the city centre with lovely sea views, restaurant and pool.
$$$ Marsal, Prat 867, T055-226 8063, www.marsalhotel.cl. Modern, very comfortable, bright and spacious rooms, Catalan owner.
$$ Dakota, Latorre 2425, T055-225 1749, floreria magnolia@hotmail.com. Popular, good value.

$$ Hostal 1127, Coquimbo 1127, T055-284 1497, www.hostal1127.com. En suite rooms with all services, in a residential neighbourhood, quiet, helpful.
$$-$ Frontera, Bolívar 558, T055-228 1219, www.fronterahotel.cl. Basic but with good hot showers and decent beds, convenient for Tur-Bus and Pullman.
$$-$ Residencial El Cobre, Prat 749, T055-226 7726. Private or shared bath, set around a central courtyard, bright and clean, but tatty.
$ Residencial La Riojanita, Baquedano 464, T09-8360 2796. Basic, very helpful, older rooms have high ceilings but are run-down, newer rooms with bath are smaller. Not a bad budget option.

Camping
To the south on the road to Coloso are: **Las Garumas**, Km 6, T055-263 7395, **$** per site

(ask for lower price out of season), **\$\$** for cabins, cold showers and beach (reservations Av Angamos 601, Av Jaime Guzmán s/n).

Around Antofagasta *p164*
\$\$ Hostería Sandokan, Juan López, T055-222 3022. Standard facilities.

🍴 Restaurants

Antofagasta *p161, map p163*
Many bars and restaurants are closed on Sun.
\$\$\$ Club de la Unión, Prat 474, p 2, T055-2428 4600, www.clubdelaunion.cl. Open to non-members, traditional atmosphere, excellent *almuerzo* and service.
\$\$\$-\$\$ Picadillo, Av Grecia 1000, T055-224 7503. Lively atmosphere, serves a wide range of dishes. Good music.
\$\$\$-\$\$ Tomodachi, Balmaceda 2355, Local 21, Mall Plaza, T055-253 3300, www.tomodachi.cl. The best of the city's sushi restaurants.
\$\$ Aromas y Sabores de la India, Argentina 1294, T055-278 0280. Indian restaurant and take-away, the only one of its kind in northern Chile.
\$\$ El Arriero, Condell 2644, T055-226 4371. Grills and traditional hearty criollo food. Good service, cheap set lunch, popular, live music.
\$\$ Panda, Condell 2505, T055-225 4827. Self-service, Chinese and Chilean, eat all you can for set price.
\$\$ Pizzante, Carrera 1857, T055-222 3344, www.pizzante.cl. Good pasta, seafood and vegetarian options.
\$\$ Rincón Oriental, Washington 2743, T055-222 6869. Excellent Cantonese, 'over the top' decor.
\$\$ Tío Jacinto, Uribe 922, T055-222 8486. Friendly atmosphere, serves good seafood.
\$\$-\$ El Chico Jaime, Mercado Central 2nd floor, local 115, T055-222 7401. Best of the restaurants in the central market, good food and friendly service.

\$ El Curicano, Simón Bolívar 607. Good value, basic set menu lunches and dinners.
Above the market are a few good places selling cheap seafood *almuerzos* and super-cheap set lunches, including El Mariscal and Toledo. Good fish restaurants in Terminal Pesquero Centro and at Caleta Coloso, which is 18 km south.

Cafés
Café Bahía, Prat 470. Open at 0900 for real coffee.
Café del Centro, Galería, Prat 482. Real coffee.

Around Antofagasta *p164*
\$\$\$ La Portada, Camino a la portada, T055-226423. Open lunchtime and afternoon only. Expensive seafood restaurant and café.

🍸 Bars and clubs

Antofagasta *p161, map p163*
Thanks to Antofagasta's student population, the city's nightlife is buzzing. The most popular bars and clubs are 16 km south of the town in Balneario El Huáscar. Take micro 103 from C Matta for there. There is also a wide choice on O'Higgins.
Moove. One of the most popular disco options at El Huáscar.
Wally's Pub, Toro 982. British expat-style with darts, pool and beer, closed Sun.

🎭 Entertainment

Antofagasta *p161, map p163*
Teatro Municipal, Sucre y San Martín, T055-259 1732, www.culturaantofagasta.cl. Modern, state-of-the art theatre.
Teatro Pedro de la Barra, Condell 2495. Theatre run by University of Antofagasta, regular programme of plays, reviews, concerts, etc, high standard, details in press.

☸ Festivals

Antofagasta *p161, map p163*
29 Jun The image of **San Pedro**, patron saint of the fishermen, is taken out by launch to the breakwater to bless the first catch of the day.
Last weekend of Oct The city's immigrant communities put on a joint festival on the seafront with national foods, dancing and music.

○ Shopping

Antofagasta *p161, map p163*
The **Mall Plaza Antofagasta**, Balmaceda y Maipú has a wide variety of shops and a pleasant promenade on the roof, with colourful flowers and views out to the ocean.

Markets
Feria Modelo O'Higgins (next to fish market on Av Pinto). Excellent fruit and veg, also restaurants. **Municipal market** is at Matta y Uribe.

○ What to do

Antofagasta *p161, map p163*
Many tour companies offer packages to the Atacama, but the office of tourism recommends booking tours in San Pedro de Atacama, as it is far cheaper. See www. surfantofagasta.cl for information on surfing in the area.
Buceo Magallanes, Balmaceda 2615, T09-9232 7932, www.buceomagallanes.cl. Regular diving trips and courses.

○ Transport

Antofagasta *p161, map p163*
Air
LAN, **PAL** and **Sky** fly daily to **Santiago**, **Copiapó**, **Iquique** and **Arica**. **LAN** also daily to La Serena.

Bus
Bus company phone numbers: **Flota Barrios**, T055-224 4626; **Géminis** and **Romani**, T055-256 1021; **Pullman Bus**, T055-223 6836; **Tur-Bus**, T600-660 6600.
To **Santiago**, many companies, 18 hrs, US$54-78; book in advance in high season. If all seats to the capital are booked, catch a bus to **La Serena** (12 hrs, US$26-42), or **Ovalle**, 14 hrs, and re-book. To **Valparaíso**, US$40-70. To **Copiapó**, 7 hrs, US$18-32. Frequent buses to **Iquique**, US$16-21, 6 hrs. To **Arica**, US$20-37, 11 hrs. To **Calama**, several companies, US$9, 3 hrs; to **San Pedro de Atacama**, Tur-Bus 6 daily, 5 hrs, US$8, or via Calama. To **Tocopilla**, 2½ hrs, US$10, many daily. Buses to **Mejillones**, every 30 mins, 1 hr, US$2, from Corsal terminal, Condell y Sucre (will drop off 2 km from La Portada); also minibuses from Latorre 2730, US$5 return. To **Juan López**, bus 129 from Condell y Sucre, summer only; these will drop you much closer to La Portada.

Car hire
First, Bolívar 623, T055-222 5777.
Plus international agencies.
Andrés Ljubetic Romo, Atacama 2657, T055-226 8851, is a recommended mechanic.

○ Directory

Antofagasta *p161, map p163*
Banks It's difficult to change TCs anywhere between La Serena and Antofagasta. There are several ATMs around the plaza and the rest of the centre. *Casas de cambio* are mainly on Baquedano. **Consulates** Argentina, Blanco Encalada 1933, T055-222 0440; **Bolivia**, Washington 2675, p 13, T055-279 4369.

North of Antofagasta

There are two routes north from Antofagasta: to Iquique along the Pan-American Highway, or along the coastal road, Ruta 1, towards Tocopilla and beyond. The coastal route is more picturesque and makes a beautiful alternative to the sterility that accompanies large stretches of the *Panamericana*.

Along the Pan-American Highway → *For listings, see page 170. Colour map 1, C1/2 and B2.*

From Antofagasta, the Pan-American Highway continues north via the former railway post of **Baquedano** (Km 68) where there is a museum and a project underway to restore the station, to **Carmen Alto** (Km 101), where there is a turning to Calama. Four kilometres' walk from the junction is **Chacabuco** (100 km northeast of Antofagasta), a large abandoned nitrate town, opened in 1924 and closed in 1938. It was used as a concentration camp by the Pinochet government between 1973 and 1975. Workers' housing, the church, theatre, stores and the mineral plants can be visited and there is a free guided tour in Spanish. If you visit Chacabuco, be sure to take water and set out early in the morning as you will probably be hitching back.

Another turning 69 km north of Carmen Alto leads to **Pedro de Valdivia**, a nitrate town abandoned in 1996, which has been declared a National Monument and can be visited. From here, a road runs north, parallel to the Pan-American Highway, crossing the Salar del Mirage to **María Elena**, the only nitrate town still functioning. After a half-century or more in the doldrums, the nitrate business is now profitable once again, because the nitrates extracted from the Atacama Desert are thought to be better for the soil than the chemical version. The town itself was badly damaged by an earthquake in 2007, but tours can be taken to see the historic buildings. Some 20 km southeast of María Elena, just off the Pan-American Highway, is the **Balneario Chacance**, where bathing and camping are available on the banks of the Río Loa. North of María Elena, meanwhile, the Highway crosses the Tocopilla–Calama road 107 km north of Carmen Alto.

At **Quillagua**, Km 81, there is a customs post where all vehicles heading south are searched. Situated 111 km further north is the southernmost and largest section of the **Reserva Nacional Pampa del Tamarugal**, which contains the **Geoglifos de Pintados** (see page 199).

Along the coastal road → *For listings, see page 170.*

Mejillones and beyond → *Colour map 1, C1.*
Located 60 km north of Antofagasta, Mejillones stands on a good natural harbour protected from westerly gales by high hills. Until 1948, it was a major terminal for the export of tin and other metals from Bolivia. Remnants of that past include a number of fine wooden buildings: the **Intendencia Municipal**, the **Casa Cultural**, built in 1866, and the **church**, 1906, as well as the **Capitanía del Puerto**. The town has been transformed in recent years by the building of the largest port in South America here – the port links Argentina, southern Brazil and Paraguay with the lucrative markets of the

Asian Pacific Rim. Although the large port buildings now dominate the northern end of the town, fishing remains important, and Mejillones comes alive in the evening when the fishermen prepare to set sail. The sea is very cold around Mejillones because of the Humboldt current.

From Mejillones, the road runs at the foot of 500-m cliffs, with shifting views of the mountains and glistening ocean. Where the cliffs break into jagged rocks on the shoreline, hundreds of cormorants can be seen swarming all over the pinnacles. There are good beach resorts at **Hornitos**, 88 km north of Antofagasta, and **Poza Verde**, 117 km north.

Behind the mountains, the coastal sierra is extensively mined for copper, often by *pirquineros*, small groups of self-employed miners. There are larger mines, with the biggest concentration inland from Michilla. Reminders of the area's mining past can be seen, principally at the ruins of **Cobija**, 127 km north of Antofagasta, founded by order of Simón Bolívar in 1825 as Bolivia's main port. A prosperous little town handling silver exports from Potosí, it was destroyed by an earthquake in 1868 and again by a tidal wave in 1877 before losing out to the rising port of Antofagasta. Adobe walls, the rubbish tip right above the sea and the wreckage of the port are all that remain. The haunting ruins of the port of **Gatico** are at Km 144, just a little way beyond, and about 4 km further north there is an amazing ransacked cemetery.

About 152 km north of Antofagasta, a very steep zigzag road winds up the cliffs a further 18 km to the mine at **Mantos de la Luna**. At the top, there are rather dead-looking groves of giant cactus living off the sea mist that collects on the cliffs. Wildlife includes foxes, or *zorros*.

Tocopilla → *Colour map 1, C1.*

Tocopilla lies 187 km north of Antofagasta via the coast road (or 365 km via the Pan-American Highway), and has one of the most dramatic settings of any Chilean town, sheltering at the foot of the coastal mountains that loom inland at heights of up to 2000 m. Tocopilla is dominated by a thermal power station, which supplies electricity to much of the far north, and by the port facilities used to unload coal and to export nitrates and iodine from María Elena. There is a run-down and slightly menacing air to the place, not helped by the 2006 earthquake, which laid waste to a sizeable part of the town. A prolonged stay is not recommended. There are, however, a few interesting early 20th-century buildings with wooden balustrades and façades, while the sloping plaza is an unlikely fiesta of palms and pepper trees amid the otherwise unremitting desert. There are two good beaches: **Punta Blanca**, 12 km south, and **Caleta Covadonga**, 3 km south, which has a swimming pool. A colony of some 20 to 30 sea turtles can often be seen about 3 km north of town. There is also fine deep-sea fishing here, if you can find a boat and a guide.

For a spectacular view, head up Calle Baquedano as far as possible until you reach a stone stairway. Walking up this, you reach a minor road, which climbs up behind the town, giving views of the cliffs to the north, the mountains reaching inland and the fishing boats bobbing up and down in the harbour.

Routes north and east of Tocopilla

The coastal road runs north from Tocopilla to **Iquique**, 244 km away, and is a highly recommended journey, offering views of the rugged coastline, sea lions and tiny fishing communities. The customs post at **Chipana-Río Loa** (Km 90) searches all

Nitrates

The rise and fall of the nitrate industry played an important role in opening up the northern desert areas between Iquique and Antofagasta to human settlement. In the second half of the 19th century, nitrates became important in Europe and the USA as an artificial fertilizer and for making explosives. The world's only known nitrate deposits were in the Atacama Desert provinces of Antofagasta in Bolivia and Tarapacá in Peru. After the War of the Pacific, Chile gained control of all the nitrate fields and thus a monopoly over world supply. Ownership was dominated by the British who controlled 60% of the industry by 1900. Taxes on the export of nitrates provided Chilean governments with around half their income for the next 40 years.

The processing of nitrates was labour intensive: at its height over 60,000 workers were employed. Using a combination of dynamite and manual labour, the workers dug the nitrate ore from the desert floor. It was then transported to nitrate plants, known as oficinas, crushed and mixed with water, allowing pure nitrates to be extracted. The mining and refining processes were dangerous and cost many lives. Wages were relatively high, but workers were paid in special tokens valid only for the particular oficina in which they worked. This not only meant that they had no means of leaving the oficina with ready cash, but also that they had to buy all their goods from the company stores which were, of course, controlled by the oficina.

The development of the Haber-Bosch process, a method of producing artificial nitrates, in Germany during the First World War, dealt a severe blow to the nitrate companies and many mines closed in the 1920s. New techniques were introduced by the Guggenheim company, but the world depression after 1929 led to a decline in demand and with it the collapse of the Chilean nitrate industry. Traces of the nitrate era can, however, still be seen: the mining ghost towns of Chacabuco, north of Antofagasta, and Humberstone, near Iquique, can be visited, as can Baquedano, the most important junction of the nitrate railways; most of the other oficinas are marked only by piles of rubble at the roadsides north of Antofagasta. Only one mine survives today, at María Elena, and its future is secure. The nitrates from the Atacama are believed to be much better for the soil than those created by the artificial process and so demand has increased again in recent years.

---

southbound vehicles for duty-free goods; this can take up to half an hour. Basic accommodation is available at **San Marcos**, a fishing village (Km 131). At **Chanaballita** (Km 184), there is a hotel, cabañas, camping, restaurant, shops. There are campsites at the former salt mining town of **Guanillos** (Km 126), **Playa Peruana** (Km 129) and **Playa El Aguila** (Km 160).

East of Tocopilla a good paved road climbs a steep, narrow valley 72 km to the Pan-American Highway. From here, the road continues eastwards to **Chuquicamata** (see page 173), which lies 16 km north of Calama, the main city of the interior.

For hotel and restaurant price codes and other relevant information, see pages 14-21.

🛏 Where to stay

Along the Pan-American Highway
p167
$ Residencial Chacance, María Elena, T055-263 9524. Run-down but the same owners provide nicer rooms round the corner.

Mejillones *p167*
Wild camping is possible on the beach.
$$$ Hotel Mejillones, M Montt 086, T055-255 5149, www.hotelmejillones.cl. 4-star, with restaurant, café and bar. One of several upper range hotels and apart-hotels.
$$ París, Pje Iquique 095, T055-262 3061. Clean, modern, good.
$ Residencial Elisabeth, Alte Latorre 440, T055-262 3738. Friendly, basic, with restaurant. Price per person.

Tocopilla *p168*
$$$ Atenas, 21 de Mayo 1448, T055-281 4247. Characterless but comfortable. With bath and cable TV. Restaurant.
$$ Croacia, Bolívar 1332, T055-281 0332. Modern, helpful. Cheaper without bath. Opposite on Bolívar is the **Sucre**, same ownership, same price.

🍴 Restaurants

Tocopilla *p168*
$$ Club de la Unión, Prat 1354. Pleasant atmosphere. Good-value *almuerzo*.

🚌 Transport

Along the Pan-American Highway
p167
Bus
Buses between Antofagasta and Calama stop at the **Carmen Alto** junction, 1½ hrs, US$8. **María Elena** is served by TurBus to/from Iquique, 6 hrs, US$15.

Mejillones *p167*
Bus
Buses to **Antofagasta**, every 30 mins, 1 hr, US$2; also minibuses.

Tocopilla *p168*
Bus
There is no bus terminal in Tocopilla. Bus offices are located on 21 de Mayo, including **Pullman Bus**, **TurBus**, **Flota Barrios** and **Pullman Carmelita**, all serving the following destinations: **Antofagasta**, many daily, 2½ hrs, US$10; **Iquique**, frequent, 3 hrs, US$11. **TurBus** also runs services to **Calama**, 3 a day, 3 hrs, US$11.50. All the above companies also serve Santiago.

Note that most buses to southern destinations are en route from Iquique, so you're unlikely to be able to leave Tocopilla before mid-morning.

🛈 Directory

Tocopilla *p168*
Banks BCI, Baquedano y Prat, has a Redbanc ATM. **Post office** 21 de Mayo y A Pinto.

Calama and around

Calama is a somewhat seedy city, set at 2265 m in the oasis of the Río Loa, with beautiful views of volcanoes in the Ollagüe area. An expensive and modern town, roughly 200 km northeast of Antofagasta, it acts as a service centre for the large nearby mines of Chuquicamata and Radomiro Tomic. Initially a staging post on the silver route between Potosí and Cobija, Calama superseded San Pedro de Atacama in importance with the development of mining activities at Chuquicamata. Most travellers use Calama as the departure point for San Pedro de Atacama; however, football fans will certainly want to make sure that their visit coincides with a home match of Cobreloa, the most successful Chilean football team outside Santiago in the past 20 years or so. Nearby are oasis villages such as Chiu Chiu and Caspana with their historic churches and altogether slower pace of life.

Arriving in Calama → *Colour map 1, B3/C2.*
Getting there and around Calama is easily reached by regular buses from Antofagasta and the south, and by less frequent buses from Iquique and Arica, which often travel overnight. The **main terminal** ① *Granaderos 3048, T055-231 3722*, is served by many companies. The modern and efficient airport is about 5 km from the city centre and is served by daily flights to/from Antofagasta and Santiago. The terminal building has Redbanc ATM, restaurant upstairs and shop with internet. Transfer services are offered by **Transfer City Express** ① *T055-234 1022, US$11*. There are also taxis to/from the airport, which are more expensive. The more upmarket hotels may offer courtesy vans. The central part of Calama is relatively compact and you should not need to take public transport. There are, however, many *colectivos* (black cabs with a number on the roof), most of which pick up on Abaroa or Vargas. Just ask which number goes in your direction and flag it down: US$0.75 by day, US$0.85 after 2400. ▸▸ *For further details, including buses to Bolivia and Argentina, see Transport, below.*

Tourist office ① *Latorre 1689, T055-253 1707, www.calamacultural.cl, Mon-Fri 0830-1300, 1400-1800*. They provide maps of the town and can book tours to Chuquicamata. English spoken, helpful staff, but don't expect any information on San Pedro.

Places in Calama
The centre of Calama is Plaza 21 de Mayo, a shady spot in which to relax. The peach-coloured **Catedral San Juan Bautista** on the west side with its copper-clad spire makes a pleasant contrast to the colours of the desert. On the northeastern side, the pedestrian walkway of Ramírez continues two blocks east, where visitors will not be able to miss the

bright red, phallic statue of **El Minero**, erected as a tribute to the bravery of the region's miners, but also an unlikely piece of kitsch in the Atacama. This is a lively area at night.

On Avenida Bernado O'Higgins, 2 km from the centre, is the **Parque El Loa** ① *daily 1000-1800*, which contains a reconstruction of a typical colonial village built around a reduced-scale reproduction of Chiu Chiu church. To get there take bus B or X or *colectivos* 8 or 18 from the centre. In the park is the **Museo Arqueológico y Etnológico** ① *Tue-Sun 1000-1300, 1500-1930, US$0.40*, which has an exhibition of local pre-Hispanic cultural history. Nearby is the new **Museo de Historia Natural** ① *Wed-Sun 1000-1300, 1500-1830, US$1*, which has an interesting collection devoted to the *oficinas* and the region's ecology and palaeontology.

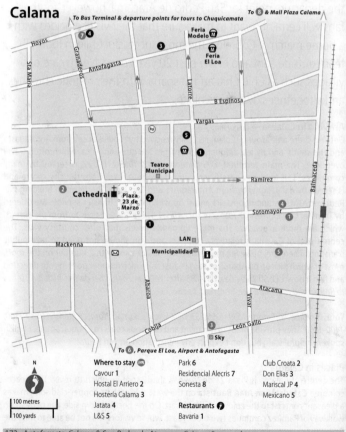

Calama

To Bus Terminal & departure points for tours to Chuquicamata

To ⑧ & Mall Plaza Calama

Where to stay 🛏
Cavour 1
Hostal El Arriero 2
Hostería Calama 3
Jatata 4
L&S 5

Park 6
Residencial Alecris 7
Sonesta 8

Restaurants 🍴
Bavaria 1

Club Croata 2
Don Elias 3
Mariscal JP 4
Mexicano 5

Chuquicamata

A visit here is truly memorable. Some 16 km north of Calama, Chuquicamata is the site of the world's largest open-cast copper mine, employing 8000 workers and operated by **Codelco**, the state copper corporation. Although copper has been mined here since pre-Inca times, it was the Guggenheim brothers who introduced modern mining and processing techniques after 1911 and made Chuquicamata into the most important single mine in Chile. In other parts of the plant, 60,000 tonnes of low-grade ore are processed a day to produce refined copper of 99.98% purity. Output is over 600,000 tonnes a year, but the diggers must cut ever-deeper into the desert, making the extraction process increasingly expensive.

In 2005 the town that surrounds the mine was closed and some 2500 families were moved from Chuqui to new neighbourhoods on the outskirts of Calama, leaving only a small historic centre for visitors. The town had always been famous in Chile for providing its miners with guaranteed housing and free healthcare in a special modern hospital. The decision to move the residents down to Calama was very sad for those who had grown up and lived in the town, but the famous hospital, which was also transferred to Calama, is now of great benefit to the city as a whole.

The removal of the town enables Codelco to exploit the copper that is buried in the earth beneath and will make Chuquicamata the latest and the largest in the Atacama's long line of ghost towns. The latest plan is to link the three mines in the area, Chuquicamata, Mina Sur and Radomiro Tomic to create a hole in the earth 14 km long producing 10% of the world's copper supplies.

A visit to the mine at Chuquicamata is highly recommended for the insight it gives into the industry that bankrolls Chile's economy. Although you don't actually go down into the mine, you can see right into it, and there are also fantastic views of the desert pampa and the volcanoes to the east. **Guided tours**, by bus, in Spanish (although guides usually speak reasonable English) leave from the **Codelco office** ① *Av Central Sur y Av Granaderos, Villa Ayquina, Calama, T055-232 2122, visitas@codelco.cl; make reservation in advance by calling the office in Calama or asking at the tourist office; passport number essential.* Wear covered shoes, long trousers and long sleeves; filming is permitted in certain areas. Tours may be cancelled without notice if there are high winds.

North and east of Calama

Chiu Chiu was one of the earliest centres of Spanish settlement in the area. Set in the shadow of the Volcán San Pedro, it is a peaceful oasis village and a nice contrast to the bustle of Calama. In the glades nearby, horses graze on surprisingly lush grasses and the local people cultivate alfalfa. Chiu Chiu's plaza, fringed with pepper trees, is a pleasant place to while away a few hours. Opposite, the church of **San Francisco**, dating from 1611, has roof beams of cactus and walls over 1 m thick – please leave a donation. Some 10 km away on the road to Caspana is a unique, perfectly circular, very deep lake, also called **Chiu Chiu** or **Icacoia**.

From the village of Chiu Chiu, the road continues north towards Ollagüe. Just beyond the oasis, a small turning branches off the main road and follows the course of the **Río Loa**. Here the canyon is green with crops, and donkeys plough the earth – it seems like a secret valley. This area has been settled for millennia and petroglyphs are clearly visible in the rocks on the right-hand side of the road heading towards **Lasana**. This small hamlet, 8 km north of Chiu Chiu, has striking ruins of a pre-Inca *pukará*, a national monument; drinks are on sale. At **Conchi**, 25 km north of Lasana, the road crosses the Río Loa via a bridge dating from 1890; there is a spectacular view over the river from the bridge, but it is a military zone, so no photographs are allowed. Access to the river is by side tracks, best at Santa Bárbara. There are interesting wildflower meadows here, as well as trout fishing in season; you can obtain a permit from Gobernación in Calama.

From Conchi, a road branches east following the valley of the **Río San Pedro**, which has been a route for herders and silver caravans for centuries, to **Inacaliri**, from where a very poor road (4WD essential) runs south to Linzor and the **El Tatio geysers** (see page 181). While there are several direct routes east from Chiu Chiu towards the geysers, only one is in good condition: just north of Chiu Chiu, turn right off the Ollagüe road and continue until you reach a fork some 22 km east of Chiu Chiu. Take the right fork, ignoring the large sign pointing left to El Tatio (this leads to another very bad track via Linzor). At Km 47 a track turns off north to Caspana; again, ignore this turning and continue along the main road as it climbs steeply up the Cuesta de Chita. At about Km 80, branch left to Tatio; this branch meets the main Tatio–San Pedro road some 5 km further north.

Caspana is beautifully set among hills with a tiny church dating from 1641 and a **museum** ① *Tue-Sun 1000-1400, 1500-1800*, with interesting displays on Atacameño culture. Basic accommodation is available. A poor road runs north and east of Caspana through valleys of pampas grass with llama herds to **Toconce**, which has extensive pre-Hispanic terraces set among some interesting rock formations. There are many archaeological sites nearby and the area is ideal for hiking, with the **Cerros Toconce**, **León** and **Paniri** – all over 5500 m – within reach.

Some 20 km west of Toconce is **Ayquina**, in whose ancient church is enshrined the statue of the Virgin of Guadalupe. Her feast day is 8 September, when pilgrims come from far and wide to celebrate and worship. ▶▶ *See Festivals, page 176.*

Six kilometres north of Ayquina are the lukewarm thermal waters of the **Baños de Turi** and the ruins of a 12th-century *pukará*, a National Monument, which was once the largest fortified town in the Atacama mountains. Close to the village of **Cupo** is a large, ruined pre-Hispanic settlement at **Paniri**, with extensive field systems, irrigation canals (including aqueducts) and a necropolis. Some of the fields are still in use. The area around Cupo is one of the best for seeing the Atacama giant cactus (*Notocereus atacamensis*); flamingos are also visible on the mudflats. Surrounding the *baños* is an oasis of ancient pastoral land, the **Vega de Turi**, now drying up due to the water consumption of the mines. It remains an important site for the llama- and sheep-herders, who believe it has curative properties. At several times in the year, especially September, herders from a wide area congregate here with their flocks.

Ollagüe

Situated 198 km north of Calama on the dry floor of the Salar de Ollagüe at 3696 m, Ollagüe is surrounded by a dozen volcanic peaks of over 5000 m. It is a cold, dusty, windswept place, but remarkable for its sense of remoteness. At this altitude, nights are cold, while the days are warm and sunny, there are only 50 mm of rain a year and water is very scarce.

The road to Ollagüe from Chiu Chiu runs north to Estación San Pedro. This first section is in poor condition, but from Estación San Pedro to a *carabinero* checkpoint at **Ascotán**, it is worse. This is the highest point of the road at 3900 m. Ask at Ascotán or Ollagüe about weather conditions before setting out, especially in December and January or August. North of Ascotán, the road improves as it crosses the **Salares de Ascotán** and **de Carcote** and **Ollagüe**. There are many llama flocks along this road and flamingos on the

Border crossings: Chile–Bolivia

Ollagüe–Uyuni → *Bolivian phone code: +591.*

A poor road leads across the Bolivian border from Ollagüe and runs to Uyuni, 170 km east. Trucks take a more northerly route across the Salar de Uyuni but motorists are warned against using this latter route into Bolivia. As well as the danger of getting lost on the many tracks leading over the salt lakes, there's no petrol between Calama and Uyuni and little hope of help with a breakdown on the Bolivian side. After rain the route is impassable and even experienced guides get lost. Maps give widely differing versions of the route. Where the road has been built up, never forsake it for the appealing soft salt beside it; the salt takes a person's weight but a vehicle breaks through the crust into unfathomable depths of plasticine mud below.
Immigration and customs is open daily 0800-2000; there is a US$3 per person charge for entry to Bolivia. For further information, see www.pasosfronterizos.gov.cl/cf_ollague.html.

salares. There is no petrol between Calama and Uyuni in Bolivia, but if you completely run out, you could try buying some from the *carabineros* at Ollagüe or Ascotán, the military at Conchi or the mining camp at Buenaventura.

Some 5 km south of Ollagüe is the sulphur mining camp of **Buenaventura**, which is situated at an altitude of 5800 m, only 150 m short of the summit of the Ollagüe volcano. Camping is possible and there are amazing views over the volcanoes and salt flats. A road leads to the sulphur camp but be wary of walking the route (unless you've come from Bolivia), as you will not yet be acclimatized for exercise at this altitude. You should also bear in mind that temperatures can drop as low as -37°C.

A road runs west from Ollagüe to the sulphur mines, now closed, of **Aucanquilcha**, where there are the ruins of an aerial tram system. A high-clearance vehicle is needed to drive to the mine but from there you can scramble to the summit of Aucanquilcha, at 6176 m, from which there are superb views. An interesting excursion can also be made north from Ollagüe to the village of **Coska** with its traditional agriculture and herds of llamas and alpacas.

Calama and around listings

For hotel and restaurant price codes and other relevant information, see pages 14-21.

Where to stay

Calama *p171, map p172*
$$$$-$$$ Park, Alcalde José Lira 1392,
T055-271 5800, www.parkcalama.cl.
On the edge of town by the airport.
First class, pool, bar and restaurant,
excursions to the salar.
$$$$-$$$ Sonesta, Av Balmaceda 2634,
T055-268 1100, www.sonesta.com. Business
hotel near Mall Plaza Calama and the

casino, with fitness centre, restaurant, bar,
Wi-Fi throughout.
$$$ Hostería Calama, Latorre 1521,
T055-234 1511, www.hosteriacalama.cl.
Comfortable heated rooms, good service;
gym and small pool. Airport transfer.
$$$ L&S, Vicuña MacKenna 1819,
T055-236 1113, www.lyshotel.cl. Business
hotel, upstairs rooms more spacious.
Often full Mon-Wed with mining
engineers. A good choice.
$$ Hotel Jatata, Sotomayor 1822, T055-236
1640, jatataexpress.hoteles@gmail.com.
Decent rooms with bath, most face onto a

corridor, but those with windows onto the street are much better and good value.

$$ Residencial Alecris, Félix Hoyos 2153, T055-234 7984. Single, double and triple rooms, private or shared bath, well maintained, very clean, family atmosphere, often fully booked with miners, safe (CCTV, near police station), no breakfast, sunny courtyard. Chatty owner Alejandro.

$$-$ Cavour, Sotomayor 1841, T055-231 4718. Hot water, TV, no breakfast, rooms off an open-air corridor, simple, hospitable but a bit run-down.

$$-$ Hostal El Arriero, Ramírez 2262, T055-231 5556, www.hostalelarriero.cl. Family run, spacious doubles and triples (with thin walls) situated around a narrow courtyard, shared bath, Wi-Fi functional most of the time, good value.

Ollagüe *p174*
There is a municipal hostel in Ollagüe, as well as a place to eat and other basic services.

❼ Restaurants

Calama *p171, map p172*
There are several cafés, juice bars, heladerías and fast food places on the pedestrian part of C Eleuterio Ramírez.

$$ Bavaria, Sotomayor 2095. Good restaurant with *cafetería* downstairs, real coffee, breakfast 0830-1130 Mon-Fri, very popular, not quiet, also cheaper café at Latorre 1935, upstairs.

$$ Mariscal JP, Félix Hoyos 2127, T055-231 2559. Closed Mon. Best seafood in town, worth that bit extra (has another branch in the Mercado Central at Latorre 1974).

$$ Mexicano, Vivar 2037. Genuine Mexican cuisine, live music at weekends.

$$-$ Club Croata, Abaroa 1869 at Plaza 23 de Marzo. Excellent value 4-course *almuerzo*, good service.

$ Don Elias, Antofagasta 2029, opposite the Frontera bus station (no sign). Open 1200 for lunch. Cheap, hearty, no-frills Chilean home-cooking. Packed at lunchtime.

North and east of Calama *p173*
$$ Café Tambo, Chiu Chiu. A nice place with old wooden furniture. Mid-range meals.

🍸 Bars and clubs

Calama *p171, map p172*
There are decent bars on Ganaderos between the town centre and the **TurBus** terminal. Calama's discos are all out of town on Av Circunvalación. There are over 10 of them, including **Kamikaze**. Anywhere called a nightclub is actually a strip-joint.

✸ Festivals

Calama *p171, map p172*
Jan Festival Internacional de Teatro, with a different dramatic production every day at the municipal theatre. In Aug, there is a Festival de Teatro de Invierno in the same theatre.
Early Feb Calama's **annual festival** is a riot of activities and celebrations – recommended for those in the area.
Feb The Parque Loa hosts Calama's annual **jazz festival**.

North and east of Calama *p173*
8 Sep The feast day of the **Virgen de Guadalupe** is celebrated in Ayquina, with day-long group dancing to indigenous rhythms on flute and drum. Towards sunset the Virgin is carried up a steep trail to a small thatched shrine, where the image and the people are blessed before the dancing recommences, continuing all the way back to the village. The poor people of the hills gather stones and make toy houses all along the route: miniatures of the homes they hope to have some day.
19 Mar The **fiesta** of San José is celebrated in Cupo, southwest of Ayquina.

Ollagüe *p174*
Mid Jun Fiesta de San Antonio de Padua celebrates the patron saint of Ollagüe, with dancing and Quechua customs, such as the sacrifice of llamas.

Shopping

Calama *p171, map p172*
There are craft stalls on Latorre 1600 block. The market, **Feria El Loa**, is on Antofagasta between Latorre and Vivar; it sells fruit juices and crafts.

What to do

Calama *p171, map p172*
Several agencies run trips to Chiu Chiu and 1-day and longer tours to the Atacama region, including San Pedro; these are usually more expensive than tours from San Pedro itself (see page 188) and require a minimum number for the tour to go ahead. Standards here are not generally very high, so be wary of agencies with poorly maintained vehicles and poor guides. Operators with positive recommendations include: **Sol del Desierto**, Caur 3486, Villa Lomas Huasi, T055-233 0428, www.soldeldesierto.cl.

Transport

Calama *p171, map p172*
Air
LAN, daily, to **Santiago**, via Antofagasta; also **Sky**. LAN also flies to **Iquique** and **Arica** twice a week.

Bus
Long distance Tur-Bus, Pullman, Flota Barrios, Géminis and Kenny Bus all use the main terminal. To **Chiu Chiu**, 4 a day, US$3. To **Santiago**, 23 hrs, US$62-120. To **La Serena**, usually with prolonged stop in Antofagasta, 16 hrs, US$35-55. To **Antofagasta**, 3 hrs, several companies, US$9. To **Iquique**, 6 hrs, via **Tocopilla**, US$22, 3 daily with **Tur-Bus**. To **Arica**, US$25, 9 hrs, usually overnight, or change in Antofagasta. To **San Pedro de Atacama**,

with **Tur-Bus** several daily, 1½ hrs, US$5.50, or with **Frontera**, 6 a day. To **Toconao**, see below. To **Ollagüe** for Bolivia, with **Intertrans** (daily) and **Atacama** (Thu, Mon 2000), US$15, 3 hrs.

International For **Uyuni**, cross the border at Ollagüe, then board bus to Uyuni (Sun, Mon, Wed, Thu). To **Salta**, Argentina, 12 hrs, with **Géminis**, **Pullman Bus** and **Andesmar**, each 3 a week, US$45-65 (check in advance as days change).

Car hire
A hired car shared between several people is an economic alternative for visiting the Atacama region. A 4WD jeep (necessary for the desert) costs US$100 a day, a car US$40-50. Hire companies include **Alamo**, T055-255 6802 (good), **Avis**, T055-256 3151, **Budget**, T055-236 1072, and **Hertz** T055-234 0018. All offices are closed Sat 1300-Mon 0900; those in the airport only open when flights arrive. If intending to drive in the border area, visit the police in San Pedro to get maps of which areas may have landmines.

Taxi
Basic fare, US$5.

Ollagüe *p174*
There is no fuel in Ollagüe.

Directory

Calama *p171, map p172*
Banks There are several cambios for US$, TCs, Argentine pesos and bolivianos but exchange rates are generally poor especially for TCs. There are many **Redbanc** ATMs on Latorre and on Sotomayor.
Consulates Bolivia, León Gallo 1985A, T055-234 1976, open (in theory anyway) Mon-Fri 0900-1230, helpful.

San Pedro de Atacama and around

Situated 103 km by paved road southeast of Calama, San Pedro is an oasis town in the valley of the Río San Pedro at 2436 m. While it is now famous among visitors as the base for excursions in this part of the Atacama, it was important as the centre of the Atacameño culture long before the arrival of the Spanish. There is a palpable sense of history in the shady streets and the crumbling ancient walls that drift away from the town into the fields and on into the dust. Owing to the clear atmosphere and isolation, there are wonderful views of the night sky from just outside town. Despite being in the desert, it does rain in San Pedro about three or four times a year, usually around March, as a result of the *invierno altiplánico*. San Pedro is a good base from which to visit Toconao, the Salar de Atacama and the geysers of El Tatio.

Arriving in San Pedro de Atacama → *Colour map 1, C3.*

Getting there and around San Pedro can be reached by multiple buses a day to/from Calama and Antofagasta with three companies: **Atacama 2000**, **Frontera** and **TurBus**. If driving, be aware there is no food, water or fuel along the Calama–San Pedro road. **Turismo Licancabur** ① *T055-2543426, www.translicancabur.cl*, run a minibus service from Calama airport to San Pedro, although the service can be unreliable. San Pedro is small so taxis (from by the football field) are only needed for out-of-town trips.

Tourist information The **tourist office** ① *Toconao y Gustavo Le Paige, T055-285 1420, sanpedrodeatacama@gmail.com, Mon-Sun 0900-2100*, is on the plaza. Staff are helpful and there's a useful suggestions book, with feedback from other visitors about agencies' tours. See also *www.sanpedrochile.com*, *www.sanpedroatacama.com* and *www. sanpedrodeatacama.net*. **Note** The main tourist season October-end February is accompanied by high prices and pressure on resources. Entry charges are levied at most of the natural attractions (around US$2-5), with the money going to the local communities.

Climate Be prepared for the harsh climate and high altitudes of the interior. Gloves, a hat and a warm coat are essential for excursions from San Pedro, especially for the early morning trip to El Tatio. High-factor suncream and a hat are necessary for the burning daytime sun; you should also take plenty of water, sunglasses and lip balm with UV protection on any excursion.

Background

The main centre for the Atacameño culture, which flourished in this region before the arrival of the Incas around 1450, San Pedro was defended by a *pukará* (fortress) at Quitor,

3 km north. The cultivable land around was distributed in 15 *ayllus* (socio-economic communities based on family networks) and irrigation channels were built. San Pedro was visited by both Diego de Almagro and Pedro de Valdivia, and the town became a centre of Spanish colonial control, with a mission established here in 1557. After Independence, the town became an important trading centre on the route between Cobija on the coast and Salta in Argentina, but the decline of Cobija and the rise of copper-mining led to San Pedro being superceded as an economic centre by Calama.

In the early 20th century, San Pedro's economy was based around mining, with salt mines in the Valle de la Luna (whose ruins are easily visible today) and sulphur mines in the high mountains. Since the 1970s, tourism has been of increasing importance; the town is now dependent on income from Chilean and foreign visitors. However, travellers should be aware that tourism is a somewhat divisive issue in San Pedro. In many ways the town has lost much of its Atacameño feel, and, with more tourists than locals, you may well feel that on entering San Pedro you are leaving Chile behind. Moreover, the tour companies are often run by outsiders and their influx has led to a tenfold increase in rents in the past ten years. Many of the local people, who still work in agriculture, have lower incomes than those who work with tourism, and there are dark (and doubtless somewhat exaggerated) rumours that some of the tour operations are fronts for money laundering and drug running, especially with Bolivia so close.

San Pedro de Atacama

Where to stay
1 Altiplánico
2 Awasi
3 Don Raul
4 Elim
6 Hostal Mamatierra
8 Hostal Miskanty
10 Hostal Sonchek
11 Hostelling International
12 Hostería San Pedro
13 Kimal
14 La Casa de Don Tomás
16 Res Chiloé
16 Res Vilacoyo
17 Takha-Takha

Restaurants
1 Adobe & Casa Piedra
2 Bendito Desierto
3 Café Etnico
4 Café Tierra Todo Natural
5 Café y Cia
6 Estrella Negra
7 La Casona
8 La Estaka
9 Milagro

Beware: minefields

An indication of the nature of General Pinochet's geopolitics in the 1970s and 1980s is provided by the numerous minefields that were placed along Chile's border with Bolivia and northern Argentina at that time. The minefields were put down to forestall any possible invasion from Chile's neighbours, which was then perceived to be a very real threat.

Following the Ottowa convention, Chile has begun the slow process of dismantling its extensive minefields. Meanwhile, the danger remains. It is not unknown for people to have been killed or maimed (often while attempting to smuggle drugs across the border). It is therefore very unwise to make any lone forays into the Altiplano without a knowledgeable local guide.

Minefields are known to affect **Parque Nacional Llullaillaco** (see page 184; check with CONAF in Antofagasta, www.conaf.cl/parques/parque-nacional-llullaillaco/) and the Chilean side of **Volcán Licancabur** (see box, page 184) to give just two examples – and there may be other areas that are not known about. Always ask first before heading off into the northern wilderness and bear in mind that local people are often more knowledgeable than officials.

The road from Calama

At **Paso Barros Arana** (Km 58) there is an unpaved turning to the left, which leads through interesting desert scenery to the small, mud-brick village of **Río Grande**. Look out for guanacos on the pass. The main road skirts the Cordillera de la Sal about 15 km from San Pedro. There are spectacular views of the sunset over the western *cordilleras*. The old unpaved road to San Pedro turns off the new road at Km 72 and crosses this range through the Valle de La Luna (see below), but should only be attempted by 4WD vehicles. This road is partly paved with salt blocks.

Places in San Pedro de Atacama

The **Iglesia de San Pedro**, dating from the 17th century, is supposedly the second oldest church in the country. It has been heavily restored and the tower was added in 1964. The roof is made of cactus; inside, the statues of Mary and Joseph have fluorescent light halos. Nearby, on the shady Plaza, is the **Casa Incaica**, the oldest building in San Pedro.

The **Museo Arqueológico** ① *www.sanpedroatacama.com, Mon-Fri 0900-1200, 1400-1800, Sat and Sun from 1000, US$3.50*, children half price, contains the collection of Padre Gustave Le Paige, a Belgian missionary who lived in San Pedro between 1955 and 1980. It is now under the care of the Universidad Católica del Norte. One of the most important museums in northern Chile, it traces the development of pre-Hispanic Atacameño society. It is well organized, each display having a card with explanations in English. The centrepiece of the collection was always the Atacameño mummies, fully clothed and perfectly preserved. However these have recently been removed from display at the behest of the local indigenous community and are gathering dust in a storeroom. Nevertheless the museum is still well worth a visit.

Archaeological sites around San Pedro

The **Pukará de Quitor** ① *3 km north of San Pedro along the river, US$3*, is a pre-Inca fortress that covers 2.5 ha on a hillside on the west bank of the river; it was restored in 1981. The fortress was stormed by 30 Spanish horsemen under Pedro de Valdivia, who vaulted the walls and overcame 1000 defenders. The road to Quitor involves fording the river several times, until the *pukará* comes into view on the hill on the left-hand side of the valley. There is a new plaza here, built in homage to the indigenous people of the region and set amid thorn trees. The road continues along the valley of the Río San Pedro as the canyon climbs further into the Atacama, passing a couple of small farmsteads sheltered by pepper trees where sheep graze in the desert sun. A further 4 km up the river, there are ruins at **Catarpe**, which was the Inca administrative centre for this region. The ruins are on top of a hill on the east side of the valley, and are difficult to find without a guide; horseback tours are offered in San Pedro.

There's another archaeological site 12 km southwest of San Pedro at **Tulor** ① *US$5.50*, where parts of a village (dated 500-800 BC) have been excavated. The road is *ripio*, and fine for 4WD vehicles. You can sleep in two reconstructed huts or take a tour, US$10. Nearby are the ruins of a 17th-century Spanish-style village, abandoned in the 18th century because of the lack of water.

Valle de la Luna
① *12 km west of San Pedro on the old San Pedro–Calama road, US$4.50.*
This is a valley of fantastic landscapes caused by the erosion of salt mountains. The valley is crossed by the old San Pedro–Calama road. Although buses on the new road will stop to let you off where the old road branches 13 km northwest of San Pedro (signposted to Peine), it is far better to travel from San Pedro on the old road, either on foot (allow three hours each way), by bicycle or high-clearance vehicle. There is a small information centre at the entrance with info in Spanish only, although there is a leaflet in English. The Valle is best seen at sunset. Take water, hat, camera and a torch. Note that camping is prohibited. Agencies in San Pedro offer tours, departing around 1600, returning around 2000, US$20 per person, but make sure the agency departs in time to arrive in the Valle before sunset. Be aware that most tour groups watch the sunset from the same spot, so do not expect a solitary desert experience. Tours usually include a visit to the **Valle de la Muerte**, a crevice in the Cordillera de la Sal near San Pedro, with red rock walls, contorted into fantastic shapes.

The geysers of El Tatio
① *US$9.*
At an altitude of 4321 m, the geysers of El Tatio are a popular attraction. From San Pedro, they are reached by a road in variable state of repair that runs northeast, past the **Baños de Puritama** ① *just under 30 km north of San Pedro, US20*, then on for a further 94 km. The geysers are said to be at their best in the morning between 0600 and 0800, although the spectacle varies; locals say the performance is best when weather conditions are stable. A swimming pool has been built nearby, along with a series of stone walls and wooden walkways, which some say has detracted from the spectacle. From El Tatio, you can hike to surrounding volcanoes if you are adapted to altitude, although it is advisable to take a guide because of the dangers of minefields.

Tours to El Tatio depart around 0400, arriving at the geysers at 0700, US$80, including breakfast. There are opportunities to swim in the hot thermal pool and to visit the Baños de Puritama on the return journey. Take very warm clothing and a swimming costume. Some agencies offer tours to El Tatio and on to Calama, via the villages of the Altiplano. There is no public transport to the geysers and hitching is impossible. If going in a hired car, make sure the engine is suitable for very high altitudes and is protected with antifreeze; a 4WD is advisable. If driving in the dark, it is almost impossible to find your way: the sign for El Tatio is north of the turn-off.

San Pedro to Toconao

The 37-km journey south from San Pedro to Toconao is on a paved road that runs through occasional groves of acacia and pepper trees. There are many tracks leading to the *pozos* (wells), which supply the intricate irrigation system. Most have thermal water but bathing is not appreciated by the local farmers. The groves of trees are havens for wildlife, especially *ñandu* (rhea) and Atacama owls; there are also some llamas. About half-way to Toconao a side road heads east to the Atacama Large Millimeter/submillimeter Array (**ALMA**), the largest astronomical project on Earth (www.almaobservatory.org); it may be open to the public by 2015.

Toconao and around

This village, at an altitude of 2600 m, is on the eastern shore of the Salar de Atacama. Unlike San Pedro, Toconao's economy is based on agriculture, not tourism. All the houses,

South of San Pedro de Atacama

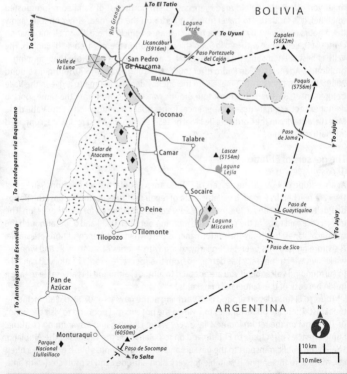

plus the 18th-century church and bell tower, are built of bricks of white volcanic stone, which gives the village an appearance totally different from San Pedro. Food is available and there are small shops selling handicrafts. The local church is cared for by nuns who give liturgies. There are no priests.

East of the village is a beautiful gorge called the **Quebrada de Jere** ⓘ *US$2*, which is almost unimaginably verdant and filled with fruit trees and grazing cattle. At the bottom of the gorge a crystal-clear stream cuts down towards Toconao. There are picnic sites but camping is prohibited. Near the head of the valley on the east side is a petroglyph of a llama. Nearby is the quarry where the stone *sillar* is worked; it can be visited. The stones sound like bells when struck. Also worth visiting are the vineyards, which produce a unique sweet wine.

About 4 km before Toconao, vehicle tracks head east across the sand to a hidden valley 2 km from the road where there is a small settlement called **Zapar**. There are some well-preserved pre-Hispanic ruins on the rocky cliffs above the cultivated valley here. The sand is very soft and a 4WD vehicle is essential.

Salar de Atacama

South of Toconao is one of the main entrances to the Salar de Atacama. Formed by deglaciation some 12,000 years ago, it encompasses some 300,000 ha, making it the third largest expanse of salt flats in the world. The air is so dry here that you can usually see right across the salar, 100 km to the north. Rich in minerals, including borax, potassium and an estimated 40% of world lithium reserves, the salar is also home to three of the world's five species of flamingo – the Andean, Chilean and James – as well as other birds, including sandpipers, the Andean gull and the Andean avocet (although these can only be seen when lakes form in winter). The flamingos live by eating algae and tiny shellfish that subsist in the small saline pools in the salar. There is a walkway over part of the salar with information boards in Spanish. You should not leave the path. Agencies in San Pedro offer excursions to Toconao and the Salar, returning via the Quebrada de Jere (see above), US$20, plus park entry, usual departure 1530, but note that the flamingos are best seen in the morning, so try to get a morning tour, or combine with visiting the Altiplano lakes (US$111).

Three areas of the salar are part of the **Reserva Nacional de los Flamencos** ⓘ *administered by CONAF, Ayllú de Solcor, San Pedro, T055-285 1608, in conjunction with local communities, US$4.50*, a seven-sector reserve covering a total of 73,986 ha.

From Toconao, a road runs 67 km along the eastern edge of the Salar de Atacama to the attractive village of **Peine**, where you'll find the offices of the lithium extraction company. It is worth asking if the company's access road can be used to visit the Salar de Atacama's spectacular salt formations. Nearby are some prehistoric cave paintings. Local guides in the village offer tours. There is also a thermal pool where you can swim. Woollen goods and knitwear are made here. To the east of the village lies a group of beautifully coloured hills, whose colours are more vibrant at sunset, with good views over the Salar de Atacama. A path leads across these hills to **Socaire**; allow two days. Other villages worth visiting include **Tilomonte** and **Tilopozo**, south and west of Peine.

South of the Salar de Atacama

From Peine, a road (64 km) crosses the Salar de Atacama and joins the road that runs south from San Pedro down the west side of the salar, continuing south to **Pan de Azúcar**, an abandoned railway station. Here it meets the paved road that runs east–west from

Into Bolivia: the Salar de Uyuni and other sights

East of San Pedro, on the border with Bolivia, lies Volcán Licancábur (5916 m), a sacred site for the Incas and the focal point of three Inca paths that crossed the Altiplano and the Salar de Atacama. The volcano can be climbed only from the Bolivian side, at any time of the year except January and February. At the foot of the volcano on the Bolivian side is Laguna Verde (4400 m), which extends over 17 sq km; its wind-lashed waters are an impressive jade, the result, it is said, of magnesium, calcium carbonate, lead or arsenic. There is a *refugio*, La Cabaña, by the ranger station near the lake (US$5 per person in comfortable but very cold dorms, solar-powered lighting, hot water seldom works, cooking facilities but take your own food, in high season book in advance – tour agencies can do this by radio).

Further north is the equally impressive Laguna Colorada (4278 m), which covers 60 sq km; its flaming red waters are the result of the effects of the wind and afternoon sun on the numerous microorganisms that live in it (up until midday the water is a fairly ordinary colour). The water is less than a metre deep but the mud is very soft, and the shores are encrusted with borax, which provides an arctic white contrast with the waters of the lake. The pink algae in the lake provides food for the rare James flamingos, along with the more common Chilean and Andean flamingos. Some 40 other bird species can also be seen.

Further north still, beyond Ollagüe, is the Salar de Uyuni, the largest and highest salt lake in the world and an increasingly popular attraction for visitors. Situated at an altitude of 3650 m and covering 9000-12,000 sq km (depending on who you believe), the Salar is twice as big as the Great Salt Lake in the United States. The depth of the salt varies from 2 to 20 m. Driving across it is one of the most fantastic experiences in South America, especially in June/July when the bright blue skies contrast with the blinding-white salt (be sure to bring good sunglasses). After particularly wet rainy seasons the Salar is covered in water, which adds to the surreal experience.

Tour operators in San Pedro (see What to do, page 188) offers tours to the Salar de Uyuni, Laguna Colorada and Laguna Verde and will drop passengers off in Uyuni. However, some travellers report that, to see the colour changes on Laguna Colorada, the trip is best done from Uyuni itself, where accommodation, money exchange and transport to La Paz, Oruro and Potosí are all available. If you are taking a tour to Bolivia from San Pedro, find out if park entrance fees are included; if not, be aware that they are payable in Bolivianos only.

the Pan-American Highway south of Antofagasta to **Socompa** on the Argentine border, via the vast **La Escondida** copper mine, which has an output of copper higher than any other mine in the world. Ten kilometres east of La Escondida at Imilac, a poor road turns off south to the **Parque Nacional Llullaillaco**. This recently created park covers 263,000 ha and includes **Cerro Llullaillaco** at 6739 m, the second highest peak in Chile, as well as three other peaks over 5000 m: **Cerro de la Pena** at 5260 m, **Guanaqueros**, 5131 m, and **Aguas Calientes**, 5070 m. The park is inhabited by large numbers of guanacos and vicuñas. Visits are by arrangement only with CONAF in Antofagasta, owing to the dangers of minefields in the area. Further along the Pan de Azúcar–Socompa road (poor condition) is **Monturaqui**, the source of the green onyx that is used for carving.

Southeast of Toconao

From Toconao, another road heads south towards the Paso de Sico border crossing (see box, page 189) through the villages of **Camar**, where handicrafts made from cactus may be bought, and **Socaire**, which has llama-wool knitwear for sale and a recently restored church built from volcanic rock. From the top of the church tower you can see agricultural land planted on traditional terraces. There are also a couple of places that serve basic lunches. The road is paved as far as Socaire. About 20 km further south, a rough road leaves the main route to the Paso de Sico and climbs a hill to the beautiful **Laguna Miscanti** (4240 m), a lake that is part of the **Reserva Nacional Los Flamencos** (see above). 'Miscanti' means 'toad' in Atacameño, and refers to the fact that the lake was full of toads until trout were introduced in the 1940s and 1950s for American fishermen working in Chuquicamata; today there are no toads left. There is a path around the lake. Allow four hours for the circuit. Nearby is the **Laguna Miñiques**. The lakes are on the site of ancient Atacameño hunting grounds and arrowheads can still be found on the shores, which are edged with whorls of calcium salt crystals. The rare Hornet coot can often be seen here. There are clear views of the volcanoes behind the lakes, often snow-capped between April and June, as well as fantastic views down to the Salar.

After the turning to the lakes, the road goes on to the mine at Laco, before proceeding to the **Paso de Sico**, which has replaced the higher, more northerly Guaytiquina pass, at 4295 m (also spelt Huaytiquina) to Argentina (see box, page 189).

Some 10 km south of Toconao, the old road branches east towards Guaytiquina. In a deep *quebrada* below Volcán Láscar is the now deserted settlement of **Talabre**, with terracing and an ancient threshing floor. Above the *quebrada* is an isolated, stone-built cemetery. Large flocks of llamas graze where the stream crosses the road below the Láscar Volcano at 5154 m. After a steep climb on a very bad road, you reach the **Laguna Lejía** at 4190 m, once full of flamingos. Mysteriously, the colony declined rapidly immediately after the eruption of Volcán Láscar in 1993. You then pass through the high plains of **Guaytiquina** (4275 m), where only a few herdsmen are found. The Guaytiquina crossing to Argentina is not open to road traffic.

◉ San Pedro de Atacama and around listings

For hotel and restaurant price codes and other relevant information, see pages 14-21.

◉ Where to stay

San Pedro de Atacama
p178, map p179

There is electricity, but take a torch for walking around at night. Rooms are scarce in Jan/Feb, and pricey all year round. There are unregistered hostels, usually **$** pp, but security is often lax.

$$$$ Altiplánico, Atienza 282, T055-285 1245, reservations T02-2958 4289, www.altiplanico.com. Comfortable boutique hotel on the edge of town

(20-min walk), adobe huts, well designed and spacious.

$$$$ Alto Atacama, Suchor s/n, reservations T02-2912 3945, www.alto atacama.com. Spacious rooms, all with private terrace, spa, observatory, packages and excursions offered.

$$$$ Awasi, Tocopilla 4, T055-285 1460, reservations T02-2233 9641, www.awasi.cl. All-inclusive packages. Just 8 luxury cabins, all built with traditional materials, fine food, excellent customer service, professional tours included.

$$$$ Explora, Atienza y Ayllú de Larache (head office Av Américo Vespucio Sur 80, 5 piso, Santiago, T02-2395 2800), www.explora.com. Luxury full board and excursion programme, solar-heated pool, sauna, jacuzzi, massages, the only lodge with its own stables and horses.

$$$$ Hostería San Pedro, Toconao 460, T055-285 1011, www.dahoteles.com. The town's oldest luxury hotel. Pool (residents only), petrol station, cabins, some rooms with satellite TV, quite comfortable.

$$$$ Kimal, Atienza 452 y Caracoles, T055-285 1152, www.kimal.cl. Small, intimate, near the centre, room size varies, pool with jacuzzi and spa. Good restaurant (open to the public). Opposite is Poblado Kimal, under same ownership.

$$$$ Tierra Atacama, Camino Séquitor s/n, T055-255 5977 (or T02-2207 8861), www.tierraatacama.com. Modern design, elegant and minimalist, somewhat removed from the village itself. Very good reports, including fine dining, spa, excursions, birdwatching.

$$$ Don Raul, Caracoles 130-B, T055-285 1138, www.donraul.cl. Pleasant, simple rooms, good value, some with kitchenette, one for the disabled.

$$$ La Casa de Don Tomás, Tocopilla s/n, T055-285 1055, www.dontomas.cl. Good rooms, bright and spacious lounge, quiet, swimming pool. Late check out/and check in. Decent value.

$$$-$$ Elim, Palpana 6, T055-285 1567, www.hostalelim.cl. Rooms sleep 1-3, nice hot showers, garden, hammock area, bicycle rental, laundry service.

$$$-$$ Takha-Takha, Caracoles 101, T055-285 1038, www.takhatakha.cl. Pretty, lovely garden and shady patio rooms with bath are nicer than those without. Also camping under trees, with hot showers.

$$$-$ Hostelling International, Caracoles 360, T055-256 4683, www.hostellingsanpedro.cl. Lively hostel, cramped shared rooms with lockers,

also private rooms. Bicycle rental, tours, sandboarding school.

$$ Haramaksi, Coya, near Tulor, 10 km southwest of San Pedro, T09-9595 7567. Simple accommodation in traditional Atacameño surroundings away from the hubbub of San Pedro. Free transfer from bus station.

$$ Hostal Mamatierra, Pachamamá 615, T055-285 1418, hostalmamatierra@ sanpedrodeatacama.com. 5 mins' walk from the centre, will pick you up from the bus terminals. Some rooms with bath, kitchen facilities, peaceful.

$$ Hostal Miskanty, Pasaje Mutulera 141, T055-285 1430, www.hostalmiskanty. cl. Simple but pleasant rooms with bath, laundry service.

$$ Hostal Sonchek, Le Paige 170, T055-285 1112, www.hostalsonchek.cl. Decent value hostel, some rooms with bath, café, English and French spoken.

$$ Residencial Chiloé, Atienza 404, T055-285 1017, www.residencialchiloe. supersitio.net. Rooms with bath much nicer than those without, good clean bathrooms, good beds, breakfast extra. Sunny veranda, laundry facilities, luggage store, parking.

$$-$ Residencial Vilacoyo, Tocopilla 387, T055-285 1006, vilacoyo@ sanpedrodeatacama.com. Shared bath, good kitchen facilities, hammock in courtyard, laundry service. One of few good budget options in the centre.

Camping
Alberto Terrazas Oasis Camping, Pozo Tres, 5 km east of town, T055-285 1042. The best facilities, including a swimming pool.
Camping Los Perales, Tocopilla 481.

Toconao and around p182
There are basic *residenciales* in the village. Camping is not possible along the Quebrada de Jere.

● Restaurants

San Pedro de Atacama
p178, map p179

Few places are open before 1000. Drink bottled water as the local supply has a high mineral content, which may not agree with some. Many San Pedro restaurants double as bars at night, although they close around midnight.

$$$-$$ Bendito Desierto, Atienza 426. Inventive food served in a kind of grotto.

$$$-$$ La Estaka, Caracoles 259, T055-285 1164, www.laestaka.cl. Wood fire, cane roof, jazz music, pizzería and other dishes, good food, bar and book exchange, lively after 2300, favoured spot of the local New Age crowd.

$$ Adobe, Caracoles 211, www.cafe adobe.cl. Open fire, internet, good atmosphere, loud music. Described as "like Greenwich Village/Islington in the Atacama".

$$ Casa Piedra, Caracoles. Open fire, also has a cheap menu, waiters sometimes play live folk music, good food and cocktails.

$$ La Casona, Caracoles. Good food, vegetarian options, cheap *almuerzo*, large portions. Interesting Cubist-style desert paintings. Check bill with care.

$$ Milagro, Caracoles 241. Good food, vegetarian options, attentive service.

$$-$ Café Etnico, Tocopilla 423, T055-285 1377. Good food, juices and sandwiches, cosy, book exchange, internet (free for diners).

$$-$ Café y Cia, Toconao 568, T055-285 1506. French run, specializing in salads, omelettes and sandwiches; also has full leaf teas, coffees and ice cream on offer.

$ Café Tierra Todo Natural, Caracoles. Excellent fruit juices, "the best bread in the Atacama", real coffee, yoghurt, best for breakfast, opens earliest.

$ Empanadium, Galería El Peral, Caracoles 317, loc 5. Over 100 varieties of *empanada* fillings.

$ Estrella Negra, Caracoles 362, in patio de comidas. Good cheap vegetarian and some vegan food.

O Shopping

San Pedro de Atacama
p178, map p179
Handicrafts
There are a couple of craft markets, one near the plaza, and the other in the **Galería el Peral**, Caracoles 317. Very little *artesanía* is produced in San Pedro itself, most comes from Bolivia.

O What to do

San Pedro de Atacama
p178, map p179
Mountain biking
Bicycles for hire all over town, by the hour or full day: 'professional' model or cheaper 'amateur'. Tracks in the desert can be really rough, so check the bike's condition and carry a torch if riding after dark.

Swimming pools
Piscina Oasis (at the campsite), Pozo Tres, 3 km southeast but walking there is tough and not recommended. Open all year Tue-Sun 0500-1730, US$2 to swim. Good showers and picnic facilities, very popular Sat-Sun.

Tour operators
Usual tours include: to Valle de la Luna, the Salar de Atacama, Altiplano lakes (including Toconao and Salar de Atacama), El Tatio (begin at 0400) with trekking (take swimming costume and warm clothing). Beware of tours to Valle de la Luna that leave too late to catch the sunset; they need to depart before 1600. Before taking a tour, check that the agency has dependable vehicles, suitable equipment (eg oxygen for El Tatio), experienced drivers, a guide who speaks English if so advertised, and that the company is well established. Always get a receipt. Report any complaints to the municipality or **Sernatur**. There are about 25 agencies, but some are temporary and/or open for only part of the year. Some operators will offer a reduction if you book a series of tours with them. For tours into Bolivia, see box, page 184.

Atacama Horse Adventure (La Herradura), Tocopilla 406, T055-285 1956, www.atacamahorseadventure.com. Horse-riding tours with good local guides, mountain bike hire.

Atacama Mística, Caracoles 238, T055-285 1956, www.atacamamistica.cl. Chilean-Bolivian company, daily tours with transfer to San Pedro de Atacama, also transfers between San Pedro and Uyuni, good service.

Azimut 360°, T09-8449 1093, www.azimut.cl. Santiago-based company offers excursions, trekking, private tours with English-, German- and French-speaking guides.

Cordillera Traveller, Toconao 447-B, T055-285 1291, www.cordilleratraveller.com. Specializes in tours to Salar de Uyuni.

Cosmo Andino Expediciones, Caracoles s/n, T055-285 1069, http://cosmoandino-expediciones.cl/. Very professional and experienced, English, French, German, Dutch spoken, good vehicles, drivers and guides, owner Martin Beeris (Martín El Holandés).

Desert Adventure, Caracoles s/n, T055-285 1067, www.desertadventure.cl. Good guides and range of trips, English spoken, modern fleet of vehicles, mostly good reports.

Rancho Cactus, Toconao 568, T055-285 1506, www.rancho-cactus.cl. Offers horse riding with good guides to Valle de la Luna and other sites (Farolo and Valerie – speaks French and English), suits inexperienced riders.

Space, Caracoles 166, T055-256 6278/09-9817 8354, www.spaceobs.com. Run by French astronomer Alain, who speaks 3 languages and has set up a small observatory in the village of Solor, south of San Pedro; gives tours 2000-2330 to study the night sky, hot drink included but wear all your warmest clothes.

Border crossings: Chile–Argentina

There are three crossings into Argentina east of San Pedro de Atacama. Immigration and customs formalities for Paso de Jama (www.pasosfronterizos.gov.cl/cf_jama. html) and Paso de Sico (www.pasosfronterizos.gov.cl/cf_sico.html) are dealt with in San Pedro de Atacama, open 0800-2300 (0800-2400 on the Argentine side). Incoming vehicles are searched for meat, fruit and dairy products. If crossing by private vehicle, check road conditions with the *carabineros* and at immigration in San Pedro, as these crossings are liable to be closed by heavy rain in summer and blocked by snow in winter. If hitching, try the immigration post in San Pedro; Spanish is essential.

San Pedro–Paso de Jama

The best crossing and the most northerly, the spectacular Paso de Jama (variously put at 4200-4400 m), is reached by a road that runs southeast from San Pedro via the Salar de Tara, which forms a sector of the Reserva Nacional de los Flamencos. The road is fully paved and is spectacular. It stays high on the puna, going by snow-capped peaks, lakes and salt pans, before reaching the Argentine border post, 165 km from San Pedro. There are no money changing facilities nor any other services here. Be prepared for cold. The road continues paved on the Argentine side to Susques and Jujuy.

San Pedro–Paso de Sico

This pass at 4079 m has replaced the higher Paso de Guaytiquina and is the main alternative to Paso de Jama. Paso de Sico lies 207 km southeast of San Pedro and is reached by a very poor road which runs via Toconao and Socaire (see page 185). The road is paved to Socaire on the Chilean side and is about 40% paved on the Argentine side to San Antonio de los Cobres. This route is hardly used by any public or heavy traffic and is slow going on the unpaved parts.

San Pedro–Paso de Socompa

The most southerly crossing is Paso de Socompa, 3876 m, which is reached by a very poor but spectacular road from Pan de Azúcar. It crosses salt flats and wide expanses of desert, but is virtually unused. Chilean immigration and customs were officialy closed in 2014 (see www.pasosfronterizos.gov.cl/cf_socompa.html), although the Argentine side was open, according to www.gendarmeria.gov.ar/pasos/chile/fichsocom.html.

Vulcano, Caracoles 317, T055-285 1023, www.vulcanochile.cl. Mountain climbs, sandboarding and other adventure tours, mountain bike hire, English-speaking guides.

⊙ Transport

San Pedro de Atacama
p178, map p179
Bus
Most buses leave from Licancábur opposite the football field. **Tur-Bus** terminal on

Atienza, north of the centre, office Licancábur 294, T055-285 1549. To **Calama**: US$5.50, **Frontera** (7 daily), 1½ hrs, **Tur-Bus**, several daily. Frequencies vary with more departures in Jan-Feb and some weekends. Book in advance to return from San Pedro on Sun afternoon. **Tur-Bus** to **Arica**, 2030, US$35-55. **Tur-Bus** to **Santiago**, several daily, 23 hrs, US$70-90. **Frontera** to **Socaire**, Mon, Thu, Fri 1930, Sun 1230, 2200, US$3; to **Toconao**, 4 a day (3 on Sun), US$1.50. **To Argentina** Géminis, on Toconao

Border crossings: Chile–Bolivia

San Pedro–Hito Cajón (Hito Cajones)

There are two crossings to Bolivia from Calama, the more northerly of which, via Ollagüe, is described on page 175. This, the more southerly crossing, is, 45 km east of San Pedro via a poor road that turns off the paved road towards Paso de Jama at La Cruz, 8 km southwest of the border. Laguna Verde (see box, page 184) is 7 km north of Hito Cajón (Hito Cajones on the Bolivian side).

Chilean immigration and customs are in San Pedro, www.pasosfronterizos.gov.cl/cf_hitocajon.html, daily 0800-2000 (may be closed at lunchtime). Bolivian immigration closes at 2100 and charges US2 for entry. Vehicles entering Chile are searched for fruit, vegetables and dairy products.

There is no public transport: do not be tempted to hitch to the border as you risk being stranded without water or shelter at sub-zero temperatures. The most practical method of crossing this border is on a tour from San Pedro (see page 188). If you intend to travel independently in this region do not underestimate the dangers of getting stuck without transport or accommodation at this altitude. Do not travel alone and seek full advice in advance.

(changes bolivianos), to **Salta**, US$45-65, 9 hrs, reserve in advance.(buses fill up early); also **Pullman** (Frontera office) and **Andesmar** 3 a week each.

Car

Expensive fuel is available in the grounds of **Hostería San Pedro**. If planning to cross the border to Bolivia, remember that octane ratings are different in the 2 countries, but diesel cars can safely be used.

❶ Directory

San Pedro de Atacama
p178, map p179

Banks ATMs come and go and are out of commission as often as they are working. If coming from inside Chile stock up on pesos before arriving. Dollars, Argentine pesos and bolivianos can be exchanged at bad rates and most companies accept credit cards, but with high charges. The tourist office recommends always changing money at banks; however, **Casa de Cambios Mazzetti**, on Toconao, Mon-Sat 0730-2230, Sun 0800-1300, is one sturdy option. Some other places change euros; ask around.

Contents

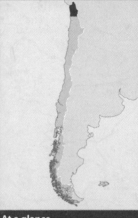

Iquique, Arica & the Altiplano national parks

At a glance

⊕ **Getting around** Good public transport links between towns. A 4WD will allow you to explore the Altiplano, though tours from Arica or Putre are an easier option.
⟲ **Time required** 4 days to do justice to the Altiplano, plus beach and relaxation time on the coast.
✿ **Weather** Moderate temperatures on the coast. Overcast but no rain. The Altiplano is cool by day and freezing at night with seasonal rain.
✕ **When not to go** Roads in the Altiplano are liable to occasional flooding in Jul and also Jan-Mar.

★ **Don't miss ...**
1 Humberstone and Santa Laura, page 199.
2 The oasis of Pica, page 200.
3 La fiesta de La Tirana, page 201.
4 Cerro Unitas, Pintados or Tiliviche, page 202.
5 The Altiplano national parks, page 217.

20 km
20 miles

PERU

Tacora
(5988m)

Visviri

BOLIVIA

Parque
Nacional
Lauca

Pomerape
(6282m)

Putre

Parinacota

Parinacota (6342m)

Socoroma

Lago
Chungará

Paso Tambo
Quemado

Capurata (5990m)

Río Lluta

Guallatiri
(6060m)

Arica

Poconchile

Belén

Tignamar

Guallatiri

San Miguel
de Azapa

Río Azapa

Tignamar
Viejo

Reserva
Nacional
Las Vicuñas

Codpa

Río Camarones

Monumento
Natural Salar
de Surire

Salar de Surire

Surire

Cuya

Geoglifos
de Chiza

Camiña

Parque Nacional
Volcán Isluga

Isluga
(5530m)

Colchane

Geoglifos
de Tiliviche

British
Cemetery

REGION I

Isluga

Cariquima

Pisagua

Zapiga

Reserva Nacional
Pampa del
Tamarugal

Chusmisa

Alto Toroni
(5982m)

Pacific
Ocean

Cta Buena

Gigante del
Atacama

Huara

Tarapacá

Lirima

Mamiña

Humberstone

Iquique

Pozo
Almonte

La Tirana

Reserva Nacional
Pampa del Tamarugal

Salar de
Huasco

Geoglifos de
Pintados

Salar de
Pintados

Pica

Matilla

Salar de
Coposa

The far north of Chile is just as forbidding as the region around Antofagasta and Calama. North of the brash city of Iquique, transport arteries head inland into the desert pampa. There is a strong sense of antiquity here in the few oases and settlements that are sprinkled across the Atacama; the profusion of geoglyphs are testament to the fact that, wherever there is water, people have been living for millennia. These geoglyphs of peoples now vanished and the countless ghost towns of former nitrate *oficinas* stand witness to both the harshness and fragility of life in the region.

Further inland still, towards the Altiplano, are some beautiful spots. Mamiña and Pica are two thermal spring resorts near Iquique, each of them remarkable for their tranquillity. There are four remote national parks in the high Andes, the northernmost of which – the Parque Nacional Lauca – offers some of the most stunning scenery in Chile, with a necklace of high lakes, snow-capped volcanoes, lava fields and varied bird life. It is easily reached from Arica, Chile's northernmost city, along the international road to Bolivia. Near Parque Nacional Lauca are small Andean villages, such as Visviri and Parinacota, where most people speak Aymará, and Spanish remains a foreign language.

Background

As elsewhere in northern Chile, there was a widespread and highly developed network of pre-Hispanic cultures in this region. The geoglyphs at sites such as Pintados and Tiliviche are thought to have been markers for caravans of traders making their way from the Altiplano to the coast and back again. Circles marked in the hillsides signalled the presence of water. The coastal peoples traded furs and fish with the more highly developed cultures of the interior, maintaining links with Tiahuanaco and the Incas.

Even after the Spanish conquest, the early Spanish settler population was small in number. Settlement was concentrated largely in the oases of the sierra, where the climate was easier and where malaria, the scourge of the coast, was not found. From an early date, Arica became one of the principal ports for the silver trade from Potosí, but the coast remained sparsely inhabited until the 19th century. At the time of Independence, the whole of this area became the Peruvian provinces of Tarapacá and Arica, with the provincial capital at the now ruined city of Tarapacá, near Huara. The region became the focal point for the War of the Pacific (1879-1883), with decisive naval battles fought at Iquique on 21 May 1879, and at Angamos, near Mejillones, on 8 October of the same year. After the war, the area as far north as Tacna came under Chilean control, and became the country's economic powerhouse following the sudden growth of the nitrate industry.

The poor conditions of workers in the nitrate mines led to the development of early left-wing and trade unionist movements in the far northern part of Chile. In 1907, a group of miners from one of the nitrate *oficinas* was executed by the army in the Santa María school in Iquique for campaigning to be paid in hard cash instead of *oficina* tokens. The legacy of the far north's radicalism can be seen in the now infamous 'caravan of death' executed in seven northern cities by one of General Pinochet's henchmen in the days following the 1973 coup (see page 509).

The region's borders were finally delineated in 1929: Tacna voted in a referendum to return to Peru, while Arica opted to remain Chilean. The collapse of the nitrate industry in the 1930s and 1940s was a regional crisis but the quick growth of the fishing industry saved the area from disaster.

The sea still provides the main source of wealth in this region: Iquique is the principal fishing port in Chile, unloading 35% of the total national catch, and has important fish-processing industries. Nowadays, mining is much less important than in other parts of northern Chile; however, silver and gold are mined at Challacollo and copper at Sagasca, near Tarapacá, while the new copper mine at Collahuasi has made a big difference to the region's economy. Over 90% of the population lives in the two coastal cities, Arica and Iquique.

Geography and climate

The Atacama Desert extends over most of the far north. The Cordillera de la Costa slowly loses height north of Iquique, terminating at the Morro in Arica: from Iquique northwards it drops directly to the sea and, as a result, there are few beaches along this coast. Inland, the central depression, the *pampa*, 1000 to 1200 m high, is arid and punctuated by salt flats south of Iquique. Between Iquique and Arica, it is crossed from east to west by numerous gorges, formed by several rivers flowing west from the sierra; the more northerly of these, the Ríos Lluta and San José, provide water for Arica and for the Valle de Azapa. The source of the former is snowmelt from Volcán Tacora. Its sulphurous waters can only support crops such as corn, alfalfa and onions. In contrast the San José

Behind the wheel

Driving on the Altiplano is a serious undertaking. Do not think of visiting this area in a cheap hire car; a 4WD is essential, with the highest clearance possible. If you wish to cross into Bolivia you will need a permit from the hire company. Note that the only safe routes between the Pan-American Highway and the Altiplano are the international route from Arica to La Paz through Parque Nacional Lauca (see page 216), from Huara to Colchane (see page 203), and from Pica or Pozo Almonte to the Salar de Huasco (see page 221).

- Tyres should not be inflated to more than 30 lbs at sea level. During the climb from Arica, you should stop several times to release excess pressure from tyres if necessary.
- Cars are much less fuel-efficient at high altitude, so take at least one spare fuel can with a tightly fitting cap. During the climb from Arica, stop several times to release excess pressure in fuel cans. There is a private petrol pump at the chemical plant at the Salar de Surire that will nearly always sell petrol or diesel in an emergency.

- For the Parque Nacional Lauca, antifreeze is essential. You should also bring plenty of warm clothes, sleeping bags, spare fuel, drinking water, food and a spade.
- In the rainy season water levels rise. If a bridge is washed away or the road/path goes through a river or laguna, get out, check the depth and make sure that your car's air vents are higher than this. At the Río Lauca crossing south of Guallatiri this can be as high as 1 m. Drive through the shallowest part.
- Do not leave the main road or well-travelled tracks. Many maps show roads ascending from the Pan-American Highway to the Altiplano at Surire and from Camiña to Colchane; do not be tempted to follow them. These roads are terrible in the dry season, dangerous and impassable in the rainy season.
- Even on main routes, drive slowly and watch out for potholes and erratic lorry drivers.
- If a vehicle is approaching in the other direction on a *ripio* track, apply pressure to the windscreen with your hand. This will prevent it from shattering if hit by a stone.

brings crystal fresh water from the Altiplano to the Azapa Valley which is well known for its olive crop and tropical fruit. On the coast, temperatures are moderated by the Pacific Ocean but, in the *pampa,* variations of temperature between day and night are extreme, ranging between 30°C and 0°C. Coastal regions receive *camanchaca* (sea mist) but the *pampa* is permanently rainless.

East of the central depression lies the sierra, the western branch of the Andes, beyond which is a high plateau, the *Altiplano* (3500-4500 m), from which rise volcanic peaks, including Parinacota (6348 m), Pomerape (6282 m), Guayatiri (6071 m), Acotango (6050 m), Capurata (5990 m), Tacora (5988 m) and Tarapacá (5825 m). There are also a number of lakes in the Altiplano, the largest of which, Lago Chungará, is one of the highest in the world. The main river draining the Altiplano, the Río Lauca, flows eastwards into Bolivia. Temperatures in the sierra average 20°C in summer and 9°C in winter. The Altiplano is much colder, averaging just 10°C in summer and -5°C in winter. Both the sierra and the Altiplano are affected by storms of rain, snow and hail (*invierno boliviano*), usually between January and March.

Iquique and around

Iquique is the capital of Región I (Tarapacá) and one of the main ports of northern Chile (with a growing population of around 200,000). The city is situated on a rocky peninsula at the foot of the high coastal mountain range, sheltered by the headlands of Punta Gruesa and Cavancha. Iquique is a brash, modern city, with a well-preserved collection of historical buildings in the centre, whose bright wooden façades make a surprising contrast to the lifeless desert and the grey coastal mist.

Inland from Iquique are several small towns that were the early centres of Spanish colonial settlement. They are less crowded than villages near Calama and Arica and are well worth visiting.

Iquique → *For listings, see pages 203-207. Colour map 1, B2.*

Although the site of present-day Iquique was used as a port in pre-Hispanic times, it remained sparsely populated throughout the colonial period. Even in 1855, when Iquique had begun to export nitrates, the population was only about 2500. The nitrate trade transformed the city, bringing large numbers of foreign traders and creating a wealthy elite. Although partly destroyed by an earthquake in 1877, the city became the centre of this trade after its transfer from Peru to Chile at the end of the War of the Pacific. Today, the fabulous wealth the nitrate industry brought to the town can be seen in some wonderful buildings. Its coastal position also means that you can enjoy some relaxing days sunning, surfing and swimming, while the hills behind the town have proved to be a perfect jumping-off point for paragliding trips.

Arriving in Iquique → *Iquique is 492 km north of Antofagasta.*
Getting there and around **Diego Aracena international airport** is 35 km south of the city at Chucumata and is served by flights to/from Arica, Antofagasta and Santiago. A taxi to the centre costs US$25; the airport transfer service, T057-231 0800, is unreliable. The bus terminal is at north end of Patricio Lynch, although not all buses leave from here; bus company offices are near the market on Sgto Aldea and B Arana. **Tur-Bus** ① *Esmeralda 594, T057-273 6656*, has a **Redbanc** ATM and luggage store. Iquique is served by all major bus companies from the south and from Arica. There are also daily buses up to Oruro and La Paz in Bolivia. The best way to get around in Iquique is by *colectivo*. Note that the area northeast of the junction of O'Higgins and Ramirez can be rough, especially at night.

Tourist information **Sernatur** ① *Serrano 145, of 303, T057-242 7686, infoiquiqe@sernatur.cl, Mon-Fri, 0830-1630*, has masses of information and is very helpful. See also www.iquique.cl.

Places in Iquique

The old town stretches south and west from **Plaza Prat** with a clock tower and bell dating from 1877. The plaza has recently been remodelled to good effect, with shady benches and newly planted trees. Every Sunday at midday there is a military parade lasting 45 minutes, while on Friday and Saturday nights there are often free theatrical or musical events. On the northeast corner of the plaza is the **Centro Español**, built in Moorish style by the local Spanish community in 1904, and unique in Chile. The ground floor is a restaurant but the upper floors show paintings of scenes from Don Quixote and from Spanish history by the Spanish artist, Vicente Tordecillas. The extravagance of its construction shows the fabulous wealth that nitrates once brought to the city.

Iquique

Pacific Ocean

To Zofri

Av Centenario

Solomayor

To Bolivia

Tur-Bus

Esmeralda

Former Aduana/
Museo Naval

Cathedral

Bolívar

Souper

Patricio Lynch

Obispo Labbé

Ramírez

Vivar

San Martín

Barros Arana

Amunátegui

Juan Martínez

Covadonga

Anibal Pinto

Serrano

Plaza Prat

Lagos

Plaza Condell

Municipalidad

Tarapacá

Thompson

Gorostiaga

Teatro Municipal

Wilson

To Pica

Sargento Aldea

Latorre

Museo Regional

Grumete Bolados

Palacio Astoreca

Anibal Pinto

Baquedano

Patricio Lynch

Obispo Labbé

Ramírez

Vivar

Barros Arana

Amunátegui

Juan Martínez

Zegers

O'Higgins

Bulnes

To Route 5 (Pan-American Highway)

N

200 metres

200 yards

To ❿ ⓭ (1 block)

To ❷ ❸ ❺ ❻ (2½ blocks),
Playa Cavancha, Tocopilla &
Antofagasta via Route 1

To ❻ (4 blocks)

To ❽

Where to stay 🛏
1 Arturo Prat
2 Atenas

3 Backpacker's Hostel Iquique
4 Cano
5 Hostal Cuneo
6 Hostal La Casona 1920
7 Hostal Li Ming
8 YMCA

Restaurants 🍴
1 Birimbao
2 Brasileña
3 Casino Español
4 Cioccolata
5 El Rincón del Cachuperto
6 El Tercer Ojito
7 El Wagon

8 Kiru
9 La Picada Curicana
10 Muselina
11 Nan King
12 Peña mi Perú
13 Ruta del Gigante

On the south side of the plaza is the **Teatro Municipal**, built as an opera house in 1890 with a façade featuring four women representing the seasons; in its heyday it played host to such famous names as Caruso. Three blocks north of the plaza is the old **Aduana** (customs house) built in 1871 and the scene, in 1891, of an important battle in the Civil War between supporters of President Balmaceda and congressional forces. Part of it now houses the **Museo Naval de Iquique** ① *Esmeralda 250, www.museonaval.cl, Tue-Sun 1000-1730, US$2,* dedicated to the War of the Pacific, and more specifically, to the naval battle of Iquique and its principal hero, Captain Prat. There is some information in English. Nearby, is the harbour; **cruises** ① *45 mins, US$5, minimum 10 people,* depart from the passenger pier. Sea lions and pelicans can be seen.

Five blocks east along Calle Sotomayor is the **railway station**, now disused, built in 1883 and displaying several old locomotives. Two blocks south of the railway station, on Bolívar, is the **cathedral**, dating from 1885. It is painted bright yellow and blue and has interesting stained-glass windows. On Amunátegui, behind the **Escuela Santa María** on Zégers, there is a memorial to the workers from the nitrate mines who were killed by the army while sheltering in the school during the strike of 1907.

On Calle Baquedano, which runs south from Plaza Prat, is the highly recommended **Museo Regional** ① *Baquedano 951, www.cormudesi.cl/Dir_Museo.html, Mon-Fri 0900-1730, Sat 0930-1800, free,* which has an excellent collection of pre-Hispanic artefacts (including several mummies). The archaeological section is very well set out, although explanations are in Spanish only, tracing the development of pre-Hispanic civilizations in the region and containing an important ethnographical collection of the Isluga culture of the Altiplano (circa AD 400) and of contemporary Aymará cultures. There is also a section devoted to the nitrate era, with exhibits including a collection of *oficina* tokens, a model of a nitrate *oficina* and the collection of the nitrate entrepreneur, Santiago Humberstone.

Elsewhere on the street are the attractive former mansions of the 'nitrate barons'. Adorned with columns, balconies and impressive old doors, these buildings date from between 1880 and 1903 and were constructed from timber imported from California. The finest of these is the **Palacio Astoreca** ① *O'Higgins 350, Tue-Fri 1000-1300, Sat 1000-1330, Sun 1100-1400, US$1,* built in 1903, subsequently the Intendencia and now a museum with fine late 19th-century furniture and exhibitions of shells. Continuing south towards the beach at Playa Cavancha, along Baquedano, Lynch or Obispo Labbé, you'll pass many beautiful old wooden houses painted blue, green, yellow and pink, with white columns and large wooden shutters and doors.

A free tram service runs intermittently up and down Baquedano. It is incredibly slow (walking would be quicker) but that is not the point. Along this stretch of the road an impromptu market often appears, selling various bits and pieces.

Playa Cavancha is very popular in summer – in spite of the Humboldt Current, the water is almost warm – although surfers and other watersports enthusiasts make for the pounding waves of **Playa Brava** further south (see page 206). Those who enjoy walking or sandboarding may want to climb the large sand dune, **Cerro Dragón**, which rises behind Iquique and gives fantastic views of the city and the sea; take a *colectivo* to Chipana y La Tirana and then walk to the base of the hill. Most paragliding trips take off from the top of the hill before circling the city and landing at Playa Cavancha.

Iquique is a major duty-free centre. North of town is the Free Zone, the **Zofri** ① *Amunategui, www.zofri.com, Mon-Sat 1100-2100, also Sun in summer, limit on tax free purchases US$1000 for foreigners, colectivo from the centre, US$1.* It is a giant shopping centre selling a wide range of duty-free imported products, including electronic and leather goods, perfumes, cars, motorcycles and good-quality camping equipment. Although better than Punta Arenas' equivalent, these days most are a similar price in Santiago. Drivers should note that all vehicles travelling south from Iquique are searched for duty-free goods at Quillagua on the Pan-American Highway and at Chipana on Route 1, the coastal road.

South and east of Iquique → *For listings, see pages 203-207.*

Nitrate towns

Humberstone ① *T057-275 1213, daily 0830-1830, entry by 'donation', US$3, guided tours Sat-Sun, leaflets available*, is a large nitrate town, abandoned in 1961, at the junction of the Pan-American Highway and the road to Iquique. At its height in 1940 the town had a population of 3700. It is now open to visitors daily; you can see the plaza, the church, a well-preserved theatre, the *pulpería* (company stores) and the Olympic-size pool complete with grandstand (built of metal plating from ships' hulls). Recently granted World Heritage status by UNESCO, the town is being slowly restored by former residents who are happy to reminisce with visitors.

Nearby are the ruins of several other mining towns, including **Santa Laura** ① *2 km from Humberstone*, which has the skeleton of a nitrate-processing plant, the machinery used to crush the minerals and a small, somewhat disorganized mining museum. Both Humberstone and Santa Laura can be visited on tours arranged by local agencies (see What to do, page 206). If you're travelling independently from Iquique, take any bus to Arica or a *colectivo* for Pozo Almonte from Sargento Aldea y Barros Arana, US$3; there's a phone near the site for booking a return or you could probably flag down an Iquique-bound bus or minibus from the highway.

Situated on the Pan-American Highway, 5 km south of the Iquique road, **Pozo Almonte** was the main service centre for the nitrate fields of the area. The **Museo Histórico Salitrero** ① *on the tree-shaded plaza, Mon-Fri 0830-1300, 1600-1900*, displays artefacts and photographs of the nitrate era.

South along the Pan-American Highway

South of Pozo Almonte, the Pan-American Highway runs to **Quillagua**, 172 km, where there is a customs post and all southbound vehicles are searched, before continuing towards Antofagasta. At Km 24, the road runs through the largest section of the **Reserva Nacional Pampa del Tamarugal** (the other two sections are around La Tirana and north of Huara), which is administered by CONAF. Covering a total of 100,650 ha, the reserve includes plantations of tamaruga, a tree species adapted to the dry climate and saline soils.

The **Geoglifos de Pintados**, some 400 figures on the hillsides, representing humans, animals and birds, as well as abstract designs, are situated some 3 km west of the Pan-American Highway; take any bus south, US$4, and get off at Km 43. Many other geoglyph sites around Iquique, including the Gigante del Atacama (see box, page 202), are difficult to visit without a vehicle.

Mamiña

Once a very popular thermal springs resort, Mamiña is reached by a good paved road, which runs 74 km east from Pozo Almonte. Situated on a ridge at 2750 m, this historic village is now dominated by the recently expanded copper mine, some 8 km to the west. Day-trips can be made from Iquique.

Mamiña has pre-Hispanic origins – its name means 'the girl of my eyes' in Aymará – and is inhabited mainly by people of Aymará origin. If you stand on the hill above the village, a circular geoglyph indicating the presence of water is clearly visible on the opposite side of the valley. Legend has it that one of Mamiña's thermal pools once cured an Inca princess; an Inca *pukará* stands on a hilltop 3 km east marked by a white cross that can be seen from the village (it's probably best to hire a guide if you want to visit it). There are also said to be the ruins of a pre-Hispanic settlement further down the valley towards the *pampa*.

The church, built in 1632, is the only colonial Andean church in Chile with twin towers, each topped by a bell tower; ascend the church by steps at the side for a view of the bells linked together by a single rope. Mamiña's abundant thermal springs and unique mud spring have meant that it has been a popular health resort since the nitrate era; the **Hotel Termas** dates from this period. The thermal springs, classified as being radioactive, are rich in sodium, potassium, sulphur, chlorides and silicates, and are acknowledged to be valuable in treating ailments, such as rheumatoid arthritis and sciatica, as well as respiratory and digestive problems. There is also a mud bath, the **Baño Los Chinos** ① *daily 0930-1300*, which is considered valuable in the treatment of many skin diseases, such as psoriasis. The bath contains radioactive mud with natural deposits of vegetal mineral mud activated by the fermentation of certain algae; the mud is allowed to dry on the skin after the bath and then washed off in one of the thermal springs.

La Tirana

Situated 10 km east of the Pan-American Highway, on a turning 9 km south of Pozo Almonte, La Tirana is famous for a religious festival dedicated to the **Virgen del Carmen**, held annually from 10 to 16 July (see box, opposite), which attracts some 150,000 pilgrims and merrymakers to the village, whose resident population is around 550. Over 100 groups dance night and day decked out in colourful costumes and spectacular masks, starting on 12 July. All the dances take place in the main plaza in front of the church; no alcohol is served. At other times of year, the church is well worth a visit, and there is a small museum.

Matilla

Some 38 km east of La Tirana, Matilla is an oasis settlement founded in 1760 by settlers from Pica (see below). The village declined after 1912 when the waters of the Quebrada de Quisma were diverted to Iquique. The church (1887) is built of blocks of borax and rears up from over the arid plain like a version of the Sacré Coeur in the desert. It was damaged by an earthquake in 2005 but has now been restored. Nearby is a **museum** ① *Lagar de Matilla, daily 0900-1800*, used in the 18th century for fermenting wine. Get a key from the kiosk in the plaza. Near Matilla, an unpaved, rough road runs southwest to meet the Pan-American Highway.

Pica

Four kilometres northeast of Matilla, Pica, with a current population of 3000, was the most important centre of early Spanish settlement in this region. In colonial times, it produced a famous wine sold as far away as Potosí. Most of the older buildings, including the church, date from the nitrate period when it became a popular resort. It is a leafy oasis, famous for its thermal baths and the fruit grown here – one of the highlights of a stay is drinking fresh fruit juices from any one of numerous stalls near the thermal springs, which lie about 1 km from the centre of the town at **Cocha Resbaladero** ① *daily*

La Tirana

The legend of La Tirana is an intriguing mix of Andean traditions and Catholicism. It is said that, when Diego de Almagro made the first Spanish foray into Chile, one of his companions was an Inca princess. She was a fierce warrior who loathed everything to do with the Spanish and escaped into the pampa to wage war against them. She was so fierce that she became known as 'La Tirana' ('The Tyrant').

La Tirana's techniques were overthrown when she fell in love with Vasco de Almeyda, a Portuguese soldier enlisted by the Spanish, who persuaded her to convert to Christianity. When her companions discovered her treachery, both the Inca princess and the warrior were killed. The legend goes that a priest, coming some years later to the area to evangelize, discovered a cross on the spot where the couple had died, and built a church there.

Today, the fiesta treads a fine line between commercialism and maintaining these hybrid traditions. The most important day and night occur on 16 July but, for up to a week beforehand, the town is awash with travelling salesmen, who come from all over Chile to sell everything that you could possibly need – clothes, music, bags, hats, cheap meals, ice creams and so on. At the same time, troupes of religious dancers and their accompanying brass bands come from as far away as Peru and Argentina to pay homage to the Virgen del Carmen. Eclecticism is the order of the day: as well as traditional Andean groups, there are also dancers who imitate the Sioux Indians from North America, as well as the 'Ali Baba Christians' dancing with imitation wooden sphinxes. The noise is deafening, day and night, as the brass bands vie with one another to produce the greatest racket. There is even an office set up by the church to perform marriages, and one of the most touching sights at the fiesta is that of happy couples being carried towards the church, amid the dancing, music and the chaos.

0700-2000 all year, US$4. There are changing rooms, a snack bar and a beautiful pool on site and a small tourist information office opposite.

A few kilometres east of Pica on the road to the Altiplano, there is a mirador with fine views. There is also a map showing where to find some fossilized dinosaur footprints. Tours are available from Pica.

North of Iquique → *For listings, see pages 203-207.*

Iquique to the Bolivian border

Some 30 km north of Pozo Almonte, **Huara** was once a town of 7000 people, serving as a centre for the nearby nitrate towns. Today, the population is reduced to 400 and little evidence remains of the town's former prosperity, apart from the railway station, which is a national monument, and a fascinating small museum preserving a pharmacy from the nitrate era with all the cures and remedies that were then on offer (ask at the municipalidad). The church is also worth a look. The town was badly damaged by the 2005 earthquake and much of it is still in ruins.

At Huara, a paved road turns off the Pan-American Highway and runs to the forlorn and windy border town of Colchane, 173 km northeast on the Bolivian frontier (see box, page 203). The town provides access to the southern entrance of the Parque Nacional

Set in stone

Found as far south as the Río Loa and as far north as the Río Azapa near Arica, as well as along the Peruvian coast as far as Nazca, geoglyphs or *geoglifos* are one of the most visible traces left by ancient civilizations in the Atacama. Dating from around AD 1000-1400, these designs were made on the rocks using two different techniques: by scraping away the topsoil to reveal different coloured rock beneath or by arranging stones to form a kind of mosaic. They exhibit three main themes: geometrical patterns; images of animals, especially camelids, birds and snakes; and humans, often holding or carrying instruments or weapons, such as a bow and arrows. They are easily visible because they were intended to be seen. They are generally located on isolated hills in the desert, on the western slopes of the Cordillera de la Costa or on the slopes of *quebradas* (gorges). Their significance is thought by some experts to be ritual, but the more current theory is that they were often a kind of signpost pointing out routes between the coast and the sierra.

The largest site is at **Pintados**, 96 km south of Iquique, reached by turning off

the Pan-American Highway at the Pica junction and then following a 4-km track west from which several panels can be seen, including representations of animals, birds and a large number of humans dressed in ponchos and feather head-dresses, as well as geometrical designs.

At **Tiliviche**, 127 km north of Iquique, a 300-m panel can be seen on the southern side of the *quebrada*, representing a drove of llamas moving from the *cordillera* to the coast. There are also two important sites near Huara: at **Cerro Rosita**, 20 km north of Huara near the Pan-American Highway, the 'Sun of Huara' (an Aymara sun emblem) is visible on the eastern side of the hill; and at **Cerro Unitas**, 15 km east of Huara, geoglyphs are visible on the western and southern sides of an isolated hill. On the western slope of Cerro Unitas is the **Gigante del Atacama** or Giant of the Atacama, probably the most famous of all the images: 86 m high, this is a representation of an indigenous leader with a head-dress of feathers and a feline mask; to his left is a reptile, thought to link him to the earth god Pachamama, to his right is his staff of office.

Volcán Isluga, some 6 km northwest (see page 221). Some 13 km east of Huara, to the north of the road, are the **Geoglifos de Cerro Unitas**, the most outstanding of which is the **Gigante del Atacama**, a human figure 86 m tall, reported to be the largest geoglyph in the world and best viewed from a distance (see box, above).

At Km 23, an unpaved road branches off south to **Tarapacá**, settled by the Spanish around 1560 and capital of the Peruvian province of Tarapacá until 1855, now largely abandoned except for the **Fiesta of the Virgen de la Candelaria** on 2 and 3 February. The major historic buildings, the Iglesia de San Lorenzo and the Palacio de Gobierno, are in ruins. At **Chusmisa** (Km 77), there are thermal springs producing water that is bottled and sold throughout northern Chile.

North towards Arica

The Pan-American Highway runs across the Atacama Desert at an altitude of around 1000 m, with several steep hills, best tackled in daylight. At night, *camanchaca* (sea mist) can reduce visibility.

Border crossings: Chile–Bolivia

Colchane

The isolated frontier town of Colchane can be reached from the west via a paved road that runs 173 km from Huara, or from the north via the Parque Nacional Volcán Isluga (see page 221). The border here is open daily 0830-2030. On the Bolivian side, the road is paved from Pisiga via Huachachalla to Opoquari (about 100 km) and from Toledo to **Oruro**, 32 km, but the rest of the 170 km road in Bolivia is unpaved.

At Zapiga, 47 km north of Huara, a road heads west for 41 km to **Pisagua**, formerly an important nitrate port, now reduced to a small fishing village. Several of the old wooden buildings are national monuments, including the **municipal theatre** (1892) and the **clock tower** (1887), but the town is now largely abandoned, although a handful of fish restaurants make it a pleasant meal stop. Pisagua was the site of a detention centre after the 1973 military coup; mass graves from that period were discovered near here in 1990.

Heading east from Zapiga, meanwhile, a poor road (deep sand and dust) leads 67 km to **Camiña**, a picturesque village in an oasis. From here, a terrible road runs to the **Tranque de Caritaya**, a dam 45 km further northeast, which supplies water for the coastal towns and which is set in splendid scenery with lots of wildlife and interesting botany (especially *llareta*).

Ten kilometres north of Zapiga is a British cemetery dating from the 19th century: note the fine wrought-iron gates. Nearby, stop for a view of the **Geoglifos de Tiliviche**, representing a group of llamas (signposted to the left and easily accessible). Further north at Km 111, the **Geoglifos de Chiza** can be seen from the bridge that carries the highway over the Quebrada de Chiza.

At Km 172, a road runs east to **Codpa**, an agricultural community in a deep gorge surrounded by interesting scenery. Poor roads continue north and east of here towards Putre (see page 218**).**

◉ Iquique and around listings

For hotel and restaurant price codes and other relevant information, see pages 14-21.

◉ Where to stay

Iquique *p196, map p197*
Accommodation is scarce in Jul and also in high summer. There's no campsite in Iquique and wild camping is forbidden on Playa Brava and Playa Cavancha.
$$$ Arturo Prat, Aníbal Pinto 695, Plaza Prat, T057-252 0000. Under new management and renovated, good location if a bit noisy, good standard, nice pool.
$$$ Atenas, Los Rieles 738, Cavancha, T057-243 1100, atenashotel2002@yahoo.es.

Pleasant, personal, good value, good service and food, pool.
$$$-$$ Cano, Ramírez 996, T057-247 0277, www.hotelcano.cl. Mostly big rooms, but also some small interior rooms to be avoided. nice atmosphere, brightly coloured, modern decor, parking.
$$ Hostal Cuneo, Baquedano 1175, T057-242 8654, www.hostalcuneo.cl. Long-established hostel, helpful, piano in the living room, good value.
$$-$ Backpacker's Hostel Iquique, Amunategui 2075 esq Hernán Fuenzalida, T057-232 0223, www.hosteliquique.cl. Seafront location at Cavancha, all the usual backpacker's services plus surfboard and

wetsuit rental, surf classes, sand duning, bicycles, roof terrace with ocean view.
$$-$ Hostal La Casona 1920, Barros Arana 1585, T057-241 3000, http://casonahostel. com. Fun, in a quiet area of town not far from the beach, English spoken.
$$-$ Hostal Li Ming, Barros Arana 705, T057-242 1912, www.hostal.cl. Simple, good value, small rooms, also beachfront apartments to rent.
$ YMCA, Baquedano 964, T057-241 5551, www.ymcaiquique.org. Impressive façade, modern interior, most rooms are dorm-style with their own bathroom. Basic, but clean and central.

Nitrate towns *p199*
$$ Estancia Inn, Comercial, Pozo Almonte. Basic, geared towards mineworkers.

Mamiña *p199*
It is extremely difficult to find lodging in Mamiña as hotels generally have exclusive contracts with the nearby mine.

La Tirana *p200*
During the festival, a bed is difficult to find other than in organized campsites (take your own tent), which have basic toilets and showers, and through a few families who rent out rooms.

Matilla *p200*
Complejo Turístico El Parabien, T057-274 1588, elparabien.blogspot.com. Fully furnished *cabañas* and a pool.

Pica *p200*
Hotels fill up at weekends, holiday times and during La Tirana's festival 10-16 Jul: book ahead.
$$ Camino del Inca, Esmeralda 14, T057-274 1008, hotelcaminodelinca@ hotmail.com. Shady patio, table football, good value.
$$ Los Emilios, Cochrane 201, T057-274 1126. Interesting old building, nice lounge and patio.

$$ Hostal Casablanca, Ibáñez 75, Cocha Resbaladero, T057-274 1410. Smallish rooms with bath and cable TV. Friendly, comfortable, cooking facilities, bright patio with pool, parking.
$$-$ O'Higgins, Balmaceda 6, T057-274 1524, hohiggins@123mail.com. Modern, well furnished.
$ Residencial El Tambo, Ibáñez 68, Cocha Resbaladero, T057-274 1041. Without bath, meals served, somewhat run-down. Also 4-person *cabañas*.
$ San Andrés, Balmaceda 197, T057-274 1319, gringa733@hotmail.com. Basic, excellent restaurant, serves good-value 4-course *almuerzos*. Safe parking.

Iquique to the Bolivian border *p201*
Basic accommodation is available in the **Restaurant Frontera** in Huara and in simple *residenciales* in Colchane.

North towards Arica *p202*
Belén Food and lodging from **María Martínez**, General Lagos y San Martín.

❼ Restaurants

Iquique *p196, map p197*
The restaurants on the wharf on the opposite side of Av Costanera from the bus terminal are poor value. There are several good, cheap seafood restaurants on the 2nd floor of the central market, Barros Arana y Latorre. There are also many restaurants on the Península Cavancha.
$$$-$$ Casino Español, Plaza Prat, T057-242 3284. Good meals well served in beautiful Moorish-style 1904 building.
$$$-$$ El Tercer Ojito, P Lynch 1420, T057-247 1448. Well-presented fish, sushi, pasta and vegetarian options with a Peruvian twist, served in a pleasant courtyard, deservedly popular.
$$$-$$ El Wagon, Thompson 85, T057-234 1428. Fish and seafood cooked to traditional northern recipes. Regarded as the best eatery in the centre.

$$$-$$ Kiru, Amunátegui 1912, Cavancha, T057-276 0795, www.kiru.cl. Mon-Sat 1300-1530, 2000-0030, Sun 1300-1600. Half elegant restaurant, half sports bar, Peruvian influenced food, fish and good pasta. Huge pisco sours.

$$$-$$ Ruta del Gigante, Baquedano 1288, T057-247 5215, www.rutadelgigante.cl. Delicious and varied food from the Andes drawn on Aymara family heritage with modern twist. Also has a hostel and can arrange tours.

$$ Brasileña, Vivar 1143, T057-276 1752. Brazilian run, serves seafood in the week, Brazilian food on Sat.

$$ La Picada Curicana, Pinto y Zegers 204, T057-276 5830, www.lapicadacuricana.cl. Tue-Sat 1100-1600, 2000-2400, Sun 1200-1700. Good hearty Central Chilean country cooking (such as oven-roasted game, served in clay pots), large portions, good value menú de la casa.

$$ Nan King, Amunátegui 533, T057-242 0434. Large portions, good value, renowned as best Chinese in town.

$ El Rincón del Cachuperto, Valenzuela 125, Península Cavancha, T057-232 9189. Famed as having the best seafood *empanadas* in Iquique.

$ Peña mi Perú, Bolívar 711. Open 24 hrs. Cheap Chilean and Peruvian staples, good value menú on weekdays.

Birimbao, Gorostiaga 419. Opens early for breakfast (0800). Fresh juices.

Cioccolata, Pinto 487, T057-242 7478 (another branch in the Zofri). Very good coffee and cakes.

Muselina, Baquedano 1406, www.muselina.cl. Mon-Fri 0900-2300, Sun 1800-2200. Café/bistro with good coffee, delicious cakes and smoothies.

Mamiña *p199*
$$ Restaurant Cerro Morado, Av Barros Chino 18. Good variety, traditional dishes, including rabbit. One of few restaurants open to the general public.

Pica *p200*
Try the local *alfajores*, delicious cakes filled with cream and mango honey.
$$ El Edén, Riquelme 12. 1st class local food in delightful surroundings, fine ice cream, best restaurant in town.
$ La Mía Pappa, Balmaceda, near plaza. Good selection of meat and juices, attractive location.
$ La Palmera, Balmaceda 115. Excellent *almuerzo*, popular with locals, near plaza.
$ La Viña, Ibáñez 70, by Cocha de Resbaladero. Good cheap *almuerzo*.

Iquique to the Bolivian border *p201*
Meals are served in the *residenciales* in Colchane.
$ La flor de Huara, Huara. Good and cheap. Much the best choice in town.

🎵 Bars and clubs

Iquique *p196, map p197*
Most discos are out of town on the road south to the airport.
Siddharta, Mall Las Américas, locales 10-11-193. Sushi.
Taberna Barracuda, Gorostiaga 601, T057-242 7969. For late-night food and drink in pleasant surroundings.

🎭 Entertainment

Iquique *p196, map p197*
There are occasional recitals in the cathedral.
Casino Dreams, Prat 2755, www.mundodreams.com.
Mall las Américas, Av Héroes de la Concepción, south of the centre, T057-239 9600, www.malllasamericas.cl. Multi-screen cinema and shopping mall.
Teatro Municipal, Plaza Prat, T057-241 1292. Plays, ballet, dance and concerts.

⊛ Festivals

Iquique *p196, map p197*
There are numerous small religious festivals in the area – ask in Iquique's tourist office for information. For La Tirana, see box, page 201.

⊙ Shopping

Iquique *p196, map p197*
Most of the city's commerce is in the **Zofri** duty-free zone.
Mall de las Américas, on Av Héroes de la Concepción, T057-239 9600, www.mall lasamericas.cl. Multi-screen cinema and shopping mall.
Unimarc, Tarapacá 579. Supermarket.

⊘ What to do

Iquique *p196, map p197*
The tourist office maintains a full list of operators. Iquique is a good place for paragliding: several agencies offer 30- to 40-min tandem flights from around US$80. It also offers some of the best surfing in Chile with numerous reef breaks on **Playa Brava**, south of the city. Surfboard rental and surf classes are available from a number of agencies.
Altazor, Flight Park, Vía 6, manzana A, sitio 3, Bajo Molle, T057-238 0110, www.altazor.cl. Parapenting; will pick you up from wherever you are staying. Also offers week-long courses including accommodation, as do many other operators.
Avitours, Baquedano 997, T057-241 3332, www.avitours.cl. Tour to Pintados, La Tirana, Humberstone, Pica, etc, some bilingual guides, day tours start at US$50.
Civet Adventure, Bolívar 684, T057-242 8483, www.civet-adventure.cl. Adventure tourism in the desert and the High Andes, photography, mountainbiking, landsailing, trekking, English, German and Spanish spoken, contact Sergio Cortez.

Extremo Norte, T057-276 0997, www. extremonorte.cl. Good tours to the Altiplano and desert, responsible.
Trans Atacama, T02-2620 9620, www. transatacama.com. A tourist excursion on Sat by train, with historic coaches, from Iquique (pick-up at hotels) to the Pintados geoglyphs. Includes meals and drinks, 2 classes of carriage: classic or premium.

⊖ Transport

Iquique *p196, map p197*
Air
LAN, PAL and Sky fly to **Arica**, **Antofagasta** and **Santiago**.

Bus
Companies include **Tur-Bus**, Esmeralda 594, T057-273 6656, and **Pullman**, in terminal, T057-242 6522. Most southbound buses take the coastal road to **Tocopilla** and are searched for duty-free goods at Chipana; those on the Pan-American Highway are stopped and searched at Quillagua.

To **Mamiña**, with **Transportes Tamarugal**, Barros Arana 897, Iquique, daily 0800, 1600, return 1800, 0800, 2½ hrs, US$7, good service. Also with **Turismo Mamiña**, Latorre 779, daily, more-or-less same prices and frequency. To **La Tirana**, in ordinary times, buses to Pica stop here; during the festival, virtually every taxi and *colectivo* in Iquique seems to be heading for La Tirana. Minibuses to **Pica**, US$4 one-way, 2 hrs, are run by 3 companies: **San Andrés**, Sgto Aldea y B Arana, daily 0930, return 1800; **Pullman Chacón**, Barros Arana y Latorre, many daily, and **Santa Rosa**, Barros Arana 777, daily 0830, 0930, return 1700, 1800. To **Colchane** (Bolivian border) daily 1300 and 2100.

To **Arica**, buses and *colectivos*, US$11, 4½ hrs. To **Antofagasta**, US$14, 6 hrs. To **Calama**, 6 hrs, US$22. To **San Pedro de Atacama** direct with **Frontera del Norte**, but with a 5-hr stop-over in Calama, 0300-0800. To **Tocopilla** along the coastal road, buses and minibuses, several companies, 3 hrs, US$11. To **La Serena**, 18 hrs, US$35-70. To **Santiago**, 25 hrs, several companies, US$65-92.

International To **Bolivia**, **Litoral**, T057-242 3670, daily 2200 to **Oruro** and **La Paz**, US$30. **Salvador** and others depart from Esmeralda near Juan Martínez around 2100-2300, same price (passengers may have a cold wait for customs to open at 0800).

Car hire
Econorent, Labbé y O'Higgins, T600-200 0000, weekend specials; **IQSA**, Labbé 1089, T057-241 7068. **Procar**, Serrano 796, T057-241 3470 (airport T057-241 0920).

Pica *p200*
There are several minibuses to Iquique daily with **San Andrés**, **Pullman Chacón** and Santa Rosa (see Iquique Transport, above, for details). Most stop at **La Tirana** en route.

ⓘ Directory

Iquique *p196, map p197*
Banks Numerous **Redbanc** ATMs in the centre and the Zofri. Best rates for TCs and cash at *casas de cambio* in the Zofri.
Consulates Bolivia, Gorostiaga 215, Departamento E, T057-252 7472, Mon-Fri 0930-1200. Peru, Zegers 570, T057-241 1466, consulperu-iquique@rree.gob.pe.
Language schools Academia de Idiomas del Norte, Ramírez 1345, T057-241 1827, www.languages.cl. Swiss-run, Spanish classes and accommodation for students.

Arica and around

Arica is the northernmost city in Chile, just 19 km south of the Peruvian border. With Peru so close and Arica being the main port for Bolivian trade, the city has a halfway house atmosphere. It is less ordered than most Chilean cities, with hundreds of street vendors and indoor markets selling cheap, imported goods and has a friendly, laid-back feel. The city centre itself is quite attractive, with long beaches, pleasant gardens and extensive networks of sand dunes all nearby. Rearing up to the south is El Morro, the rock that marks the end of the Chilean coastal range. Inland is the verdant Valle de Azapa with olive groves and a museum housing the world's oldest mummies. Day trips can easily be made across the border to Tacna, the southernmost city in Peru.

Arriving in Arica → *Colour map 1, A1.*

Getting there and around Arica is a long way from most of Chile; buses take 30 hours to reach Santiago to the south and all major bus companies serving the north make this their final stop. Long-distance buses use two adjacent **terminals** ① *Av Portales y Santa María, northeast of the centre, T058-224 1390, terminal tax US$0.40.* The terminals are served by numerous buses, *colectivos* (eg Nos 8, 18), US$0.80, and taxis, US$2. Arica is a centre for connections to Bolivia and Peru, with a train service (not running in 2014) and frequent *colectivos* north to Tacna in Peru and buses east to La Paz in Bolivia. There is also quite a wide-ranging bus service to villages in the sierra and the Altiplano. The airport is 18 km north of city at Chacalluta, T058-221 1116, and is served by **Sky** and **LAN** with flights to/from Santiago via Iquique and Antofagasta. A taxi from the airport to town costs US$10-15; *colectivos* charge US$5 per person. Be wary if your taxi driver suggests 'a good hotel', as many are paid commission to do so. Arica is quite a large city, and you may need to transport to get to more out-of-the-way places, particularly the clubs, many of which are on the road out to the Azapa valley. Taxis are black and yellow and are scarce; hire a *colectivo* instead, US$2-3, from Maipú between Velásquez y Colón (all are numbered).

Tourist information Sernatur ① *San Marcos 101, T058-223 3993, infoarica@sernatur.cl, Mon-Fri 0830-1300, 1500-1830,* is situated in a kiosk next to the Casa de la Cultura. Staff are very helpful and can supply a list of tour companies and a good map. There's a municipal kiosk opposite (www.muniarica.cl), and an office of **CONAF** ① *Av Vicuña MacKenna 820, T058-220 1200, aricayparinacota.oirs@conaf.cl. Mon-Fri 0830-1300, 1430-1630 (take colectivo 1).*

Background

During the colonial period, Arica was important as the Pacific end of the silver route from Potosí. Independence from Spain and the re-routing of Bolivian trade through Cobija led to a decline, but the city recovered with the building of rail links to Tacna (1855) and La Paz (1913) when it became the port of choice for those two cities. The city came under Chilean control at the end of the War of the Pacific. The Morro in Arica was the site of an important Chilean victory over Peru on 7 June 1880.

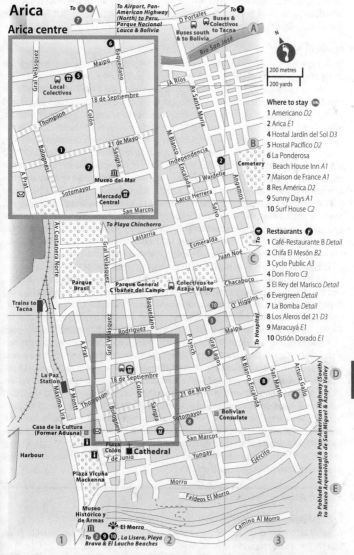

Arica

Arica centre

Where to stay
1 Americano *D2*
2 Arica *E1*
4 Hostal Jardín del Sol *D3*
5 Hostal Pacífico *D2*
6 La Ponderosa
   Beach House Inn *A1*
7 Maison de France *A1*
8 Res América *D2*
9 Sunny Days *A1*
10 Surf House *C2*

Restaurants
1 Café-Restaurante B *Detail*
2 Chifa El Mesón *B2*
3 Cyclo Public *A3*
4 Don Floro *C3*
5 El Rey del Marisco *Detail*
6 Evergreen *Detail*
7 La Bomba *Detail*
8 Los Aleros del 21 *D3*
9 Maracuyá *E1*
10 Ostión Dorado *E1*

Arica remains an important route centre and port. Now linked to the Bolivian capital La Paz by road and an oil pipeline, it handles almost half of Bolivia's foreign trade and attracts Bolivians, as well as locals, to its beaches. There are also road and rail connections with the Peruvian city of Tacna, 54 km north. Most of the large fishmeal plants have moved to Iquique, leaving several rusting hulks of trawlers in the bay, now home to a significant local crow population. Regrettably, there are indications that Arica is also becoming a key link in the international drugs trade.

Places in Arica

Unlike in most Chilean cities, life is not centred around the main square, but Avenida 21 de Mayo, a mostly pedestrianized street full of banks, shops, restaurants and cafés. Just south of this is the **Plaza Colón**, on which stands the Gothic-style cathedral of **San Marcos**, built in iron by Eiffel. Although small, it is beautifully proportioned and attractively painted. It was brought to Arica from Ilo in Peru as an emergency measure after a tidal wave swept over Arica in 1868 and destroyed all its churches; inside the cathedral is a Christ figure dating from the 12th century. Eiffel also designed the nearby Aduana (customs house), which is now the **Casa de la Cultura** ① *Mon-Fri 0830-2000, ask for permission to go up into the altillo.* Just north of the Aduana is the La Paz railway station; outside is an old steam locomotive (made in Germany in 1924) once used on this line, while inside is a memorial to John Roberts Jones, builder of the Arica portion of the railway. The Casa Bolognesi, Colón y Yungay, is a fine old building painted blue and white. It holds temporary exhibitions. Hidden away on a small side street behind the cathedral is the private **Museo del Mar** ① *Pasaje Sangra 315, www.museodelmardearica.cl, Mon-Sat 1100-1900, US$2,* which has over 1000 exhibits from around the world, well-displayed. If the owner is there he will explain everything to you in English.

To climb **El Morro**, 130 m high, walk to the southernmost end of the Calle Colón, past a small in situ museum displaying a number of recently uncovered Chinchorro mummies, and then follow the pedestrian walkway up to the summit; there are fine views of the city from here. The **Museo Histórico y de Armas** ① *daily 0800-2000, US$1,* on the summit, contains a selection of weapons and military uniforms as well as displays on the War of the Pacific. There's basic information in English but most of the exhibits speak for themselves.

A coastal road heads out of Arica to the south. There is no public transport but it makes a pleasant cycle ride. Past the Morro, to the right, is the former Island of Alacrán, now connected to the mainland and a favourite surfing destination. The road passes La Lisera, a beach, crowded in summer, and with a natural pool. Past the empty Playa Brava the air fills with the pungent smell of fishmeal from the processing plant here. At Km 7, past further rocky and sandy beaches and a natural blowhole is Playa Corazones, a pleasant beach, quiet except at weekends and in summer. Good cheap seafood is available. Shortly after, the road runs out but a path continues for a further kilometre, past guano-covered rocks, pools full of crabs, starfish and shellfish to the Cuevas de Anzota, a series of caves and fantastic rock formations with crashing waves, a small secluded beach and a sea-lion colony on a small island off-shore.

East of Arica → *For listings, see pages 212-216.*

Valle de Azapa

A highly recommended excursion is up the Azapa Valley, a beautiful oasis east of Arica. Several groups of geoglyphs of humans and llamas can be seen to the south of the road.

Border crossing: Chile–Peru

Chacalluta–Santa Rosa

The border is 20 km north of Arica along the Pan-American Highway. There are no exchange facilities at the border.

Chilean immigration at Chacalluta, is open Sunday to Thursday 0800-2400, 24 hours Friday and Saturday. Immigration is usually fairly uncomplicated, although crossing the border into Peru with a hire car is difficult: make sure you have the correct papers.

The **Peruvian border post** at Santa Rosa is open daily 0900-2200. Drivers entering Chile are required to file a form, Relaciones de Pasajeros, giving details of passengers, obtained from a stationery store in Tacna, or at the border in a booth near Customs. You must also present the original registration document for your car from its country of registration. The first checkpoints outside Arica on the road to Santiago also require the Relaciones de Pasajeros form.

Tacna is 36 km north of the border. The city was in Chilean hands from 1880 to 1929, when its citizens voted by plebiscite to return to Peru. There is a wide variety of hotels and restaurants here, as well as exchange facilities and bus and air services to the rest of Peru. Many Chileans travel to Tacna for optical and dental treatment, which is much cheaper than in Chile, but of dubious quality. For more information, see: www.turismotacna.com.

Note that between September and April Peru is one hour behind Chile (the date of the time change differs annually).

At Km 12 is the **Museo Arqueológico San Miguel de Azapa** ① *T058-220 5555, www.uta.cl/masma, Jan-Feb daily 0900-2000, Mar-Dec daily 1000-1800, US$5*, part of the University of Tarapacá and well worth a visit. Set in a pleasant, shady part of the valley, the museum contains a fine collection of pre-Columbian tools, weaving, pottery, woodcarving and basket work from the coast and the valleys as well as four mummified humans from the Chinchorro culture (8000-10,000 BC), the most ancient mummies yet discovered. In the final room there is an exhibition about the olive oil produced in the valley, including a huge old press. In the forecourt of the museum are several boulders with pre-Columbian petroglyphs and opposite is a garden full of tropical plants and birds. Comprehensive explanations are provided by booklets in English, French, German and Spanish, loaned free at the entrance. Most multi-day tours to the Altiplano make a stop here on the way up or you can take a yellow *colectivo* from P Lynch y Chacabuco and 600 block of P Lynch in Arica for US$1.50.

In the nearby village of San Miguel, there are several restaurants with a wide range of prices. The village cemetery is worth a visit, its simple, well-maintained graves protected from the sun by roofs and awnings and decorated with plastic flowers are a stark reminder of the unique conditions here. If you have the energy, a good walk is to climb the desert hill behind the valley, 45 minutes, giving wonderful views of the green oasis and the desolation beyond – running back down the hill takes three minutes and is an exhilarating experience. On the opposite side of the valley at San Lorenzo are the ruins of a *pukará* (pre-Inca fortress) dating from the 12th century.

Lluta Valley

Route 11 turns off the Pan-American Highway, 12 km north of Arica and runs through the Lluta Valley to the Bolivian border at Chungará (see box, page 216). The **Geoglifos de Lluta** – four groups of geoglyphs representing llamas and humans – can be seen on the hillsides between Km 14 and Km 16. At Km 35 at Poconchile there is a Hari Krishna community offering accommodation and good vegetarian food. Further on, at Km 73 is a *centro magnético*, an optical illusion that makes the climbing road seem as if it going downhill. There is a stunning mirador overlooking Copaquilla at Km 89. At Km 90, there is a pre-Inca *pukará* (fortress) and, a few kilometres further, is an Inca tambo (inn). Turn off at Km 99 for the village of Belén, which was founded by the Spanish in 1625 on the silver route between Potosí and the coast. It has two colonial churches: the **Iglesia de Belén** is one of the oldest (and smallest) churches in Chile; the other, the **Iglesia de Carmen**, dates from the 18th century. There are many pre-Hispanic ruins in the area, with four *pukarás* and a well-preserved stretch of the Camino del Inca. (South of Belén a poor road continues through **Tignamar and Tignamar Viejo**, where there is another colonial church, to Codpa; see page 203.)

The village of **Socoroma**, meanwhile, lies 9 km up the Lluta Valley, 4 km north of the main road, at an altitude of 3000 m. It is a pretty Aymara settlement with a well-ordered plaza and bright flowers. The traditional straw and leather roofs, which were havens for the bug that causes Chagas disease, have been replaced with corrugated zinc, making the houses look rather odd. Past Socoroma the road continues to Putre (see page 218).

◉ Arica and around listings

For hotel and restaurant price codes and other relevant information, see pages 14-21.

● Where to stay

Arica *p208, map p209*
For apartment rental on the beach, see local newspapers.
$$$$ Arica, San Martín 599, about 2 km along shore (frequent micros and *colectivos*), T058-225 4540, www.panamericana hoteles.cl. 4-star, best, price depends on season, decent restaurant, tennis court, pool, lava beach (not safe for swimming).
$$$ Americano, General Lagos 571, T058-225 7752, www.hotelamericano.cl. Airy, spacious rooms, pleasant patio, rooms on upper floor have views to the Morro. Gym and sauna (extra charge).
$$ Hostal Jardín del Sol, Sotomayor 848, T058-223 2795, www.hostaljardindelsol.cl. Comfortable, beds with duvets, good value, bike hire. Large kitchen area (US$1 charge).

$$ Sunny Days, Tomás Aravena 161 (a little over halfway along P de Valdivia, 800 m from bus terminal, transport to hotel), T058-224 1038, www.sunny-days-arica.cl. Run by a New Zealander and his Chilean wife. Rooms with shared or private bath, English spoken, cosy atmosphere, lots of info, book exchange, bike rental. Convenient for the beach. One of the best hostels in the north of Chile.
$$-$ La Ponderosa Beach House Inn, Av Las Dunas, north of town, T09-6539 4445, www.chilloutbeachhouse.com. Ocean-front hotel with surfer dorms and private rooms. Restaurant, laundry service, Wi-Fi, guest kitchen, barbecue areas and rental of sports equipment. Pick-up service from airport, bus terminal and town centre. Camper garage with showers and toilets. All bookings taken online.
$$-$ Maison de France, Aurelio Valdivieso 152, pob Chinchorro, T058-222 3463, atchumturist@hotmail.com. Owned

by Frenchman Cristian, good meals, information on tours and self-guided trips, convenient for beach and nightlife.
$$-$ Residencial América, Sotomayor 430, T058-225 4148, www.residencialamerica. com. Variety of room sizes, shared or private bath, hospitable, good value.
$$-$ Surf House, O'Higgins 661, T058-231 2213, www.aricasurfhouse.cl. Surfers' hostel (the owner also runs a surf school), decent beds and showers, large common areas.
$ Hostal Pacífico, Gen Lagos 672, T058-225 1616, hostalpacifico672@hotmail.com. Good option in the city centre, private of shared bath.

Valle de Azapa *p210*
$$$ Saucache, Sánchez 621, Valle de Azapa, T058-224 1458. Fully equipped *cabañas*, sleep 2 or 4.
$$$ Sol de Arica, Avalos 2041, T058-224 6050, www.hotelsoldearica.cl. Set in large grounds on the edge of the city on the way to Azapa. Sauna, jacuzzi, pool. Recommended.

🍴 Restaurants

Arica *p208, map p209*
Many good places on 21 de Mayo offering meals, drinks, real coffee, juices and outdoor seating.
$$$ Don Floro, V MacKenna 847, T058-223 1481. Good seafood, steaks and Peruvian specialities, good service, popular, cosy little place.
$$$ Los Aleros del 21, 21 de Mayo 736, T058-225 4641. One of the city's longest-established restaurants, specializing in southern Chilean cuisine, large portions, lots of pork dishes.
$$$ Maracuyá, San Martín 0321, at the northern end of Playa El Laucho south of the centre, T058-222 7600. Arica's premier restaurant specializing in fish and seafood. Expensive, but worth it. Has a sports bar on the top floor.

$$ Chifa El Mesón, Santa María 1364. One of several good-value Chinese restaurants in the area. Generous portions and clean kitchen.
$$ Cyclo Public, Diego Portales 1364, T058-226 2098. Open from 2030. Fashionable seafood and pasta restaurant, vegetarian options, reasonably priced.
$$ El Rey del Marisco, Colón 565, p 2, T058-222 9232. Seafood specialities. A timeless sort of place, in business for 35 years, very good.
$$ Mata Rangi, on the pier. Good food in fishy environment, good-value *menú de casa*.
$$-$ Café-Restaurant e B, 21 de Mayo 233. Very good, extensive menu including seafood.
$$-$ Ostión Dorado, Playa Corazones. A small shack selling fabulous *empanadas* and other super-fresh seafood.
$ Evergreen, Baquedano entre O'Higgins y Maipú. Lunch only, vegetarian with good menu options and lots of fruit drinks. They also sell tofu and dried mushrooms.
$ La Bomba, Colón 357, at fire station, T058-225 5626. Good value *almuerzo* and friendly service.
$ Mercado Colón, Maipú y Colón. Several stalls offering tasty good-value lunches and fresh juices.

Valle de Azapa *p210*
$$ La Picada del Muertito, Los Yaganes s/n, by the cemetery, San Miguel de Azapa, T058-226 4189. Closes 2100. Known as the best traditional restaurant in the valley. Simple no-frills decor, famed for its *pastel de choclo*, but many other options. Fills up on Sun with locals. You won't go hungry here unless you are a vegetarian. Recommended.
$$ Las Tejas de Azapa, Km 1.5, No 4301, T058-224 6817. *Parrillada* and other options.

🍷 Bars and clubs

Arica *p208, map p209*
Chill Out, 18 Sep y Lynch. Open till 0400, doesn't get going until 2400, popular bar. Also **Bar Central**, next door.

Soho, Buenos Aires 209, Playa Chinchorro, T09-8905 1806. Opens at 1800, closed Wed. Pub, bar, nightclub, see Facebook for special nights.

Valle de Azapa *p210*
Several options, all around 3-4 km out of town. Open weekends, usually from late in the evening.

🎭 Entertainment

Arica *p208, map p209*
Teatro Municipal de Arica, Baquedano 234. Wide variety of theatrical and musical events, as well as exhibitions.

🎉 Festivals

Arica *p208, map p209*
End-Jan/Feb Con la Fuerza del Sol, a festival of Andean dance and music that is a slightly more debauched version of the festival at La Tirana, www.aricafuerzadelsol.cl.
Jun Festival of Arica and the national cueca dance championships.
7 Jun Anniversary of the Chilean victory in the **Battle of the Morro**, with parties and fireworks.
29 Jun San Pedro, religious service at fishing wharf and boat parades.
1st weekend of Oct Virgen de las Peñas, pilgrimage to the site of the Virgin, some 90 km inland near Livilcar.

🛍 Shopping

Arica *p208, map p209*
Calle 21 de Mayo is pedestrianized, with many shops, restaurants and internet cafés. **Feria Turística Dominical** is a Sun market, along Chacabuco between Valásquez and Mackenna, mostly bric a brac. **Mercado Central**, Sotomayor y Sangra, between Colón and Baquedano. Mostly fruit and vegetables, mornings only. A smaller fruit and veg market, with food stalls, is on Colón between 18 de Septiembre and Maipú.

Poblado Artesanal, Plaza Las Gredas, Hualles 2825 (take bus 2, 3 or 7). Craft shop that's expensive but especially good for musical instruments, Tue-Sun 0930-1300, 1530-1930, peña Fri and Sat 2130; shop not always open out of season.

⚙ What to do

Arica *p208, map p209*
Surfing
There's good surfing at **Playa Las Machas** (good waves, relatively few people) and **Playa Chinchorro**, north of the city (good for beginners), and at **La Ex Isla Alacrán**, see www.arica-info.com. **La Ponderosa Beach House Inn**, see above, north of town near Playa Las Machas and the Lluta estuary, has surf shop, equipment rental, kitesurfing. Also for surfing lessons and equipment rental, try **Magic Chile Surf School**, T058-231 1120, www.surfschool.cl. English spoken, best to call before 0900.

Swimming
Olympic pool in **Parque Centenario**, Tue-Sat. Take No 5A bus from 18 de Septiembre. The best beach for swimming is **Playa Chinchorro**, north of town (bus 24). Buses 7 and 8 run to beaches south of town – the first 2 beaches, **La Lisera** and **El Laucho**, are both small and mainly for sunbathing. **Playa Brava** is not good for swimming due to dangerous currents.

Tour operators
Clinamen Safaris y Expediciones, Sotomayor 361, piso 2, T058-231 3289, www.clinamen.cl. Bespoke small-group expeditions (maximum 3 people) to the Altiplano. Guide Christian Rolf speaks fluent Spanish, English, German and French.
Latinorizons, Bolognesi 449, T058-225 0007, www.latinorizons.com. Specializes in tours to Parque Nacional Lauca and the Altiplano, small groups in 4WD; also tourist train rides from Arica, bike rental, not cheap, but good. Also run hostel in Putre.

Parinacota Expeditions, Thompson y Bolognesi, T058-225 6227, www. parinacotaexpediciones.cl. One of the oldest operators in Arica for Altiplano tours. **Raíces Andinas**, Héroes del Morro 632, T058-223 3305, www.raicesandinas.com. Specializes in Altiplano trips, English spoken. **Suma Inti**, Gonzalo Cerda 1366, T058-222 5685, www.sumainti.cl. Tours to the Altiplano.

⊖ Transport

Arica *p208, map p209*
Air
Flights to **Santiago**, **LAN** and **Sky** (daily) via Iquique and, less frequently, Antofagasta. To **Lima**, **LanPerú** and others from Tacna (Peru), enquire at travel agencies in Arica.

Bus
Bus company offices at the bus terminal include **Pullman**, T058-222 3837, and **Tur-Bus**, T058-224 1059.

To **Iquique**, frequent, US$10, 4½ hrs, also *colectivos*, several companies, all in the terminal. To **Antofagasta**, US$20-32, 11 hrs. To **Calama**, 10 hrs, US$25, several companies, all depart 2000-2200. To **San Pedro de Atacama**, 2200, 11½ hrs, US$35-55. To **La Serena**, 23 hrs, US$40-75. To **Santiago**, 30 hrs, a number of companies, US$76-98 (most serve meals of a kind, somewhat better on the more expensive services; student discounts available). To **Viña del Mar** and **Valparaíso**, 29 hrs, US$55.

To **Putre**, **La Paloma** (Flota Paco) buses leave from Germán Riesco 2071, T058-222 2710 (bus U from centre) daily 0700, 3-4 hrs, US$6, returning from La Paloma supermarket in Putre at 1400 (book in advance as the bus is often full – beware overcharging and note that drivers may be overworked); also **Gutiérez**, Esteban Ríos 2140, T058-222 9338, depart Arica Mon, Wed, Fri 0700, return same days at 1700. **Note** if you take an Arica–La Paz bus for Putre, it is 3 km from

the crossroads to the town at some 4000 m; hitching from here is usually easy with the army or *carabineros*, but to walk is tough if you've come straight up from sea level. **Buses La Paloma** (see above) also run a service to Belén, but not every day.

To **Peru** *Colectivos* run from the international bus terminal on Diego Portales to **Tacna**, US$4 pp, 1½ hrs. There are many companies and you will be besieged by drivers. For quickest service take a Peruvian *colectivo* heading back to Peru. Give your passport to the *colectivo* office where your papers will be filled. After that, drivers take care of all the paperwork. There are also buses from the same terminal, US$2, 1 hr longer than journey by *colectivo*. For **Arequipa** it is best to go to Tacna and catch an onward bus there.

To **Bolivia** There are daily buses between Arica and **La Paz**, via the border towns of **Chungará** (Chile) and **Tambo Quemado** (Bolivia), 8-10 hrs: **Buses Cuevas** depart 0**900**, 0300, US$14-18; **Pullman** departs 1000, US16.50. If you are going to Putre, these will drop you off 3 km away.

Car hire
A 4WD is required for road trips to the **Altiplano**, see Behind the wheel, page 195, for precautions and tips. Hire companies include: **American**, Gen Lagos 559, T058-225 7752, servturi@entelchile.net; **Cactus**, Baquedano 635, T058-225 7430, cactusrent@latinmail.com; **Hertz**, Baquedano 999, T058-223 1487, and at airport, good service; **Klasse**, Velásquez 760, piso 2, Loc 25, T058-225 4498, good deals. Several others at Chacalluta airport.

Hitchhiking
Trucks from Arica to La Paz sometimes give lifts, a good place to try is at the Poconchile control point, 37 km from Arica, but to get to this point can cost more than taking a direct bus from the terminal.

Border crossings: Chile–Bolivia

There are two routes from Arica to the Bolivian border.

Chungará–Tambo Quemada

Route 11 (paved as far as La Paz, although seriously worn in places by overloaded juggernauts) turns off the Pan-American Highway, 12 km north of Arica and runs through the Lluta Valley (see page 212) via Putre and the Parque Nacional Lauca to the border at Chungará. This is the route followed by most transport to Bolivia, including buses and trucks. It is a relatively speedy crossing, but very cold; if you're travelling by bus, take a blanket or sleeping bag, food, water and a sense of humour. Estimated driving time from Arica to La Paz is six hours.
Chilean immigration is at Chungará, 7 km west of the border, daily 0800-2000.
Bolivian immigration and customs is at Tambo Quemado, 7 km east of the border, also daily 0800-2000.

Over the border, Route 108 passes through the **Parque Nacional Sajama**, which covers 60,000 ha and contains the world's highest forest, consisting mainly of the rare queñal tree (polylepis tarapacana), which survives at altitudes of up to 5200 m. The scenery is wonderful and includes views of three volcanos: Parinacota (6348 m) and Pomerape (6282 m), both of which are on the border, and Sajama (6530 m), which is Bolivia's highest peak, but can be seen from Lauca national park. Park administration is at Sajama village, 14 km off Route 108 (altitude 4200 m), where there is basic accommodation. There is also accommodation at **Carahuara de Carangas**, 111 km northeast of Tambo Quemado, and at **Patacamaya**, 104 km south of La Paz, where Route 108 joins the main Oruro–La Paz highway. Note that Route 108 is unpaved and should not be attempted in wet weather.

Visviri–Charaña

A minor road from Arica follows the La Paz–Arica railway line east and then north to Visviri (altitude 4069 m), 3 km from the Bolivian border and 12 km from Peru (no crossing). Cheap accommodation is available in Visviri at **Alojamiento Aranda**.

Chilean immigration in Visviri, T058-224 1322, is open daily 0800-2000.
Bolivian immigration is at **Charaña**, just over the border. There is a charge of US$2 for crossing with a private vehicle, Monday to Friday 1300-1500 and 1850-2000 and all day on Saturday, Sunday and holidays. There is no fuel or accommodation in Charaña, although there is a local barter market every other Friday. Two routes, both poor, continue from Charaña towards La Paz, both of which meet at **Viacha**.

❶ Directory

Arica p208, map p209
Banks Many Redbanc ATMs on 21 de Mayo and by Plaza Colón. Money changers on 21 de Mayo and its junction with Colón, some accept TCs. **Consulates** Bolivia, P Lynch 298, T058-258 3390, colivian_arica@yahoo.es. Peru, Av 18 de Setiembre 1554, T058-223 1020, conperarica@terra.cl.
Language classes SW Academia de Artes y Lenguas, 21 de Mayo 483, p 3, T058-225 8645, www.spanishinchile.blogspot.com. Chilean/British school.

Altiplano national parks

In the Andes and stretching from the border with Bolivia, Parque Nacional Lauca is one of the most spectacular national parks in Chile. Declared a Biosphere Reserve by UNESCO, it is renowned for its bird life, but is equally remarkable for the extraordinary views of snow-capped volcanoes set against the backdrop of Lago Chungará, one of the world's highest lakes, and the profusion of vicuñas and viscachas that live here. The brilliant quality of the light gives colours an intensity that is not easily forgotten and there are many deserted tracks across the Altiplano that provide a unique sense of the space and beauty of one of the world's last great wildernesses.

South of Parque Nacional Lauca are three further parks, covering areas of the western range of the Andes. They are best visited from Arica or Putre, as this permits acclimatization (Colchane and Enquelga, the alternatives, are too high). Furthermore, during the winter months, moving from north to south means you will not have the sun in your eyes as you travel. Tours in this area, lasting two or four days, can be arranged in Putre; guides charge a fixed price per vehicle per day, so for groups of three or four, arranging a tour from here can be better value than from Arica.

Arriving in the Altiplano national parks
Getting there and around Access to Parque Nacional Lauca is easy as Route 11, the main Arica–La Paz road, runs through the park. In January and February, during the rainy season, and in August, when snowfall can occur, some roads in the park may be impassable; check in advance with **CONAF** or with the *carabineros* in Arica or Putre. If you're heading for Putre, buses on the Arica–La Paz route will drop passengers at the crossroads, 3 km from the village, at some 4000 m; hitching from here is usually easy with the army or carabineros, but to walk is tough if you've come straight up from sea level. Maps are available from the **Instituto Geográfico Militar** in Santiago. Much of the water in the park is drinkable but you should take bottled water as well.

Parque Nacional Lauca → *For listings, see pages 221-224.*

Situated 145 km east of Arica, the park covers 137,883 ha and includes a large lake, **Lago Chungará**, a system of smaller lakes, the **Lagunas Cotacotani**, and lava fields. Ranging in altitude from 3200 m to four peaks of over 6000 m, Lauca brings significant risks of *soroche*, or altitude sickness (unless you are coming from Bolivia). Because of this, it is best to ascend to the Altiplano in stages, spending a night in Putre before going on to Lago Chungará; one-day tours from Arica are not the best way of seeing the park.

Often, when ascending from Arica, it may seem as though the weather is overcast; but vehicles soon gain altitude, climbing through the mist into a sort of lost world above, where the sky is a piercing blue and you can gaze down at the grey clouds huddled in the valley as if looking into a different plane of reality.

Putre

Putre is a scenic Aymará village, 15 km west of the park entrance at 3500 m, and provides an ideal base for exploring and acclimatization. Situated at the base of **Volcán Tarapacá** (known as Nevadas de Putre in Spanish; 5824 m), it is surrounded by terracing dating from pre-Inca times, which is now used for cultivating alfalfa and oregano. It has a church dating from 1670. The main street, Baquedano, has several shops, restaurants and *residenciales*, and there is a tourist information office on the plaza that will help arrange tours (some English is spoken) but is otherwise not particularly useful. There is also an office of **CONAF** ① *Teniente del Campo 301, T058-258 5704 (in Arica), Mon-Fri 0830-1730*, which provides information on the parks as well as bookings for the CONAF *refugios* on the Altiplano.

The village, with a population of 1200, is a good centre for hiking: an extensive network of trails lead to numerous villages in the mountains, which provide great opportunities to explore, for those with the necessary time and fitness. In the vicinity are four archaeological sites with cave paintings up to 6000 years old. About 11 km east by road are the hot springs of **Jurasi** ① *US$2*, with very hot water, a red mud bath and views of vicuñas and alpacas. Transport can be organized in Putre. Weather can be poor in January and February, with fog and rain.

Exploring the park

From Putre, the road continues to climb and soon enters the park. Some 23 km from Putre is the *sector* **Las Cuevas**, where there is a path and a wooden bridge leading to some rustic thermal springs with water at 40°C. Vizcachas are a common sight. Near here there is a turning south past a *chaku* (corral for llamas) to Cerro El Milagro, a hill ablaze with an incredible range of colours. Back on the main road, past the Cuevas there is a CONAF ranger station.

Parinacota (4392 m), a small village of whitewashed adobe houses, lies 26 km into the park and 41 km from Putre on two ancient trading routes, one from Potosí to Arica and the other from Belén into Bolivia. Today, an unpaved road heads north from Parinacota 90 km to the Bolivian border at Visviri (see box, page 216). The village's interesting 17th-century **church** – rebuilt in 1789 – has frescoes, silver religious objects and the skulls of past priests. Señor Sipriano keeps the key: ask for him at the kiosks and make sure you leave a donation. The **CONAF office** ① *daily 0830-1730*, which administers the national park is also here and maintains a nature trail that covers most plant and bird habitats, beginning at the pond and ending back in the village. **Cerro Guaneguane** (5300 m) can be climbed from Parinacota; ask one of the villagers to accompany you as a guide (and pay them). There is also a path to the **Lagunas de Cotacotani**, a walk that would make a good day hike. There is a small shop in Parinacota with basic supplies, but most of the handicrafts sold here are from Bolivia or Peru: a better place to buy locally made products is **Chucuyo**, 36 km further east, where local residents weave and knit from their own high-quality alpaca wool.

Some 20 km southeast of Parinacota is **Lago Chungará**, one of the highest lakes in the world, at 4512 m, a must for its views of the Parinacota, Pomerape, Sajama and Guallatiri

Wildlife of Lauca National Park

Although the park lies very close to the Atacama Desert, its altitude ensures it receives more rain, which creates a fairyland of volcanoes and highland lakes surrounded by brilliant-green wetlands and vast expanses of puna grassland. The Río Lauca rises near Lago Chungará, then laces slowly through the park leaving marshy cushion bogs and occasional raceways and providing an array of habitats for the varied wildlife of the Altiplano.

The **camelids** are the stars of the park; thousands of domesticated llamas and alpacas, as well as the dainty, graceful, wild vicuña, which now number over 18,000. The charming viscacha, seemingly a long-tailed rabbit, but in fact belonging to the chinchilla family, can be seen perched sleepily on the rocks in the mornings, backside toward the rising sun. Pumas, huemules (deer), foxes, skunks and armadillos are the more elusive **mammals**, some nocturnal, occupying the more remote reaches.

Lauca **birdlife** is spectacular, with over 120 species either resident or migrant here. Lago Chungará is home to more than 8000

giant coots, distinguished by their bright orange legs, never-ending nest building and primordial cackling. In addition to coots, ducks and grebes, the wetlands provide a fine habitat for the puna plover, the rare diademed sandpiper plover, the puna ibis, Andean species of avocet, goose and gull, and an assortment of migratory shorebirds. Occasionally, three species of flamingo can be seen at once: the Andean, the James (locally called *parinas*) and the more common Chilean flamingo.

Trips through the drier grasslands can produce glimpses of the puna tinamou, always in groups of three, and the puna rhea, seen in October and November with 20 or 30 miniatures scooting along behind. Passerines occupy all the habitats in the park, some to 5000 m and above. There are also Sierra finches, black siskins, earthcreepers, miners, canasteros, cinclodes, tit-spinetails – new names for most birders. And in the skies above, keep your eyes peeled for Andean condors, mountain caracaras, aplomado falcons, black-chested buzzard eagles and buteo hawks.

---

volcanoes. Overlooking the lake is a CONAF *refugio* and campsite; vicuñas, llamas and alpacas can be seen grazing nearby. From here, it is 3 km to the Chilean passport control point at Chungará and 10 km to the Bolivian border at Tambo Quemado. ▸▸ *See page 216 for border crossing information.*

Heading south → *For listings, see pages 221-224.*

A dirt road (A235) turns south off the Arica–La Paz highway, 1 km east of the **Las Cuevas** park-ranger post. It is signed to Chilcaya and Colchane and ends at Huara on the Pan-American Highway, near Iquique (see page 201). There is no public transport on this route, and between Las Cuevas and Isluga the only traffic you will see is the occasional tour group and the odd truck from the Borax plant (see below). The road is open all year round, but between December and February and in August it may be impassable because of deep mud and water, which can wash out the bridges. If you are planning to travel then, you will find a spade useful. Although many maps show roads descending from the Altiplano from Surire to the Pan-American Highway and from Colchane to Camiña, do not be tempted to follow them; they are in a terrible condition and if stranded you could wait weeks for help to arrive. See also Behind the wheel, page 195.

Acclimatization for the Altiplano

Unless you are entering Chile from Bolivia, the high altitude of the Altiplano encountered in the national parks presents specific health problems for the traveller. The risks should not be underestimated; anyone with circulation or respiratory problems should avoid the area.

One-day trips to the national park from Arica cannot really be recommended, either for health or for enjoyment: what should be an unforgettable trip amid incredible scenery can become an unpleasant endurance exercise in a minibus full of passengers all suffering from the dreaded *soroche* (altitude sickness). Instead, visitors to the park are advised to spend at least one night, preferably more, in Putre before moving on to higher altitudes.

To minimize symptoms of altitude sickness the following tips should be followed during the day before the climb to the Altiplano:

• Eat plain food, avoiding anything that could be hard to digest, such as shellfish, dairy products or rich sauces.

• Do not drink any fizzy drinks or excessive alcohol. A glass of wine is fine but travelling to the Altiplano with a hangover is a recipe for disaster.
• Take lip balm, sunblock, a sun hat, woolly hat and windproof clothing with you.

Once you're at altitude, you can avoid getting that familiar headache associated with soroche by doing the following:

• Drink lots of water and/or *mate de coca* to compensate for the loss of body fluid.
• Take it easy, limiting exercise, especially for the first day.
• Avoid smoking and take steps to get as much fresh air as possible, particularly if spending the night in a *refugio*.
• In popular *refugios* there can be six to 10 people breathing the same air all night in a small room: to avoid the 0300 headache that often develops in such conditions leave a window open and keep the water bottle nearby. Sleeplessness is a common first-night problem but is not a cause for concern.

Reserva Nacional Las Vicuñas

Split off from Parque Nacional Lauca in order to permit mining, this reserve, reached by Route A235 (entrance free), stretches across 209,131 ha, most of it rolling Altiplano at an average altitude of 4300 m. The reserve is bisected by the Río Lauca, along which riverine vegetation alternates with *puna tola* (an upland plant) and grasslands, and many camelids can be seen. Keep an eye open, too, for condors, rheas and migrating peregrine falcons. **Mina Choquelimpie** (not operating), one of the world's highest gold and silver mines, can be reached by a 7-km detour (clearly marked) off Route A235. The park administration is in **Guallatiri**, a village 96 km south of Las Cuevas at the foot of the smoking Guallatiri Volcano (6060 m); the village has a lovely 17th-century Altiplano church and a *carabinero* control post.

Monumento Natural Salar de Surire

At Km 139, the road reaches the Salar de Surire, situated at 4300 m and covering 17,500 ha. The Salar de Surire is a desolate, spectacular drying salt lake split into two sections. The first, with windy and sulphurous thermal springs (together with a picnic site) and a year-round population of 12,000 to 15,000 flamingos of three species (nesting season is January) is protected and administered by CONAF. It is open all year, but see advice above.

Administration is in **Surire**, 45 km south of Guallatiri and 138 km south of Putre. The other half of the *salar* is mined for borax; sometimes Surire may be reached by getting a ride in a borax truck from Zapahuira, a road junction at Km 100 on the road from Arica to La Paz.

Parque Nacional Volcán Isluga

ⓘ *Park administration at Enquelga, 10 km north of the entrance, no entry fee but see Where to stay below for prices at the refugio.*

This park includes some of the best volcanic scenery of northern Chile and covers 174,744 ha at altitudes above 2100 m. Peaks over 5000 m in the park are Volcán Isluga (5501 m), Quimsachata (5400 m), Tatajachura (5252 m) and Latamara (5207 m). Wildlife varies according to altitude; there are large numbers of camelids and birds but fewer than in Parque Nacional Lauca. Although the lower parts of the park, at its southwestern end, lie in the hills of the *precordillera*, the heart of the park is situated between **Laguna Aravilla**, with its flamingos, and the village of **Isluga**, where there is a beautiful 18th-century Andean church and bell tower. Route A235 crosses the park, from the northern entrance, 40 km south of Surire, to the southern near Isluga. Northeast of Isluga under the **volcano** is the village of **Enquelga**, where Aymaran weavers can be seen working in the sand behind wooden wind breaks. This is also the location of the park administration. Just 1 km south of the village is a turn-off to some warm natural thermal springs with changing rooms and a picnic area.

South of the park is the border village of Colchane (see box, page 203) with basic services and transport from both Iquique (1300 and 2100 daily) and Oruro in Bolivia. From here a mostly good road runs southwest 180 km to join the *Panamericana* at Huara. Alternatively a *ripio* road continues south. After 20 km or so there is a turning to the right leading to a hill of giant *Cardón* cactuses. Towering up to 8 m, they flower in September and produce an edible fruit, like a cross between a kiwi and a prickly pear. The road south passes the village of Cariquima and continues on to **Lirima** through a pass at over 5000 m. This road is new and may not be marked on some maps, but has some of the most spectacular views of the Altiplano over the shrubland below. Lodging is available in Lirima, and there are thermal springs 6 km west, with accommodation with a thermal pool in each room. The road from Lirima continues south for 53 km, with microplants turning the flat terrain a radioactive green, before arriving at the **Salar de Huasco**. On the west side there is a radio station in contact with Iquique, and a *refugio* has been built. The view of the sun or full moon rising here is spectacular. In theory it is possible to continue south on the Altiplano to Ollagüe and on to San Pedro, but there are also decent roads west to Pica or Pozo Almonte.

⦿ Altiplano national parks listings

For hotel and restaurant price codes and other relevant information, see pages 14-21.

⦿ Where to stay

Note that many 'villages' marked on maps in the Altiplano are uninhabited. Do not expect even the most basic services. CONAF *refugios* should be booked and paid for in advance in the regional office

in Arica, T058-201201. CONAF *refugios* do not provide sheets or blankets.

Putre *p218*
$$ Kukulí, Canto y Baquedano, T09-9161 4709, www.translapaloma.cl. 10 decent rooms with bath, in town.
$$ La Chakana, Cochrane s/n, T09-9745 9519, www.la-chakana.com. Cabins on the edge of town sleep up to 4, private

bath, with pleasant views, English spoken, good breakfast, lots of hiking and mountaineering info, tours, involved with social projects, Aymara museum on site. A good choice.

$$ Terrace Lodge & Tours, Circunvalación, T058-258 4275, www.terracelodge.com. Small lodge with café, 5 rooms, heating, comfortable, helpful owner, Flavio, runs excellent tours by car, pick-up from Arica can be arranged.

$$-$ Hostal Cali, Baquedano 399, T09-8536 1242, krlos_team@hotmail.com. Private or shared bath, pleasant, no heating, warm water, good restaurant, supermarket. Also has transport to Bolivia.

$$-$ Hostal Pachamama, Lord Cochrane s/n y Parinacota, T058- 258 5814, www. hostalpachamama.cl. Rooms sleep up to 3, shared bath, or self-contained cabin sleeps 5. Pleasant inner courtyard, basic rooms.

$$-$ Parinacota Trek, Baquedano 501, T056-9282 6194, www.parinacotatrek.cl. Hostel rooms and dorm, private or shared bath, washing machine, parking, open all year, near La Paloma and Gutiérrez buses. Also has travel agency for tours and treks throughout the region.

$$-$ Residencial La Paloma, O'Higgins 353, T09-9197 9319, www.translapaloma.cl. Some rooms with bath, hot showers after 0800 unless requested, no heating but lots of blankets, good food in large, warm restaurant, indoor parking; supermarket opposite.

Camping

Sra Clementina Cáceres, blue door on C Lynch, allows camping in her garden and offers lunch.

Parque Nacional Lauca *p217*
The **CONAF** office at Lago Chungará has 4 beds which may be available for visitors. Advance booking in Arica is essential, or ask at the Parinacota or Putre offices. Accommodation is available with various families in Parinacota; ask at the food and

artesanía stands. You can also camp behind the **CONAF** office for free, great site.

Reserva Nacional Las Vicuñas *p220*
There is accommodation for up to 7 people at the park administration in Guallatiri, T058-225 0570, www.conaf.cl/parques/ reserva-nacional-las-vicunas/. Imperative to reserve at least 5 days in advance or you will find it closed.

$ Sra Clara Blanca, 1 km east off A235, 10 km after Chuquelimpie turn-off. Price per person. An Aymaran weaver offers overnight accommodation, food typical of the region and allows travellers to help with llamas and alpacas.

Monumento Natural Salar de Surire *p220*
At Surire, the **CONAF** office has 4 beds available, prior application to **CONAF** in Arica is essential.

Parque Nacional Volcán Isluga *p221*
$ CONAF refugio, Encuelga. 8 beds, US$9.50 pp, and cooking facilities, reservation advised, contact **CONAF**, T057-243 2085, tarapaca.oirs@conaf.cl.

There are also several basic *residenciales* in Colchane, which lies 6 km south of the southern entrance.

❼ Restaurants

Putre *p218*
$ Kuchamarka, Baquedano between La Paloma supermarket and Hostal Cali. Popular, good value, specializes in local dishes, including alpaca, as well as vegetarian options.

⊛ Festivals

Putre *p218*
Nov Feria de la Voz Andina takes place every year, attracting top Andean groups, as well as cultural exhibitions. If going, book accommodation in advance.

○ Shopping

Parque Nacional Lauca *p217*
Buy all food for the park in Putre, which has markets where bottled water, fresh bread, vegetables, meat, cheese and canned foods can be obtained. Fuel (both petrol and diesel) is available from the **Cali** and **Paloma** supermarkets; expect to pay a premium. **Sra Daria Condori**'s shop on O'Higgins sells locally made *artesanía* and naturally coloured alpaca wool. Other than a small shop with limited supplies in Parinacota, no food is available outside Putre. Take drinking water with you as water in the park is not safe.

○ What to do

Parque Nacional Lauca *p217*
One-day tours are offered by most tour operators and some hotels in Arica, daily in season, according to demand at other times, but some find the minibuses cramped and dusty. You spend all day in the bus (0730-2030) and you will almost certainly suffer from soroche. You can leave the tour and continue another day as long as you ensure that the company will collect you when you want (tour companies try to charge double for this). Much better are 1½-day tours, leaving Arica at 1400 and arriving back at 1800 the following day (eg **Latinorizons**). These include a night in Putre and a stop on the ascent at the Aymara village of Socoroma. For 5 or more, the most economical proposition is to hire a vehicle.

Climbing
Aug-Nov is best season for mountain climbing; permits are needed for summits near borders. Either go to the governor's office in Putre, or contact **Dirección Nacional de Fronteras y Límites del Estado (DIFROL)**, Teatinos 180, piso 7, Santiago, T02-2827 5900, www.difrol.cl, in advance, listing the mountains you wish to climb.

Putre *p218*
Alto Andino Nature Tours, Baquedano 299 (Correo Putre) T09-9890 7291, www.birdingaltoandino.com. Specialist private birdwatching tours of the area and also walking tours along the Camino del Inca. All tours personalized and customized, English spoken, owner is an American biologist/naturalist.
Parinacota Trek, see Where to stay, above.
Tour Andino, C Baquedano 340, T09-9011 0702, www.tourandino.com. Comfortable 4WD tours from 1 to 4 days with Justino Jirón (owner) to Lauca and other areas, excellent, knowledgeable, flexible.

○ Transport

Parque Nacional Lauca *p217*
Bus
To **Arica**, **La Paloma** buses, T058-222 2710, leave from La Paloma supermarket in Putre daily 1400 (book in advance as the bus is often full – beware overcharging and note that drivers may be overworked); also **Gutiérez** buses from Putre, T058-222 9338, Mon, Wed, Fri 1700. **Hostal Cali** (see Where to stay) runs buses from Putre to Bolivia. Otherwise, a bus to **La Paz** from the Putre crossroads (3 km from the village) or from Lago Chungará can be arranged in Arica (same fare as from Arica).

Car
For 5 or more, the most economical proposition is to hire a vehicle in Arica to explore the Altiplano but bear in mind that driving in this area is a serious undertaking. See Behind the wheel, page 195, for precautions and tips. Remember that, if you wish to cross into Bolivia, you will need a permit from the hire company.

Hitchhiking
Hitching back to Arica from the national park is not difficult, with lots of carabineros coming and going; you may also be able to bargain your way on to one of the tour

buses. Trucks between Arica and La Paz also sometimes give lifts. The Chungará border post is a good place to try; truck transport to La Paz leaves in the afternoon.

Putre *p218*
Banks The bank in Putre changes dollars but commission on TCs is very high. The ATM does not take international cards.

Contents

At a glance

⊖ **Getting around** Good bus
and train links between cities.
Buses also serve national parks in
season. Private transport or tours
required to visit most vineyards.

⟳ **Time required** A couple of
days to get a sense of the region
and to visit a few wineries. Many
more days can be spent trekking
in national parks or relaxing
on the coast in summer.

☁ **Weather** Hot summers inland.
Cooler on the coast. Winter rains are
stronger the further south you go.

✖ **When not to go** This area
can be visited all year round,
although the national parks are
often snowed out in winter.

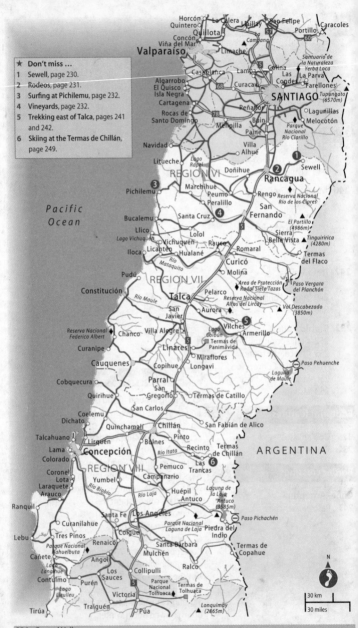

Pacific Ocean

REGION VI

REGION VII

REGION VIII

ARGENTINA

N

30 km
30 miles

The Central Valley is the heart of Chile. Stretching from just north of Santiago south to the Río Biobío, this wonderful region climbs from secluded tracks and beaches along the coast to the high Andes in the east, with the fertile valley itself in between.

On clear days, the snowy mountains can easily be seen from the coast, across the woods, fields and vineyards of Chile's agricultural heartland. It is here that the most enduring images of Chilean village life can be found: *huasos* (cowboys) with their long spurs; green valleys speckled with grazing horses, and whitewashed houses in colonial style, hinting at a bygone age.

Background

The peoples of the Central Valley did not prove as fierce as their Mapuche neighbours and were conquered by the Incas in about 1470. On his second visit to Chile, Pedro de Valdivia led an expedition southwards, founding Concepción in 1550 and a further seven cities south of the Río Biobío. The Mapuche insurrection of 1598 and the Spanish defeat at Curalabo in 1599 led the Spanish to withdraw north of the Río Biobío and concentrate their efforts in the Central Valley.

Here, the land and its inhabitants were divided up among the colonists to create the forerunner of the hacienda, which was to dominate social and economic life in Chile. The hacienda was a self-contained unit, producing everything it needed. There were no towns in the area but, from the 1740s, the Spanish crown attempted to increase its control over the region by founding settlements, including Rancagua (1743), San Fernando (1742), Curicó (1743), Talca (1742), Cauquenes (1742) and Linares (1755).

After Independence, the Río Biobío continued to be the southern frontier of white settlement until, in 1862, Colonel Cornelio Saavedra led an army south to build a line of 10 forts, each 4 km apart, between Angol and Collipulli. Following the occupation of the coast around Arauco in 1867, another line of forts was built across the Cordillera de Nahuelbuta. By 1881, the railway from Santiago had reached Angol, from where Chilean troops set out on the final campaign against the Mapuche.

Today, the Central Valley is the agricultural heartland of Chile, transformed in the past 40 years by the growth of commercial agriculture, fishing, forestry and wine production.

Geography and climate

Encompassing three of the administrative regions of Chile, Regions VI (O'Higgins), VII (Maule) and VIII (Biobío), the Central Valley is a wide depression located between the Andes to the east and the Cordillera de la Costa to the west. The Andes gradually lose height as they continue southwards, although there are a number of high peaks east of Rancagua: Alto de los Arrieros (5000 m), El Palomo (4986 m), Tingiririca (4280 m). The northern parts of the region enjoy a Mediterranean climate, with a prolonged dry season, but with more rain than Santiago. Rainfall increases gradually from north to south, until around Concepción there is usually some rainfall each month. The Central Valley receives less rain than the coastal mountains, but temperatures vary more inland than in coastal areas. The coastal range is generally under 500 m, but south of the Río Biobío it forms a range of high peaks known as the Cordillera de Nahuelbuta. Five major rivers cross the Central Valley: the Rapel, Mataquito, Maule, Itata and Biobío. This is also a region plagued by earthquakes, most recently on 27 February 2010 when the cities of Curicó, Talca, Chillán, Concepción and Talcahuano were very badly damaged, as were many other towns, villages and vineyards. Worst affected was the coast where tsunamis almost obliterated the resorts of Constitución, Pichilemu, Iloca and others. By 2014 most services were back to normal.

Rapel Valley

The damming of the Río Rapel has created Lago Rapel, a very popular destination for Santiaguinos taking their summer holidays. There are numerous small and pleasant towns, and several large *fundos* (farms) south of the town of Rapel, in an area of green hills and stunted thorn trees. Open roads by the coast have wonderful views of the high Andes east of Rancagua, while the beach at Pichilemu is one of the best in Chile for surfing.

Rancagua → *For listings, see pages 233-235. Colour map 3, B3.*

The capital of Región VI, Rancagua lies 82 km south of Santiago, on the Río Cachapoal. The city was founded in 1743 and in October 1814 was the scene of an important battle during the Wars of Independence, when Bernardo O'Higgins and his 1700 Chilean patriots were surrounded in the centre of the town by 4500 Royalist (pro-Spanish) troops. O'Higgins managed to break out and escape but was forced into exile in

Rancagua

Where to stay 🛏
Aguila Real **1**
Hostal El Parrón **4**
Mar Andino **8**

Restaurants 🍴
La Cocina Artesanal **1**

Bars & clubs 🍸
La Notta **2**

Argentina, only to return within a few years finally to defeat the Spanish forces in Chile (see also page 503).

Arriving in Rancagua

Getting there and around Rancagua is accessible by bus and train from Santiago (both hourly). There are also connections to the towns further south, especially Talca, Chillán, Concepción, Temuco and Puerto Montt (several daily). While the centre of Rancagua is compact, some of the outlying barrios are quite a distance and you may wish to take one of the numerous *colectivos*.

Tourist information ① *Germán Riesco 277, T072-223 0413, inforancagua@sernatur.cl, English spoken.* Also municipal office in the Municipalidad on Plaza de los Héroes.

Places in Rancagua

At the heart of the city is an attractive tree-lined plaza, the **Plaza de los Héroes** and several streets of single-storey colonial-style houses. In the centre of the plaza is an equestrian statue of O'Higgins. The double-spired cathedral on the south side of the plaza was restored in the 1860s, the original building having been destroyed in the battle of Rancagua, together with most of the other buildings around the plaza. There are several plaques in the city centre marking the sites of the battle and a diagram in the plaza shows the disposition of the troops. One block north is the **Merced** church, from where O'Higgins commanded his beleaguered forces. It dates from 1758 but has been restored several times. The main commercial area lies along Avenida Independencia, which runs west from the plaza towards the bus and rail terminals. **Museo Regional** ① *Estado 685 y Ibieta, T072-222 1524, www.museorancagua.cl, Tue-Fri 1000-1800, Sat and Sun 0900-1300*, housed in a colonial mansion, contains collections of religious art and late 19th-century furniture. There is also a **Casa de la Cultura** ① *corner of Milán and Cachapoal, T072-230976, www.rancaguacultura.cl, daily 0830-1330, 1500-1700*, directly south of Plaza de Los Héroes, which houses temporary exhibitions. In the station there is a small gallery with paintings by local artists for sale.

Around Rancagua → *For listings, see pages 233-235.*

Lago Rapel

West of Rancagua, this lake is 40 km long and feeds the Rapel hydroelectric plant. Most facilities at this popular summer resort are on the east shore around El Manzano, the main town, while the tourist information office is in Las Cabras. There are watersports at Bahía Skorpios, including windsurfing, yachting, waterskiing and fishing.

East of the city

The **El Teniente** copper mine, one of the biggest in the country, is 67 km east of Rancagua. Owned by **Codelco**, it can only be visited by prior arrangement with the company. Nearby, on a private road above El Teniente, is the small **Chapa Verde ski resort** ① *T072-221 7651, www.chapaverde.cl, lift tickets US$35 per day in high season (Jul-Aug), US$29 in low season.* The resort offers equipment rentals and lessons, and it has restaurant and cafeteria. There is no accommodation.

Also part of the Codelco facility is the former mining complex and UNESCO World Heritage Site of **Sewell**, www.sewell.cl. The town with its steep stair-cased paths is now a ghost town, and the mine is practically deserted. The mine once laid claim to having

Rodeo

During the summer months, rodeo is one of the most popular sports in central and southern Chile, second only to the inevitable: football. Teams (or *colleras*) of two riders on horseback compete throughout the season, culminating in the national championships in Rancagua at the end of March. Elimination rounds are held in Osorno, Temuco, San Carlos, San Fernando, Vallenar and Los Andes, but most small towns in central southern Chile have their own *media lunas* (stadia, with their own corrals and horseboxes), often used once a year only.

Rodeo owes its origins to the colonial period, when cattle roamed openly and were rounded up once annually to be identified and marked by their owners in a rodeo. Based on the traditional view that heifers need to be broken in, the modern sport of rodeo is a test of the ability of two horses and their riders to work together and control the cattle.

The event takes place inside a stockade of thick upright timbers; although now circular, this is known as a *media luna*

(crescent) after the design of the early rings: at two points the walls of the ring are covered by padded sections, with a flag at either end of the section. Each *collera* competes by manoeuvring a heifer around the edge of the ring between the padded sections, stopping it at each padded section by pinning its hindquarters against the fence, before turning it in the opposite direction. This is done three times before the animal is released from the ring.

Three judges give points (on a scale of one to seven) for elegance and horsemanship. It is one of the principles of rodeo that no heifer should be put through this performance more than once; the event should come as a complete surprise to the animal.

Rodeo is a good opportunity to see traditional Chilean rural customs: the *huasos* (cowboys) wearing brightly coloured ponchos, wide-brimmed hats and carved wooden stirrups that were common in the 19th century; the fine horses, and the *cuecas* (traditional dances) that sometimes follow the main event.

---

the biggest underground machine room in the world and it has unusually inverted shafts leading upwards from the main entrance in the mountainside. Visits are by guided tour only; contact **VTS** ⓘ *Manuel Montt 192, T072-295 2692, www.vts.cl*. See for more information.

South of El Teniente and 28 km east of Rancagua are the thermal springs of **Cauquenes** ⓘ *www.termasdecauquenes.cl*, which have been known since before colonial times and visited by, among others, Charles Darwin in 1835. The 2010 earthquake wrecked the supply of natural hot water and a complete remodeling of the resort, hotel and restaurant were taking place in 2014. Some 5 km north is the village of **Coya**, and to the south is the **Reserva Nacional Río de los Cipreses** ⓘ *T072-220 4610, US$4*. Situated 50 km southeast of Rancagua, the reserve covers 36,882 ha of the valley of the Río de los Cipreses at altitudes ranging from 900 m to 4900 m. Park administration is at the entrance at the north end of the park.

San Fernando and around

San Fernando lies on the Río Tingiririca, 51 km south of Rancagua. Founded in 1742, it is capital of Colchagua Province and a service town for this fertile valley. There is a small local museum in the **Casa Patronal de Lircunlauta** ⓘ *Jiménez 1595 y Alameda, T072-271 7326, closed Mon, US$0.35*, a 17th-century colonial mansion, with local history exhibits.

From San Fernando, a road runs east towards the *cordillera* and divides: the southern branch of the road goes to the resort of **Sierra Bellavista**, a private *fundo* where many Santiago businesspeople have holiday houses, and where there are rodeos in October and November. The northern branch, a treacherous 75 km, runs to the **Termas del Flaco** near the Argentine border, where there are camping facilities, *cabañas* and several hotels and *hospedajes*. The thermal springs are only open in the warmer months (October-Easter). Some 500 m from the Termas del Flaco are '*Las huellas de dinosaurios*', dinosaur footprints preserved in the rock, dating from over 120 million years ago. There are good one-day treks starting from the baths, and a four-hour horse ride leads to the site of the Uruguayan plane crash immortalized in the film *Alive*.

Heading west → *For listings, see pages 233-235.*

West of San Fernando, dry thorn trees gradually give way to more fertile land, with swathes of vineyards and the first signs of *copihues* and forests. Ridges high above the valleys provide beautiful routes for cyclists, walkers and horse riders.

Santa Cruz

Some 50 km southwest of San Fernando, Santa Cruz is surrounded by some of the country's best vineyards and is the site of the offices of the **Ruta del Vino del Valle de Colchagua** ① *Plaza de Armas 298, of 6, T072-282 3199, www.rutadelvino.cl.* For further details, see box, page 18. In the town is **Museo de Colchagua** ① *Errázuriz 145, T072-282 1050, www.museocolchagua.cl, daily 1000-1800, US$11,* an excellent small museum with exhibits on local history and prehistory as well as winemaking. In summer, a steam train links Santa Cruz with many of the wineries in the Colchagua valley. For reservations, see www.trendelvinochile.cl.

Pichilemu

Pichilemu is a coastal resort with a great many hotels and *residenciales*, 120 km west of San Fernando. It was founded by Agustín Ross Edwards in the 19th century in the style of a European resort. The town is on two levels, one at sea level and the main town above. In summer it is a popular destination for Chileans, while, for the rest of the year, there is a steady flow of foreigners who come to enjoy some of the best surf in South America. This is reflected in the number of shops along the main drag selling surfing accessories. The town is now fully back in business after the 2010 earthquake. For further information, consult the tourism pages of the online newspaper www.pichilemunews.cl; see also www.pichilemu.cl and www.depichilemu.cl, for lodgings.

There is a small go-kart-style motorbike circuit on the south end of the *costanera*, and further along there are three surf schools that also hire equipment. Among several beaches is **Punta Los Lobos**, where international surfing competitions are held. The former train station, made of wood in 1925, is a national monument, and now home to the tourist information office. There is also a small museum, the **Museo del Niño Rural de Ciruelos**, a few kilometres south of town, with three rooms of interesting exhibits from the pre-Hispanic cultures of the region. Fishing is good in nearby lakes. Some 20 km southeast along a *ripio* road is **Pañul**, where interesting pottery is produced using the local clay. Nearby is a watermill, dating from 1904, which locals still use to grind their wheat into flour. It can be visited for US$1. Unless you go by taxi or with a guide, prepare to get lost on the way.

⦿ Rapel Valley listings

For hotel and restaurant price codes and other relevant information, see pages 14-21.

⦿ Where to stay

Rancagua *p229, map p229*
$$$ Aguila Real, Brasil 1045, T072-222 2047, hotelaguilareal@terra.cl. Modern 3-star, with restaurant. Some English spoken.
$$$ Mar Andino, Bulnes 370, T072-264 5400, www.hotelmarandino.cl. New, modern, comfortable, decent restaurant, business centre, pool.
$$ Hostal El Parrón, San Martín 135, T072-275 8550, www.hostalelparron.cl. 2-storey artdeco-style house in the centre, singles, doubles, triples, parking, patio.

Lago Rapel *p230*
$$ Hostería La Finca, Sector La Carmen caminio Llallauquén, Km 3, T09-335 6855. Pleasant hostel with a pool and restaurant.

Camping
The eastern shore of Lago Rapel around El Manzano is lined with campsites.
Camping Punta Arenas, 3 km north of El Manzano, is basic and cheap.

East of the city *p230*
There is a campsite at **Los Maitenes**, 12 km south of the entrance to the Reserva Nacional Río de los Cipreses.

San Fernando and around *p231*
$$$$ Hacienda Los Lingues, Panamericana Sur, Km 124.5, 22 km north of San Fernando, T072-297 7080, www.loslingues.com. A hacienda with its roots in the colonial period, it offers luxury accommodation, fine dining and outdoor activities such as riding and mountain biking, swimming pool Nov-Mar. Day tours and other excursions arranged. The hacienda has been completely refurbished after major damage in the 2010 earthquake.

$$$$ Viña Casa Silva, Hijuela Norte, T072-271 6519, www.casasilva.cl. Upmarket accommodation in a colonial building in this well-known vineyard north of San Fernando. Only 7 rooms. Pool, spacious grounds with pleasant views. Relaxing ambiance. Good restaurant.
$$$-$$ Español, Av Rodríguez 959, San Fernando, T072-271 1098, hotelespanol6@ terra.cl. 3-star, with parking and pool.

Santa Cruz *p232*
Prices are cheaper Apr-Dec.
$$$$ Santa Cruz Plaza, Plaza de Armas 286, T072-220 9600, www. hotelsantacruzplaza.cl. 4-storey building in colonial style on the Plaza. There is a gym, pool and spa as well as a fine restaurant and casino. Spacious rooms and luxurious suites, though some bathrooms on the small side. Disabled-friendly. Tours and visits to wineries arranged. Occasional internet-only specials.
$$$$ Viña la Playa, Camino a Quelluque s/n, Peralillo, T072-282 2174, www.hotel vinalaplaya.cl. Luxurious lodge some 30 km northwest of Santa Cruz. Pool, tennis court, good meals. Attentive staff.
$$$$-$$$ Vendimia, Ismael Valdés 92, T072-282 2464, www.hotelvendimia.cl. Filled with antiques, clean, spacious rooms and very attentive staff who can help arrange wine tours. Good breakfast. Recommended.
$$$ Hostal Casa Familia, Los Pidenes 421, T072-282 5766, www.hostalcasafamilia. cl. Charming upmarket bed and breakfast. Some rooms a on the small side.
$$$ Vino Bello, Camino Los Boldos s/n, T072-282 5788. Lovely guesthouse in the heart of wine country, some 2 km west of Santa Cruz. Friendly staff, spacious rooms, good breakfasts. Recommended if you have your own transport.

Pichilemu p232

There are dozens of cheap places to stay.
$$$$ Alaia, Punta de Lobos 681, T09-5701 5971, www.hotelalaia.com. "Boutique" surfers' lodge, with single, double and triple rooms, surf classes, SUP, mountain biking and other activities, hot tub, restaurant.
$$$ Chile-España, Ortúzar 255, T072-284 1270, www.chileespana.cl. Good option close to the beach. Ample space for storing surf boards. The rooms with bath have cable TV and electric blankets. There is also a café.
$$$ Rocas del Pacífico, Gaete 244, T072-284 1346, www.hotelrocasdelpacifico.cl. With breakfast. Spacious rooms with good bathrooms. Some rooms on the top floor have a decent sea view. Comfortable, if a little plastic.
$$$ Surf Hostal, Eugenio Díaz Lira 167, Playa Infernillo, T907-492 6848, www.pichilemusurfhostal.cl. Cheaper on weekdays and in low season (Apr-Nov), **$** per person in shared rooms. Comfortable rooms with bath. Some with sea view. Dutch-owned. Good surfing information.
$$$-$ Asthur, Ortúzar 540, T072-284 1072, www.hotelasthur.cl. Traditional hotel dating from the 1930s but redesigned since then. Small comfortable rooms with bath and cable TV. The best rooms back on to the terrace with extensive views to the north. There is a pleasant bar/breakfast area where meals are served in summer and an unheated pool outside. Recommended.
$$$-$$ Waitara, Av Costanera 1039, T072-284 3026, www.waitara.cl. Cabins on the seafront with fully equipped kitchens. Also slightly cheaper rooms with bath. Discounts for longer stays.
$$-$ La Sirena Insolente, Camino Punta de Lobos 169, T09-5856 5784, www.sirenainsolentehostel.cl. In same group as **La Princessa Insolente** and **La Casa Roja** in Santiago, private and shared rooms, surf and wetsuit rental, lessons, bike rental, Spanish classes, 5 mins from beach.

Camping

Pichilemu has several campsites; the cheapest charge from about US$7 per pitch, but others are more expensive than the cheaper *residenciales*.

🍴 Restaurants

Rancagua *p229, map p229*
$ La Cocina Artesanal, O'Carroll 60, T072-224 1389. Traditional meat and seafood dishes.

San Fernando and around *p231*
$ Club Social San Fernando, Rodríguez 787. Good local food.
$ Restaurante La Carreta, O'Higgins 262. Traditional cuisine.
$ Arenspastycaf, Chillán y Manuel Rodríguez, www.arenpastycaf.cl. The best sandwiches for miles around.

Pichilemu *p232*
$ There a number of basic restaurants serving fish and traditional Chilean dishes.

🍸 Bars and clubs

Rancagua *p229, map p229*
La Notta, San Martin 550. Mon-Wed 0900-1800, Thu-Fri 0900-1800 and 2100-0300, Sat 2100-0300 only. Bar with restaurant; lunch menus from US$2.50-8.50.

Pichilemu *p232*
Many people come here for the nightlife; there is a good atmosphere after dark, with a dozen or so discos open in summer, and at weekends off season.
Delerium Tremens, Ortúzar 215, is one of a growing number of micro-brew pubs in Chile.

🎉 Festivals

Rancagua *p229, map p229*
April National Rodeo Championships are held in the Complejo Deportivo, north of

the centre. There are plenty of opportunities for purchasing cowboy items; watch out especially for the fantastic spurs, which are much more important to horsemanship in Chile than elsewhere in Latin America.

Santa Cruz *p232*
Early Mar Fiesta de la Vendimia (harvest celebration) is held in Santa Cruz around the town's main plaza, where local wine and food can be sampled.

O Shopping

Rancagua *p229, map p229*
There's a shopping mall at Cuevas 483, and a supermarket at **Hipermercado Independencia**, Av Miguel Ramírez 665.

O Transport

Rancagua *p229, map p229*
Bus
The terminal for regional buses is at Doctor Salinas y Calvo, T072-223 6938, just north of the market. The thermal springs of **Cauquenes** are served by daily buses with **Buses Termas**, US$3, or a *colectivo* from Rancagua market.

Frequent services to **Santiago** from Tur-**Bus** terminal at O'Carroll 1175, T072-223 0482, US$5.45, 1¼ hrs. Main terminal for long-distance buses is at Av O'Higgins 0484, T072-222 5425.

Car
Car hire available from **Weber Rentacar**, Membrillar 40, of 2, T072-232 0435; and **Comercial O'Carrol**, O'Carrol 1120, T072-258 3190, ocarrolrentacar@yahoo.com.

For parts, try **Aucamar**, Brasil 1177, T072-223 7103, and several others around Brasil 1100-1200, although the selection and prices are better in Santiago. **Automóvil Club de Chile**, Ibieta 09, T072-232 0486.

Train
Train station on Av Viña del Mar and Av Estación, at the end of Carrera Pinto, T072-223 8530, T0600-585 5000 for tickets. Mainline services between **Santiago** and **Chillán** stop here, US$3, 1 hr. Also regular services to/from **Santiago** on **Metrotren**, 1¼ hrs.

San Fernando and around *p231*
Bus
Many companies have buses to **Santiago**, US$7, including **Andimar** and **Pullman del Sur**. To **Pichilemu**, US$5.50, with **Nilahue** and **Galbus**; to **Termas del Flaco**, US$16 return, with **Amistad**, **Andibus** and others. Lots of competition to the south, with services running as far as **Chiloé**, with **Cruz del Sur**, and most intermediate destinations with **TurBus**, T072-271 9643, and **Buses Lit**.

Train
The station is at Quecheregua s/n, T600 585 5000. **Metrotren** runs 10 trains daily to **Santiago**, www.tmsa.cl, US$3.55.

Pichilemu *p232*
Andimar and **Nilahue** run buses to **Santiago**, 4 hrs, US$10.

O Directory

Rancagua *p229, map p229*
Banks Exchange at **Cambios Afex**, Cuevas 483; also several banks on Independencia.

Mataquito Valley

The Río Mataquito, formed by the confluence of the Ríos Lontué
and Teno, flows through the peaceful heart of Chilean wine country,
reaching the Pacific at a wide and serene estuary near Iloca. The Andes
can clearly be seen from the cliffs above the largely deserted coast.

Curicó → For listings, see pages 238-239.

Curicó, which means 'black water' in the Mapuche language, lies between the rivers
Lontué and Teno, 54 km south of San Fernando. Founded in 1743, it is the only town
of any size in the Mataquito Valley and is the service centre for the region's vineyards
(see box, page 18). The town centre offers good views towards the mountains and

Curicó

Where to stay 🛌
Comercio 1
Prat 3
Raices 11
Residencial Colonial 6

Residencial Ensueño 7

Restaurants 🍴
Centro Italiano
Club Social 3

Club de la Unión 4
Los Cisnes 6
Sant' Angelo 7
Tortas Montero 1

a friendly atmosphere after dark, but most of the historic centre was destroyed in the February 2010 earthquake.

Arriving in Curicó

Getting there and around Curicó is easily accessible by bus from Santiago (many times daily). There are also some connections to the towns further south, especially Talca, Chillán, Temuco and Puerto Montt (several daily). The bus terminal is at the west end of Prat, four blocks west of Plaza de Armas, and is used by most local and long-distance companies except **Tur-Bus** ① *M de Velasco y Castellón, T075-231 2115*, and **Pullman del Sur** ① *Henríquez y Carmen*. Opposite the bus terminal is the **train station** ① *T075-231 0028; tickets available from Maipú 657, T0600-585 5000*. While the centre of Curicó is quite compact, some of the outlying barrios are quite a distance away, and you may wish to take one of the numerous *colectivos*.

Tourist information **Gobernación Provincial** ① *Carmen 925 Mon-Fri 0900-1400*, helpful, has street map. **CONAF** ① *Argomedo 380, T075-231 0231*.

Places in Curicó

The **Plaza de Armas** is surrounded by about 40 Canary Island palms and has lovely fountains with sculptures of nymphs, black-necked swans and a monument to the Mapuche warrior, **Lautaro**, carved from the trunk of an ancient beech tree. The steel **bandstand** was built in New Orleans in 1904 and is now a national monument. On the western side of the plaza is the church of **La Merced**, which was badly damaged by the earthquakes in 1986 and 2010 but has been restored. Five blocks east is the neo-Gothic church of **San Francisco**, a national monument, which was wrecked by the 2010 earthquake. At the junction of Carmen and Avenida San Martín is the imposing **Iglesia del Carmen**, being rebuilt after the 2010 earthquake.

To the east of the city is the Avenida Manso de Velasco, with statues of various national heroes, and also a bust of Mahatma Gandhi. Nearby is **Cerro Condell** offering fine views of the surrounding countryside and across to the distant Andes; it is an easy climb to the summit, from where there are a number of short walks.

The **Miguel Torres bodega** ① *5 km south of the city, T075-256 4100, www.miguel torres.cl, Apr-Oct daily 1000-1700, Nov-Mar daily 1000-1900, tours in Spanish only*, is one of the biggest wine *bodegas* in Chile and well worth a visit. To get there, take a bus for Molina from the local terminal or from outside the railway station and get off at Km 195 on the Pan-American Highway. For details of other *bodegas* and vineyards in the area, contact the **Ruta del Vino del Valle de Curicó** ① *Prat 301-A, T075-232 8972, www. rutadelvinocurico.cl, Mon-Fri 0900-1400, 1530-1930*.

Around Curicó → *For listings, see pages 238-239.*

Parque Nacional Radal Siete Tazas

① *Oct-Mar, US$4. Buses Hernández and Buses Radal from Molina to Radal village, Mar-early Dec daily 1700, return 0800, mid Dec-Feb, 6 daily, 3 hrs, US$3.20. It's a further 2 km to La Vela de la Novia and 4 km to Siete Tazas. It's 9 km from Radal to Parque Inglés, US$3.40. Access by car is best as the road through the park is paved.*

This park is in two sectors, one at **Radal**, 65 km east of Curicó, the other at **Parque Inglés**, 9 km further east and the site of the park administration. The most interesting sector is at Radal, where the Río Claro flows through a series of seven rock 'cups' (the *siete tazas*) each with a pool emptying into the next by means of a waterfall. The river then passes through a canyon, 15 m deep but only 1.5 m wide, which ends abruptly in a cliff and a beautiful waterfall. There is excellent trekking in the park, through beautiful woods and scenery, similar to that found further south, but with a better climate.

Towards the coast

From Curicó, a road runs west through the small town of **Licantén** towards the mouth of the Río Mataquito and the popular resort of **Iloca**, set in a wide bay with great views south along the coastline. Some 5 km north of Iloca is **Puerto Duao**, a fishing village with a good campsite, while beyond is the resort of **Llico**, a long, narrow, one-street town with a pleasant dark-sand beach and windsurfing facilities. It is reached either by the coastal route or by an unpaved inland road, which branches off at Hualañe, 74 km east of Curicó.

Six kilometres west of Licantén a bridge crosses the Río Mataquito, leading to a road south along the coast to **Putú**, past kilometres of rolling sand dunes, a kind of mini Sahara. Further south, the road reaches the Río Maule, where a ferry crosses to Constitución (see page 242).

Lago Vichuquén and around

Just east of Llico and 114 km west of Curicó, Lago Vichuquén is a large, peaceful lake, set in a bowl surrounded by pinewoods. It is very popular with the wealthy and with watersports enthusiasts and, although parts of the eastern shore of the lake are inaccessible by road, there are full facilities on the western shore, particularly at Aquelarre. The nearby town of **Vichuquén** has some well-preserved colonial architecture and a recommended small **museum** ① *Tue-Sun, 1000-1330, 1600-2000*, set in a beautiful house with a portico, in the town centre. The area was badly hit by the 2010 earthquake and tsunami.

Just north of Lago Vichuquén, 120 km west of Curicó, is the **Reserva Nacional Laguna Torca** ① *T071-220 9517, talca.oirs@conaf.cl,* The reserve covers 604 ha and is a natural sanctuary for over 80 species of bird, especially black-necked swans and other water fowl. To get there take any bus from Curicó to Llico and get out near the administration.

⊛ Mataquito Valley listings

For hotel and restaurant price codes and other relevant information, see pages 14-21.

⊜ Where to stay

Curicó *p236, map p236*
$$$ Comercio, Yungay 730, T075-231 0014, www.hotelcomercio.cl. 3-star, with pool, gym, restaurant, Wi-Fi and car hire.
$$$ Raíces, Carmen 727 y Prat, T075-254 3440, www.hotelraices.cl. Curicó's best hotel has suites, a pleasant garden and a good restaurant with an extensive wine list.
$$ Prat, Peña 427, T075-231 1069, www. facebook.com/HotelPratCurico. Rooms

with or without bath. Pleasant patio with grapevines and fig trees, friendly, clean, hot water, laundry facilities, breakfast extra, parking. Recommended.
$$-$ Residencial Colonial, Rodríguez 461, T075-231 4103. Clean, patio, friendly, some rooms with bath. Full board available. Good value.
$$-$ Residencial Ensueño, Rodríguez 442, T075-222 1788. Basic lodging, some rooms with bath. Includes breakfast.

Parque Nacional Radal Siete Tazas *p237*
$$ Hostería Flor de la Canela, Parque Inglés, Km 9 al interior de El Radal, T075-

249 1613. Open all year, breakfast extra, good food, good value.

Camping
$$$-$ Valle de las Catas, Camino Radal Parque Inglés (Fundo Frutillar), T09-1689 7820. Cabins for 4-6 people or camping, hot showers, good service, convenient.
$ Los Robles, Parque Inglés, Km 7 al interior de El Radal, T075-222 8029. Open all year, toilets, hot showers, tables and benches, good.

Towards the coast *p238*
$$$ Hotel Iloca, Besoain 221, Iloca, T075-198 3751, www.hoteliloca.cl. Rooms with bath, breakfast, good views. Several *cabañas*, many open in summer only.

Camping
El Peñón, 6 km south of Iloca, T09-9751 9928. Phone ahead for reservation.
La Puntilla, 2 km north of Iloca, T09-9741 5585. Also *cabañas*.

Lago Vichuquén and around *p238*
$$$ Marina Vichuquén, T075-240 0265, www.marinavichuquen.cl. Fully equipped resort, good. Lots of activities including watersports, tennis, mountain biking, horse riding.

Camping
Vichuquén, east shore of lake, T075-240 0062, www.campingvichuquen.cl. Full facilities.
El Sauce, north shore of lake, T075-240 0203, www.elsaucedevichuquen.cl/informacion.htm. Good facilities, US$45 per site for 5 people, also cabins, **$$$**.

🍴 Restaurants

Curicó *p236, map p236*
There are several seriously cheap restaurants with varying standards of cleanliness outside the market on C Donoso. **Hotels Raíces** and **Comercio** both have decent restaurants.

$$$-$$ Club de la Unión, Plaza de Armas. Innovative food in elegant surroundings. Recommended.
$$ Los Cisnes, Rodríguez 1186. *Parilladas* and cheaper *almuerzos*.
$ Centro Italiano Club Social, Estado 531. Good, cheap meals.
$ Sant' Angelo, Prat 442. Excellent patisserie, also serving good-value set lunches.
$ Tortas Montero, Prat 669. *Salón de té*, restaurant and manufacturer of traditional *tortas de manjar* and *dulce de alcayotas*.

✹ Festivals

Curicó *p236, map p236*
Mid-Mar Fiesta de la Vendimia (wine harvest festival) has displays on traditional winemaking and the chance to try local food and wine. A similar event is also held in nearby Molina at the same time.

⊖ Transport

Curicó *p236, map p236*
Bus
Many southbound buses bypass Curicó, but can be caught by waiting outside town. To **Santiago**, US$7.25, 2½ hrs, several companies, frequent. To **Talca**, every 15 mins, US$3.40, 1 hr. To **Temuco**, Alsa and Tur-Bus, US$16-24, 7 hrs. Minibuses to **Molina**, 26 km south, for connections to Parque Nacional Radal Siete Tazas, US$1;

Train
To/from **Santiago**, 5-6 a day, 2 hrs 20 mins, US$5.

ⓘ Directory

Curicó *p236, map p236*
Banks Major banks located around Plaza de Armas. **Casa de Cambio**, Merced 255, Local 106, no TCs. **Laundry** Lavacentro, Yungay 437; expensive, good. **Post office** Plaza de Armas.

Maule Valley

The Río Maule flows for 240 km from Laguna Maule in the Andes to the sea at Constitución. Its waters have been dammed east of Talca, providing power for the region and creating Lago Colbún. The river itself is particularly beautiful near the coast at Constitución.

Talca → *For listings, see pages 244-246.*

Situated on the south bank of the Río Claro, a tributary of the Maule, Talca lies 56 km south of Curicó. The most important city between Santiago and Concepción, it is a major manufacturing centre and the capital of Region VII, Maule. Founded in 1692, it was destroyed by earthquakes in 1742, 1928 and 2010. Today, it is a busy, dusty town, with a lively atmosphere day and night.

Arriving in Talca
Getting there and around Talca is easily accessible by bus and train from Santiago (both many times daily). The **station** ① *Av 2 Sur y 11 Oriente, T0600-585 5000,* is one block west of the bus terminal, which has frequent connections to the towns further south, especially Chillán, Concepción, Temuco and Puerto Montt (several daily). Talca is a sizeable city and some of the barrios are quite a distance from the centre. Buses and *colectivos* ply the routes to these areas, with their destinations marked in the window.

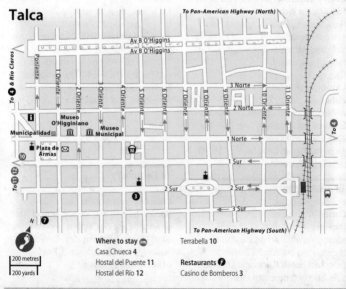

Talca

Where to stay
Casa Chueca **4**
Hostal del Puente **11**
Hostal del Río **12**
Terrabella **10**

Restaurants ❼
Casino de Bomberos **3**

Tourist information Sernatur ① *1 Poniente 1150 p 1 y 4, T071-223 3669, infomaule@ sernatur.cl, Mon-Fri 0830-1730.* See also www.talca.cl. **CONAF** ① *C 4 Norte 1673, T071-220 9517, maule.oirs@conaf.cl.*

Places in Talca

In the **Plaza de Armas** are statues that were looted by the Talca Regiment from Peru during the War of the Pacific. Just off the plaza is a **colonial mansion** that belonged to Juan Albano Pereira, tutor to the young Bernardo O'Higgins, who lived here as a child. The house was later the headquarters of O'Higgins' Patriot Government in 1813-1814, before his defeat at Rancagua and is now **Museo O'Higginiano** ① *1 Norte 875, T071-261 5880, www.museodetalca.cl, currently closed to the public.* In 1818, O'Higgins signed the declaration of Chilean Independence here: the room Sala Independencia is decorated and furnished in period style. The museum also houses a collection of regional art. The **Casino de Bomberos** ① *2 Sur y 5 Oriente,* has a small museum room with two old fire engines, old firefighting equipment and, for those with an interest in little-known conflagrations, information on important fires in Talca's history. **Paseo peatonal** ① *C 1 Sur entre 3 y 6 Oriente,* is a pleasant place for a stroll, with handicrafts, cafés, bookstalls and shops

About 8 km southeast of the centre is **Villa Huilquilemu** ① *T071-241 3641,* a 19th-century hacienda, now part of the Universidad Católica del Maule, housing four museums of religious art, handicrafts, agricultural machinery and wine. The **Ruta de Vino del Valle del Maule** ① *Camino a San Clemente, Km 10, Restaurant Corral Victoria, 09-8157 9951, www.valledelmaule.cl,* arranges tours to several vineyards, tastings, meals at typical restaurants and other events. See also box, page 18.

East of Talca → *For listings, see pages 244-246.*

Lago Colbún and around

From Talca a good paved road runs 175 km southeast along **Lago Colbún** and up the valley of the Río Maule, passing through some of the finest mountain scenery in Chile to reach the Argentine border at **Paso Pehuenche** (see box, page 243). Off this road, beyond the town of **Armerillo**, is the private Belgian/Chilean-administered **Parque Natural Tricahue** ① *open all year, US$3.65,* a great place for trekking, with snowshoes in winter, cycling and fishing. There's a good refugio in the park but no restaurant, so take your own food or walk 500 m to El Fosforito.

Another route, south of Talca, is paved for the first 65 km, running east from the Panamericana to Colbún at the western end of the lake, from where another road leads south and west to join the Pan-American Highway at Linares. After 5 km it passes through **Panimávida**, where there are thermal springs. While at Panimávida, try the local 'Bebida Panimávida', made from spring water, flavoured with lemon or raspberry. Artesanal goods are better and cheaper here than in Linares. Further on towards Linares is **Quinamávida**, 12 km south of Colbún, where there are more thermal springs and an upmarket hotel.

Vilches and around

Some 63 km east of Talca, Vilches is the starting point for the climb to the volcanoes **Quizapu** (3050 m) and **Descabezado** (3850 m). For walks on Descabezado Grande and Cerro Azul, ice axe, crampons and an experienced guide are required. There is also great horse riding in this area. ▸▸ *See What to do, page 245.*

Situated just east of Vilches, the **Reserva Nacional Altos del Lircay** ① *entrance 2 km from Alto Vilches bus stop, US$7,* covers 12,163 ha and includes peaks up to 2228 m as well as several small lakes. Much of the park is covered with mixed forest including lenga, ñirre, coigüe, roble, raulí and copihue. Near the entrance are the CONAF administration and visitor centre with full information on trails and activities. Nearby are the **Piedras Tacitas**, a stone construction supposedly built by the indigenous inhabitants of the region, and the **Mirador Del Indio** from where there are fine views over the Río Lircay. There are well-signed trails and horses can be hired in Alto Vilches. See www.ecoturismovilches.cl for hiking and horse riding guides, accommodation and other community tourism. Two stand-out treks are to **Enladrillado** (10 km), a mysterious 800 m by 60 m rock platform with fabulous views of Descabezado and Cerro Azul; it is the subject of many outlandish theories, including UFO landings. A further 1.5 km is **Laguna del Alto**. Allow eight to 10 hours to the lake and back. A second walk goes to Mirador del Venado from where you can descend to the river and the lovely Valle del Venado. From here you can continue to Descabezado Grande and Quizapú (five to six days overall).

South of Talca → *For listings, see pages 244-246.*

Linares
Fifty-three kilometres south of Talca on the *Panamericana*, Linares is a peaceful town with a distinctly *huaso* feel. It boasts the remarkable **Cathedral de San Ambrosio**, built between 1934 and 1967 in a Byzantine romantic style. On Letelier 572, in the middle of a row of colonial houses, is the **Museo de Arte y Artesanía Nacional** ① *www.museodelinares.cl, Mon-Fri 1000-1730, Sat 1000-1400, Sun 1200-1700, US$1.10, Sun free.* Here are exhibits of local, military and prehistoric history, including a 2-ft-long decorative curved spanner, an exploded cannon, horsehair artefacts from the village of Rari, local paintings, petrified wood, old toys and everyday utensils. In the **Mercado Municipal** on Chacabuco, it is possible to buy horsehair art from Rari. Tourist information is available from the Gobernación and Municipalidad, both on the plaza.

West of Talca → *For listings, see pages 244-246.*

Constitución
Lying west of Talca at the mouth of the Río Maule, Constitución is reached by road (89 km) and by a **narrow-gauge railway** line from Talca, which offers fine views over the wooded Maule Valley. The railway, packed with chatting locals (and as often as not their goats and chickens) is unique in Chile and offers travellers a microcosm of life in the Central Valley. It is not unusual for trains to be flagged down like buses and for the driver to stop in order to share gossip and a coffee with a farmer.

Founded in 1794, the city is situated in a major commercial logging area and has naval shipyards, a giant cellulose factory and a fishing fleet. Its main appeal, however, is as a seasonal seaside resort. While the town itself is relatively uninteresting, the beach, an easy walk from the centre, is surrounded by picturesque rocks, and the coast both to the north and south is beautiful. The seafront was almost completely destroyed by the tsunami and earthquake of February 2010 but has since been remodelled with restaurants open all year.

There are good views from **Cerro Mutrún**, at the mouth of the river, accessed via Calle O'Higgins; the **Playa El Cable**, www.playaelcable.cl, with *cabañas*, is 5 km south. For a

Border crossing: Chile–Argentina

Paso Pehuenche

Paso Pehuenche (2553 m) lies 175 km southeast of Talca along a good paved road. The border is open daily 0800-1800, but may be closed in bad weather. Chilean customs is at La Mina, 106 km from Talca, 60 km from the border. On the Argentine side the road continues as good *ripio* to Malargüe and San Rafael. See www.gendarmeria.gov.ar/pasos/chile/fichpehuenche.html for detailed information (in Spanish).

pleasant walk or drive, take the quiet track along the south bank of the Maule 8 km east of Constitución to a disused railway bridge over the river; the bridge is open to vehicles, and has great views of the river valley.

Chanco and around

A paved road runs from Constitución along the coast, through thick forest and past a large logging factory, via deserted beaches and fishing villages to the small, peaceful town of Chanco. Chanco is famous for its cheese and its traditional colonial architecture. Sadly, the charming adobe-built **Iglesia San Ambrosia** was destroyed in February 2010. There is a pleasant 3-km walk to the coast and the unspoilt **Playa Monolito** The land just north of Chanco is the prettiest in this area, with rolling hills, small farmsteads and a small park: the **Reserva Nacional Federico Albert** ① *Apr-Nov 0830-1800, Dec-Mar 0830-2000, US$3.65*, which covers 145 ha of dunes planted with eucalyptus and cypresses in experiments to control the shifting sands. It has a visitor centre and campsite facilities.

Further south

South of Chanco are two more small resorts at **Pelluhue** and **Curanipe**, 83 km south of Constitución. Both were severely damaged in February 2010. From Curanipe a mostly paved road leads 50 km through wild country past the village of **Buchupureo** to the small seaside town of **Cobquecura**. This was, the closest place to the epicentre of the earthquake: 95% of the historic centre was wrecked. It remains, however, a tranquil, friendly town, with a good beach, a pretty plaza, accommodation and several good seafood restaurants. About 1 km north of the village is a long curved beach with a large colony of sea lions offshore. At low tide the beach almost extends as far as the rock on which they live and their yelps can clearly be heard. It is worth a detour to see. About 5 km to the north is an impressive *portada* or arch in the cliffs. There are also a few good surfing beaches nearby.

This coast can also be reached by paved road from Parral via Cauquenes. Just north of the road between Cauquenes and Chanco is the **Reserva Nacional Los Ruiles** ① *Dec-Mar daily 0830-2000, Apr-Nov daily 0830-1730, US$3.65, buses from Constitución or Cauquenes*, which covers 45 ha of native flora, including the *ruil* (*Nothofagus alessandri*), an endangered species of southern beech.

For hotel and restaurant price codes and other relevant information, see pages 14-21.

⊜ Where to stay

Talca *p240, map p240*
$$$ Terrabella, 1 Sur 641, T071-222 6555, terrabella@hotel.tie.cl. Good service, *cafetería* and swimming pool.
$$$-$$ Casa Chueca, Camino Las Rastras, 4 km from Talca by the Río Lircay, T071-197 0096, T09-9419 0625, www.trekkingchile. com. Closed Jun-Aug. Phone *hostal* from bus terminal for directions on how to get there. From suites to rooms with shared bath. Vegetarian restaurant, Austrian and German owners, many languages spoken, lovely setting, pool, mountain bikes, good trekking, riding and climbing tours.
$$ Hostal del Puente, 1 Sur 401, T071-222 0930, www.hostaldelpuente.cl. Family-owned, parking in central courtyard, lovely gardens, English spoken, pleasant atmosphere and surroundings.
$$ Hostal del Río, 1 Sur 407, T071-251 0218, www.hostaldelrio.cl. Rival to **Del Puente** next door, a little cheaper, also good.

Lago Colbún and around *p241*
$$$$ Hotel Termas de Panimávida, Panimávida, T073-221 1743, www.termas depanimavida.cl. Full board and access to thermal pools. In the grounds is a small fountain, where you can drink the sulphourous *agua de la mona*.
$$$$ Hotel Quinamávida, Quinamávida, T073-262 7100, www. termasdequinamavida.cl. In the hotel there are thermal baths, Turkish baths, reflexology, and massage.
$$-$ Refugio Tricahue, Parque Natural Tricahue, east of Armerillo, www.refugio-tricahue.cl. Cabins, sauna, pool, bicycle hire and kitchen (bring your own food).

Camping
There are several campsites about 12 km east of Colbún on the south shore of Lago Colbún. There are also sites near Panimávida.

Vilches and around *p241*
$$ Refugio Galo, Vilches Altos, www. refugiodegalo.com. Open all year for food and lodging, warm welcome, good service, horse riding.
$$-$ pp Refugio Biotamaule, T09-9609 3644, www.biotamaule.blogspot.co.uk. Open in summer only, meals available.

Camping
Antahuaras, 500 m from Reserva Altos de Lircay administration, at 1300 m, hot showers, good services, light at each site, beautiful location.

Linares *p242*
$$$ Hotel Curapalihue, Curapalihue 411, T073-221 2516. Breakfast and bath, cable TV, conference facilities.
$$$ Hotel Turismo, Manuel Rodríguez 522, T073-221 0636. Breakfast and bath, restaurant, cable TV.

Constitución *p242*
$$$ Casa Puccllana, Los Hibiscus 1855, Villa Copihue, T071-267 3393. Sea view, perched above the Piedra de la Iglesia, modern rooms, parking.
$$$ Las Azucenas, Alameda 910, T071-267 1933, http://lasazucenashotel.com. Colonial style, 6 well-equipped and spacious rooms. Local cuisine and wines offered.
$$ Cabañas Playa el Cable, 3 km from Constitución on Playa el Cable, T071-267 0595, www.playaelcable.cl. Beachfront rooms and restaurant, pool, timber and glass, modern and light.

Further south *p243*
$$$$ La Joya del Mar, Buchupureo, T042-197 1733, www.lajoyadelmar.com.

Small boutique resort on the coast, accommodation in independent villas, excellent restaurant.
$$$-$$ Cabañas Campomar, north of Curanipe, T073-2541000, www.cabanascampomar.cl. Prices for up to 8 people, kitchen, sea views, swimming pool. English spoken.

There are other *cabañas* and a few *hostales* in Curanipe and Pelluhue.

🍴 Restaurants

Talca *p240, map p240*
There are cheap local restaurants and fresh food on sale at the **Mercado Municipal** entrance on C 1 Norte.
$ Casino de Bomberos, 2 Sur y 5 Oriente. Good value, open every day. It has the Museo Bomberil Benito Riquelme attached.

Linares *p242*
$$ Las Parrillas de Linares, Lautaro 350. Typical grill.
$ Estadio Español, León Bustas 01242, www.estadioespanolinares.cl. Traditional food.

🍷 Bars and clubs

Talca *p240, map p240*
Wurlitzer, 5 Oriente 960. Deservedly popular pub above a pool hall.

🎉 Festivals

Talca *p240, map p240*
4 Oct Fiesta San Francisco, an important *huaso* festival, takes place in Huerta del Maule (southwest of Talca).
1st week of Nov Feria del Vino y la Viticultura (TECVIN) is enjoyable for those with an interest in Chilean wine.
Last week in Nov Feria Regional de Folklore y Artesanía is held at Villa Cultural Huilquilemu.

⚙ What to do

Talca *p240, map p240*
Trekking Chile, see **Casa Chueca**, above, www.trekkingchile.com. Excellent touring information, plus kayaking, trekking and horse-riding trips. Also run a CO2-offset scheme.
Leonardo Cáceres Rencoret, T09-9641 5582. Good mountain guide, works for **CONAF**. See www.trekkingchile.com for details.

🚌 Transport

Talca *p240, map p240*
Bus
To **Santiago**, US$6.60. To **Chillán**, frequent, US$5.40. To **Temuco**, US$13.50, 6 hrs. To **Puerto Montt**, US$22-37, 10½ hrs. To **Alto Vilches** (for Altos del Lircay), bus from platform 23, US$3.40, 6 a day in summer 0715-1730, 3-4 from 0715 (0800 on Sun) Mar-Dec. To **Lago Colbún**, Pullman del Sur, 2 a day, US$2. To **Linares**, frequent, US$2.

Car hire
Trekker Ltda, Casilla 143, T071-197 2757, T09-8501 6211, www.trekkerchile.com. Camper vans, trucks and 4WD vehicles available for routes throughout Chile and into Argentina.

Train
To/from **Santiago**, 5-6 a day, 3 hrs, US$6. To **Constitución**, daily 0715, return 1615, 3½ hrs, US$4 one way, preference given to local residents.

Lago Colbún and around *p241*
Buses Villa Prat runs direct services to **Quinamávida** from Santiago's Terminal Sur.

Linares *p242*
Linares' **bus** terminal is at Espinoza 530. To **Talca**, frequent, US$2. The **railway** station is at Brasil y Independencia, T09-7568 1126. Trains run to **Santiago**, 3¼ hrs, US$12-US$24; to **Chillán**, 1 hr, US$13.75.

Constitución *p242*
Bus
To **Santiago**, **Pullman del Sur**, US$12.75.

❶ Directory

Talca *p240*, *map p240*
Banks **Banco Santander**, Uno Sur 853 and Oriente 1085; **Edificio Caracol**, of 15, 1 Sur 898. For US$ cash. **Laundry** Lavaseco Donini, Colin 0237; **Lavaseco Flash**, 1 Norte 995. **Post office** 1 Oriente s/n.

Linares *p242*
Banks On plaza; Banco Santander, Independencia 336. **Post office** Rodríguez 610.

Itata Valley

The Río Itata and its longer tributary, the Río Ñuble, flow west reaching the Pacific 60 km north of Concepción. This is a tranquil valley with some native woods along the banks near the mouth of the river at the tiny hamlet of Vegas de Itata. There is no bridge here, although boats can be hired to make the short crossing in summer; in winter the river swells and no one attempts the crossing.

Chillán → *For listings, see pages 250-251. Colour map 3, C2.*

Chillán, 150 km south of Talca, is a busy but friendly place. Founded in 1580 and destroyed by the Mapuche, the city has been moved several times, most recently following an earthquake in 1833. Although the older site, now known as Chillán Viejo, is still occupied, further earthquakes in 1939, 1960 and 2010 ensured that few old buildings have survived. Nevertheless, this is one of the more interesting cities south of Santiago and has a shady plaza, numerous interesting churches and several museums, as well as a mural of the life of Bernardo O'Higgins. Pleasantly hot in summer, the city is filled with local *campesinos* on market days, creating an atmosphere that is the essence of the Central Valley.

Arriving in Chillán

Getting there and around Chillán is served by several trains and buses daily from Santiago. There are also frequent bus connections to the towns further south, especially Concepción, Temuco and Puerto Montt, but no train services. There are two long-distance bus terminals: Northern on Ecuador y O'Higgins, for all companies to major destinations, and Central on Brasil y Constitución (for Línea Azul buses in the Central Valley). Local buses leave from Maipón y Sgto Aldea. Opposite the Central terminal is the **train station** ① *Av Brasil, 5 blocks west of Plaza Bernardo O'Higgins, T0600-585 5000.* Chillán is a reasonably large city and some of the outlying barrios and attractions are quite a distance from the centre. Buses and *colectivos* are numerous, with their destinations marked in the window, but taxis are most useful for arranging excursions out of the city.

Tourist information Tourist office ① *Centro de Gestión Turística Chillán, Edif Los Héroes, of 324, T042-243 3349, www.municipalidadchillan.cl.*

Places in Chillán

Chillán was the birthplace of Bernardo O'Higgins and today's city is centred around the Plaza O'Higgins and its modern **cathedral**, designed to resist earthquakes. The **San Francisco** church, three blocks northeast contains a **museum** ① *www.museosanfrancisco.com, Mon-Fri 0930-1330, 1500-1800, Sat-Sun 1000-14000 US$2,* of religious and historical artefacts. Above the main entrance is a mural by Luis Guzmán Molina, a local artist, which is an interpretation of the life of San Francisco but placed in a Chilean context. The adjoining **convent** (1835) was a big centre for missionary work among the Mapuche.

Five streets west of the plaza is the neo-Gothic **Iglesia Padres Carmelita** (damaged in the 2010 earthquake), while to the northwest, on Plaza Héroes de Iquique, is the **Escuela México**, donated to the city after the 1939 earthquake. In its library are outstanding murals by the great Mexican artists David Alvaro Siqueiros and Xavier Guerrero depicting allegories of Chilean and Mexican history. The murals were restored in 2009, only to be damaged again in February 2010. With help from the Mexican government, they were repaired in 2013. Southwest of the Plaza is the **Museo Interactivo Claudio Arrau** ⓘ *Arrau 568, T042-243 3390, Tue-Fri 0830-1330 and 1500-1930, Sat 1000-1300 and 1600-1930, Sun 1000-1400, free entry*, built in honour of the life of the world-famous pianist

Chillán
To Talca & Santiago via Pan-American Highway (north)
Northern Terminal
To 5
Av Ecuador
Itata
Gamero
Vega de Saldias
Bulnes
Av Libertad
Constitución
El Roble
Maipón
Arturo Prat
Cocharcas
Purén
Av Collín
Escuela México
Plaza Héroes de Iquique
Santo Domingo
Plaza General Lagos
San Francisco
Gobernación
Municipalidad
Plaza Bernardo O'Higgins
Cathedral
Central Terminal
Padres Carmelita
Museo Arrau
Plaza El Roble Shopping Centre
Mercado y Feria Municipal
Local Terminal
La Merced
Plaza Segunda Independencia
San Vicente
Museo Naval El Chinchorro
Estero las Toscas
To Termas de Chillán
Isabel Riquelme
Sgto Aldea
Independencia
5 de Abril
Arauco
18 de Septiembre
Carrera
Claudio Arrau
Av B O'Higgins
Rosas
Av Brasil
To Capilla San Juan de Dios, Chillán Viejo, Concepción & Los Angeles via Pan-American Highway (south)
N
200 metres
200 yards
Where to stay
Cordillera 2
Gran Isabel Riquelme 7
Libertador 8
Ventura 4
Restaurants
Arcoiris 1
Café Europa 3
Club Comercial 4
El Sureño 2
Jai Yang 6
La Copucha 8
La Motoneta 1 5
Bars & clubs
Onde'l Pala 7

who was born here. It includes many of the musician's personal effects as well as a small interactive music room.

Five minutes' walk to the southeast is **Museo Naval El Chinchorro** ① *Riquelme y Collín, T042-221 1275*, which contains naval artefacts and models of Chilean vessels.

In Chillán Viejo, southwest of the centre, is a monument and park marking the birthplace of Bernardo O'Higgins; a 60-m-long mural depicts his life (an impressive, but sadly faded mosaic of various native stones), while the **Centro Histórico y Cultural** has a gallery of contemporary paintings by regional artists. Halfway between the centre and Chillán Viejo at Avenida O'Higgins 1661 is the **Capilla San Juan de Dios**, a small chapel dating from 1791 (closed since the 2010 earthquake).

Around Chillán → *For listings, see pages 250-251.*

Quinchamalí

Quinchamalí is a small village of little houses hidden under large fruit trees, located 27 km southwest of Chillán, at the halfway point of the new motorway to Concepción. The village is famous for the originality of its crafts in textiles, basketwork, guitars, primitive paintings and especially black ceramics. These are all on sale in Chillán market and at a handicraft fair in the village during the second week of February.

Termas de Chillán

Situated 82 km east of Chillán by good road (paved for the first 50 km), 1850 m up at the foot of the double-cratered Chillán volcano, are two open-air thermal pools, officially for hotel guests only, and a health spa with jacuzzi, sauna, mud baths and other facilities. There are several trekking opportunities from the *termas*, including a good one- or two-day return hike past some natural hot mud baths (free of charge) to the **Valle de Aguas Calientes**, where there are yet more hot springs, spectacular scenery and solitude.

Above the thermal baths is the largest ski resort in southern Chile, with 11 ski lifts and 32 ski runs (the longest is 13 km in length), rental shops, restaurants, bars, ski school, first aid and a nursery. Experienced skiers can take advantage of Nordic skiing, alpine randonnée and heli-skiing, but Chillán is also suitable for families and beginners and is a little cheaper than centres nearer Santiago, although accommodation can be pricey. For further information, contact the **Termas de Chillán Resort de Montaña** ① *Barros Arana 261, T042-243 4200, www.termaschillan.cl.*

San Fabián de Alico

This pleasant mountain village on the banks of the Río Nuble lies 67 km northeast of Chillán (via San Carlos, daily buses). In summer it is very lively and full of young Chileans. There are several campsites and *hospedajes*, and many opportunities for trekking up the valley. Horses can readily be hired. Tourist information is available in the plaza or from the Municipalidad.

Viña Chillán

① *T042-197 1573, www.vinachillan.com.*

Some 35km south of Chillán on the Bulnes–Yungay road is this Swiss-run vineyard, the southernmost in Chile to produce good quality red (and white) wines. Guided tours are available with advance notice, and there is also comfortable accommodation and a good restaurant. If you are driving this is a good place to break the journey on the long trip down to the lakes.

⦿ Itata Valley listings

For hotel and restaurant price codes and other relevant information, see pages 14-21.

⦿ Where to stay

Chillán *p247, map p248*
$$$ Gran Hotel Isabel Riquelme,
Constitución 576, T042-243 4400,
www.hotelisabelriquelme.cl. Central
business hotel, with restaurant, parking.
$$$ Libertador, Libertad 85, T042-
222 3255, www.hlbo.cl. Quite spacious
rooms, parking.
$$$-$$ Cordillera, Isabel Riquelme 652,
T042-287 6730, hotelcordillera@hotmail.cl.
3-star, central, small, all rooms with
heating, good.
$$ Ventura, O'Higgins 638, T042-222 7588,
www.hotelventura.cl. 3 star, pleasant garden,
good home cooked food in restaurant.

Termas de Chillán *p249*
$$$ Cabañas La Piedra, Los Coihues 1143,
Km 48 on road to Termas de Chillán, Recinto,
T09-9673 4250, www.cabanaslapiedra.cl.
5 *cabañas* sleeping 2, 4 or 8 are nestled in
forest, with a "tranquil and rejuvenating",
pool, hiking trips to the mountains, music
performances outdoors around the pool
under stars, good restaurants close by.
Manager Jacqueline van Nunen speaks
English, German, Dutch, Spanish.
$$$ Robledal, Las Trancas, on the road to
the Termas, Km 72 from Chillán, T042-243
2030, www.hotelrobledal.cl. Pleasant
rooms, bar, restaurant, sauna and jacuzzi,
tours offered.
$$$-$$ MI Lodge, T09-9321 7567,
www.misnowchile.com. Small lodge
with fine views, hot tub and good
restaurant. Price depends on season.

There are many *cabañas* in Las Trancas,
70 km southeast of Chillán. Usually **$$$** pp
for up to 6, see www.vallelastrancas.cl.

$ Hostelling International, Km 73.5, T042-
242 3718, hostellinglastrancas@gmail.com.
Camping available, 2 km from the slopes.

⦿ Restaurants

Chillán *p247, map p248*
The Chillán area is well known for its *pipeño*
wine (very young) and *longanizas* (sausages).
There are many cheap restaurants in and
around the Mercado Municipal.
$$$-$$ El Sureño, 5 de Abril y Gamero.
Meat and fish dishes well prepared.
Nothing extraordinary, probably the
best restaurant here.
$$ Arcoiris, El Roble 525. Vegetarian.
$$ Café Europa, Libertad 475.
Recommended.
$$-$ La Motoneta 1, Av Padre Hurtado
242, T042-227 6693. North of the town
centre, this *picada* is famous for its hearty
home-cooked food. If you are feeling
adventurous try the *guatitas españolas*.
Do not confuse with the restaurant over
the road under the same ownership that
has a different menu.
$ Club Comercial, Arauco 399. Popular at
lunchtime, good value *almuerzo*, popular
bar at night. Recommended.
$ Jai Yang, Libertad 250.
Good-value Chinese.
$ La Copucha, 18 de Septiembre y
Constitución. Inexpensive meals and snacks.

⦿ Bars and clubs

Chillán *p247, map p248*
Onde'l Pala, Flores Millan 31, T042-
232 0705, www.ondelpala.cl. Old-time
chichería full of character with rustic
wooden benches and brick walls.
Fills up with locals who come to drink
chicha or *borgoña*. Good live music at
weekends. Recommended. Note there
is no sign outside.

⊛ Festivals

Chillán *p247, map p248*
Jan Encuentro International de Teatro,
plays are performed in various public spaces.
3rd week in Mar Fiesta de la Vendemia is
an annual wine festival.

O Shopping

Chillán *p247, map p248*
Casa Rabie, 5 de Abril 758. Supermarket.
Mercado y Feria Municipal, Riquelme y
Maipón. Large market selling regional arts
and crafts.
Plaza El Roble, El Roble y Riquelme.
A modern shopping centre.

⊖ Transport

Chillán *p247, map p248*
Bus
To **Santiago**, 5½ hrs, US$17-36. To
Concepción, every 30 mins, 1½ hrs,
US$4. To **Temuco**, 3½ hrs, US$16.

Train
To/from **Santiago**, 5-6 a day, 5 hrs,
US$10.75-23.50. No trains go south

beyond Chillán and no date has been
set for a resumption of services.

Termas de Chillán *p249*
Ski buses run Jun-Sep from Libertador 1042
in Chillán at 0800, US$60 (includes lift pass).
Rem Bus, Maipón 890, of, 15, T042-222 9377,
also runs a service Fri, Sat, Sun and holidays
0750, 1320, with return at 0940, 1650, US$12
return, book in advance. Also **Montecinos**,
Sgto Aldea 647, T042-222 1105. Direct bus
from Santiago with **Nilahue** (Porto Seguro
4420, Santiago, T02-2776 1139, www.buses
nilahue.cl, in Chillán T042-270569). At busy
periods hitching may be possible between
Chillán Ski Centre and the thermal baths.

⊕ Directory

Chillán *p247, map p248*
Banks On the Plaza Bernardo O'Higgins
are **Banco BCI**, **Banco Santander** and
Banco de Chile, with ATMs; better rates at
Casa de cambio, Constitución 550. **Post
office Gobernación**, Plaza Bernardo
O'Higgins.

Biobío Valley

The Río Biobío flows northwest from the Andes to reach the sea near Concepción. At 407 km, it is the second longest river in Chile. Its more important tributaries include the Laja, Duqueco and Renaico rivers. Apart from Concepción and Talcahuano on the coast, the valley includes several other important cities, notably Los Angeles. This is the southernmost end of the Central Valley, and while you will find grapes and other Mediterranean fruit being cultivated, there are also hints of what the Lake District has to offer to the south, with forests of araucaria and snow-capped volcanos inland.

Concepción and around → For listings, see pages 258-261.

The capital of Región VIII (Biobío), Concepción is the third biggest city in Chile, with a population of nearly a quarter of a million. Founded in 1550, it was a frontier stronghold in the war against the Mapuche after 1600. The city was destroyed by an earthquake in 1751 and moved to its present site in 1764, but suffered another destructive earthquake and a tidal wave in 1835. It was severely damaged again in the February 2010 earthquake. Today, it is one of the country's major industrial centres and, at first sight, does not have many attractions. Those staying for a long period or getting involved with students at the important university will find doors opening, but otherwise a visit to the port of Talcahuano, Chile's most important naval base (15 km north), is the highlight, although it too was a casualty of the February 2010 earthquake.

Arriving in Concepción
Getting there and around Concepción is 15 km from the estuary of the Río Biobío, 516 km south of Santiago. The airport is north of the city, off the main road to Talcahuano. There are flights daily to Concepción from Santiago and Puerto Montt, one or two of which continue on to Punta Arenas. Concepción is the transportation hub of the region and is served by buses to and from Santiago, Temuco, Valdivia and Puerto Montt, as well as to and from other smaller destinations such as Cañete and Lota. There are two long-distance bus terminals and neither is located in the city centre. **Terminal Collao** ① *2 km east, on Av Gral Bonilla*, is next to the football and athletics stadium. As well as long-distance services, it also runs buses to Lota, Cañete and Contulmo. From the terminal, several city buses run to the centre, US$0.75; a taxi costs US$5. **Tur-Bus**, **Línea Azul** and **Buses Bío Bío** services leave from **Terminal Camilo Henríquez** ① *2 km northwest of main terminal off J M García, reached by buses from Av Maipú in centre*, via **Terminal Collao**. To get to nearby destinations such as Dichato and Talcahuano, it is easiest to take a *colectivo*. *Colectivos* and buses abound; the destinations are signed on the window or roof. Fares are US$0.60 for buses, slightly more for *colectivos*. There is also a suburban rail service, **Bío Tren** ① *ticket office, Av Padre Hurtado 570, T041-286 8015, www.biotren.cl.*

Tourist information **Sernatur** ⓘ *Aníbal Pinto 460 on Plaza de la Independencia, T041-274 1337, infobiobio@sernatur.cl*, provides regional information. Other useful addresses include **CONAF** ⓘ *Barros Arana 215, p 2, T041-262 4000, biobio.oirs@conaf.cl*, and **CODEF** ⓘ *Portales 508, T041-239 163*.

Places in Concepción

In the centre of the city is the attractive **Plaza de la Independencia**, where, in January 1818, Bernardo O'Higgins proclaimed the Independence of Chile. Nearby are many official buildings, including the modern cathedral, the Municipalidad and the Palacio de la Justicia. Also on the plaza is the **Museo de Arte Sagrado** ⓘ *Caupolicán 441*, containing many fine sacred Christian objects, including priests robes embroidered with gold, and a marble Christ. Southeast of the plaza is the **Parque Ecuador**, where the **Galería de la**

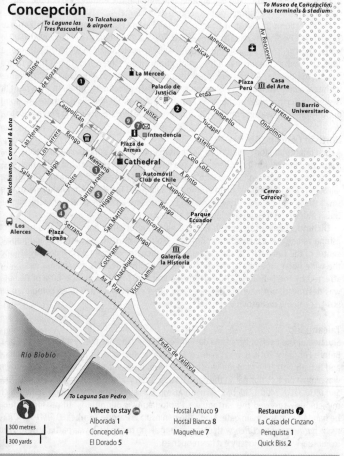

Concepción

Where to stay
Alborada 1
Concepción 4
El Dorado 5

Hostal Antuco 9
Hostal Bianca 8
Maquehue 7

Restaurants
La Casa del Cinzano
  Penquista 1
Quick Biss 2

Historia ① *Lincoyán y V Lamas, T041-285 3759, www.ghconcepcion.cl, Mon 1500-1830, Tue-Fri 1000-1330, 1500-1830, Sat-Sun 1000-1400, 1500-1900, free*, contains a pictorial history of the region; upstairs is a collection of Chilean painting. From the Parque Ecuador you can climb **Cerro Caracol**, to the south, from where there are views over the city and the river.

A few blocks north is the **Casa del Arte** ① *Chacabuco y Paicaví, by the Plaza Perú, T041-220 4290, Tue-Fri 1000-1800, Sat 1000-1600, Sun 1000-1300, free*, which contains the University art collection and temporary exhibitions; the entrance hall is dominated by *La Presencia de América Latina* by the Mexican Jorge González Camerena (1965), an impressive allegorical mural depicting Latin American history, famous throughout Chile and often depicted on postcards. Note especially the pyramid representing the continent's wealth, the figures of an armoured warrior and an Indian woman and the wounded cactus with parts missing, representing Mexico's defeat by the USA in 1845-1848. University art students are on hand to provide explanations. There is another fine mural in the entrance hall of the railway station, *La Historia de Concepción* by Gregorio de la Fuente.

Sixteen kilometres west of Concepción, the Parque Museo, **Pedro del Río Zañartu** ① *T041-241 7386, www.parquepedrodelrio.cl, Tue-Sun 1000-1900 in summer, 0900-1800 in winter, US$4 per car*, is a house and garden that is now a National Monument. Built around 1885, the house contains beautiful exhibits from all over the world. To get there take a city bus to Hualpencillo from Freire; ask the driver to let you out, then walk for 40 minutes (or hitch) along Avenida Las Golondrinas to the Enap oil refinery; turn left, then right (it is signed). Further west in the park, near the mouth of the Río Biobío, there are good opportunities for walking on the hills and several fine beaches including **Playa Rocoto**.

North of Concepción

A road (nightmare for cyclists) runs north from Concepción along the coast through the suburbs of **Penco** (Km 12), where there is a fine beach, and **Lirquén**, Km 15, a small, old, pretty town of wooden houses with a beach that can be reached by walking along the railway. There is plentiful cheap seafood for sale here. **Tomé**, 13 km further north, is a small town set in a broad bay with long beaches and an interesting cemetery, Miguel Gulán Muñoz, on the cliff overlooking the ocean.

Dichato, 9 km further north along a hilly road offering fine views, is a beautiful fishing village and a busy summer holiday resort. It is also the site of the oceanographic centre of the University of Concepción. From Dichato you can take a local bus around the wide horseshoe bay to the tiny village of **Cocholgüe**. This whole area was badly affected by the February 2010 earthquake and tsunami; for instance, 80% of Dichato was destroyed, but new sea defences and other repair work had been completed by 2014. See www.dichatovive.cl.

Talcahuano

Situated at the neck of Península de Tumbes, Talcahuano has the best harbour in Chile. Before February 2010, it was Chile's main naval station and an important commercial and fishing port. The tsunami wrecked the naval base and port, but by 2014 the town was almost back to normal. In the naval base you can visit the great ship **Huáscar** ① *Tue-Sun 0930-1200, 1400-1730, US$2, www.huascar.cl*, a relic of the War of the Pacific which miraculously survived the earthquake. Photography is permitted, but passports must be handed in at the main gate. Along the peninsula is **Parque Tumbes** ① *T041-227 0156, www.parquetumbes.cl, free*, with paths leading along the coast. It was partially destroyed in February 2010; ask locally if it has reopened.

South of the Río Biobío is the **Costa del Carbón**, until recently the main coalmining area of Chile. The road is busy, noisy and polluted by trucks plying to and from the numerous local industries; it is linked with Concepción by two bridges over the Biobío. This is another area recovering from the 2010 earthquake and tsunami.

Towards Lota

Just across the Río Biobío from Concepción is the **Laguna Grande**, a watersports centre, and **Laguna San Pedro Chica**, which is good for swimming. **Coronel**, 29 km from Concepción, was the scene of a British naval defeat in 1914, when the *Good Hope* and *Monmouth* were sunk by the German ship *Scharnhorst*. A monument commemorating the defeat was erected in November 1989. The defeat was later avenged at the Battle of the Falklands/Malvinas with the destruction of the German squadron. Close to town on the Bahía de Coronel are the small **Playa Negra**, which has few people and black sand, and **Playa Blanca**, which is bigger with white sand.

Forty-two kilometres south of Concepción, **Lota** was, until recently, the site of the most important coal mine in Chile, originally the property of the Cousiño family. Even before the mine's closure in April 1997, the town was known to be one of the poorest in Chile and, although the government has invested in retraining for the miners and in trying to open up Lota to tourism, the city still suffers greatly from poverty and neglect. The town is in two parts: **Lota Alto**, on the hill, is the original mining town, while **Lota Bajo**, below, is more recent. The tunnels of the **coal mine** ① *T041-287 1549, 0900-1800, US$7.25*, run almost entirely under the sea (the longest is 11 km) and can be visited on guided tours led by former miners; at the entrance is a small **Museo Minero**.

The **Parque de Lota Isidora Cousiño**, covering 14 ha on a promontory to the west of the town, was the life's work of Isadora Cousiño. Laid out by English landscape architects in the 19th century, it contained plants from all over the world, ornaments imported from Europe, romantic paths and shady nooks offering views over the sea. The mansion, which was Isadora's home during her stays in Lota, was destroyed in the 1960 earthquake, and sadly, the garden suffered badly in 2010. Near the entrance to the park is the **Museo Historíco de Lota**.

Towards Lebu

South of Lota the road runs past the seaside resort of **Laraquete**, where there are miles of golden sands and lots of Chilean holidaymakers in summer. The road passes a large cellulose factory and then, at Carampangue, Km 64 south of Concepción, it forks: one branch running west to **Arauco**, the site of a great beach but also two pungent cellulose factories; the other branch continuing south, 52 km, to Tres Pinos, where there is a turning towards Lebu.

A fishing port and coal washing centre, **Lebu** lies at the mouth of the Río Lebu, 149 km south of Concepción, and is the capital of Arauco province. There are enormous beaches to both the north and south, popular on summer weekends. About 3 km north, at **Playa Millaneco**, are steep hills and caves offering good walks and majestic views.

Cañete, Contulmo and Lago Lanalhue

Twenty-four kilometres south of Tres Pinos is the small town of Cañete. It is located on the site of the historic **Fort Tucapel** (being restored), where Pedro de Valdivia and 52 of his men were killed by Mapuche warriors in 1553. About 1 km south on the road to Contulmo, in a modern building supposedly inspired by the traditional Mapuche *ruca*, is the **Museo Mapuche Juan Antonio Ríos** ① *T041-261 1093, www.museomapuchecanete.cl, Jan-Feb Mon-Fri 0930-1730, Sat-Sun 1100-1730, Sun 1300-1730; rest of year Tue-Fri 0930-1730, Sat-Sun 1300-1730; US$1.25*. Displays include Mapuche ceramics and textiles. Behind the museum is a reconstruction of a *ruca*.

South of Cañete, **Lago Lanalhue** is surrounded by forested hills from which there has been extensive logging. Much less popular than the Lake District, this area offers good opportunities for walking. A road runs south from Cañete along the north side of the lake to **Contulmo**, a sleepy village at the foot of the cordillera. The **Monumento Natural Contulmo**, 8 km south of the village and administered by CONAF, covers 82 ha of native forest. Access to the lake shore is restricted, as much of it is private property, but **Playa Blanca**, 10 km north of Contulmo, is a popular beach in summer (take any bus between Contulmo and Cañete). The wooden **Casa y Molino Grollmus**, 3 km along the southern side of the lake, are well worth a visit. The splendid garden has a fine collection of *copihue*, the national flower, and the mill, built in 1928, still contains its original wooden machinery. Twenty kilometres further east, **Purén** is reached by crossing the cordillera through dense forest (do this journey in daylight). Located in a major logging area, Purén was the site of a fortress built by Pedro de Valdivia in 1553 and destroyed soon after. It was again a key stronghold of the Chilean army in the last campaign against the Mapuche (1869-1881) and there is now a full-scale reconstruction of the wooden fort on the original site.

Lago Lleulleu and Tirúa

Lago Lleulleu lies 34 km south of Cañete. It is a peaceful lake covering 4300 ha and offers sandy beaches, many opportunities for camping, fine views of the coastal mountain range and the chance to interact with the local Mapuche community, but there are few facilities. Further south, at the mouth of the Río Tirúa is the town of **Tirúa**, largely destroyed in February 2010, but close to some wonderful country for walking and riding and with a beach that is calm and deserted. The island of **Mocha**, visited by Juan Bautista Pastenes in 1544 and later by Sir Francis Drake, lies 32 km offshore. The 2010 tsunami washed away all coastal habitation.

Los Angeles and around → *For listings, see pages 258-261.*

Situated on the Pan-American Highway, 110 km south of Chillán, Los Angeles is the capital of Biobío province and lies at the heart of a wine, fruit and timber-producing district. Founded in 1739 as a fort, it was destroyed several times by the Mapuche. Here, too, severe damage was recorded in February 2010.

Arriving in Los Angeles

Getting there Los Angeles is easily accessible from north and south by bus; the most common destinations are Santiago, Puerto Montt and Concepción, but all intermediate destinations are also served. The long-distance bus terminal is on the northeast outskirts of town; the local terminal at Villagrán y Rengo in the centre, by the market.

Tourist information Tourist office ① *Caupolicán p 3, of 6, T043-231 7107;* **CONAF** ① *J Manzo de Velasco 275, T043-232 1086.*

Places in Los Angeles

Most visitors find themselves in Los Angeles on their way to Parque Nacional Laguna de Laja and, although there isn't much here in the way of sights, it is a pleasant, expanding city, with a large Plaza de Armas. Colón is the main shopping street and there is a good daily market. The **Museo de la Alta Frontera** ① *Colón 195, closed for renovation in 2014*, has some Mapuche silver and colonial artefacts. Swimming is possible in the nearby **Río Duqueco**, 10 minutes south by bus, US$1.

Salto del Laja, 25 km north of Los Angeles, is a spectacular waterfall where the Río Laja plunges 15 m over the rocks. Numerous tour groups stop here, and the place is filled with tourist kiosks selling pap. Boat trips are available on the **Buenaventura** ① *www.buenaventura.saltosdellaja.com, US$4.50*.

Parque Nacional Laguna de Laja

① *Information from CONAF, J Manzo de Velasco 275, T043-232 1086. To get there, take the ERS Bus from Villagrán 507 in Los Angeles (by market) to Abanico, then it's a 2-hr/4-km walk to park entrance; hitching is also possible from Antuco. For details, see Transport, page 260.*
A road, paved for the first 64 km, runs east from Los Angeles for 93 km, past the impressive rapids of the Río Laja, to the Parque Nacional Laguna de Laja. Covering 11,600 ha, the park is dominated by the scree slopes of the **Antuco Volcano** (2985 m), which is still active, and the glacier-covered **Sierra Velludac**. There is no clear path to the summit of Antuco. Start out early (0500) from the Refugio Digeder at 1400 m to allow about six hours to ascend, and leave plenty of time for the descent, which is exhausting. The volcano slopes are made of black scorias blocks, which are razor sharp, so wear good strong boots and take water; be warned that this sort of terrain is very demanding and can catch out those who are unaware of its severity. From the sulphur fume-cloaked summit of the volcano are fine views over the glaciers and south to the smoking Villarrica Volcano. The valley below is green and wooded, very pleasant and sparsely visited, even in high season. The **visitor centre** is 1 km from the park administration (4 km from the entrance).

Club de Esquí de los Angeles ① *May-Aug*, has two ski-lifts, giving a combined run of 4 km on the Antuco Volcano. Passing the ski station, the road reaches the turquoise waters of the **Laguna de la Laja**, with views of the Andes stretching towards Argentina; note, however, that it is a walk of several hours from the park entrance to the lake and there is very little passing traffic. The laguna was created by the damming of the Río de Laja by a lava flow and is surrounded by stark scenery. Trees include a few surviving araucarias, and there are 47 species of birds including condors and the rare Andean gull. From the lake, the road continues to the Argentine border at **Paso Pichachén**, which is only open between December and April, depending on snowfall.

Angol

Although of limited interest to travellers, Angol is the main base for visiting the Parque Nacional Nahuelbuta, further west. Reached from the Pan-American Highway by roads from Los Angeles and Collipulli, the town is situated at the confluence of the Ríos Rehue and Picolquén, at the foot of the Cordillera de Nahuelbuta, and is the capital of the province of Malleco. It was founded by Pedro de Valdivia in 1552 and was destroyed seven times by the Mapuche. There's an excellent **tourist office** ① *O'Higgins s/n, across bridge from bus terminal, T045-271 1255*, and an office of **CONAF** ① *Prat 191, piso 2, T045-271 1870*.

Northwest of the attractive Plaza de Armas is the church and convent of **San Buenaventura**. Built in 1863, it became the centre for missionary work among the Mapuche.

Also worth visiting is **El Vergel** ① *5 km southeast of Angol, T045-271 2103, www.fundoel vergel.cl, Mon-Fri 0900-1900, Sat and Sun 1000-1900, US$2, colectivo No 2*, which was founded in 1919 by Methodists as an experimental fruit-growing nursery but now incorporates an attractive park with a wide range of trees and the Museo Dillman Bullock with displays on archaeology and natural history. It also has a hostel (**$$** without breakfast) and café.

Parque Nacional Nahuelbuta

① *Visitor centre: Pehuenco, 5 km from the entrance, www.parquenahuelbuta.cl. Park daily all year (snow Jun-Sep); visitor centre spring and summer daily 0800-1300, 1400-2000. US$8 for foreigners. Rough maps US$0.25. There is a direct bus from Angol Dec-Feb Sun 0800, return 1700; otherwise, take the bus to Vegas Blancas (27 km west of Angol) and get off at El Cruce, from where it is a steep 7 km walk to park entrance.*

Situated in the coastal mountain range at an altitude of 800-1550 m, the park covers 6832 ha of forest and offers views over both the sea and the Andes. There are some good walks: one heads 4 km west of the visitor centre to the **Piedra el Aguila** at 1158 m, where there is a mirador on top of a huge boulder; another goes to **Cormallín**, 5 km north of the visitor centre, from where you may continue to Cerro Anay, 1402 m, and another mirador. Although the forest includes many species of trees, the araucaria is most striking; some are over 2000 years old, 50 m high and with trunks 2 m in diameter. There are also seven species of orchid. Animals include pudú, Chiloé foxes, pumas, kodkod, black woodpeckers and parrots.

⊙ Biobío Valley listings

For hotel and restaurant price codes and other relevant information, see pages 14-21.

⊙ Where to stay

Concepción *p252, map p253*
$$$ Alborada, Barros Arana 457, T041-291 1121, www.hotelalborada.cl. Good 4-star with all mod cons, disabled-friendly, tours offered.
$$$ El Dorado, Barros Arana 348, T041-222 9400, www.hoteleldorado.cl. Comfortable, spacious rooms, central, bar, cafeteria, parking.
$$ Concepción, Serrano 512, T041-222 8851, www.hotelconcepcion.cl. Central, comfortable, heating, English spoken.
$$ Hostal Antuco, Barros Arana 741, flats 31-33, T041-223 5485, hostalantuco@ hotmail.com. Entry via Galería Martínez. Some rooms with bath. Simple and spartan, but clean and reasonable value.
$$ Hostal Bianca, Salas 643-C, T041-225 2103, www.hostalbianca.cl. Private or shared bath, food available, parking, student discounts.

$$ Maquehue, Barros Arana 786, p 7, T041-221 0261, www.hotelmaquehue.cl. Good services, with restaurant, laundry.

Talcahuano *p254*
$$$$ Sonesta, C A No 809, Brisas del Sol, Talcahuano, T041-210 9500, www.sonesta. com. Close to airport, attached to casino Marina del Sol, rooms and suites with all facilities, business centre.
$$ Hostal De La Costa, Jordán Valdivieso 24, T041-246 7151, www.hostaldelacosta.cl. Rooms for 1 to 4 people, with bath, TV, Wi-Fi, heating, also has a *comedor* and parking.
$$ France, Av Pinto 44, T041-292 0090. Standard 2-star hotel with café and internet access.
$$-$ Residencial San Pedro, Rodríguez 22, T041-254 2145. With breakfast. Some rooms with bath.

Towards Lota *p255*
$$ Angel de Peredo, Cousiño 149, Lota, T041-287 6824. With bath and breakfast. Good value.

Towards Lebu *p255*

For places to stay in Lebu, see http://tursimolebu.cl.

$$ Hostería Arauco, Esmeralda 80, Arauco, T041-255 1131, www.pymesdechile.cl/hosteriaarauco/. Good restaurant, bar, laundry and parking.

$$ Plaza, Chacabuco 347-B, Arauco, T041-255 1265. Cheaper rooms without bath.

$$-$ Hostal La Quinta, Gabriela Mistral 45, Laraquete, T041-257 2245. Helpful, basic, good breakfast.

$ Residencial Los Abedules, Los Abedules 40, Laraquete, T041-257 1953. Friendly, small rooms, poor bathrooms.

Cañete, Contulmo and Lanalhue *p255*

See also www.lanalhueturismo.cl.

$$$-$$ Hostal Licahue, 4 km north of Contulmo towards Cañete, T09-9779 7188, www.licahue.cl. Hotel rooms, cabins and pool, attractively set overlooking the lake.

$$ Nahuelbuta, Villagrán 644, Cañete, T041-261 1073, hotelnahuelbuta@lanalhueturismo.cl. Private or shared without bath, pleasant, parking.

$$-$ Gajardo, 7° de la Línea 817 (1 block from plaza), Cañete. Shared bath, old fashioned, pleasant rooms.

$ Central, Millaray 131, Contulmo, T041-261 8089, hotelcentral@lanalhueturismo.cl. Shared bath, no sign, very hospitable.

Camping

Sites include **Camping Huilquehue**, 15 km south of Cañete on lakeside; Elicura in Contulmo and **Playa Blanca**, 10 km north of Contulmo.

Los Angeles *p256*

$$$ Salto del Laja, T043-232 1706, www.saltodellaja.cl. Good rooms, fine restaurant, 2 pools, on an island overlooking the falls.

$$$-$$ El Rincón, Panamericana Sur, Km 494 (20 km north of Los Angeles), exit Perales/El Olivo, 2 km east, T09-9441 5019,

www.elrinconchile.cl. New English/German owners, private or shared bath. Beautiful, beside a small river, restful, fresh food from organic garden, good base for excursions, English, French, German, Italian and Spanish spoken, cash only.

$$-$ Complejo Turístico Los Manantiales, Salto del Laja, T043-231 4275, www.losmanantiales.saltosdellaja.com. Hotel rooms, cabins and camping. Private or shared bathrooms, even for tents

Parque Nacional Laguna de Laja *p257*

$$-$ Cabañas Lagunillas, T232 1086, 2 km from park entrance. Open all year, cabins sleep 6, lovely spot close to the river among pine woods, restaurant, also camping.

$ Refugio Digeder, 11 km from the park entrance, and Refugio Universidad de Concepción, both on slopes of Volcán Antuco, T041-222 9054.

Parque Nacional Nahuelbuta *p258*

Camping is available near the visitor centre (US$24); there are many other campsites along the road from El Cruce to the entrance, at Km 20 and Km 21.

🍴 Restaurants

Concepción *p252, map p253*

$$ La Casa del Cinzano Penquista, Castellón 881. Characterful restaurant, decorated with movie memorabilia and old photos, Chilean food, jazz and blues music.

$ Quick Biss, O'Higgins 960, entre Tucapel y Castellón. Salads, real coffee, good lunches and service.

Los Angeles *p256*

$$ Donde Juanito, Lientur 260. Good value, simple fish and seafood. Often packed full. Recommended.

$$ El Arriero, Colo Colo 235. Good *parrillas* and international dishes.

$ Julio's Pizzas, Colón 452. Good pizzeria.

⊛ Festivals

Cañete, Contulmo and Lanalhue
p255

Jan Semana Musical (music week) is held in Contulmo.
20 Jan Fiesta de Piedra Santa is a major Mapuche festival, held in Lumaco.

O Shopping

Concepción *p252, map p253*
The main shopping area is north of Plaza de Armas.
Feria Artesanal, Freire 777, for handicrafts.
Mercado Municipal, 1 block west of the Plaza de Armas. Seafood, fruit and veg.

⊙ What to do

Concepción *p252, map p253*
Hello Chile, T09-8433 0101, www.hello-chile.com. For tours of the Biobío region and further afield, Austrian/Chilean-run, Spanish courses, car hire arranged, lots of information.

Los Angeles *p256*
Strong Visión, Caupolicán 506, T042-241 2295, www.strongvisionaventura.co.cl. Trekking, mountain biking, rafting, kayaking, bungee jumping, fishing.

⊖ Transport

Concepción *p252, map p253*
Air
In summer flights daily to and from **Santiago** (LAN and Sky), fewer in winter; connections to **Temuco**, **Puerto Montt** and **Punta Arenas**.

Bus
To **Santiago**, 6½ hrs, US$25-36. To **Los Angeles**, US$4. To **Loncoche**, 5½ hrs, US$12. To **Pucón**, direct in summer only, 7 hrs, US$18. To **Valdivia**, 7 hrs, US$16-34.

To **Puerto Montt**, several companies, US$21-36, about 9 hrs. Best direct bus to **Chillán** is **Línea Azul**, 2 hrs, US$3. To **Lota**, 1½ hrs, US$2; many buses bypass the centre of Lota; catch them from the main road.

Train
Direct long-distance services to **Santiago** are suspended.

Cañete, Contulmo and Lanalhue
p255
Bus
Cañete Buses leave from 2 different terminals: **J Ewert** and **Inter Sur** from Riquelme y 7° de la Línea; **Jeldres**, **Erbuc** and other companies from the **Terminal Municipal**, Serrano y Villagrán. To **Santiago**, 9 hrs, US$36-47. To **Concepción**, 3 hrs, US$6. To **Angol**, US$6. To **Contulmo**, frequent, US$2.

To **Concepción**, US$7, 4 hrs; to **Temuco**, **Erbuc**, US$6.50.

Los Angeles *p256*
Bus
To **Salto de Laja**, every 30 mins with **Bus Bío Bio**, US$2 return. To **Santiago**, 6½ hrs, US$25-40. To **Viña del Mar** and **Valparaíso**, 8 hrs, US$27. Every 30 mins to **Concepción**, US$4, 2 hrs. To **Temuco**, US$7, hourly. To **Curacautín**, daily at 0945, 1600, 3 hrs, US$9 (otherwise change in Victoria). To **Antuco**, 2 hrs, Mon-Sat 5 daily, Sun and hols 2 daily, last return 1730, US$3. To **Abanico** (for Parque Nacional Laguna de Laja), **ERS Bus** from Villagrán 507 (by market), 6 a day, US$2.

Angol *p257*
Bus
To **Santiago**, US$27-42. To **Los Angeles**, US$3. To **Temuco**, **Trans Bío-Bío**, frequent, US$5. To **Parque Nacional Nahuelbuta**, direct Dec-Feb only, Sun 0800, return 1700; otherwise, to **Vegas Blancas** (7 km from park entrance), daily 0700 and 1600, return 0900 and 1600, 1½ hrs, US$2.

ℹ Directory

Concepción *p252, map p253*
Banks ATMs at banks on Av O'Higgins;
high commission; several *cambios*
in **Galería Internacional**, Barros
Arana 565 and Caupolicán 521, check
rates first. **Consulates** Argentina,
O'Higgins 420, of 82, T041-223 0257.
Laundry Lavandería Radiante, Salas 442,
very good. **Police** Station at Salas y San
Martín. **Post office** O'Higgins y Colo Colo.

Los Angeles *p256*
Banks Several around the Plaza; best rates
at **Agencia Interbruna**, Caupolicán 350.
Post office Plaza de Armas.

Angol p257
Banks Banco Santander, Lautaro 399.

Contents

Lake District

At a glance

⊖ **Getting around** Extensive bus
network and many tour operators.
Hiring a car will make things easier.
⊃ **Time required** You could do
a different activity every day for a
week and still have tons left to see.
❀ **Weather** Pleasant daytime
temperatures during summer
and autumn; a bit chilly at
night. Can rain at any time.
✖ **When not to go** Winter is
seriously wet. More popular
destinations are crowded in Feb.

★ **Don't miss ...**
1 Parque Nacional Conguillio, page 272.
2 Temuco's *feria*, page 277.
3 Adventure tourism around Pucón, page 289.
4 Lago Llanquihue, page 313.
5 The journey from Puerto Montt to Bariloche in Argentina, page 327.
6 Eating at Angelmó, pages 332 and 334.

Extending from the Río Biobío south to the city of Puerto Montt, the Lake District is one of the most popular destinations for both Chilean and overseas visitors. The main cities are Temuco, Valdivia, Osorno and Puerto Montt, but the most attractive scenery lies further east where a string of lakes stretches down the western side of the Andes. Much of this region has been turned into national parks and the mixture of forests, lakes and snow-capped volcanoes is unforgettable.

Between Temuco and the Pacific coast, meanwhile, is the indigenous heartland of Chile, home to the largest Mapuche communities. Here you will find *rucas* (traditional thatched houses) and communities still fiercely proud of their traditions, hinting at the sort of country that the first *conquistadores* might have found.

The major resorts include Pucón on Lago Villarrica and Puerto Varas on Lago Llanquihue. The cities of Temuco and Puerto Montt are also popular: Temuco for excursions into the Mapuche communities towards the coast and Puerto Montt as the starting point for longer voyages south to Puerto Natales, Puerto Chacabuco and the San Rafael glacier, as well as east across the lakes and mountains to the Argentine resort of Bariloche.

Border crossings: Chile–Argentina

There are several main routes from the Chilean Lake District into Argentina:

1 From Curacautín and Lonquimay to Zapala via Paso Pino Hachado, or Paso de Icalma (see page 274).
2 From Pucón and Curarrehue to Junín de los Andes via Paso Mamuil Malal (also known as the Paso Tromen – see page 285).
3 From Lago Pirehueico to San Martín de los Andes via Paso Hua Hum (see page 295).
4 From Paso Samoré (formerly Puyehue) to Bariloche (see page 310).
5 The lakes route, from Puerto Varas via Ensenada, Petrohué and Lago Todos los Santos to Bariloche (see page 327).

Background

After the Mapuche rebellion of 1598, Spanish settlement south of the Río Biobío was limited to Valdivia, although the Spanish had a right of way north from Valdivia along the coast to Concepción. At independence the only other Spanish settlement in this region was Osorno, refounded in 1796. The Chilean government did not attempt to extend its control into the Lake District until the 1840s. In 1845, all land south of the Río Rahue was declared the property of the state and destined for settlement and, in 1850, Vicente Pérez Rosales was sent to Valdivia to distribute lands to arriving European colonists.

The southern Lake District was settled from the 1850s onwards, mainly by German immigrants (see box, page 315). Further north, Chilean troops began occupying lands south of the Biobío after 1862, but the destruction of Mapuche independence did not occur until the early 1880s when Chilean forces led by Cornelio Saavedra founded a series of forts in the area including Temuco (1881), Nueva Imperial (1882), Freire (1883) and Villarrica (1883). A treaty ending Mapuche independence was signed in Temuco in 1881.

White settlement in the area was further encouraged by the arrival of the railway, which reached Temuco in 1893, reducing the journey time from Santiago to 36 hours; the line was later extended to Osorno (1902) and Puerto Montt (1912). In the 1930s the area became popular as a destination for rich Santiaguinos and foreign fishermen.

Today, agriculture is the most important sector of the local economy and the main industries are connected to the region's produce. Proof of Chile's position as a timber producer of international standing is provided by wood-chip piles and cellulose plants dotted along the coast. Fishing is particularly important in the south of the region, where farmed salmon regularly appears on restaurant menus. Tourism is a mainstay in summer (from mid-December to mid-March), when Chileans flock to the Lake District resorts, prices are high, and it is best to book well in advance, particularly for transport. Out of season, however, many facilities are closed.

Geography

The region between the cities of Temuco and Puerto Montt is one of the most picturesque lake regions in the world. There are 12 great lakes, and dozens of smaller ones, as well as imposing waterfalls and snow-capped volcanoes. This landscape has been created by two main geological processes: glaciation and volcanic activity. The main mountain peaks are volcanic: the highest are Lanín (3747 m) and Tronador (3460 m), both on the

The Mapuche

The largest indigenous group in southern South America, the Mapuche take their name from the words for 'land' (*mapu*) and 'people' (*che*). They were known as Araucanians by the Spanish.

Never subdued by the Incas, the Mapuche successfully resisted Spanish attempts at conquest. At the time of the great Mapuche uprising of 1598 they numbered some 500,000, concentrated in the area between the Río Biobío and the Reloncaví estuary. After 1598, two centuries of intermittent war were punctuated by 18 peace treaties. The 1641 Treaty of Quilín recognized Mapuche autonomy south of the Río Biobío.

Although tools and equipment were privately owned, the Mapuche held land in common, abandoning it when it was exhausted by repeated use. This relatively nomadic lifestyle helps explain their ability to resist the Spanish. Learning from their enemies how to handle horses in battle, they became formidable guerrilla fighters. They pioneered the use of horses by two men, one of whom handled the animal, while the other was armed with bow and arrows. Horses also enabled the Mapuche to extend their territory to the eastern side of the Andes and the Argentine *pampas*.

The conquest of the Mapuche was made possible by the building of railways and the invention of new weapons, especially the breach-loading rifle (which had a similarly disquieting effect in Africa and Asia). The settlement of border disputes between Chile and Argentina enabled Argentine troops to occupy border crossings, while the Chileans subjugated the Mapuche.

Under the 1881 treaty, the Mapuche received 500,000 ha from the government, while 500,000 ha were kept for Chile. The Mapuche were confined to reservations, most of which were situated near large estates for which they provided a labour force. By the 1930s, the surviving Mapuche, living in more than 3000 separate reservations, had become steadily more impoverished and dependent on the government.

The agrarian reforms of the 1960s provided little real benefit to the Mapuche since they encouraged private landholding – indeed some communal lands were sold off at this time – and the military government made continued encroachments on Mapuche communities, which remain among the poorest in Chile.

It is estimated that the Mapuche now occupy only about 1.5% of the lands they inhabited at the time of the Spanish conquest, mainly in communities south of the Biobío and in reserves in the Argentine *cordillera* around Lago Nahuel Huapi.

Argentine border. The most active volcanoes include Llaima and Villarrica, which erupted 22 and 10 times respectively in the 20th century.

Seven main river systems drain the Lake District, from north to south the ríos Imperial, Toltén, Valdivia, Bueno, Maullín, Petrohué and Puelo. The Río Bueno drains Lago Ranco and is joined by the ríos Pilmaiquén and Rahue, thus receiving also the waters of Lagos Puyehue and Rupanco: it carries the third largest water volume of any Chilean river. In most of the rivers there is excellent fishing.

Rain falls all the year round, most heavily further south, but decreases as you go inland: some 2500 mm of rain fall on the coast compared to 1350 mm inland. There is enough rainfall to maintain heavy forests, mostly of southern beech and native species, though there are increasingly large areas of eucalyptus and other introduced varieties to cater for the booming timber industry.

Temuco and around

At first sight, Temuco may appear a grey, forbidding place. However, in reality it is a lively industrial and university town. For visitors, it is perhaps most interesting as a contrast to the more European cities in other parts of Chile. Temuco is proud of its Mapuche heritage, and it is this that gives it a distinctive character, especially around the *feria* (outdoor market). North and east of the city are five national parks and reserves, and several hot springs, while to the west, in the valley of the Río Imperial, are the market towns of Nueva Imperial and Carahue and, on the coast, the resort of Puerto Saavedra.

Arriving in Temuco → *Colour map 4, A2/3.*

Getting there and around **Manquehue Airport** is 6 km southwest of city. There are several daily flights to/from Santiago, Concepción and Puerto Montt. There is no public bus into the city but a transfer service is run by **Transfer Temuco** ⓘ *T045-233 4033, www.transfertemuco.cl, US$4.25, book 24 hrs in advance*; it also goes to hotels in Villarríca and Pucón in season, US$15. Taxis charge US$9-11.

Temuco is the transport hub for the Lake District, and its municipal bus station serves much of the region, as well as the communities towards the coast. The long-distance terminal (Rodoviária) is north of city at Pérez Rosales y Caupolicán, and is served by city bus 2, 7 or 10; *colectivo* 11P, or taxi US$3-5. JAC ⓘ *Balmaceda y Aldunate, T045-246 5465, www.jac.cl*, has its own efficient terminal 7 blocks north of the Plaza, which also serves neighbouring towns. NarBus and Igi-Llaima are opposite. The city is easily accessible by bus from Santiago (many daily) and has connections to large towns both north and south, especially Talca, Chillán, Concepción, Valdivia and Puerto Varas and Puerto Montt (many daily). Train connections to/from Santiago and south as far as Puerto Montt are currently suspended.

Temuco is a large city. *Colectivos* and buses serve the outlying barrios. However, the centre is relatively compact, and few places are more than a 30-minute walk away. When looking for a specific address, be careful not to confuse the streets Vicuña MacKenna and General MacKenna. ▸▸ *For further information, see Transport, page 277.*

Tourist information Sernatur ⓘ *Bulnes 590, T045-240 6200, infoaraucania@sernatur.cl, Mon-Fri 0900-1900, Sat 0900-1300, 1400-1800, Sun 1100-1500*, has good leaflets in English. There is also a tourist information kiosk in the municipal market, T045-297 3628, and an office of **CONAF** ⓘ *Bilbao 931, p2, T045-229 8100, temuco.oirs@conaf.cl*. Contact **Sernap** ⓘ *Vicuña Mackenna 51, T045-223 8390, for fishing permits*. Also see www.temucochile.com.

Places in Temuco → *For listings, see pages 274-278.*

The city is centred on the recently redesigned **Plaza Aníbal Pinto**, around which are the main public buildings including the cathedral and the municipalidad; the original cathedral was destroyed by the 1960 earthquake, when most of the old wooden buildings in the city were also burnt down. On the plaza itself is a monument to La Araucanía featuring figures from local history. Nearby are fountains and a small **Sala de Exposiciones**, which stages exhibitions. More compelling, though, is the *feria*, the huge produce market at Lautaro y Aníbal Pinto, always crammed with people (many of them Mapuche), who have come from the countryside to sell their produce (see page 277).

West of the centre, the **Museo de la Araucanía** ⓘ *Alemania 84, www.museoregional araucania.cl, Tue-Fri 0930-1730, Sat 1100-1700, Sun 1100-1400, US$1 (half price for students and seniors), take bus 1 from the centre,* houses a well-arranged collection devoted to the history and traditions of the Mapuche nation; there's also a section on German settlement.

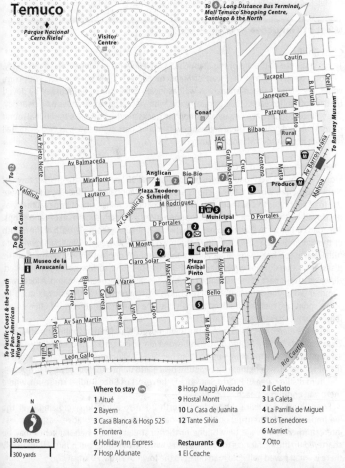

Temuco

Where to stay 🏠
1 Aitué
2 Bayern
3 Casa Blanca & Hosp 525
5 Frontera
6 Holiday Inn Express
7 Hosp Aldunate
8 Hosp Maggi Alvarado
9 Hostal Montt
10 La Casa de Juanita
12 Tante Silvia

Restaurants 🍴
1 El Ceache
2 Il Gelato
3 La Caleta
4 La Parrilla de Miguel
5 Los Tenedores
6 Marriet
7 Otto

A couple of kilometres northeast of the centre is the **Museo Nacional Ferroviario Pablo Neruda** ① *Barros Arana 565, T045-297 3941, www.museoferroviariotemuco.cl, Tue-Fri 0900-1800, Sat 1000-1800, Sun 1100-1700 (1000-1800 Oct-Mar), US$2, take micro 1 Variante, 9 Directo, 4b, taxi from centre US$2, the national railway museuem*. Exhibits include over 20 engines and carriages (including the former presidential carriage) dating from 1908 to 1953. The grounds contain rusting hulks and machinery, while the annex houses temporary exhibitions.

On the northern edge of the city is the **Monumento Natural Cerro Nielol** ① *daily 0800-1900, US$1.50*, offering views of the city and surrounding countryside. It is a good spot for a picnic. There is an excellent **visitor centre** run by CONAF and a fine collection of native plants in their natural environment, including the copihue rojo, the national flower. A tree marks the spot where peace was finally made with the Mapuche. Note that the hill has a one-way system for drivers (entry by Prat, exit by Lynch).

West of Temuco → *For listings, see pages 274-278.*

Chol Chol

To get a flavour of the life of the Mapuche, it is well worth making a trip to this dusty, friendly country town in the heart of Mapuche country. Daily buses, laden with corn, vegetables, charcoal and animals as well as locals make the 30-km journey by paved road from Temuco across rolling countryside, with views of five volcanoes on a clear day. You will see people travelling by ox cart on the tracks nearby, and a few traditional round *rucas* (thatched houses). There are also several cheap bars in the town, as well as a small museum dedicated to Mapuche culture.

Puerto Saavedra and around

From Temuco a paved road follows the Río Imperial 35 km west to the market town of **Nueva Imperial**, where cattle auctions are held on Mondays and Tuesdays. From here the road continues to **Carahue**, the site of the Spanish colonial city of Imperial that was destroyed by the Mapuche. It has accommodation, a market, supermarkets and shops. The road continues to **Puerto Saavedra**, which lies behind a sandspit south of the mouth of the Río Imperial. Founded in 1897, the town was destroyed in 1960 by a *maremoto* (tidal wave; see box, page 300). Fortunately the local population was warned of the disaster by the sight of water draining from the bay, and so few people were killed. However, the impact of the *maremoto* on folktales cannot be overestimated. A local man commented to one of the authors of this book, "We thought it was the end of the world, so we spent two months drunk on the hills until the water receded". One of Chile's most famous films, *La Frontera*, was filmed here.

After the *maremoto*, the centre of the town moved inland and its former site at **Maule**, 2 km south, became a fishing port. Just beyond Maule is a track to the incredibly narrow sandspit created by the *maremoto*. It stretches several kilometres north to the mouth of the Río Imperial, where there s a beautiful beach and uninterrupted views of the ocean. The third distinct area of Puerto Saavedra is the resort of **Boca Budi**, 4 km south, where there's an enormous beach.

From Puerto Saavedra a track leads north 2 km to a free ferry crossing over the Río Imperial to **Nehuentue**, on the north bank (there is an alternative, easier but less interesting crossing via a new bridge further upstream). From here launches may be chartered up the Río Moncul to the pleasant town of **Trovolhue**, four hours. Alternatively there is a half paved half *ripio* road north to the town of **Tirúa**, 70 km away.

Lago Budi

The only inland saltwater lake in Chile, Lago Budi lies south of Puerto Saavedra and is visited by over 130 species of water bird, including black-necked swans. Although the lake is marked on maps as having an outlet to the sea, this is dried up for most of the year, when there is a continuous track along the expanses of sandy beach from Puerto Saavedra south to Porma and Toltén. This was the old right of way for the Spanish between Concepción and Valdivia before their final defeat of the Mapuche; wild and remote, it passes many isolated Mapuche communities.

On the east shore of Lago Budi, 40 km by road south of Carahue, is **Puerto Domínguez**, a picturesque little town famous for its fishing. On the west shore is **Isla Huapi** (also spelt Guapi), a peninsula with a Mapuche settlement of *rucas* and fine views of the lake and the Pacific. This is one of the poorest spots in Chile, but is ideal for camping. It can be reached by *balsa* (ferry) either from 10 km south of Puerto Saavedra or from Puerto Domínguez.

North and east of Temuco → *For listings, see pages 274-278.*

Curacautín and around

Some 30 km north of Temuco a paved road branches off the Pan-American Highway and runs east to the Argentine border at Pino Hachado (see page 274), passing through Curacautín. A small town situated on the Río Cautín, Curacautín lies 84 km northeast of Temuco and 56 km southeast of Victoria by good paved roads. Deprived by new, stricter deforestation laws of its traditional timber industry, Curacautín is trying to recreate itself as a centre for tourism; it is a useful base for visiting the nearby national parks and hot springs, including the indoor **Termas de Manzanar** ① *17 km east of Curacautín, www.termasdemanzanar.cl, open all year daily 1000-2000, US$18 for the swimming pool, discounts for children; reached by bus from Temuco and Victoria*. The building dates from 1954. On the way, at Km 6, the road passes a turn-off to **Laguna Blanca** (25 km north, take fishing gear) and the **Salto del Indio** ① *Km 13 (Km 71 from Victoria), US$33 for up to 5 people*, a 30-m-high waterfall, where there are *cabañas*. Some 3 km beyond Manzanar is the **Salto de la Princesa**, a 50-m waterfall, with camping and *hostería*.

Termas Malleco and Parque Nacional Tolhuaca

The beautiful pine-surrounded **Termas Malleco (formerly Tolhuaca)** ① *www.termas malleco.cl, open all year, US$18, taxi from Curacautín US$20-30*, are 35 km to the north of Curacautín by *ripio* road, or 57 km by unpaved road from just north of Victoria; a high-clearance 4WD is essential out of season. Just 2 km further north is the **Parque Nacional Tolhuaca** ① *open Dec-Apr, taxi from Curacautín US$15-20*, which covers 6374 ha of the valley of the Río Malleco at altitudes of 850 to 1830 m and includes the waterfalls of Malleco and Culebra, and two lakes, Laguna Malleco and Laguna Verde. There's superb scenery and good views of the volcanoes from Cerro Amarillo. Park administration is near Laguna Malleco and there is a campsite nearby. Unfortunately, much of the park, together with the neighbouring **Reserva Nacional Malleco**, was damaged by forest fires in 2002, and will take several decades fully to recover, although some half-day trails are open.

Volcán Lonquimay and around

Situated northeast of Curacautín is **Lonquimay Volcano** (2865 m), which began erupting on Christmas day 1988; the resulting crater was named 'Navidad'. The 31,305-ha Reserva Nacional Nalcas Malalcahuello lies on the slopes of the volcano and is much less

The monkey puzzle tree

The *Araucaria araucana*, known in Chile as the araucaria or *pehuén* and elsewhere called variously the Chilean pine, the umbrella tree, the parasol tree and the monkey puzzle tree, is the Chilean national tree and has flourished in this area for 200 million years. Very slow growing, it can reach up to 40 m in height and live for 1200 years. The characteristic cones can weigh up to 1 kg so take care sitting underneath! Though its natural habitat is on both sides of the Andes between 37° and 39° south, it is much more widespread in Chile than in Argentina.

The araucaria was revered by the Mapuche, who ate both its cones and its sharp leathery leaves. Some isolated trees are still seen as sacred by the Mapuche, who leave offerings to the tree's spirit.

crowded than the nearby Parque Nacional Conguillío. Useful information about the park is available from the **CONAF** office on the main road in Malalcahuello (east of Curacautín) and from **La Suizandina** (see Where to stay, below), which is also a good base for treks and for the ascent of the volcano. Several marked trails (varying from one hour to two days) leave from the CONAF office. From Malalcahuello it is a one-day hike to the Sierra Nevada (see below), or a two-day hike to Conguillío national park; less experienced climbers should hire a guide.

Corrolco ski resort ① *T02-2206 0741, www.corralco.com, season Jun-Oct*, on the southeast side of Volcán Lonquimay, is a high-end resort with four lifts servicing 18 runs that are suitable for beginner, intermediate and advanced skill levels.

Los Arenales ski resort ① *access from Lonquimay town, T045-289 1071, www.arenales park.cl, season Jun-Sep, Sat-Tue only, ski pass US$25, equipment hire US$23*, is at Las Raíces Pass on the road from Malalcahuello to Lonquimay town. It is a pleasant, small resort with a nice restaurant and four lifts that go up to 2500 m with great views. In winter the pass is usually snowed out, and the road from Malalcahuello to Lonquimay town is diverted via the **Túnel Las Raíces** ① *toll US$1.50*. This former railway tunnel was, until recently, the longest in South America at 4.8 km. There is talk of repairing the tunnel, but for the moment it is in poor condition, unlit and with constant filtration. If travelling by bicycle it is wiser to hitch through the tunnel in a pickup than cycling through yourself.

Access to climb Lonquimay is either from Malalcahuello, 15 km south, or from from the ski resort from where it is a one-hour walk to the municipal *refugio* at the base of the mountain. Walk towards the ski lift and from there head to the spur on the left. Allow four hours for the ascent, one hour for the descent. Crampons and ice-axe are necessary in winter, but in summer it is a relatively simple climb.

Parque Nacional Conguillío
① *Entry US$8 in high season. Visitor centre at the park administration by Lago Conguillío, Dec-Mar daily 0830-1800. CONAF runs free slide lectures and short guided walks during the summer, covering flora and fauna, Volcán Llaima and other subjects.*

Situated 80 km east of Temuco and covering 60,833 ha, the park is one of the most popular in Chile though it is deserted outside January and February and at weekends. In the centre is the **Llaima Volcano** (3125 m), which is still active and can be climbed. There are two craters: the western crater was blown out in 1994 and began erupting again in March 1996. The volcano came to life again on New Year's day 2008 and the effects are visible in the massive lava-flow to the north. The last eruption was in April 2009. There are two large lakes, Laguna Verde and Lago Conguillio, and two smaller ones, Laguna Arco Iris and Laguna Captrén. North of Lago Conguillio rise the snow-covered peaks of extinct volcano **Sierra Nevada**, which reaches 2554 m.

Much of the park is covered in forests of southern beech but it is also the best place in Chile to see native **araucaria forest**, which used to cover extensive areas of land in this part of the country (see box, opposite). Mature araucaria forest can be found around Lago Conguillio and on the slopes of Llaima. Other trees include cypress and *canelo* (winter's bark). Among the park's wildlife are condors, black woodpeckers, the marsupial *monito del monte*, pumas, foxes, pudú and many waterfowl.

There are three **entrances** to the park: the northern entrance is reached by *ripio* road from Curacautín, 28 km north; the southern entrance at Truful-Truful is reached by a *ripio* road from Melipeuco, 13 km southwest, while the western entrance is reached by *ripio* road from Cherquenco (high-clearance vehicle essential). Close by is the **Araucarias ski resort** ① *T045-223 9999, www.skiaraucarias.cl, US$43 (high season)*, with four ski lifts, a café, restaurant, bar, *refugio* and equipment rental (US$27).

Trails within the park range from 1 to 22 km in length. Details are available from the park administration or from CONAF in Temuco. One of the best trails is a path round the east side

Parque Nacional Conguillio

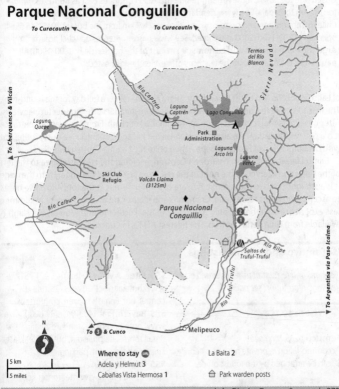

Where to stay 🛌
Adela y Helmut **3**
Cabañas Vista Hermosa **1**

La Baita **2**

🏠 Park warden posts

Border crossings: Chile–Argentina

Paso Pino Hachado

A paved road runs southeast from Lonquimay to the border at Paso Pino Hachado (1864 m). Temuco lies 145 km southwest of Lonquimay. On the Argentine side the largely paved Route 22 continues 115 km east to Zapala. Buses from Temuco to Zapala and Neuquén use this crossing.

Chilean immigration and customs Licura, 24 km west of the border, open daily 0800-1900 (2000 in summer). Very thorough searches and two- to three-hour delays reported. (See www.pasosfronterizos.gov.cl/cf_pinohachado.html.)

Argentine immigration and customs 9 km east of the border, open daily 0900-2000. There are toilets and a kiosk. For more information, see www.gendarmeria.gov.ar/pasos/chile/fichpihacha.html.

Paso de Icalma

Paso de Icalma (1303 m) lies 53 km east of Melipeuco via an unpaved road. This border is used as an alternative crossing when other crossings at higher altitude are closed due to snow. On the Argentine side this road continues east as Route 13 (*ripio*) for 132 km to Zapala. See www.gendarmeria.gov.ar/pasos/chile/fichicalma.html.

Chilean immigration and customs The police post is 3 km from the border, T045-246 6554, open daily 0800-1900 (2000 in summer). See www.pasosfronterizos.gov.cl/cf_icalma.html.

Argentine immigration and customs 9 km east of the border, daily 0800-1900. All paperwork is carried out at the customs office, clearly signposted.

---

of Lago Conguillío and north towards the Sierra Nevada (allow a full day for the round-trip). The first 10 km are reasonably easy, with two or three miradors offering spectacular views. After this it gets much more difficult for the final 5-km climb. From the western entrance it is a two- to three-day hike around Volcán Llaima to Lago Conguillío – a dusty route, but with beautiful views of Laguna Quepe – then on to the Laguna Captrén *guardería*.

Climb **Llaima** south from **Guardería Captrén**, avoiding the crevassed area to the left of the ridge and keeping to the right of the red scree just below the ridge. From the ridge it is a straight climb to the summit. Beware of sulphur fumes at the top. Allow five hours to ascend, two hours to descend. Crampons and ice-axe are essential except in summer; less experienced climbers should also hire a guide. Further information on the climb is available from **Guardería Captrén**. The nearest ATM is in Cunco.

◉ Temuco and around listings

For hotel and restaurant price codes and other relevant information, see pages 14-21.

◍ Where to stay

Temuco *p268, map p269*
Accommodation in private houses, category
$, can be arranged by the tourist office.

$$$ Aitué, A Varas 1048, T045-221 2512, www.hotelaitue.cl. Business standard, central, bar, English spoken, comfortable.
$$$ Bayern, Prat 146, T045-227 6000, www.hotelbayern.cl. Standard 3-star. Small rooms, helpful staff, buffet breakfast, *cafetería*/restaurant, parking.
$$$ Frontera, Bulnes 733-726, T045-220 0400, www.hotelfrontera.cl.

Good business standard and comfortable rooms.

$$$ Holiday Inn Express, Av R Ortega 01800, T045-222 3300, www.holidayinn express.cl. A member of the Chileanized version of this chain, good value, gym, pool, out of town but convenient for the bus terminal, worth considering if driving.

$$ Hostal Montt, M Montt 637, T045-298 2488. Comfortable if overpriced, some rooms with bath, parking, gym.

$$ La Casa de Juanita, Carrera 735, T045-221 3203, www.lacasadejuanita. co.cl. Private or shared bath, quiet, good bathrooms, parking, lots of information.

$$-$ Casa Blanca, Montt 1306 y Zenteno, T045-227 2677, hostalcasablancatemuco@gmail.com. Slightly run-down, but good value for rooms with bath.

$$-$ Hospedaje 525, Zenteno 525, T045-223 3982. Some rooms with bath, good value, older part has poor beds.

$$-$ Hospedaje Aldunate, Aldunate 187, T045-227 0057, cristorresvalenzuela@hotmail.com. Cooking facilities, some rooms with TV and bath.

$$-$ Hosp Maggi Alvarado, Recreo 209, off Av Alemania, T045-226 3215, cppacl@gmail. com. Small rooms, helpful, nice atmosphere. Also has a good-value *cabaña* sleeping 4.

$$-$ Tante Silvia, Pinto Puelma 259, T045-248 4442. Rooms or dorms, meals available, for students and groups.

Puerto Saavedra *p270*
$$$ Hotel Boca Budi, Boca Budi, T045-197 2989, www.bocabudi.cl. With bath and breakfast. Sea views, heating, room service, heated swimming pool. Tours offered. Mid-price restaurant.

$$ Cabañas Miramar, Miramar 4, Puerto Saavedra, T045-263 4290, www.miramar chile.com. Fully equipped *cabañas* for 2-8 people, with picnic and barbecue areas.

$ Hospedaje Santa Rita, Las Dunas 1511, T045-263 4171, ritasandovalm@hotmail. com. Lovely, knowledgeable host, home-cooked food served.

Curacautín and around *p271*
$$ Hostal Las Espigas, Prat 710, T045-288 1138, rivaseugenia@hotmail.com. Good rooms, dinner available on request.

$$ Plaza, Yungay 157 (main plaza), T045-288 1256, www.rotondadelcautin.cl. With **La Cabaña** restaurant, pricey. Also has **Hostería La Rotunda del Cautín**, Termas de Manzanar, T045-288 1569. Rooms and good mid-range restaurant.

$ Turismo, Tarapacá 140, T045-288 1116, hotelturismocuracautin@gmail.com. Good food, hot shower, comfortable, good value if old-fashioned.

Termas de Manzanar *p271*
$$$$-$$$ Termas de Manzanar, T045-288 1200, www.termasdemanzanar.cl. Over-priced rooms, also has suites with thermal jacuzzi.

$$$-$ Andenrose, Carr Int Km 68.5, 5 km west of Manzanar, Curacautín, T09-9869 1700, www.andenrose.com. Cosy rooms, cabins and camping, restaurant serving international and Bavarian food, bike, horse, kayak rental, jeep tours arranged, German/Chilean-run.

$ Hostería Abarzúa, Km 18, T045-287 0011. Simple, cheaper rooms without bath, full board available (good food), also campsite.

Termas Malleco and Parque Nacional Tolhuaca *p271*
$$$$-$$ Termas Malleco, Km 33, T045-241 9488, www.termasmalleco.cl. With breakfast or full board, including use of baths and horse riding, very good; jacuzzi and massage. Camping, good facilities and unlimited use of pools.

$ Residencial Rojas, Tarapacá 249. Hot water, food, camping near the river.

Volcán Lonquimay and around *p271*
$$$-$ La Suizandina, 3 km before Malalcahuello village, Km 83 Carretera Internacional a Argentina (Erbuc bus from Temuco 2½ hrs), T045-2197 3725 or T09-9884 9541, www.suizandina.com. Hostel

offering a range of rooms, in main house, guesthouse, dorm, cabin or camping. Large Swiss breakfast with home-baked bread, half board available, credit cards accepted, laundry, book exchange, bike and ski rental, horse riding, hot springs, travel and trekking information, German and English spoken. "Like being in Switzerland".

$$ Hostal Lonquimay, Pinto 555, Lonquimay, T045-289 1324. Basic rooms with shared bath.

$$-$ Residencial Los Sauces, Estación 510, Malalcahuello village, T09-7497 8706. Doubles and singles with shared bath and good-value *cabañas*. Full board available.

Parque Nacional Conguillio
p272, map p273

$$$ La Baita, in the park, 3 km south of Laguna Verde, T045-258 1073, www.labaita conguillio.cl. *Cabins* with electricity, hot water, kitchen and wood stoves, charming, lots of information, Italian/Chilean-owned.

$$$-$$ Cabañas Vista Hermosa, 10 km from the southern entrance, T09-9444 1630, www.vistahermosaconguillio.cl. Clean but spartan wooden cabins, each with a wood stove and fantastic views to the volcano. Electricity in afternoon only. Run by a horse-riding guide (former champion rider). Good food.

$$ Adela y Helmut, Faja 16000, Km 5 Norte, Cunco, T09-8258 2230, www.adelay helmut.com. Guesthouse and restaurant on a Mapuche/German-owned farm, English spoken, room for families and for backpackers in 6-bed dorm, breakfast and dinner available, kitchens, hot showers, solar heating, mountain bike rental, good reports. They run year-round tours to Conguillio National Park, visiting lakes, waterfalls, with hikes adapted to physical ability. They can also arrange fly-fishing packages and golf. The guesthouse is 16 km from Cunco on the way to Melipeuco; website has directions and you can phone for a pick-up from the bus stop; **Nar-Bus**,

Cruzmar and **InterSur** buses from Santiago and Temuco pass the Faja and will drop passengers. Alternatively, a pick-up from Temuco costs US$49 for up to 4 people.

$ Hospedaje Icalma, Aguirre Cerda 729, Melipeuco, T09-9280 8210, www.melipeuco hospedaje.cl. Spacious, basic rooms. There are other *hostales* and restaurants in Melipeuco.

Camping
Cabañas y Camping La Caseta y El Hoyón, administered by **CONAF**, T065-297 2336, reservas@parquenacionalconguillio.cl.

🍴 Restaurants

For places to eat in Puerto Saavedra, Curacautín and the national parks, see Where to stay, above.

Temuco *p268, map p269*
Many good restaurants around Av Alemania and Mall Mirage, about 10 blocks west of centre. For a cheap lunch, make for the **Mercado Municipal** on Aldunate y Portales, or the rural bus terminal, where there are countless restaurants serving very cheap set meals.

$$ La Caleta, Mercado Municipal, Aldunate y Portales, T045-221 3002. One of the better choices in the covered market serving fish and seafood.

$$ La Parrilla de Miguel, Montt 1095, T045-227 5182. Good for meat, large portions, and wine; one of the better restaurants.

$$ Otto, V MacKenna 530. German food, sandwiches, cakes, etc.

$ El Ceache, Cruz 231. Simple food such as chicken and fries, good value set lunch.

$ Los Tenedores, San Martín 827. Good-value lunch.

Cafés
Il Gelato, Bulnes 420. Delicious ice cream.
Marriet, Prat 451, loc 9, www.marriet.cl. Excellent coffee.

🍸 Bars and clubs

Temuco *p268, map p269*
Banana bliss, Montt 1031. Bar and disco.
El Túnel, Caupolicán y M Blanco. Restaurant with dancing.

🎭 Entertainment

Temuco *p268, map p269*
Dreams, Av Alemania 945, www.mundo dreams.com. Casino and hotel holds concerts by local and international artists.

🛍 Shopping

If you're heading to the Parque Nacional Conguillio, buy supplies in Temuco, Curacautín or Melipeuco, where they are much cheaper than in the shop in the national park.

Temuco *p268, map p269*
Crafts
Best choice is in the **indoor municipal market** at Aldunate y Portales, and in the Agrupación de Mujeres Artesanas, Claro Solar 1005 y Aldunate, T045-7790 3676, wanglenzomo@gmail.com, Mon-Fri 1000-1800, which sells many items, including textiles made by a Mapuche weavers' cooperative, all with traditional designs. It also offers design classes for traditional dresses (US$73).
Fundación Chol-Chol, Sector Rengalil, Camino Temuco–Nueva Imperial Km 16, T045-261 4007, http://en.cholchol.org. This non-profit organization sells traditional Mapuche textiles, naturally dyed and hand woven by local women. Book in advance to sample some traditional, freshly made Mapuche fare.

Market
Temuco Feria, Lautaro y Aníbal Pinto. This is one of the most fascinating markets in Chile, with people bringing excellent fruit and vegetables from the surrounding countryside, including spices, fish, grains,

cheese and honey. Also many cheap bars and restaurants nearby.
Frutería Las Vegas, Matta 274, sells dried fruit (useful for climbing/trekking).

⛰ What to do

Temuco *p268, map p269*
Most companies in Temuco offer tours to **Parque Nacional Conguillio**, 1 day, US$180; to **Puerto Saavedra** and **Villarrica volcano** (US$100), but unless you are in a hurry it is better and cheaper to book a tour closer to the destination. Some also offer skiing and snowboarding trips.
Amity Tour, Bucalemu 01220, T045-244 4574, www.amity-tours.com. A wide range of tours throughout the region.

Curacautín and around *p271*
Turismo Tolhuaca, Calama 230, T045-288 1211, www.termasdetolhuaca.cl. Agency for accommodation, restaurants and riding in the area.

🚌 Transport

Temuco *p268, map p269*
Air
LAN has flights from **Manquehue Airport**, to **Santiago**, **Concepción**, **Osorno**, **Puerto Montt** and **Balmaceda**. Sky to **Santiago**, **Concepción**, **Osorno** and **Puerto Montt**.

Bus
Local Buses to neighbouring towns leave from **Terminal Rural**, Pinto y Balmaceda, or from bus company offices nearby. To **Coñaripe**, 3 hrs, and **Lican Ray**, 2 hrs. To **Panguipulli**, with **Power** and **Pangui Sur**, 3 hrs, US$6.50. **Pangui Sur** also run to **Loncoche**, US$4, **Los Lagos**, US$8, **Mehuin** in summer only. To **Curacautín** via Lautaro, with **Erbuc**, US$6.50, 4 daily, 2½ hrs. To **Lonquimay**, with **Erbuc**, 4 daily, 3½ hrs, US$8. To **Contulmo**, US$6.50, and **Cañete**, US$6, with **Erbuc** and **Igi Llaima**.

Long distance The long-distance terminal (Rodoviária) is north of city at Pérez Rosales y Caupolicán. **JAC, NarBus** and **Igi-Llaima** services depart from Balmaceda y Aldunate, 7 blocks north of the Plaza. To **Santiago**, many overnight, 8-9 hrs, US$23-62. To **Concepción**, with Bío Bío (Lautaro entre Prat y Bulnes), US$13, 4 hrs. To **Chillán**, 3½ hrs, US$16. **Cruz del Sur** run 3 buses a day to **Castro**, 10 a day to **Puerto Montt** (US$11.50-28, 5-6 hrs). To **Valdivia**, with **JAC, Narbus/Igi Llaima**, several daily, US$7, 2½ hrs. To **Osorno**, US$9, 4¼ hrs. To **Villarrica** and **Pucón**, with **JAC**, many between 0705 and 2045, 1½ hrs, and 2 hrs, US$9.

To Argentina El Valle and **Caraza** have buses to **Zapala** and **Neuquén**, via Paso Pino Hachado. To reach **Bariloche**, change in Osorno.

Car hire
Ace, Carrera 940 (in terminal), T045-231 8585. **Automóvil Club de Chile**, San Martín 278, T045-291 0521. **Euro**, MacKenna 399, T045-221 0311, helpful, good value. **Full Famas**, at airport and in centre T045-221 5420.

Puerto Saavedra *p270*
To **Temuco** (Terminal Rural), with **Narbus**, hourly, 3 hrs, US$4.

Lago Budi *p271*
There are buses from **Puerto Domínguez** to Temuco, 3 hrs. The Carlos Schalchli ferry leaves Puerto Domínguez for **Isla Huapi**, Mon and Wed 0900 and 1700, returning 0930 and 1730, free, 30 mins.

Curacautín and around *p271*
Bus Terminal on the main road, by the plaza. Buses to/from **Temuco**, **Los Angeles** and **Santiago**.

Volcán Lonquimay and around *p271*
Bus **Erbuc** runs 4 services from **Temuco** via Lautaro to **Malalcahuello**, US$3, 2½ hrs, and **Lonquimay town**, US$4, 3½ hrs. **Buses Bio Bio** has daily services from Temuco via Lautaro and Curacautín to **Malalcahuello**, 3 hrs, US$6, and **Lonquimay** town, 3½ hrs (or 4 hrs via Victoria), US$7.75.

Parque Nacional Tolhuaca *p271*
There are bus services from Victoria to **San Gregorio** (19 km from park entrance).

Parque Nacional Conguillio
p272, map p273
Private transport or taking a tour are the best ways to see the area. For touring, hire a 4WD vehicle in Temuco (essential in wet weather). See also **Adela y Helmut**, under Where to stay, above.

To the **northern entrance**, poor *ripio* road: **taxi** from Curacautín to Laguna Captrén, US$70-80 one way. To **Melipeuco** (paved road, stops at **Hospedaje Icalma**), buses every hour from Balmaceda bus terminal, **Temuco** (or flag down at Mackenna y Varas), 2½ hrs, US$7, and once a day to **Icalma** when no snow on road. From May to end-Dec the only access is via Melipeuco. Transport can be arranged from Melipeuco into the park (ask in grocery stores and *hospedajes*, US$50-60 one way). To **Cunco**, every 20 mins from same terminal. To the **western entrance**: daily **buses** from Temuco to **Cherquenco**, from where there is no public transport to the park.

ℹ Directory

Temuco *p268, map p269*
Banks Many ATMs at banks on Plaza Aníbal Pinto. Also at the JAC bus terminal (Visa). Many *cambios* around the plaza, all deal in dollars and Argentine pesos.

Lago Villarrica and around

Wooded Lago Villarrica, 21 km long and about 7 km wide, is one of the most beautiful lakes in the region, with the active and snow-capped Villarrica Volcano (2840 m) to the southeast. Villarrica and Pucón, resorts at the lake's southwest and southeast corners, are among the more expensive in the region, but are definitely worth a visit.

Villarrica → *For listings, see pages 286-291. Colour map 4, B2.*

Pleasantly set at the extreme southwest corner of the lake, Villarrica can be reached by a paved road southeast from Freire, 24 km south of Temuco on the Pan-American Highway, or from Loncoche, 54 km south of Freire, also paved. Less significant as a tourist resort than nearby Pucón, it is a little cheaper. Founded in 1552, the town was besieged by the Mapuche in the uprising of 1599: after three years the surviving Spanish settlers, 11 men and 13 women, surrendered. The town was refounded in 1882; the **Museo Leandro Penchulef** ① *O'Higgins 501, T045-241 1667, Dec-Jan Mon-Fri 1000-1800, Feb 0900-1700, free,* in the striking Universidad Católica, focuses on this event. There is a small museum, **Museo Histórico** ① *Pedro de Valdivia 1050 y Zegers, Mon-Sat 0900-1300, 1800-2200, reduced hrs in winter,* containing a collection of Mapuche artefacts. Next to it is the

Lagos Villarrica, Caburga & Colico

Muestra Cultural Mapuche, featuring a Mapuche *ruca* and stalls selling good quality handicrafts in summer. The **tourist office** ① *Valdivia 1070, T045-241 1162, summer daily 0800-2300, off season daily 0800-1330, 1430-1800,* has information and maps.

There are good views of the volcano from the *costanera*; for a different perspective over the lake, go south along Aviador Acevedo and then Poniente Ríos towards the **Hostería de la Colina**. Just south of town (500 m along Avenida Matta), there is a large working farm, **Fundo Huifquenco** ① *T045-241 5040,* with trails, horse riding, carriage rides and meals (book in advance).

Villarrica

Where to stay 🛏
Bungalowlandia 1
Chito Fuentes 7
El Ciervo 5
Hospedaje Nicolás 11
Hostería Bilbao 9
Hostería de la Colina 10
Hotel y Cabañas El Parque 6

Hotel-Yachting Kiel 12
La Torre Suiza 13
Villarrica Park Lake 16

Restaurants 🍴
Café 2001 1
Casa Vieja 6
El Marítimo 7

El Tabor 2
El Turismo 8
Juanito 4
La Cava del Roble 3
La Vecchia Cucina 9
The Travellers Resto Bar 5

On the southeastern corner of the lake, 26 km east of Villarrica, Pucón is one of the most popular destinations in the Lake District, famous above all as a centre for visiting the 2840 m Villarrica Volcano, which dominates the view to the south. Built across the neck of a peninsula, the town has two black-sand beaches, which are popular for swimming and water sports. Whitewater rafting is also offered on the nearby rivers and excursions can be made into the Parque Nacional Huerquehue or the Cañi Nature Reserve as well as a number of thermal springs, all of which lie east of the town. Other activities include winter sports and ziplining (see What to do, page 289).

Arriving in Pucón
Getting there and around Pucón is served by daily buses from Puerto Montt and Valdivia and several daily (many overnight) from Santiago. There are regular services from Temuco and Villarrica. The airport is 2 km east of Pucón on the Caburga road. Pucón is small enough to walk around. Taxis are available for out-of-town trips.

Tourist information Do not confuse the **Municipal Tourist Office** ① *Municipalidad, O'Higgins 483, T045-229 3002, ofturismo@municipalidadpucon.cl*, which provides information and sells fishing licences, with the **Chamber of Tourism** ① *at the entrance to Pucón from Villarrica, Brazil 315, T045-244 1671, www.puconturismo.cl*, and other private operators displaying 'Tourist Information' signs. The town also has a **CONAF** office ① *Lincoyan 336*, with leaflets and information on the national parks.

Places and what to do in Pucón
The Pucón of today is very different from the town of 30 years ago, when it was a small, pleasant, quiet village with some seasonal Chilean tourism, but no foreign backpackers. It is now a thriving tourist centre, full of Chileans in summer and gringos in the autumn. Within easy reach of town is an active climbable volcano where you can also ski in winter, plus rivers for whitewater rafting and fly-fishing, canopy tours in native forests, quadbike excursions, lakes and waterfalls, two national parks and a private nature sanctuary as well as a dozen thermal springs. This makes Pucón an excellent base for visiting the northern Lake District.

Every other house in the town centre seems to offer accommodation, while the main drag is awash with tour operators. Neon signs are forbidden and road signs and telephone kiosks are made of wood, but the streets are full of bars, restaurants, boutiques and *artesanía*. The commercial centre lies between **Avenida O'Higgins**, the main thoroughfare, and the **Gran Hotel Pucón**. Private land (ask for permission at the entrance) leads west from the centre of town to **La Península**, where there are fine views of the lake and volcano, as well as a golf course. There is also a pleasant walk, along the **Costanera Otto Gudenschwager**, starting at the northern end of Calle Ansorena (beside Gran Hotel Pucón) and following the lakeside north.

Boat trips ① *5 a day in summer only, 2 hrs, US$9*, on the lake leave from the landing stage at La Poza at the western end of O'Higgins. Walk a couple of kilometres north along the beach from here to the mouth of the Río Trancura for views of volcanoes. Or take a **boat** ① *summer only, US$15*, to the mouth of the river from near the **Gran Hotel**.

To cross the Río Pucón, head east out of Pucón along the main road, then turn north on an unmade road leading to a bridge. There are pleasant walks from here along the north shore of the lake to the Mapuche settlement of **Quelhue** and the beach at **Río Plata**, or northeast towards **Caburga** (the round trip makes a perfect day's outing by mountain bike). You can also strike up into the hills through farms and agricultural land, with views of three volcanoes and the lake (if possible, ask permission to cross first).

From the road to the Villarrica Volcano, a *ripio* road branches off for 5 km to some privately managed **Cuevas Volcánicas** (volcanic caves) ① *T045-244 2002, www. cuevasvolcanicas.cl, US$21.50*, surrounded by a small attractive park with tunnels and a museum, as well as paths through the forest. Entry to the site is expensive, but it's recommended as a bad-weather option. Snowmobile tours are also offered.

Pucón

100 metres / 100 yards		
Where to stay		
Antumalal **2** *C1*	Donde Germán **6** *C3*	Interlaken **24** *C1*
Cabañas Rucamalal **1** *B3*	El Refugio **4** *C2*	La Bicicleta **7** *B2*
	Hospedaje Irma **5** *C1*	La Poza **9** *C1*
	Hospedaje Victor **11** *C2*	La Tetera **29** *B2*
	Hostal Backpackers **3** *C2*	
	Hostal Gerónimo **26** *B3*	**Restaurants**
	Hostería ¡école!	Arabian **1** *B2*
	& restaurant **21** *B3*	Café de la P **2** *B1*

Café Lounge Brasil **3** *C3*	
Cassis **4** *B2*	
Il Baretto **5** *B2*	
La Maga **7** *B2*	
Puerto Pucón **10** *B2*	
Rap Hamburguesa **9** *B3*	
Senzo **11** *B2*	

East of Lago Villarrica → *For listings, see pages 286-291.*

Within easy reach of Villarrica and Pucón are two more lakes, two national parks and several hot springs. Busy with Chilean tourists in summer, these are among the most dramatic spots in the Lake District and well worth a visit for those in the area.

Parque Nacional Villarrica

This park, which covers 61,000 ha, stretches from Pucón to the Argentine border near Puesco. There are three sectors: Villarrica Volcano sector ① *entry fee US$1.75, ascent fee US$7.50*; Quetrupillán Volcano sector (see page 285); and the Puesco sector, which includes the slopes of the Lanín Volcano on the Argentine border. Each sector has its own entrance and ranger station.

The **Villarrica Volcano**, 2840 m high and still active, lies 8 km south of Pucón. Access to this sector is in theory restricted only to groups with a guide and to individuals who can show proof of membership of a mountaineering club in their own country. There is no public transport, although several agencies offer trips. Entry is refused if the weather is poor. Good boots, crampons and ice picks are essential; these can be rented from tour operators for US$12.50, but will generally be included in the price of a tour. You should also take sunglasses, sun block, plenty of water and chocolate or some other snack; equipment is checked at the park entrance. ▶ *See What to do, page 289.*

It is a three- to four-hour trek to the summit, but you can skip the first part of the ascent by taking the **ski lift** ① *US$16*. In summer this is recommended as it saves 400 m climbing scree. If the conditions are right, at the summit you can look down into the crater at the bubbling molten lava below, but beware of the sulphur fumes; take a cloth mask moistened with lemon juice. On exceptionally clear days you will be able to see six or more other volcanoes. Conditions permitting, groups may carry ski and snowboard equipment for the descent; otherwise just slide down the many toboggan chutes.

The **Pucón ski resort** ① *T045-244 1901, www.skipucon.cl*, owned by the Gran Hotel Pucón, is on the eastern slopes of the volcano, reached by a track, 35 minutes. The ski season is July to September, occasionally longer. Information on snow and ski-lifts (and, perhaps, transport) is available from the tourist office or Gran Hotel Pucón. The centre offers equipment rental, ski instruction, first aid, restaurant and bar as well as wonderful views from the terrace. The centre is good for beginners; more advanced skiers can try the steeper areas

Lagos Caburga and Colico

Lago Caburga (spelt locally Caburgua) is a very pretty lake in a wild setting 25 km northeast of Pucón. It is unusual for its beautiful white-sand beach (other beaches in the area have black volcanic sand), and is supposedly the warmest lake in the Lake District. The western and much of the eastern shores are inaccessible to vehicles, but the village of **Caburga**, at the southern end of the lake, is reached by a turning off the main road to Argentina, 8 km east of Pucón. If walking or cycling, there is a very pleasant alternative route: turn left 3 km east of Pucón, cross the Puente Quelhue, then turn right and follow the track for 18 km through beautiful scenery. Just off the road from Pucón, at Km 15, are the **Ojos de Caburga** ① *US$1; ask the bus driver to let you off, or go by mountain bike from Pucón via the Puente Quelhue*, beautiful pools fed from underground, particularly attractive after rain. The northern tip of the lake can be reached by a road from Cunco, which runs east along the northern shore of **Lago Colico**. This is one of the less accessible lakes and lies north of Lago Villarrica in a remote setting.

Parque Nacional Huerquehue

① Daily 0800-2000 but often closed after heavy snowfall, US$3.50. To get there: take the Caburga road from Pucón; 3 km before Caburga turn right along a ripio road to Paillaco, from where another road leads 7 km to the park administration, free parking 1.5 km along the track. Buses Caburga has services from Pucón.

Located a short distance east of Lago Caburga, Parque Nacional Huerquehue covers 12,500 ha at altitudes rising to 1952 m at Cerro San Sebastián in the **Nevados del Caburga**. It also encompasses about 20 lakes, some of them very small, and many araucaria trees. The entrance and administration is on the western edge, near **Lago Tinquilco**, the largest lake in the park. From the entrance there is a well-signed track north up a steep hill to **Lago Chico**, where the track divides left to **Lago Verde** and right to **Lago Toro**. Both paths eventually meet up, making a circuit. The lakes are surrounded by trees and are very beautiful. At **Lago Huerquehue**, a further 20 km of trails begin. None of the routes is particularly taxing, making the park a good warm-up for the Volcán Villarrica hike. An adequate map may or may not be provided at the entrance. The warden is generally very helpful. People in the park rent horses and boats, but you should take your own food.

Termas de Quimey-co, de Huife and los Pozones

South of Parque Nacional Huerquehue and reached via turning off the Pucón–Caburga road are three sets of thermal baths. The most expensive and ostentatious are the **Termas de Huife** ① Km 33, T045-244 1222, www.termashuife.cl, US$25 in high season (Dec-Mar), where entry includes the use of one modern, pleasant pool. Closer to Pucón are the recently refitted **Termas de Quimey-co** ① Km 29, T09-8775 2113, www.termasquimeyco. com, US$21.50 in high season, while further on are the **Termas los Pozones** ① Km 35, US$6.30 per day, US$8 at night, which have six natural rock pools but little infrastructure and are very popular with travellers, especially at night. The road here is rough.

Reserva Forestal Cañi

① Park entry US$3.50. There is a self-guided trail, US$8 plus transport. For tours with English-speaking guide, contact the Cañi Guides Program, www.ecole.cl.

Situated south of Parque Nacional Huerquehue and accessed from the road to the Termas de Huife, this is a private nature reserve covering 500 ha, owned by the non-profit **Fundación Lahuén**. It is a three- to four-hour trek to its highest peak, **El Mirador**. The first part of the trek to a basic *refugio* at the park entrance is straightforward, along a wide path winding upwards through ancient native forests of coigue and lenga, with occasional views back to Lagos Villarrica and Caburga. Inside the reserve there are 17 small lakes, snow-covered for much of the year. Between these lakes are dotted millennial araucaria trees. From here it is a steep climb to **El Mirador** (1550 m) from where there are panoramic views over neighbouring parts of Argentina and Chile, including four volcanoes: **Lanín**, **Villarrica**, **Quetrupillán** and **Llaima**. As the reserve is above the snowline for much of the year, independent visits are normally restricted to summer, although guided visits are possible off season. ▶▶ See also What to do, page 289.

Towards Argentina

From Pucón a road runs southeast along the southern bank of the valley of the Río Trancura to **Curarrehue** and the Argentine border, providing access en route to thermal springs and a number of hikeable *saltos* (waterfalls).

Border crossings: Chile–Argentina

Paso Mamuil Malal

Paso Muil Malal (also known as Paso Tromen) is 76 km southeast of Pucón. There is free CONAF camping with no facilities at Puesco. A bus from Pucón to Puesco takes two hours, US$4. The border is open all year, but is closed during heavy rain or snow (phone to check: in Chile, Cautín provincial government, T045-296 8126; in Argentina, gendarmería, T02972-427339). The road (very hard for cyclists) continues south through Parque Nacional Lanín in Argentina to Junín de los Andes, San Martín de los Andes and Bariloche.

Chilean immigration and customs 17 km before the border at Puesco, open daily 0800-2000 (until 1900 mid-March to mid-October; see www.pasosfronterizos.gov.cl/cf_puesco.html).

Argentine immigration and customs Puesto Tromen, 3 km east of the pass, open daily 0900-2000 all year, see www.gendarmeria.gov.ar/pasos/chile/fichmamal.html.

At Km 18, a *ripio* road heads south 10 km to the **Termas de Palguín** ① *T045-244 1968, termasdepalguin@gmail.com, US$8,* and a series of spectacular **waterfalls** ① *US$3.50.* A hidden 200-m path leads to **Salto Palguín** (which can be seen from the road), and beyond that is the impressive **Salto China**, where there's a restaurant and camping. **Saltos del Puma** and **del León** are 800 m from the Termas. From Pucón take Bus Regional Villarrica from Palguín y O'Higgins at 1100 to the junction (10 km from Termas); last bus from junction to the Termas at 1500, so you may have to hitch back. Taxi US$20.

From the springs, a rough dirt road runs south to Coñaripe, with access to the Volcán Quetrupillán section of the **Parque Nacional Villarrica**. If you're driving, a high-clearance 4WD vehicle is necessary to reach the national park, and the road is often impassable in winter; but travelling on horseback is best. The treks in this sector are not physically demanding. Palguín is also the starting point for a three-day hike to Puesco, with vistas over the Villarrica and Lanín volcanoes. Further along the road, on the other side of the park are the **Termas Geométricas** (see page 294). Because of the poor state of the road, access is easier from Coñaripe.

Back on the Curarrehue road, at Km 23, a turning leads north to the indoor and outdoor pools at **Termas de San Luis** ① *T045-241 2880, www.termasdesanluis.cl, US$9,* and **Termas Trancura** ① *www.termastrancura.com, US$9 or US$18 including transport from Pucón,* from where it is 30 minutes' walk to **Lago del León**. At Km 35 another turning leads north for 15 km to the **Termas de Panqui** ① *US$9,* where there are three pools beautifully situated in the mountains as well as accommodation (T045-211 2039).

Beyond the small town of Curarrehue, 36 km east of Pucón, where there is a small but interesting Mapuche museum, the road continues unpaved, climbing south past Puesco to Lago Quellelhue, a beautiful area for trekking, tranquil and with well-marked trails. This is probably the easiest area to see araucaria forest close-up from the comfort of a car. Six kilometres southeast is the border at **Paso Mamuil Malal** (also known as Paso Tromen), see box, above. To the south of the pass rises the graceful cone of **Volcán Lanín** (3747 m), one of the world s most beautiful mountains. Currently dormant, Lanín is geologically one of the youngest volcanoes in the Andes and is climbed from the Argentine side. A four-hour hike from Argentine customs leads to a *refugio* at 2400 m. The climb from here to the summit is not difficult but crampons and ice axe are needed.

Lago Villarrica and around listings

For hotel and restaurant price codes and other relevant information, see pages 14-21.

Where to stay

Villarrica *p279, map p280*
Lodging in private homes in our **$$-$** range can be found on Muñoz blocks 400 and 500, Koerner 300 and O'Higgins 700 and 800. More upmarket accommodation is on the lakefront.

$$$$ Villarrica Park Lake, Km 13 on the road to Pucón, T045-245 0000, www.starwoodhotels.com. 5-star, all rooms with balconies overlooking the lake, spa with pools, sauna, solarium, fishing trips.

$$$ El Ciervo, Koerner 241, T045-241 1215, www.hotelelciervo.cl. Comfortable rooms, pleasant grounds, German-style breakfasts, German and some English spoken, pool, terrace.

$$$ Hostería de la Colina, Las Colinas 115, overlooking town, T045-241 1503, www.hosteriadelacolina.com. Large gardens, good restaurant (the US owner makes fresh ice cream every day), fine views, very attentive service. Fishing, horse riding and dog sledding can be organized from the *hostería* as well.

$$$ Hotel y Cabañas El Parque, Camino Villarica, Km 2.5, T045-241 1120, www.hotelelparque.cl. Lakeside with beach, tennis courts, good restaurant set meals.

$$$ Hotel Yachting Kiel, Koerner 153, T045-241 1631, www.restaurantkiel.cl. Small hotel with 3 rooms, all with views across the lake to the volcano. Spacious bathrooms, heating. German and some English spoken. Good restaurant.

$$$ Parque Natural Dos Ríos, 13 km west of Villarrica, Putue Alto s/n, Casilla 535, T09-9419 8064, www.dosrios.de. B&B rooms or self-catering cabins. Tranquil 40-ha nature park on the banks of the Río Toltén (white-sand beach), birdwatching, child-friendly, German and English spoken.

$$ Bungalowlandia, Prat 749, T045-241 1635, www.bungalowlandia.cl. *Cabañas*, dining room, good facilities, pool.

$$ Hostería Bilbao, Henríquez 43, T045-241 1186, www.interpatagonia.com/bilbao. Small rooms, pretty patio, good restaurant.

$$ La Torre Suiza, Bilbao 969, T045-241 1213, www.torresuiza.com. Rooms and dorms, camping, cycle rental, book exchange, lots of info, reserve in advance. German and English spoken.

$$-$ Hospedaje Nicolás, Anfion Muñoz 477, T045-241 2637. Simple rooms with bath. Good value, but thin walls.

$ Chito Fuentes, Vicente Reyes 665, T045-241 1595. Basic rooms above a restaurant.

Camping

Many sites east of town on Pucón road, open in season only and expensive.

Pucón *p281, map p282*
In summer (Dec-Feb) rooms may be hard to find. Plenty of alternatives (usually cheaper) in Villarrica. Prices below are Jan-Feb. Off-season rates are 20-40% lower and it is often possible to negotiate. Many families offer rooms, look for the signs or ask in bars/restaurants. Touts offer rooms to new arrivals; check that they are not way out of town.

$$$$ Antumalal, 2 km west of Pucón, T045-244 1011, www.antumalal.com. Small, luxury, picturesque chalet-type boutique hotel, magnificent views of the lake (breakfast and lunch on terrace), 5 ha of gardens, with meals, open year round, indoor pool, hot tub, sauna, spa, jacuzzis and private beaches.

$$$$ Interlaken, Caupolicán 720, T045-244 3965, www.hotelinterlaken.cl. Chalets with full facilities, water skiing, pool, no restaurant.

$$$ Cabañas Rucamalal, O'Higgins 770, T045-244 2297, www.rucamalal.cl. Lovely cabins (with satellite TV) in a pretty garden, spacious, well equipped and decorated, various sizes, pool.

\$\$\$-\$\$ Hostal Gerónimo, Alderete 665, T045-244 3762, www.geronimo.cl. Open all year. Quiet, smart, multilingual staff, bar, restaurant.

\$\$\$-\$\$ Hostería ¡école!, General Urrutia 592, T045-244 1675, www.ecole.cl. Rooms and dorms, shop, vegetarian and fish restaurant, forest treks (departure for Lahuén Foundation's Cani Forest Sanctuary), rafting and biking, information, language classes, massage.

\$\$ Donde Germán, Las Rosas 590, T045-244 2444, www.dondegerman.cl. Single, double or triple rooms with private or shared bath. Fun, organizes tours, book in advance.

\$\$ El Refugio, Palguín 540, T045-244 1596, www.hostalelrefugio.cl. Dorm or double room, shared bath, small, convenient, cosy, Dutch/Chilean-owned. Trips sold, but shop around.

\$\$ Hostal Backpackers, Palguín 695, T045-244 1417, www.backpackerspucon.com. With or without bath, quiet, next to JAC buses, lots of activities, **Navimag** reservations, tourist info.

\$\$ La Tetera, Urrutia 580, T045-246 4126, www.tetera.cl. 6 rooms, some with bath, English spoken, book swap, information centre, good Spanish classes, car rental, book in advance. Nearby bar music is audible on weekends.

\$\$-\$ Hospedaje Irma, Lincoyán 5 45, T045-244 2226, http://hirma.cl. Private or shared bath, tourist information, bicycle hire.

\$\$-\$ Hospedaje Víctor, Palguín 705, T045-244 3525, www.pucon.com/victor. Rooms sleep 2-4 with private or shared bath, laundry. A decent choice.

\$\$-\$ La Bicicleta, Palguín 361, T045-244 4679. Cosy budget hostel offering excursions and bike tours. Owner José can help with all the details.

\$ pp Etnico Hostel and Adventures, Colo Colo 36, T045-244 2305, www.etnico.hostel.com. Owner is mountain guide. Double rooms and mixed dorms, car and bike parking, lots of activities and keen on recycling.

Camping

There are many camping and cabin establishments. Those close to Pucón include **La Poza**, Costanera Geis 769, T045-244 1435, campinglapoza@hotmail.com, hot showers, good kitchen. Several sites en route to volcano, including: **L'Etoile**, Km 2, T045-244 2188, www.letoilepucon.com, in attractive forest.

Lagos Caburga and Colico *p283*

\$\$\$\$-\$\$\$ Trailanqui, 20 km west of Lago Colico (36 km north of Villarrica), T045-257 8219, www.trailanqui.com. Luxurious hotel on the riverbank, with suites and restaurant, also equipped *cabañas*, campsite, horse riding, pool, Sunday lunch buffet.

\$\$\$ Landhaus San Sebastián, Camino Pucón a Caburga, Pucón 2222, T045-2197 2360, www.landhaus.cl. With bath and breakfast, good meals, laundry facilities, English and German spoken, Spanish classes, good base for nearby walks.

Parque Nacional Huerquehue *p284*

\$\$\$-\$\$ Puerto Parque Tinquilco, T045-244 1480, www.parquehuerquehue.cl. Hotel, cabins, camping and motorhome parking, restaurant, kayaks, boats for hire.

\$\$ Inés Braatz, German speaking family offers accommodation, no electricity, food and camping (US\$18-22 depending on season); also rents rowing boats on the lake.

\$\$ Refugio Tinquilco, 2 km from park entrance, where forest trail leads to lakes Verde and Toro, T02-2278 9831, T09-9539 2728, www.tinquilco.cl. Range of cabins, bunk beds or doubles, cheapest without sheets, bring sleeping bag, private or shared bath, meals available, heating, 24-hr electricity, sauna.

Camping

\$\$-\$ Camping Olga, T045-244 1938, camping in the park, 2 km from park entrance, with hot water.

Termas de Quimey-Co, de Huife and los Pozones *p284*

\$\$\$\$ Hostería Termas de Huife, Termas de Huife, T045-2441222, www.termashuife.cl. The most upmarket of the spa hotels.

$$$ Hotel Termas de Quimey-Co, Termas de Quimey-Co, T09-8775 2193, www.termasquimeyco.com. Also a campsite and 2 cabins.

Towards Argentina p284
$$ Kila Leufu/Ruk a Rayen, 23 km east on road to Curarrehue, T09-9711 8064, www.kilaleufu.cl. 2 adjacent guesthouses run by the same Austrian/Mapuche owners. **Kila Leufu** offers rooms on the Martínez family farm, contact Irma or Margot at Ruka Rayen in advance, home-grown food, boat tours. **Ruka Rayen** is on the banks of the Río Palguín, 15 mins' walk from the main road (regular buses to Pucón). Some rooms with bath, English-speaking hosts (Margot's parents own Kila Leufu), mountain-bike hire. Both serve meals, offer horse-riding, trekking information and camping. The perfect choice if you want to avoid the hustle and bustle of Pucón.
$$ Rancho de Caballos, Palguín Aito Km 32, T09-8346 1764 (limited signal), www.rancho-de-caballos.com. Restaurant with vegetarian dishes; also *cabañas* and camping, self-guided trails, horse-riding trips ½-7 days, English and German spoken.

● Restaurants

For eating options in the national parks and lakes east of Pucón, see Where to stay, above.

Villarrica p279, map p280
$$$ El Tabor, S Epulef 1187, T045-241 1901. Fish and seafood specialities, excellent but pricey.
$$$ La Cava del Roble, Valentín Letelier 658, p 2, T045-241 6446. Excellent grill, specializes in exotic meat and game, extensive wine list.
$$ La Vecchia Cucina, Pedro de Valdivia 1011, T045-241 1798. Good Italian serving a range of pizzas and pastas.
$$ The Travellers Resto Bar, Letelier 753, T045-241 3617. Varied menu including vegetarian and Asian food, bar, English spoken.

$$-$ Juanito, Vicente Reyes 678. Closed Sun. Good, and cheap end of the range.
$ Casa Vieja, Letelier 609. Good-value set lunch, family-run.
$ El Marítimo, Alderete 769, T045-241 9755. Generally first-rate, unpretentious, serving traditional fish and seafood.
$ El Turismo, Epulef 1201 y Rodriguez. No frills, good Chilean dishes.
Café 2001, Henríquez 379, T045-241 1470, www.cafebar2001.cl. Best coffee in town. Also good cakes and friendly service at a reasonable price. For ice cream, try the stall next door.

Pucón p281, map p282
See Where to stay for other options.
$$$ Puerto Pucón, Fresia 246, T045-244 1592. One of Pucón's older restaurants, Spanish, stylish.
$$$-$$ La Maga, Alderete 276 y Fresia, T045-244 4277, www.lamagapucon.cl. Uruguayan *parrillada* serving excellent steak. So good that several imitations have opened up nearby to take the overspill.
$$$-$$ Senzo, Fresia 284, T045-244 9005. Fresh pasta and risotto prepared by a Swiss chef.
$$ Arabian, Fresia 354-B, T045-244 3469. Arab specialities, including stuffed vine leaves, falafel, etc.
$$ ¡école!, in Hostería of same name, General Urrutia 592, T045-244 1675. Good vegetarian restaurant.
$$ Il Baretto, Fresia 124, T045-244 3515. Stone-baked pizzas.
$ Rap Hamburguesa, O'Higgins 625. Open late. Freshly made hamburgers, chips and Chilean fast food.

Cafés
Café de la P, O'Higgins y Lincoyán, T045-244 3577. Real coffee.
Café Lounge Brasil, Colo Colo 485, T045-244 4035, www.cafeloungebrasil.com. Gourmet cafeteria which also has a 'boutique' hostel. Meals include vegetarian options, Jamaican coffee.

Cassis, Fresia 223, T045-244 4715, www.chocolatescassis.com. Chocolates, ice creams, pancakes and snacks as well as coffee.

🍸 Bars and clubs

Pucón *p281, map p282*
At weekends in summer, there are discos 2-3 km east of town, near the airport, at **Kamikaze** and **La Playa**, plus several more in the same area. There are several bars on O'Higgins.

✹ Festivals

Villarrica *p279, map p280*
Jan and **Feb** Villarrica has a summer programme with many cultural and sporting events (www.villarrica.org), such as the **Fiesta Costumbrista de Chaillupen Alto** and the official rodeo.

Pucón *p281, map p282*
Jul Pucón is home to an **international triathlon competition**, www.ironman pucon.com, every year as well as mountain-bike races and other events.

🛍 Shopping

Pucón *p281, map p282*
Camping equipment is available from **Eltit supermarket**, O'Higgins y Fresia, and from **Outdoors & Travel**, Lincoyán 36, which also sells outdoor clothing, equipment and maps. There is a **handicrafts market** just south of O'Higgins on Ansorena; local specialities are painted wooden flowers.

☉ What to do

Villarrica *p279, map p280*
Fundo Huifquenco, just south of town (500 m) along Av Matta, T045-241 2200, www.fundohuifquenco.cl. Working farm, trails, horse riding, carriage tours, bicycle hire, meals (book in advance).

Novena Región, Parque Ecológico 3 Esteros, 20 km from Villarrica towards Panguipulli, T09-8901 2574, www.novena-region.com. Mushing and husky trekking on the winter snow and in summer with Siberian Huskies. Unique in Chile.
Ríos Family, T045-241 2408. Birdwatching and fishing trips.
Rodrigo Puelma, T09-9625 1345. Private guide, speaks basic English.
Villarica Extremo, Valdivia 910, T045-241 0900, www.villaricaextremo.com. Good excursions featuring the usual suspects like volcano tours, rafting, thermal pools and paintball.

Pucón *p281, map p282*
Canopy ziplining
Several agencies can arrange this activity (sliding from platform to platform among the treetops along a metal cord). The best (and most safety conscious) is **Bosque Aventura**, Arauca 611 y O'Higgins, T09-9325 4795, www.canopypucon.cl.

Climbing
Sierra Nevada, O'Higgins 524-A, T045-244 4210. Offers *Vía Ferrata*, a kind of climbing up sheer rock faces for beginners using metal hand- and footholds embedded in the rock.

Fishing
Pucón and Villarrica are celebrated as centres for fishing on Lake Villarrica and in the beautiful Lincura, Trancura and Toltén rivers. Local tourist office will supply details on licenses and open seasons, etc. 2 fishing specialists are **Mario's Fishing Zone**, O'Higgins 580, T09-9760 7280, www.fly fishingpucon.com (expensive but good), and **Off Limits**, O'Higgins 560, T045-244 3741, www.offlimits.cl (English and Italian spoken).

Horse riding
Centro de Turismo Ecuestre Huepilmalal, Camino a Termas de Huife, Km 25, T09-9643 2673, www.huepilmalal.cl. Rodolfo Coombs and Carolina Pumpin, 40 mins from town,

also with lodging; from riding lessons (US$31) to 10-day treks.

Rancho de Caballos, see Where to stay, above. Average hire costs about US$31 half day, US$70 full day (transfer from Pucón extra).

Mountain biking
Bike hire from US$2.50 per hr to US$200 per day for cross-country excursions with guide. Available from several travel agencies on O'Higgins.

Tour operators
Tour operators arrange trips to thermal baths, trekking to volcanoes, whitewater rafting, etc. For falls, lakes and *termas* it's cheaper for groups to flag down a taxi and bargain. There are many agencies, so shop around: prices vary at times, as do quality of guides and equipment. In high season, when lots of groups go together, individual attention may be lacking.

Aguaventura, Palguín 336, T045-244 4246, www.aguaventura.com. French-run, in summer kayaking and rafting specialities, in winter 'snowshop' for ski and snowboard rental, volcano climbing, trekking.

Elementos, Pasaje Las Rosas 640, T045-244 1750, www.elementos-chile.com. Provider covering the entire country and specializing in sustainable tourism. Has its own **EcoHostel**. Good option for volcano treks.

Mountain Life Adventure, T09-7472 3665, mountainlifeadventure@hotmail.com. Villarrica hike plus treks and climbs up other volcanoes in the region, Chilean/ Swiss-owned (ask here about new location of the owners' **Hostel One Way**).

Politur, O'Higgins 635, T045-244 1373, www.politur.com. Well-established and responsible, good for volcano trek and rafting; a little pricier than others.

Pucón Tours, O'Higgins 615, T09-9273 0208. Small-group quad-bike excursions US$28, good fun. Also hires out good quality bicycles and offers a wide range of other tours.

Travel Aid, Ansorena 425, loc 4, T045-244 4040, www.travelaid.cl. Helpful general travel agency, sells trekking maps, guidebooks, lots of information, agents for **Navimag** and other boat trips, English and German spoken.

Volcán Villarica, O' Higgins 555, T09-9002 4587, volcan.villarica@hotmail.com. Specializes in group excursions to Volcán Villarrica as well as a number of other activities, including rafting, canyoning and paintball. English spoken, good equipment.

Watersports
Waterskiing, sailing, rowing boats and windsurfing at Playa Grande beach by **Gran Hotel** and at **La Poza beach** at the end of O'Higgins (this is more expensive than Playa Grande and not recommended).

Whitewater rafting and kayaking
Very popular on the Río Trancura: Trancura Bajo (grade 3), US$30; Trancura Alto (grades 3 and 4), US$50. Many agencies offer trips, including **Rafting Kayak Chile**, O'Higgins 524, http://raftingkayakchile.com; see also **Pucón Kayak Hostel** (10 km from town on road to Caburga), http://puconkayakhostel.co.

Parque Nacional Villarrica *p283*
Tours from Pucón cost US$65-85, including park entry, guide, transport to park entrance and hire of equipment (no reduction for those with their own equipment). Bargain for group rates. Travel agencies will not start out if the weather is bad and some travellers have experienced difficulties in obtaining a refund: establish in advance what terms apply in the event of cancellation and be prepared to wait a few days. For information on independent guides, all with equipment, ask for recommendations at the tourist office.

Towards Argentina *p327*
Escape, in Curarrehue, T09-9678 5380, www.patagonia-escape.com. Owned by John 'LJ' Groth, specializing in SUP, private

kayak guiding trips and rafting on some beautiful sections of the Río Trancura and around. Safe, responsible, environmentally aware and different.

Reserva Forestal Cañi *p284*
Hostería ¡école!, General Urrutia 592, T045-244 1675, www.ecole.cl. See Where to stay, above, offers good tours.

Transport

Villarrica *p279, map p280*
Bus
Terminal at Pedro de Valdivia y Muñoz. **JAC** terminal at Bilbao 610, T045-241 1447, and opposite for Pucón and Lican-Ray. **Terminal Rural** for other local services at Matta y Vicente Reyes. To **Santiago**, 10 hrs, US$27-50, several companies. To **Pucón**, with **Vipu-Ray** (main terminal) and **JAC**, in summer every 15 mins, 40 mins' journey, US$1.50; same companies to **Lican-Ray**, US$1.50. To **Valdivia**, JAC, US$8, 5 a day, 2½ hrs. To **Coñaripe** (US$3) and **Liquiñe** at 1600 Mon-Sat, 1000 Sun. To **Temuco**, JAC, US$3-4. To **Loncoche** (Ruta 5 junction for hitching), US$2.25. To **Panguipulli**, go via Lican-Ray, occasional direct buses.

To Argentina Buses from Valdivia to **San Martín de los Andes** pass through **Villarrica**, fares are the same as from Valdivia, T045-241 2733, book in advance. Note that if the Mamuil Malal pass is blocked by snow buses go via Panguipulli instead of Villarrica and Pucón.

Pucón *p281, map p282*
Air
Check with airlines for summer flights from **Santiago** via Temuco.

Bus
No municipal terminal: each company has its own terminal: **JAC**, Uruguay y Palguín; **Tur-Bus**, O'Higgins 910, east of town; **Igi**

Llaima and **Cóndor**, Colo Colo y O'Higgins. JAC to **Villarrica** (very frequent, US$1.50) and **Valdivia** (US$9, 3 hrs). **Tur-Bus** direct to **Valdivia**, **Osorno** and **Puerto Montt**, 6 hrs, US$14-17, daily. To **Santiago**, 10 hrs, US$27-50, many companies, early morning and late evening. *Colectivos* to **Villarrica** from O'Higgins y Palguín. **Buses Caburgua** run minibuses to many local destinations, including: **Parque Nacional Huerquehue**, 3 daily, 1½ hrs, US$3.50; **Caburga**, every 30 mins, US$1.50 (there are also *colectivos* to Caburga from Ansorena y Uruguay); **Los Pozones**, 5 daily, passing by the termas and Reserva Forestal Cani on the way (**Termas de Huife and de Quimey co** have their own transport and will pick people up from Pucón, US$36.) There are several minibuses daily to **Curarrehue** and buses weekly to **Puesco**.

To Argentina Buses from Valdivia to **San Martín** pass through Pucón.

Car hire
Hire prices start at US$35 per day; **Avis**, Arauco 302, T045-246 5328, www.avis.cl; **Hertz**, in the Gran Hotel, T045-244 1664; **Kilómetro Libre**, Alderete 480, T045-244 4399, www.rentaarkilo metrolibre.com; **Pucón Rent A Car**, Colo Colo 340, T045-244 3052, www.puconrentacar.cl.

Taxi
Araucaria, T045-244 2323.

Directory

Villarrica *p279, map p280*
Banks ATMs at banks on Pedro de Valdivia between Montt and Alderete.

Pucón *p281, map p282*
Banks There are 3 or 4 banks with ATMs and several *casas de cambio* on O'Higgins, although *cambio* rates are universally poor. Much better to change money in Temuco.

The Seven Lakes

These lakes, situated south of Lago Villarrica, form a beautiful necklace of water, surrounded by thick woods and with views of distant snows giving a picture-postcard backdrop. Six of the lakes lie in Chile, with the seventh, Lago Lácar, in Argentina. After the final peace settlement of 1882 the area around these lakes was reserved for Mapuche settlements. Lago Riñihue is most easily reached from Valdivia and Los Lagos and is dealt with in a later section (see page 302). Most of the lakes have black-sand beaches, although in spring, as the water level rises, these can all but disappear.

Lago Calafquén → *For listings, see pages 295-297.*

The most northerly of the seven lakes, Lago Calafquén is a popular tourist destination for Chileans, readily accessible by a paved road from Villarrica, along which there are fine

The Seven Lakes

The legend of Lican-Ray

At the height of the wars between the Spanish and the Mapuche, a young Spanish soldier lost the rest of his unit and strayed into the forests near Lago Calafquén. Suddenly he saw a beautiful young Mapuche woman drying her hair in the sun and singing. As he did not want to frighten her he made himself visible at a distance and began to sing along. Singing, smiling and exchanging glances, they fell in love. She called him Allumanche, which means white man in Mapuche, and, pointing to herself, indicated that her name was Lican-Rayan, meaning the flower of magic stone. They began to live together near the lake.

Lican Rayan's father, Curtilef, a powerful and fearsome chief, feared she might be dead. One day a boy came to him and said: "Lican Rayan is alive. I have seen her near the lake with a white man but she is not a prisoner: it is clear they are in love".

Lican Rayan saw the warriors coming to look for her. Knowing her father she feared what might happen, so she persuaded the soldier that they should flee. They escaped by riding on logs to one of the islands. There they felt safe, but they could not light a fire against the cold because the smoke would give them away. The weather grew cooler, the north wind blew and it rained heavily. After several days, unable to bear the cold and thinking that the warriors would have given up the search, they lit a fire. The smoke was spotted by Curtilef's men, so Lican Rayan and the solider fled to another island but again they were discovered and had to escape. This happened so many times that, although they were never caught, they were never seen again.

In the town of Lican-Ray, it is said that on spring afternoons it is sometimes possible to see a distant column of smoke from one of the islands, where Lican Rayan and the soldier are still enjoying their love after over 400 years.

Abridged and translated from *Lengua Y Costumbres Mapuches* by Orietta Appelt Martin, Imprenta Austral, Temuco, 1995.

---

views of the Volcán Villarrica. Wooded and dotted with small islands, the lake is reputedly one of the warmest in the region and is good for swimming. A mostly paved road runs around the lake.

Lican-Ray

Situated 30 km south of Villarrica on a peninsula on the north shore, Lican-Ray is the major resort on the lake and is named after a legendary Mapuche woman (see box, above). There are two beaches, one on each side of the peninsula. Boats can be hired for US$5 per hour, and there are **catamaran trips**. Although crowded in season, Lican-Ray can feel like a ghost town by the end of March, when most facilities have closed. Some 6 km to the east is the river of lava formed when Volcán Villarrica erupted in 1971. There is a **tourist office** ① *daily in summer, Mon-Fri in winter,* on the plaza.

Coñaripe

Lying 21 km southeast of Lican-Ray at the eastern end of Lago Calafquén, Coñaripe is another popular Chilean tourist spot. At first sight the village is dusty and nondescript, but its setting, with a 3-km black-sand beach surrounded by mountains, is beautiful. Most services are on the Calle Principal. The **tourist office** ① *on the plaza, T063-231 7378, daily 15 Nov to 15 Apr, otherwise weekends only,* can arrange trips to local thermal springs.

From Coñaripe a road (mostly *ripio*) around the lake's southern shore leads to **Lago Panguipulli**, see below, 38 km west, and offers superb views over Volcán Villarrica, which can be climbed from here. Another dirt road heads northeast through the Parque Nacional Villarrica to Pucón, see page 281; the first few kilometres are good *ripio*. There are several thermal springs here. **Termas Vergara**, 14 km northeast of Coñaripe by a steep *ripio* road which continues to Palguín, has nice open-air pools. **Termas Geométricas** ① *3 km beyond Termas Vergara, T09-7477 1708, www.termasgeometricas.cl*, has 17 pools, geometrically shaped and linked by wooden walkways. There is a small café. After the Termas Geométricas the road worsens and is suitable for high-clearance 4WD only.

Southeast of Coñaripe

From Coñaripe a road runs southeast over the steep Cuesta Los Añiques offering views of **Lago Pellaifa**, a tiny lake with rocky surroundings covered with vegetation and a small beach. **Termas de Coñaripe** ① *Km 15, 2 km from the lakeshore, T045-241 9498, www.termasconaripe.cl, US$30*, has six pools, accommodation, restaurant, cycles and horses for hire. Transport can be organized from Coñaripe.

Further south are the **Termas Río Liquiñe** ① *Km 32, T063-197 1301, www.termasrioliquine.cl*, with eight thermal springs and accommodation (but little other infrastructure), surrounded by a small native forest. About 8 km north of Liquiñe is a road going southwest for 20 km along the southeast shore of **Lago Neltume** to meet the Choshuenco–Puerto Fuy road.

Lago Panguipulli → For listings, see pages 295-297.

Covering 116 sq km, Lago Panguipulli, the largest of the seven lakes, is reached either by paved road from Lanco or Los Lagos on the Pan-American Highway or by *ripio* roads from Lago Calafquén. A road leads along the beautiful northern shore, which is wooded with sandy beaches and cliffs, but most of the lake's southern shore is inaccessible by road.

Panguipulli

The site of a Mapuche settlement, Panguipulli, meaning 'hill of pumas', is situated on a hillside at the northwest corner of the lake. It grew as a railway terminal and a port for vessels carrying timber from the lakesides, and is now the largest town in the area.

On Plaza Prat is the **Iglesia San Sebastián**, built in Swiss style with twin towers by the Swiss Padre Bernabé; its belltower contains three bells from Germany. By the plaza there is a **tourist office** ① *T063-231 0436, www.sietelagos.cl, also www.municipalidadpanguipulli.cl, daily Dec-Feb, otherwise Mon-Fri*.

From Plaza Prat the main commercial street, Martínez de Rozas, runs down to the lakeshore. In summer, catamaran trips are offered on the lake and excursions can be made to Lagos Calafquén, Neltume, Pirehueico and to the northern tip of Lago Riñihue, see page 302. The road east to Coñaripe, on Lago Calafquén, offers superb views of the lake and of Volcán Villarrica.

Choshuenco and around

Choshuenco lies 45 km east of Panguipulli on the Río Llanquihue, at the eastern tip of the lake and can only be reached by road from Panguipulli or Puerto Fuy. Call T063-231 8305 for tourist information. To the south is the **Reserva Nacional Mocho Choshuenco** (7536 ha), which includes two volcanoes: Choshuenco (2415 m) and Mocho (2422 m).

Border crossings: Chile–Argentina

Paso Hua Hum

Paso Hua Hum (659 m) lies 11 km southeast of Puerto Pirehueico. The border is usually open all year 0800-2000 and is an alternative to the route via Paso Mamuil Malal (Tromen), see page 285. On the Argentine side, the *ripio* road (very tough going for cyclists) continues along the north shore of Lago Lacar to San Martín de los Andes. There are buses from Puerto Pirehueico to San Martín. For more information, see www.gendarmeria.gov.ar/pasos/chile/fichhuahum.html.

On the slopes of Choshuenco the **Club Andino de Valdivia** runs a small ski resort and three *refugios*. (The resort is reached by a turning from the road that goes south from Choshuenco to Enco at the east end of Lago Riñihue, see page 302.) From Choshuenco a road leads east to **Neltume** and **Lago Pirehueico**, via the impressive waterfalls of **Huilo Huilo**. The falls are a three-hour walk from Choshuenco, or take the Puerto Fuy bus and get off at **Alojamiento Huilo Huilo** (see Where to stay, below), from where it is a five-minute walk to the falls. Huilo Huilo is a biological reserve, with lots of outdoor activities and a variety of lodgings in the trees; see www.huilohilo.com.

Lago Pirehueico → *For listings, see pages 295-297.*

East of Choshuenco, Lago Pirehueico is a 36-km long, narrow and deep glacial lake surrounded by virgin *lingue* forest. It is beautiful and largely unspoilt, although there are plans to build a huge tourist complex in Puerto Pirehueico.

There are two ports on the lake: **Puerto Fuy** at the northern end and **Puerto Pirehueico** at the southern end. The ports are linked by a ferry service (see page 297), a beautiful crossing that is comparable to the more famous lakes crossing from Puerto Montt to Bariloche (see page 327), but at a fraction of the price. They can also be reached by the road that runs east from Neltume to the Argentine border crossing at Paso Hua Hum (see box, above). The road south from Puerto Fuy, however, is privately owned and closed to traffic. This is a shame because it is a beautiful route passing around Volcán Choshuenco and through rainforest to Río Pillanleufú, Puerto Llolles on Lago Maihue and Puerto Llifén on Lago Ranco.

⦿ The Seven Lakes listings

For hotel and restaurant price codes and other relevant information, see pages 14-21.

⦿ Where to stay

Lican-Ray *p293*
$$ Cabañas Los Nietos, Manquel 125, Playa Chica, T09-5639 3585, www.losnietos.cl. Self-catering cabins.

$ Residencial Temuco, G Mistral 517, Playa Grande, T045-243 1130. Shared bath, with breakfast, good.

Camping
Las Gaviotas, Km 5 Camino Lican-Ray, T09-9030 1153, www.campinglasgaviotas.cl. Beach camping with many amenities, such as hot showers, mini market and volleyball area.

Coñaripe p293

$$-$ Hospedaje Chumay, Las Tepas 201, on plaza, T063-231 7287, turismochumay@hotmail.com. With restaurant, tours, some English spoken, good.

Camping

Sites on beach charge US$20, but if you walk half a kilometre from town you can camp on the beach for free; there are cold municipal showers on the beach, US$0.35. There is another site with *cabañas* on **Isla Llancahue** in the Río Llancahue, 5 km east, T09-9562 0437.

Southeast of Coñaripe p294

$$$$ Termas de Coñaripe, T063-241 1111, www.termasconaripe.cl. Excellent hotel with 4 pools, good restaurant, spa with a variety of treatments, cycles and horses for hire. Full board available.

$$$ Termas de Liquiñe, T063-2197 1301. Full board, cabins, restaurant, hot pool, small native forest.

$$ Hospedaje Catemu, Camino Internacional, T063-197 1629, neldatrafipan@yahoo.es. Known as much for its restaurant as its cosy, wood-panelled cabins, this option can arrange excursions to the Termas.

Panguipulli p294

See www.sietelagos.cl for list of lodgings.
$$ La Casita del Centro, J M Carerra 674, T063-231 1812, B&B, refurbished, safe, with restaurant, parking.

$ Hospedaje Familiar, JP Segundo 801, T063-231 1483. English and German spoken, helpful.

$ pp Hostal Orillas del Lago, M de Rosas 265, T063-231 1710 (or T063-231 2499 if no reply; friends have key). From plaza walk towards lake, last house on left, 8 blocks from terminal. Backpacker place with good views.

Camping

El Bosque, P Sigifredo 241, T063-231 1489. Small, good, but not suitable for vehicle camping, hot water. Also 3 sites at Chauquén, 6 km southeast on lakeside.

Choshuenco and around p294

$$$ Hostería Ruca Pillán, San Martín 85, T063-231 8220, www.rucapillan.cl. Family-run hotel rooms and cabins overlooking the lake, restaurant, English spoken, tours.

$$ Cabañas Choshuenco, Bernabé 391, T063-231 8316, www.choshuencochile.cl. *Cabañas*, fully equipped, self-contained, for 6-8 people.

$ pp Cabañas Huilo Huilo, Km 9 east from Choshuenco, on Camino Internacional (1 km before Neltume). Basic but comfortable and well situated for walks, good food.

Lago Pirehueico p295

Camping is possible on the beach (take own food).

$$ Hospedaje y Cabañas Puerto Fuy, Puerto Fuy, www.cabañaspuertofuy.cl. Hot water, good food in restaurant.

$ Hostal Kay Kaen, Puerto Fuy, T063-197 1562. Meals, use of kitchen, bike rental. One of several private houses offering accommodation.

$ pp Restaurant San Giovanni, Puerto Fuy, T063-2197 1562. Family atmosphere, good rooms.

Restaurants

For eating options in Coñaripe, Choshuenco and around, see Where to stay.

Lican-Ray p293

$$ Cábala, Urrutia 201, nice centre location; good pizzas and pastas.

$$-$ The Ñaños, Urrutia 105. Good café, reasonable prices, helpful owner. Service can be patchy.

Panguipulli p294

$$-$ Café Central, M de Rosas 750. Fixed menu, good and cheap at lunchtimes, expensive in evenings.

$$-$ El Chapulín, M de Rosas 639. Good food and value. Several cheap restaurants in O'Higgins 700 block.

✪ Festivals

Panguipulli *p294*
2nd half of Feb La Semana de Rosas, with dancing and sports competitions.

♻ What to do

Coñaripe *p293*
Hospedaje Chumay, see Where to stay, organizes hikes to Villarica volcano and trips to various thermal springs.
Rucapillán Expediciones, Martínez de Rosas 519, T063-231 8220, www.rucapillan.cl. Rafting in the rivers Fuy, Enco and San Pedro as well as volcano treks.

Panguipulli *p294*
Fishing
The following fishing trips on Lago Panguipulli are recommended: Puntilla Los Cipreses at the mouth of the Río Huanehue, 11 km east of Panguipulli, 30 mins by boat; the mouth of the Río Niltre, on east side of lake. Licences from the **Municipalidad**, **Librería Colón**, O'Higgins 793; or from the **Club de Pesca**.

Rafting
Good rafting opportunities on the Río Fuy, Grade IV-V; Río San Pedro, varying grades, and on the Río Llanquihue near Choshuenco.

⊖ Transport

Lican-Ray *p293*
Bus
Buses leave from offices around plaza. To **Villarrica**, 1 hr, US$1.50, **JAC** frequent in summer. In summer, there are direct buses to/from **Santiago** (Tur-Bus US$20, 10 hrs,

salón cama US$45-80) and **Temuco** (2½ hrs, US$7). To **Panguipulli**, Mon-Sat 0730.

Coñaripe *p293*
Bus
To **Panguipulli**, 7 a day (4 off season), US$3 and 16 daily to **Villarrica**, US$2.75. Nightly bus direct to **Santiago**, **Tur-Bus** and **JAC**, 11½ hrs, US$30-60.

Panguipulli *p294*
Bus
Terminal at Gabriela Mistral y Portales. To **Santiago** daily, US$21-50. To **Valdivia**, frequent (Sun only 4), several companies, 2 hrs, US$5. To **Temuco** frequent, **Power** and **Pangui Sur**, US$6, 3 hrs. To **Puerto Montt**, US$12. To **Choshuenco**, **Neltume** and **Puerto Fuy**, 3 daily, 3 hrs, US$7. To **Coñaripe** (with connections for Lican-Ray and Villarrica), 7 daily, 4 off season, 1½ hrs, US$3.

Lago Pirehueico *p295*
Bus
Puerto Fuy to **Panguipulli**, 3 daily, 3 hrs, US$7. Buses between Puerto Pirehueico and **San Martín de los Andes (Argentina)** are run by **Ko Ko** in San Martín, T+54 (0)2972-427422, and connect with the ferry service across the lake.

Ferry
The **Hua Hum** sails from **Puerto Fuy** to **Puerto Pirehueico** at 0800, 1300, 1800 (Jan-Feb), 1400 (rest of year), returns 2 hrs later, foot passengers US$1.50, cars US$30, motorbikes US$9; to take vehicles reserve in advance on T063-2197 1871, or see **Somarco**'s website, www.barcazas.cl.

⊙ Directory

Panguipulli *p294*
Banks ATM at the **BCI**, M de Rozas y Matta.

Valdivia and around

Surrounded by wooded hills, Valdivia is one of the most pleasant cities in southern Chile and a good place to rest after arduous treks in the mountains. In the summer tourist season the city comes to life with activities and events, while off season this is a pleasant verdant city with a thriving café culture. With a high student population (its total population is 127,000), it is also one of the best cities for meeting young Chileans, who will be at the pulse of anything in the way of nightlife in the city. Valdivia lies nearly 839 km south of Santiago at the confluence of two rivers, the Calle Calle and Cruces, which form the Río Valdivia. To the northwest of the city is a large island, Isla Teja, where the Universidad Austral de Chile is situated. West, along the coast, are a series of important Spanish colonial forts, while to the north are two nature reserves with native forests and a wide range of birdlife. Inland there are two lakes off the beaten tourist path.

Valdivia city → *For listings, see pages 303-306. Colour map 4, B2.*

Arriving in Valdivia
Getting there and around There are daily flights north to Santiago and Concepción. The city has a well-organized bus terminal at Muñoz y Prat, by the river. The bus network is very wide, with numerous daily services to Santiago and south to Puerto Montt, as well as to cities such as Temuco, Pucón, Concepción and Chillán. By road, access to the Panamericana is north via Mafil or south via Paillaco. Valdivia is quite sizeable: *colectivos* and buses serve the outlying barrios. However, like many Chilean cities, the centre is relatively compact, and few places are beyond walking distance, even those across the river on the Isla Teja.

Tourist information The **tourist office** ① *Prat 675, by dock, T063-223 9060, infolosrios@ sernatur.cl, daily in summer, weekdays off season,* has good maps of the region and local rivers, a list of hotel prices and examples of local crafts with artisans' addresses. There is a **Municipal tourist office** ① *Av Prat (Costanera) at the north side of the Feria Fluvial, T063-222 0490, www.turismolosrios.cl, Mon-Fri 0900-1800 in winter, 0900-2100 in summer, Sat-Sun 1000-2030;* also upstairs in the bus terminal and other locations. There's also a **CONAF office** ① *Los Castaños 100, T065-224 5200.*

Background
Valdivia was one of the most important centres of Spanish colonial control over Chile. Founded in 1552 by Pedro de Valdivia, it was abandoned as a result of the Mapuche insurrection of 1599 and was briefly occupied by Dutch pirates. In 1645 it was refounded as

a walled city and the only Spanish mainland settlement south of the Río Biobío. The Spanish continued to fortify the area around Valdivia throughout the 1600s, developing the most comprehensive system of defence in the South Pacific against the British and Dutch navies. Seventeen forts were built in total. They were reinforced after 1760, but proved of little avail during the Wars of Independence, when the Chilean naval squadron under Lord Cochrane seized control of the forts in two days. From independence until the 1880s Valdivia was an outpost of Chilean rule, reached only by sea or by a coastal route through Mapuche territory. In 2007 it became capital of the newly created Región XIV, Los Ríos.

Places in Valdivia

The city is centred around the tree-lined **Plaza de la República**. In the cathedral, the **Museo de la Catedral de Valdivia** ① *Independencia 514, Mon-Sat 1000-1300, US$1*, covers four centuries of Christian history. Three blocks east is the **Muelle Fluvial**, the dock for boat trips down the river. From the Muelle Fluvial there is a pleasant walk north along the *costanera* (Avenida Prat) and under the bridge to Isla Teja and on round the bend in the river (as far as the bus terminal).

On the western bank of the river, **Isla Teja** has a botanical garden and arboretum with trees from all over the world. West of the botanical gardens is the **Parque Saval** ① *open daylight hours, US$0.75*. Covering 30 ha it has areas of native forest as well as a small lake, the Lago de los Lotos. There are beautiful flowers in spring. It often hosts events like Rodeos, and a Mapuche market and craft market in summer. Also on the island are two museums. The **Museo Histórico y Antropológico** ① *T063-221 2872, www.museosaustral.cl,*

Valdivia

Universidad Austral de Chile
Botanic Garden
Av Prat (Costanera)
Main Bus Terminal
C Anwandter
ISLA TEJA
Colectivo No 20 to Niebla
Puente Pedro de Valdivia
Hotel y Casino Valdivia
Carampangue
Caupolicán
Ismael
Av Alemania
Chacabuco
Valdés
Picarte
Encinas
Municipalidad
O'Higgins
Independencia
Plaza de la República
Cathedral
Arauco
G Reyes
Anfion Muñoz
P De Valdivia
Marti
To the south
Los Robles
Museo Histórico y Antropológico & Museo de Arte Moderno Contemporáneo
Muelle Fluvial (Dock)
Yungay
Av Prat (Costanera)
San Carlos
Río Valdivia
Pérez Rosales
C Henríquez
Esmeralda
Beauchef
Supermarket
Shopping Mall
Beneficencia
Bertolotto
Laurel
Gral Lagos
Y Buenas
San Francisco
Cochrane
Carrillo
N
100 metres
100 yards

Where to stay 🛏
1 Airesbuenos Central
4 Encanto del Río
5 Hostal Ana María
6 Hostal Anwandter
7 Hostal Arlense House
8 Hostal Casagrande
9 Hostal Torreón
10 Hostal Totem
11 Hostal y Cabañas Internacional
12 Melillanca
13 Puerta del Sur

Restaurants 🍴
1 Agridulce
2 Café Haussmann
3 Café Moro
4 Cervecería Kunstmann
6 Entrelagos
7 La Baguette
8 La Calesa
9 Lomodetoro
10 Mi Pueblito
11 Volcán

The 1960 earthquake

Southern Chile is highly susceptible to earthquakes: severe quakes struck the area in 1575, 1737, 1786 and 1837, but the tremor that struck around midday on 22 May 1960 caused the most extensive damage throughout southern Chile and was accompanied by the eruption of four volcanoes and a *maremoto* (tidal wave) that was felt in New Zealand and Japan.

Around Valdivia the land dropped by 3 m, creating new lagunas along the Río Cruces to the north of the city. The *maremoto* destroyed all the fishing villages and ports between Puerto Saavedra in the north and Chiloé in the south. The earthquake also provoked several landslides. The greatest of these blocked the Río San Pedro, near the point where it drains Lago Riñihue, and the lake rose 35 m in 24 hours. Over the next two months all available labour and machinery was used to dig channels to divert the water from the other lakes and to drain off the waters of Lago Riñihue, thus averting the devastation of the San Pedro Valley.

Mar-Dec Tue-Sun 1000-1300, 1400-1800, Jan and Feb daily 1000-2000, US$2.75, is beautifully situated in the former mansion of Carlos Anwandter, a leading German immigrant. Run by the university, it contains sections on archaeology, ethnography and German colonization. Next door, in the former Anwandter brewery, is the **Museo de Arte Moderno Contemporáneo** ① *T063-222 1968, www.macvaldivia.cl, Tue-Sun 1000-1300, 1400-1900, US$2.25, times change according to the exhibition*. Boat trips can be made around Isla Teja, offering views of birds and seals.

Kunstmann Brewery ① *just out of town on the Niebla road, T063-222 2570, www.cerveza-kunstmann.cl*, offers tours of the working brewery and its beer museum; it also has a good restaurant.

Every Sunday during January and February there is a special **steam train service** ① *T063-257 8259, returns from Antilhue 2 hrs later, US$11 return, advance booking essential*, from the train station on Equador to **Antilhue**, 20 km to the east. The train is met by locals selling all sorts of culinary specialities. The engine dates from 1913. Special additional trips are often made on public holidays; check departure times before travelling.

Along the Río Valdivia to the coast → *For listings, see pages 303-306. Colour map 4, B1/2.*

The various rivers around Valdivia are navigable: rent a motor boat to explore the Ríos Futa and Tornagaleanes south of town around the **Isla del Rey**, or visit the interesting and isolated villages at the mouth of the Río Valdivia by road or river boat. The two main centres are **Niebla** on the north bank and **Corral** opposite on the south bank, site of two of the most important 17th-century Spanish forts (see page 298). There is a frequent boat service between the two towns. Midstream between Niebla and Corral is **Isla Mancera**, a small island dominated by the Castillo de San Pedro de Alcántara, the earliest of the Spanish forts. Inside is a small church and convent. The island is a pleasant place to stop over on the boat trips, but it can get crowded when an excursion boat arrives.

Niebla and around

Some 18 km west of Valdivia, **Niebla** is a resort with seafood restaurants and accommodation. To the west on a promontory is the **Fuerte de la Pura y Limpia**

Concepción de Monfort de Lemus ⓘ *closed for renovation in 2014*, with a museum on Chilean naval history, a tourist information office and a telephone office. Around Niebla the north bank is dotted with campsites and *cabañas*. About 6 km further round the coast is **Los Molinos**, a seaside resort set among steep wooded hills. There is a campsite and lots of seaside restaurants. The road continues, rising and falling along the coast, with fine views of beaches deserted outside summer. The paved road runs out about 6 km north of Los Molinos but a *ripio* road continues past Curiñanco as far as the Parque Oncol.

Corral and around

Corral lies 62 km west of Valdivia by road and is the main port serving the city. It is much quieter and more pleasant than Niebla, and its fort, **Castillo de San Sebastián** ⓘ *US$5 Jan-Feb, US$3 off season*, has a dilapidated, interesting atmosphere. It was built in 1645 as one of the main fortifications on the estuary, and during the 17th century its 3-m-thick walls were defended by a battery of 21 guns. Inside is a museum, and in summer (15 December to 15 March) there are re-enactments in period costume of the 1820 storming of the Spanish fort by the Chilean Republican forces (daily 1600, 1730, 1830).

Further north near the mouth of the river are pleasant beaches and the remains of two other Spanish colonial forts, the **Castillo San Luis de Alba de Amargos** and the **Castillo de San Carlos**. The coastal walks west and south of Corral, along very isolated and forested roads above the ocean, are splendid and very rarely visited. The friendly tourist office on the pier can provide some trekking information.

North of Valdivia → *For listings, see pages 303-306.*

Some 27 km to the northwest is the **Parque Oncol** ⓘ *T800-370222, www.parqueoncol.cl, US$4.50, students, children and seniors US$1, anyone on a bike US$2, daily buses in summer, US$5.50 including park entry*. It consists of 754 ha of native Valdivian forest with several easy trails and lookouts with fine views, canopy zip-lines (US$27, daily 1130-1600), a picnic area, a good café and campsite.

Stretching from the outskirts of the city along the Río Cruces for 30 km north is the **Santuario de la Naturaleza Carlos Anwandter**, which was flooded as a result of the 1960 *maremoto* and now attracts many bird species. Boat trips are available from Valdivia aboard the **Isla del Río** ⓘ *Embarcaciones Bahía, on the riverfront near the fish market, T063-234 8727, www.embarcacionesbahia.cl, daily 1600-2015, US$18 per person*.

Further along the Río Cruces, 42 km north of Valdivia, lies the small town of **San José de la Mariquina**. From the town an unpaved road leads west along the north side of the river to the **Fuerte de San Luis de Alba de Cruces** (22 km), a colonial fortification built in 1647 and largely rebuilt according to the original plans.

West of San José, **Mehuín** is a small, friendly resort and fishing port with a long beach. The fishermen here are usually willing to take people out to see the nearby sealion and penguin colonies, and with a little luck dolphins can also be spotted. A clifftop *ripio* road, with fantastic views north and south along the coastline, leads 6 km north to **Queule**, which has a good beach, but which is dangerous for bathing at high tide because of undercurrents. (Bathing is safer in the river near the ferry.) From Queule, a pretty road leads north again to **Toltén**; numerous small ferry crossings provide access to isolated Mapuche communities and there are wonderful beaches along the coast.

The route east from Valdivia to the lakes passes through what is, perhaps, the least interesting part of the Lake District, consisting largely of wheatfields and dairy farms. Some 93 km east of Valdivia, beyond Antilhue and Los Lagos, is **Lago Riñihue**, the southernmost of the Seven Lakes. **Riñihue**, a beautiful but small and isolated village at its western end, is worth visiting but the road around the southern edge of the lake from Riñihue to Enco is poor and there is no road around the northern edge of the lake.

Lago Ranco

South of Lago Riñihue is **Lago Ranco**, one of the largest lakes, covering 41,000 ha, and also one of the most accessible as it has a road, poor in many places, around its edge. The road is characterized by lots of mud and animals. However it is worth taking the opportunity to escape the gringo trail and witness an older lifestyle while admiring the beautiful lake, starred with islands, and the sun setting on the distant volcanoes. There is excellent fishing on the southern shore; several hotels organize fishing expeditions.

From the Pan-American Highway the north side of the lake can be reached either from Los Lagos or from a better road 18 km further south. These two roads join and meet the road around the lake some 5 km west of **Futrono**. This is the main town on the northern shore and has a daily boat service to **Huapi**, the island in the middle of the lake. From Futrono the road (paved at this point) curves round the north of the lake to **Llifén**, Km 22, a picturesque place on the eastern shore. From Llifén, it is possible visit **Lago Maihue**, 33 km further east, the south end of which is surrounded by native forests. From Llifén the road around Lago Ranco continues via the Salto de Nilahue (Km 14) to **Riñinahue**, Km 23, at the southeast corner, with access to beaches. Further west is **Lago Ranco**, Km 47, an ugly little town on the south shore, which has a museum with exhibits on Mapuche culture. Paved roads lead from here to Río Bueno and the Pan-American Highway. On the western shore is **Puerto Nuevo**, where there are watersports and fishing on the Río Bueno. Further north, 10 km west of Futrono, is **Coique**, where there are more good beaches.

Lagos Ranco & Maihue

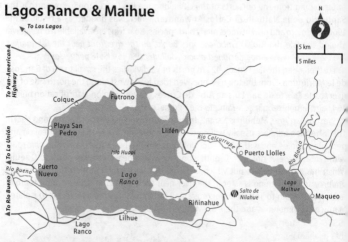

Lord Cochrane

Lord Thomas Alexander Cochrane (1775-1860) was born into a Scottish aristocratic family and began his career in the British navy during the Napoleonic Wars, rising rapidly through the officer ranks. He was elected to Parliament in 1806 as MP for Honiton and in 1807 as MP for Westminster. Cochrane had never been on good terms with his naval superiors, and when he used his position in the House of Commons to accuse the naval commander, Lord Gambier, of incompetence, he precipitated his own downfall. Gambier was court-martialled and acquitted; Cochrane was retired on half-pay and spent the next three years exposing corruption and abuses in the navy. His links with a financial scandal in 1814 provided his enemies with an opportunity for revenge: he was dismissed from the navy, expelled from Parliament and sentenced to 12 months' imprisonment.

Cochrane was recruited for the Chilean armed forces by an agent in London and quickly became friendly with Chile's independence leader Bernardo O'Higgins. He was put in command of the new republic's 'navy', a few ill-equipped vessels that relied on foreign adventurers for experienced sailors, and with this fleet harassed the Spanish-held ports along the Chilean coast. His audacious storming of the fortresses of Corral, San Carlos and Amargos led to the capture of the key Spanish base of Valdivia (see page 298).

Later that year Cochrane transported Peruvian liberation troops, led by José de San Martín, along the Pacific coast to invade Peru, but his relations with San Martin were poor and he became very critical of the Peruvian's cautious strategy. Afterwards Cochrane continued to attack Spanish shipping in the Pacific, sailing as far north as Mexico in 1822.

In 1823 the new government of Brazil appointed Cochrane to head its navy in the struggle for independence from Portugal. Once again leading a motley collection of boats manned largely by foreigners, Cochrane drove the colonial fleet from Bahia and pursued it back to Portugal. In 1825 he fell out with the Brazilian government and returned to Britain. Two years later he volunteered to help the Greeks in their struggle for independence from Turkey. He was reinstated in the British navy in 1832, was promoted to Rear-Admiral and spent much of the rest of his life promoting developments in the use of steam power in shipping.

⊚ Valdivia and around listings

For hotel and restaurant price codes and other relevant information, see pages 14-21.

🛏 Where to stay

Valdivia *p298, map p299*
Accommodation is often scarce during Semana Valdiviana. In summer, rooms are widely available in private homes, usually **$$**, or **$** for singles.
$$$$-$$$ Puerta del Sur, Los Lingües 950, Isla Teja, T063-222 4500, www.hotelpuerta delsur.com. 5 star, with all facilities and extensive grounds.
$$$ Encanto del Río, Prat 415, T063-222 4744, www.hotelencantodelrio.cl. Small, comfortable, rooms on the middle floor have balconies and river views, disabled access, heating.
$$$ Melillanca, Alemania 675, T063-221 2509, www.hotelmelillanca.cl. 4-star, decent business standard, with restaurant, sauna.
$$ Hostal y Cabañas Internacional, García Reyes 660, T063-221 2015,

www.hostalinternacional.cl. Self-catering cabins sleep 5, hostel rooms and dorms with private or shared bath, helpful, English and German spoken, book exchange, excursions to the ocean and rainforest.

$$ Hostal Torreón, P Rosales 783, T063-221 2622, mrprelle@gmail.com. Old German-style villa, nice atmosphere, rooms on top floor are airy, parking.

$$ Hostal Totem, Anwandter 425, T063-229 2849, www.turismototem.cl. Simple rooms, French and basic English spoken, tours arranged, credit cards accepted.

$$-$ Airesbuenos Central, García Reyes 550, T063-222 2202, www.airesbuenos.cl. Eco-conscious hostel. Private rooms and dorms, private or shared bath, garden with friendly duck named Gardel, yoga space, tours, many languages spoken by volunteers, HI affiliated.

$ Hostal Arlense House, Camilo Henríquez 749, Casa 6, T063-243 1494/9-7984 5597, arlene_ola@hotmail.com. Charming tumbledown mansion, endearingly wonky floors (after-effect of 1960 earthquake), large rooms, some English spoken.

Around the bus terminal

$$ Hostal Ana María, José Martí 11, 3 mins from terminal, T063-222 2468, anamsandovalf@hotmail.com. Good value, also *cabañas*.

$$ Hostal Anwandter, Anwandter 601 and García Reyes 249, T063-221 8587, www.hostalanwandter.cl. Rooms sleep 1-4, private or shared bathroom, meals available, usual hostel facilities.

$$ Hostal Casagrande, Anwandter 880, T063-220 2035, www.hotelcasagrande.cl. Heated but small rooms, some gloomy, in attractive house, convenient, great views from breakfast room.

Camping

Camping Centenario, in Rowing Club on España. **$** per tent, overlooking river.

Niebla *p300*

$$$ El Castillo, Antonio Ducce 750, T063-228 2061, www.hotelycabanaselcastillo.com. Typical Germanic 1920 mansion, lots of character. Rooms and apartments. parking, playground, pool.

$$ Cabañas Fischer, Del Castillo 1115, T063-228 2007, rosemarief24@gmail.com. Cabins and 2 campsites. Worth bargaining out of season.

East of Valdivia *p302*

Some of the houses around Lago Ranco are available for let in summer.

$$$$ Hostería Huinca Quinay, 3 km east of Riñihue, Lago Riñihue, T063-197 1811, www.cabanasrinihue.cl. 4-star *cabañas* for 5-6 people with restaurant and lots of facilities.

$$$ Hotel Puerto Nuevo, Puerto Nuevo, Lago Ranco, T063-249 1376, www.hotel puertonuevo.cl. Leisure complex in large grounds by the lake, with restaurant.

$$$ Hostería Chollinco, 3 km out of Llifén, on the road towards Lago Maihue in the Lago Ranco area, T063-197 1979, www.hosteria chollinco.cl. Remote country lodge with swimming pool, trekking, horse riding, fishing, hunting and other activities.

$$$ Riñimapu, northwest edge of Lago Riñihue, T063-231 1388, www.rinimapu.cl. Comfortable rooms and suites with views over the lake, gardens, excellent food.

$$ Hospedaje Futronhue, Balmaceda 90, Futrono, T063-248 1265. Good breakfast.

Camping

There are campsites all around Lago Ranco as well as several on Lago Maihue, though many are open in summer only and prices are high.

Bahía Coique, 9 km west of Futrono, T02-2422 7310, www.bahiacoique.cl. Autocamping Nov-Mar and cabins.

Bahía Las Rosas, 1 km east of Futrono. US$22 per site.

Camping Lago Ranco. US$20 per site.

Maqueo, eastern shore of Lago Maihue, US$20 per site.

Nalcahue, 1 km west of Futrono, T063-248 1663. US$20 per site.

Restaurants

For places to eat in the coastal resorts and around the lakes, see Where to stay, above.

Valdivia *p298, map p299*
$$$-$$ Agridulce, Prat 327, T063-221 6765, www.agridulcevaldivia.cl. Perfect mix of sophisticated dishes using local produce, tapas and generous sandwiches. Good service and good value.
$$$-$$ Lomodetoro, Los Robles 170, Isla Teja, T063-234 6423. Probably the best steak in town. Good wine list.
$$ Cervecería Kunstmann, Ruta T350, No 950, T063-229 2969, www.cerveza-kunstmann.cl. On road to Niebla. German/Chilean food, brewery with 5 types of beer, beautiful interior, museum. Open from 1200 for visits; yellow *colectivo* from outside the Mercado Municipal.
$$ La Calesa, O'Higgins 160, T063-222 5467. Elegant, intimate, Peruvian and international cuisine. Good pisco sours.
$ Volcán, Caupolicán y Chacabuco, T063-221 2163. *Pichangas*, *cazuelas*, great food at a good price.

Cafés
Café Haussmann, O'Higgins 394, T063-221 3878. A Valdivia institution. Good tea, cakes and *crudos*.
Café Moro, Independencia y Libertad, T063-221 2345. Airy café with a mezzanine art gallery. Good for breakfast, good value lunches, popular bar at night.
Entrelagos, Pérez Rosales 622. Ice cream and chocolates.
La Baguette, Yungay 518, T063-221 2345. Panadería with French-style cakes, brown bread.
Mi Pueblito, San Carlos 190, T063-224 5050. Wholemeal bread and vegetarian snacks to take away.

Niebla *p300*
$$ Las Delicias, Ducce 583, T063-221 3566. A restaurant with 'a view that would be worth the money even if the food wasn't good'. Also *cabañas* and camping.

Bars and clubs

Valdivia *p298, map p299*
Bunker, Av Los Robles 1345, Isla Teja. Lively student bar.
La Bomba, Caupolicán. Pleasant old Valdivian bar, serves *empanadas* and other dishes.
La Ultima Frontera, Pérez Rosales 787 (in Centro Cultural 787). Fills up with alternative 20- and 30-something crowd. Cheap beer as well as a large variety of sandwiches (including falafel) and filling soups. Friendly but slow service and very smoky.
Ocio Restobar, Arauco 102, loud music. Popular with young professionals.
Santo Pecado, Yungay 745. Refined but laid-back bar also serving a variety of sandwiches and exotic dishes.

Entertainment

Valdivia *p298, map p299*
There's a cinema in the Mall on Calle Arauco.
Cine Club UACH, on the university campus on Isla Teja, www.2013.cineclubuach.cl. Shows films at the weekend (not in summer).

Festivals

Valdivia *p298, map p299*
Mid-Feb Semana Valdiviana, with a series of sporting and cultural activities such a as a triathlon, theatre and music, culminates in **Noche Valdiviana** on the Sat with a procession of elaborately decorated boats that sail past the Muelle Fluvial.
Sep A well-regarded **film festival**.

Niebla *p300*
Mid-Feb Feria Costumbrista, with lots of good food including *pullmay*, *asado* and *paila marina*.

O Shopping

Valdivia *p298, map p299*
Feria Fluvial is a colourful riverside market selling livestock, fish, etc. The separate **municipal market** building opposite has been restored and is occupied mainly by *artesanía* stalls. On the river-side of the market building there are several fish restaurants serving cheap, tasty food in a nice atmosphere.

O What to do

Valdivia *p298, map p299*
Boat trips
Kiosks along the Muelle Fluvial offer trips to **Corral**, **Niebla** and elsewhere. Boats will only leave with a minimum of 10 passengers, so organize your trip in advance during the off-season. A full list of operators is available from the tourist information office.
Tourist House, Camilo Henríquez 266, T063-243 3115, offers a range of trips and gives good advice.

Sea kayaking
Pueblito Expediciones, San Carlos 188, T063-224 5055, www.pueblito expediciones.cl. Offer classes and trips in the waters around Valdivia.

O Transport

Valdivia *p298, maps p299*
Air
LAN to/from **Santiago** daily, via Temuco or Concepción.

Bus
To **Niebla**, orange bus No 20 from outside bus station or along calles Anwandter and Carampangue, regular service 0730-2100, 30 mins, US$1.20 (bus continues to **Los Molinos**). There are occasional buses from Valdivia to **Corral**. To **Llifén** via Futrono, with **Cordillera Sur**, daily; also frequent services to **Riñihue** via Paillaco and Los Lagos.

To **Santiago**, several companies, 10 hrs, most services overnight, US$30-80. To **Osorno**, every 30 mins, 2 hrs, several companies, US$8. To **Panguipulli**, **Empresa Pirehueico**, about every 30 mins, US$5. Many daily to **Puerto Montt**, US$9, 3 hrs. To **Puerto Varas**, 3 hrs, US$10. To **Frutillar**, US$6, 2½ hrs. To **Villarrica**, with **JAC**, 6 a day, 2½ hrs, US$8, continuing to **Pucón**, US$9, 3 hrs. To **Bariloche (Argentina)** via Osorno, 7 hrs, **Andesmar**, US$35-50.

Ferry
The tourist boats to **Isla Mancera** and **Corral** offer a guided ½-day tour (US$25-75, some with meals) from the Muelle Fluvial, Valdivia, or the Marqués de Mancera (behind the tourist office on Av Prat).

Niebla *p300*
Somarco vehicle ferry to **Corral**, every 2 hrs, US$1.25.

O Directory

Valdivia *p298, maps p299*
Banks Several banks with ATMs in the centre. **Turismo Cochrane**, Prat 723; **Casa de Cambio**, Carampangue 325, T063-213305; **Turismo Austral**, Arauco y Henríquez, Galería Arauco, accepts TCs. **Laundry** Au Chic, Arauco 436; **Lavazul**, Chacabuco 300, slow; coin laundry at **Lavamatic**, Schmidt y Picarte.

Osorno and around

Situated at the confluence of the Ríos Rahue and Damas, 921 km south of Santiago, Osorno was founded in 1553 before being abandoned in 1604 and refounded by Ambrosio O'Higgins and Juan MacKenna O'Reilly in 1796. It later became one of the centres of German immigration; their descendants are still of great importance in the area. Although Osorno is an important transport hub and a reasonable base for visiting the southern lakes, it is a drab uninspiring city, and is likely to be a place that you will just pass through.

Arriving in Osorno → *Colour map 4, B2.*

Getting there and around Osorno is a key crossroads for bus routes in southern Chile. Passengers heading overland to Bariloche, Neuquén, Coyhaique or Punta Arenas will pass through here before making for the Samoré (formerly Puyehue) Pass into Argentina (see box, page 310); travellers from Santiago may well change buses here. The main terminal is four blocks from the Plaza de Armas at Errázuriz 1400. Left luggage open 0730-2030. A bus to the city centre costs US$0.50. Local buses to **Entre Lagos**, **Puyehue** and **Aguas Calientes** leave from the **Mercado Municipal terminal**, one block west of main terminal. There are also hourly local services to Puerto Montt, as well as frequent services north to Temuco and Valdivia. Most of the places visitors

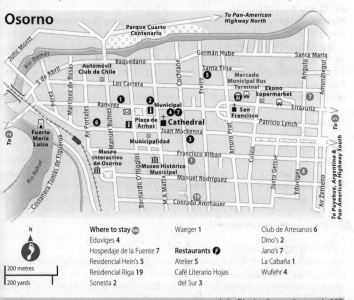

Osorno

N

200 metres
200 yards

Where to stay	Waeger 1	Club de Artesanos 6
Eduviges 4		Dino's 2
Hospedaje de la Fuente 7	**Restaurants**	Jano's 7
Residencial Hein's 5	Atelier 5	La Cabaña 1
Residencial Riga 19	Café Literario Hojas	Wufehr 4
Sonesta 2	del Sur 3	

are likely to visit are within easy walking distance. Taxis or *colectivos* may be useful for longer trips.

Tourist information Information is available from the provincial government office of **Sernatur** ① *Plaza de Armas, O'Higgins 667, piso 1, T064-223 7575, Mon-Thu 0900-1300 and 1400-1700, Fri 0900-1300 and 1400-1600, Sat-Sun 1400-1900.* The municipal tourist office is based in the bus terminal and in a kiosk on the Plaza de Armas, www.municipalidadosorno.cl, both open December to February. There is also a **CONAF** office ① *Rosas 430, T064-222 1304.*

Places in Osorno
On the large **Plaza de Armas** stands the modern, concrete and glass cathedral, with many arches and a tower that is itself an open, latticed arch with a cross superimposed. West of the centre on a bend overlooking the river is the **Fuerte María Luisa**, built in 1793 and restored in 1977; only the river front walls and end turrets are still standing. East of the main plaza along Calle MacKenna are a number of late 19th-century wooden mansions built by German immigrants, now preserved as national monuments. Two blocks south of the Plaza is the **Museo Histórico Municipal** ① *Matta 809, entrance in Casa de Cultura, www.interpatagonia.com/paseos/museo_osorno/, Mon-Thu 0930-1730, Fri 0930-1630, Sat 1400-1900, free,* which has displays on natural history, Mapuche culture, the refounding of the city and German colonization. Three blocks southwest of the plaza, in the former train station is the **Museo Interactivo de Osorno (MIO)** ① *Portales 901, T064-221 2997, www.municipalidadosorno.cl, Mon-Thu 0900-1300, 1400-1700, Fri 0900-1300, 1400-1600, Sat-Sun 1400-1900,* an interactive science museum designed for both children and adults.

North and west of Osorno
Río Bueno, 30 km north, is celebrated for its scenery and fishing. The Spanish colonial fort, dating from 1777, is situated high above the river and offers fine views. Just over 20 km further west on the Río Bueno is **Trumao**, a river port with a river launch service to La Barra on the coast. There are beaches at **Maicolpue**, 60 km west of Osorno, and **Pucatrihue**, which are worth a visit in the summer. Further north is the **Monumento Natural Alerce Costero**, a park covering 2307 ha of the coastal mountain range and protecting an area of alerce forest (though a fire in 1975 destroyed some of the forest). Access is by a poor *ripio* road which runs northwest for 52 km from La Unión. There is a CONAF *guardería* and *refugio* at the entrance, from which a 3-km trail leads to a 3500-year-old alerce tree.

East of Osorno
From Osorno Route 215 runs east to the Argentine border at the Samoré (Puyehue) Pass via the south shore of Lago Puyehue, Anticura and the Parque Nacional Puyehue. **Auto Museo Moncopulli** ① *Route 215, 25 km east of Osorno, T064-210744, www.moncopulli. cl, daily 1000-2000, in summer, 1000-1800 in winter, US$2, bus towards Entre Lagos,* is the best motor museum in Chile. Exhibits include a Studebaker collection from 1852 to 1966. There is also a 1950s-style cafetería.

Lago Puyehue and the Parque Nacional
Surrounded by relatively flat countryside, 47 km east of Osorno, **Lago Puyehue** extends over 15,700 ha. The southern shore is much more developed than the northern shore, which is accessible only by unpaved road from **Entre Lagos** at the western end. On the

eastern side of the lake are the **Termas de Puyehue** ⓘ *www.puyehue.cl, day or night passes from US$74.*

Stretching east from Lago Puyehue to the Argentine border, Parque Nacional Puyehue covers 107,000 ha, much of it in the valley of the Río Golgol. On the eastern side are several lakes, including Lago Constancia and Lago Gris. There are two volcanic peaks: **Volcán Puyehue** (2240 m) in the north (access via a private track, US$10) and **Volcán Casablanca** (also called Antillanca, 1900 m). Leaflets on walks and attractions are available from the park administration at Aguas Calientes and from the ranger station at Anticura.

On the edge of the park, 4 km south of the Termas de Puyehue, **Aguas Calientes** ⓘ *www.termasaguascalientes.cl, daily 0830-2000, day passes US$38-45*, has indoor and very hot open-air thermal pools in a thickly forested valley beside the **Río Chanlefú**, with camping, cabins, massages and other therapies.

From Aguas Calientes the road continues 18 km southeast past three small lakes and through forests to the small ski resort of **Antillanca** (see What to do, page 312) on the slopes of Volcán Casablanca. In winter a one-way traffic system may operate on the last 8 km. There is no public transport between Aguas Calientes and **Antillanca**, but it is not a hard walk. This is a particularly beautiful section, especially at sunrise, with views over Lago Puyehue to the north and Lagos Rupanco and Llanquihue to the south, as well as the snow-clad peaks of Calbuco, Osorno, Puntiagudo, Puyehue and Tronador forming a semicircle. The tree-line on Casablanca is one of the few in the world made up of deciduous trees (*nothofagus* or southern beech). From Antillanca it is possible to climb Casablanca for even better views of the surrounding volcanes and lakes; there's no path and the hike takes about seven hours there and back; information from **Club Andino** in Osorno. On the south side of the volcano there are caves (accessible by road, allow five hours from **Hotel Antillanca**; see Where to stay).

Lagos Puyehue & Rupanco

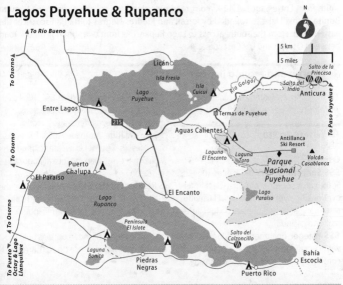

Border crossing: Chile–Argentina

Paso Samoré (formerly Puyehue)

The Chilean border post is 4 km east of Anticura at Pajaritos (T064-231 1563, www. pasosfronterizos.gov.cl/cf_cardenalsamore.html). Immigration is normally open daily 0800-2000. From here it's a further 22 km east to the border at Paso Samoré, although this route is liable to closure after snow. For private vehicles entering Chile, formalities are quick (about 15 minutes), but include a search for fruit, vegetables and the spraying of tyres. Shoes have to be wiped on a mat. On the Argentine side the road continues to Bariloche. Cyclists should know that there are no supplies between Entre Lagos and La Angostura (Argentina).

The paved Route 215, meanwhile, continues from the Termas de Puyehue to **Anticura**, northeast of Aguas Calientes. In this section of the park are three waterfalls, including the spectacular 40-m wide **Salto del Indio**. Legend has it that an Indian, enslaved by the Spanish, was able to escape by hiding behind the falls. Situated just off the road, the falls are on a marked path through dense forest which includes a 800-year-old Coigüe tree known as 'El Abuelo'. For details of the Argentine border crossing east of Anticura, see box, above.

Lago Rupanco

Lying south of Lago Puyehue and considerably larger, this lake covers 23,000 ha and is far less accessible and less developed for tourism than most of the other larger lakes. Access to the northern shore is via two unpaved roads that branch off Route 215. **El Paraíso** (aka Marina Rupanco), at the western tip of the lake, can be reached by an unpaved road south from Entre Lagos. A 40-km dirt road runs along the southern shore, via **Laguna Bonita**, a small lake surrounded by forest, and **Piedras Negras** to **Bahía Escocia** at the eastern end. From the south, access to Lago Rupanco is from two turnings off the road between Osorno and Las Cascadas.

⦿ Osorno and around listings

For hotel and restaurant price codes and other relevant information, see pages 14-21.

⦿ Where to stay

Osorno *p307, map p307*
$$$ Sonesta, Ejercito 395 Rahue, T064-255 5000, www.sonesta.com. First-class hotel overlooking river, all amenities, **El Olivillo** restaurant, attached to Plaza de los Lagos mall and casino.
$$$ Waeger, Cochrane 816, T064-223 3721, www.hotelwaeger.cl. 4-star, restaurant, comfortable but room sizes vary greatly.

$$$-$$ Eduviges, Eduviges 856, T064-223 5023, www.hoteleduviges.cl. Spacious, quiet, attractive, gardens, also *cabañas*.
$$ Hostal Riga, Amthauer 1058, T064-223 2945, resiriga@surnet.cl. Pleasant, good value, quiet area, parking, heavily booked in season.
$ Residencial Hein's, Errázuriz 1757, T064-223 4116. Private or shared bath, old-fashioned, spacious, family atmosphere.

There are plenty of cheap options near the bus terminal, for instance on Los Carrera.

North and west of Osorno *p308*
$$$-$$ Hostería Miller, Maicolpue,
60 km west of Osorno, T064-255 0277/197
5630, www.hosteriamiller.com. On the
beach, clean, with good service, also a
recommended campsite.

**Lago Puyehue and the Parque
Nacional** *p308, map p309*
$$$$ Hotel Antillanca, Antillanca, T02-
2946 2900, www.chileanski.com. Full board.
Located at the foot of Volcán Casablanca
and offering skiing and snowboarding
in the winter, outdoor sports in summer:
hiking, caving, climbing and rappelling.
Pool. Friendly club-like atmosphere; also
has a *refugio*.
$$$$ Hotel Termas de Puyehue, at
the Termas de Puyehue, T064-233 1400,
www.puyehue.cl. All inclusive: meals,
drinks, use of thermal pools and all
activities (spa extra), well maintained,
in beautiful scenery, heavily booked
Jan-Feb, cheaper May to mid-Dec.
$$ Hospedaje Millaray, Ramírez 333,
Entre Lagos, T09-9761 6625, bernarda_
ro@hotmail.cl. Very good place to stay.
$$ Hostal y Cabañas Miraflores,
Ramírez 480, Entre Lagos, T064-
237 1275, www.hostal-miraflores.cl.
Pleasant rooms and cabins.

Camping
Camping Los Copihues, Km 58, T09-9344
8830, on south shore of Lake Puyehue.
Restaurant, spa, camping (US$8) and *cabañas*.
Camping Los Derrumbes, 1 km from
Aguas Calientes, no electricity.
Camping No Me Olvides, Ruta 215,
Km 56, on south shore of Lake Puyehue,
T09-9128 3002, www.nomeolvides.cl.
Tent site and *cabañas*.
CONAF refugio, Volcán Puyehue. Check
with CONAF in Anticura whether it is open.

Lago Rupanco *p310, map p309*
There is no accommodation on the
northern shore of the lake.

$$$ Puntiagudo Lodge, Bahía Escocia,
T09-9643 4247, www.puntiagudolodge.
com. With breakfast, very comfortable,
good restaurant, fly-fishing, horse riding,
boat excursions. Advance bookings only.
$$ Refugio Club de Pesca y Caza,
Sector Islote, 7 km east of Piedras
Negras, T064-223 2056. Basic *refugio*
with breakfast and bath.

Camping
There are several campsites on the southern
shore, including at Puerto Rico.
Desague del Rupanco, just south of
El Paraíso. No facilities.
Puerto Chalupa, on northern shore,
T064-223 2680. US$21.50 per site.

🍴 Restaurants

For other eating options in the area,
see Where to stay above.

Osorno *p307, map p307*
There are good cheap restaurants in the
municipal market.
$$$ Atelier, Freire 468. Fresh pasta and
other Italian delights, good.
$$ Dino's, Ramírez 898, on the plaza.
Restaurant upstairs, bar/cafeteria
downstairs, good.
$$ Wufehr, Ramírez 959 loc 2, T064-222
6999. Local raw meat specialities and
sandwiches. Popular with locals. Also
Rincón de Wufehr, Manuel Rodríguez 1015.
$$-$ Club de Artesanos, MacKenna 634.
Decent and hearty traditional Chilean fare.
$ Café Literario Hojas del Sur, MacKenna
1011 y Cochrane. More like a living room
than a café, cosy, Wi-Fi.
$ La Cabaña, Ramírez 774, T064-227 2479.
Wide variety of cheap lunches ranging
from Chinese to home-cooked Chilean.
Excellent value.
$ Jano's, Ramírez 977, T064-221 1828.
Bakery with fresh juices and lunch/dinner
options. Many vegetarian options as well.

Lago Puyehue and the Parque Nacional *p308, map p309*
$$$-$$ Jardín del Turista, Ruta 215, Km 46, Entre Lagos, T064-437 1214, www.interpatagonia.com/jardindelturista/. Very good, also has *cabañas* and suites.

○ Shopping

Osorno *p307, map p307*
There is a mall on C Freire 542 with 3 internet cafés and a bookshop, **CM Books**, which sells some English titles.
Alta Artesanía, MacKenna 1069. Excellent handicrafts, not cheap.
Climent, Angulo 603. Fishing tackle.
Ekono, Colón y Errázuriz. Supermarket.
The Lodge, Los Carrera 1291, local 5. Fishing tackle.

○ What to do

Osorno *p307, map p307*
Club Andino, O'Higgins 1073, T064-223 8877. Information and advice on climbing and skiing in the area.

Lago Puyehue and the Parque Nacional *p308, map p309*
Skiing
Hotel Antillanca, see Where to stay, above, is attached to one of Chile's smaller ski resorts; 17 pistes are served by 3 lifts, ski instruction and first-aid available. Piste preparation is unreliable. Skiing is not difficult but quality depends on the weather: rain is common. See www.skiantillanca.cl for information on the state of the pistes.

Lago Rupanco *p310, map p309*
Fishing
Lago Rupanco is very popular for fishing.
Bahía Escocia Fly Fishing offers excursions from the **Puntiagudo Lodge** (see Where to stay). Advance booking required.

○ Transport

Osorno *p307, map p307*
Air
LAN, daily to **Santiago**, via Concepción and/or Temuco.

Bus
Expreso Lago Puyehue and **Buses Barria** leave from the Mercado Municipal terminal to **Entre Lagos**, frequent in summer, reduced service off-season, 1 hr, US$2.75. Some of these buses continue to **Aguas Calientes** (off-season according to demand), 2 hrs, US$5 but do not stop at Lago Puyehue (unless you want to get off at **Hotel Termas de Puyehue** and clamber down). Daily service with **Empresa Ruta 5** to **Lago Ranco**. To **Anticura**, 2-3 buses daily, 3 hrs, US$5-11.
To **Santiago**, frequent, US$23, salón cama US$55-64, 11 hrs. To **Concepción**, US$22-33. To **Temuco**, US$9. To **Pucón** and **Villarrica**, frequent, US$13. To **Frutillar** (US$2), **Llanquihue**, **Puerto Varas** (US$3) and **Puerto Montt** (US$3), services every 30 mins. To **Puerto Octay**, US$3, every 20 mins. To **Bariloche** (Argentina), 4 companies, US$30.

North and west of Osorno *p308*
River launches run between **Trumao** on the Río Bueno, 22 km west of Osorno, to **La Barra** on the coast.

○ Directory

Osorno *p307, map p307*
Banks Several banks with ATMs around the plaza. Casas de cambio include **Cambio Tur**, MacKenna 1004; **Turismo Frontera**, Ramírez 949, local 11 (Galería Catedral); if stuck try **Travels** bar in bus terminal. **Laundry** Limpec, Prat 678, allow at least a day. **Post office** O'Higgins 645.

Lago Llanquihue

The second largest lake in Chile and the third largest natural lake in South America, Lago Llanquihue is one of the highlights of the Lake District. Three snow-capped volcanoes can be seen across the vast expanse of water: the perfect cone of Osorno (2680 m), the shattered cone of Calbuco (2015 m), and the spike of Puntiagudo (2480 m), as well as, when the air is clear, the distant Tronador (3460 m). On a cloudless night with a full moon, the snows reflect eerily in the lake and the peace and stillness are hard to match.

Arriving at Lago Llanquihue → *Colour map 4, C2.*

Getting there and around Access from the south is from nearby Puerto Montt, while there are direct transport links with Santiago along the Pan-American Highway. The northern tip of the lake is also easily reached from Osorno. The largest towns, Puerto Varas, Llanquihue and Frutillar are all on the western shore, linked by the Pan-American Highway. Although there are roads around the rest of the lake, the eastern shore is difficult to visit without transport, and beyond Las Cascadas, the road is narrow with lots of blind corners, necessitating speeds of 20-30 kph at best in places (see below). Beware of lorries that ply the route servicing the salmon farms. There is no public transport between Las Cascadas and Ensenada and hitching is very difficult.

Puerto Octay to Ensenada → *For listings, see pages 318-323.*

Puerto Octay

Puerto Octay is a peaceful and picturesque small town at the northern tip of the lake 56 km southeast of Osorno, set amid rolling hills, hedgerows and German-style farmhouses with views over Volcán Osorno. Founded by German settlers in 1852, the town enjoyed a boom period in the late 19th century when it was the northern port for steamships on the lake: a few buildings survive from that period, notably the church and the enormous German-style former convent. Since the arrival of railways and the building of roads, the town has declined. Much less busy than Frutillar or Puerto Varas, Puerto Octay offers an escape for those seeking peace and quiet. Rowing boats and pedalos can be hired for trips on the lake.

Museo el Colono ① *Independencia 591, T064-264 3327, http://museoelcolono.jimdo. com, daily 1000-1300, 1500-1900, US$2,* has displays on German colonization. Another part of the museum, housing agricultural implements and machinery for making *chicha*, is just outside town on the road towards **Centinela**. This peninsula, about 3 km south (taxi US$3 one way) along an unpaved road, has accommodation, camping, a launch dock, bathing beaches and watersports. It is a very popular spot in good weather, especially for picnics, with fine views of the Osorno, Calbuco and Puntiagudo volcanoes.

Puerto Octay to Volcán Osorno

The eastern lakeside, with Volcán Osorno on your left is very beautiful. From Puerto Octay two roads run towards Ensenada, one *ripio* along the shore, and one paved. (They join up after 20 km.) At Km 10 along the lakeside route is **Playa Maitén**, a lovely beach, often deserted, with a marvellous view of Volcán Osorno. Continue for another 24 km past **Puerto Fonck**, which has fine 19th-century German-style mansions, and you'll reach **Las Cascadas**, surrounded by picturesque agricultural land, old houses and German cemeteries. To reach the waterfalls that give the village its name turn east at the school along a *ripio* road to a car park, continue along a footpath over two or three log bridges over a stream before arriving at an impressive jungle-like 40-m-high natural cauldron, with the falls in the middle. The round trip takes about 1½ hours.

Volcán Osorno

The most lasting image of Lago Llanquihue is the near-perfect cone of Volcán Osorno, situated north of Ensenada on the eastern edge of the lake. Although the peak is on the edge of the Parque Nacional Pérez Rosales (see page 324), it is climbed from the western side, which lies outside the park. Access is via two roads that branch off the Ensenada–Puerto Octay road along the eastern edge of Lago Llanquihue. The northern one is at Puerto Klocker, 20 km southeast of Puerto Octay and only suitable for 4WDs, while the main entrance is 2 km north of Ensenada along a good paved road.

Lago Llanquihue

German colonization in the Lake District

The most important area of German agricultural colonization in Chile was around Lago Llanquihue. The Chilean government declared the area as destined for colonization in 1845, and to encourage settlement, gave each adult male 75 *cuadras* of land, an extra 12 *cuadras* for each son, a milking cow, 500 planks of timber, nails, a yoke of oxen, a year's free medical assistance and Chilean citizenship on request.

The first groups of German colonists arrived in the area in 1852: one group settled around Maitén and Puerto Octay, another helped found Puerto Montt. The lives of these early settlers were hard and the risks great, yet within 10 years the settlers had cleared much of the forest round the lake and soon they were setting up small industries. In 1880, when the offer to colonists ended, unsettled land was auctioned in lots of 400-800 ha. By then the lake was ringed

by a belt of smallholdings and farms. The legacy of this settlement can be seen in the German-looking farmhouses around Puerto Octay and in many of the older buildings in Frutillar and Puerto Varas.

Valdivia was another centre for German colonization. A small number of German and Swiss colonists settled in the city, exerting a strong influence on the architecture, agricultural methods, education, social life and customs of the area. They established most of the industries that made Valdivia an important manufacturing centre until the 1950s. According to an 1884 survey of Valdivia, all breweries, leatherworks, brickworks, mills, bakeries, and machine shops belonged to families with German surnames.

Little of the architectural heritage of this period survived the 1960 earthquake, but the city's German heritage can still be seen in some of its best cafés and restaurants and in the names of its streets.

Guided ascents of the volcano (organized by agencies in Puerto Varas) set out from the *refugio* at **La Burbuja** where there is a small ski centre in winter and pleasant short walks in summer to a couple of craters and with great views of the lake and across to Puerto Montt. From here it is six hours to the summit. The volcano can also be climbed from the north at La Picada (the refugio here burnt down some years ago); this route is easier and may be attempted without a guide, although only experienced climbers should try to climb right to the top as ice-climbing equipment is essential, and there are many craters hidden below thin crusts of ice.

Ensenada

Despite its lack of a recognizable centre, Ensenada is beautifully situated at the southeast corner of Lago Llanquihue, almost beneath the snows of Volcán Osorno. A good half-day trip from Ensenada itself is to **Laguna Verde**, about 30 minutes from **Hotel Ensenada**, along a beautiful circular trail behind the lake (take first fork to the right behind the information board), and then down the road to a secluded campsite at Puerto Oscuro on Lago Llanquihue.

The western shore → For listings, see pages 318-323.

Frutillar

Lying about half-way along the western side of the lake, Frutillar is in fact two towns: **Frutillar Alto**, just off the main highway, and **Frutillar Bajo**, beautifully situated on the lakeside, 4 km away. The latter is possibly the most attractive and expensive town on the lake, with superb views from the *costanera* over the water with volcanoes Osorno and Tronador in the background. The town's atmosphere is very German and somewhat aloof, but the **tourist office** ① *on the Costanera, Filippi 753, T065-242 1261 www.munifrutillar.cl and www.frutillar. com*, is helpful. In the square opposite is an open-air chess board and the **Club Alemán** restaurant. After eight years of construction work, the new, state-of-the-art concert hall on the lakeside, **Teatro del Lago** (www.teatrodellago. cl), is now complete and hosts a highly regarded classical music festival (www. semanasmusicales.cl) in late January to early February.

Away from the waterfront, the appealing **Museo Colonial Alemán** ① *Vicente Pérez Rosales s/n, T065-242 1142, www.museosaustral.cl, daily 0900-1930 summer, 0900-1730, winter, US$4*, is set in spacious gardens, with a watermill, replicas of two German colonial houses with furnishings and utensils of the period, and a blacksmith's shop selling personally engraved horseshoes for US$9. It also has a *campanario*, a circular barn with agricultural machinery and carriages inside, as well as a handicraft shop. At the northern end of the town is the **Reserva Forestal Edmundo Winckler**, run by the Universidad de Chile and extending over 33 ha, with a guided trail through native woods. Named after one of the early German settlers, it includes a very good collection of native flora as well as plants introduced from Europe.

Frutillar Bajo

To Reserva Forestal Edmundo Winckler

To Frutillar Alto & Pan-American Highway

To ⑧ ⑪, Playa Maqui & Puerto Octay (Ripio)

Caupolicán

S Junginger

18 de Septiembre

Carlos Richter

Av Philippi

🏛 Museo Colonial Alemán

Prat

⑬

Av Alemania

Balmaceda

✝

Lago Llanquihue

San Martín

④

Municipalidad ✉ ℹ

O'Higgins

Pier

J Montt

①

Las Piedras

A Varas

Pérez Rosales

① ②

Teatro del Lago

M Rodríguez

②

P Aguirre

⑦

21 de Mayo

N

Lautaro

To Llanquihue

200 metres
200 yards

Where to stay 🛏
Ayacara 7
Hospedaje Tía Clarita 4
Hostería Trayen 1
Lagune Club 8
Residenz am See 13
Salzburg 11

Winkler 2

Restaurants 🍴
Andes 1
Casino de Bomberos 2

Llanquihue

Twenty kilometres south of Frutillar, Llanquihue lies at the source of the Río Maullín, which drains the lake. The site of a large dairy processing factory, this is the least touristy town on the lake, and makes a cheaper alternative to Puerto Varas and Frutillar. It has uncrowded beaches. Just north of town is the **Colonos brewery**, which has a restaurant and can be visited.

Puerto Varas and around → *For listings, see pages 318-323.*

Situated on the southwestern corner of the lake, Puerto Varas, with a population of 25,000, is the commercial and tourist centre of Lago Llanquihue. It also serves as a residential centre for Puerto Montt, 20 km to the south. The self-styled "city of the roses" has in the past been voted the best place to live in Chile. In the 19th century, Puerto Chico (on the eastern outskirts) was the southern port for shipping on the lake. With the arrival of the railway the settlement moved to its current location and is now a resort, popular with Chilean as well as foreign tourists; in February especially, the town clogs up with oversized jeeps from Santiago. Despite the numbers of visitors, though, it has a friendly, compact feel, and is one of the best bases for exploring the southern Lake District, near centres for trekking, rafting, canyoning and fly-fishing.

Where to stay
Amancay **3** *B1*
Bellavista **2** *B3*
Cabañas del Lago **27** *A2*
Canales del Sur **25** *A3*
Casa Kalfu **1** *B3*
Casa Azul **5** *B3*
Casa Margouya **7** *B2*

Compass del Sur **8** *B1*
Hospedaje Don Raúl **12** *C1*
Hostería Outsider **21** *B2*
Weisserhaus **6** *B2*

Restaurants
Bravo Carrera **1** *A3*
Café Danés **3** *B2*

Cassis **5** *B2*
Di Carusso **11** *B2*
Donde El Gordito **4** *B2*
El Barrista **7** *B2*
La Chamaca Inn **8** *B3*
La Olla **2** *A3*
Mediterráneo **6** *A2*
Xic Dalí **8** *C2*

Arriving in Puerto Varas

Getting there Puerto Varas is served by many buses from Puerto Montt; there are also connections north to Osorno, Valdivia, Temuco and all the way to Santiago. A taxi from Puerto Montt airport costs US$25-35. Minibuses from the airport are cheaper but will often stop in Puerto Montt first. The bus terminal is on the southwestern outskirts. Only local minibus services enter the town centre.

Tourist information There's a municipal **tourist office** ① *Del Salvador 320, T065-236 1194, aboegel@ptovaras.cl, see www.ptovaras.cl.* The information office on the pier belongs to the chamber of tourism and does not give wholly impartial advice. Many places close in the off-season. Information is available on the **Parque Pumalín** ① *Klenner 299, T065-225 0079, www.pumalinpark.org*, see page 366.

Places in Puerto Varas

Puerto Varas is small and easily navigable on foot. **Parque Philippi**, on top of a hill, is a pleasant place to visit, although the views are a bit restricted by trees and the metal cross at the top is unattractive. Also in the park is an electric clock that chimes the quarter-hours during daylight hours. To reach the summit walk up to **Hotel Cabañas del Lago** on Klenner, cross the railway and the gate is on the right. The centre lies at the foot of the hill, but the town stretches east along the lake to **Puerto Chico**, where there are hotels and restaurants. The imposing **Catholic church** was built by German Jesuits in 1918 in baroque style as a copy of the church in the Black Forest. North and east of the former **Gran Hotel Puerto Varas** (1934) are a number of German-style mansions.

Puerto Varas is a good base for trips around the lake. A paved road runs along the south shore to Ensenada on the southwestern corner of the lake. Two of the best beaches are **Playa Hermosa**, Km 7, and **Playa Niklitschek**, Km 8, where an entry fee is charged. At Km 16, narrow channels overhung with vegetation lead south from Lago Llanquihue to the little lake of **La Poza**. There are boat trips (US$5) to the beautiful **Isla Loreley**, an island on the lake, and a channel leads from La Poza to yet another lake, the **Laguna Encantada**. At Km 21 there is a watermill and a restaurant run by the **Club Alemán**.

Just past the village of Nueva Braunau, 9 km west of Puerto Varas, is the remarkable **Museo Antonio Felmer** ① *T065-233 0831, www.museoaleman.cl, summer daily 1100-2000, otherwise weekends 1100-1300, 1500-1800 or by appointment, US$4.50,* a huge private collection of machinery, tools and household items used by the first Austrian immigrants to the area, some with English descriptions. On quiet days staff may give demonstrations of the more ingenious objects.

⊙ Lago Llanquihue listings

For hotel and restaurant price codes and other relevant information, see pages 14-21.

⊜ Where to stay

Wild camping and barbecues are forbidden on the lake shore.

Puerto Octay *p313*
$$$$-$$$ Hotel Centinela, Centinela, T064-239 1326, www.hotelcentinela.cl. Built in 1914 as a summer mansion, Edward VIII once stayed here. Rooms and cabins in idyllic location with superb views, excellent restaurant, bar, open all year.
$$$-$$ Zapato Amarillo, 35 mins' walk north of town, T064-221 0787,

www.zapatoamarillo.cl. **$** pp in dorms.
Book in advance in high season, private
or shared bath, home-made bread, meals,
German/English spoken, mountain bikes,
sailboats, tours, house has a grass roof.
$$ Hostería La Baja, Centinela, T09-8218
6897, www.hosterialabaja.cl. Beautifully
situated at the neck of the peninsula.
Good value.
Camping El Molino, beside lake, T064-
239 1375. East of Puerto Octay.

Puerto Octay to Volcán Osorno *p314*
Several farms on the road around the
north and east side of the lake offer
accommodation; look for signs. Camping
is possible at the **Centro de Recreación
Las Cascadas**, T02-2863 2010, and at
Playa Maitén.
$ Hostería Irma, 1 km south of
Las Cascadas, T064-239 6227. Very
pleasant, good food; also farmhouse
accommodation and camping.

Volcán Osorno *p314*
There are 2 *refugios* (**$** pp), both of them
south of the summit and reached from
the southern access road: **La Burbuja**,
the former ski-club centre, 14 km north of
Ensenada at 1250 m, and **Refugio Teski
Ski Club**, T09-9700 3700, just below the
snowline, with café. **CONAF runs a good
campsite** at Puerto Oscuro, beneath the
road to the volcano.

Ensenada *p315*
$$$$ Hotel Ensenada, Km 45, T065-221
2028, www.hotelensenada.cl. Olde-worlde,
half-board, good food, good view of lake
and Osorno Volcano, mountain bikes and
tennis for guests.
$$$ Cabañas Brisas del Lago, Km 42,
T065-221 2012, www.brisasdellago.cl.
Chalets for up to 6 and rooms for up to
3 on beach; good restaurant nearby,
supermarket next door.
$$$-$$ Casa Ko', Km 37, T09-7703 6477,
www.casako.com. 3 km off Puerto Varas–

Ensenada road, ask bus to drop you at sign
and walk or phone in advance for pick-up.
Traditional house, helpful owners, lovely
surroundings and views, good meals. Plenty
of outdoor activities plus programme for
artists and photographers.
$$ Hospedaje Ensenada, Km 43, T065-
221 2050, www.hospedajensenada.cl.
Typical old house, rooms sleep 1-4,
private or shared bath, beach, parking.

Camping
Montaña, central Ensenada, T065-221
2088. Fully equipped, nice beach sites.
Also at Playa Larga, 1 km further east,
and at Puerto Oscuro, 2 km north. Trauco,
4 km west, T065-223 6262. Large site with
shops, fully equipped.

Frutillar *p315, map p316*
During the annual music festival
accommodation should be booked well
in advance; alternatively stay in Frutillar
Alto or Puerto Varas. In most cases on Av
Philippi you are paying a premium for the
view. If you are staying here, try and ensure
your room has one. There are several cheap
options along Carlos Richter (main street)
in Frutillar Alto and at the school in Frutillar
Alto in Jan-Feb (sleeping bag required).
$$$$ Ayacara, Av Philippi 1215, Frutillar
Bajo, T065-242 1550, www.hotelayacara.cl.
Beautiful rooms with lake view,
welcoming, have a pisco sour in
the library in the evening.
$$$$-$$$ Salzburg, Camino Playa Maqui,
north of Frutillar Bajo, T065-242 1589, www.
salzburg.cl. Excellent, spa, sauna, restaurant,
mountain bikes, arranges tours and fishing.
$$$ Lagune Club, 3 km north of Frutillar
Bajo, T065-233 0033, www.interpatagonia.
com/laguneclub. In an old country house
in 16 ha of land, private beach, fishing trips,
free pickup from terminal. Disabled-visitor
friendly, discounts for the over-65s. Also
cabañas. Good value in dollars.
$$$ Residenz/Café am See, Av Philippi
539, Frutillar Bajo, T065-242 1539, www.

hotelamsee.cl. Good breakfast, café has German specialities.

$$$ Winkler, Av Philippi 1155, Frutillar Bajo, T065-242 1388. Much cheaper (**$**) in low season. Also sells cakes from the garage, **Kuchen Laden**.

$$ Hospedaje Tía Clarita, Pérez Rosales 648, Frutillar Bajo, T065-242 1806, hospedajetiaclarit@hotmail.com. Kitchen facilities, very welcoming, good value.

$$ Hostería Trayen, Av Philippi 963, Frutillar Bajo, T065-242 1346, tttrayen33@ hotmail.com. Nice rooms with bath.

Camping

Los Ciruelillos, 1.5 km south of Frutillar Alto, T065-242 0163, losciruelillos@surnet.cl. Most services.

Playa Maqui, 6 km north of Frutillar Bajo, T065-233 9139. Fancy, expensive.

Llanquihue *p316*
Camping

Baumbach, 1 km north of Llanquihue, T065-224 2643. On lakeside, meals available.

Playa Werner, 2 km north of Llanquihue, T065-224 2114. On lakeside.

Puerto Varas *p317, map p317*

$$$$ Cabañas del Lago, Luis Welmann 195, T065-220 0100, www.cabanasdellago.cl. On hill overlooking lake, upper floor rooms have the best view in town. Service not up to much. Also self-catering cabins sleeping 5, heating, sauna, swimming pools and games room. Often full with package groups.

$$$$ Cumbres, Imperial 0561, T065-222 2000, www.cumbrespatagonicas.cl. Best hotel in town. All rooms look out over the lake, attentive staff, good restaurant. Spa and small pool with great views.

$$$ Bellavista, Pérez Rosales 60, T065-223 2011, www.hotelbellavista.cl. 4-star hotel, king-size beds; cheerful, restaurant and bar, overlooking lake and main road, sauna, parking.

$$$ Casa Kalfu, Tronador 1134, T065-275 1261, www.casakalfu.cl. Characterful blue

wooden building remodelled in traditional style. Helpful owners, English spoken, good value.

$$$ Weisserhaus, San Pedro 252, T065-234 6479, www.weisserhaus.cl. Central, cosy, family-run, German-style breakfast, good facilities, very helpful, central heating, very pleasant.

$$$-$$ Amancay, Walker Martínez 564, T065-223 2201, www.cabanahostal amancay.cl. Nice *cabañas* with log-burning stoves or hostel rooms, good, German spoken.

$$ Canales del Sur, Pérez Rosales 1631A, 1km east of town, T065-223 0909, www.canalesdel sur.cl. Pleasantly set on the lakeside. Very helpful, family-run, tours arranged, garden, car hire.

$$ Casa Azul, Manzanal 66 y Rosario, T065-223 2904, www.casaazul.net. Wooden building, variety of rooms and dorms, heating, beautiful Japanese garden, book exchange, German and English spoken, excursions offered. Reserve in advance in high season.

$$ Casa Margouya, Santa Rosa 318, T065-223 7640, www.margouya.com. Bright, colourful hostel, lots of information, French-run, English spoken.

$$ Compass del Sur, Klenner 467, T065-223 2044, www.compassdelsur.cl. Chilean/Swedish-run hostel, all rooms with shared bath, comfy lounge, helpful, German, English, Swedish spoken, excursions offered. Reserve in advance in high season.

$$ Hostería Outsider, San Bernardo 318, T065-223 1056, www.turout.com. Rooms sleep 1-3, private bath, comfortable, heating, helpful, restaurant, travel agency, English and German spoken, book in advance.

$$-$ Hospedaje Don Raúl, Salvador 928, T065-231 0897, www.informatur.com. Shared rooms and bath, hostel facilities, spotless, helpful, camping.

Camping

Wild camping and use of barbecues is not allowed on the lake shore.

Casa Tronador, Tronador y Manzanal, T09-9078 9631. Expensive but central.
Playa Hermosa, Km 7, T065-233 8283, fancy (negotiate in low season), take own supplies.
Playa Niklitschek, Km 8, T09-8257 0698, www.playaniklitschek.cl. Full facilities.

🍴 Restaurants

Puerto Octay p313
$$ El Rancho del Espantapajaros, 6 km south on the road to Frutillar, T065-233 0049, www.espantapajaros.cl. In a converted barn with wonderful views over the lake, serves spit roasted meat. All-you-can-eat, with salad bar and drinks included.
$$ Fogón de Anita, 1 km out of town, T065-239 1276, www.fogondeanita.blogspot.co.uk. Mid-priced grill. Also German cakes and pastries.
$ Restaurante Baviera, Germán Wulf 582, T065-239 1460. Cheap and good, salmon and *cazuelas*.

Ensenada p315
Most eating places close off season. There are a few pricey shops. Take your own provisions.
$$$ Latitude 42, Yan Kee Way Resort, T065-221 2030. Expensive, excellent and varied cuisine, very good quality wine list. Lake views.
$ Canta Rana for bread and *küchen*.

Frutillar p315, map p316
$$ Andes, Philippi 1057, Frutillar Bajo. Good set menus and à la carte.
$ Casino de Bomberos, Philippi 1060, Frutillar Bajo. Upstairs bar/restaurant, memorable painting caricaturing the firemen in action (worth studying while awaiting your meal), good value.

Cafés
Many German-style cafés and tea-rooms on C Philippi (the lakefront) in Frutillar Bajo.

Puerto Varas p317, map p317
$$$-$$ Mediterráneo, Santa Rosa 068, T065-223 7268, www.mediterraneo puertovaras.cl. On the lakefront, international and local food, interesting varied menu, often full.
$$$-$$ Xic Dalí, Purísima 690, T065-223 4424. Intimate Catalan bistro. Inventive menu, top quality preparation and service, good wine list.
$$ Bravo Cabrera, Pérez Rosales s/n, 1 km east of centre, T065-223 3441, www.bravocabrera.cl. Popular bar/ restaurant opposite the lake, big portions, good value, varied menu, lively bar.
$$ Di Carusso, San Bernardo 318. Italian trattoria, good fresh pasta dishes on Fri.
$$ Donde El Gordito, San Bernardo 560, T065-223 3425, downstairs in market. Good range of meat dishes, no set menu.
$$ La Chamaca Inn, Del Salvador y San Bernard, T065-223 2876, Good choice for traditional Chilean seafood. Larger than life owner.
$$ La Olla, Ruta 225, 4 km east of town towards Ensenada, T065-223 4605. Good, popular for seafood, fish and meat, traditional Chilean cuisine.
$ There are a couple of little snack bars along the coast on Santa Rosa at the foot of Cerro Philippi, serving, amongst other things, tasty vegetarian burgers.

Cafés
Café Danés, Del Salvador 441. Coffee and cakes.
Cassis, San Juan 431 y San José. Sweet cakes, generous ice creams and great brownies.
El Barista, Walker Martínez 211A, T065-223 3130, www.elbarista.cl. Probably the best place for a coffee. Good value set lunches and bar.

🍸 Bars and clubs

Puerto Varas p317, map p317
Club Orquídea, San Pedro 537, T065-223 3024, www.cluborquidea.cl. Popular club

with tables dotted around several small rooms and alcoves. Occasional live music, huge pizzas.

⊛ Festivals

Frutillar *p315, map p316*
Jan/early Feb A highly regarded **classical music festival** is held in the town; tickets must be booked well in advance from the Municipalidad, T065-242 1261, www.munifrutillar.cl.

Llanquihue *p316*
End Jan A German-style **beer festival** with oom-pah music is held here.

⊙ Shopping

Ensenada *p315*
There are several shops selling basic supplies. Most places are closed off season, other than a few pricey shops, so take your own provisions.

Frutillar *p315, map p316*
Services and shops are generally much better in Frutillar Alto, although in Frutillar Bajo, seek out **Der Volkladen**, O'Higgins y Philippi, for natural products, including chocolates, cakes and cosmetics.

Puerto Varas *p317, map p317*
Líder, Gramado 565. Supermarket with a good selection, reasonably priced.
Mamusia, San José 316. Chocolates.
Santa Isabel, Salvador 451. Supermarket.

⊙ What to do

Most tours operate in season only (Sep-May).

Volcán Osorno *p314*
Weather permitting, agencies in Puerto Varas organize climbing expeditions with a local guide, transport from Puerto Montt or Puerto Varas, food and equipment, payment in advance (minimum group

2, maximum 6 with 3 guides). Weather conditions are checked the day before. A full refund is given if the trip is cancelled, and a 50% refund is available if the trip is abandoned due to weather before the real climbing begins. Those climbing from La Burbuja must register with **CONAF** at La Burbuja, and show they have suitable equipment. Those climbing from the north (La Picada) are not subject to any checks.

Also based at **La Burbuja** is a small skiing centre, with 11 pistes and 5 ski lifts, usually open Jun-Sep. Ski ticket US$43, equipment rental US$34, ski school. See www.volcanosorno.com for conditions.

Ensenada *p315*
Southern Chile Expeditions, T065-212 3030, www.southernchilexp.com. Expensive fly-fishing tours.

Puerto Varas *p317, map p317*
Horse riding
Quinta del Lago, Km 25 on road to Ensenada, T065-233 0193. All levels catered for, US$35-85 for 2-5 hrs, also accommodation. See also **Campo Aventura**, below.

Kayaking
Al Sur, Aconcagua e Imperial, T065-223 2300, www.alsurexpeditions.com. Sea kayak, rafting and trekking tours, good camping equipment, English spoken, official tour operators to Parque Pumalín.
Ko'kayak, San Pedro 210 and Ruta 225, Km 40, T065-223 3004, www.kokayak.cl. Kayaking and rafting trips, good equipment and after-trip lunch, French/Chilean-run.
Miralejos, San Pedro 311, T065-223 4892, www.miralejos.cl. Kayaking in northern Patagonia, also trekking, horse riding and mountaineering. Associated is **Trekking Cochamó**, same address, www.trekkingcochamo.cl, which concentrates on adventure sports in Cochamó. Both are part of the **www.secretpatagonia.cl** group of operators who specialize in the area.

Yak Expediciones, owner Juan Federico Zuazo (Juanfe), T09-8332 0574, www.yak expediciones.cl. Experienced and safe kayaking trips on lakes and sea, in the fjords of Pumalín, enthusiastic and excellent, small groups, also runs courses.

Ziplining
Ziplining (*canopy*), is offered by several operators.

⊖ Transport

Puerto Octay *p313*
Bus

To **Osorno** every 20 mins, US$3; to **Frutillar** (1 hr, US$1.50), **Puerto Varas** (2 hrs) and **Puerto Montt** (3 hrs, US$4) with **Thaebus**, 5 a day. Around the east shore to **Las Cascadas (34 km)**, Mon-Fri 1730, returns next day 0700.

Ensenada *p315*
Frequent minibuses run to/from **Puerto Varas** in summer. Buses from Puerto Montt via Puerto Varas to **Cochamó** also stop here. Hitching from Puerto Varas is difficult.

Frutillar *p315, map p316*
Bus

Most buses use the small bus terminal at Alessandri y Richter in Frutillar Alto. To **Puerto Varas** (US$1.50) and **Puerto Montt** (US$3), frequent, with **Full Express**. To **Osorno**, Turismosur 1½ hrs, US$2. To **Puerto Octay**, Thaebus, 6 a day, US$1.50.

Puerto Varas *p317, map p317*
Bus

Pullman is the only long-distance company to have its terminal in the town centre (Diego Portales). Other companies have ticket offices dotted around the centre but buses leave from the outskirts of town (**Turbus**, **Jac** and **Cóndor** from Del Salvador 1093; **Cruz del Sur** from San Fransisco 1317).

To **Santiago**, US$46-63, several companies, 12 hrs. To **Osorno** hourly, US$3, 1 hr. To **Valdivia** US$9, 3 hrs.

Minibuses run to the following destinations leave from San Bernardo y Walker Martínez: **Puerto Montt**, **Thaebus** and **Full Express** every 15 mins, US$1.70, 30 mins. Same frequency to **Frutillar** (US$1.50, 30 mins). To **Ensenada,** hourly.

Ferry
Cruce Andino, www.cruceandino.com, operates the bus and ferry crossing from Puerto Varas 0830 to **Bariloche** (Argentina), arriving 2015, US$280 one way (low season price), half price on the return. From 1 May to 30 Aug this trip is done over 2 days with an overnight stay in Peulla at **Hotel Peulla** or **Hotel Natura**. You may break the journey at any point and continue the next day (see box, page 327).

❶ Directory

Frutillar *p315, map p316*
Banks Banco Santander, Philippi, at the lakeside, with **Redbanc** ATM taking Visa and other cards. **Post office** Alessandri Palma 430, Mon-Fri 0900-1600, Sat 0900-1200.

Puerto Varas *p317, map p317*
Banks Several banks with ATMs in the town centre. *Casas de cambio* include **Afex Transferencias**, San Pedro 414, www. afex.cl, **Travel Sur**, San Pedro 451, **Turismo Los Lagos**, Del Salvador 257 (Galería Real, local 11), accepts TCs, good rates. **Laundry** Lavandería Delfín, Martínez 323, expensive. **Medical services** Clínica Alemana, Otto Bader 810, T065-239100, usually has English-speaking doctors. **Post office** San José y San Pedro; Del Salvador y Santa Rosa.

Parque Nacional Vicente Pérez Rosales and around

Established in 1926, this is the oldest national park in Chile, stretching east from Lago Llanquihue to the Argentine border. The park is covered in woodland and contains a large lake, Lago Todos los Santos, plus three major volcanic peaks: Osorno, Puntiagudo and Tronador. Several other peaks are visible, notably Casablanca to the north and Calbuco to the south. Near the lake are the Saltos de Petrohué, impressive waterfalls on the Río Petrohué. A memorable journey by road and water takes you through the park from Puerto Varas to Bariloche in Argentina. South of the park is the beautiful Seno de Reloncaví.

Arriving in Parque Nacional Vicente Pérez Rosales → *Colour map 4, C2/3.*
Getting there and around In season, take one of the hourly minibuses from Puerto Montt and Puerto Varas via Ensenada to Petrohué. They generally allow you to break your journey at the waterfalls at no extra cost. It is impossible to reach the national park by public transport out of season: there are buses only as far as Ensenada, little traffic for hitching and none of the ferries take vehicles. Entrance to the park is free. A combination of walking and hitching rides in locals' boats is the best way to explore the park. In wet weather many treks in the park are impossible and the road to Puerto Montt can be blocked.

Tourist information The park is open 0900-2000 (1830 in winter), US$2.75. **CONAF** has an office in Petrohué with a visitor centre, small museum and 3D model of the park. There is also a *guardaparque* office in Puella. No maps of treks are available in the park; buy them from a tour operator in Puerto Varas (see page 322). Note that the park is infested by horseflies in December and January: cover up as much as possible with light-coloured clothes which may help a bit.

Lago Todos los Santos → *For listings, see pages 328-329.*

The most beautiful of all the lakes in southern Chile, Lago Todos los Santos is a long, irregularly shaped sheet of emerald-green water, surrounded by a deeply wooded shoreline and punctuated by several small islands that rise from its surface. Beyond the hilly shores to the east are several graceful snow-capped mountains, with the mighty Tronador in the distance. To the north is the sharp point of **Cerro Puntiagudo**, and at the northeastern end **Cerro Techado** rises cliff-like out of the water. The lake is fed by several rivers, including the Río Peulla to the east, the ríos Techado and Negro to the north, and the Río Blanco to the south. At its western end the lake is drained by the Río Petrohue. The lake is warm and sheltered from the winds, and is a popular location for watersports, swimming and for trout and salmon fishing. There are no roads round the lake, but private launches can be hired for trips around the lake.

Petrohué and around

At the western end of the lake, 16 km northwest of Ensenada, Petrohué is a good base for walking tours with several trails around the foot of Volcán Osorno, or to the miradors that look over it, such as Cerro Picada. Near the Ensenada–Petrohué road, 6 km west of Petrohué, is the impressive **Salto de Petrohué** ⓘ *US$3*, which was formed by a relatively recent lava flow of hard volcanic rock. Near the falls are a snack bar and two short trails, the **Sendero de los Enamorados** and the **Sendero Carileufú**. In Petrohué, boats can be hired to visit Cayetué on the lake's southern shore (see below) or the **Termas de Callao** – actually two large Alerce tubs in a cabin – north of the lake. The boat will drop you at the uninhabited El Rincón (arrange for it to wait or collect you later), from where it's a 3½-hour walk to the baths through forest beside the Río Sin Nombre. The path twice crosses the river by rickety hanging bridges. Just before the baths is a house, doubling as a comfortable *refugio*, where you collect the keys and pay. From the termas there is a two-day trail northwards to Lago Rupanco.

Peulla and around

Peulla, at the eastern end of the lake, is a good starting point for hikes in the mountains. The **Cascadas Los Novios**, signposted above the **Hotel Peulla**, are a steep walk away,

Parque Nacional Pérez Rosales & the lakes route to Argentina

but are stunning once you reach them. There is also a good walk to **Laguna Margarita**, which takes four hours.

Cayutué and around

On the south shore of Lago Todos Los Santos is the little village of Cayutué, reached by hiring a boat from Petrohué. From Cayutué (no camping on the beach but there are private sites) it is a three-hour walk to **Laguna Cayutué**, a jewel set between mountains and surrounded by forest, where you can camp and swim. From the laguna it is a five-hour hike south to Ralún on the Reloncaví Estuary (see below): the last half of this route is along a *ripio* road built for extracting timber and is part of the old route used by missionaries in the colonial period to travel between Nahuel Huapi in Argentina and the island of Chiloé.

Seno de Reloncaví → *For listings, see pages 328-329.*

The Seno de Reloncaví, situated east of Puerto Montt and south of the Parque Nacional Pérez Rosales, is the northernmost of Chile s glacial inlets. It is a quiet and beautiful estuary, often shrouded in mist and softly falling rain, but stunning nonetheless, and recommended for its wildlife, including sea lions and dolphins, and for its peaceful atmosphere. It is relatively easily reached by a road that runs along the wooded lower Petrohué Valley south from Ensenada and then follows the eastern shore of the estuary for almost 100 km to join the Carretera Austral.

Ralún and around

A small village situated at the northern end of the estuary, Ralún is 31 km southeast from Ensenada by a poorly paved road. There is a village shop and post office, and on the outskirts are **thermal baths** ① *US$2, reached by boat across the Río Petrohué, US$4 per person*. From Ralún you can either travel along the eastern shore of the estuary to Cochamó (see below) or take the road that branches off and follows the western side of the estuary south, 36 km to Lago Chapo and the Parque Nacional Alerce Andino (see page 364).

Cochamó and the Gaucho Trail

Some 17 km south of Ralún along a poor *ripio* road is the pretty village of Cochamó (www. cochamo.com). It's situated in a striking setting, on the east shore of the estuary with the volcano behind, and has a small, frequently deserted waterfront, where benches allow you to sit and admire the view. Cochamó's fine wooden church dates from 1900 and is similar to those on Chiloé. It has a clock with wooden hands and an unusual black statue of Christ.

The Gaucho Trail east from Cochamó to **Paso León** on the Argentine border was used in the colonial period by the indigenous population and Jesuit priests, and later by *gauchos*. Four kilometres south of the village a road branches inland for about 3 km, following the course of the Cochamó valley. At the end of the road is the head of the trail up the valley to La Junta (five hours), described as Chile's Yosemite for its imposing granite peaks and now becoming a popular centre for many outdoor activities in and around the alerce forests (trekking, climbing, kayaking, riding, birdwatching and fishing). Beyond La Junta the trail runs along the north side of Lago Vidal, passing waterfalls and the oldest surviving alerce trees in Chile at El Arco. The route takes three to four days by horse or five to six days on foot, depending on conditions and is best travelled between December and March. From the border crossing at Paso León it is a three-hour walk to the main road towards Bariloche.

Border crossing: Chile–Argentina

Three Lakes Crossing

This popular and ever-more expensive route from Puerto Montt to Bariloche, involving ferries across Lago Todos los Santos, Lago Frías and Lago Nahuel Huapi, is outstandingly beautiful whatever the season, though the mountains are often obscured by rain and heavy cloud. Cruce Andino (www.cruceandino.com) has the monopoly on this crossing, although tickets are sold by various operators. The mid-2014 season price was US$280 one way, 50% on return ticket; check the website before booking as prices alter with the season.

The journey starts by bus via Puerto Varas, Ensenada and the Petrohué falls (20-minute stop) to Petrohué, where you board the catamaran service (1¾ hours) across Lago Todos Los Santos to Peulla. During the summer there is a two-hour stop in Peulla for lunch and for **Chilean customs**, open daily 0900-2000. This is followed by an hour-long bus ride through the **Paso Pérez Rosales** (www.gendarmeria.gov.ar/pasos/chile/fichperezro.html) to **Argentine customs** in Puerto Frías. Then it's a 20-minute boat trip across Lago Frías to Puerto Alegre, and a short bus journey (15 minutes) to Puerto Blest. A catamaran departs from Puerto Blest for the beautiful one-hour trip along Lago Nahuel Huapi to Puerto Panuelo (Llao Llao), from where there is a 30-minute bus journey to Bariloche. (The bus drops passengers at hotels, camping sites or in the town centre.)

Bariloche is a popular destination and centre for exploring the Argentine Lake District. Beautifully situated on the south shore of Lago Nahuel Huapi, the streets rise steeply along the edge of a glacial morraine. Boat excursions can be made from Bariloche to other parts of the Argentine Lake District. There is a wide range of accommodation as well as air and bus connections to Buenos Aires and other destinations in Argentina.

Puelo and beyond

Further south, on the south bank of the Río Puelo (crossed by a new bridge), is **Puelo**, a very peaceful place with some expensive fly fishing lodges nearby. Here the road forks. One branch (very rough) continues to Puelche (see page 364) on the Carretera Austral, while the other heads southeast, past Lago Tagua Tagua (ferry 0900, 1300, return 1130, 1630, US$3 one way, US$12 for vehicles) to the peaceful village of Llanada Grande, nestled in the Andes, with basic accommodation. The road continues to the village of Primer Corral.

An alternative route to Argentina starts with a 45-minute walk to Lago Azul from the road between Llanada Grande and Primer Corral. A 25-minute boat trip across Lago Azul is followed a 45-minute hike through pristine forest to Lago Las Rocas, where another 25-minute boat ride ends at the Carabineros de Chile post on Lago Inferior. Go through immigration then navigate Lagos Inferior and Puelo as far as the pier on Lago Puelo.

For hotel and restaurant price codes and other relevant information, see pages 14-21.

◐ Where to stay

Lago Todos los Santos *p324*

$$$$ Hotel Petrohué, Ruta 225, Km 64, Petrohué, T065-221 2025, www.petrohue. com. Excellent views, half-board available, also has cabins, cosy, restaurant, log fires, sauna and heated pool; hiking, fishing and other activities.

$$$$ Natura Patagonia, Peulla, T065-297 2289, www.hotelnatura.cl. Rooms and suites, disabled facilities, lots of activities offered, restaurant.

$$$ Hotel Peulla, Peulla, T065-297 2288, www.hotelpeulla.cl. Half board. Beautiful setting by the lake and mountains, restaurant and bar, cold in winter, often full of tour groups (older partner of **Natura**).

Camping

Camping wild and picnicking in the national park is forbidden. There's a basic site with no services and cold showers at Petrohué beside the lake; locals around the site sell fresh bread (local fishermen will ferry you across). There's also a good campsite 1½ hrs' walk east of Peulla, but you'll need to take your own food. A small shop in Peulla sells basic goods, including fruit and veg. There's an *albergue* in Petrohué school in summer. The CONAF office can help find cheaper family accommodation.

Ralún *p326*

Lodging is available with families and at restaurant **Navarrito** (**$**, basic).

$ pp Posada Campesino, very friendly, clean and simple accommodation without breakfast.

Cochamó *p326*

For details of *cabañas*, campsites and eateries, see http://cochamo.com.

$$$ Cochamó Aventura Riverside Lodge, 4 km south of Cochamó in Valle Rio Cochamó, http://campoaventura.cl. Full board available (great breakfast), local food and very fresh milk from their own cow. Also have the Mountain Lodge further up the valley at La Junta. For details of their multi-day riding and trekking tours, see What to do.

$$$-$ Refugio Cochamó, La Junta, Cochamó valley, www.cochamo.com. Oct-Apr. The perfect base for outdoor activities in the Cochamó valley, only accessible on foot (4-6 hrs) or horseback. Private rooms have bed linen, bring sleeping bag for dorm beds.

$$ Hostal Cochamó, Av Aeródromo s/n, T09-5828 5231, www.hostalcochamo.com. Private rooms and shared dorms, price pp, local meals available, activities arranged as well as transport.

$$ Hostal Maura, JJ Molina 12, T09-9334 9213, www.experienciapatagonia.cl. Beautiful location overlooking the estuary, rooms with shared bath, meals served, kayaks, horse riding, good information, sauna and hot tub (at extra cost).

$$-$ Edicar, Prat y Sgto Aldea, T09-7445 9230, on seafront by the dock/ramp. With breakfast, hot shower, good value.

Puelo and beyond *p327*

$$$ Posada Martín Pescador, Lago Totoral, 2 km from Llanada Grande on road to Primer Corral, www.posadamartin pescador.cl. Rooms with bath and hot water, plus meals, barbecues, horse riding, trekking, fishing, canoeing and rafting.

Basic lodging is available at the restaurant in Puelo, or with families – try Roberto and Olivia Telles, who offer rooms with no bath/shower but meals on request, or Ema Hernández Maldona.

🍴 Restaurants

Lago Todos los Santos *p324*
See Where to stay, above, for hotel restaurants. There is a small shop in the ferry building in Petrohué, with basic supplies and some of the houses sell fresh bread, but if you're camping it's best to take your own food.

Seno de Reloncaví *p326*
Eateries in Cochamó include **Donde Payi**, opposite the church, and **Reloncaví**, on the road down to the waterfront. On the seafront there is a cheap fish/seafood restaurant, which also hires out canoes.

🎣 What to do

Seno de Reloncaví *p326*
Fly fishing guides in Puelo generally charge around US$80 per hour, boat included.
Cabalgatas Cochamó, Cra Principal, Cochamó, T09-7764 5289, http://cabalgatas cochamo.wix.com/chile. On a farm by the water, riding trips from 1 to 8 days, also boat trips, climbing and fishing.
Cochamó Aventura, T09-9289 4314, T09-9289 4318, http://campoaventura.cl. Specializes in tailor-made horse riding and trekking tours between the Reloncaví Estuary and the Argentine border including accommodation at their 2 lodges (see Where to stay, above).
Sebastián Contreras, C Morales, Cochamó, T065-221 6220. An independent guide who offers tours on horseback and hires out horses.

🚌 Transport

Lago Todos los Santos *p324*
Boat
The **Cruce Andino service** (see page 323) is the only regular sailing between Petrohué and Peulla, although local fishermen may make the trip across the lake for a group.

Bus
Minibuses run every 30 mins in summer between **Petrohué** and Puerto Montt via Puerto Varas (US$4, 1¼ hrs), much less frequent off season. Last bus to **Ensenada** at 1800.

Seno de Reloncaví *p326*
Boat
In summer boats sail up the Estuary from **Angelmó**. The **Sernatur** office in Puerto Montt has details of scheduled trips.

Bus
Transhar (T065-225 4187) and **Buses Río Puelo** (T065-254 4226) run buses from Puerto Montt, via Puerto Varas and Ensenada, to **Ralún** (US$3), **Cochamó** (2½ hrs, US$4) and **Puelo**, 3 a day Mon-Sat, 2 on Sun. The first bus of the day continues to **Llanada Grande** (5 hrs, US$6). Minibus services from Puerto Montt airport cost between US$12.50 and US$30 pp depending on size of vehicle (see http://cochamo.com).

Puerto Montt and around

The capital of Región X (Los Lagos), Puerto Montt lies on the northern shore of the Seno de Reloncaví, 1016 km south of Santiago. The jumping-off point for journeys south to Chiloé and Patagonia, it is a busy, modern and often windy city, flourishing with the salmon-farming boom. As the fastest growing city in Chile, it sometimes seems as if it is buckling under the pressure, with infrastructure struggling to keep up with population growth. It was founded in 1853, as part of the German colonization of the area, on the site of a Mapuche community known as Melipulli, meaning four hills. Good views over the city and bay are offered from outside the Intendencia Regional on Avenida X Región. There is a wide range of accommodation, but most people will prefer to stay in Puerto Varas, more picturesque and only 20 minutes away by bus.

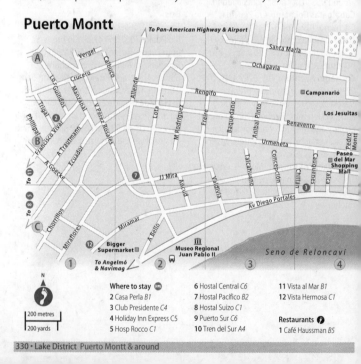

Puerto Montt

Where to stay 🛏
2 Casa Perla *B1*
3 Club Presidente *C4*
4 Holiday Inn Express *C5*
5 Hosp Rocco *C1*
6 Hostal Central *C6*
7 Hostal Pacífico *B2*
8 Hostal Suizo *C1*
9 Puerto Sur *C6*
10 Tren del Sur *A4*
11 Vista al Mar *B1*
12 Vista Hermosa *C1*

Restaurants 🍴
1 Café Haussman *B5*

Puerto Montt → *For listings, see pages 333-336. Colour map 4, C2.*

Arriving in Puerto Montt

Getting there and around El Tepual Airport ① *13 km northwest of town, T065-248 6200*, has ATMs, a tourist information desk and car hire desks. **ETM buses** ① *T065-229 0100, www.etm.cl, US$3.75*, run between the terminal and the city centre. **ETM** also has a minibus service to/from hotels, US$11 per person, or US$27.50 for two people to Puerto Varas. A taxi to the town centre costs US$22, or US$37 to Puerto Varas. There are several daily flights north to Santiago and south to Chaitén, Coyhaique and Punta Arenas. Ferries and catamarans serve Chaitén and Puerto Chacabuco; there's also a weekly service south to Puerto Natales.

Puerto Montt is the departure point for bus services north to Santiago, and all the intermediate cities, and south to Punta Arenas. The bus terminal (www.terminalpm.cl) is on the sea front at Portales y Lota with rural buses leaving from one side and long-distance buses from the other. The terminal has also telephones, restaurants, ATMs, a *casa de cambio* and left luggage service (US$1-1.75 per item for 24 hrs). There is an official taxi rank on level 1.

Puerto Montt is quite a large city, with many *colectivos* and buses serving the *barrios* on the hill above the town. The cental area is down by the port, though, and everything here is within walking distance.

2 Cafés Central and Real *B4*
3 Club Alemán *B5*
4 Club de Yates *C5*
5 Cotele *C5*
6 Pazos *C5*

Tourist information For information and town maps, contact **Sernatur** ① *just southwest of the Plaza de Armas, Antonio Varas 415 y San Martín, T065-222 3016, infoloslagos@sernatur.cl, Mon-Fri 0830-1300, 1500-1730.* See www.puertomonttchile.cl for information on the web. There are information desks at the airport and the bus station. **CONAF** ① *Ochogavía 458, T065-248 6102, loslagos.oirs@conaf.cl*, has information but cannot supply details of conditions in the national parks.

Places in Puerto Montt

The **Plaza de Armas** lies at the foot of steep hills, one block north of Avenida Diego Portales, which runs east-west parallel to the shore. Near the plaza, the **Casa del Arte Diego Rivera** ① *Varas y Quillota, T065-226 1836, www.corporacion culturalpuertomontt.cl*, has a theatre and holds regular exhibitions. Two blocks west of the square, on Calle Gallardo, is the **Iglesia de los Jesuitas**, dating from 1872, which has a fine blue-domed ceiling; behind it on a hill is the **campanario** (clock tower). Further west, near the bus terminal, is the **Museo Regional Juan Pablo II** ① *Diego Portales 997, 1030-1800, closed weekends off season, US$1,* documenting local history. It has a fine collection of historic photos of the city and memorabilia of Pope John Paul II's visit in 1988. Next to the museum is a small park with an old crane and a couple of rusting steam engines. The **Casa Pauly** ① *Rancagua 210, T065-248 2611, Mon-Fri 1000-1700,* is one of the city's historic mansions, now in a poor state, which holds temporary exhibitions.

The little fishing port of **Angelmó**, 2 km west along Avenida Diego Portales, has become a tourist centre thanks to its dozens of seafood restaurants and handicraft shops (reached by Costanera bus along Portales and by *colectivos* Nos 2, 3, 20 from the centre, US$0.30). Launches depart from Angelmó (US$1 each way), for the wooded **Isla Tenglo** offshore. It's a favourite place for picnics, with views from the summit. The island is famous for its *curanto*, served by restaurants in summer. Boat trips round the island from Angelmó last for 30 minutes and cost US$5. A longer boat trip (two hours) will take you to **Isla Huar** in the Seno de Reloncaví. If you are lucky you can stay at the island's church, but it may be best to camp.

Around Puerto Montt → *For listings, see pages 333-336.*

West of Puerto Montt
Parque Provincial Lahuen Nadi ① *T065-248 6101 or T065-248 6400, US$2.65,* lies along a *ripio* road signed 'Lagunillas', which branches north off the main road, 5 km before the airport. There is a pleasant, short and easy (30-minute) trail through mixed native forest. This is perhaps the most easily accessible place in Chile to see alerce forests, although they are nowhere near as old or impressive as in other parts. Note that it is easy to get lost on the way back to the main road from the park.

The old coast road west from Puerto Montt is very beautiful. **Chinquihue** (the name means 'place of skunks'), beyond Angelmó, has many seafood restaurants, oysters being a speciality. Further south is **Calbuco**, scenic centre of the fishing industry. It is situated on an island linked to the mainland by a causeway and can be visited direct by boat or by road. West of here is the Río Maullín, which drains Lago Llanquihue, and has some attractive waterfalls and good salmon fishing. At its mouth is the little fishing village of **Maullín**, founded in 1602. On the coast to the southeast is **Carelmapu**, with an excellent beach and *cabañas* at windswept Playa Brava, about 3 km away.

Sea routes south of Puerto Montt
Puerto Montt is the departure point for several popular voyages along the coast of southern Chile. All sailings are from Angelmó; timetables should be checked carefully in advance as schedules change frequently. ▸▸ *See Transport, page 336.*

To Puerto Natales One of the classic journeys in Chile is the 1460-km voyage between Puerto Montt and the southern port of Puerto Natales, made by Navimag ferries. It is quicker and cheaper to fly or even to go by bus via Argentina, but the voyage by boat is spectacular given a little luck with the weather. The route south from Puerto Montt crosses the Seno de Reloncaví and the Golfo de Ancud between the mainland and the large island of Chiloé, then continues south through the Canal Moraleda and the Canal Errázuriz, which separate the mainland from the outlying islands. It then heads west through the Canal Chacabuco to Bahía Anna Pink and across the infamous Golfo de Peñas (Gulf of Sorrows), 12 to 17 hours, where seasickness pills come in more than handy; if you haven't brought any, you can buy them on board – you'll be advised when to take them! After this stretch of open sea you reach a series of channels – Canal Messier, Angostura Inglesa, Fiordo del Indio and Canal Kirke – which provide one of the narrowest routes for large shipping in the world. There are spectacular views of the wooded fjords, weather permitting, particularly at sunrise and sunset, and a sense of peace pervades everything except the ship, which is filled with people having a good time.

The only regular stop on this route is at the fishing village of **Puerto Edén** on Isla Wellington, one hour south of the Angostura Inglesa. It has three shops (scant provisions), one off-licence, one café, and a *hospedaje* for up to 20 people (open intermittently). The population of 180, includes five *carabineros* and a few remaining native Alacaluf people. Puerto Edén is the drop-off point for exploring **Isla Wellington**, which is largely untouched, with stunning mountains. If you do stop here, take all food; maps (not very accurate) are available in Santiago.

These ferries also carry freight (including live animals); they aren't cruise liners. Standards of service and comfort vary, depending on the number of passengers, weather conditions and the particular vessel running the service. On-board entertainment consists of a book exchange, bingo, film screenings and bilingual talks on fauna, botany, glaciation and history. Food is good and plentiful and includes vegetarian options at lunch and dinner. Passengers tend to take their own alcohol and extra food.

To Puerto Chacabuco Navimag also runs a twice-weekly ferry service between Puerto Montt and **Puerto Chacabuco**, 80 km west of Coyhaique. This beautiful voyage passes forested cliffs, seemingly within touching distance, and offers glimpses of distant snows. However, taking this route south means that travellers miss out on the attractions of much of the Carretera Austral. From Puerto Chacabuco there are further services to visit **Laguna San Rafael**; see page 373, for more information.

To Laguna San Rafael The luxury ship m/n *Skorpios 2* cruises for six days and five nights from Puerto Montt to San Rafael, via Chiloé and Puerto Aguirre. Generally service is excellent, the food superb, and, at the glacier, you can chip ice off the face for your whisky. After the visit to San Rafael the ship visits **Quitralco Fjord**, where there are thermal pools and boat trips on the fjord, and **Chiloé**.

◉ Puerto Montt and around listings

For hotel and restaurant price codes and other relevant information, see pages 14-21.

◉ Where to stay

Puerto Montt *p331, map p330*
Accommodation is often much cheaper off season. Check with the tourist office.
$$$$ Club Presidente, Av Portales 664, T065-225 1666, www.presidente.cl. 4-star, very comfortable, rooms, suites, some with sea view. Often full Mon-Fri with business travellers.

$$$ Holiday Inn Express, Mall Paseo Costanera, T065-256 6000, www.holiday inn.cl. Good business standard. Spacious rooms with desks and great views, some with balcony. Slightly pokey bathrooms but the best in its category.
$$$ Puerto Sur, Huasco 143, T065-235 1212, www.hotel puertosur.cl. Small business oriented hotel in a quiet part of town. 4 floors, no lifts or views but otherwise good value, parking.
$$$ Tren del Sur, Santa Teresa 643, T065-234 3939, www.trendelsur.cl. 'Boutique'

hostal with pleasant public areas, objects recycled from the old railway, some rooms without windows, café, heating, helpful English-speaking owner.

$$ Hostal Pacífico, J J Mira 1088, T065-225 6229, www.hostalpacifico.cl. Comfortable, some rooms a bit cramped. Parking, transfers.

$$ Hostal Suizo, Independencia 231, T065-225 2640, rossyoelckers@yahoo.es. Private or shared rooms and bath. Painting and Spanish classes, German and Italian spoken. Convenient for **Navimag** ferry.

$$ House Rocco, Pudeto 233, T065-227 2897, www.hospedajerocco.cl. Doubles or 4-bed dorms, shared bath. English spoken, quiet residential area, convenient for **Navimag**.

$$ Vista al Mar, Vivar 1337, T065-225 5625, hospedajevistaalmar@yahoo.es. Impeccable small guest house, good breakfast, peaceful, great view from the double en suite.

$$ Vista Hermosa, Miramar 1486, T065-231 9600, http://hostalvistahermosa.cl/. Simple hostel, ask for front room for best views (10 mins' walk uphill from terminal), also has a fully equipped cabin.

$$-$ Casa Perla, Trigal 312, T065-226 2104, www.casaperla.com. French, English spoken, helpful, meals, Spanish classes offered off season, pleasant garden, good meeting place.

$$-$ Hostal Central, Huasco 61, T065-226 3081, hostalcentralpm@hotmail.com. Small, neat rooms in an old wooden house, peaceful neighbourhood, no breakfast, kitchen facilities, midnight curfew. A couple of rooms with nice views. A good choice.

Camping

Camping Los Alamos, Chinquihue-Panitao Bajo Km 14.5, T065-226 4666, losalamos@surnet.cl. Others on this road.

West of Puerto Montt *p332*
$$ Hotel Colonial, Calbuco, T065-246 1546. One of several decent hotels.

🍽 Restaurants

Puerto Montt *p331, map p330*
In Angelmó, there are several dozen small seafood restaurants in the old fishing port, past the fish market; these are very popular but serve lunch only except in Jan-Feb when they are open until late. Local specialities include *picoroco al vapor*, a giant barnacle whose flesh looks and tastes like crab, and *curanto*. To accompany your meal ask for *'té blanco'* (white wine); they are not legally allowed to serve wine. There are other seafood restaurants in Chinquihue, west of Angelmó.

$$$ Club Alemán, Varas 264, T065-229 7000. Old fashioned, good food and wine.

$$$ Club de Yates, Juna Soler s/n, Costanera, east of centre, T065-228 4000. Excellent seafood, fine views from a pier.

$$$-$$ Cotele, Juan Soler 1611, Pelluco, 4 km east, T065-227 8000. Closed Sun. Only serves beef, but serves it as well as anywhere in southern Chile. Reservations advised.

$$$-$$ Pazos, Pelluco, T065-225 2552. Serves the best *curanto* in the Puerto Montt area.

$$ Café Haussman, San Martín 185. German cakes, beer and *crudos*.

$ Café Central, Rancagua 117. Spartan decor, generous portions (sandwiches and *pichangas* – savoury salad snack). Giant TV screen.

$ Café Real, Rancagua 137. For *empanadas*, *pichangas*, *congrío frito*, and lunches.

West of Puerto Montt *p332*
$$ Kiel, Chinquihué, T065-225 5010, www.kiel.cl. Good meat and seafood dishes.

🛍 Shopping

Puerto Montt *p331, map p330*
Woollen goods and Mapuche-designed rugs can be bought at roadside stalls in Angelmó and on Portales opposite the bus terminal. Prices much the same as on

Chiloé, but quality often lower. There is a **supermarket** opposite the bus terminal, open 0900-2200 daily, and in the **Paseo del Mar** shopping mall, Talca y A Varas. **Paseo Costanera** is a big mall on the seafront.

○ What to do

Puerto Montt *p331, map p330*
Diving
Ecosub, Panamericana 510, T065-226 3939, www.ecosub.cl. Scuba-diving excursions.

Sailing
Club de Deportes Náuticas Reloncaví, Camino a Chinquihue Km 7, T065-225 5022, www.nauticoreloncavi.com. Marina, sailing lessons.
Marina del Sur (MDS), Camino a Chinquihue, Km 4.5, T065-225 1958, www.marinadelsur.cl. All facilities, restaurant, yacht charters, notice board for crew (*tripulante*) requests, specialists in cruising the Patagonian channels.

Tour operators
There are many tour operators. Some companies offer 2-day excursions along the Carretera Austral to Hornopirén, including food and accommodation. Most offer 1-day excursions to Chiloé and to Puerto Varas, Isla Loreley, Laguna Verde and the Petrohué falls: both are much cheaper from bus company kiosks inside the bus terminal. **Eureka Turismo**, Gallardo 65, T065-225 0412, www.chile-travel.com/eureka.htm. Helpful, German and English spoken.

○ Transport

Puerto Montt *p331, map p330*
Air
LAN and **Sky** have several flights daily to **Santiago**, **Balmaceda** (for Coyhaique) and **Punta Arenas**. Flights to **Chaitén** (or nearby Santa Bárbara) leave from the Aerodromo la Paloma on the outskirts of town. Charters, sightseeing trips and air taxi services can

be arranged with **Aerocord**, La Paloma aerodrome, T065-226 2300, www.aerocord. cl; **Aerotaxis del Sur**, A Varas 70, T065-233 0726, www.aerotaxisdelsur.cl; **Cielo Mar Austral**, Quillota 245 loc 1, T065-226 4010.

Bus
To **Puerto Varas** (US$1.70), **Llanquihue** (US$2), **Frutillar** (US$3; minibuses every few mins), **Puerto Octay** (US$4), 5 daily, with **Expreso Puerto Varas**, **Thaebus** and **Full Express**. To **Ensenada** and **Petrohué**, Buses JM several daily. To **Cochamó**, US$4, 3 hrs. To **Hornopirén**, 5 hrs, US$7.25, with **Kémel** (which also runs daily to **Chaitén**) and M&M. To **Osorno** US$3, 2 hrs. To **Valdivia**, US$9, 3½ hrs. To **Pucón**, US$14-17, 6 hrs. To **Temuco**, US$11.50-28. To **Concepción**, US$21-36. To **Valparaíso**, 14 hrs, US$45-63. To **Santiago**, 12 hrs, US$46-63, several companies including **Tur-Bus**.

To **Bariloche (Argentina)**, daily services via Osorno and the Samoré pass are run by **Vía Bariloche** and others, 7 hrs. US$30; out of season, services are reduced. Buy tickets for international buses from the bus terminal; book well in advance in Jan and Feb. Ask for a seat on the right-hand side for the best views. To **Punta Arenas** (through Argentina via Bariloche), with **Pacheco**, **Turibus** and others, 1-3 a week, 32-38 hrs; take US$ cash for Argentina expenses en route and take plenty of food for this "nightmare" trip; book well in advance in Jan-Feb and check if you need a multiple-entry Chilean visa; also book any return journey before setting out. For services to **Chiloé**, see page 343.

Car hire
Autovald, Sector Cardenal, Pasaje San Andrés 60, T065-221 5366, www.autovald.cl. Cheap rates. **Full-Car**, O'Higgins 525, T065-223 3055, www.full-car.cl. **Hunter**, T065-225 1524 or T09-9920 6888; office in Puerto Varas, San José 130, T065-223 7950, www. interpatagonia.com/hunter/. Good service. **Salfa Sur**, Pilpilco 800, also at airport, T600-

600 4004, or T065-229 0201, www.salfasur.cl. Good value, several regional offices.

Sea routes south of Puerto Montt *p332*

Navimag (Naviera Magallanes SA), Terminal Transbordadores, Angelmó 1735, T065-243 2360 or T02-2442 3120, www.navimag.com, sails to **Puerto Natales** throughout the year leaving Puerto Montt usually on Mon (check in 0900-1400, board 1600, depart 2000), arriving Thu. The return from Puerto Natales is on Fri (check-in Thu 1500-1800, board Thu 2000, dep Fri 0600), arriving in Puerto Montt Mon morning (Thu dinner is not included). Service was resumed in 2014 after several months' hiatus; always confirm times and booking well in advance. In winter especially days and vessels may change. The fare, including meals, ranges from US$400 pp for a bunk in a shared cabin on the *Amadeo* in low season, to US$1512 for 2 people in AAA double cabin. First class is recommended, but hardly luxurious. Check the website for discounts and special offers. Cars are carried for US$525, motorcycles for US$150. Tickets can be booked by credit card through many travel agencies, in **Navimag** offices throughout the country, or direct from www.navimag.com. Book well in advance for departures between mid-Dec and mid-Mar. It is well worth going to the port on the day of departure if you have no ticket. Departures are frequently delayed by weather conditions.

    Navimag's ferry sails twice a week to **Puerto Chacabuco** (80 km west of Coyhaique). The cruise to Puerto Chacabuco lasts about 24 hrs. Cabins sleep 4 or 6 (private bath, window, bed linen and towel) with a berth costing US87-101 in low season. Cars, motorcycles and bicycles are also carried. There is a canteen; long queues if the boat is full. Food is expensive so take your own.

    Skorpios Cruises, Augusto Leguía Norte 118, Santiago, T02-2477 1900, www.skorpios.cl, sail from Puerto Montt to **Laguna San Rafael**, via Chiloé and Puerto Aguirre. The fare varies according to season, type of cabin and number of occupants: double cabin from US$2000 pp.

    Naviera Austral, Angelmó 1673, T065-227 0430, www.navieraustral.cl, runs to **Chaitén**, via Ayacara, as well as Hornopirén–Ayacara, but check with the company for schedules. It also has services Chacabuco–Quellón and Chaitén–Quellón and, in Jan-Feb only, Chaitén–Castro on Chiloé.

ⓘ Directory

Puerto Montt *p331, map p330*
Banks Many ATMs in the city. Commission charges vary widely. This is the last city on the mainland with Visa ATM before Coyhaique. Obtain Argentine pesos before leaving Chile. There is a *cambio* at the bus terminal, **Borex**, G Gallardo 65. **Consulates** Argentina, Pedro Montt 160, p 6, T065-225 3996, http://cpmon.cancilleria.gov.ar, quick visa service. **Cycle repairs** Kiefer, Pedro Montt 129, T065-225 3079. 3 shops on Urmeneta, none very well stocked. **Motorcycle repairs** Miguel Schmuch, Urmeneta 985, T065-225 8877.

Contents

Footprint features

At a glance

⊖ **Getting around** Good public transport between towns. Private transport needed for some out-of-the-way places, be it a sturdy car or mountain bike.

⟳ **Time required** A day for a brief glimpse, 3 or 4 to see most of the sights and at least a week to begin to appreciate something of Chilote culture.

☁ **Weather** Lots of rain. Showers in summer and prolonged downpours the rest of the year.

✕ **When not to go** Winter (May-Aug) is generally dark and very wet. *Tábanos* (horseflies) can be a problem in Dec and Jan.

Chiloé

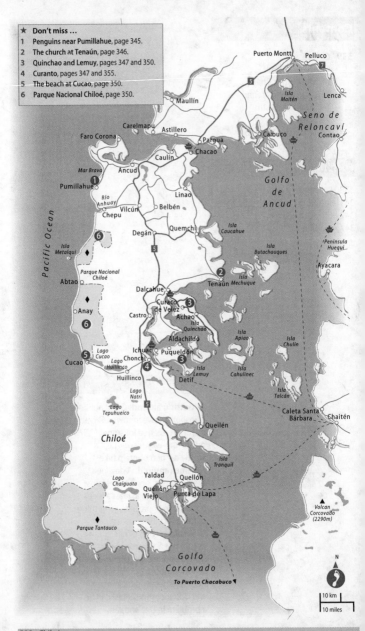

★ **Don't miss ...**
1 Penguins near Pumillahue, page 345.
2 The church at Tenaún, page 346.
3 Quinchao and Lemuy, pages 347 and 350.
4 Curanto, pages 347 and 355.
5 The beach at Cucao, page 350.
6 Parque Nacional Chiloé, page 350.

Puerto Montt
Pelluco
Lenca

Seno de Reloncaví

Calbuco
Contao

Maullín
Carelmapu
Astillero
Pargua
Chacao

Faro Corona
Caulín

Mar Brava
Ancud

Pumillahue ①

Río Anhuay
Vilcún
Chepu
Linao
Belbén

Golfo de Ancud

Degán
Quemchi

Isla Caucahue

Isla Butachauques

Peninsula Huequi

⑥

Isla Metalqui

Parque Nacional Chiloé

Abtao

Dalcahue

Tenaún ②

Isla Mechuque

Ayacara

Anay ⑥

Curaco de Velez ③
Achao
Isla Quinchao

Castro

Aldachildo

Isla Apiao

Isla Chulín

Ichuac
Puqueldón ③

Lago Cucao
Cucao ⑤

Lago Huillinco

Chonchi ④

Isla Lemuy

Isla Cahulinec

Huillinco

Detif

Isla Talcán

Lago Natri

Lago Tepuhueico

Queilén

Caleta Santa Bárbara
Chaitén

Chiloé

Isla Tranquil

Lago Chaiguata

Yaldad
Quellón

Quellón Viejo
Punta de Lapa

▲ *Volcan Corcovado (2290m)*

Parque Tantauco

Golfo Corcovado

To Puerto Chacabuco ▼

Pacific Ocean

N

10 km
10 miles

Chiloé

The mysterious archipelago of Chiloé is one of the most fascinating areas of Chile. Consisting of one main island, officially known as La Isla Grande de Chiloé, and numerous islets, its rolling hills, covered in patchwork fields and thick forest, provide a lasting sense of rural calm. Here you are almost always within sight of the sea, with dolphins playing in the bay and, on a clear day, there are views across to the twisting spire of Volcán Corcovado on the mainland.

Just under half the population of 155,000 live in the two main towns, Ancud and Castro, and there are also many fishing villages. The Cordillera de la Costa runs at low altitudes along the Pacific side of the island. South of Castro a gap in the range is filled by two connected lakes: Lago Huillinco and Lago Cucao. Thick forests cover most of the sparsely populated western and southern parts of the island; elsewhere hillsides are covered with wheat fields and dark green plots of potatoes and the roads are lined with wild flowers in summer. East of the main island are several groups of smaller islands, where the way of life is even more peaceful.

Chiloé is famous for its legends and rich mythology; here witches are said to fly around at night, identifiable as lights in the dark sky. Chiloé is equally well known for its painted wooden churches, some of them dating back to the late colonial period. In January and February, towns and villages celebrate their annual fiestas costumbistas, good events at which to capture the spirit of the place. Traditional dishes, such as *curanto*, are served and there are rodeos and dancing, as well as much drinking of local *chicha*.

Background

History

The original Chilotes (inhabitants of Chiloé) were the Chonos tribe, who were pushed south by the Huilliches, invading from the north. The first Spanish sighting of the islands was by Francisco de Ulloa in 1553 and, in 1567, Martín Ruiz de Gamboa took possession of the islands on behalf of Spain. The small settler population divided the indigenous population and their lands between them, but the Huilliche uprising after 1598 drove the Spanish out of the mainland south of the Río Biobío, isolating the 200 Spanish settlers on Chiloé. Following a violent earthquake in 1646, the Spanish population asked the viceroy in Lima for permission to leave, but this was refused. Much of Chiloé's distinctive character derives from 200 years of separation from mainstream Spanish colonial development.

The islanders were the last supporters of the Spanish Crown in South America. When the Chilean patriot leaders rebelled, the Spanish governor fled to the island and, in despair, offered it to Britain. George Canning, the British foreign secretary, turned the offer down; Chiloé finally surrendered to the patriots in 1826. Visiting less than a decade later, Charles Darwin still clearly distinguished Chiloé from the rest of Chile, saying that here the Andes were not nearly "so elevated as in Chile".

Throughout the 19th and the first part of the 20th century, Ancud was the capital of Chiloé. All that changed with the earthquake and *maremoto* (tidal wave) of 1960. This drastically altered the landscape in Ancud, bringing petrified trees to the surface and causing forests to submerge. The whole of the lower town was destroyed, except for the cathedral, which was badly damaged and then blown up rather than renovated; until then, this had been the second largest cathedral in South America. The capital was moved back to its former site at Castro, which is the only place in Chiloé that really feels urban today. The *maremoto*, and the rivalry between Ancud and Castro that it spawned, have never entirely been forgotten.

The relatively high birth rate and the shortage of employment in Chiloé have led to regular emigration, with Chilotes settling across Chile; they were prominent as shepherds in late 19th-century Patagonia and as sailors and fishermen along the coast. However, with the recent growth in the salmon farming industry, a major source of employment, more Chilotes are choosing to stay. Also see www.chiloe.cl.

Climate

The appalling climate of Chiloé is almost as legendary as the witches that are said to live there. The west coast has particularly vile conditions – it can rain here for three weeks at a time – while the sheltered east coast and offshore islands are only a little drier. Some of the best weather is in early December and late March. The main benefits of the climate are culinary: the Humboldt Current and the sheltered east coast ensure a wide variety of fresh shellfish is available all year. Chiloé also has indigenous elephant garlic, which is used to make a very tasty garlic sauce, as well as several dozen endemic varieties of potato.

Art and architecture

The availability of wood and the lack of metals on the islands have left their mark on Chilote architecture. Some of the earliest churches were built entirely of wood, using pegs instead of nails. These churches often displayed German influence as a result of the missionary work of Bavarian Jesuits. Four notable features were the *esplanada* or porch that ran the length of the front of the church, the not-quite semi-circular arches, the

Jesuits in Chiloé

The Jesuits arrived in Chiloé in 1608 and the first Jesuit residence was established four years later. Although in Chiloé they introduced few of the missions for which they became famous in Paraguay, at their expulsion in 1767 there were 79 churches on the island.

The key to the Jesuits' influence lay in their use of *fiscales*: indigenous people who were trained to teach Christian doctrine and to ensure that everyone observed religious duties. One *fiscal* was appointed for every 50 inhabitants. On 17 September each year, two missionaries set sail from Castro in small boats, taking with them statues of saints and essential supplies. They spent the next eight months sailing around the islands of Chiloé, visiting all the parishes in a set order. In each parish they would spend three days officating at weddings and baptisms, hearing confessions and reviewing the work of the *fiscales*.

Most of the old churches for which Chiloé is famous date from after the expulsion of the Jesuits, but some writers claim that their influence can still be seen, for example in the enthusiasm for education on the island, which has long boasted one of the highest literacy rates in the world. Many villages in Chiloé still have *fiscales* who are, according to tradition, responsible for keeping the church keys.

central position of the tower directly above the door and the fact that they have three levels representing the Holy Trinity. Few of the oldest churches have survived, but there are still over 150 on the islands and even small villages almost invariably have churches with pretty cemeteries – in 2001, UNESCO declared them World Heritage Sites.

The *rucas* (houses) of the indigenous population were thatched; thatch continued in widespread use throughout the 19th century. The use of thin *tejuelas* (shingles) made from alerce wood was influenced by the German settlers around Puerto Montt in the late 19th century; these tiles, which are nailed to the frame and roof in several distinctive patterns, overlap to form effective protection against the rain. *Palafitos*, or wooden houses built on stilts over the water, were once popular in all the main ports, but are now mainly found at the northern end of Castro, to the west of the *Panamericana*.

The islands are also famous for their traditional handicrafts, notably woollens and basketware, which can be bought in all the main towns and on some of the smaller islands, as well as in Puerto Montt and Angelmó.

Arriving in Chiloé

Getting there

Air An airport outside Castro opened in late 2012, with LAN flights from Santiago, via Puerto Montt on Wednesday, Friday, Saturday and Sunday.

Bus It is possible to travel direct to Chiloe from many cities, including Santiago, Osorno, Valdivia, Temuco and Los Angeles. Buses from Puerto Montt to the ferry terminal in Pargua are frequent (US$3, one hour); most continue via the ferry to Ancud (3½ to four hours) and Castro. Transport to the island is dominated by **Cruz del Sur** | Panamericano 500, at end of Avenida Salvador Allende, Puerto Montt, T065-248 3127, www.busescruzdelsur.cl, who also own **Trans Chiloé** and have their own ferries. Cruz del Sur run frequent services

Chilote folklore

Chiloé's distinctive history and its maritime traditions are reflected in the strength of its unique folklore. There is widespread belief in witches, who are said to meet at caves near Quicaví (between Dalcahue and Quemchi); and legend has it that Chiloé's dead are rowed along the reaches of Lago Huillinco and Lago Cucao in a white ship, out into the Pacific. For further information about the myths associated with the islands, read *Casos de Brujos de Chiloé* by Umiliana Cárdenas Saldivia (1989, Editorial Universitaria) and *Chiloé, Manual del Pensamiento Mágico y Creencia Popular* by Renato Cárdenas and Catherine Hall (1989, El Kultrún).

Visitors to Chiloé should beware of these four unlikely mythological hazards.

El Trauco A small, ugly and smelly man who wears a little round hat made of bamboo and clothing of the same material; he usually carries a small stone hatchet, with which he is reputed to be able to fell any tree in three strokes. He spends much of his time haunting the forests, sitting on fallen tree trunks and weaving his clothes.

El Trauco specializes in seducing virgins and is – conveniently – held to be responsible for unwanted pregnancies. He uses his magic powers to give them erotic dreams while they are asleep; they wake and go to look for him in the forest and are seduced by his eyes. Despite his ugliness, he is irresistible and the girl throws herself on the ground. You should be careful not to disturb the Trauco while he is thus occupied: those who do so are immediately deformed beyond recognition and sentenced to die within 12 months.

La Fiura A small ugly woman who lives in the forests near Hualdes, where she is reputed to bathe in the streams and waterfalls, combing her hair with a crystal comb. Known as the indefatigable lover of bachelors, she attracts her victims by wearing colourful clothes. As the man approaches he is put to sleep by her foul breath. After La Fiura has satisfied her desire, the unfortunate man goes insane. Refusing her advances is no escape either: those who do so, whether animals or men, become so deformed that they are unrecognizable.

La Sirena and **El Caleuche** A dangerous double act for those travelling by sea. La Sirena is a mermaid who lies alluringly on rocks and entices sailors to their deaths. Once shipwrecked, sailors are whisked into the bowels of *El Caleuche*, the ghost ship that is said to patrol the channels of the archipelago. Both the Chilean navy and merchant ships have reported sightings of the *Caleuche*. One of the authors of this book has also met several people on Chiloé who claim to have seen the ghost ship; but a word of warning was sounded by an old cynic in Castro: "I knew a fisherman who used to walk along the beach shouting 'I've seen La Sirena'. All the other fishermen fled, and then he stole their fish."

from Puerto Montt to Ancud (US$10) and Castro (US$11.50), plus six services a day to Chonchi (US$11.25) and Quellón (US$12.75); their fares are highest but they are faster than other operators because their buses have priority over cars on Cruz del Sur ferries. The main independent long-distance bus operator to the island is **Queilen Bus** (cheaper but less regular). A bridge to the island across the Chacao channel was approved in 2014; it is scheduled to be built by 2019.

Ferry There are about 24 ferry crossings daily (30 minutes) between Pargua, 55 km southwest of Puerto Montt on the mainland, and Chacao on Chiloé, operated by several companies including Transmarchilay and Cruz del Sur; all ferries carry buses, private vehicles (*cars US$19.50 one way, motorcycles US$14.75, bicycles US$4.20*) and *foot passengers* (US$1.30). Sea lions, penguins, birds and occasionally dolphins can be seen in the straits of Pargua. There are also **ferry services** to the island from Chaitén on the Carretera Austral, mostly in summer.

Getting around

Provincial bus services are crowded, slow and often wet, but provide a good picture of life in rural Chiloé. Mountain bikes and horses are ideal for travelling slowly through remote parts of the archipelago.

Ancud and around → *For listings, see pages 352-358. Colour map 4, C1.*

Situated on the northern coast of Chiloé, 34 km west of the Straits of Chacao, Ancud lies on a great bay, the Golfo de Quetalmahue. It is a little less characterful than some of the other towns on the island but is nevertheless the best centre for visiting the villages of northern Chiloé. There is a friendly small-town feel; everyone knows each other and everything happens in its own time. Tourism is slowly reviving Ancud's fortunes following the disaster of the maremoto in 1960. Within striking distance are white-sand beaches, Spanish colonial forts and an important colony of Magellanic and Humboldt penguins.

Arriving in Ancud

Getting there and around There are buses every 30 minutes from Castro and Quellón, and hourly from Puerto Montt. **Cruz del Sur** have buses to and from Valdivia, Temuco and Santiago (several daily). There are two long-distance bus terminals: the Terminal Municipal, on the outskirts of town, 1.5 km east of the centre, at Av Prat y Marcos Vera, reached by bus 1 or Pudeto *colectivos*, and the much more convenient Cruz del Sur terminal at Los Carrera 850, T065-262 2249. The Terminal Rural for local services is on Colo Colo, up a ramp behind the Unimarc supermarket. Timetables are posted on the door to the admin office and toilet. Ancud is big enough for you to want to take the occasional *colectivo*; there are many of these, with their destinations signed on the roof (US$0.70, US$0.90 after 2100). Rural buses serve nearby beaches and villages.

Tourist information **Sernatur** ① *Libertad 665, on the plaza, T065-262 2800, infochiloe@ sernatur.cl. Mon-Thu 0830-1800, Fri 0830-1700, in summer Mon-Fri 0830-1900, Sat-Sun 0930-1900.* Ask here about the Agro Turismo programme, staying with farming families. There is another tourist office in the Feria Municipal. Other useful contacts include **CONAF** ① *Errázuriz 300 block, Mon-Fri 0830-1400*, and **Fundación Amigos de las Iglesias de Chiloé** ① *Errázuriz 227, T262 1046, open daily, suggested donation US$1*, in a precinct off the street, which has an exhibition of various churches and styles of construction, a shop and El Convento café.

Places in Ancud

By the Plaza de Armas is the **Museo Regional** ① *Libertad 370, T065-262 2413, www. museoancud.cl, Mar-Dec Tue-Fri 1000-1730, Sat-Sun 1000-1400, Jan-Feb daily 1000-1900,*

US$1.30, half price for seniors and children, with an interesting collection on the early history of Chiloé. It also displays a replica of a traditional Chilote thatched wooden house and of the small sailing ship, *Ancud*, which claimed the Straits of Chacao for Chile, pipping the French to the post by a day. In the patio is a skeleton of a blue whale. Beside it is the Centro Cultural, with details of events and handicrafts outside. The modern cathedral stands on the plaza, built anew after the 1960 tsunami. Two kilometres east is a mirador offering good views of the island and across to the mainland, even to the Andes on a clear day.

The small fishing harbour at Cochrane y Prat is worth a visit, especially towards the end of the morning when the catch is landed. The port is overlooked by the **Fuerte San Antonio** ① *Mon-Fri 0800-2100, Sat and Sun 0900-2000, free*, the fort where the Spanish surrendered Chiloé to Chilean troops in 1826. It has a few cannon and a surrounding wall. Close to it are the unspectacular ruins of the Polvorín del Fuerte. A lovely 1-km walk north of the fort is a secluded beach, **Arena Gruesa**, where public concerts are held in summer. Heading in the other direction, along the coast road to the west, you can see concrete pillars, remnants of the old railway, destroyed by the 1960 earthquake.

Ancud

To Polvorín del Fuerte & Playa Arena Gruesa

To Mar Brava, Pumillahue & Faro Corona

Where to stay		Restaurants
13 Lunas 3	Hostal Altos de Bellavista 2	El Cangrejo 3
Balai 1	Hostal Lluhay 14	El Embrujo 1
Don Lucas 11	Hostal Vista al Mar 13	El Pingüinito 4
Galeón Azul 4	Hostería Panamericano 12	La Pincoya 8
Hospedaje Austral 7	Mundo Nuevo 17	La Ñaña 5

The **Faro Corona** lighthouse lies 34 km west of Ancud along a beach, which, although unsuitable for swimming (absolutely freezing water and dangerous currents), offers good views with interesting birdlife and dolphins. The best time of day to see birds is early morning or late afternoon/evening. The duty officer may give a tour. There isn't much there, so take something to eat and drink. To the south is **Fuerte Ahuí**, an old fort with good views of Ancud.

Chacao and around

Most people travelling to Chiloé will arrive in **Chacao** on the north coast. The town has a small, attractive plaza; and there's a pretty church and old wooden houses in Chacao Viejo, east of the port. Black-necked swans arrive here in summer from their winter habitat in Paraguay and Brazil. The *Panamericana* heads west from here to Ancud, while a coastal road branches south, towards Quemchi. Turn north off the *Panamericana* along the coast to reach **Caulín**; the road is only passable at low tide. There are good beaches here; in Caulín you can see many black-necked swans in summer and flamingos in autumn.

Pumillahue

Pumillahue is 27 km southwest of Ancud, on the Pacific coast. About 10 km before is **Mar Brava**, a vast, deserted curved beach, wonderful for horse riding. About 3 km away from Pumillahue at Puñihuil, there is colony of both Humboldt and Magellanic penguins as well as sea otters, sea lions and a wide range of marine birdlife, situated on an island facing the beach. Local fishermen will provide a guided tour in Spanish, often with exaggerated hand gestures to make up for the lack of informed commentary. The penguins are there from October to late March. The best time to see them is in the early morning or evening. For an account of penguin-watching at Puñihuil, read Ben Richards' *The Mermaid and the Drunks* (Weidenfeld, 2003). To get there, catch one of the two or three buses that leave daily from Ancud, take a tour (US$26 per person, twice a day, 3½ hours including short boat trip; several agencies run trips), hire a taxi, or hitch.

South of Pumillahue a poor road continues south some 5 km to Duhatao. From here it is a wild coastal walk of seven hours to Chepu (see below). The route is difficult to follow so take extra food and a tent and wear light-coloured clothes in summer to protect against *tábanos* (horseflies).

Chepu and around

Twenty-six kilometres south of Ancud, a dirt road heads west from the Pan-American Highway to the coast at Chepu, famed for its river and sea fishing. (There's a bus on Monday, Wednesday and Friday; taxi US$32). It is a base for exploring the drowned forest and the waterways of the Río Chepu and its tributaries (a result of the 1960 *maremoto*). There is a wide range of birdlife here and excellent opportunities for kayaking, boat trips and horse riding. Chepu is also the entrance to the northern sector of the **Parque Nacional Chiloé** (see page 350). From here, it is a 1½-hour walk to Playa Aulén, which has superb forested dunes and an extinct volcano. At **Río Anguay** (also known as Puerto Anguay), there is a campsite and *refugio*.

Boat trips can be organized in Río Anguay to **Laguna Coluco**, one hour up the Río Butalcura (a tributary of the Río Chepu). Two-day trips, navigating the ríos Grande, Carihueco and Butalcura, usually start further inland and finish at Río Anguay. These can be arranged in Ancud (see page 356), or contact Javier Silva, at Puente Anhuay, T09-9527 8719, turismo_riochepu@hotmail.com.

The Mirador de Chepu information centre gives views of the wetlands and has information about the flora, fauna and tourist options. It also has a café, kayaks (electric) for hire and accommodation in cabins or dorms.

Towards Castro → For listings, see pages 352-358.

There are two alternative routes from Ancud to Castro: direct along the Pan-American Highway, crossing rolling hills, forest and agricultural land, or the more leisurely route via the east coast. This is a dramatic journey on roads that plunge up and down forested hills. The road is paved to Huillinco, a few kilometres before Linao, then is *ripio* to Quemchi. The route passes through small farming and fishing communities and offers a real insight into rural life in Chiloé. The two main towns along the coastal route, Quemchi and Dalcahue, can also be reached by paved roads branching off the Pan-American Highway.

Quemchi and around

South of Chacao is the small village of **Hueihue**, where fresh oysters can be bought. Further south, before Quemchi, is a small lake with model sailing boats, which are made in the town. Quemchi itself is a quiet place with long beaches, overlooking a bay speckled with wooded islands. There is a small **tourist office** ① *in the plaza, www. muniquemchi.cl, Mon-Fri 0900-2100, Sat-Sun 1000-2000*. Every summer cultural events are held. Boat trips are offered in January and February from Restaurante Barloventos (barloventos.quemchi@gmail.com). A short walk up the road north towards **Linao** leads to high ground from where there are views to the temperate rainforest on the mainland. Some 4 km from Quemchi is **Isla Aucar**, once linked by bridge (now ruined), where black-necked swans can be seen.

The road from Quemchi to Dalcahue (50 km) passes many places that are the essence of Chiloé. The road rises up and down steep forested hills, rich with flowers, past salmon farms and views of distant bays. Some 20 km from Quemchi is a turn-off to **Quicaví**, legendary as the home to the witches of Chiloé. A few kilometres further brings you to the beautiful village of **Tenaún**, whose church with three towers, dating from 1837, is a UNESCO World Heritage Site.

Offshore is Isla Mechuque in the **Chauques Archipelago** (www.turismoislamechuque. blogspot.co.uk). This is a group of 16 islands east of Dalcahuen that are interconnected by sandbars which are accessible at low tide. **Mechuque** has two small museums of island life and there are palafito houses in the town, plus beautiful views of the mainland in good weather. Boats go from Tenaún (45 minutes), Quicaví and Dalcahue (not daily), but the easiest way to get there is on a tour from Castro, with **Turismo Pehuén** or **Turismo Mi Tierra** (see What to do, page 357).

Beyond Tenaún, you will pass numerous small communities with churches and views to the coast before you reach Dalcahue.

Dalcahue and around

Some 74 km south of Ancud via the Pan-American Highway, Dalcahue is more easily reached from Castro, 30 km further south. The wooden church on the main plaza dates from the 19th century (under repair in 2014). There is a large *artesanía* market on the waterside, near which are several restaurants. A good-quality market is held near the handicraft market on Sunday mornings. There is a tourist kiosk in season and various

Curanto

Particularly associated with Puerto Montt and Chiloé, *curanto* is a very filling fish, meat and seafood stew, which is delicious despite the rather odd combination of ingredients. Though of pre-Hispanic origins, it has developed by adding new ingredients according to new influences. In its original pre-Conquest form, a selection of fish was wrapped in leaves and baked over hot stones in a hole – some specialists wonder if this way of cooking may have come from the Pacific islands, where pit baking is still practised. With the arrival of the Spanish, the dish was modified to include pork, chicken and white wine. Today, it is often cooked in a large pan and advertised as *pullmay* or *curanto en olla*, to distinguish it from the pit-baked form.

hotels. Between Dalcahue and Castro is the Rilán peninsula, with several traditional villages but also a growing number of upmarket hotels, golf and agrotourism.

Quinchao → *Population: 3500.*

The island of Quinchao is a 10-minute ferry journey from Dalcahue. Passing the pretty village of Curaco de Velez (handicrafts sold on the plaza in summer), you reach the main settlement, **Achao**, 25 km southeast of Dalcahue. This is a large fishing village serving the smaller islands offshore, with a boarding school attended by pupils from outlying districts. Its wooden church, built in 1730, is the oldest surviving church in Chiloé. In 1784 a fire destroyed much of the town, but the church was saved by a change in the wind direction. It is a fine example of Chilote Jesuit architecture and contains a small **museum** ① *US$1*. Achao has a seasonal **tourist office** ① *Serrano y Progreso, Dec-Mar only*. A beautiful road leads 9 km south of Achao to the small village of **Quinchao** in a secluded bay at the foot of a hill; an important religious festival is held in the fine church here on 8 December (see page 356). For more information, see www.islaquinchao.com.

 With patience and persistence, boats can be found to take you from Achao to outlying islands, where facilities are basic and shops non-existent but lodging can be found with families; ask around. It is recommended to go with a local friend, if possible.

Castro → *For listings, see pages 352-358.*

The capital of Chiloé, with a population of just under 30,000, lies 88 km south of Ancud on a fjord on the east coast. Founded in 1567, it is a small, friendly town, full of bars and seafood restaurants. It is far livelier and more commercial than other towns and is the major tourist centre on the island. The centre is on a promontory, from which there is a steep drop to the port.

Arriving in Castro

Getting there and around Castro is Chiloé's transport hub. There are many buses south to Quellón (hourly) and north to Ancud and Puerto Montt. **Cruz del Sur** have buses continuing north to Valdivia, Temuco and Santiago (several daily). There are two bus terminals: the crowded Terminal Municipal, San Martín 667, from which all buses and micros to island and long-distance destinations leave; and Cruz del Sur terminal, San Martín 486, T065-263 5152. **Trans Chiloé**'s office is in Terminal Municipal. Although most passenger ferries leave from Quellón, Castro is occasionally used as a port services to Chaitén and Puerto Montt. There are some *colectivos* and public buses serving the barrios high above the town near the *media luna*, but it is unlikely that you will need to use these. It is only a half-hour walk up there in any case.

Tourist information A kiosk on the Plaza de Armas, opposite the cathedral, has a list of accommodation, prices and other information. **CONAF** is at Gamboa 424, behind the Gobernación building.

Places in Castro

On the Plaza de Armas is the large wooden **cathedral**, unmissable in bright lilac and yellow, designed by the Italian architect, Eduardo Provosoli, and dating from 1906. It contains models of other churches on the islands. One block south is the **Museo Municipal**

Castro

To Mercado Municipal & Museo de Arte Moderno
To Ancud

G Riveros
Magallanes
Gabriela Mistral
Los Carrera
Sargento Aldea
Unimarc Supermarket
Monjitas
Municipal Terminal
San Martín
Chiloé Natural
Plazuela del Tren
Ramírez
Freire
O'Higgins
Palafitos
Pedro Montt
Sotomayor
Barros Arana
Serrano
Cruz del Sur
Cathedral
Port
Gamboa
CONAF Gobernación
Prat
Latorre
Turismo Pehuén
Plazuela Gamboa
Plaza de Armas
Boat trips
Portales
Blanco Encalada
Balmaceda
Esmeralda
Museo Regional
Feria de Artesanía
Chacabuco
Colectivos to Chonchi
Thompson
Lillo
Palafitos
Cemetery
Río Gamboa
To Mirador la Virgen, Cerro Millantuy
Riquelme Palafitos
To Quellón & Chonchi

N
200 metres
200 yards

Where to stay
Alerce Nativo **9** *A2*
Cabañas Trayen **5** *C1*
Casita Española **4** *C2*
Hospedaje América **16** *C3*
Hospedaje El Mirador **12** *B3*
Hospedaje El Molo **17** *B3*
Hostel de Castro **18** *C3*
Hostel Don Camilo **2** *B2*
Palafito Hostel **10** *C1*
Unicornio Azul **25** *B3*

Restaurants
Brisas del Mar, El Caleuche,
 El Curanto, La Pincoya **4** *C3*
Café Blanco &
 Ristretto Caffé **1** *C2*
Café del Puente **2** *C1*
Donde Eladio **3** *C3*
Don Octavio **8** *B3*
La Brújula del Cuerpo **5** *C2*
La Playa **6** *C3*
Sacho **7** *C3*

ⓘ C Esmeralda, T065-263 5967, closed in 2014, with displays on the history, handicrafts and mythology of Chiloé, as well as photos of the effects of the 1960 earthquake. Further south, on the waterfront, is the **Feria de Artesanía**, where local woollen articles, such as hats, sweaters, gloves, can be bought. Behind it are four traditional *palafito* restaurants, built on stilts above the water. More traditional *palafitos* can be seen on the northern side of town and by the bridge over the Río Gamboa (Calle Riquelme, with a number of *hostales*, cafés and handicraft shops).

There are good views of the city from **Mirador La Virgen** on Millantuy hill above the cemetery. **Museo de Arte Moderno** ⓘ *T065-263 5454, www.mamchiloe.cl, daily 1000-1700, until 1800 during exhibitions, donations welcome*, is in the Parque Municipal near the river, about 3 km northwest of the centre, and is reached by following Calle Galvarino Riveros up the hill west of town (or take a bus marked 'Al Parque'), from where there are fine views. Passing the Parque Municipal, Calle Galvarino Riveros becomes a small track heading out into the thick forests of the interior, with several small farmsteads. There is also a pleasant two-hour circular walk through woods and fields to **Puntilla Ten Ten** and the Rilán peninsula (see above); turn off the Pan-American Highway 2 km north of town.

On the southern outskirts of town is **Nercón**, whose UNESCO-recognized church is signed off Ruta 5. From the ceiling of the nave hang models of sailing boats. The community holds its Fiesta Costumbrista at the end of January.

Chonchi to Quellón → For listings, see pages 352-358.

The Pan-American Highway continues south to Quellón, the southernmost port in Chiloé, with paved side roads leading east to Chonchi and west to Cucao. From Chonchi, a partially paved road continues southeast to Queilen. Winding across forested hills, this is probably the most attractive route on the island; numerous tracks branch off to deserted beaches where you can walk for hours and hear nothing but the splashing of dolphins in the bay. The ferry to Lemuy sails from a port just south of Chonchi on this road.

Chonchi

A picturesque fishing village 23 km south of Castro, Chonchi is a good base for exploring the island. Known as the *Ciudad de los Tres Pisos* (city built on three levels), it was, until the opening of the Panama Canal in 1907, a stopping point for sailing ships. In the years that followed, it was the cypress capital of Chile: big fortunes were made in the timber industry and grand wooden mansions were built in the town. In the 1950s, Chonchi boomed as a free port but, in the 1970s, it lost that status to Punta Arenas. Its harbour is now a supply point for salmon farms almost as far south as Coyhaique.

On the main plaza is the wooden church (if it's closed, ask for the key from the small handicraft market next door), built in 1754 and remodelled in neoclassical style in 1859 and 1897. The nave roof is painted blue and dotted with stars. Its impressive tower was blown off in a storm in March 2002 and has been rebuilt.

There is a **tourist information kiosk** at the crossroads one block uphill from here in summer (there's also an information desk in the market). From the plaza, **Calle Centenario** drops steeply to the harbour, lined with several attractive but sadly neglected wooden mansions. The small **Museo de Tradiciones Chonchinas** ⓘ *Centenario 116, T065-267 2802, US$1, Tue-Sun 1000-1330, 1500-1845*, is housed in a former residence, laid out to give an idea of domestic life in the first decade of the 20th century, when Chonchi was the most important port in Chiloé. It shows videos on the churches of Chiloé. Fishing boats bring in the early morning catch, which is carried straight into the new **market** on the seafront. The tiny **Museo del Acordeón of Sergio Colivor Barria** ① *Andrade 183 next to Restaurant La Quila, daily,* has some 50 instruments on display. There is another, undecorated 18th-century church at Vilupulli, 5 km north (sign on Ruta 5, *ripio* road). The woman who has a tiny handicraft stall behind the church holds the key.

Lemuy
① *Ferry departs 4 km south of Chonchi on the road to Queilen every 30 mins, cars US$5, foot passengers free (micro from Castro).*
In the bay opposite Chonchi lies the island of **Lemuy**. It covers 97 sq km and offers many good walks along quiet unpaved tracks through undulating pastures and woodland. From the ferry dock, a road runs east across the island, passing a fine 19th-century wooden church at **Ichuac** before reaching **Puqueldón**. This is the main settlement on the island and is built on a very steep hill stretching down to the port. There's a post office and a telephone centre here, as well as a small private park, **Parque Yayanes** ① *T09-8861 6462, www.parqueyayanes.cl,* which offers a 30-minute walk across a hanging bridge and through mixed forest, has lodging in cabins and serves traditional food. From Puqueldón, the road continues a further 16 km on a ridge high above the sea, passing small hamlets, with views of the water and the patchwork of fields. There are old churches at **Aldachildo**, 9 km east of Puqueldón, and at **Detif**, in the extreme south of the island.

Queilen
Some 46 km southeast of Chonchi, **Queilen** is a pretty fishing village on a long finger-shaped peninsula. On the north side is a sandy beach, which curves round the head of the peninsula, while on the south side is the old wooden pier, which doubles as the port. There are fine views across the straits to Tanqui Island and the mainland, as well as the **Museo Refugio de Navegantes** ① *Pres Alessandri s/n, T065-236 7149, Jan and Feb 1100-2000.* Also here are places to stay and several restaurants including Restaurant Melinka, Alessandri 126, for good food.

West of Chonchi
West of Chonchi at Km 12 is **Huillinco**, a charming village on Lago Huillinco, with *cabañas* and cafés. Beyond here the narrow and sinuous paved road continues west to **Cucao**, one of the few settlements on the west coast of Chiloé. The immense 20-km-long beach is battered by thundering Pacific surf and dangerous undercurrents, making it one of the most dramatic places along the whole coast of Chile. Cucao is divided by a creek. The landward side is beside the lake and has the small church, a helpful tourist information desk (www.turismocucao.cl) and a couple of traditional restaurants, plus places to stay. Cross the bridge to the newer sector, with *hostales*, eating places, adventure sports agencies (horse riding, trekking, kayaks, SUP) and the road to the national park (see below). Beyond the park entrance the rough road continues to Canquín, with a bridge shaped like a boat. Over the bridge, on the left, is a track through private property to the beach (US$2 to park car). It's about 30 minutes' walk from Cucao bridge to Canquín bridge.

Parque Nacional Chiloé
① *T09-9932 9193, parque.chiloe@conaf.cl, daily 0900-2000 (until 1800 in winter, US$2.75.*
The park, divided into three sections, covers extensive areas of the wild and uninhabited western side of the island, much of it filled by temperate rainforest. Wildlife includes the

Chilote fox and pudú deer. There are over 110 species of bird resident here, including cormorants, gulls, penguins and flightless steamer ducks. The northern sector, covering 7800 ha, is reached by a path which runs south from Chepu (see page 345). The second section is a small island, Metalqui, off the coast of the northern sector. The southern sector (35,207 ha) is entered 1 km north of Cucao, where there is an **administration centre**, small museum, restaurant Fogón, *cabañas* (**$$$** for five to six people) and camping (US$9 per person). The centre provides maps of the park, but they are not very accurate and should not be used to locate *refugios* within the park. From the administration centre six short trails ranging from 108 m to 1700 m run along the lakeside and through dunes to the beach.

A path, affording great views, runs 3 km north from the administration centre to **Laguna Huelde** and then north for a further 12 km to **Cole Cole**. Once you reach **Río Anay**, 9 km beyond Cole Cole, you can wade or swim across the river to reach a beautiful, secluded beach from where you can enjoy the sight of dolphins playing in the huge breakers. The journey can also be made on horseback; allow nine hours for the round trip. Take lots of water and your own food. There are several other walks in the national park, but signposts are limited so ask at the administration centre or at horse riding agencies about excursions further into the park. *Tábanos* are bad in summer, so wear light-coloured clothing.

Quellón and around

The southernmost port in Chiloé, located 92 km south of Castro, Quellón has suffered its fair share of misfortunes in recent years. In 2002, the arrival of the lethal *marea roja* microorganism caused the collapse of the shellfish industry, provoking demonstrations from fishermen and dockers who destroyed part of the pier. There is not much to interest the traveller here, and the **tourist information office** ① *Vargas y García, is often closed, even in summer*. Another source of information is the **Cámara de Turismo Quellón** ① *T09-9191 2150, www.turismoquellon.cl, www.muniquellon.cl*. Note that the street numbering system in Quellón is unfathomable.

Museo Amador Cárdenas Paredes ① *Pedro Montt 309, T065-268 3452, Mon-Fri 0930-1800*, has an odd collection of antique typewriters and sewing machines. There are pleasant beaches nearby: **Viejo**, 4 km west, where there is an old wooden church; **Punta de Lapa**, 7 km west, and **Yaldad**, 9 km west along a pretty road over the hills.

Boat trips go to Isla Cailín in summer from the pier, US$42 for a full day (www.turismochiloe.cl). A trip can also be made to **Chaiguao**, 11 km east, where there is a small Sunday morning market. The Golfo de Corcovado, between southern Chiloé and the mainland is visited by blue whales from December to April.

The far south of the island has been bought by a private foundation and has been turned into a nature sanctuary known as the **Parque Tantauco** ① *information from Av La Paz 034, Quellón, T065-277 3100, or E Riquelme 1228, Castro, T065-263 0951, http://parquetantauco.cl, US$6.50, children US$1*. Covering some 120,000 ha of native woodland, wetlands, lagoons and rivers, it is home to a range of endangered wildlife. There are two campsites (no electricity), a casa de huéspedes and a refugio. There are 120 km of trails from three hours to five days. Access is by road or by a three-hour boat trip from Quellón to **Inio** ① *US$50, Mon, Wed, Fri*.

Chiloé listings

For hotel and restaurant price codes and other relevant information, see pages 14-21.

Where to stay

Ancud *p343, map p344*

$$$ Don Lucas, Salvador Allende (Costanera) 906, T065-262 0950, www.hoteldonlucas.cl. Nice rooms, some with sea view, disabled access, restaurant. A good choice.

$$$ Galeón Azul, Libertad 751, T065-262 2567, www.hotelgaleonazul.cl. Small heated rooms, rather basic for the price but excellent views. Bright restaurant.

$$$ Panamericana, San Antonio 30, T065-262 2340, www.panamericana hoteles.cl. Nice views of the bay, attractive, very comfortable, helpful, restaurant, tours offered, English spoken.

$$ Balai, Pudeto 169, T065-262 2966, www.hotelbalai.cl. With heating, parking, restaurant, interesting local paintings, models and artefacts on display. Tours arranged.

$$ Hostal Lluhay, Cochrane 458, T065-262 2656, www.hostal-lluhay.cl. Attentive, sea views, heating, meals, nice lounge, kayak and bicycle rental, tours with Ancud Mágico.

$$ Hostal Vista al Mar, Salvador Allende (Costanera) 918, T065-262 2617, www.vistaalmar.cl. Close to Cruz del Sur buses, cabins for 2-5, also private rooms with or without bath. Views over the bay, safe, heating, parking.

$$-$ 13 Lunas, Los Carrera 855, T065-262 2106, www.13lunas.cl. Opposite Cruz del Sur bus terminal, single-sex and mixed dorms, private rooms, wheelchair accessible, very helpful, *asados* and ping pong in the basement, parking, great penguin tour and other activities.

$$-$ Mundo Nuevo, Salvador Allende (Costanera) 748, T065-262 8383, www.backpackerschile.com. Comfortable hostel, dorms, rooms with and without bath, one

room has a boat-bed, great views over the bay, lots of info, heating, good showers, car and bicycle hire, English and German spoken.

$ pp Hospedaje Austral, A Pinto 1318, T065-262 4847, www.ancudchiloechile.com. Cosy wooden house, near long-distance bus station, with small breakfast, lots of bathrooms, double room (**$$**), family of Mirta Ruiz, very welcoming and caring, lots of information.

$ pp Hostal Altos de Bellavista, Bellavista 449, T065- 262 2384, cecilia2791@gmail. com. Rooms for 1-5, with or without bath, family atmosphere, long stay available, tatty outside but welcoming inside. Several other places to stay on Bellavista.

Camping

Hostal y Cabañas Arena Gruesa, Av Costanera Norte 290, T065-262 3428, www.hotelarenagruesa.cl. US$8-9.75 for campsite, also mobile homes, with light, water and services, also cabins for 2-10 and hotel.

East of Ancud *p345*

$$$-$$ Caulín Lodge, Caulín, T09-9643 7986, www.caulinlodge.cl. Native Chilote trees grow in the garden, *cabañas* and a sauna available. Decent restaurant. Horse riding and other trips offered.

Chepu and around *p345*

Armando Pérez and **Sonia Díaz**, T09-9899 8914, www.agroturismochepu.cl, offer agrotourism stays. Make cheese, tend cattle and sheep, and go for good walks in the Chepu area. To get there from Ancud, travel 26 km south on Route 5, turn right (east) for 5 km to Coipomó, there turn left, and after 3.5 km turn right. The farm is on the left after 2 km.

$$$-$ Mirador de Chepu, Chepu Adventures, T09-9227 4517, www.chepu.cl. Cabins or dorms; no children under 14.

Quemchi and around *p346*
$$ Hospedaje y Cabañas Costanera, D Bahamonde 141, Quemchi, T065-269 1230, www.chiloe.cl/hospedajecostanera/. *Cabañas* for up to 5 people, as well as bed and breakfast in rooms with shared bath. Other basic places to stay include **Hostal Backpackers**, beside bus stop, T09-764 2038/9440 1321, and **Camping La Casona**, T09-909 9015.

Quemchi to Dalcahue *p346*
$ Hospedaje, Rural María Humilde, Isla Mechuque, T09-9012 6233, http://turismoislamechuque.blogspot.co.uk.

Dalcahue and around *p346*
$ Residencial Playa, Rodríguez 9. Price per person. Basic.
$ Hospedaje Putemun, Freire 305, T065-264 1330. Price per person. Clean, basic.
$ Residencial San Martín, San Martín 1. Price per person. Basic, clean, also meals.

Quinchao *p347*
$$ Hostería La Nave, Prat y Aldea, Achao, T065-266 1219. Breakfast provided, cheaper rooms without bath, restaurant with fine views over bay.
$$ Hostal Plaza, Amunátegui 20, Achao, T065-266 1283. With bath and breakfast, clean, good.
$ Hospedaje Achao, Serrano 061, Achao, T065-266 1373. Without bath, good, clean.
$ Hospedaje Chilhue, Zañartu 021, Achao, www.chiloe.cl/hospedajechilhue/. Without bath, with breakfast, clean.
$ Hospedaje São Paulo, Serrano 54, Achao, T065-266 1245. Basic, hot water.

Castro *p347, map p348*
There is an **Asociación Hospedajes Castro**, approved by the Municipalidad, ask at the tourist office.
$$$$-$$$ Cabañas Trayen, Nercón, 5 km south of Castro, T065-263 3633, www.trayenchiloe.cl. Lovely views, cabins for 4 to 6.

$$$$-$$$ Hotel de Castro, Chacabuco 202, T065-263 2301, www.hosteriadecastro.cl. The newer section is spacious and comfortable, with wonderful views and nice suites. Spa, pool. Good restaurant and bar.
$$$ Unicornio Azul, Pedro Montt 228, T065-263 2359, www.hotelunicornioazul.cl. Striking pink and blue building climbing the hillside from the waterfront, good views over bay, comfortable, restaurant.
$$$-$$ Palafito Hostel, Riquelme 1210, T065-253 1008. In a restored traditional *palafito* building on stilts over the water, downhill from centre and across bridge. Helpful staff, good breakfast, tours arranged. (On same street are places with similar names: Palafito Azul, No 1242, www.palafitoazul.cl, and Palafito 1326, No 1326, www.palafito1326.cl.)
$$ Casita Española, Los Carrera 359, T065-263 5186, www.hosteriadecastro.cl. Heating, parking, good, in same group as **Hostería de Castro**.
$$ Hostal Don Camilo, Ramírez 566, T065-263 2180, hostaldoncamilo@gmail.com. Pleasant accommodation in functional rooms with all services, good value restaurant, secure parking.
$$-$ Hospedaje El Mirador, Barros Arana 127, T065-263 3795, maboly@yahoo.com. Private or shared bath, rooms a bit small, cosy, relaxing, kitchen (shared with family).
$ pp Hospedaje América, Chacabuco 215, T065-263 4364, hosameri@telsur.cl. Good location, family welcome, shared bath, comfortable. They offer an evening meal service: you buy, they cook, everyone shares.
$ pp Hospedaje El Molo, Barros Arana 140, T065-263 5026, www.elmolochiloe.cl. The oldest hostel in Castro, comfortable, safe, welcoming, good location on steps down to seafront, nice view. Several others on this passageway.

Camping
Camping Pudú, Ruta 5, 10 km north of Castro, T065-263 2286, www.chiloeweb.com/chwb/pudu/. Cabins, showers with

hot water, sites with light, water, kids' games. Several sites on road to Chonchi, including **Llicaldad**, Esmeralda 269, T065-263 2380, apachecocornejo@gmail.com, also has *cabañas*.

Chonchi and around *p349*
$$$ Cabañas Treng Treng, José Pinto Pérez 420, T065-267 2532, www.treng treng.cl. Impeccable fully furnished cabins sleeping 2-7. Splendid views, some English spoken.
$$ Hostal Emarley, Irarrázabal 191, T065-267 1202. Near market, cheaper rooms with shared bath.
$$ Hostal Esmeralda, Esmeralda con Irarrázabal 267, T065-235 5035, T09-9504 4944/9597 9401, abraniff@gmail.com. Beyond market, access from road or beach. Completely renovated, family atmosphere, quiet, suite on top floor, or rooms with and without bath, breakfast extra, small garden, parking, kitchen and Wi-Fi to follow.
$$ Hostal La Tortuga, Pedro Montt 241, T09-9098 2925, www.hostallatortuga.com. In a historic house on the main plaza, comfortable rooms, cafeteria, laundry.
$$ Huildín, Centenario 102, T065-267 1388, www.hotelhuildin.com. Old-fashioned, decent rooms with good beds but windows are onto interior passages, also *cabañas*, garden with superb views.

West of Chonchi *p350*
Most lodgings and restaurants in Cucao are open Jan-Mar, but you can camp all year.
$$$-$$ Hostal Palafito Cucao, 300 m from national park entrance, T065-297 1164, www.hostelpalafitocucao.cl. Open all year. Built from native timber and with large windows for great views of Lake Cucao. Transfers and excursions arranged. Private rooms and a 6-bed dorm, comfortable, good breakfast and kitchen, meals available.
$$ La Paloma, behind the church on lakeshore, T09-9313 1907. *Cabañas* and camping (US$6.50 pp) open all year.

$ pp **Jostel**, T09-8242 3007/9833 4830, jostle.chiloe@gmail.com. Open summer only for lodging, but also kayaks US$9 per hr, SUP US$18, pedal boats US$14.50.

Camping
There are campsites, some with restaurants and shops, on the road to the national park, others on the road east of Cucao. There are minimarkets on the little street behind Jostel and another before the tourist office.

Quellón *p351*
$$ El Chico Leo, P Montt 325, T065-268 1567, www.turismochiloe.cl/ hotelelchicoleo. Private or shared bath, heating, games room, restaurant. There are several other places to stay including *cabañas* and campsites: see www. muniquellon.cl and www.turismochiloe.cl.

❼ Restaurants

Ancud *p343*, map *p344*
$$ La Pincoya, Prat 61, near the dock entrance, T065-262 2613. Good seafood, service and views.
$$ Quetalmahue, 12 km west of Ancud on the road to Faro Corona and Fuerte Ahui, T09-9033 3930, www.quetalmahue.cl. The best place for traditional *curantos al hoyo* (cooked in the ground, daily in summer).
$ El Cangrejo, Dieciocho 155. Has a good reputation for its seafood.
$ El Embrujo, Maipú 650. Café serving teas, coffees, sandwiches, cakes, beers and tragos. Above the handicrafts in the Mercado Municipal are 2 restaurants, **Los Artesanos**, loc 71, and **Rincón Sureño**, loc 53, both serving comida típica. Walking up Dieciocho towards the Feria Municipal there are many eating places behind the Mercado, including **La Ñaña**, which is cheap and good. All serve much the same local fare. In an alley from Dieciocho to Prat is a row of even cheaper lunch spots, including **El Pingüinito**, decent lunches, but more basic than others. In

the Feria Municipal there are 4 restaurants upstairs, all much the same with lunch specials at US$4.50-6.75.

East of Ancud *p345*
$$$-$$ Ostras Caulín, Caulín, T09-9643 7005, www.ostrascaulin.cl. Excellent, very fresh oysters served in any number of ways.

Pumillahue *p345*
There are restaurants at Puñihuil, all with similar menus and prices. The best of these is probably **Bahía Puñihuil**, T09-9655 6780, punihuil@gmail.com, who also offer trips to see the penguins.

Towards Castro *p346*
There are numerous small restaurants along the harbour and around the market in Dalcahue, serving excellent and cheap seafood. Note that if you ask for *té*, you will be served a mug of white wine.
$ Fogón La Pincoya, Isla de Mechuque, T09-6287 7400. For traditional meals and handicrafts.

$ Hostería La Nave, Quinchao, see Where to stay, above.

$ Restaurant La Dalca, Freire 502, Dalcahue. Good cheap food. Recommended.

Castro *p347, map p348*
Breakfast before 0900 is difficult to find. There are several eating places and bars on the south side of the Plaza, on Portales and Balmaceda. By the market many places offer set lunch, usually fish dishes. In the market, try *milcaos*, fried potato cakes with meat stuffing. Also licor de oro like Galliano.
$$$-$ Donde Eladio, Lillo 97. Meat and seafood specialities on offer.
$$$-$ La Playa, Lillo 41, www.playa chiloe.cl. Good seafood, also meat dishes.
$$ Don Octavio, Pedro Montt 261. Good food and nice views over bay, specializes in seafood.
$$ Palafito restaurants near the **Feria de Artesanía** on the waterfront offer good

food and good value: **Brisas del Mar**, **El Caleuche**, **El Curanto** and **La Pincoya**.
$$-$ Descarriada, Esmeralda y Blanco, corner of the Plaza. Good local dishes, meat and fish, nice atmosphere, also desserts, tea and coffee, ice cream cart outside.
$$-$ Sacho, Thompson 213. Tue-Sat 1200-1530, 2100-2330, Sun 1200-1530. Good sea views and good food.

Cafés
Café Blanco, Blanco 268. Busy little place for coffee, teas, juices, sandwiches, cakes, *piscos*, beers and wine. Similar, at No 264, is Ristretto Caffé.
Café del Puente, Riquelme 1180-B, T065-263 4878. Tue-Sun 0900-2100. Smart café over the water serving breakfast, lunches, afternoon tea (30 varieties of tea), coffee, sandwiches, cakes, juices and ice cream.
La Brújula del Cuerpo, O'Higgins 308, Plaza de Armas. Fast food, grill, snacks, drinks and coffee.

Chonchi and around *p349*
There are a few places to eat on Av Irrarrázabal. Most places close on Sun, even in summer, although Iscamar, Centenario 66 y P J Andrade, is open on Sun. **Supermercado Economar**, Irrarrázabal 49, far end of Costanera from Mercado, has a café. Next door is **Chocolatería Pastelería Alejandra**.
$$-$ Tres Pisos, Pedro Andrade 296 y Esmeralda, near the market. Serves good food.
$ Café Sueños de la Pincoya, P J Andrade 135. Daily 1000-2200. For sweet empanadas, cakes, teas and coffee.

West of Chonchi *p350*
In Huillinco try Café de Lago, on the lakeshore by Camping Huillinco, for teas, coffees, cakes, sandwiches (Jan to mid-Mar daily and weekends to Semana Santa); or Los Coihues, above Huillinco, for more substantial fare.

$$-$ Las Luminarias, Cucao, T09-9487 9847, sells excellent *empanadas de machas* (*machas* are local shellfish). It also has accommodation (**$**) with breakfast and hot shower. There are several other restaurants and cafés in Cucao across the bridge on the road towards the national park, among them **El Fogón de Cucao** (also has accómmodation), **Las Terrazas de Cucao** (with shop and campsite), **Maervi** and others.

Quellón *p351*
$$ Tierra del Fuego, P Montt 445, T065-268 2079. For fish, seafood and other local dishes. In hotel of same name.
$ Fogón Onde Agüero, La Paz 307, T065-268 3653. Good cheap traditional food. Popular at lunchtime.

🍸 Bars and clubs

Ancud *p343, map p344*
Lumière, Ramírez 278, The place to be seen for the younger crowd. Also serves good food.
Retro's Pub, Maipú 615, off Pudeto, T065-626410. Appealing ambience, food (including vegetarian fare) and good cocktails.

Castro *p347, map p348*
Kaweshkar Lounge, Blanco Encalada 31. Minimalist bar with wide range of cocktails and occasional live music. Also serves food.

🎉 Festivals

Quinchao *p347*
8 Dec People come from all over Chiloé for **Día de la Virgen** and watch as a huge model of the Virgin is carried with great reverence to the church.

Chonchi and around *p349*
2nd week of Feb La Semana Chonchina is one of the series of Chilote festivals.

🛍 Shopping

Ancud *p343, map p344*
Mercado Municipal is on Libertad between Dieciocho and Prat. The **Feria Municipal** (or Rural) is at Pedro Montt y Prat, selling local produce, fish and handicrafts on the 2nd floor. Also has a tourist office. Opposite is a huge **Unimarc** supermarket.

Dalcahue *p346*
Dalcahue's weekly market is held on Sun. It has quality goods, but bargaining is practically impossible, and in recent years it has become somewhat overrun with tourists. It's good for *curantos*, though.

Castro *p347, map p348*
Feria de Artesanía, Lillo on the wharf, sells good-value woollens. The **Mercado Municipal** is on Yumbel, off Ulloa, uphill northwest of town, for fish and veg. **Unimarc** supermarket, O'Higgins y Aldea, bakes good bread.

Chonchi and around *p349*
Handicrafts (woollens, jams, liqueurs) are sold at the **Feria Artesanal**, on the waterfront and from the *parroquia*, next to the church (open Oct-Mar only).

Quellón *p351*
Traditional wooden carvings are sold at **Tallados Noly**, Gómez García 361, www.turismochiloe.cl/noly/. Other handicrafts can be bought from the **Feria Artesanal** on Ladrilleros y Gómez García.

🎯 What to do

Ancud *p343, map p344*
Aki Turismo, patio of Mercado Municipal, T065-254 5253, www.akiturismochiloe.cl. Good-value trips to the penguin colony and other tours. Car rental in the same office, www.chiloerentacar.cl.

Austral Adventures, Salvador Allende (Costanera) 904, T065-262 5977, www.austral-adventures.com. Bespoke small-group tours of the archipelago and northern Patagonia (including Parque Pumalín) on land and sea. Good English-speaking guides, lots of interesting choices; director Britt Lewis.
Mistyk's, Los Carrera 823, T09-9644 3767, www.turismomistyks.com. For local tours and diving.
Viajes Nativa, in Cruz del Sur bus terminal, T065-254 6390, www.viajesnativa.cl or www.chiloetour.com. Tours to the penguin colony.

Chepu and around *p345*
This area offers great opportunities for horse riding, with long beaches that are perfect for a windswept gallop. Ask around for independent guides who offer riding, fishing and kayaking. See also **Mirador de Chepu**/Chepu Adventures, www.chepu.cl.

Dalcahue and around *p346*
Altue Active Travel, 3 km south of Dalcahue, office for reservations in Santiago at Encomenderos 83, piso 2.
Las Condes, T02-232 1103, www.altue.com. Sea kayaking.

Castro *p347, map p348*
Mar y Magia, cabin on the dockside or at Chacabuco 202, T065-253 1048, www.marymagia.cl. Fjord trips by boat, US$12.50 pp, longer trips in summer.
Chiloé Natural, P Montt next to Unicornio Azul, T065-6319 7388, tours@chiloenatural.cl. Lots of activities, trips to islands and boat trips.
Turismo Mi Tierra, San Martín 473-A, T09-863 2667, www.turismomitierra.cl. Trips to Isla Mechuque, including a meal of *curanto al hoyo* and a visit to waterfalls at Tocoihue on the main island.
Turismo Pehuén, Latorre 238, T065-263 5254, www.turismopehuen.cl. **Naviera Austral** agency, kayak and boat trips, trips to national park, penguin colony, around the island and car hire.

West of Chonchi *p350*
Many houses in Cucao rent horses. It usually costs US$140 for two people per day for the round trip on horseback to **Río Anay**. Bear in mind that the horses will be of varied temperament, and that if you hire a guide, you pay for his horse too.

⊙ Transport

Ancud *p343, map p344*
Bus
To **Castro**, US$3.75, frequent (see below), 1½ hrs. To **Puerto Montt**, frequent services, see Arriving in Chiloé, above. To **Quemchi**, most via Degán, 2 hrs, US$2.75; to Dalcahue US$3.

Dalcahue and around *p346*
Bus
To **Castro**, frequent services, US$1.50; daily bus to **Puerto Montt**, via Ancud.

Ferry
To **Quinchao**, 10 mins, frequent, in summer it runs till 0100, cars US$4.55, free for pedestrians

Quinchao *p347*
Ferry to **Dalcahue**, 10 mins, frequent, in summer it runs till 0100, cars US$4.55, free for pedestrians. San Cristóbal buses to **Ancud** and Castro (11 a day, 7 at weekends, US$3).

Castro *p347, map p348*
Bus
Frequent services to **Ancud**, Chonchi and **Puerto Montt** by Cruz del Sur, Queilén Bus and others. **Cruz del Sur** goes as far as Santiago, US$56-76, and all cities in between. Isla de Chiloé and Ojeda both run to **Cucao**, almost hourly in summer, 2-3 a day in winter, 1½ hrs, US$2.75, US$5.40 return to national park. To Dalcahue frequent services, US$1.50. To **Achao** (Quinchao) via Dalcahue and Curaco de Vélez, see above. To **Puqueldón** on the island of Lemuy, Gallardo, 4 daily Mon-Fri, fewer Sat-Sun,

US$3.50. To Quemchi, daily with **Queilén Bus**, 1½ hrs, US$2.55. To Queilén, Queilén Bus and others, 6 a day, US$3.

Ferry
Naviera Austral, Latorre 238, T065-263 5254, www.navieraustral.cl, has occasional services to **Chaitén** when Quellon's port is out of action.

Chonchi and around *p349*
Buses and taxis to **Castro**, frequent, US$1.45, from main plaza. Services to **Quellón** (US$2), Cucao and **Queilén** from Castro and Puerto Montt also call here.

West of Chonchi *p350*
There are buses to **Cucao** from Castro, via Chonchi and Huillinco.

Quellón *p351*
Bus
To **Castro**, 2 hrs, frequent, Quellón Expreso, US$3, and **Cruz del Sur** (Pedro Aguirre Cerda 052, T065-268 1284), US$3.25; also to **Ancud**, US$7.25, and **Puerto Montt**.

Ferry
Naviera Austral, Pedro Montt 457, T065-268 2207, www.navieraustral.cl, runs ferries from Quellón to **Chaitén** once a week (more in high season), 5 hrs, seat US$29, bunk US$56-62, US$11 bicycle, US$36 motorbike, US$156 car. To **Puerto Chacabuco** (via Melinka, Raul Marin Balmaceda, Santo Domingo, Melimoyu, Puerto Gala on Isla Toto, Puerto Cisnes, Puerto Gaviota and Puerto Aguirre) twice weekly, 28 hrs, reclining seat US$27, bunk US$66-68, cars US$214. All services leave from Castro when Quellón's port is out of commission and schedules are subject to last-minute changes due to inclement weather. Check with the company for current schedules and fares.

⊙ Directory

Ancud *p343, map p344*
Banks ATM at **Banco BCI**, Ramírez, 1 block from the plaza; *casa de cambio* on same block. **Police** Baquedano y O'Higgins. **Post office** Pudeto y Blanco Encalada, corner of Plaza de Armas.

Castro *p347, map p348*
Banks Banco de Chile, Plaza de Armas, ATM, accepts TCs (at a poor rate); **BCI**, Plaza de Armas, MasterCard and Visa ATM. There are places to exchange or obtain cash on Blanco Encalada and on Portales (south side of Plaza de Armas). **Laundry** Clean Centre, Balmaceda 220; **Lavandería Magic Matic**, Gamboa 385. **Medical services** Hospital de Castro, Freire 852, www.hospitalcastro. gov.cl. **Post office** On west side of Plaza de Armas.

Chonchi *p349*
Banks Banco del Estado, Centenario 28.

Quellón *p351*
Banks Banco del Estado, Veintidós de Mayo 399. **Banco de Chile**, Ladrilleros 315, ATM accepts Visa. **Laundry** Lavandería Ruck-Zuck, Ladrilleras 392.

Contents

Footprint features

Border crossings

Chile–Argentina

At a glance

⊖ **Getting around** Boat, minibus,
air taxi, or ideally mountain bike.
You will need a lot of patience.
⊘ **Time required** At least a week
and twice as much as you think.
◈ **Weather** Cold in winter, wet
on the coast but surprisingly
pleasant in summer.
⊗ **When not to go** Winter is
unforgiving, while the road is liable
to flooding in spring and autumn.

Puerto Montt
Cochamó
Carelmapu
La Arena
Parque Nacional
Alerce Andino
Parga
Puelche
Parga Chacao
Hornopirén
Parque Nacional
Hornopirén
Degán
Ayacara
Parque
Pumalín
Dalcahue
Castro
Nercón
Lepetepu
Fiordo Largo
Caleta
Gonzalo
Parque
Pumalín
Queilen
Chaitén
Chiloé
Amarillo
Quellón
Puerto
Cárdenas
Corcovado
(2290m)
Futaleufú
Lago
Espolón
Lago
Yelcho
Villa
Santa Lucía
Puerto
Piedra
Paso Futaleufú
Nevada
(2042m)
Puerto
Ramírez
Golfo de Corcovado
Puerto Raúl
Marín
Balmaceda
Palena
Paso Palena
Melinka
Río Palena
Lago
Palena
La Junta
Reserva
Nacional
Rosselot
Lago
Verde
Puyuhuapi
Parque Nacional
Queulat
La Tapera
Puerto
Cisnes
Villa
Amengual
Reserva Nacional
Lago Las Torres
Villa
Mañihuales
Termas de
Chiconal
Puerto
Aisén
Reserva
Nacional
Coyhaique
Coyhaique
Alto
Coyhaique
Puerto
Chacabuco
Reserva Nacional
Río Simpson
El
Blanco
Monumento Natural
Dos Lagunas
Balmaceda
Paso
Huemules
Reserva Nacional
Cerro Castillo
Villa Cerro
Castillo
Puerto
Grosse
Puerto Ibáñez
Lago
General
Carrera
Lago
Buenos Aires
Bahía
Murta
Chile Chico
Los Antiguos
Laguna
San Rafael
Río
Tranquilo
Jeinimeni
(2600m)
Reserva Nacional
Lago Jeinimeni
Parque
Nacional
Laguna
San Rafael
Puerto Guadal
El Maitén
Reserva
Nacional
Tamango
Paso
Roballos
Campo de Hielo
San Valentín
Villa Chacabuco
Cochrane
Lago
Cochrane
REGION XI
Campo de
Hielo Norte
Río Baker
Lago
Puerredón
ARGENTINA
Tortel
Puerto Yungay
N
Campo de
Hielo Sur
Villa
O'Higgins
Lago
O'Higgins
Candelario
Mancilla
40 km
40 miles

Travelling along the Carretera Austral is one of the greatest journeys South America has to offer. It is a largely unpaved *ripio* road stretching almost 1200 km through spectacular ever-changing scenery and with a similar length of branch roads heading either to the fjords or the mountains and Argentinian Patagonia beyond. Before the opening of the road, this part of Chile was largely inaccessible; it remains breathtaking. The journey will take you past trees growing up out of vertical cliffs; impenetrably thick millennial forests; burned pastures dotted with glacial debris; innumerable waterfalls rushing right down to the road's edge, while spiralling volcanoes and sparkling glaciers feed turquoise lakes and fast-flowing rivers, all rich with southern Chile's unique flora.

The only town of any size, Coyhaique, lies in the valley of the Río Simpson. South of Coyhaique are Lago General Carrera, the largest lake in Chile, and the Río Baker, one of the longest rivers in the country, which reaches the sea at Caleta Tortel. Further south still is Villa O' Higgins and the icefields of the Campo de Hielo Sur, which feed several magnificent glaciers and prevent further road building, although a route (by boat and on foot or mountain bike) exists that goes on to El Chaltén in Argentina. Coyhaique enjoys good air connections with Puerto Montt and Santiago, while nearby Puerto Chacabuco can be reached by ferry or catamaran from Puerto Montt, Chaitén and Chiloé. The most appealing parts of this region, however, can only be visited by travelling along the Carretera Austral.

Background

The original inhabitants of northern Patagonia were Alacalufes (Kaweshkar or *canoeros*), who were coast dwellers living off the sea (see page 501), and Tehuelches (Tzónecas, or Patagones), who lived on the pampa hunting guanacos, *ñandúes* (rheas) and *huemules* (see box, page 386).

The Spanish called the region Trapalanda, but initially explored little more than the coast. This was the last territory to be occupied by the Chilean state after Independence from Spain. In the late 19th century, expeditions up the rivers led by George Charles Musters (1869) and Enrique Simpson Baeza (1870-1872) were followed by a failed attempt to found a settlement at the mouth of the Río Palena in 1884. Fearing that Argentina might seize the territory, the Chilean government appointed Hans Steffen to explore the area. His seven expeditions (1892-1902) were followed by an agreement with Argentina to submit the question of the frontier to arbitration by the British crown.

The Chilean government granted concessions to three large cattle companies in an attempt to occupy the area. Until the 1920s, there were few settlers; early pioneers settled along the coast and brought supplies from Chiloé. Although the first town, Baquedano (modern-day Coyhaique), was founded in 1917, followed by Puerto Aysén in 1924, the first road, between Puerto Aysén and Coyhaique, was not built until 1936. It was not until the 1960s that this region began to be integrated with the rest of the country. Although the road has helped transform the lives of many people in this part of Chile, the motivation behind its construction was mainly geopolitical. Ever since Independence, Chilean military and political leaders have stressed the importance of occupying the southern regions of the Pacific coast and preventing any incursion by Argentina.

Begun in 1976, the central section of the Carretera Austral, from Chaitén to Coyhaique, was opened in 1983. Five years later, the northern section, linking Chaitén with Puerto Montt, and the southern section, between Coyhaique and Cochrane, were officially inaugurated. Since then, the Carretera has been extended south of Cochrane to Puerto Yungay and Villa O'Higgins. Work is continuing, building branch roads (which currently amount to around 1300 km) and widening and paving the most important sections. The road is the work of the army corps of engineers and dotted along the route are memorials to the dozens of young recruits who died during its construction.

Despite recent growth, this remains one of the most sparsely populated areas of Chile, with barely 100,000 inhabitants, most of whom live in Coyhaique or in nearby Puerto Aysén. Agriculture is limited by the climate and poverty of the soil, but fishing, forestry and mining are key industries. A project for a huge aluminium plant was abandoned after continued protests. Similarly, plans for damming some of Chile's most spectacular rivers, including the Baker and Futaleufú, were scuttled in 2014.

Geography and climate

South of Puerto Montt the sea has broken through the coastal cordillera and drowned the central valley. The higher parts of the coastal cordillera form a maze of islands, stretching for over 1000 km and separated from the coast by tortuous fjords and *senos* (inlets). There is no real dry season near the coast, with annual rainfall of over 2000 mm on the offshore islands. Westerly winds are strong and temperatures vary little day to night.

The Andes are much lower in this region than they are further north, and eroded by glacial action; inland they form a high steppe around 1000 m, where the climate is drier, warm in summer and cold during the winter months. To the south of Coyhaique are two areas of highland covered by ice, known as *campos de hielo* (icefields). The Campo de Hielo Norte, over 100 km from north to south and some 50 km from east to west, includes the *ventisqueros* (glaciers) San Rafael, Montt and Steffens. The Campo de Hielo Sur covers a larger area, stretching south from the mouth of the Río Baker towards Puerto Natales.

Five main rivers flow westwards: from north to south these are the Futaleufú or Yelcho, the Palena, the Cisnes, the Simpson or Aysén and the Baker. The three largest lakes in this region, Lagos General Carrera, Cochrane and O'Higgins, are shared with Argentina.

Travelling along the Carretera Austral

The road can be divided into three sections: **Puerto Montt to Chaitén** (143 km), plus two ferry crossings; **Chaitén to Coyhaique** (445 km); and **Coyhaique to Villa O'Higgins** (559 km), plus one ferry crossing. There is also a main branch that runs along the southern shore of **Lago General Carrera** from Puerto Guadal to Chile Chico, as well as important branches to Futaleufú, Palena, Raúl Marín Balmaceda, Lago Verde, Puerto Cisnes, Puerto Aysén, Bahía Exploradores and Tortel. The Puerto Montt–Chaitén section can only be travelled in summer, when the ferries are operating, but three alternative routes exist year round, either direct by ferry from Puerto Montt to Chaitén, through Chiloé and then by boat to Chaitén, or overland through Argentina via Osorno, Bariloche, Esquel and Futaleufú. The road is paved just south of Chaitén and around Coyhaique, from just north of Villa Amengual to Villa Cerro Castillo and Puerto Ibáñez.

The condition of the road can vary dramatically depending on the time of year and amount of traffic. January and February are the best months to travel, with strong westerly winds but plenty of sunshine too. Some sections can be difficult or even impossible after heavy rain or snowfall, and widening/paving/repair work is constantly being undertaken. If you are driving, take a 4WD vehicle and fill up your tank whenever possible. Drivers should carry adequate fuel and spares, especially if intending to detour from the main route, and should protect their windscreens and headlamps. After heavy rain, parts of the Carretera are liable to flood, so check the weather carefully and be prepared to be stuck in one place for a few days while conditions improve.

Most of the **buses** that ply the Carretera Austral are minibuses (and in more than one case, converted transit vans) operated by small companies, and often they are driven by their owners. Services are less reliable than elsewhere in Chile and timetables change frequently. Booking your ticket in advance means that if your bus does not leave, for whatever reason, the company is liable to pay for your accommodation until the bus is ready to depart. Complaints should be directed to SERNAC, in Coyhaique.

Hitching is popular in summer, but extremely difficult out of season, particularly south of Cochrane. Watching the cloak of dust thrown up by the wheels from the back of a pickup, while taking in the lakes, forests, mountains and waterfalls, is an unforgettable experience, but be prepared for long delays, carry a tent and plenty of food and allow at least three days from Chaitén to Coyhaique.

The Carretera Austral is highly recommended for **cycling** as long as you have enough time and are reasonably fit. A good mountain bike is essential and a tent is an advantage. Most buses will take bicycles for a small charge.

Be sure to take enough cash. While there are Cirrus and MasterCard ATMs in Chaitén, Puerto Aysén and Cochrane, Coyhaique is the only place between Puerto Montt and Villa O'Higgins with Visa ATMs.

Puerto Montt to Chaitén

This 242-km section of the Carretera Austral is perhaps the most inaccessible and secluded stretch along the entire route, passing through two national parks and the private Parque Pumalín. Beautiful old trees close in on all sides, the rivers and streams sparkle, and on (admittedly rare) clear days, there are beautiful views across the Golfo de Ancud to Chiloé. The 2008-2009 eruptions of Volcán Chaitén caused considerable damage around the town of Chaitén, the effects of which can still be seen today.

Travelling from Puerto Montt to Chaitén → *Colour map 4, C2.*
This section of the route includes two ferry crossings at La Arena and Hornopirén. Before setting out, it is imperative to check when the ferries are running (weather conditions can alter itineraries) and, if driving, to make a reservation for your vehicle: do this in Puerto Montt (not Santiago), on the website of Transportes Austral, www.taustral.cl, which is a consortium of the three ferry companies that operate the routes, or at the offices of the ferry companies listed in Transport, page 368. Hitching to Chaitén takes several days, and there is a lot of competition for lifts: you must be prepared for a day's wait if you find yourself out of luck. The experience of riding in the back of a pickup, however, will make the hanging around worthwhile. An alternative route to Chaitén is by ferry from Puerto Montt or Castro/Quellón (see page 358).

South of Puerto Montt
The Carretera Austral (Ruta 7) heads east out of Puerto Montt through **Pelluco**, where there is a polluted bathing beach with black sand and some good seafood restaurants, and then follows the shore of the beautiful Seno de Reloncaví (Reloncaví Estuary, see page 326).

Between the sound to the south and west and Lago Chapo to the northeast is **Parque Nacional Alerce Andino** ① *entrances 2.5 km from Correntoso (35 km west of Puerto Montt) and 7 km west of Lenca (40 km south of Puerto Montt), T065-248 6101, loslagos.oirs@conaf.cl, US$2.65.* The park covers 39,255 ha of steep forested valleys rising to 1500 m and containing ancient alerce trees, some over 1000 years old (the oldest are estimated to be 4200 years old). There are also some 50 small lakes and many waterfalls in the park. Wildlife includes pudú, pumas, *vizcachas*, condors and black woodpeckers. **Lago Chapo** (5500 ha) feeds a hydroelectric power station at Canutillar, east of the park. There are ranger posts at Río Chaicas, Lago Chapo, Laguna Sargazo and at the north entrance. These can provide very little information, but a map is available from **CONAF** in Puerto Montt. To get to the north entrance, take a Fierro or Río Pato bus from Puerto Montt to Correntoso (or a **Lago Chapo** bus which passes through Correntoso) – there are several daily except Sunday – then walk. To reach the south entrance, take any bus from Puerto Montt to **Chaicas**, **La Arena**, **Contau** and **Hornopirén**, US$2.50, getting off at **Lenca** sawmill, then walk (signposted).

Some 45 km south of Puerto Montt (allow one hour), **La Arena** is the site of the first ferry, across the Reloncaví Estuary to **Puelche**. From Puelche there is an unpaved road east to Puelo, from where transport can be found north to Cochamó and Ralún (see page 326).

Hornopirén and around

Also called Río Negro, Hornopirén lies 54 km south of Puelche at the northern end of a fjord. Although a branch of the Carretera Austral runs round the edge of the fjord to Pichanco, 35 km further south, that route is a dead-end. Instead, to continue south you have to catch a ferry to Leptepu, travel 10 km by road to Fiordo Largo and then catch another ferry to Caleta Gonzalo. There is excellent fishing in the area and Hornopirén is a base for excursions to the **Hornopirén Volcano** (1572 m) and to **Lago Cabrera**, which lies further north. At the mouth of the fjord is **Isla Llancahué**, a small island with a hotel and thermal springs, good for hiking in the forests amid beautiful scenery. The island is reached from Hornopirén by **boat** ⓘ *US$60 one way shared between passengers, 50 mins;* look out for dolphins and fur seals on the crossing.

Parque Nacional Alerce Andino

Some 16 km by *ripio* road east of Hornopirén and covering 48,232 ha, **Parque Nacional Hornopirén** includes the **Yates Volcano** (2187 m) as well as the basins of two rivers, the Blanco and the Negro. The park protects some 9000 ha of alerce forest as well as areas of mixed native forest including lenga and coigue. From the entrance a path leads 8 km east up along the Río Blanco to a basic *refugio*.

Parque Pumalín and around

① *Information from Klenner 299, Puerto Varas, T065-225 0079; (in USA T415-229 9330), www.pumalinpark.cl. Open all year, free.*

Situated on the southern edge of the Fiordo Reñihue, Caleta Gonzalo is the base for visiting Parque Pumalín. Created by the US billionaire Douglas Tompkins and seen by many as one of the most important conservation projects in the world, this private reserve extends over 700,000 ha and is in two sectors: one just south of the Parque Nacional Hornopirén and the other stretching south and east of Caleta Gonzalo to the Argentine border. Much of this section of the park was covered in ash after the 2008-2009 eruptions of Volcán Chaitén. Its purchase aroused controversy, especially in the Chilean armed forces, who saw it as a threat to national sovereignty. Initially Tompkins was frustrated by stonewalling from the Chilean government, but progress has been made and the park now has nature sanctuary status.

Covering large areas of the western Andes, most of the park is occupied by temperate rainforest. The park is intended to protect the lifestyles of its inhabitants as well as the physical environment. Tompkins established a native tree nursery, producing 100,000 saplings of native endangered species, and developed apiculture. There are treks ranging from short trails into the temperate rainforest to hikes lasting for several days (these are very arduous). The trail heads are all on the main road. Three marked trails lead to a waterfall, **Cascadas Escondidas**; to an area of very old alerce trees; and to **Laguna Tronador**. The road through these forests was only built in the 1980s, meaning that, unlike areas to the north and south, endangered trees have been protected from logging (laws protecting alerces, araucaria and other native species were passed in the 1970s). As a result, Parque Pumalín is home to perhaps the most diverse temperate rainforest in the world, and is the only place where alerce forests remain intact just a few metres from the main road. It is a truly humbling experience looking up from the base of a 3000-year-old, 3-m-wide alerce, and this, in itself, is a reason to visit the park. There are weekly buses and hitching is not difficult in season.

The Carretera Austral runs through the park, climbing steeply before reaching two lakes, **Lago Río Negro** and **Lago Río Blanco**. The coast is reached at **Santa Bárbara**, 48 km south, where there is a black sand beach. Towards sunset dolphins often swim right up to the beach. You can join them, although the water is very cold.

Chaitén

Chaitén lies in a beautiful spot, with a forest-covered hill rising behind it, and a quiet inlet leading out into the Patagonian channels. In many ways Chaitén is a cultural crossroads. Until relatively recently, the town had more contact with Argentina than the central Chilean mainland, while a Chilote influence is clear in the town's architecture. Indeed until the construction of the Carretera this area was known as Chiloé Continental and was governed as part of the island opposite.

In May 2008, Volcán Chaitén, previously thought to be extinct, erupted, spewing a 20-cm layer of ash over the surrounding countryside and causing the Río Blanco to shift its banks. It flooded most of the town of Chaitén, destroying many buildings and covering much of the town with a thick layer of volcanic mud. A further eruption followed in February 2009. The government decided to abandon Chaitén, cutting off utilities, moving the seat of provincial government to Futaleufú and starting to rebuild the town 10 km north at Santa Bárbara. Chaitén, however, survived with running water, generators and fuel, and in 2011 the government reversed former decisions and the town was reestablished in the northern part of the old town. There are shops, *hospedajes* and *cabañas* and good transport links: ferries to Puerto Montt and Chiloé (see page 368), flights and buses. See www.camaraturismochaiten.cl (in English) and www.munichaiten.cl.

There is excellent fishing nearby, especially to the south in the Ríos Yelcho and Futaleufú and in Lagos Espolón and Yelcho.

⊙ Puerto Montt to Chaitén listings

For hotel and restaurant price codes and other relevant information, see pages 14-21.

◉ Where to stay

South of Puerto Montt *p364*
There are basic *refugios* at Río Pangal, Laguna Sargazo and Laguna Fría in the Parque Nacional Alerce Andino; no camping is permitted inside the boundaries of the park.

$$$$ Alerce Mountain Lodge, Km 36 Carretera Austral, T065-228 6969, www. mountainlodge.cl. In Los Alerces de Lenca private reserve, beside Parque Nacional Alerce Andino, remote lodge, rooms and cabins, all-inclusive 2- to 4-night packages, with hiking, guides speak English, good food.

Hornopirén and around *p365*
$$$$ Hotel Termas de Llancahué, Isla Llancahué, T09-9642 4857, www.termas dellancahue.cl. Full board (excellent food), hot spring at the hotel, excursions by boat, fishing, kayaking.
$$ Hornopirén, Carrera Pinto 388, T065-221 7256, h.hornopiren@gmail.com. Rooms with shared bath, also *cabañas* and restaurant at the water's edge.
$$ Hostería Catalina, Ingenieros Militares s/n, T065-221 7359, www.hosteriacatalina.cl. Comfortable rooms and *cabañas*, meals, excursions, a good place to stay.
For a full list, see www.hornopiren.net.

Camping
There's a good site on Ingenieros Militares, and more sites south of Hornopirén on the road to Pichanco.

Parque Pumalín and around *p366*
There is a restaurant, *cabañas* and a campsite in Caleta Gonzalo, as well as a visitor centre (not always open) and demonstrations of agricultural techniques in the region. Camping is available in the park at several well-run sites from US$4.50 per tent.

Chaitén *p366*
Among many places to stay are: **Cabañas Brisas del Mar** (Corcovado 278, T09-9115 8808, cababrisas@telsur.cl); **Cabañas Pudú** (Corcovado 668, T09-8227 9602, puduchaiten@hotmail.com); **Casa de Rita** (Riveros y Prat, T09-9778 2351, ritagutierrezgarcia@hotmail.es); **El Refugio** (Corcovado y Juan Todesco); **Hostería Corcovado** (Corcovado 408, T09-8868 4922); **Hospedaje Don Carlos** (Riveros 53, T09-9128 3328, doncarlos.palena@gmail. com); **Hostería Llanos** (Corcovado 378, T09-8826 0498), and **Shilling** (Corcovado 258, T065-226 0680, hotelschilling@hotmail. com). See www.camaraturismochaiten.cl.

◑ What to do

Chaitén *p366*
Chaitur, O'Higgins 67, T09-7468 5608, www.chaitur.com. Nicholas La Penna runs this agency making bus, boat, plane and hotel reservations, tours to hot springs, glaciers, beaches, Carretera Austral, photography trips. Still the place for local information. English and French spoken, helpful, book exchange, internet.

⊖ Transport

South of Puerto Montt *p364*
Bus
There are buses from Puerto Montt to **Correntoso** and **Lago Chapo**, with **Fierro** or **Río Pato**, several daily Mon-Sat. There are also services to **Chaicas**, **La Arena**, **Contau** and **Hornopirén**.

Ferry
From La Arena, 2 roll-on, roll-off ferries cross the Reloncaví Estuary to **Puelche**, every 45 mins daily 0645-0030, 30 mins, US$17 for a car, US$12.50 for motorcycle, US$5 for bicycle, US$1 for foot passengers. Arrive at least 30 mins early to guarantee a place; buses have priority. See www. taustral.cl, or contact **Naviera Puelche**, Av Italia 2326, Parque San Andrés, Puerto Montt, T065-227 0761, www. navierapuelche.cl, or **Naviera Paredes**, T065-227 6490, www.navieraparedes.cl.

Hornopirén and around *p365*
Bus
To **Puerto Montt**, **Kémel** (T065-225 3530) has 4 services daily Mon-Sat, 2 on Sun; **M&M** has 2 daily Mon-Sat, 1 on Sun, US$7.25.

Ferry
Hornopirén to **Chaitén** via Leptepu (once daily each way, twice in high season) and Fiordo Largo to **Caleta Gonzalo** (twice

daily each way, 4 in high season): check on www.taustral.cl, or with **Naviera Puelche** (T065-221 7266 in Hornopirén, T07-475 1168 in Ayacara) for updated schedules. If driving your own car, it is essential to reserve a place: cars US$54.50, motorbikes US$13.65, bicycles US$9, car passengers US$9, bus passengers US$4.50; one fare covers both ferries.

Chaitén *p366*
Air
Daily flights (except Sun) between Puerto Montt and Santa Bárbara with **Aerocord** (19 passengers), US$75.

Bus
Terminal at Chaitur, O'Higgins 67. **Kémel** (as above) have a daily bus/ferry service from **Puerto Montt**, 0700, US$25, 9 hrs, return from Chaitén 1200. To **Coyhaique**, twice a week direct with **Becker**, also **Terraustral**, direct in summer, 12 hrs; otherwise travel via **La Junta** (overnight stop), Mon, Tue, Fri, Sat 0930, with connections to **Puyuhuapi** and **Coyhaique** next day. Minibuses usually travel full, so can't pick up passengers en route. Buses to **Futaleufú**, Fri-Wed 0930; change here for buses to the Argentine border.

Ferry
The ferry port is about 1 km north of town. Schedules change frequently and ferries are infrequent off season. Check with **Naviera Austral**, Corcovado 466, T065-273 1011, www.navieraustral.cl or on www.taustral.cl for all future sailings.

To **Chiloé**, Naviera Austral operates ferry services to **Quellón** or **Castro** (Jan-Feb only), once a week, more in summer (Dec-Mar); fares given under Quellón, see page 358.

To **Puerto Montt**, Naviera Austral, Mon-Fri via Ayacara, 10 hrs, passengers US$29, cabin US$55-62, car US$156, motorbike US$36, bicycle US$11.

Chaitén to Coyhaique

This section of the Carretera Austral, 422 km long, runs through long stretches of virgin rainforest, passing small villages, the perfectly still waters of Lago Yelcho, and the Parque Nacional Queulat, with its glaciers and waterfalls. Roads branch off east to the Argentine border and west to Puerto Cisnes. Near Coyhaique, the road passes huge tracts of land destroyed by logging, where only tree stumps remain as testament to the depredations of the early colonists.

Amarillo

At Amarillo, 25 km south of Chaitén, there is a turning to the **Termas de Amarillo** ① *5 km east*, which consists of two wooden sheds with a very hot pool inside, and an outdoor swimming pool – worth a visit. There is superb salmon fishing in the nearby rivers. From here, it is possible to hike along the old trail to Futaleufú (see below). The hike takes four to seven days and is not for the inexperienced; be prepared for wet feet all the way. The trail follows the Río Michinmawida, passing the volcano of the same name, to **Lago Espolón** (see below). A ferry with a sporadic schedule crosses the lake, taking cargo, foot passengers and bicycles to Futaleufú.

Puerto Cárdenas and Lago Yelcho

Situated 46 km south of Chaitén and surrounded by forest, **Puerto Cárdenas** lies on the northern tip of **Lago Yelcho**, a beautiful glacial lake on the Río Futaleufú, surrounded by hills and with views of the stunning Yelcho glacier. The lake is frequented by anglers for its salmon and trout. Further south at Km 60, a path leads to the **Yelcho glacier**, a two-hour walk each way (there is a viewing station halfway up). There is a campsite here. The administrator charges people US$3.50 to walk to the glacier; whether he is legally allowed to do this is a contentious issue.

Towards Argentina → *For listings, see pages 374-376.*

Southeast of Chaitén the Argentine border is reached in two places, Futaleufú and Palena, along a road that branches off the Carretera Austral at **Villa Santa Lucía** (Km 81), named after General Pinochet's wife, where there are 30 houses, a military camp and one small shop; bread is available from a private house. The road to the border is *ripio* of variable standard, passable in a regular car, but best with a good, strong high-clearance vehicle. The scenery is beautiful. At **Puerto Ramírez**, at the southern end of **Lago Yelcho**, the road divides: the north branch runs along the valley of the Río Futaleufú to Futaleufú, while the southern one continues to Palena. See box, page 371.

Futaleufú

Futaleufú has established itself as the centre for the finest whitewater rafting in the southern hemisphere. Every year, hundreds of fanatics travel to spend the southern summer here and there is no shortage of operators offering trips. The river is an incredible deep blue and offers everything from easy Grade II-III sections downstream to the extremely challenging Grade V Cañón del Infierno (Hell Canyon). Although the town is only at 350 m, the spectacular mountain scenery makes you feel as if you were up in the High Andes. The Río Espolón provides a peaceful backdrop to this pleasant town, with wide streets lined with shrubs and roses and Chilote-style houses. There is **tourist information** ① *on the plaza at O'Higgins and Prat, T065-272 1629, www.futaleufu.cl, Oct-Apr, 0900-2100*, which sells fishing licences. **Lago Espolón**, west of Futaleufú, is reached by a turning 41 km northeast of Puerto Ramírez. It is a beautiful lake and enjoys a warm microclimate, regularly reaching 30°C in the day in summer. The lake is even warm enough for a quick dip, but beware of the currents.

Futaleufú

Where to stay 🛏
Adolfo B&B **1**
Cabañas Río Espolón **2**
Continental **4**
El Barranco **5**
Hostería Río Grande **6**

Restaurants 🍴
Futaleufú **1**
Martín Pescador **2**
Sur Andes **3**

La Junta and around

From Villa Santa Lucía, the Carretera Austral follows the Río Frío and then the Río Palena to La Junta, a tranquil, nondescript village at the confluence of Río Rosselot and Río Palena, 151 km south of Chaitén. La Junta has a service station for fuel and a minimarket. Some 9 km east is **Lago Rosselot**, surrounded by forest and situated at the heart of a *reserva nacional* (12,725 ha) with a well-equipped campsite and cabins. From here, the road continues east for 74 km, to the border crossing at picturesque **Lago Verde** ① *summer 0800-2200, winter 0800-2000*, and on to Las Pampas in Argentina. There is also a road leading northwest from La Junta, past some rustic thermal springs (not always open), across the broad expanse of the Río Palena (four ferry crossings daily) and on to **Puerto Raúl Marín Balmaceda** on the coast, a tranquil fishing village with more than its share of rainfall. Different species of dolphin can be seen, and when it is clear there are wonderful views of Volcán

Border crossing: Chile–Argentina

Paso Futaleufú

Chilean immigration Open 0800-2000, is on the border, 8 km east of Futaleufú (see www.pasosfronterizos.gov.cl/cf_futaleufu.html). The border is just west of the bridge over the Río Grande: straightforward crossing. There is nowhere to change money at the border but you can pay the bus fare to Esquel (Argentina) in US dollars. If entering Chile, change money in Futaleufú (poor rates), and then continue from Futaleufú towards Puerto Ramírez; outside Ramírez, take the right turn to Chaitén, otherwise you'll end up back at the border in Palena.

Paso Palena

Chilean immigration Open 0800-2000, is 8 km west of the border. It is much quieter than the crossing at Futaleufú. Note If entering from Argentina, no fresh produce may be brought into Chile. Check conditions locally before crossing at this border.

Trevelin is 45 km east of Futaleufú, 95 km east of Palena. It is an offshoot of the Welsh Chubút colony on the Atlantic side of Argentine Patagonia, as featured in Bruce Chatwin's *In Patagonia*. It has accommodation, restaurants, tea rooms and a tourist office, but there is a much wider range of services at Esquel, 23 km northeast. Esquel is a base for visiting the Argentine Parque Nacional Los Alerces. There are also transport connections to Bariloche and other destinations in Argentine Patagonia.

Melimoyu from the beach. Accommodation is available and camping is possible. Raúl Marín forms one apex of the blue whale triangle, and the giant cetacean can sometimes be sighted on the ferry to Quellón in the summer.

Puyuhuapi and around → *For listings, see pages 374-376.*

From La Junta, the Carretera Austral runs south along the western side of Lago Risopatrón, past several waterfalls, to Puyuhuapi (also spelt Puyuguapi), 45 km further south. Located in a beautiful spot at the northern end of the Puyuhuapi fjord, the village is a tranquil stopping place, about halfway between Chaitén and Coyhaique with phone, fuel, shops, but no banks (some hotels may change dollars). It was founded by four Sudeten German families in 1935, and its economy is based around fishing, ever-increasing tourism and the factory where Puyuhuapi's famous handmade carpets are produced and which can be visited: **Alfombras de Puyuhuapi** ① *T067-632 5131, www.puyuhuapi.com, daily in summer 0830-1930, closed lunch, English spoken.* By the municipalidad on the main street there is a decent **tourist information office** ① *www.puertopuyuhuapi.cl, in season Mon-Sat 1000-1400, 1600-1900.* A bus timetable is pinned up here. If you are travelling in your own vehicle, ask at the police station about road conditions and temporary road closures.

From Puyuhuapi, the road follows the eastern edge of the fjord along one of the most beautiful sections of the Carretera Austral, with views of the **Termas de Puyuhuapi** ① *18 km southwest of Puyuhuapi; day packages including lunch and transfer, US$87.50.* This resort is on the western edge of the fjord and is accessible only by boat. It has several 40°C springs filling three pools near the beach. The resort can be visited as part of a three- to five-day package with **Patagonia Connection SA/Puyuhuapi Lodge & Spa** (see page 374) and day trips are possible from Puyuhuapi. More easily accessible are the **Termas del Ventisqero** ⓘ *6 km south of Puyuhuapi by the side of the Carretera overlooking the fjord, T09-7966 6862, www.termasventisqueropuyuhuapi.cl, daily until 2300 in season, US$14.50.* A café is open during the day.

Parque Nacional Queulat

ⓘ *Administration at the CONAF office in La Junta, T067-221 2225, aysen.oirs@conaf.cl, Dec-Mar daily 0830-2100, rest of year 0830-1830, US$7, reductions for Chileans and children.*

Covering 154,093 ha of attractive forest around Puyuhuapi, the **Parque Nacional Queulat** is, supposedly, the former location of the legendary Ciudad de los Césares, a fabulously wealthy mythological city built between two hills made of gold and diamonds and inhabited by immortal beings. According to legend, the city was protected by a shroud of fog and hence was impossible for strangers to discover. The Carretera Austral passes through the park, close to **Lago Risopatrón** north of Puyuhuapi, where boat trips are available. Some 22 km south of Puyuhapi, a road turns off to the main entrance of the park, continuing for 3.5 km past the guardaparques' hut to a campsite and car park. Three walks begin from here: a short stroll through the woodland to a viewpoint of the spectacular **Ventisquero Colgante** hanging glacier; or cross the river where the path begins to **Laguna Tempanos**, where boats cross the lake in summer. The third trail, 3.25 km, takes 2½ hours to climb to a panoramic viewpoint of the **Ventisquero**, where you can watch the ice fall into huge waterfalls.

The Carretera Austral climbs out of the Queulat valley towards the Portezuelo de Queulat pass through a series of narrow hairpin bends surrounded by an impressive dense jungle-like mass of giant Nalcas. There are fine views of the forest and several glaciers. Near the pass (250 m off the main road) is the **Salto Pedro García** waterfall, with the **Salto del Cóndor** waterfall some 5 km further on. Steep gradients mean that crossing the park is the hardest part of the Carretera for those travelling by bicycle.

On the southern side of the pass there is a sign labelled **Bosque Encantado** with a small parking area. A path leads west through a forest of Arayanes, like something out of a fairytale. After crossing a series of small bridges the path runs out at the river. Follow the river bank around to the right to get to a beautiful laguna with floating icebergs and a hanging glacier. The trek to the laguna and back should not take more than three hours and is well worth the effort.

The Río Cisnes and further south

Stretching 160 km from the Argentine border to the coast at Puerto Cisnes, the Río Cisnes is recommended for rafting or canoeing, with grand scenery and modest rapids – except for the horrendous drop at Piedra del Gato, about 60 km east of Puerto Cisnes. Good camping is available in the forest. Possibly the wettest town in Chile, **Puerto Cisnes** is reached by a 33-km winding road that branches west off the Carretera Austral about 59 km south of Puyuhuapi. Once a peaceful fishing port where traditional knitted clothes were made, it is now an important salmon-farming centre. Fuel is available.

Fifteen kilometres further on, at Km 92, south of **Villa Amengual**, a road branches west for 104 km to the **Argentine border** via La Tapera, see box, page 376.

Reserva Nacional Lago Las Torres is 98 km south of Puyuhuapi and covers 16,516 ha. There are no trails, but it includes the wonderful **Lago Las Torres**, which offers good fishing and a small *hospedaje* and campsite. Further south, at Km 125, a road branches east to **El Toqui**, where zinc is mined.

Laguna San Rafael

Situated west of Lago General Carrera and some 200 km south of Puerto Aysén, Laguna San Rafael is one of the highlights for many travellers to Chile. The **Ventisquero San Rafael**, one of a group of four glaciers that emanate in all directions from Monte San Valentín in the giant **Campo de Hielo Norte**, flows into the Laguna, which, in turn, empties into the sea northwards via the Río Tempano. About 45 km in length and towering 30 m above water level, the deep blue glacier groans and cracks as it calves icebergs, which are carried across the Laguna and out to sea. Around the shores of the lake is thick vegetation and above are snowy mountain peaks.

Laguna San Rafael and the Campo de Hielo Norte are part of the **Parque Nacional Laguna San Rafael**, which extends over 1,740,000 ha, and is a UN World Biosphere Reserve. In the national park are puma, pudú, foxes, dolphins, occasional sea lions and sea otters, and many species of bird. Walking trails are limited (about 10 km in all) but a lookout platform has been constructed, with fine views of the glacier. There is also a small ranger station that provides information, and a pier. The rangers are willing to row you out to the glacier in calm weather, an awesome three-hour adventure, past icebergs and swells created when huge chunks of ice break off the glacier and crash into the Laguna. Sadly, the glacier is disintegrating and is predicted to disappear entirely; some suggest that the wake from tour boats is contributing to the erosion.

The only access is by plane or boat; either provides spectacular views. Official cruises from Puerto Montt are run by Skorpios (see page 336) and Compañía Naviera Puerto Montt; various private yachts for six to 12 passengers can also be chartered. From Puerto Chacabuco, cruises to the Laguna are run throughout the year by Navimag (www.navimag.com), and from Septermber to April by Catamaranes del Sur (www.catamaranesdelsur.cl), see page 383 for company contact details. Local fishing boats from Puerto Chacabuco and Puerto Aysén take about 18-20 hours each way and charge a little less than the tourist boats; ask at the port. Note that these unauthorized boats may have neither adequate facilities nor a licence for the trip. Trips to Laguna San Rafael out of season are very difficult to arrange.

Villa Mañihuales, at Km 148, is a small, nondescript town with a Copec petrol station and several basic *residenciales* and restaurants. Most buses stop here for 15 to 30 minutes. Nearby is the **Reserva Forestal Mañihuales**. The reserve covers 1206 ha and encompasses a huemul sanctuary. Fires largely destroyed the forests in the 1940s but reforestation is being studied here.

For hotel and restaurant price codes and other relevant information, see pages 14-21.

Where to stay

Amarillo *p369*
$ Residencial Marcela, Amarillo, T065-226 4442. Also *cabañas* and camping.

Puerto Cárdenas and Lago Yelcho *p369*
There are no shops or restaurants in Puerto Cárdenas, but Viola, T09-9884 2946, a bungalow next to the old carabinero post, offers half board (**$$**) with excellent food.
$$$ Cabañas Yelcho en La Patagonia, Lago Yelcho, 7 km south of Puerto Cárdenas, T065-257 6005, www.yelcho.cl. Cabins and rooms on the lake shore. Also expensive campsite and cafeteria.
$$ Residencial Yelcho, Puerto Cárdenas, T09-8243 5928. Clean, full board available.

Towards Argentina *p369*
$ Residencial La Chilenita, Pudeto 681, Palena, T065-274 1212. Simple rooms.
$ Sra Rosalía Cuevas de Ruiz, No 7, Villa Santa Lucía. Basic, meals available. One of several options on the main street in Villa Santa Lucía; none has hot water.

Futaleufú *p369, map p370*
$$$$ El Barranco, O'Higgins 172, T065-272 1314, www.elbarrancochile.cl. Elegant rustic rooms, luxurious, pool, sauna, good restaurant, and expert fishing guides, horses and bikes for hire.
$$$ Río Grande, O'Higgins y Aldea, T065-272 1320, www.pachile.com. Also upmarket, spacious attractive rooms, international restaurant, popular with rafting groups.
$$$ Cabañas Río Espolón, follow Cerda to the end, T065-272 1423. Cosy *cabañas* in secluded riverside setting, restaurant overlooking Río Espolón, *parrilla*, bar. Popular with river-rafting groups, book ahead.

$$-$ Adolfo B&B, O'Higgins 302, T065-272 1256, lodeva@surnet.cl. Best value in this range, comfortable rooms in family home, shared hot showers.
$ pp Continental, Balmaceda 595, T065-272 1222. Oldest in town, no breakfast, basic, but clean and welcoming.

Camping
Aldea Puerto Espolón, Sector La Puntilla, 400 m from town, T065-272 1509, www.aldeapuertoespolon.blogspot.com. Teepees, dome-tents or your own tent, take sleeping bag, hot showers. Several other campsites.

La Junta and around *p370*
$$$ Espacio y Tiempo, T067-231 4141, www.espacioytiempo.cl. Spacious rooms, warm and cosy atmosphere, restaurant, attractive gardens, fishing expeditions.
$$ Residencial Copihue, Varas 611, T067-231 4184. Some rooms with bath, good meals.
$$-$ Hostería Valdera, Varas s/n, T067-231 4105, luslagos@hotmail.com. Private bath, meals served. Excellent value.
$$-$ Residencial Patagonia, Lynch 331, T067-231 4120. Good meals, small rooms, limited bathrooms.

Puyuhuapi and around *p371*
$$$$ Puyuhuapi Lodge and Spa, reservations T02-2225 6489, www.puyuhuapilodge.com. Splendidly isolated on a nook in the sea fjord, the hotel owns the outdoor thermal baths and indoor spa complex. Good packages for de-stressing with riding, fishing, kayaking, trekking, mountain biking, yoga and the thermals included.
$$$-$$ Casa Ludwig, Otto Uebel 202, T067-232 5220, www.casaludwig.cl. Cheaper with shared bath. Open Oct-Mar; enquire in advance at other times. In a beautiful 4-storey house built by first German settlers, wonderful views, a range of rooms, good breakfast, comfortable;

charming owner Luisa is knowledgeable about the area, speaks German and English.
$$ Aonikenk, Hamburgo 16, T067-232 5208, aonikenkturismo@yahoo.com. Pleasant heated rooms or *cabañas* (not sound-proofed), good beds, meals, helpful, informative, bike hire.
$$ Hostería Alemana, Otto Uebel 450, T067-232 5118, www.hosteriaalemana.cl. A large traditional wooden house on the main road by the water, very comfortable, lovely lake views and garden.

Parque Nacional Queulat *p372*
$$$ El Pangue, 18 km north of Puyuhuapi, Km 240, at end of Lago Risopatrón, T067-252 6906, www.elpangue.com. Rooms and luxurious *cabañas* for 4 to 7 in splendid rural setting, fishing, horse riding, trekking, mountain bikes, pool, sauna, hot tubs, great views, restful.

Camping
There's a **CONAF** campsite at Lago Risopatrón.

The Río Cisnes and further south *p372*
$$$-$$ Cabañas Río Cisnes, Costanera 101, Puerto Cisnes, T067-234 6404, andromeda346@hotmail.com. Cabins sleep 4 to 8. Owner, Juan Suazo, offers sea fishing trips in his boat.
$$ Hostería El Gaucho, Holmberg 140, Puerto Cisnes, T067-234 6514. With bath and breakfast, dinner available. Puerto Cisnes also has various *cabañas* and *residenciales*.
$ pp Hospedaje El Encanto, Pasaje Plaza 3, Villa Amengual, T09-9144 8662, hugomancillaopazo@hotmail.com. With restaurant and café, one of several cheap options in Villa Amengual.

⑦ Restaurants

Futaleufú *p369, map p370*
$$ Futaleufú, Cerda 407, T065-272 1295. Serves typical Chilean meat dishes and local foods.

$$ Martín Pescador, Balmaceda y Rodríguez, T065-272 1279. For fish and meat dishes, rustic.
$$-$ Sur Andes, Cerda 308, T065-272 1405. Café serving cakes, sweets, light meals and real coffee. Also sells handicrafts.

Puyuhuapi and around *p371*
$$ Café Rossbach, Costanera. Run by the descendants of the original German settlers, an attractive place by the water for delicious salmon, tea and *Küchen*.
$$ Lluvia Marina, next to Casa Ludwig, veronet@entelchile.net. The best café, also selling handicrafts. Superb food in relaxed atmosphere, a great place to just hang out, owner Veronica is very helpful.

The Río Cisnes and further south *p372*
$ K-Cos Café Restaurante, Prat 270, Puerto Cisnes. Good snacks.

⊛ Festivals

Futaleufú *p369, map p370*
Late Feb Futa Festival. Rafting and kayaking races on the river.

⦿ What to do

Puerto Cárdenas and Lago Yelcho *p369*
Martín Pescador Lodge, www.martinpescadorfishing.com. Offers packages at 3 lodges, on Lago Yelcho, near La Junta and on Lago Verde.

Futaleufú *p369, map p370*
Tour operators arrange whitewater rafting trips, prices starting from US$75 pp. There are good fishing opportunities on Río Futaleufú and Lago Espolón (ask for the Valebote family's motorboat on the lake); local fishing guides can also be found in the village.
Expediciones Chile, Mistral 296, T065-256 2639 (in US T1-208-629 5032), www.exchile.com. Whitewater rafting, kayaking, etc.

Border crossing: Chile–Argentina

La Tapera

Chilean immigration is 12 km west of the border and is open summer 0800-2200, winter 0800-2000. For information on the Argentine side, see http://www.gendarmeria.gov.ar/pasos/chile/fichriofrias.html.

On the Argentine side, the road continues, unmade, through the village of Apeleg to meet up with Route 40, the main north–south road at the foot of the Andes. This stretch of road has few services for fuel or food and there is no public transport.

Offers the best multi-day trips, book in advance. Day trips can be booked at office. **Futaleufú Explore**, O'Higgins 772, T09-7433 4455, www.futaleufuexplore.com. A respected rafting company.
Rancho Las Ruedas, Pilota Carmona 337, T09-7735 0989, guide.stallion@gmail.com. The best horse riding in the area.

The Río Cisnes and further south *p372*
There's good fishing around Puerto Cisnes; contact **Cabañas Río Cisnes** (see Where to stay, above).

⊙ Transport

Futaleufú *p369, map p370*
Bus
To **Chaitén**, 6 days a week, information from **Chaitur** in Chaitén (see page 368). A Jacobsen bus departs from west side of plaza to the Argentine border, 3 times a week Mar-Dec, and Mon-Fri in Jan-Feb, US$4, 30 mins, connecting with services to **Trevelin** and **Esquel**. Frontera del Sur buses run between Futaleufú and **Palena**, T065-272 1360.

La Junta and around *p370*
Bus
To **Chaitén**, 4 a week, information from Chaitur (see page 368). To **Coyhaique**,

with **Daniela** (T09-9512 3500), **Becker** (T067-224 2626), and **Aguilas Patagónicas**, 7 hrs, US$18.50-22. To **Puerto Cisnes**, with **Empresa Entre Verde** (T067-231 4275), US$10.

Puyuhuapi and around *p371*
Bus
Daily to **Coyhaique**, US$14.50-16.50, 6 hrs, plus 2 weekly to **Lago Verde**.

The Río Cisnes and further south *p372*
Bus
Aguilas Patagónicas and **Sao Paulo**, run daily between Puerto Cisnes and **Coyhaique** (on Sun towards Coyhaique only), US$9-11.

⊙ Directory

Futaleufú *p369, map p370*
Banks **Banco del Estado**, ATM accepts MasterCard but not Visa. Changing foreign currency is difficult, but US dollars and Argentine pesos are accepted in many places. **Medical services** Hospital, Balmaceda y Aldea, T065-272 1231.

Coyhaique and around

Located 420 km south of Chaitén, Coyhaique (also spelt Coihaique) lies in the broad green valley of the Río Simpson. The city is encircled by a crown of mountains and, for a few hours after it has rained, the mountainsides are covered in a fine layer of frost – a spectacular sight. Founded in 1929, it is the administrative and commercial centre of Región XI and is the only settlement of any real size on the Carretera Austral (with a population of just nearly 60,000). The constant call of chickens in people's gardens gives away the fact that much of the population are recent arrivals from a very distinct and slowly disappearing lifestyle in the surrounding countryside, while the number of bow-legged elderly men making their way slowly about town is indicative of a generation who feel more comfortable on horseback than on foot. A rapidly growing and increasingly lively city, it also provides a good base for day excursions in the area. Rafting down the Río Simpson is a memorable experience, while in the Reserva Nacional Río Simpson there are picturesque waterfalls and the occasional sighting of the elusive huemul. Note that there are no Visa ATMs south of Coyhaique, so stock up on cash here if you are heading south.

Arriving in Coyhaique → *Colour map 5, B3.*

Getting there There are two airports in the Coyhaique area: **Teniente Vidal** ① *5 km southwest of town*, handles only smaller aircraft; **Balmaceda** ① *56 km southeast of Coyhaique via paved road, 5 km from the Argentine border at Paso Huemules, 1 hr*, is the most direct way into Coyhaique from Santiago or Puerto Montt, with several flights daily. However, there is no bus service between Balmaceda and Coyhaique; instead minibuses, known as *transfers*, ply this route, stopping at hotels; contact **Transfer & Turismo** ① *Cochrane 387, T067-225 6600*, or **Transfer Valencia** ① *Lautaro 828, T067-223 3030, www.transfervalencia.cl; both charge US$9 per person and sell tickets at the airport baggage carousel*. A taxi from Balmaceda to Coyhaique takes one hour and costs US$30. Car rental agencies at the airport are very expensive and closed on Sunday.

Ferries (one or two a week) make the journey from Puerto Montt or Chiloé to Puerto Chacabuco, 77 km west of Coyhaique.

Within Región XI, Coyhaique is the transport hub. There is a **main bus terminal** ① *Lautaro y Magallanes, T067-225 5726*, but most buses leave from their own offices. **Buses** (several weekly) to Puerto Montt have to take the route via Argentina, which is long and expensive. There are also one or two weekly buses to Comodoro Rivadavia and south to Punta Arenas. There are regular minibuses north to Chaitén or Futaleufú, and daily services south to Cochrane, as well as minibuses connecting with the ferry at Puerto Ibáñez for Chile Chico (daily; see page 382).

Tourist information English is spoken at the very helpful **Sernatur office** ① *Bulnes 35, T067-223 1752, infoaisen@sernatur.cl, Mon-Fri 0830-1730, high season Mon-Fri 0830-2000, Sat-Sun 1000-1800,* which has up-to-date bus timetables. There's also a privately run information kiosk on the plaza in summer, as well as **CONAF** ① *Ogana 1060, T067-221 2109, aysen.oirs@conaf.cl, Mon-Fri 0830-1730.*

Places in and around Coyhaique

Although a visit to the tourist office will throw up far more attractions outside Coyhaique than in the town itself, this is a pleasant, friendly place, perfect for relaxing for a couple of days or as a base for day trips. The town centre is an unusual pentagonal plaza, on which stand the cathedral, the Intendencia and a handicraft market. The plaza was built in 1945, supposedly inspired by the Place de l'Étoile in Paris. Two blocks northeast of the plaza at Baquedano y Ignacio Serrano, there is a monument to El Ovejero (the shepherd). Further north on Baquedano is a display of old military machinery outside the local regimental

Coyhaique

200 metres

200 yards

N

Where to stay
1 Belisario Jara
2 Cabañas Baquedano
3 Cabañas Mirador
4 Cabañas Río Simpson
5 Cabañas San Sebastián
6 El Reloj
8 Hostal Bon
9 Hostal Las Quintas
11 Las Salamandras
13 San Sebastián

Restaurants
1 Café Oriente
2 Casino de Bomberos
3 Club Sandwich Patagonia
4 Donde Ramiro
5 El Mastique
6 Histórico Ricer & Café Ricer
7 La Casona
8 Pizzería La Fiorentina

Bars & clubs
9 Pepe le Pub
10 Piel Roja

Border crossings: Chile–Argentina

Coyhaique Alto

This crossing is 43 km east of Coyhaique. Chilean immigration is 6 km west of the border, open summer 0800-2200, winter 0800-2000 (www.pasosfronterizos.gov.cl/cf_coyhaiquealto.html). It is reached by a *ripio* road that runs east of Coyhaique past the **Monumento Natural Dos Lagunas**, US$3.50, a small park that encompasses Lagos El Toro and Escondido with black-necked swans among the wildlife that can be seen from the short interpretive trails.

On the Argentine side, the road leads through Río Mayo and Sarmiento to Comodoro Rivadavia on the Atlantic seaboard.

Paso Huemules

This crossing is 61 km southeast of Coyhaique, open summer 0800-2200, winter 0800-2000 (www.pasosfronterizos.gov.cl/cf_balmaceda.html). It is reached by a paved road, Route 245, which runs southeast from Coyhaique, via Balmaceda airport. There is no accommodation at the frontier or at the airport and no public transport between the border and the airport. On the Argentine side, a *ripio* road runs via Lago Blanco (has fuel) to join Route 40, 105 km east of Paso Huemules.

headquarters. In the Casa de Cultura the **Museo Regional de la Patagonia Central** ① *Lillo 23, T067-221 3175, Tue-Sun summer 0900-2000, winter 0830-1730, US$1*, has sections on history, mineralogy, zoology and archaeology, as well as photos of the construction of the Carretera Austral (no information in English). Near the city, on the east bank of the Río Simpson, is the **Piedra del Indio**, a rock outcrop which, allegedly, looks like a face in profile. This is best viewed from the Puente Simpson, west bank of the Río Simpson.

There are two national reserves close to Coyhaique. Five kilometres northwest off the Carretera Austral is **Reserva Nacional Coyhaique** ① *information from CONAF, Oct-Apr daily 0830-1700, US$5.50, camping (US$8)*, which covers 2150 ha of forest (mainly introduced species) and has a number of well-marked trails of between 20 minutes and five hours. The walks to Laguna Verde and Laguna Venus are particularly recommended. Follow Baquedano to the end, over the bridge, and past the guardeparque's hut to where all the trails begin.

Around the valley of the Río Simpson west of Coyhaique (take any bus to Puerto Aysén) is the **Reserva Nacional Río Simpson** ① *administration office is 32 km west of Coyhaique, just off the road, campsite opposite turning to Santuario San Sebastián (US$7)*, covering 40,827 ha of steep forested valleys and curiously rounded hills rising to 1878 m. One of these, near the western edge of the park, is known as '*El Cake Inglés*'. There are beautiful waterfalls, lovely views of the river and very good fly-fishing here, as well as trekking options. Wildlife includes pudú, pumas and huemul, as well as a variety of birds, ranging from condors to several species of duck. On the southern side of the Reserva, 12 km west of Coyhaique reached by a separate *ripio* road, is the **Cerro Huemules**, where lots of wildlife can be seen including 23 bird species, foxes, wildcats and of course, the huemul.

Puerto Aysén and around

Puerto Aysén lies at the confluence of the rivers Aysén and Palos. First developed in the 1920s, the town grew as the major port of the region although it has now been replaced by Puerto Chacabuco, 15 km downriver. Few vestiges of the port remain today: boats lie high and dry on the riverbank when the tide is out and the foundations of buildings by the river are now overgrown with fuchsias and buttercups. To see any maritime activity you have to walk a little way out of town to **Puerto Aguas Muertas**, where the fishing boats come in.

The town is linked to the south bank of the Río Aysén by the Puente Presidente Ibáñez, once the longest suspension bridge in Chile. From the far bank a paved road leads to **Puerto Chacabuco**; a regular bus service runs between the two. There is a helpful **tourist office** ① *Prat y Sgto Aldea, Dec-Feb only*, in the Municipalidad. For information on shipping, see www.chacabucoport.cl.

A good 10-km walk north along a minor road from Puerto Aysén leads to **Laguna Los Palos**, calm, deserted and surrounded by forested hills. En route is a bridge over a deep, narrow river; it's freezing cold but offers the chance for a bracing swim. **Lago Riesco**, 30 km south of Puerto Aysén, can be reached by an unpaved road that follows the Río Blanco. In season, the *Apulcheu* sails regularly from Puerto Chacabuco to **Termas de Chiconal** ① *US$26.50, 1 hr, on the northern shore of the Seno Aysén*, offering a good way to see the fjord; take your own food.

⊚ Coyhaique and around listings

For hotel and restaurant price codes and other relevant information, see pages 14-21.

⊚ Where to stay

Coyhaique *p377, map p378*

$$$$-$$$ El Reloj, Baquedano 828, T067-223 1108, www.elrelojhotel.cl. Tasteful, in a former sawmill, with a good restaurant, charming, comfortable wood panelled rooms, some with wonderful views, nice lounge, the best in town.

$$$ Belisario Jara, Bilbao 662, T067-223 4150, www.belisariojara.cl. Most distinctive and delightful, an elegant and welcoming small place.

$$$ Cabañas Mirador, Baquedano 848, T067-223 3191. Attractive, well-equipped *cabañas*, also rooms, in lovely gardens with panoramic views of the Reserva Forestal, and Río Coyhaique below.

$$$ San Sebastián, Baquedano 496, T067-223 3427. Modern, spacious rooms with great views over the Reserva. Also **Cabañas San Sebastián**, Freire 554, T067-223 1762, www.cabsansebastian.cl. Central, very good.

$$$-$$ Cabañas Río Simpson, 3 km north on road to Pto Aysén, T067-223 2183, riosimpsoncab@hotmail.com. Fully equipped cabins for 2-6 people. Horse riding, fishing and tours. Tame alpacas in grounds.

$$ Cabañas Baquedano, Baquedano 20, T067-223 2520, Patricio y Gedra Guzmán, http://balasch.cl. Welcoming, well-maintained, lovely place, 7 *cabañas* of varying standards, with splendid views over the Reserva Forestal, very helpful hosts who speak English, access to river, great value.

$$ Hostal Bon, Serrano 91, T067-223 1189, hostal_bon@hotmail.com. Simple but very welcoming place, with multilingual owner. They also have *cabañas* near Reserva Forestal, 1 km away.

$$ Hostal Las Quintas, Bilbao 1208, T067-223 1173, nolfapatagonia@hotmail.com. Spartan, but clean and very spacious rooms (some in very bizarre design) with bath.

$$-$ Las Salamandras, Sector Los Pinos, 2 km south in attractive forest, T067-221 1865, www.backpackerschile.com. Variety of rooms, dorms cabin and camping, kitchen facilities, trekking and other sports and tours.

Many more *hospedajes* and private houses with rooms; ask tourist office for a list.

Camping

Tourist office on plaza or **Sernatur** in Coyhaique has a full list of all sites in XI Región. There are numeourus sites in Coyhaique and on the road between Coyhaique and Puerto Aysén, including **Camping Alborada**, at Km 2, T067-223 8868, hot shower, and **Camping Río Correntoso**, Km 42, T067-223 2005, showers, fishing.

Puerto Aysén and around *p379*
Accommodation is hard to find, most is taken up by fishing companies in both ports. There are several places to eat along Tte Merino and Aldea in Puerto Aysén.
$$$$ Loberías del Sur, José Miguel Carrera 50, Puerto Chacabuco, T067-235 1112, www.loberiasdelsur.cl. 5-star hotel, whose restaurant serves the best food in the area (handy for meal or a drink before boarding ferry – climb up steps direct from port). Same owner as Catamaranes del Sur (see Transport, below), which also has a nearby nature reserve, Parque Aiken del Sur.
$$$ Patagonia Green, 400 m from bridge (on Pto Chacabuco side), T067-233 6796, www.patagoniagreen.cl. Nice rooms or cabins for up to 5, kitchen, heating, gardens, arranges tours to Laguna San Rafael, fishing, mountain biking, riding, trekking, etc, English spoken.
$$$-$$ Caicahues, Michimalonco 660, Puerto Aysén, T067-233 6623, hcaicahues@ puertoaysen.cl. Popular business hotel, with heating, book ahead.

Restaurants

Coyhaique *p377, map p378*
$$$ Histórico Ricer, Horn 48 y 40, p 2, T067-223 2920. Central, warm and cosy, serving breakfast to dinner, regional specialities, with good vegetarian options, historical exhibits. Also has Café Ricer at No 48, serving light food.
$$ La Casona, Obispo Vielmo 77, T067-223 8894. Justly reputed as best in town, a

charming family restaurant serves excellent fish, congrio especially, but best known for grilled lamb.
$$-$ Casino de Bomberos next to the fire station, Gral Parra 365, T067-223 1437. For great atmosphere and a filling lunch, can be slow when serving groups.
$$-$ Donde Ramiro, Freire 319, T067-225 6885. Good set lunches, big screen TV.
$ Club Sandwich Patagonia, Moraleda 433. 24-hr fast food and huge Chilean sandwiches, a local institution.
$ El Mastique, Bilbao 141. Cheap but good pasta and Chilean food.
$ Pizzería La Fiorentina, Prat 230. Tasty pizzas, good service.

Cafés
Café Oriente, Condell 201. Serves a good lunch and tasty cakes.

Puerto Aysén and around *p379*
There are many cheap places on Aldea, between Municipal and Dougnac.
$$ Café Restaurante Ensenada, O'Higgins 302, Puerto Chacabuco. Basic grub.
$$ Restaurante La Cascada, Km 32 between Coyhaique and Puerto Aysén. Waterfalls nearby. Recommended for meat and fish.

Bars and clubs

Coyhaique *p377, map p378*
El Boliche, Moraleda 380. A beer-drinkers' bar. Many bars on the same street.
Pepe le Pub, Parra 72. Good cocktails and snacks, relaxed, live music at weekends.
Piel Roja, Moraleda y Condell. Good music, laid back, open Wed, Fri, Sat 1000-0500 for dancing, pub other nights.

Festivals

Puerto Aysén and around *p379*
2nd week of Nov Local festival of folklore is held in Puerto Aysén.

⚙ Shopping

Coyhaique *p377, map p378*
Handicrafts
Artesanía Manos Azules, Riquelme 435. Sells fine handicrafts. **Feria de Artesanía** on the plaza. **Kaienk**, Plaza 219-A, T067-224 5216, sells good-quality locally made knitwear.

⚙ What to do

Coyhaique *p377, map p378*
Many tours operate Sep to Apr, some Dec-Mar only. The surrounding area is famous for trout fishing with several estancias offering luxury accommodation and bilingual guides. Most tour operators also offer specialist fishing trips.
Andes Patagónicos, Horn 48 y 40, loc 11, T067-221 6711, www.ap.cl. Trips to local lakes, Tortel, historically based tours and bespoke trips all year round. Good, but not cheap.
Aysén Tour, Pasaje Río Backer 2646, T067-223 7070, www.aysentour.cl. Tours along the Carretera Austral, also car rental.
Camello Patagón, Carlos Cardell 149, T067-224 4327, www.camellopatagon.cl. Daily trips to Cavernas de Marmol in Río Tranquilo, among others, also car rental and other services.
Casa del Turismo Rural, Odeón Plaza de Armas, T067-221 4031, www.casaturismo rural.cl, Mon-Fri 1000-1330, 1530-2000 (also weekends in high season). An association of 40 families, mostly in the countryside, who offer activities such as horse riding and fishing. Many do not have telephones or internet, make reservations here.
Expediciones Coyhaique, Portales 195, T067-223 1783, www.coyhaiqueflyfishing. com. Fly-fishing experts.
Geo Turismo, José de Moraleda 480, T067-258 3173, www.geoturismo patagonia.cl. Offers wide range of tours, English spoken, professional.
Turismo Prado, 21 de Mayo 417, T067-223 1271, www.turismoprado.cl. Tours of local

lakes and other sights, Laguna San Rafael trips and historical tours.

Skiing
El Fraile, near Lago Frío, 29 km southeast of Coyhaique, www.chileanski.com/eng/el-fraile/. This ski resort has 5 pistes, 2 lifts, a basic café and equipment hire (season Jun-Sep).

⚙ Transport

Coyhaique *p377, map p378*
Air
Tte Vidal airport has flights with **Don Carlos** to **Chile Chico** (Mon-Sat), **Cochrane** (Mon, Thu) and **Villa O'Higgins** (Mon, Thu, for those who like flying, with strong stomachs, or in a hurry).

Balmaceda airport has daily flights to **Santiago** with LAN, mostly via **Puerto Montt**, and Sky, which sometimes makes several stops. Landing can be dramatic owing to strong winds. **Sky** also flies to **Punta Arenas**, 3 flights weekly.

Bicycle
Rental available from **Manuel Iduarte**, Parra y Bulnes; check condition first. Bicycle repairs at Tomás Madrid Urrea, Pasaje Foitzich y Libertad, T067-225 2132.

Bus
Full list of buses from tourist information. Minibuses (**Alí**, Dussen 283, T067-223 2788, www.busesali.cl; **Suray**, A Prat 265, T067-223 8387) run every 45 mins to **Puerto Aysén**, 1 hr, US$2.75-3.35; change here for **Puerto Chacabuco**, 20 mins, US$1. Also several minibus companies (**Yamil Ali**, Prat y Errázuriz, T067-221 9009; **Miguel Acuña**, M Moraleda 304, T067-225 1579 or T067-241 1804) to **Puerto Ibáñez** on Lago Gral Carrera to connect with ferry to Chile Chico, pick up 0530-0600 from your hotel, 1½ hrs; book the day before.

Buses on the Carretera Austral vary according to demand, and they are always full so book early. Bikes can be taken by arrangement. North towards Chaitén: twice a week direct with **Becker** (Parra 335, T067-223 2167), US$44, also **Terraustral**; otherwise change in La Junta (with an overnight stop in winter). To **Futaleufú**, with **Daniela**, 3 a week, US$34. To **Puerto Cisnes**, **Sao Paulo** (at terminal, T067-233 2918) and **Aguilas Patagónicas** (Lautaro 104, T067-221 1288, www. aguilaspatagonicas.cl), US$9-11. South to **Cochrane**, daily in summer with **Don Carlos** (Subteniente Cruz 63, T067-223 1981), **Sao Paulo**, Aguilas Patagónicas, or **Acuario 13** (at terminal, T067-255 2143), US$23.50. All buses stop at **Villa Cerro Castillo** (US$8), **Bahía Murta** (US$12), **Puerto Tranquilo** (US$14.50) and **Puerto Bertrand** (US$16).

Car hire

If renting a car, a high 4WD vehicle is recommended for the Carretera Austral. There are several rental agencies in town, charging at least US$150 a day, including insurance, for 4WD or pickup. Add another US$50 for paperwork to take a vehicle into Argentina. Buy fuel in Coyhaique.

Ferry offices

Navimag, Paseo Horn 47 D, T067-223 3306, www.navimag.com. **Naviera Austral**, Paseo Horn 40, of 101, T067-221 0727, www.navieraustral.cl.

Taxi

US$7.50 to Tte Vidal airport (US$2 if sharing). Fares in town US$3, 50% extra after 2100. Taxi *colectivos* (shared taxis) congregate at Prat y Bilbao, average fare US$1.

Puerto Aysén *p379*
Bus

Minibuses (**Alí**, Aldea 1143, T067-233 3335, www.busesali.cl; **Suray**, T067-223 8387) run every 45 mins to **Coyhaique**, 1 hr, US$2.75-3.35. To **Puerto Chacabuco**, 20 mins, US$1.

Ferry

Navimag (Terminal de Transbordadores, Puerto Chacabuco, T067-235 1111, www. navimag.com) sails twice a week from Puerto Chacabuco to **Puerto Montt**, taking about 24 hrs (for details, see page 332). **Catamaranes del Sur** (J M Carrera 50, T067-235 1115, www.loberiasdel sur.cl) have sailings to **Laguna San Rafael** (see page 373). It is best to make reservations in these companies' offices in Puerto Montt, Coyhaique or Santiago. Other shipping offices: **Agemar** (Tte Merino 909, Puerto Aysén, T067-233 2716); **Naviera Austral** (Terminal de Transbordadores, T067-235 1493, www.navieraustral.cl).

ℹ Directory

Coyhaique *p377, map p378*
Banks Several with **Redbanc** ATMs in the centre. **Language school** Baquedano International Language School, Baquedano 20, T067-223 2520, www. balasch.cl, US$600 per week including lodging and meals.

Puerto Aysén *p379*
Banks BCI, Prat, for Visa; Banco de Chile, Plaza de Armas, only changes cash, not TCs. There's a **Redbanc** ATM in Puerto Chacabuco. **Post office** South side of bridge. **Telephone** Plaza de Armas, next to Turismo Rucuray; **ENTEL**, Aldea 1202, internet access.

Lago General Carrera

The section of the Carretera Austral around the north and western sides of Lago General Carrera is reckoned by many people to be the most spectacular stretch of all. Straddling the border with Argentina, this is the largest lake in South America after Lake Titicaca and is believed to be the deepest lake on the continent; soundings in 1997 established its maximum depth as 590 m.

The lake is a beautiful azure blue, surrounded at its Chilean end by predominantly alpine terrain and at the Argentine end by dry pampa. The region prides itself on having the best climate in southern Chile, with some 300 days of sunshine a year; much fruit is grown as a result, especially around Chile Chico, where rainfall is very low for this area. In general, the climate here is more similar to Argentine Patagonia than to the rest of the Carretera Austral region.

Arriving at Lago General Carrera → *Colour map 5, B3.*

The main towns, Puerto Ibáñez on the north shore and Chile Chico on the south, are connected by a ferry, *La Tehuelche*. Overland routes between Coyhaique and Chile Chico are much longer, passing either through Argentina, or along the Carretera Austral, which runs west around the lake (this route is described below). Minibuses run along the Carretera Austral in summer and air taxis link the small towns of the region.

Reserva Nacional Cerro Castillo and around

Beyond Coyhaique, the Carretera Austral runs through slightly wilder, more rugged land, with the occasional cow or wild horse feeding by the side of the road. Some 40 km south of Coyhaique, it enters the **Reserva Nacional Cerro Castillo** ① *US$3.55*, which extends over 179,550 ha. The park is named after the fabulous **Cerro Castillo** (2675 m), which resembles a fairy-tale castle with rock pinnacles jutting out from a covering of snow. It also encompasses Cerro Bandera (2040 m) just west of Balmaceda and several other peaks in the northern wall of the valley of the Río Ibáñez. There is a *guardería* at the northeastern end of the park, 50 m to the left of the main road (as you head south), opposite Laguna Chinguay to the right, with access to walks and a **campsite** ① *T067-221 2225, Nov-Mar, US$8.65 per site; take equipment – there are no refugios*. The picnic ground is open summer 0830-2100, winter to 1830. The park offers a number of excellent day treks and some of the best self-contained multi-day trekking in Patagonia. A truly challenging four-day trek goes around the peaks of Cerro Castillo, starting at Las Horquetas Grandes, a bend in the river Río Ibáñez, 8 km south of the park entrance, where any bus driver will let you off. It follows Río La Lima to the gorgeous Laguna Cerro Castillo, then follows animal trails around the peak itself, returning to Villa Cerro Castillo (see below). This is a challenging walk: attempt it only if fit, and ideally, take a guide, as trails are poorly marked (IGM map essential, purchase in advance in Coyhaique). Another equally spectacular five-day trek goes around Lago Monreal; ask in Villa Cerro Castillo for details.

At Km 83 the Carretera Austral crosses the **Portezuelo Ibáñez** (1120 m) and drops through the **Cuesta del Diablo**, a series of bends with fine views over the Río Ibáñez. Beyond the turning to Puerto Ibáñez (see below) the road goes through **Villa Cerro Castillo** (Km 8), a quiet village in a spectacular setting beneath the striking, jagged peaks of Cerro Castillo, overlooking the broad valley below. There's a petrol station, public phone, several food shops and a tiny tourist information kiosk by the road side (January and February only), with details of trekking guides and horse rides. The village is a good place to stop for a few days to explore the reserve. There is also a small **local museum** ① *2 km south of Villa Cerro Castillo, Dec-Mar daily 0900-1200*, and a few kilometres further south is the **Monumento Nacional Manos de Cerro Castillo** ① *open all year, US$1 payable Dec-Apr*. In a shallow cave, a few handprints have been made on the side of vertical rocks high above the Río Ibáñez. There's no clue to their significance, but they're in a beautiful place with panoramic views. This makes a delightful two-hour walk and is signposted clearly from the road.

Lago General Carrera

Native deer

The Andean **huemul** (*Hippocamelus bisulcus*) is a mountain deer native to the Andes of southern Chile and Argentina. Sharing the Chilean national crest with the Andean condor, the huemul (pronounced 'way-mool') is a medium-sized stocky cervid adapted to survival in rugged mountain terrain. Males grow antlers and have distinctive black face masks.

Human pressures have pushed the huemul to the brink of extinction and current numbers are estimated at less than 1500. The huemul has become the focal point of both national and international conservation efforts, carried out primarily by CONAF and the Comité pro la Defensa de la Fauna y Flora de Chile (CODEFF).

Your best chance of seeing the huemul is in one of two reserves managed by CONAF: the Reserva Nacional Río Claro, which lies on the southeastern corner of the larger Reserva Nacional Río Simpson

just outside Coyhaique, and the Reserva Nacional Tamango, near Cochrane. To visit either of these you will need to be accompanied by a warden: ask in Coyhaique or Cochrane to make sure someone is available.

The Carretera Austral area is also one of the best places for trying to spot the equally rare **pudú**. This miniature creature, around 40 cm tall and weighing only 10 kg, is the smallest member of the deer family in the world. Native to southern Argentina and Chile, the pudú is listed in Chile as vulnerable to extinction, largely due to habitat loss, but also because its unique appearance (the males grow two short spiked antlers) has made it a target for poaching for zoos. Reddish-brown in colour, the pudú is ideally adapted to the dense temperate rainforests of Chile and Argentina, scooting along on trails through the undergrowth, leaving behind minuscule cloven tracks.

Puerto Ibáñez

The principal port on the Chilean section of the lake, **Puerto Ibáñez** (officially Puerto Ingeniero Ibáñez) is reached by taking a paved branch road, 31 km long, from La Bajada, 97 km south of Coyhaique. You will probably just pass through Puerto Ibáñez to reach the ferry. It is, however, a centre for distinctive pottery, leather production and vegetable growing (you can visit potters and buy salad from greenhouses). Local archaeology includes rock art and the largest Tehuelche cemetery in Patagonia. There are some fine waterfalls, including the **Salto Río Ibáñez**, 6 km north. There is also a road from Puerto Ibáñez to **Perito Moreno** in Argentina. It is poor-quality *ripio*, suitable for 4WD only, and there is no public transport.

The western shore

Beyond Villa Cerro Castillo, the road climbs out of the valley, passing the emerald-green **Laguna Verde** and the Portezuelo Cofré. It descends to the boggy Manso Valley, with a good campsite at the bridge over the river; watch out for mosquitoes. Some 5 km from the Carretera Austral, at Km 203, is **Bahía Murta**, situated on the northern tip of the central arm of Lago General Carrera. This sleepy, almost forgotten village dates from the 1930s, when it exported timber to Argentina via Chile Chico. There is a tiny **tourist information hut**① *summer daily 1000-1430, 1500-1930 (in theory)*. Petrol is available from a house with a sign just before Puerto Murta.

Back on the Carretera, the road follows the lake's western shore. At Km 207 from Coyhaique is a small privately owned forest of ancient and gnarled *arrayanes* that is worth a visit. Some 20 km further south is **Río Tranquilo**, where the buses stop for lunch and fuel is available. The lake reflects the mountains that surround it and the clouds above. Close to Río Tranquilo is the unusual **Capilla y Catedral de Mármol**, a peninsula made of marble, with fascinating caves that can be visited by **boat** ① *2 hrs, group tours US$20, private boat with guide US$67*; go early in the morning when the lake is calmer and prepare to get wet. The village also has an unusual cemetery made up of mausolea in the form of miniature Chilote-style houses. A new branch of the Carretera Austral heads northwest from Río Tranquilo to **Puerto Grosse** on the coast at Bahía Exploradores. At Km 52 on this road is a *refugio* from which a well-maintained path leads to a lookout opposite the Exploradores glacier. **Guided hikes** ① *6 hrs including 2-3 hrs on the glacier, US$89 per person, crampons provided*, are available. The hike can be treacherous in bad weather. Book though **El Puesto** in Río Tranquilo, www.elpuesto.cl.

South to Puerto Bertrand

The road continues along the edge of the azure lake, with snow-covered mountains with pointed peaks visible in the distance. At the southwestern tip of Lago General Carrera, at Km 279, is **El Maitén**, from where a road branches off east along the south shore of the lake towards Chile Chico. South of El Maitén, meanwhile, the Carretera Austral becomes steeper and more winding; in winter this stretch is icy and dangerous. The picturesque, tranquil village of **Puerto Bertrand**, 5 km away, is a good place for fishing and the best base in the region for whitewater rafting and kayaking. Day hikes are possible along decent trails. Nearby is a sign showing the *Nacimiento del Río Baker*: the place where the turquoise Río Baker begins. This area is home to the most impressive hydrological system in Chile, with its most voluminous river, its biggest lake to the north and a huge icefield to the west. Beyond Puerto Bertrand, the road climbs up to high moorland, passing the confluence of the ríos Neff and Baker, before winding south along the east bank of the Río Baker. On a sunny day it is hard to imagine more pleasant surroundings. The road is rough but not treacherous and the scenery is splendid all the way to Cochrane. Watch out for cattle and hares on the road (and the occasional huemul) and take blind corners slowly.

The southern shore of Lago General Carrera

Some 10 km east of El Maitén, **Puerto Guadal** is a friendly, picturesque town that is a centre for fishing. It also has shops, accommodation, restaurants, a post office, petrol and a lovely stretch of lakeside beach. Further east along the shore, just past the nondescript village of **Mallín Grande**, Km 40, the road runs through the **Paso de las Llaves**, a 30-km stretch carved out of the rock face on the edge of the lake. The south side of the lake is much drier than the rest of the Carretera but there are still gorges and waterfalls dotted along the route. The landscape is more open as there is less of an influence from the icefields. The road climbs and drops, narrow and poor in places, offering wonderful views across the lake and the icefields to the west. At Km 74, a turning runs to **Fachinal**. A further 5 km east is the **Garganta del Diablo**, an impressive narrow gorge of 120 m with a fast-flowing stream below. Further on there is an open-cast mine, which produces gold and other metals.

Chile Chico and around → www.chilechico.cl.

Chile Chico is a quiet, friendly but dusty town situated on the lake shore 122 km east of El Maitén, close to the Argentine border (for details of the border crossing, see

Border crossings: Chile–Argentina

Chile Chico

A road runs 2 km east from Chile Chico to **Chilean immigration**, open September-April daily 0730-2200, May-August 0800-2000 (www.pasosfronterizos.gov.cl/cf_chilechico. html). **Argentine immigration** is open daily 0900-1300 and 1400-2100. See www. gendarmeria.gov.ar/pasos/chile/fichjeimeni.html. From the border, the road continues on for 5 km to **Los Antiguos**, a town with a cherry festival in January. There are daily buses from Chile Chico to Los Antiguos in summer, taking one hour, US$4. **Perito Moreno**, 67 km east of the border, has accommodation, a restaurant and money exchange services. Remember that you can't take fresh food across in either direction, and you'll need ownership papers if crossing with a car. If entering Argentina here you will not have to fill in an immigration form (ask if you need entry papers).

Paso Roballos

Some 17 km north of Cochrane, a road runs east through Villa Chacabuco and continues east for 78 km to enter Argentina at Paso Roballos. **Chilean immigration** open summer 0800-2200, winter 0800-2000. The road continues on to Bajo Caracoles. There isn't any public transport along this route and, although the road is passable in summer, it is generally in a poor state and often flooded in spring.

box, above). The town dates from 1909 when settlers crossed from Argentina and occupied the land, leading to conflict with cattle ranchers who had been given settlement rights by the Chilean government. In the showdown that followed (known as the war of Chile Chico) the ranchers were driven out by the settlers, but it was not until 1931 that the Chilean government finally recognized the town's existence. Now the centre of a fruit-growing region, it has an annual festival at the end of January and a small **museum** (summer only). There are fine views from the **Cerro de las Banderas** at the western end of town. The **tourist office** ⓘ *Casa de la Cultura, O'Higgins, T067-241 1303, infochilechico@sernatur.cl*, is helpful but usually closed. An unofficial purple tourist kiosk, on the quay where the ferry arrives, sells bus tickets for Ruta 40 (Argentina) and has some accommodation information.

To the south and west of Chile Chico is good walking terrain, through weird rock formations and dry brush scrub. The northern and higher peak of **Cerro Pico del Sur** (2168 m) can be climbed by the agile from Los Cipres (beware dogs in the farmyard). You will need a long summer's day and the 1:50,000 map. Follow the horse trail until it peters out, then navigate by compass or sense of direction until the volcano-like summit appears. After breaching the cliff ramparts, there is some scrambling and a 3-m pitch to the summit, from where you'll enjoy indescribable views of the lake and the Andes.

About 20 km south of Chile Chico towards Lago Jeinimeni is the **Cueva de las Manos**, a cave full of Tehuelche paintings, the most famous of which are the *manos azules* (blue hands). From the road, climb 500 m and cross the Pedregoso stream. The path is difficult, and partly hidden, so it is recommended to take a guide.

Reserva Nacional Lago Jeinimeni

ⓘ *52 km south of Chile Chico, open all year but access may be impossible Apr-Oct due to high river levels, US$3.50, camping US$6; contact the CONAF office for lifts from Chile Chico.* This park covers 160,000 ha and includes two lakes, **Lago Jeinimeni** and **Lago Verde**,

388 • Carretera Austral Lago General Carrera

which lie surrounded by forests in the narrow valley of the Río Jeinimeni. Impressive cliffs, waterfalls and small glaciers provide habitat for huemul deer, pumas and condors. Activities include fishing for salmon and rainbow trout, trekking and rowing. Access is via an unpaved road, which branches south off the road to the Argentine border at Los Antiguos and crosses five rivers, four of which have to be forded. At Km 42, there is a small lake, **Laguna de los Flamencos**, where large numbers of flamingos can be seen. The park entrance is at Km 53; just beyond is a ranger station, a campsite and fishing area at the eastern end of Lago Jeinimeni. Take all supplies, including a good map.

⦿ Lago General Carrera listings

For hotel and restaurant price codes and other relevant information, see pages 14-21.

⦿ Where to stay

Reserva Nacional Cerro
Castillo and around *p386*
$ Cabañas Don Niba, Los Pioneros 872, Villa Cerro Castillo, T067-241 9920. Friendly but basic *hospedaje*, good value.
$ Hostería Villarrica, O'Higgins 59, next to Supermercado Villarrica, Villa Cerro Castillo, T067-241 9500. Welcoming, basic, hot showers and meals too, kind owners can arrange trekking guides and horse riding. There are other *residenciales* in town.

Puerto Ibáñez *p386*
$$ Cabañas Shehen Aike, Luis Risopatrón 55, T067-242 3284, info@aike.cl. Swiss/Chilean-owned, large cabins, lots of ideas for trips, bike rental, organizes tours, fine food, welcoming, English spoken, best to phone in advance.
$ pp Hospedaje Don Francisco, San Salvador y Lautaro, T09-8503 3626. Very hospitable, lunch or dinner extra, good food round the clock, camping US$5.50, tents and bikes for hire.
$ Vientos del Sur, Bertrán Dixon 282, T067-242 3208. Good, nice family, dorms, cheap meals (restaurant open till late); also arranges adventure activities.

The western shore *p386*
$$$ Hostal El Puesto, Pedro Lagos 258, Puerto Río Tranquilo, T09-6207 3794,

www.elpuesto.cl. No doubt the most comfortable place in Río Tranquilo, with breakfast, also organizes tours.
$$$ Hostal Los Pinos, Godoy 51, Puerto Río Tranquilo, T067-241 1576. Family-run, well maintained, good mid-price meals.
$$ Cabañas Jacricalor, Carretera Austral 245, Puerto Río Tranquilo, T067-241 9500 (public phone). Tent-sized *cabañas*, hot shower, good meals, good information for climbers.
$$ Campo Alacaluf, Km 44 towards Río Tranquilo-Bahía Exploradores, T067-241 9500. Wonderful guesthouse hidden away from civilization. Run by very friendly German family.
$$ Hostal Carretera Austral, 1 Sur 223, Río Tranquilo, T067-241 9500. Also serves meals (**$$-$**).
$ Residencial Patagonia, Pje España 64, Bahía Murta, T067-241 9600. Comfortable, and serves food. There is also free camping by the lake at Bahía Murta.

South to Puerto Bertrand *p387*
$$$$ Hacienda Tres Lagos, Carretera Austral Km 274, just west of cruce El Maitén, T067-241 1323, T02-2333 4122 (Santiago), www.haciendatreslagos.com. Small, boutique resort on the lake-shore with bungalows, suites and cabins. Good restaurant, wide range of excursions offered, sauna, jacuzzi, good service. English spoken.
$$$$ Mallín Colorado Ecolodge, Carretera Austral Km 273, 2 km west of El Maitén, T09-7137 6242, www.mallincolorado.cl. Comfortable *cabañas* in sweeping gardens,

complete tranquility, charming owners, packages available, including transfers from Balmaceda, horse riding, estancia trip, superb meals, open Oct-Apr.

$$$ Patagonia Baker Lodge and Restaurant, 3 km from Puerto Bertrand, towards the south side of the lake, T067-241 1903, www.pbl.cl. Stylish *cabañas* in woodland, fishing lodge, birdwatching, fabulous views upriver towards rapids and the mountains beyond.

$$ Hostería Puerto Bertrand, Puerto Bertrand, T067-241 9900. With breakfast, other meals available, also *cabañas*, activities.

$ Hospedaje Doña Ester, Casa No 8, Puerto Bertrand, T09-9990 8541. Rooms in a pink house, good.

$ Turismo Hospedaje Campo de Hielo Norte, Ventisquero Neff s/n. Owned by Anselmo Soto, open tourist season only, hospitable, helpful.

The southern shore of Lago General Carrera *p387*

$$$ El Mirador Playa Guadal, 2 km from Puerto Guadal towards Chile Chico, T09-9234 9130, www.elmiradordeguadal. com. *Cabañas* near beach, excursions and activities with or without guide, walks to nearby waterfalls, restaurant.

$$$-$$ Terra Luna Lodge, on lakeside, 2 km from Puerto Guadal, T09-8449 1092, www.terra-luna.cl. Welcoming well-run place with lodge, bungalows and camping huts, also has restaurant, sauna, cinema, private disco, climbing wall, many activities offered.

$$-$ Eco Hostal Un Destino No Turístico, Camino Laguna La Manga, off road to Chile Chico 1.5 km from Puerto Guadal, www. destino-noturistico.com. Open from Sep. Private rooms and dorms, also camping and tent hire, with eco initiatives, workshops, tours and information. Transfers arranged.

$ Hostería Huemules, Las Magnolias 382, Puerto Guadal, T067-243 1212. Good views, meals.

Camping
Camping El Parque, Km 1 on road to Chile Chico, T067-243 1284.

Chile Chico *p387*

$$ Hospedaje Don Luis, Balmaceda 175, T09-8441 4970. Meals available, laundry, helpful.

$$ Hostería de la Patagonia, Camino Internacional s/n, T067-241 1337. Camping or full-board available. Good food, English, French and Italian spoken, trekking, horse riding, whitewater rafting.

Camping
Free site at **Bahía Jara**, 5 km west of Chile Chico, then turn north for 12 km.

🍴 Restaurants

Most *hosterías* and *residenciales* will serve meals (see Where to stay, above).

Chile Chico *p387*

Café Refer, O'Higgins 416. Good, despite the exterior.

Cafetería Loly y Elizabeth, PA González 25, on plaza. Serves coffee, as well as delicious ice cream and cakes.

🍸 Bars and clubs

Chile Chico *p387*

Pub El Minero, Carrera 205. Recommended for a drink.

🎉 Festivals

South to Puerto Bertrand *p387*
3rd weekend of Feb Semana de Bertrand. 3 days of drunken revelry.

Chile Chico *p387*
Last week of Jan The town hosts the Festival Internacional de la Voz.

☀ What to do

The western shore *p386*
El Puesto Expediciones, Lagos 258, Río
Tranquilo, T09-6207 3794, www.elpuesto.cl.
Fishing, ice hiking, kayaking and other trips.

South to Puerto Bertrand *p387*
Horse riding, fishing guides and whitewater
rafting on the Río Baker (generally easy with
a few Grade-III rapids) can all be arranged
at the tourist information office, T067-241
9900 (public phone). Advance booking
helpful. **Hacienda Tres Lagos**, see Where
to stay, also offers various excursions.
Patagonia Adventure Expeditions,
T09-8182 0608, www.adventurepatagonia.
com. Professional outfit running exclusive
fully supported treks to the Campo de
Hielo Norte and the eastern side of Parque
Nacional Laguna San Rafael. Expensive but
a unique experience. Also rafting on the Río
Baker and general help organizing tours,
treks and expeditions.

The southern shore *p387*
Turismo Kalem Patagonia, cabalgasur
@hotmail.com, leads trips to nearby
fossil fields.

☐ Transport

**Reserva Nacional Cerro
Castillo and around** *p386*
There are weekly buses in summer from
Villa Cerro Castillo to both **Coyhaique**
(US$8) and **Cochrane** (see Coyhaique
Transport, above).

Puerto Ibáñez *p386*
Bus
Minibuses and jeeps meet the ferry
in Puerto Ibáñez for connections to
Coyhaique, 2 hrs.

Ferry
The ferry, *La Tehuelche*, sails from **Puerto
Ibáñez** to **Chile Chico** daily, cars US$31.50,

passengers US$3.55. The number of foot
passengers is limited to 75 plus 5 cars.
Reserve at least 2 days in advance through
Turismo Ayacara (www.ayacara.cl) and
arrive 30 mins before departure. This is a
very cold crossing even in summer: take
warm clothing.

The western shore *p386*
All buses from Coyhaique to Cochrane
stop at **Bahía Murta** (US$12) and **Puerto
Tranquilo** (US$14.50).

South to Puerto Bertrand *p387*
All buses from Coyhaique to Cochrane stop
1 km from **Puerto Bertrand** on the main
carretera (US$16).

The southern shore *p446*
Buses between Coyhaique and Los
Antiguos (Argentina) travel via **Puerto
Guadal: ECA** (T067-243 1224/252 8577)
on Tue and Fri, **Seguel** (T067-243 1214/
224 5237) on Wed.

Chile Chico *p387*
Bus
Several minibuses daily to **Cochrane**,
US$23.50, 5 hrs. In summer, minibuses
to **Los Antiguos** (Argentina) 0800-2200,
US$4 (in Chilean pesos), ½-1 hr including
formalities: 3 companies at B O'Higgins 426,
and **La Porteña** at Santiago Ericksen 150.
See above for ferry to **Puerto Ibáñez** and
connecting minibus to Coyhaique. Ferry
and minibus tickets from **Miguel Acuña**,
Sector Muelle, T067-223 1579.

☐ Directory

Chile Chico *p387*
Banks It's best to change money in
Coyhaique. ATM in the middle of O'Higgins
for Mastercard and Cirrus, not Visa. Dollars
and Argentine pesos can be changed
in small amounts in shops and cafés,
including **Loly y Elizabeth**, at poor rates.
Hospital Lautaro s/n, T067-241 1334.

Cochrane and further south

Travelling by bus along the final 224-km stretch of the Carretera Austral from Cochrane to Villa O'Higgins can be frustrating, as you will undoubtedly want to stop every 15 minutes to marvel at the views. This is a beautiful trip through thick forest, with vistas of snow-capped mountains and waterfalls.

Arriving in Cochrane → *Colour map 5, C2/3.*
Getting there Cochrane can be reached by air taxi or bus from Coyhaique, or on a poor unpaved road from Perito Moreno in Argentina. The southern tip of the Carretera at Villa O'Higgins is linked in summer by a ferry service to Calendario Mansilla, from where it is a day long journey to/from El Chaltén in Argentina. Public transport is scarce. Only two weekly buses ply the route from Cochrane to Villa O'Higgins. Hitching is a possibility in summer (be prepared for long waits), but a pick-up or 4WD vehicle will make getting around much easier. Better still, travel by mountain bike. ▶▶ *See Transport, page 396.*

Tourist information ① *On corner of plaza on Dr Steffen, T067-252 2115, www. cochranepatagonia.cl, summer Mon-Fri 0830-2000, Sat-Sun 1100-2000, off season Mon-Fri 0830-1730.* **CONAF** ① *Río Neff 417, T067-252 2164, piero.caviglia@conaf.cl.*

Cochrane and around
Sitting in a hollow on the northern banks of the Río Cochrane, 343 km south of Coyhaique, Cochrane is a simple place. With its pleasant summer climate, it is a good base for walking and fishing in the nearby countryside. There is a small **museum** ① *San Valentín 555, Mon-Fri 0830-1400, 1500-1745,* with displays on local history. On the same street is an odd, *mate*-shaped house. Fuel is available and there is an ATM for MasterCard only.

Just 4 km northeast of Cochrane is the entrance to the **Reserva Nacional Tamango** ① *Dec-Mar 0830-2100, Apr-Nov 0830-1830, US$6.30, plus guided visits to see the huemules Tue, Thu, Sat, US$80 for up to 6 people;* ask in the CONAF office (see above) before visiting. The reserve covers 6925 ha of lenga forest and is home to one of the largest colonies of the rare huemul as well as guanaco, foxes and lots of species of bird, including woodpecker and hummingbird. There are marked paths for walks between 45 minutes and five hours, up to **Cerro Tamango** (1722 m) and **Cerro Temanguito** (1485 m). Take water and food, and windproof clothing if climbing the *cerros*. The views from the reserve are superb, over the town, the nearby lakes and to the Campo de Hielo Norte to the west. Tourist facilities, however, are rudimentary and it is inaccessible in the four winter months.

Excursions can also be made to **Lago Cochrane**, which straddles the frontier with Argentina (the Argentine section is called **Lago Puerredón**). The lake, which covers over 17,500 ha, offers excellent fishing all year round, and there are boats for hire. Some 17 km north of Cochrane, a road runs east through Villa Chacabuco and continues east for 78 km to enter Argentina at Paso Roballos.

Border crossing: Chile–Argentina

Villa O'Higgins–El Chaltén

With the opening of this route it is possible to do the Carretera Austral and go on to Argentina's Parque Nacional Los Glaciares and Chile's Torres del Paine without doubling back on yourself. Note that the route is closed from late April to Oct.

From Villa O'Higgins, the road continues 7 km south to Bahía Bahamóndez on Lago O'Higgins (minibus/bus US$4), from where the boat Quetru leaves for **Chilean immigration** at **Candelario Mancilla**. The boat service runs daily from November to April, 2¾ hours, US$44; for an extra US$73, you can make a detour from Candelario Mancillo to Glaciar O'Higgins (five-hours return) before continuing to the border. The number of departures varies each year, but there is usually one a week in November, two a week in December, four a week throughout January/February, and two in March. There may be other departures in November and April, but exact dates should be checked in advance, and sailings may be cancelled if the weather is bad.

From Calendario Mansilla, it's 14 km to the border and a further 5 km to Argentina immigration at Punta Norte on Lago del Desierto. The first part can be done on foot, on horseback, or by 4WD service (US$18 for two to four passengers and luggage, US$9 luggage only). The next 5 km is a demanding hike, or you can take a horse for the whole 19 km (US$36), with an extra horse to carry bags. The route descends sharply towards Lago de Desierto, with breathtaking panoramas, including of Cerro Fitz Roy. Note, however, that bridges are sometimes washed away; make sure to wear good boots for crossing wetland. A short detour to Laguna Larga (on the left as you walk towards the border) is worth it if you have the energy.

The 40-minute boat crossing of Lago de Desierto aboard the Huemul (Tue-Sun, US$30) passes glaciers and ice fields. Several minibus companies, including Transporte Las Lengas and JR Turismo, await the boat for the final hour-long journey on a gravel road to El Chaltén (37 km, US$28, US$5.50 extra for luggage). There is no food available on either side of the lake, but the Argentine immigration officials at Punta Norte are friendly and, if you are cold, may offer you coffee.

The best combination is to take 4WD from Candelario Mancilla to the border and then continue on horseback. This ensures that the trip can be done in a day (depart Villa O'Higgins 0800, arrive El Chaltén 2115). Allow for delays, though, especially if horses aren't available for hire. It's a good option to pay for each portion of the route separately.

Full details of the crossing and up-to-date itineraries and prices are available from Villa O'Higgins Expeditions (aka Robinson Crusoe), T067-243 1811/1821, www.villaohiggins.com, who also own **Robinson Crusoe Deep Patagonia Lodge** in town (Ctra Austral, Km 1240, T067-243 1909, www.robinsoncrusoe.com).

Tortel and Puerto Yungay

A branch of the Carretera Austral, beginning 2 km south of Vagabundo and continuing south for 23 km, was completed in early 2003, making the village of Tortel accessible by road. Built on a hill at the mouth of the river 135 km from Cochrane, Tortel has no streets, the village being connected by 7 km of stairs and walkways made of cypress wood. There are a couple of beaches and two plazas built on stilts, roofed for protection from the almost constant drizzle. Its main industries are wood, for trade with Punta Arenas, shellfish, and now tourism. At the entrance to the village is a small tourist office with information on the dozen or so *residenciales* and a useful map. From Tortel, you can hire a boat to visit two spectacular glaciers: **Ventisquero Jorge Montt**, five hours southwest by boat, or **Ventisquero Steffens**, north on the edge of the Parque Nacional San Rafael, 2½ hours by boat (US$190 for 10 people) and then a three-hour trek on a very wet, but well-signed trail including a river crossing by rowing boat to a viewing point from which the glacier can be seen across the lake. Trips can also be made to the nearby **Isla de los Muertos** (boat for 10 people US$70), where some 100 Chilote workers died in mysterious circumstances early in the 20th century.

The main spine of the Carretera, meanwhile, continues southwards to **Puerto Yungay** (allow 1¼ hours by car from Tortel under normal conditions), a tiny village with a military post and a pretty church. This section of the road is hilly and in places very bad; it is not advisable to drive along here at night. From Puerto Yungay, there is an army-run **ferry crossing** ①*www.barcazas.cl, 2 or 3 daily, 45 mins, free*, to Río Bravo, with capacity for four to five cars; check timetables locally off season. If you miss the last boat the *carabineros* will help you find accommodation. Beyond the ferry crossing, the road continues south. After 9 km there is a turn-off marked 'Ventisquero Montt'. Carry on through more spectacular scenery – lakes, moors, dense forest, swamps, rivers and waterfalls, often shrouded in mist – before arriving at the Carretera's final destination, Villa O'Higgins.

Note: the road beyond Río Bravo is very beautiful but very remote, with few people and few vehicles for hitching, and it is often closed by bad weather. Take food and fuel, as there are no shops or service stations on the entire route.

Villa O'Higgins

Villa O'Higgins lies 2 km from the northeastern end of an arm of **Lago O'Higgins**, which straddles the Argentine border (it's known as **Lago San Martín** in Argentina; see box, page 393, for border crossing information). With a population of around 500, the town is friendly with something of a frontier feel. There is a tiny museum, the **Museo de la Patagonia Padre Antonio Ronchi**, on the plaza, where you'll also find **tourist information** ① *in summer*. Information is also available from the **Municipalidad** ① *Lago Christie 121, www.municipalidadohiggins.cl*, which can provide trekking guides, or online at www.villaohiggins.com. Fuel is available from the ECA store (Monday to Saturday).

On rare sunny days, Villa O'Higgins' pleasant setting can be fully appreciated. Half way up a wooded hill behind the town, a mirador affords spectacular views of nearby mountains, lakes and glaciers. There are large numbers of icebergs in Lago O'Higgins, which have split off the glaciers of the Campo de Hielo Sur to the west. A six-hour trek from the town goes through native forest to the **Mosco Glacier**; allow two days for a return trip. Fresh water is plentiful and there is a *refugio* on the way, but the route is difficult after heavy rain. From Villa O'Higgins, the road continues 7 km south to **Bahía Bahamóndez** on the shores of Lago O'Higgins.

Cochrane and further south listings

For hotel and restaurant price codes and other relevant information, see pages 14-21.

Where to stay

Cochrane *p392*
In summer it is best to book rooms in advance.
$$$ Wellmann, Las Golondrinas 36, T067-252 2171, hotelwellmann@gmail.com. Comfortable, warm, hot water, good meals.
$$$-$$ Cabañas Rogeri, Río Maitén 80, T067-252 2264, rogeri3@hotmail.cl. *Cabañas* with kitchen for 4.
$$ Residencial Cero a Cero, Lago Brown 464, T067-252 2158, ceroacero@hotmail.com. Welcoming.
$$ Residencial Rubio, Tte Merino 871, T067-252 2173. Very nice, meals available.
$$ Residencial Sur Austral, Prat 334, T067-252 2150. Private or shared bath, hot water, very nice.
$ pp Residencial Cochrane, Dr Steffen 451, T067-252 2377, pquintana13@gmail.com. Good meals, hot shower, camping.

Tortel and Puerto Yungay *p393*
There are several *hospedajes*; for all, call T067-223 4815 (public phone) or T067-221 1876 (municipality). Prices are cheaper in the low season. There is camping at sector Junquillo at the far end of town.
$$$ Entre Hielos Lodge, sector centro, Tortel. T02-2196 0271, www.entrehielos tortel.cl. Upmarket place in town, excursions, boat trips.
$$ Estilo, Sector Centro, Tortel, tortelhospedajeestilo@yahoo.es. Warm and comfortable, good food. Entertaining, talkative host (Spanish).
$$ Hospedaje Costanera, S ra Luisa Escobar Sanhueza, Tortel. Cosy, warm, lovely garden, full board available.

Villa O'Higgins *p394*
$$ Cabañas San Gabriel, Lago O'Higgins 310. Nice cabins. A good choice for small groups.
$$-$ El Mosco, at the northern entrance to the town, T067-243 1819, patagoniaelmosco@yahoo.es. Rooms, dorms or camping. Spanish-run hostel. English spoken, trekking maps and information. Can help with bike repairs. More expensive than the rest, but nothing else competes in terms of infrastructure.

Restaurants

For other eating options, see Where to stay, above.

Cochrane *p392*
Residencial El Fogón, San Valentín 65, T09-7644 7914. Its pub is the only eating place open in low season, and it's the best restaurant at any time of year. Rooms available.

Tortel and Puerto Yungay *p393*
Café Celes Salom, Tortel. Bar/restaurant serving basic, cheap meals, disco on Sat, occasional live bands.

Villa O'Higgins *p394*
$$ Entre Patagones, at the northern entrance to the town, T067-243 1810, www.entrepatagones.cl. The only restaurant in town with any sort of style.

What to do

Cochrane *p392*
Excursions can be arranged through Guillermo Paso at **Transportes Los Nadis** (see Transport); fishing tours are available from **Hotel Ultimo Paraíso** (see Where to stay).
Casa del Turismo Rural, Dussen 357-B, Coyhaique, T067-252 4929, www.casaturismo rural.cl. Has many members in this area.

Tortel and Puerto Yungay *p393*
Charter boats can easily be arranged in Tortel to **Ventisquero Jorge Montt** and **Isla de los Muertos** for up to 8 people The standard of the boats varies; check first. In theory the harbourmaster will only allow boats out in good weather, however conditions can change very quickly and occasionally boats will have to turn back mid-trip. Make sure you agree beforehand with your guide whether you get any sort of refund if this happens.

Villa O'Higgins *p394*
Hielo Sur, www.hielosur.com (contact Hans Silva) runs a catamaran to Calendario Mancilla, 2½ hrs, US$76.25; with glacier visit 8½ hrs, US$100.
Nelson Henríquez, Lago Cisnes 5. Fishing trips on Lagos Ciervo, Cisnes and El Tigre.
Villa O'Higgins Expeditions, T067-243 1821, www.villaohiggins.com. Treks and expeditions, including the route to El Chaltén in Argentina.

⊖ Transport

Cochrane and around *p392*
Air
Don Carlos to **Coyhaique**, Mon, Thu.

Bus
There are buses every day between Coyhaique and Cochrane; check with companies for current timetables, US$23.50. To **Río Tranquilo**, US$11. To **Villa O'Higgins** with **Katalina** (T067-252 2020/243 1823) Sun, Thu 0800, 6-7 hrs, US$22. To **Tortel** with **Buses Aldea** (Steffen y Las Golondrinas, T067-252 2448/2020), Tue, Thu, Fri, Sat, 0930, return 1500, US$11. Minibuses, including **Bus Ale** (Las Golondrinas 399, T067-252 2242), run daily to **Chile Chico**, US$23.50. Other companies include: **Don Carlos** (Prat 344, T067-252 2150); **Aguilas Patagónicas** (Las Golondrinas 399, T067-252 2020); **Acuario 13** and **Sao Paulo** (Río

Baker 349, T067-252 2143). Petrol is available at the **Esso** and **Copec** servicentros.

Tortel and Puerto Yungay *p393*
Bus
Tortel to **Cochrane** with **Buses Aldea** (see above), Tue, Thu, Fri, Sat 1500, US$11. Tortel to **Villa O'Higgins**, Dec-Mar only Sun 1630, 4 hrs, US$30, T067-243 1821.

Villa O'Higgins *p394*
Air
Don Carlos air taxi flies to Villa O'Higgins from **Coyhaique**, via Cochrane, Mon, Thu.

Boat
For details of the boat service across Lago O'Higgins to **Candelario Mancilla**, see the border box, page 393.

Bus
Bus terminal at Residencial Cordillera, Lago Salto 302, T06-243 1829. If you have a return bus ticket northwards, reconfirm on arrival at Villa O'Higgins. There are 1 or 2 buses weekly to **Cochrane**, with **Katalina** (T067-243 1823) Mon, Fri 1000, 6-7 hrs, US$22. A local fortnightly bus goes to **Lago Cristi**. To **Tortel**, Dec-Mar only Sun 0830 (1630 return to Villa O'Higgins), 4 hrs, US$30, T067-243 1821.

⊕ Directory

Cochrane and around *p392*
Banks Banco del Estado, on the plaza, changes dollars. **Internet** On the western side of the plaza. **Supermarket** Melero, Las Golondrinas 148.

Tortel and Puerto Yungay *p393*
Banks There is no bank in Tortel but a mobile bank comes twice a month. **Medical services** Medical centre staffed by doctors, nurses and dentists visits Tortel monthly. **Post office** Mon-Fri 0900-1300, 1530-1730, Sat 0900-1300; post leaves Tortel weekly by air.

Contents

Footprint features

Border crossings

Far South

At a glance

⊕ **Getting around** Good bus links between the 2 main towns and to Torres del Paine. Hiring a 4WD will give you a little more freedom, but mostly you will be travelling on foot.
⏱ **Time required** A couple of days for a whistlestop tour, 5 or 6 to make the most of your trip, and more if you want to hike the circuit.
☁ **Weather** Unpredictable. Can range from gorgeous sun to bitingly cold frozen rain in a few hours. Winter is calmer but cold.
✖ **When not to go** Winter is beautiful, but trekking is complicated due to the short days and snowfall that closes many (but not all) trekking routes in Torres del Paine.

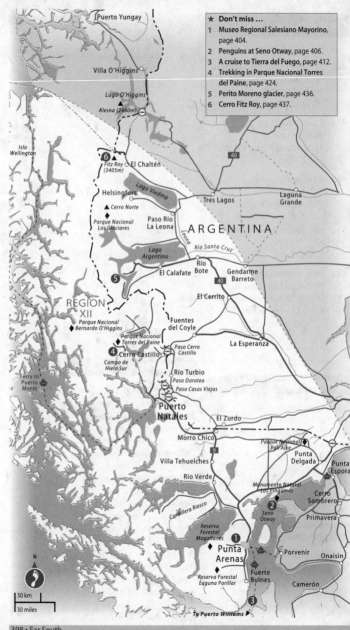

Puerto Yungay

Villa O'Higgins

Lago O'Higgins
▲ Alesna (2480m)

Isla Wellington

▲ Fitz Roy (3405m) El Chaltén

Helsingfors Lago Viedma

▲ Cerro Norte

Parque Nacional Los Glaciares Paso Río La Leona

Lago Argentino

El Calafate Río Bote

ARGENTINA

Río Santa Cruz

Leona

Tres Lagos

Laguna Grande

40

Gendarme Barreto
40

El Cerrito

REGION XII
Parque Nacional Bernardo O'Higgins

Parque Nacional Torres del Paine

Cerro Castillo

Campo de Hielo Sur

Fuentes del Coyle

Paso Cerro Castillo

La Esperanza

Ferry to Puerto Montt

Río Turbio
Paso Dorotea
Paso Casas Viejas

Puerto Natales El Zurdo

Morro Chico

9 Villa Tehuelches

Río Verde

Parque Nacional Pali Aike

Punta Delgada

Punta Espora

Monumento Natural Los Pingüinos

Cordillera Riesco

Seno Otway

Cerro Sombrero

Primavera

Reserva Forestal Magallanes

Punta Arenas

Reserva Forestal Laguna Parillar

Porvenir

Onaisin

Fuerte Bulnes

Camerón

To Puerto Williams

N

30 km
30 miles

A spectacular land of fragmenting glaciers and teetering icy peaks, southern Patagonia feels like nowhere else on earth. Although Chileans posted here will often say that they are a 'long way from Chile', this is the country's most popular destination for visitors. The jewel in the crown is the Parque Nacional Torres del Paine, a natural magnet for travellers from all over the world. The 'towers', three massif-like fingers after which the park is named, point vertically upwards from the Paine, surrounded by glaciers, turquoise-coloured lakes and thick forests of native trees.

Puerto Natales is the base for exploration of Torres del Paine and for boat trips to the glaciers in the Parque Nacional Bernardo O'Higgins. It also provides access to El Calafate and the Parque Nacional Los Glaciares in Argentina. Further south, Punta Arenas is a European-style city with a lively Chilote community and remnants of earlier English and Croatian influences.

Background

Southern Patagonia was inhabited from the end of the Ice Age, mainly by the Tehuelche people, who roamed from the Atlantic coast to the mountains (see box, page 402). The first Europeans did not visit until the 16th century. When Magellan sailed through the Straits in 1520, the strategic importance was quickly recognized: soon Spanish ships were using the route, as were mariners from other countries, including Francis Drake on his world voyage (1578). The route became less important after 1616 when Dutch sailors Jacob le Maire and Cornelius van Schouten discovered a quicker route into the Pacific round Cape Horn.

At Independence, Chile claimed the far southern territories along the Pacific coast but little was done to carry out this claim until 1843 when, concerned at British activities in the area and at rumours of French plans to start a colony, President Bulnes ordered the preparation of a secret mission. The expedition, on board the vessel *Ancud*, established Fuerte Bulnes; the fort was abandoned in 1848 in favour of a new settlement 56 km north, called Punta Arenas. The development of sheep farming in Patagonia and on Tierra del Fuego (with the help of arrivals from the nearby Falkland Islands), and the renewed importance of the Magellan Straits with the advent of steam shipping, led to the rapid expansion of Punta Arenas at the end of the 19th century, when it took the first steps towards being the city that it is today.

Sheep farming remains vital to the local economy, although wool exports have dropped in recent years. Forestry has become more important, but is controversial, as native forests are used for woodchips to export to Japan, Taiwan and Brazil. This is especially serious on Tierra del Fuego. Although oil production has declined, large quantities of natural gas are now produced and about 33% of Chilean coal comes from large open-cast coal mines on the Brunswick Peninsula. Tourism is growing rapidly, making an increasingly important contribution to the local economy.

Geography and climate

Chilean southern Patagonia stretches south from the icefields of the Campo de Hielos Sur to the Estrecho de Magallanes (Straits of Magellan), which separate continental South America from Tierra del Fuego. The coastline is heavily indented by fjords; offshore are numerous islands, few of which are inhabited. The remnants of the Andes stretch along the coast, seldom rising above 1500 m, although the Cordillera del Paine has several peaks over 2600 m and Cerro Balmaceda is 2035 m. Most of the western coast is covered by thick rainforest but further east is grassland, stretching into the arid Patagonian plateau across the Argentine border. Together with the Chilean part of Tierra del Fuego, Isla Navarino and Chilean Antarctica, this part of Chile is administered as Región XII (Magallanes); the capital is Punta Arenas. The region covers 17.5% of Chilean territory, but the population is only around 150,000, less than 1% of the Chilean total.

People from Punta Arenas say they often have four seasons in one day. Frequently, however, the only season appears to be winter. Cold winds, often exceeding 100 kph, blow during the summer bringing heavy rain to coastal areas. Further east, the winds are drier; annual rainfall at Punta Dungeness at the east end of the Straits is only 250 mm compared to over 4000 mm on the offshore islands. Coastal temperatures seldom rise above 15°C in summer. In winter, snow covers the whole region, except those parts near the sea, making many roads impassable. Moreover there is little wind in the winter months, and this means that tourism remains possible for most of the year.

Punta Arenas and around

Capital of Región XII, Punta Arenas lies 2140 km due south of Santiago. The city was originally named 'Sandy Point' by the English, but adopted the Hispanic equivalent under Chilean colonization. A centre for natural gas production, sheep farming and the fishing industry as well as an important military base, it is also the home of Polar Austral, one of the most southerly breweries in the world. Although Punta Arenas has expanded rapidly, it remains a tranquil and pleasant city. The climate and architecture give it a distinctively northern European atmosphere, quite unlike anywhere else in Chile.

Arriving in Punta Arenas → *Colour map 7, B1. Population: 116,000.*

Getting there and around Punta Arenas is cut off from the rest of Chile. Puerto Natales, 247 km north, is easily reached on a paved road, with many buses daily, but other than that the only road connections are via the Argentine towns of Comodoro Rivadavia and Río Gallegos, either from Coyhaique on the Carretera Austral (20 hours; buses weekly in summer) or from Puerto Montt via Bariloche (36 hours, daily buses in summer); it is quicker, and often cheaper, therefore to take one of the many daily flights to/from Puerto Montt or Santiago instead.

Carlos Ibáñez del Campo Airport is 20 km north of town. A minibus service is run by **Transfer Austral** ⓘ *Av Independencia 595-B, T061-272 3358, www.transferaustral.com, US$6.* Alternatively, a taxi costs US$14 to the city or US$10 to the airport. Note that in most taxis much of the luggage space is taken up by natural gas fuel tanks. Buses from Puerto Natales to Punta Arenas will only stop at the airport if they are scheduled to drop passengers there.

There is a daily ferry service aboard the **Melinka** between Punta Arenas and Porvenir on Tierra del Fuego, but buses to Tierra del Fuego use the more northerly ferry crossing at Punta Delgada (many daily) to Puerto Espora. There are also direct flights to Porvenir, Puerto Williams and Ushuaia.

Punta Arenas is not a huge city and walking about is a pleasant way of getting to know it. Buses and *colectivos* are plentiful and cheap (US$0.60): a taxi is only really necessary for out-of-town excursions. Be careful not to confuse the streets Pedro Montt with Jorge Montt and Carrera with Carrera Pinto. ▶▶ *For further details, see Transport, page 410.*

Tourist information Sernatur ⓘ *Lautaro Navarro 999 y Pedro Montt, T061-222 5385, infomagallanes@sernatur.cl, www.patagonia-chile.com, Mon-Fri 0830-2000, Sat-Sun 0900-1300 and 1400-1800.* There is also a **municipal tourist information** ⓘ *opposite Centro Español, T061-220 0610, www.puntaarenas.cl (Spanish only), Mon-Fri 0800-2000, Sat-Sun 0900-1800,* kiosk in the plaza with experienced, English-speaking staff and a good town map with all hotels marked. There is also a **CONAF office** ⓘ *Av Bulnes 0309, p 4, T061-223 8554, magallanes.oirs@conaf.cl.*

The original big foots

The dry Patagonian plateau was originally inhabited by one principal indigenous group, the **Tehuelches**, who lived along the eastern side of the Andes, as far north as modern-day Bariloche, and were hunters of guanaco and rheas. In the 18th century, they began to domesticate the wild horses of the region and sailed down the Patagonian rivers to reach the Atlantic coast.

The Tehuelches were very large: it is said that when the Spanish first arrived in this area, they discovered Tehuelche footprints in the sand, exclaiming '*qué patagón*' ('what a large foot'), hence the name Patagonia.

In the 18th and early 19th centuries, the Tehuelche interacted with European whalers and were patronizingly described as 'semi-civilized'. The granting by the Chilean government of large land concessions in the late 19th century, combined with Argentine President Julio Roca's wars of extermination against Patagonian native peoples in the 1870s, spelled the end for the Tehuelches. They were hunted and persecuted by settlers and only a few survived diseases and the radical change of lifestyle.

Towards the end of the 20th century, a belated sense of moral guilt arose among the colonizers, but it was too late to preserve the Tehuelche way of life. Today, only a few isolated groups remain in Argentine Patagonia.

For details of the indigenous groups further south and in the Patagonian fjords, see the Tierra del Fuego chapter.

Background

After its foundation in 1848, Punta Arenas became a penal colony modelled on Australia. In 1867, it was opened to foreign settlers and given free-port status. From the 1880s, it prospered as a refuelling and provisioning centre for steam ships and whaling vessels. It also became a centre for the new sheep estancias as it afforded the best harbour facilities. The city's importance was reduced overnight by the opening of the Panama Canal in 1914. Although immigrants from Britain and Croatia were central in the growth of Punta Arenas (their influence can be seen to this day), most of those who came to work in the estancias were from Chiloé; many people in the city have relatives in Chiloé and feel an affinity with the island (the barrios on either side of the upper reaches of Independencia are known as Chilote areas); the Chilotes who returned north took Patagonian customs with them, hence the number of *maté* drinkers on Chiloé.

Places in Punta Arenas → *For listings, see pages 407-413.*

Around the attractive **Plaza Muñoz Gamero** are a number of mansions that once belonged to the great sheep-ranching families of the late 19th century. A good example is the **Palacio Sara Braun** ① *Mon-Sat 1000-1300, 1700-2030, US$2*, built between 1894 and 1905 with materials from Europe. The Palacio has several elegantly decorated rooms open to the public and also houses the Hotel José Nogueira. In the centre of the plaza is a statue of Magellan with a mermaid and two Fuegian Indians at his feet. According to local wisdom, those who rub or kiss the big toe of one of the Indians will return to Punta Arenas.

Just north of the plaza is the fascinating **Museo Regional de Magallanes** ① *Palacio Braun Menéndez, Magallanes 949, T061-224 4216, www.museodemagallanes.cl, Wed-Mon 1030-1700 (May-Sep closes 1400), US$2*, the opulent former mansion of Mauricio Braun,

Punta Arenas

Where to stay 🛏

1 Backpackers' Paradise *B3*
2 Cabo de Hornos *C2*
4 Chalet Chapital *C1*
5 Diego de Almagro *C3*
7 Ely House *A3*
8 Hosp Independencia *D1*
9 Hostal Al Fin del Mundo *C3*
10 Hostal Ayelen *B3*
12 Hostal de la Patagonia *B3*
13 Hostal del Sur *B1*
14 Hostal Dinka's House *A3*
16 Hostal La Estancia *B3*
17 Hostal Sonia Kuscevic *A2*
18 Hostal Taty's House *A3*
19 Hostel Keoken *A2*

20 José Nogueira
(Palacio Sara Braun) *C2*
23 Patagonia Pionera *C1*

Restaurants 🍴

1 Café Inmigrante *B3*
2 Café Montt *C3*
3 Damiana Elena *A2*
5 Kisoco Roca *C2*
6 La Piedra *C3*
7 Imago Café *C3*
8 La Luna *C3*
9 La Marmita *B3*
10 La Tasca *D2*
11 Lomit's/Lomito's *C2*
12 Mercado Municipal *D2*

13 Remezón *D2*
15 Sotitos *D3*

Bars & clubs 🍸

16 La Taberna del
Club de la Unión *C2*
18 Santino *C2*
19 Sky Bar at Dreams
Hotel *D3*

built in 1905. A visit is recommended. Part of the museum is set out as a room-by-room regional history; the rest of the house has been left with its original furniture. Guided tours are in Spanish only, but a somewhat confusing information sheet in English is also available. In the basement there is a permanent exhibition dedicated to the indigenous people of southern Patagonia, somewhat ironic considering the leading part the Braun Menéndez family played in their demise.

Three blocks east of the plaza, the **Museo Naval y Marítimo** ⓘ *Pedro Montt 981, T061-220 5479, www.museonaval.cl/en/museo-de-p-arenas.html, Tue-Sat, 0930-1230, 1400-1700, US$2*, houses an exhibition of local and national maritime history with sections on naval instruments, cartography, meteorology, and shipwrecks. There is a video in Spanish and an information sheet in English.

West of the plaza Muñoz Gamero on Waldo Seguel are two reminders of British influence in the city: the **British School** and **St James's Anglican Church** next door. Nearby on Calle Fagnano is the **Mirador Cerro de La Cruz** offering a view over the city and the Magellan Straits complete with its various shipwrecks.

Three blocks further west is the **Museo Militar** ⓘ *Zenteno y Balmaceda, T061-247133, Tue-Fri, 0900-1700, Sat-Sun 0900-1200, 1400-1700, free*, at the Regimiento Pudeto. Lots of knives guns, flags and other military memorabilia are displayed here plus many items brought from Fuerte Bulnes. There are explanatory notes in excruciating English.

North of the centre along Bulnes is the **Museo Regional Salesiano Mayorino Borgatello** ⓘ *Colegio Salesiano, Av Bulnes 336, entrance next to church, T061-222 1001, www.museomaggiorinoborgatello.cl, Tue-Sun 1000-1230, 1500-1730, hours change frequently, US$5*, an excellent introduction to Patagonia and easily the most complete and fascinating regional museum in Chile. It covers the fascinating history of the indigenous peoples and their education by the Salesian missions, alongside an array of stuffed birds and gas extraction machinery. The Italian priest, Alberto D'Agostini, who arrived in 1909 and presided over the missions, took wonderful photographs of the region and his 70-minute film can be seen on video (ask).

Three blocks further on, the **cemetery** ⓘ *Av Bulnes 029, daily 0800-1800, 0730-2000 in summer, US$4*, is one of the most interesting places in the city, with cypress avenues, gravestones in many languages that bear testimony to the cosmopolitan provenance of Patagonian pioneers, and many mausolea and memorials to pioneer families and victims of shipping disasters. Look out for the statue of Indicito, the little Indian, on the northwest side, which is now an object of reverence, bedecked with flowers. Further north still, the **Instituto de la Patagonia** houses the **Museo del Recuerdo** ⓘ *Av Bulnes 1890, Km 4 northeast (opposite the university), T061-224 4216, outdoor exhibits Mon-Fri 0830-1130, 1430-1830, Sat 0830-1230, US$4*, an open-air museum with 3000 artefacts used by the early settlers, pioneer homes and botanical gardens. Opposite is the Zona Franca with a mall and ice rink (see Shopping, below).

On 21 de Mayo, south of Independencia, is a small ornate Hindu temple, one of only two in Chile, while further along the same street, on the southern outskirts of the city, the wooded **Parque María Behety** features a scale model of Fuerte Bulnes, a campsite and children's playground, popular for Sunday picnics. In winter, there is an ice rink here.

Reserva Nacional Magallanes ⓘ *7 km west of town, US$3, taxi US$7.50*, known locally as the Parque Japonés, extends over 13,500 ha and rises to 600 m. Although getting there by taxi is the easiest option, it can also be reached on foot or by bike: follow Independencia up the hill and take a right for Río de las Minas, about 3 km from the edge of town; the entrance to the reserve is 2 km beyond. Here you will find a self-guided nature trail through lenga and coigue trees. The road continues through the woods for 14 km passing several picnic sites. From the top end of the road a short path leads to a lookout over the **Garganta del Diablo** (Devil's Throat), a gorge with views over Punta Arenas and Tierra del Fuego. From here a slippery path leads down to the Río de las Minas Valley and then back to Punta Arenas. Within the reserve, 8 km west of Punta Arenas, Cerro Mirador is one of the few places in the world where you can ski with a sea view. In summer there is a good two-hour walk on the hill, with labelled flora; contact **Club Andino** ① T061-224 1479, www.clubandino.cl.

Around Punta Arenas → For listings, see pages 407-413.

Reserva Forestal Laguna Parrillar

About 25 km south of Punta Arenas, there is a fork in the road to the right; 21 km further on is the very peaceful Parrillar reserve, covering 18,814 ha and surrounded by snow-capped hills. It has older forest than the Magallanes Reserve and sphagnum bogs, and offers excellent salmon and trout fishing. There is a three-hour walk to the treeline (and others along poorly marked, boggy paths) and fine views from the mirador. There are CONAF-administered campsites and picnic sites. Note that there is no public transport to the reserve and hitching is virtually impossible; a radio taxi will cost about US$80-140.

Fuerte Bulnes and further south

Some 56 km south of Punta Arenas, Fuerte Bulnes (US$24) is a replica of the wooden fort erected in 1843 by the crew of the Chilean vessel *Ancud*. Built in the 1940s and originally designed to house a museum, nearly all the interesting exhibits and artefacts were moved to museums in Punta Arenas and Santiago in 1986 and now only the empty shells of the various buildings remain. Several agencies run half-day tours to here, but hitching is not difficult at weekends or in summer, as there are many holiday camps in the area.

Nearby is **Puerto Hambre**, where there are ruins of the church built by Sarmiento de Gamboa's colonists in 1584 (see box, page 406). This is a very beautiful area with views towards the towering ice mountains near Pico Sarmiento; it was of Puerto Hambre that Darwin wrote: "looking due southward … the distant channels between the mountains appeared from their gloominess to lead beyond the confines of this world". Southern dolphins can often be seen in the straits around this point.

At the intersection of the roads to Puerto Hambre and Fuerte Bulnes, 51 km south of Punta Arenas, is a small monolith marking the **Centro Geográfico de Chile**, the midway point between Arica and the South Pole. Bypassing Fuerte Bulnes, the road continues past a memorial to Captain Pringle Stokes, Captain of the *Beagle*, who committed suicide here in 1829, being replaced as captain by Fitz Roy. The road carries on, past San Juan to the lighthouse at San Isidro. The last part of this journey can only be done in summer in a high-clearance vehicle and at low tide, as it involves crossing an estuary at the mouth of the Río San Pedro. Alternatively leave your vehicle on the north side of the estuary, ford the river (at low tide) and walk 2½ hrs to San Isidro. From here, it is a day hike to **Cape Froward**, the southernmost point of the continent of South America, marked by a 24-m-high cross. There is no path, and a guide is essential (this can be arranged by the hostería at San Isidro with advance notice). Some 70 km west of Cape Froward along the Magellan Straits is *Isla Carlos III*, a popular base for humpback whale watching.

Port Famine (Puerto Hambre)

In 1582, Felipe II of Spain, alarmed by Drake's passage through the Straits of Magellan, decided to establish a Spanish presence on the Straits. A fleet of 15 ships and 4000 men, commanded by Pedro Sarmiento de Gamboa, was despatched in 1584. Before the ships had left the Bay of Biscay, a storm arose and scattered the fleet, sinking seven ships and killing 800 people. Further depleted by disease, the fleet of three remaining ships at length arrived at the Straits, with just 300 men on board. Led by Sarmiento this small force founded two cities: Nombre de Jesús on Punta Dungeness at the eastern entrance to the Straits and Rey Don Felipe near Puerto Hambre.

Disaster struck when their only remaining vessel broke its anchorage in a storm near Nombre de Jesús; the ship, with Sarmiento on board, was blown into the Atlantic, leaving many of Sarmiento's men stranded on land. After vain attempts to re-enter the Straits, Sarmiento set sail for Río de Janeiro where he organized two rescue missions: the first ended in shipwreck, the second in mutiny. Captured by English corsairs, Sarmiento was taken to England where he was imprisoned. On his release by Elizabeth I, he tried to return to Spain via France, but was jailed again. Until his death in 1608, Sarmiento besieged Felipe II with letters urging him to rescue the men stranded in the Straits.

When the English corsair Thomas Cavendish sailed through the Straits in 1587 he found only 18 survivors at Rey Don Felipe. With the English and Spanish at war, only one – Tomé Hernández – would trust Cavendish when he first arrived. A sudden spell of fine weather arose, and Cavendish set sail, leaving the rest of the men to die. He named the place Port Famine as a reminder of their grisly fate.

North of Punta Arenas

Some 70 km north of Punta Arenas, **Seno Otway** ① *Oct to mid-Mar, US$11*, is the site of a colony of around 11,000 Magellanic penguins that can be viewed from walkways and bird hides; rheas, skunks and foxes can also be seen. There are beautiful views across the sound to the mountains to the north, and it is also becoming a popular area for sea kayaking and other adventure sports. Several agencies offer trips to the colony lasting five hours (US$20 plus entry fees at peak season); if you wish to visit independently, a taxi from Punta Arenas will cost US$50-70 return or there are daily buses with Fernández. It is best to go early in the day. Try to avoid going at the same time as the large cruise ship tours – it is not much fun having to wait behind 200 people for your turn at the viewing stations. Access to the colony is via a private road where a toll of US$2.50 per person is charged.

A small island, 30 km northeast, **Isla Magdalena** is the location of the **Monumento Natural Los Pingüinos** ① *US$10*, a colony of 80,000 pairs of Megallanic penguins, administered by **CONAF**. Deserted apart from during the breeding season from November to early February, Magdalena is one of a group of three islands visited by Drake (the others are Marta and Isabel), whose men killed 3000 penguins for food. Boat trips to the island are run by **Comapa** and **Sólo Expediciones**, while the Australis cruise ships also call here (see What to do, page 410). Take a hat, coat and gloves.

Beyond, Route 255 heads northeast towards the Argentine border (see box, page 407), passing Kamiri Aike where a road branches southeast towards Punta Delgada for ferries to Tierra del Fuego (see page 506). There is also a turn-off north

Border crossing: Chile–Argentina

Integración Austral

The border is located 30 km north of Kamiri Aike via Route 255 (190 km from Punta Arenas) and is open daily 24 hours in summer and 0900-2300 from 1 April to 3 October. On the Argentine side the road continues as Route 3 for 67 km northeast to Río Gallegos. For bus passengers the border crossing is easy, although you have about a 30-minute wait at each border post as luggage is checked and documents are stamped. Hire cars from Argentina need special documents in order to cross the border. For more information see www.gendarmeria.gov.ar/pasos/chile/fichaust.html.

---

along a *ripio* road for 26 km to **Parque Nacional Pali Aike** ① *managed by CONAF, T061-223 8554, magallanes.oirs@conaf.cl, US$2*, a fantastic volcanic landscape dotted with small cones and craters. It's one of the oldest archaeological sites in Patagonia, with evidence of aboriginal occupation from 10,000-12,000 years ago. (Pali Aike means 'desolate place of bad spirits' in Tehuelche.) There are five easy, marked trails, all of which can be done in a day. Tour operators offer full day trips, US$70-80.

⊙ Punta Arenas and around listings

For hotel and restaurant price codes and other relevant information, see pages 14-21.

⊖ Where to stay

Punta Arenas *p401, map p403*
Hotel prices are lower during winter months (Apr-Sep). A few streets, in particular Caupolicán and Maipú, some 10-15 mins' walk from the centre have become a "hotbed of hostels", most of them with similar facilities and similar prices (**$$**). These include **Ely House, The Pink House, Shangri-la, Maipú Street** and **Hostal Dinka's House**; the latter is painted bright-red and run by the indomitable Dinka herself. The area is also full of car repair places, which can make it noisy day-time and occasionally at night. For accommodation in private houses, usually **$** pp, ask at the tourist office. There are no campsites in or near the city.

$$$$-$$$ Cabo de Hornos, Plaza Muñoz Gamero 1025, T061-271 5000, www.hoteles-australis.com. 4-star, comfy, bright and spacious rooms, with good views from 4th floor up.

$$$$-$$$ Diego de Almagro, Av Colón 1290, T061-220 8800, www.dahoteles puntaarenas.com. Very modern, good international standard, on waterfront, many rooms with view, heated pool, sauna, small gym, big bright rooms, good value.
$$$$-$$$ José Nogueira, Plaza de Armas, Bories 959 y P Montt, in former Palacio Sara Braun, T061-271 1000, www.hotel nogueira.com. Best in town, stylish rooms, warm atmosphere, excellent service. Smart restaurant in the beautiful *loggia*. A few original rooms now a 'small museum'.
$$$ Chalet Chapital, Sanhueza 974, T061-273 0100, www.hotelchaletchapital.cl. Small well-run hotel, smallish rooms, helpful staff, a good choice in this price range.
$$$ Hostal de la Patagonia, O'Higgins 730, T061-224 9970, www.ecotour patagonia.com. Rooms with heating, good services, dining room, 10 mins' walk from centre. Organizes a variety of tours, including fly fishing.
$$$ Patagonia Pionera, Arauco 786, T061-222 2045, www.hotelpatagoniapionera.cl. Beautiful 1930s wooden casona now a

comfortable high-end B&B. Helpful staff, onsite parking.

$$ Hostal Al Fin del Mundo, O'Higgins 1026, T061-271 0185, www.alfindelmundo. hostel.com. Rooms and dorms, bright, cosy, shared baths, central, helpful, pool table, English spoken.

$$ Hostal Ayelen, Lautarro Navarro 763, T061-224 2413 www.ayelenresidencial.com. 120-year-old house with some new rooms at the back, bathroom a bit small but super clean, comfy.

$$ Hostal del Sur, Mejicana 151, T061-222 7249, www.hostaldelsurmag.com. Impeccable old house with modern rooms in residential area, welcoming, with charming reception areas.

$$ Hostel Keoken, Magallanes 209, T061-224 4086/6376, www.hostelkeoken.cl. Light, wooden, spacious building on 3 floors each with its own entrance up rickety outside staircases. Some rooms with small bath. Good value, some info. Top floor rooms with shared bathroom have paper thin walls. Currently expanding into an even bigger, rambling place.

$$ Hostal La Estancia, O'Higgins 765, T061-224 9130, www.estancia.cl. Simple but comfortable rooms, some with bath. **$** pp in dorms. English spoken, small shop attached, music and games room recently opened.

$$ Hostal Sonia Kuscevic, Pasaje Darwin 175, T061-224 8543, www.hostalsk.cl. One of the city's oldest guesthouses, with heating and parking. Better value for longer stays, good discount if you have a Hostelling International card.

$$ Hostal Taty's House, Maipu 1070, T061-224 1525, www.hostaltatyshouse.cl. Nice rooms with good beds, decent choice in this price bracket, basic English spoken.

$$-$ Backpackers' Paradise, Carrera Pinto 1022, T061-224 0104, backpackersparadise@ hotmail.com. Popular good kitchen, 1 private and 5 shared rooms. Facilities much improved in recent years.

$ Hostal Independencia, Independencia 374, T061-222 7572, www.chileaustral.com/ independencia. Rooms, dorms and camping with use of kitchen and bathroom. Trekking equipment rental, parking, fishing and other tours, lots of information.

Fuerte Bulnes and further south *p405*
$$$$ Hostería Faro San Isidro, 75 km south of Punta Arenas, booking office Lautaro Navarro 1163, Punta Arenas, T09-934 93862, www.hosteriafarosanisidro.cl. The southernmost lodging on the American continent and within striking distance of Cape Froward. Excursions offered.

🍴 Restaurants

Punta Arenas *p401, map p403*
Many eating places close on Sun. There are seasonal bans on *centolla* (king crab) fishing to protect dwindling stocks; out of season *centolla* served in restaurants will probably be frozen. Note that *centolla* is caught illegally by some fishermen using dolphin, porpoise and penguin as live bait. If there is an infestation of red tide (*marea roja*), a disease which is fatal to humans, bivalve shellfish must not be eaten. Mussels should not be picked along the shore because of pollution and the *marea roja*. Sernatur and the Centros de Salud have leaflets.

$$$ Remezón, 21 de Mayo 1469, T061-224 1029. Regional specialities such as krill. Very good, but should be, given the prices.

$$$-$$ Damiana Elena, Magallanes 341, T061-222 2818. Mon-Sat from 2000. Stylish restaurant serving Mediterranean food with a Patagonian touch, popular with locals, book ahead at weekends.

$$$-$$ La Tasca, Plaza Muñoz Gamero 771, above Teatro Cervantes in Casa Español. Large helpings, limited selection, decent set lunch, views over the plaza.

$$$-$$ Sotitos, O'Higgins 1138. Daily (Sun 1200-1500 only). An institution, famous for seafood in elegant surroundings, excellent.

Book ahead in season. New 2nd floor serving local specialties and Italian food.
$$ La Luna, O'Higgins 1017, T061-222 8555. Fish, shellfish and local specialities, huge pisco sours, popular, quirky decor, friendly staff. Recommended.
$$ La Marmita, Plaza Sampiao 678, www.marmitamaga.cl. Mon-Sat 1230-1500, 1830-2330. Regional dishes with international twist, vegetarian options, good sized portions, prettily presented, chatty owner, generally very good.
$$-$ La Piedra, Lautaro Navarro 1087. Mon-Sat 1200-0100. Meat dishes, fish, soups, salads, good burgers and sandwiches, daily lunch specials, housed over 2 floors.
$ Lomit's/Lomito's, Menéndez 722. A fast-food institution with bar attached, cheap snacks and drinks (local beers are good), open when the others are closed, good food.
$ Mercado Municipal, 21 de Mayo 1465. Wide range of cocinerías offering cheap empanadas and seafood on the upper floor of the municipal market.
$ Kiosco Roca, Roca 875, unassuming sandwich bar, voted best in Punta Arenas. Mon-Fri 0800-1900, Sat 0800-1300, always packed. Take-away or a few seats available at the counter.

Cafés
Café Inmigrante, Quillota 599 (esq Mejicana), T061-222 2205, www.inmigrante. cl. Daily afternoons and evenings. Hugely popular cafe run by 3rd generation Croatian expats. Beautifully prepared sandwiches, daily changing cake menu, huge portions, family history on menus. Quirky and popular. Book in advance if possible. Highly recommended.
Café Montt, Pedro Montt 976. Coffees, teas, cakes, pastries and snacks, Wi-Fi. Cosy, friendly. Recommended.
Imago Café, Costanera y Colón. Tiny, laid back café hidden away in a beachfront bunker overlooking the straits.

🎵 Bars and clubs

Punta Arenas *p401, map p403*
La Taberna del Club de la Unión, on the plaza in the basement of the **Hotel Nogueira**. Mon-Sat from 1830. Atmospheric bar, good for evening drinks.
Santino, Colón 657, www.santino.cl. Open 1800-0300. Also serves pizzas and other snacks, large bar, good service, live music Sat.
Sky Bar, O'Higgins 1235. Bar with panoramic views on the top floor of the luxury Dreams hotel and spa. Open from 1830.

⊛ Entertainment

Punta Arenas *p401, map p403*
There is a single-screen **cinema** at Mejicana 777, www.cinesalaestrella.cl. The **casino**, www.mundodreams.com, is on O'Higgins just north of the port.

⊛ Festivals

Punta Arenas *p401, map p403*
Late Jan/Early Feb Muestra custumbrista de Chiloé, when the Chilote community celebrates its culture.
Late Jun Carnaval de invierno The winter solstice is marked by a carnival on the weekend closest to 21 Jun.

O Shopping

Punta Arenas *p401, map p403*
Punta Arenas has certain free-port facilities:
Zona Franca, 3.5 km north of the centre, opposite Museo del Recuerdo (Instituto de la Patagonia), is cheaper than elsewhere. The complex now has over 100 shops and is open daily from 1000 (www.zonaustral. cl); to get there take bus E or A from Plaza Muñoz Gamero or catch one of the many *colectivos*; taxi US$3.

Handicrafts
Chile Típico, Carrera Pinto 1015,
T061-222 5827. Beautiful knitwear
and woollen ponchos.
Mercado Municipal (see Restaurants,
above). Excellent handicrafts and souvenirs
on the lower floors, recently enlarged.

⚙ What to do

Punta Arenas *p401, map p403*
Skiing
Cerro Mirador in the Reserva Nacional
Magallanes has skiing Jun-Sep, weather
and snow permitting. Midway lodge
with food, drink and equipment rental.
Taxi US$8; local buses at weekends from
Punta Arenas main square.

Tour operators
Most tour operators organize trips to Torres
del Paine, Fuerte Bulnes, the *pingüineras*
on Isla Magdalena and Otway Sound, and
Tierra del Fuego; shop around.
Adventure Network International, T+1-801
266 4876, www.adventure-network.com.
Antarctic experiences of a lifetime, operating
out of Punta Arenas, flying to the interior of
the Antarctic Continent. Flights to the South
Pole, guided mountain climbing and fully
guided skiing expeditions. Camping with
Emperor Penguins in Nov.
Arka Patagonia, Manuel Señoret 1597,
T061-224 8167, www.arkapatagonia.com. All
types of tours, whale-watching, trekking.
Solo Expediciones, Nogueira 1255, T061-
224 3354, www.soloexpediciones.com.
Operate their own service to Monumento
Natural Los Pingüinos on a small, fast boat,
also passing by Isla Marta, half-day tour,
mornings only.
Turismo Aventour, Patagonia 779, T061-
222 0174, http://aventourpatagonia.cl.
Specialize in fishing trips, organize tours to
Tierra del Fuego, helpful, English spoken.
Turismo Comapa, Magallanes 990,
T061-220 0200, www.comapa.com.

Tours to Torres del Paine (responsible,
well-informed guides), Tierra del Fuego and
to see penguins at Isla Magdalena. Agents
for Australis Expedition Cruises (see below).
Turismo Laguna Azul, Menéndez 786,
T061-222 5200, www.turismolagunaazul.
com. Full-day trips to a colony of king
penguins on Tierra del Fuego. Trips run
all year round. Also city tours, trips to
glaciers and others.
Turismo Yamana, Errázuriz 932, T061-
222 2061, www.yamana.cl. Conventional
and deluxe tours, trekking in Torres del
Paine, kayaking the fjords of Parque
Nacional De Agostini (Tierra del Fuego),
multilingual guides.
Whale Sound, Lautaro Navarro 1191, T09-
9887 9814, www.whalesound.com. Whale-
watching trips in the Magellan Straits.

⊖ Transport

Punta Arenas *p401, map p403*
Most transport is heavily booked from
Christmas to Mar: advance booking
strongly advised.

Air
To **Santiago**, **LAN**, via Puerto Montt, and
Sky (several stops) daily. To **Porvenir**,
Aerovías DAP (O'Higgins 891, T061-261
6100, www.aeroviasdap.cl) 3 times daily
Mon-Fri, 2 on Sat, 9 passengers, 12 mins.
To **Puerto Williams**, daily except Sun,
1¼ hrs (book a week in advance for
Porvenir, 2 in advance for Puerto Williams).

  To **Ushuaia**, 1 hr, LAN 3 a week in
summer (schedules change frequently).
Take passport when booking tickets to
Argentina. To **Falkland Islands/Islas
Malvinas**, with **LAN**, once a week; for
information contact **International Tours &
Travel Ltd**, 1 Dean St, PO Box 408, Stanley,
T+500 22041, www.falklandislands.travel,
who are the Falkland Islands agents for LAN.
They also handle inbound tourist bookings,
book FIGAS flights and arrange tours.

Bus

The bus terminal is at the northern edge of town by the Zona Franca. To book all tickets visit the **Central de Pasajeros**, Colón y Magallanes, T061-224 5811, also *cambio* and tour operator. At the time of writing bus companies were maintaining their own offices in the city centre: **Cruz del Sur**, **Fernández**, and Turibus, Sanhueza 745, T061-224 2313/222 1429, www.busesfernandez.com; **Pacheco**, Colón 900, T061-224 2174, www.busespacheco.com; **Pullman**, Colón 568, T061-222 3359, www.pullman.cl, tickets for all Chile; **Bus Sur**, Menéndez 552, T061-222 2938, www.bus-sur.cl; **Ghisoni** and **Tecni Austral**, Lautaro Navarro 975, T061-261 3422.

To **Puerto Natales**, 3-3½ hrs, **Fernández**, **Bus Sur** and **Pacheco**, up to 8 daily, last departure 2015, US$10, look out for special offers and connections to Torres del Paine. Buses may pick up at the airport with advance booking and payment. To **Otway Sound**, with **Fernández** daily 1500, return 1900, US$13.50.

To **Tierra del Fuego** via Punta Delgada (see Arriving on Tierra del Fuego, page 452; no buses via Porvenir) **Pacheco**, **Sur**, **Tecni-Austral** and others (check with companies for schedules); to **Río Grande**, 8-10 hrs, US$42, heavily booked; to **Ushuaia**, 12 hrs, US$70-85; some services have to change in Río Grande for Ushuaia, others are direct; book well in advance in Jan-Feb.

To **Río Gallegos** (Argentina), via Route 255, **Pacheco**, Sun, Mon, Tue, Fri; **Ghisoni**, Mon, Wed, Thu, Fri, Sat; fares US$24, 5-8 hrs, depending on customs: 15 mins on Chilean side, up to 2 hrs on Argentine side (see also box, page 407).

Car hire

Note that you need a hire company's authorization to take a car into Argentina. This takes 24 hrs (not Sat or Sun) and involves mandatory international insurance at US$30 per week, plus notary fees. In addition to the multinationals, there are some local companies: **EMSA**, Kuzma Slavic 706, T061-261 4378, www.emsarentacar.cl; **Payne**, Menéndez 631, T061-224 0852, www.payne.cl, also tours, treks, birdwatching, etc.

Ferry and cruise services

To Tierra del Fuego The ferry dock is 5 km north of Punta Arenas centre, at Tres Puentes. For all ferry services to the island, see Arriving in Tierra del Fuego, page 452.

To **Puerto Montt** Contact **Navimag**, at Turismo Comapa, Magallanes 990, T061-220 0200, www.navimag.com, and see page 336. For **Australis Expecition Cruises**, see box, page 412.

To **Antarctica** Most cruise ships leave from Ushuaia, but a few operators are based in Punta Arenas. Try **Adventure Network International** (see above) or **Antarctica XXI**,

A cruise at the end of the world

From September to April, Australis Expedition Cruises have two vessels running cruises between Punta Arenas and Ushuaia, the *Vía Australis* and the newer *Stella Australis*. Vía Australis has capacity for 136 passengers, while Stella Australis can accommodate 210. Passengers sail in comfort, treated to fine food and expert service, through the Straits of Magellan and the channels and fjords between Tierra del Fuego and the islands that cling to its southern shore. These were the waters fished by the Yámana and Kawéskar people and surveyed by Robert Fitzroy and his crew.

The cruise takes four nights each way. Each includes a visit to Cape Horn where, sea conditions permitting, you can land to see the monuments and to sign the visitors' book in the lighthouse, manned by a Chilean naval officer and his family. The landing follows a rigorous procedure: everyone is togged up in waterproofs and lifejackets, and is transferred from ship to Zodiac, before disembarking with the aid of crew standing in the surf. From the shore, 160 wooden steps lead up the cliff to wooden walkways. On a relatively benign day – sunny, with an icy breeze – it's hard to imagine the tragedies of so many mariners lost, to remember the many souls that, according to legend, have become albatrosses, and to accept that this is the last piece of terra firma before Antarctica.

Other shore trips are followed by a whisky or hot chocolate. You need the sustenance, especially after a visit to Piloto and Nena glaciers in the Chico fjord. The blue ice of Piloto calves into the water, while Nena is scarred by rocky debris. All around water pours off the mountains; sleet and rain drive into your face as the Zodiac powers away.

En route from Ushuaia to Punta Arenas (the itinerary varies according to the route and the weather), there are other landings. At Wulaia Bay on Isla Navarino two walks are available, up a hill or along the shore to look for birds and flora. A museum, in an old radio station, tells the history of the place. It was here that one of Fitzroy's Fuegians, Jemmy Button, who was briefly a celebrity in England in the 1830s, was reportedly present at the massacre of missionaries in 1859. Another visit is to Isla Magdalena, just off Punta Arenas. Here, between November and January, 60,000 pairs of Magellanic penguins breed in burrows.

At all times the ship is accompanied by giant petrels, black-browed albatross and king cormorants. Occasionally, dolphins ride the wake. If it is too cold on deck, you can go onto the bridge and be entertained by the navigator. The bar is open almost all the time; stewards and guides are on hand at any hour; and there are lectures and films, visits to the engine room and cookery lessons to fill the hours at sea. Everything runs like clockwork thanks to clear instructions for safety and fine-tuned organization: when the captain says you'll dock at 1100, dock at 1100 you will.

For more information on these cruises, see www.australis.com, and **Australis Expedition Cruises**, at Turismo Comapa, Magallanes 990, T061-220 0200, www.australis.com (in Santiago: Av El Bosque Norte 0440, p 11, T02-2442 3115; in Buenos Aires: T011-5199 6697).

O'Higgins 1170, T061-261 4100, www.antarcticaxxi.com, for flight/cruise packages. See also Santiago Tour operators, page 61. Otherwise, another possibility is with the Chilean Navy vessels *Galvarino* and *Lautaro*, which sail regularly (no schedule;

see isotop@mitierra.cl, www.armada.cl). Note that the navy does not encourage passengers, so you must approach the captain direct; Spanish is essential.

Taxi

Ordinary taxis have yellow roofs. *Colectivos* (all black) run on fixed routes and pick up from taxi stands around town, US$2 flat fee.

❶ Directory

Punta Arenas *p401, map p403*
Banks Several on or around Plaza Muñoz Gamero many 24 hrs, all have ATMs. Banks open Mon-Fri 0800-1400, *casas de cambio* open Mon-Fri 0900-1230, 1500-1900, Sat 0900-1230; good rates at **Cambio Gasic**, Roca 915, of 8, T061-224 2396. German spoken; **La Hermandad**, Lautaro Navarro 1099,

T061-224 3991, excellent rates; **Sur Cambios**, Lautaro Navarro 1001, T061-222 5656.
Consulates Argentina, 21 de Mayo 1878, T061-226 1912, Mon-Fri 0900-1800, visas take 24 hrs. **Laundry** Lavaseco Josseau, Carrera Pinto 768; **Lavasol**, O'Higgins 969, the only self-service laundry. **Medical services** Dentist Rosemary Robertson Stipicic, Roca 932, T061-222 3768, speaks English. **Hospital Regional Lautaro Navarro**, Angamos 180, T061-220 5123/224 4040, public hospital, for emergency room ask for *urgencias*; **Clínica Magallanes**, Bulnes 01448, T061-220 7200, www.clinicamagallanes.cl, private clinic, medical staff the same as in the hospital but fancier surroundings and more expensive. A list of English-speaking doctors is available from Sernatur. **Post office** Bories 911 y Menéndez, Mon-Fri 0900-1830, Sat 1000-1300.

Puerto Natales and around

From Punta Arenas, a good paved road runs 247 km north to Puerto Natales through forests of southern beech and prime pastureland; this is the best area for cattle- and sheep-raising in Chile. Nandúes and guanacos can often be seen en route. Puerto Natales lies between Cerro Dorotea (which rises behind the town) and the eastern shore of the Seno Ultima Esperanza (Last Hope Sound), over which there are fine views, weather permitting, to the Peninsula Antonio Varas and the jagged peaks and receding glaciers of the Parque Nacional Bernardo O'Higgins beyond. Founded in 1911, the town grew as an industrial centre and, until recent years, the town's prosperity was based upon employment in the coal mines of Río Turbio, Argentina. Today, Puerto Natales is the starting point for trips to the magnificent O'Higgins and Torres del Paine national parks, and tourism is one of its most important industries; the town centre has a prosperous if somewhat touristy atmosphere.

Arriving in Puerto Natales → *Colour map 6, B3. Population 19,000.*

Getting there and around Puerto Natales is easily reached by many daily buses from Punta Arenas. In theory buses from Punta Arenas to Puerto Natales will also pick passengers up at Punta Arenas airport as long as reservations and payment have been made in advance through an agency in Puerto Natales; in practice, though, they are often unreliable. There are also buses from Río Turbio and El Calafate in Argentina (two to four daily) and weekly buses from Río Gallegos. Note that buses from Argentina invariably arrive late. All buses use the new bus terminal 20 minutes outside town at Avenida España 1455. *Colectivos* to/from the centre cost US$0.60 (US$0.70 Sun); taxis charge a flat fee of US$2 throughout Puerto Natales. The town is the terminus of the *Navimag* ship to Puerto Montt. In summer, there are also flights from Santiago via Puerto Montt. If driving between Punta Arenas and Puerto Natales, make sure you have enough fuel. Puerto Natales itself is small, so taxis are only needed for journeys out of town. ▶▶ *For further details, see Transport, page 421.*

Tourist office Good leaflets in English on Puerto Natales and Torres del Paine, as well as bus and boat information is available from the **Sernatur office** ① *on the waterfront, Av Pedro Montt 19, T061-241 2125, infonatales@sernatur.cl, Oct-Mar Mon-Fri 0830-1900, Sat-Sun 1000-1300 and 1430-1800, Apr-Sep Mon-Fri 0830-1800, Sat 1000-1300 and 1400-1800.* The **Municipal tourist office** ①*Av España 1455*, is located at the bus station. **CONAF** ① *Baquedano 847, T061-241 1438, patricio.salinas@conaf.cl.*

Border crossing: Chile–Argentina

There are three crossing points east of Puerto Natales. For further information, see www.pasosfronterizos.gov.cl and www.gendarmeria.gov.ar, which gives details of all three crossings in its Santa Cruz section.

Paso Casas Viejas/Laurita

This crossing, 16 km east of Puerto Natales, is reached by turning off Route 9 (towards Punta Arenas) at Km 14. **Chilean immigration** is open daily 0800-2200 (0700-2100 in winter). **Argentine immigration** is open daily 0900-0100. On the Argentine side the route joins the road north to Río Turbio (33 km) and La Esperanza or southeast to Río Gallegos.

Paso Dorotea/Mina Uno

This crossing is reached by branching off Route 9 (towards Punta Arenas) 9 km east of Puerto Natales and continuing north for a further 11 km. **Chilean immigration** is open daily 0700-2300. On the Argentine side the road continues to a junction, where you can head north to Río Turbio (5 km) and La Esperanza, or south to Río Gallegos. This is the crossing used by buses between Río Turbio and Puerto Natales.

Paso Río Cerro Castillo/Don Guillermo

Chilean immigration, open daily 0800-2200, is 7 km west of the border in the small settlement of Cerro Castillo, which lies 65 km north of Puerto Natales on the road to Torres del Paine. Cerro Castillo is well-equipped with toilets, ATM, tourist information, souvenir shop, several *cafeterías* and *hospedajes*, including $ pp Hospedaje Loreto Belén, Km 60, T061-269 1932 ext 278, which offers rooms for four and good home cooking. There's sheep shearing in December, and a rodeo and rural festival in January. **Argentine immigration**, open daily 0900-2300, is at Cancha Carrera, a few kilometres east of the border, where there are few facilities. The road continues east to La Esperanza or south to Río Turbio. All buses between Puerto Natales and El Calafate go via Cerro Castillo, making it the most convenient route for visiting the Parque Nacional Los Glaciares from Chile. Travelling into Chile, it is possible to stop in Cerro Castillo and transfer to a bus passing from Puerto Natales to Torres del Paine.

Places in Puerto Natales

The **Museo Histórico Municipal** ① *Bulnes 285, T061-241 1263, Mon 0800-1700, Tue-Fri 0800-1900, Sat 1000-1300 and 1500-1900, US$2,* houses a small collection of archaeological and native artefacts as well as exhibits on late 19th-century European colonization, with reasonable descriptions in English.

The colourful old steam train in the main square was once used to take workers to the meat-packing factory at **Puerto Bories**, 5 km north of town. It is a pleasant hour-long walk along the shore to Bories with glimpses of the Balmaceda Glacier across the sound. In its heyday the plant was the biggest of its kind in Chile with a capacity for 250,000 sheep. Bankrupted in the early 1990s, much of the plant was dismantled in 1993. Belatedly the plant was given National Monument status and is slowly being restored. The remaining buildings and machine rooms can be visited. It's also the site of **The Singular Hotel** (see Where to stay, below).

The slab-like **Cerro Dorotea** dominates the town, with superb views of the whole Seno Ultima Esperanza. It can be reached on foot or by any Río Turbio bus or taxi (recommended, as the hill is further away than it seems). The trail entrance is marked by a sign that reads 'Mirador Cerro Dorotea'. Expect to be charged US$5-8 in one of the local houses, where you will be given a broomstick handle which makes a surprisingly good walking stick. It is a 1½-hour trek up to the 600-m lookout along a well-marked trail. In theory you can continue along the top of the hill to get better views to the north, but the incredibly strong winds often make this dangerous.

Puerto Natales

Seno Ultima Esperanza

To Punta Arenas &
Parque Nacional Torres del Paine

Pier for
Balmaceda
Glacier

Pier for
Puerto Montt

Plaza de
Armas

Museo
Municipal

N

200 metres

200 yards

Where to stay
1 Aquaterra C2
4 Casa Cecilia B2
5 Casa Teresa C2
6 Costaustralis C1
7 Hosp Casa Lili B1
8 Hosp Nancy C3
9 Hostal Las Carretas C3
10 Hostal Sir Francis Drake A2
11 Hostel Natales B1
12 Indigo Patagonia B1
13 Josmar 2 Camping C2
14 Keoken B1

16 Lili Patagónico's C3
17 Martín Gusinde B2
20 Patagonia Adventure B2
21 Remota A2
23 The Singing Lamb C3
24 Weskar Patagonian
  Lodge A2

Restaurants
1 Afrigonia B2
3 Angelica's B2
4 Cormorán de las Rocas A2
5 El Asador Patagónico B2

6 El Living B2
7 La Mesita Grande B2
8 La Picada de Carlitos C3
9 Parrilla Don Jorge B2
10 Patagonia Dulce B1
11 Ultima Esperanza B2

Bars & clubs
12 Baguales Brewery B2
13 El Bar de Ruperto B2

Around Puerto Natales → *For listings, see pages 417-421.*

Monumento Nacional Cueva Milodón

ⓘ *25 km north, daily 0800-2000, US$4-8, getting there: regular bus from Prat 517, T061-241 2540, leaves 0945 and 1500, returns 1200 and 1700, US$8; taxi US$30 return or check if you can get a ride on a Torres del Paine tour bus; some stop at the cave.*

This is the end point of Bruce Chatwin's travelogue *In Patagonia* (see page 541). The cave, a massive 70 m wide, 220 m deep and 30 m high, contains a plastic model of the prehistoric ground-sloth whose remains were found there in 1895. The remains are now in London, although there is talk of returning them to the site. Evidence has also been found here of occupation by Patagonians some 11,000 years ago. Nearby, a visitor centre has summaries in English. There's also a good restaurant and handicraft store.

Parque Nacional Bernardo O'Higdón

ⓘ *US$10, only accessible by boat from Puerto Natales summer daily 0800, returning 1730 (Sun only in winter), US$125-150, minimum 10 passengers, heavily booked in high season; book through a Tour operator, see page 419.*

Often referred to as the **Parque Nacional Monte Balmaceda**, this park covers much of the Campo de Hielo Sur, plus the fjords and offshore islands further west. A three-hour boat trip from Puerto Natales up the Seno de Ultima Esperanza takes you to the southernmost section, passing the Balmaceda Glacier, which drops from the eastern slopes of **Monte Balmaceda** (2035 m). The glacier is retreating; in 1986 its foot was at sea level. The boat docks further north at **Puerto Toro**, from where it is a kilometre walk to the base of the Serrano Glacier on the north slope of Monte Balmaceda. On the trip, dolphins, sea lions (in season), black-necked swans, flightless steamer ducks and cormorants can often be seen. Take warm clothes, including a hat and gloves.

There is a route from Puerto Toro on the eastern side of the Río Serrano for 35 km to the Torres del Paine administration centre (see page 422); guided tours are available on foot or on horseback. It is also possible to continue to the southern edge of Torres del Paine by boat or zodiac. ▸▸ *For further details, see What to do, page 419.*

◉ Puerto Natales and around listings

For hotel and restaurant price codes and other relevant information, see pages 14-21.

◉ Where to stay

Puerto Natales *p414, map p416*
In season cheaper accommodation fills up quickly. Hotels in the countryside are often open only in the summer months. Good deals in upper-range hotels may be available, out of season especially, when prices may be 50% lower.

$$$$ Costaustralis, Pedro Montt 262, T061-241 2000, www.hoteles-australis.com. Very comfortable, tranquil, lovely views (but not from inland-facing rooms), lift, English spoken, waterfront restaurant Paine serves international and local seafood.

$$$$ Indigo Patagonia, Ladrilleros 105, T02-2432 6800, www.indigopatagonia.cl. Relaxed atmosphere, on the water front, great views, a boutique hotel with roof-top spa, rooms and suites, café/restaurant serves good seafood and vegetarian dishes. Tours organized.

$$$$ Remota, Ruta 9 Norte, Km 1.5, Huerto 279, T061-241 4040, www.remota.cl. Modernist design with big windows, lots of trips, activities and treks offered, spa, all-inclusive packages, good food, first-class.

$$$$ The Singular, Km 5 Norte, Puerto Bories, T061-272 2030, www.thesingular.com. Luxury hotel in recently converted warehouses a short distance from the town centre, in a scenic spot overlooking the Ultima Esperanza Sound. Spa, gourmet restaurant and varied excursions offered.

$$$$-$$$ Martín Gusinde, Bories 278, T061-271 2180, www.hotelmartingusinde.com. Modern 3-star standard, smart, parking, laundry service, excursions organized.

$$$$-$$$ Weskar Patagonian Lodge, Ruta 9, Km 05, T061-241 4168, www.weskar.cl. Quiet lodge overlooking the fjord, standard or deluxe rooms with good views, 3-course dinners served, lunch boxes prepared for excursions, many activities offered, helpful.

$$$ Aquaterra, Bulnes 299, T061-241 2239, www.aquaterrapatagonia.com. Good restaurant with vegetarian options, 'resto-bar' downstairs, spa, warm and comfortable but not cheap, very helpful staff. Excursions and tours.

$$$ Hostal Sir Francis Drake, Phillipi 383, T061-241 1553, www.hostalfrancisdrake.com. Calm and welcoming, tastefully decorated, smallish rooms, good views.

$$$ Keoken, Señoret 267, T061-241 3670, www.keokenpatagonia.com. Cosy, upmarket B&B, spacious living room, some rooms with views. All rooms have bathroom but not all are en suite, English spoken, helpful staff, tours.

$$$-$$ Hostel Natales, Ladrilleros 209, T061-241 4731, www.hostelnatales.cl. Private rooms or dorms in this high-end hostel, comfortable, cash only (pesos, dollars or euros).

$$ Casa Cecilia, Tomás Rogers 60, T061-241 2698, www.casaceciliahostal.com. Welcoming, popular, with small simple rooms, private or shared bath. English, French and German spoken, rents camping and trekking gear, tour agency and information for Torres del Paine.

$$ Hospedaje Nancy, Ramírez 540, T061-241 0022, www.natateslodge.cl.

Warm and hospitable, information, tours, equipment rental.

$$ Hostal Las Carretas, Galvarino 745, T061-241 4584. Tastefully decorated and spotless B&B 15 mins' walk to the centre, comfortable rooms, some with bath, good beds, English spoken.

$$ Lili Patagónico's, Prat 479, T061-241 4063, www.lilipatagonicos.com. **$** pp in dorms. Small but pleasant heated rooms, helpful staff. Lots of information, good quality equipment rented. Tours offered. Indoor climbing wall.

$$ Patagonia Adventure, Tomás Rogers 179, T061-241 1028, www.apatagonia.com. Lovely old house, bohemian feel, shared bath, **$** pp in dorms, equipment hire, bike and kayak tours and tour arrangements for Torres del Paine.

$$-$ pp **The Singing Lamb**, Arauco 779, T061-241 0958, www.thesinginglamb.com. Very hospitable New Zealand-run backpackers, dorm accommodation only but no bunks. Home-from-home feel. Good information.

$ Casa Teresa, Esmeralda 463, T061-241 0472, freepatagonia@hotmail.com. Good value, but thin walls and no heating in rooms, tours to Torres del Paine arranged.

$ Hospedaje Casa Lili, Bories153, T061-241 4063, lilinatales@latinmail.com. Dorms or private rooms, small, family-run, rents equipment and can arrange tickets to Paine.

Camping

Josmar 2, Esmeralda 517, in centre, T061-241 1685, www.josmar.cl. Family-run, convenient, hot showers, parking, barbecues, electricity, café, tent site or double room.

Around Puerto Natales *p417*

$$$$ Hostería Monte Balmaceda, Parque Nacional Bernardo O'Higgins; contact Turismo 21 de Mayo (see Tour operators, below). Although the park is uninhabited, guest accommodation is available in the southern section by the mouth of the Serrano river.

$$$$-$$$ Estancia Tres Pasos, 40 km north of town, T09-9644 5582, www. hotel3pasos.cl. Simple and beautiful lodge between Puerto Natales and Torres del Paine. Horse-riding trips offered.
$$$ Cabañas Kotenk Aike, 2 km north of town, T061-241 2581, www.kotenkaike.cl. Sleeps 4, modern, very comfortable, great location.
$$$ Hostería Llanuras de Diana, Ruta 9, Km 215 (30 km south of Puerto Natales), T061-241 0661. Hidden from road, beautifully situated. Recommended.

🍴 Restaurants

Puerto Natales *p414, map p416*
$$$ Afrigonia, Eberhard 343, T061-241 2232. An unexpected mixture of Patagonia meets East Africa in this Kenyan/Chilean-owned fusion restaurant, considered by many to be the best, and certainly the most innovative, in town.
$$$ Angelica's, Bulnes 501, T061-241 0007, www.angelicas.cl. Elegant Mediterranean style, well-prepared pricey food with quality ingredients.
$$$-$$ Cormorán de las Rocas, Miguel Sánchez 72, T061-261 5131-3, www. cormorandelasrocas.com. Patagonian specialities with an innovative twist, wide variety of well-prepared dishes, pisco sours, good service and attention to detail, incomparable views.
$$$-$$ El Asador Patagónico, Prat 158 on the Plaza. Spit-roast lamb, salads, home-made puddings.
$$$-$$ Parrilla Don Jorge, Bories 430, on Plaza, T061-241 0999, www.parrilladon jorge.cl. Also specializes in spit-roast lamb, but serves fish too, good service.
$$ La Mesita Grande, Prat 196 on the Plaza, T061-241 1571, www.mesitagrande.cl. Fresh pizzas from the wood-burning oven, also pasta and good desserts.
$$ Ultima Esperanza, Eberhard 354, T061-241 1391. One of the town's classic seafood restaurants.

$$-$ El Living, Prat 156, Plaza de Armas, www.el-living.com. Comfy sofas, good tea, magazines in all languages, book exchange, good music, delicious vegetarian food, British-run, popular, Wi-Fi. Recommended.
$$-$ La Picada de Carlitos, Blanco Encalada y Esmeralda. Good, cheap traditional Chilean food, popular with locals at lunchtime, when service can be slow.

Cafés
Patagonia Dulce, Barros Arana 233, T061-241 5285, www.patagoniadulce.cl. Mon-Sat 1400-2030. For the best hot chocolate in town, good coffee and chocolates.

🍸 Bars and clubs

Puerto Natales *p414, map p416*
Baguales Brewery, Bories 430, on the plaza, www.cervezabaguales.cl. Sep-Mar Mon-Sat 1800-0300. Pub with microbrewery attached. Also serves hamburgers and other snacks.
El Bar de Ruperto, Bulnes 371, T09-9218 9535, daily 2130-0330. Lively place with DJs, live music, lots of drinks and some food.
Murciélagos, Bulnes 731. Popular bar with late-night music and dancing.

🛍 Shopping

Puerto Natales *p414, map p416*
Casa Cecilia, **Lili Patagónico's**, **Sendero Aventura** and **Erratic Rock** (see Where to stay, above, and What to do, below) all hire out camping equipment (deposit required). Always check the equipment and the prices carefully. Camping gas is widely available in hardware stores. There are several supermarkets in town and the town markets are also good.

⏱ What to do

Puerto Natales *p414, map p416*
It is better to book tours direct with operators in Puerto Natales than through

agents in Punta Arenas or Santiago. There are many agencies along Eberhard. Several offer single-day tours to the Perito Moreno glacier in Argentina, US$80-100 for a 14-hr trip, including 2 hrs at the glacier, not including food or park entry fee; reserve 1 day in advance. You can then leave the tour in Calafate to continue your travels in Argentina.

Baguales Group, Barros Araña 66, T061-241 2654, www.bagualesgroup.com. Specialists in the route from Torres del Paine back to Puerto Natales. Tailor made multi-activity tours that can incorporate zodiacs, horse riding, kayaking and trekking, mostly off the beaten track.

Blue Green Adventures, M Bulnes 1200, T061-241 1800, www.bluegreenadventures. com. Adventure tour specialist and travel agent, with trekking, riding, kayaking, fishing and multi-activity options, estancia, whale watching, wine and yoga programmes. Also caters for families.

Chile Nativo, Eberhard 230, T061-241 1835, T1-800 6498 7776 (toll-free in US and Canada), www.chilenativo.travel. Specializes in 'W' trek, Paine circuit trek, horse riding, multi-sport options and tailor-made tours.

Comapa, Bulnes 541, T061-241 4300, www.comapa.com. Large regional operator offering decent day tours to Torres del Paine.

Encuentro Gourmet, Bories 349, T09-6720 3725, www.encuentrogourmet.com. Patagonian cookery workshops at lunch and dinner-time, US$44 pp, book at least 24 hrs in advance.

Erratic Rock, Baquedano 719 and Zamora 732, T061-241 4317, www.erraticrock.com. Trekking experts offering interesting expeditions from half a day to 2 weeks. Also B&B lodge, good-quality equipment hire, daily trekking seminar at 1500.

Estancia Travel, Casa 13-b, Puerto Boris, T061-241 2221, www.estanciatravel.com. Based at the Estancia Puerto Consuelo, 5 km north of Puerto Natales, offers horse-riding trips from 1 to 10 days around southern Patagonia and Torres del Paine, with accommodation at traditional estancias. Also kayaking trips, British/Chilean run, bilingual, professional guides, at the top of the price range.

Punta Alta, Blanco Encalada 244, T061-241 0115, www.puntaalta.cl. Sailings in a fast boat to the Balmaceda glacier and the possibility to continue by zodiac to Pueblito Serrano at the southern edge of Torres del Paine national park (from US$160 one way). You can return to Natales on the same day by minibus along the southern access road, thus avoiding Torres del Paine entry fees. Also offers car hire.

Sendero Aventura, Carlos Bories 349, T09-6171 3080, www.senderoaventura. com. Adventure tours by land rover, bike or kayak.

Skorpios Cruises, Augusto Leguía Norte 118, Santiago, T02-2477 1900, www. skorpios.cl. The *Skorpios 3* sails from

Puerto Natales to Glaciar Amalia and Fiordo Calvo in the Campo de Hielo Sur, 4 days, fares from US$1690 pp, double cabin. An optional first day includes a visit to Torres del Paine or the Cueva del Milodón. No office in Puerto Natales; book online or through an agency.
Turismo 21 de Mayo, Eberhard 560, T061-614420, www.turismo21demayo.com. Sailings to the Balmaceda glacier and the possibility to continue by zodiac to Pueblito Serrano at the southern edge of Torres del Paine national park (from US$160 one way from Puerto Natales).

⊖ Transport

Puerto Natales *p414, map p416*
Air
Aerodromo Teniente Julio Gallardo, 7 km north of town. **Sky** airline has services in summer from **Santiago** via **Puerto Montt**. Also charter services from **Punta Arenas** and onward connections to Argentina with **Aerovías DAP**. Other airlines use Punta Arenas airport, see page 401.

Bus
In summer book ahead. All buses leave from the new bus terminal 20 mins outside town at Av España 1455, but tickets can be bought at the individual company offices in town: **Bus Fernández**, E Ramírez 399, T061-241 1111, www.busesfernandez. com; **Pacheco**, Ramírez 224, T061-241 4800, www.busespacheco.com; **Bus Sur**, Baquedano 668, T061-261 4220, www. bussur.com; **Zaahj**, Prat 236, T061-241 2260, www.turismozaahj.co.cl.

To **Punta Arenas**, several daily, 3-3½ hrs, US$9.50, with **Fernández**, **Pacheco**, **Bus Sur**

and others, comfortable *Pullman* service with **Zaahj**, US$24. For buses to **Torres del Paine**, see page 430.

To Argentina To **Río Gallegos** direct, with **Bus Sur**, and **Pacheco**, 2-3 weekly each, US$28, 4-5 hrs. To **Río Turbio**, hourly with **Cootra** and other companies, US$8, 2 hrs (depending on customs at Paso Dorotea – change bus at border; see box, page 415). To **El Calafate**, US$35, with **Cootra** via Río Turbio, daily, 4 hrs; with **Pacheco**, 3 weekly; or with **Zaahj** via Cerro Castillo, 3 weekly, 4½ hrs; otherwise travel agencies run several times a week depending on demand (see above). To **Ushuaia**, with **Bus Sur**, Oct-Apr 4 buses a week, 15 hrs, US$70.

Car hire
Hire agents can arrange permission to drive into Argentina; it takes 24 hrs to arrange and extra insurance is required. Try **EMSA**, Eberhard 577, T061-261 4388, www.emsarentacar.cl, or **Punta Alta**, Blanco Encalada 244, T061-241 0115, www.puntaalta.cl.

Ferry
Navimag, Pedro Montt 308, T061-241 1642, www.navimag.com, runs ferries to/from **Puerto Montt**; for details, see page 332.

⊕ Directory

Puerto Natales *p414, map p416*
Banks There are several ATMs. *Casas de cambio* on Blanco Encalada, Bulnes and Prat. **Bicycle repairs** El Rey de la Bicicleta, Ramírez 540. Good, helpful.

Parque Nacional Torres del Paine

Covering 242,242 ha, 145 km northwest of Puerto Natales, this national park is a UNESCO Biosphere Reserve and a huge, huge draw for its diverse wildlife and spectacular surroundings. Taking its name from the Tehuelche word 'Paine', meaning 'blue', the park encompasses stunning scenery, with constantly changing views of peaks, glaciers and icebergs, vividly coloured lakes of turquoise, ultramarine and grey, and quiet green valleys filled with wild flowers. In the centre of the park is one of the most impressive mountain areas on earth, a granite massif from which rise oddly shaped peaks of over 2600 m, known as the 'Torres' (towers) and 'Cuernos' (horns) of Paine.

Arriving in Parque Nacional Torres del Paine → *Colour map 6, B2.*

Getting there
The most practical way to get to Torres del Paine, www.torresdelpaine.com, is with one of the many bus or tour companies that leave Puerto Natales daily. Hiring a pickup truck is another option. There are two *ripio* roads to the park from Puerto Natales. The old road goes via Cerro Castillo and Lago Sarmiento, entering the park at Laguna Amarga and continuing through the park to the administration building on Lago del Toro, 147 km northwest of Puerto Natales (3½ hours); this is the route taken by public buses. The new road, 85 km, links Natales to the south side of the park via the Pueblito Serrano. While it is a more direct route – total journey time to the administration is around 1½ hours – the road is narrow with lots of blind corners and sudden gusts of wind and can be rough in patches. An alternative way to access the park is on a three-hour zodiac trip up the Río Serrano from Parque Nacional Bernardo O'Higgins, see page 417.

There are entrances at Laguna Azul in the northeast, Laguna Amarga and Lago Sarmiento in the east and at the Puente Serrano in the south. As well as paying the park entrance fees – foreigners US$36 (low season US$20), payable in Chilean pesos only – you are required to register and show your passport when entering the park, since rangers (*guardaparques*) keep a check on the whereabouts of all visitors. If you are based outside the park and plan on entering and leaving several times, explain this to the rangers in order to be given a multiple-entry stamp valid for three consecutive days. ►► *See Transport, page 430.*

Getting around
Allow a week to 10 days to see the park properly. The park is well set up for tourism, with frequent bus services from Puerto Natales running through the park to pick up and drop off walkers at various hotels and trailheads and to connect with boat trips (see Transport, page 430). In season there are also boats and minibus connections within the park itself: from Laguna Amarga to **Hotel Las Torres**, US$5, and from the administration centre

Torres tips

Torres del Paine has become increasingly popular with foreigners and Chileans alike, receiving well over 100,000 visitors a year. Efforts to manage this ever-growing influx have been poor and the impact is showing. Do your best to ensure your visit does not have a negative effect on this unique landscape.

• The summer months (January and February) should be avoided due to the unpredictability of the weather and the overcrowding, especially at *refugios* and campsites. Try to visit the park either side of the peak season: late November/early December or mid-April are best.
• Bring sufficient clothes and proper equipment to protect you from cold, wind and rain.
• Bring your own food and equipment as supplies within the park are expensive and limited.
• When trekking, keep to the trails; cross-country trekking is not permitted.

• Try to start treks early in the morning to catch the sunrise, and also to arrive early at the next camping ground.
• Search for campsites that are less popular which may mean extending your trek by a day, but it will be worth it.
• Most campsites are riddled with field mice. These guys eat everything so string up all your food including toothpaste and chewing gum in a couple of plastic bags, and hang it from a tree so they aren't tempted to nibble through your tent or backpack.
• Litter is an increasing problem, especially around *refugios* and camping areas on the 'W'; take all your rubbish out of the park, including toilet paper.
• Forest fires are a serious hazard. Open fires are prohibited throughout the park. If you are using your own cooking stove, only cook in designated areas. Unauthorized campfires in 2005 and 2011 led to the destruction of 160 sq km and 110 sq km respectively.

to **Hostería Lago Grey**, US$15. Other than these routes, getting around the park without your own transport is difficult and expensive. When public services are reduced, travel agencies run buses subject to demand; arrange your return date with the driver and try to coincide with other groups to keep costs down.

Park information

The **CONAF administration centre** ① *in the southeast of the park, at the northwest end of Lago del Toro, T061-223 8959/269 1931, magallanes.oirs@conaf.cl, www.parquetorresdel paine.cl, summer daily 0830-2030, winter daily 0830-1230, 1400-1830,* has interesting videos and exhibitions, as well as the latest weather forecast. There are 13 ranger stations (*guarderías*) staffed by *rangers*, who offer help and advice. The outlying *guarderías* are open October to April only. Luggage can be stored for US$3 per day. On payment of the park entry fees (proceeds are shared between all Chilean national parks) you will receive a reasonable trail map to take with you (not waterproof). Climbing the peaks requires two permits, first from DIFROL (can be obtained free online, www.difrol.cl), then from CONAF in the park itself (take passports, DIFROL permit, insurance and route plan).

Best time to visit

Do not underestimate the severity of the weather here. The park is open all year round, although snow may prevent access to some areas in the winter. The warmest time is

December to March, but this is when the weather is the most unstable: strong winds often blow off the glaciers, and rainfall can be heavy. The park is most crowded in the summer holiday season, January to mid-February, less so in December or March. October and November are recommended for wild flowers. Visiting in winter (April to September) is becoming increasingly popular as, although the temperature is low, there can be stable conditions with little wind, allowing well-equipped hikers to do some good walking. However, some treks may be closed and boats may not be running.

Safety in the park

It is vital to be aware of the unpredictability of the weather (which can change in a few minutes) and the arduousness of some of the longer hikes. Rain and snowfall are heavier the further west you go and bad weather sweeps off the Campo de Hielo Sur without warning. The only means of rescue are on horseback or by boat; the nearest helicopter is in Punta Arenas and high winds usually prevent its operation in the park. An Argentine visitor disappeared as recently as Christmas 2013 and was not found, despite extensive searches. It is vital to take adequate equipment/clothing and report your route to staff. Do not be tempted to stray off the marked trails. Mobile phone coverage is erratic. Forest fires are a serious hazard; campfires are not allowed within the park. See also Torres tips, page 423.

Landscape and wildlife

There are 15 peaks above 2000 m, of which the highest is **Cerro Paine Grande** (3050 m). Few places can compare to its steep, forested talus slopes topped by 1000-m vertical shafts of basalt with conical caps; these are the remains of frozen magma in ancient volcanic throats, everything else having been eroded. On the western edge of the park is the enormous **Campo de Hielo Sur** icefield. Four main *ventisqueros* (glaciers) – Grey, Dickson, Zapata and Tyndall – branch off it, their meltwater forming a complex series of lakes and streams, which lead into fjords extending to the sea. Two other glaciers, Francés and Los Perros, descend on the western side of the central massif.

A micro-climate exists that is especially favourable to plants and wildlife. Over 200 species of plant have been identified and, although few trees reach great size, several valleys are thickly forested and little light penetrates. The grassland here is distinct from the monotony of the pampa and dispersed sclerophyl forest. Some 105 species of bird call the park home, including 18 species of waterfowl and 11 birds of prey. Particularly noteworthy are condors, black-necked swans, rheas, kelp geese, ibis, flamingos and austral parakeets. The park is also one of the best places on the continent for viewing rheas and guanacos. Apart from the 3500 guanacos, 24 other species of mammal can be seen here, including hare, fox, skunk, huemul and puma (the last two only very rarely).

Trekking

There are about 250 km of well-marked trails. Visitors must keep to the trails: cross-country trekking is not permitted. Some paths are confusingly marked and it is all too easy to end up on precipices with glaciers or churning rivers awaiting below; be particularly careful to follow the path at the Paso John Gardner on El Circuito (see below). In addition to those mentioned below there are also plenty of shorter walks in the park; see www.torresdelpaine.com for details.

Equipment

It is essential to be properly equipped against the cold, wind and rain. A strong, streamlined, waterproof tent is essential if doing El Circuito (although you can hire camping equipment for a single night at the *refugios* on the 'W'). Also essential are protective clothing, strong

Parque Nacional Torres del Paine

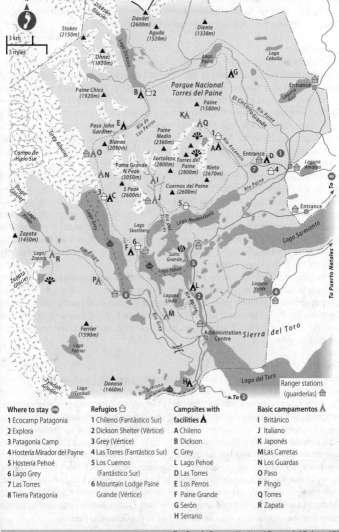

Where to stay 🛏
1 Ecocamp Patagonia
2 Explora
3 Patagonia Camp
4 Hostería Mirador del Payne
5 Hostería Pehoé
6 Lago Grey
7 Las Torres
8 Tierra Patagonia

Refugios ⌂
1 Chileno (Fantástico Sur)
2 Dickson Shelter (Vértice)
3 Grey (Vértice)
4 Las Torres (Fantástico Sur)
5 Los Cuernos (Fantástico Sur)
6 Mountain Lodge Paine Grande (Vértice)

Campsites with facilities ▲
A Chileno
B Dickson
C Grey
D Las Torres
E Los Perros
F Paine Grande
G Serón
H Serrano

Basic campamentos ▲
I Británico
J Italiano
K Japonés
M Las Carretas
N Los Guardas
O Paso
P Pingo
Q Torres
R Zapata

waterproof footwear, sunscreen, compass, good sleeping bag and sleeping mat. In summer also take shorts. Do not rely on availability of food at the *refugios* within the park; the small shops at the *refugios* (see below) and at the **Posada Río Serrano** are expensive and have a limited selection. You are strongly advised to bring all necessary equipment and your own food from Puerto Natales, although all running water within the park is fine to drink. You are not allowed to make open fires in the park, so take a camping stove. A decent map is provided with your park entrance ticket; other maps (US$7) are obtainable in many places Puerto Natales but most have one or two mistakes. The map produced by **Patagonia Interactiva** has been recommended as more accurate.

El Circuito

The park's most emblematic trek is a circuit round the Torres and Cuernos del Paine. Although most people start at the *guardería* at **Laguna Amarga**, it is probably best done anticlockwise starting from Lodge Paine Grande at the western edge of Lago Pehoe. Some walkers advise doing the route clockwise so that you climb to Paso John Gardner with the wind behind you. The route normally takes between five days and a week. The circuit is often closed in winter because of snow; major rivers are crossed by footbridges, but these are occasionally washed away. From Laguna Amarga the route is north along the western side of the Río Paine to **Lago Paine**, before turning west to follow the pastures of the valley of the Río Paine to the southern end of **Lago Dickson** (it is possible to add a journey to the *campamento* by the Torres on day one of this route); the *refugio* at Lago Dickson lies in a breathtaking position in front of the icy white lake with mountains beyond. From Lago Dickson the path runs along the wooded valley of the **Río de los Perros**, past the Glaciar de los Perros, before climbing through bogs and up scree to **Paso John Gardner** (1241 m, the highest point on the route), then dropping steeply through forest to follow the Grey Glacier southeast to **Lago Grey**, continuing to **Lago Pehoé** and the administration centre. There are superb views en route, particularly from the top of Paso John Gardner.

The longest stretch is between Refugio Laguna Amarga and Refugio Dickson (30 km, 10 hours in good weather; two campsites on the way at Serón and Cairon), but the most difficult section is the very steep, slippery slope from Paso John Gardner down to the Campamento Paso; the path is not well signed at the top of the pass, and some hikers have got dangerously lost. Camping gear must be carried, as many of the campsites do not have *refugios*.

The W

A more popular alternative to El Circuito, this four- to five-day route can be completed without camping equipment as there is accommodation in *refugios* en route. In summer this route is very crowded and far from being the solitary Patagonian experience many people expect. It combines several of the hikes described separately below. From Refugio Laguna Amarga the first stage runs west via **Hostería Las Torres** and up the valley of the **Río Ascensio** via Refugio Chileno to the base of the **Torres del Paine** (see below). From here return to the **Hostería Las Torres** and then walk along the northern shore of **Lago Nordenskjold** via Refugio Los Cuernos to **Campamento Italiano**. From here climb the **Valley of the Río del Francés** (see below) before continuing to **Lodge Paine Grande**. From here you can complete the third part of the 'W' by walking west along the northern shore of **Lago Grey** to **Refugio Grey** and the Grey Glacier before returning to **Lodge Paine Grande** and the boat back across the lake to the **Guardería Pudeto**.

To the base of the Torres del Paine

From **Refugio Laguna Amarga**, this six-hour route follows the road west to **Hostería Las Torres** (1½ hours), before climbing along the western side of the **Río Ascensio** via **Refugio Chileno** (two hours) and **Campamento Chileno** to **Campamento Las Torres** (two hours), close to the base of the **Torres del Paine** (be careful when crossing the suspension bridge over the Río Ascensio near **Hostería Las Torres**, as the path is poorly marked and you can end up on the wrong side of the ravine). The path alongside the Río Ascensio is well marked, and the **Campamento Las Torres** is in an attractive wood (no *refugio*). A further 30 minutes up the morraine takes you to a lake at the base of the towers themselves; they seem so close that you almost feel you could touch them. To see the Torres lit by sunrise (spectacular but you must have good weather), it's well worth carrying your camping gear up to **Campamento Torres** and spending the night. One hour beyond **Campamento Torres** is **Campamento Japonés**, another good campsite.

Valley of the Río del Francés

From **Lodge Paine Grande** this route leads north across undulating country along the western edge of **Lago Skottberg** to **Campamento Italiano** and then follows the valley of the Río del Francés, which climbs between Cerro Paine Grande and the Ventisquero del Francés (to the west) and the Cuernos del Paine (to the east) to **Campamento Británico**; the views from the mirador, a half-hour's walk above **Campamento Británico**, are superb. Allow 2½ hours from **Lodge Paine Grande** to **Campamento Italiano**, 2½ hours further to **Campamento Británico**.

Treks from Guardería Grey

Guardería Grey, 18 km west by road from the administration centre, is the starting point for a five-hour trek to **Lago Pingo**, recommended if you want to get away from the crowds, and one of the best routes in the park for birdwatching. It can only be undertaken with a certified CONAF guide. To reach the lake from the *guardería*, follow the **Río Pingo**, via **Refugio Pingo** and **Refugio Zapata** (four hours), with views south over Ventisquero Zapata; look out for plenty of wildlife and for icebergs in the lake. **Ventisquero Pingo** can be seen 3 km away over the lake. Note the bridge over a river here, marked on many maps, has been washed away. The river can be forded when it is low, however, allowing access to the glacier.

Two short signposted walks from Guardería Grey have also been suggested: one is a steep climb up the hill behind the ranger post to **Mirador Ferrier**, from where there are fine views; the other is via a suspension bridge across the Río Pingo to the peninsula at the southern end of **Lago Grey**, from where there are good views of the icebergs on the lakes.

To Laguna Verde

From the administation centre follow the road north 2 km, before taking the path east over the **Sierra del Toro** and then along the southern side of Laguna Verde to the Guardería Laguna Verde. Allow four hours. This is one of the easiest walks in the park and may be a good first hike.

To Laguna Azul and Lago Paine

This route runs north from Laguna Amarga to the western tip of **Laguna Azul**, from where it continues across the sheltered **Río Paine** valley past Laguna Cebolla to the Refugio Lago Paine at the eastern end of Lago Paine. Allow 8½ hours. Good birdwatching opportunities.

For hotel and restaurant price codes and other relevant information, see pages 14-21.

● Where to stay

Parque Nacional Torres del Paine *p422, map p425*

Accommodation is available on 3 levels: hotels, which are expensive, not to say overpriced (over US$300 for a double room per night); privately run *refugios*, which are generally well equipped and staffed, offering meals and free hot water for tea, soup, etc, and basic *campamentos*. All options fill up quickly in Jan and Feb, so plan your trip and book in advance. Pay in dollars to avoid IVA (VAT). Agencies in Puerto Natales offer accommodation and transfers or car hire.

$$$$ Ecocamp Patagonia, reservations T02-2923 5950, www.ecocamp.travel. Luxurious, all-inclusive accommodation is provided in geodesic domes, powered by renewable energy. This is the only environmental sustainability-certified hotel in Chile. Offers 4- to 10-day hiking, wildlife-watching and multi-sport trips. Their partner, **Cascada Expediciones**, page 62, offers eco-friendly tours and custom trips to Torres del Paine and other destinations.

$$$$ Explora (Hotel Salto Chico Lodge), T061-241 1247 (reservations: Av Américo Vespucci Sur 80, p 5, Santiago, T02-2395 2800, www.explora.com). The park's priciest and most exclusive place is nestled into a nook at Salto Chico on edge of Lago Pehoé, superb views. It's all included: pool, gym, horse riding, boat trips, tours. Arrange packages from Punta Arenas.

$$$$ Hostería Mirador del Payne, Estancia Lazo, 52 km from Sarmiento entrance, reservations from Fagnano 585, Punta Arenas, T061-222 8712, www.miradordelpayne.com. Comfortable, meals extra, riding, hiking, birdwatching. Lovely location on Laguna Verde on east edge of the park, but inconvenient for most of the park. Private transport essential, or hike there from the park.

$$$$ Hostería Pehoé, T061-296 1238, www.pehoe.cl, 5 km south of Pehoé ranger station, 11 km north of park administration. Beautifully situated on an island with spectacular view across Lago Pehoé, restaurant.

$$$$ Hotel Lago Grey, head office Lautaro Navarro 1077, Punta Arenas, T061-271 2100, www.turismolagogrey.com. Great views over Lago Grey, superior rooms worth the extra, glacier walks.

$$$$ Hotel Las Torres, T061-261 7450, www.lastorres.com. Comfortable rooms, beautiful lounge with wood fire and great views of the Macizo, excellent evening buffet, good service, horse riding, transport from Laguna Amarga ranger station, spa,

disabled access. Visitor centre and *confitería* open to non-residents.

$$$$ Patagonia Camp, reservations from Eberhard 230, Puerto Natales, T061-241 5149, T02-2882 1610, www.patagoniacamp.com. Luxury yurts outside the park at Lago Toro, 15 km south of the administration.

$$$$ Tierra Patagonia, T02-2207 8861, www.tierrapatagonia.com. Excellent, environmentally sensitive luxury hotel with spa, pool and outdoor jacuzzi on the edge of the national park overlooking Lago Sarmiento. Full- and half-day guided trips by minibus, on foot or on horseback. Gourmet dining in panorama restaurant overlooking the lake and mountains. Highly recommended.

Refugios

Two companies, **Fantástico Sur** and **Vértice Refugios**, between them run the *refugios* in the park, which provide comfortable dormitory or *cabaña* accommodation with hot showers; bring your own sleeping bag, or hire sheets for US$8-10 per night. Prices start from US$46pp bed only and go up to US$200 pp in a *cabaña* with full board. Meals can be bought individually (US$11, US$15 and US$21) and restaurants are open to non-residents. Kitchen facilities are available in some Vértice Refugios but Fantástico Sur will not let you prepare your own hot food unless you are camping. Refugios also have space for camping, US$8-16 and hire tents for US$13-15 per night, plus US$3 per sleeping mat (book in advance for Vértice Refugios as they have very few tents available). Most close in winter, although 1 or 2 may stay open, depending on the weather. Advance booking essential in high season.

Fantástico Sur Book through agencies in Puerto Natales or direct at Esmeralda 661, Puerto Natales, T061-261 4184, www.fslodges.com.

Refugio El Chileno, in the valley of Río Ascencio, at the foot of the Torres.

Refugio Las Torres (Torre Central, Torre Norte), 2 refugios next to the Hotel Las Torres (see above), good facilities, especially in the newer **Torre Central**.

Refugio Los Cuernos, on the northern shore of Lago Nordenskjold. Also has 8 cabins (US$155 double occupancy without board, US$251 full board).

Vértice Refugios Book through agencies in Puerto Natales, or direct at Bulnes 1200, Puerto Natales, T061-241 2742, www.verticepatagonia.com.

Mountain Lodges Paine Grande, on the northwest tip of Lago Pehoé, with kitchen facilities and internet.

Vértice Grey, on the northeast shore of Lago Grey.

Vértice Dickson Shelter, southern end of Lago Dickson. Basic.

Camping

Equipment is available to hire in Puerto Natales (see above). The wind tends to rise in the evening so pitch your tent early. Mice can be a problem; do not leave food in packs on the ground. Fires may only be lit at organized campsites, not at campamentos. The *guardaparques* expect people to have a stove if camping. There are 4 sites run by **Vértice Patagonia**: **Camping Los Perros**, **Paine Grande**, **Dickson** and **Grey** (from US$8 pp). **Camping Chileno**, **Serón** and **Las Torres** (by the **Refugio Las Torres**) are run by **Fantástico Sur** (US$9-11), hot showers. **Lago Pehoé**, www.campingpehoe.com, US$16 pp, tent rental US$24 for 2 including sleeping mat, also pre-pitched dome tents, hot showers, shop, restaurant.

Camping Río Serrano, just outside the park's southern entrance on a working estancia, www.campingchile.com, also has horse rides and hikes.

Free camping is permitted in 9 other locations in the park: these sites are known as *campamentos* and are generally extremely basic.

☉ What to do

Parque Nacional Torres del
Paine *p422, map p425*
See under Puerto Natales, What to do, page 419 for Tour operators. Before booking a tour, check the details carefully and get them in writing.

☉ Transport

Parque Nacional Torres del
Paine *p422, map p425*
Boat
Catamarán Hielos Patagónicos, Los Arrieros 1517, Puerto Natales, T061-241 1380, info@hielospatagonicos.cl, runs boats from Guardería Pudeto to **Refugio Paine Grande**, 30 mins, US$24 one way with 1 backpack (US$8 for extra backpacks), US$38 return, leaving Pudeto 0930, 1200, 1800, returning from Paine Grande 1000, 1230, 1830; reserve in advance. Services are reduced off season with only 1 sailing at 1200 1 Apr-15 Nov. At all times check in advance that boats are running. There are also boats from **Hotel Lago Grey** to the face of the glacier, 2-4 times daily, 3½ hrs, US$90 return, and from the hotel via the glacier face to/from Refugio Grey for US$60 one-way.

Bus
After mid-Mar there is little public transport and trucks are irregular. **Bus Gómez** (Prat 234, T061-241 1971), **JBA** (Prat 258, T061-241 0242) and **Trans Vía Paine** (Bulnes 518, T061-241 3672) run daily services into the park, leaving **Puerto Natales** between 0630 and 0800, and again (Dec-Feb) at 1430, using the old road, with a 20-min stop at Cerro Castillo

(see box, page 415), 2½ hrs to **Laguna Amarga**, 3½ hrs to **Guardería Pudeto** and 4½ hrs to the administration centre, all charge US$17 one way, US$32 open return (return tickets are not interchangeable between different companies). Buses will stop anywhere en route, but all stop at Laguna Amarga entrance, Salto Grande del Paine and the administration centre. Return buses to Puerto Natales stop at Laguna Amarga from 1430 to 2000. In high season the buses fill quickly so it is best to board at the administration for the return to Puerto Natales. All buses wait at Guardería Pudeto until the boat from **Refugio Paine Grande** arrives.

To **El Calafate** (Argentina) Either return to Puerto Natales for onward connections (see page 414), or take a bus from the park to **Cerro Castillo** (106 km east of the administration centre) then catch a direct service to Calafate. **Zaahj** has a very comfortable Super Pullman service Cerro Castillo–El Calafate, US$28. Beware that the border crossing can take up to several hours in peak season (see box, page 415).

Car hire
Hiring a pick-up in Punta Arenas is an economical proposition for a group (up to 9 people): US$400-420 for 4 days. A more economical car can cope with the roads if you go carefully; ask the rental agency's advice. If driving to the park yourself, note that the shorter road from Puerto Natales is narrow with lots of blind corners and sudden gusts of wind and can be rough in patches. In the park, the roads are also narrow and winding with blind corners: use your horn a lot. Always fill up with fuel in Puerto Natales.

Into Argentina: Parque Nacional Los Glaciares

Of all Argentina's impressive landscapes, the sight of the immense glaciers stretching out infinitely and silently before you, may stay with you longest. This is the second largest national park in Argentina, extending along the Chilean border for over 170 km. Almost half of it is covered by the Southern Ice Cap; at 370 km long, it's the third largest in the world. From it, 13 major glaciers descend into two great lakes: Lago Argentino in the southeast and Lago Viedma to the northeast.

There are two main areas to explore: the glaciers can be visited by bus and boat trips from El Calafate, while from El Chaltén, 230 km northwest, there is superb trekking around the dramatic Fitz Roy massif and ice climbing near its summit. The central section, between Lago Argentino and Lago Viedma, is the Ice Cap National Reserve, inaccessible to visitors apart from a couple of estancias.

East of the ice fields, there's southern beech forest before the land flattens to the wind-blasted Patagonian steppe. Birdlife is prolific; often spotted are black-necked swans, Magallenic woodpeckers, and, perhaps, even a torrent duck diving in the rivers. Guanacos, grey foxes, skunks and rheas (a large flightless bird) can be seen on the steppe, and the rare huemul (a deer-like animal) inhabits the forest.

Parque Nacional Los Glaciares

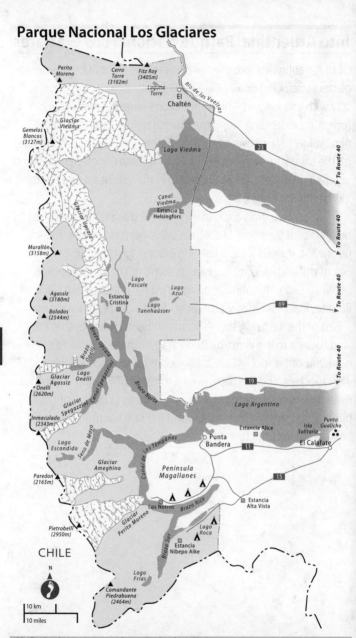

Arriving in Parque Nacional Los Glaciares → *Colour map 6, A2. Telephone country code: +54.*
Getting there Access to the park is via El Calafate, 50 km from the park's eastern boundary, for the glaciers, or via El Chaltén, 230 km northwest, for trekking near Fitz Roy on the northeastern edge of the park. There are buses from Río Gallegos and Puerto Natales to El Calafate. El Chaltén is three hours' drive north then west, with several buses daily from El Calafate and Río Gallegos. El Chaltén can also be reached from Villa O'Higgins on the Carretera Austral in Chile. ▶▶ *See Transport, page 447.*

Park information ① *Jan-Feb daily 0800-2100, rest of the year daily 0800-1600, US$27.50 for non-Argentines.* There are national park offices, known as **Intendencia del Parque** ① *Av del Libertador 1302, T02902-491005, www.losglaciares.com, Dec-Mar daily 0800-2000, Apr-Nov daily 0800-1800,* in El Calafate, and across the bridge at the entrance to the town, *T02962-493004, opening times as above,* in El Chaltén. Both hand out helpful trekking maps of the area, with paths and campsites marked, showing distances and walking times. An informative talk about the national park and its paths is given to all incoming bus passengers. Note that the hotel, restaurant and transport situation in this region changes greatly between high and low season.

Best time to visit Although this part of Patagonia is generally cold, there is a milder microclimate around Lago Viedma and Lago Argentino, which means that summers can be reasonably pleasant, with average summer temperatures between 5°C and 22°C, though strong winds blow constantly at the foot of the cordillera. In the forested area, around 1500 mm of rain falls annually, mainly between March and late May. In winter, the whole area is inhospitably cold and most tourist facilities are closed. The best time to visit, therefore, is between November and April, avoiding January and early February, when Argentines take their holidays, campsites are crowded and accommodation is hard to find.

Río Turbio → *Colour map 6, B3.*

You're only likely to visit this charmless place if you've crossed the border into Argentina via Paso Casas Viejas or Paso Dorotea (see box, page 415). The site of Argentina's largest coalfield hasn't recovered from the recent depression hitting the industry. It has a cargo railway connecting it with Punta Loyola, and visitors can see Mina 1, where the first mine was opened. Tourist information is available in the **Municipalidad** ① *Plazoleta Castillo, T029202-421950.* There's a small ski centre nearby, **Valdelén**, which has six pistes and is ideal for beginners; there's also scope for cross-country skiing between early June and late September.

El Calafate and around → *For listings, see pages 441-448. Colour map 6, A3.*

The town sits on the south shore of Lago Argentino and exists almost entirely as a tourist centre for the Parque Nacional los Glaciares, 50 km away. In both El Calafate and El Chaltén most of the inhabitants hail from Buenos Aires and other provincial cities. With the recent decline in tourism as a result of global recession, many people have returned north and the local population has fallen. The town has been known to get packed out in January and February, but it is empty and quiet all winter. It's certainly not cheap, but pleasant enough, with picturesque wooden architecture and a bustling main drag. Lago Argentino's stunning turquoise waters nearby add further charm.

From El Calafate, tours take you on boat trips and to walkways right beside the wall of Perito Moreno glacier. Highly recommended is the **mini-trekking** walk on the glacier's surface, or the more intrepid six-hour **Big Ice** hike. All these can be booked in town, or by your hotel. You could also head further north by boat to see the Spegazzini and Upsala glaciers, or stay a night at the remote **Estancia Cristina**, see box, page 442, which offers superb hiking and horse riding to see the Upsala glacier from above, and down a fossil-filled canyon. Whatever else you do, this is an unmissable part of any trip to Patagonia.

Arriving in El Calafate

Getting there and around Bus travel is convenient, with buses from Río Gallegos and Ushuaia and from Puerto Natales, via Cerro Castillo, if you want to get directly to/from Torres del Paine. The bus terminal is centrally located up a steep flight of steps off the main street. There is also an **airport** ⓘ 23 km east of town, T02902-491220, with flights from Buenos Aires and seasonal services to other destinations. A transfer service to town is run by **Transpatagonia Expeditions** ⓘ T02902-493766, US$10 open return, or take a **taxi** ⓘ T02902-491655/491745, US$13. The centre is so small that it's easy to get around on foot.
▶▶ See Transport, page 447.

El Calafate

Where to stay
1 Albergue y Hostal Lago Argentino
2 Alto Verde
3 América del Sur
4 Ariel
5 Cabañas Nevis
6 Calafate Hostel & Hostería
7 Camping AMSA
8 Casa de Grillos B&B
10 El Quijote
11 Hostel Buenos Aires
12 Hostel del Glaciar 'Libertador'
13 Hostel del Glaciar 'Pioneros'
14 i Keu Ken Hostel
15 Kau Yatún
16 Kosten Aike
17 Los Alamos
18 Marcopolo Inn Calafate
19 Michelangelo
20 Patagonia Rebelde
21 Sir Thomas
22 Vientos del Sur

Restaurants 🍴
1 Borges y Alvarez
2 Casablanca
4 Heladería Aquarela
5 La Lechuza
6 La Tablita
7 La Vaca Atada
9 Pura Vida
10 Rick's Restaurante
11 Viva la Pepa

Francisco Moreno, El Perito

You can't miss the name of Argentina's favourite son as you travel around Patagonia. Francisco Pascasio Moreno (1852-1919) is commemorated by a national park, a town, countless streets and a world-famous glacier. Moreno, a naturalist and geographer, explored areas previously unknown to the authorities. At the age of 20, he travelled up the Río Negro to Lago Nahuel Huapi, along the Río Chubut, and then up the Río Santa Cruz to reach the giant lake which he named Lago Argentino. Expeditions such as these were dangerous: apart from physical hardships, relations with the indigenous population were poor. On one expedition, Moreno was seized as a hostage, but escaped on a raft which carried him for eight days down the Río Limay to safety.

His fame established, Moreno was elected to congress and became an expert (*perito*) adviser to the Argentine side in the negotiations to draw the border with Chile. His reward was a grant of land near Bariloche, which he handed over to the state to manage, the initial act in creating the national parks system in Argentina, and an inspiring gesture at a time when anyone who could was buying up land as fast as possible. Moreno's remains are buried in a mausoleum on Isla Centinela in Lago Nahuel Huapi. For a good read while you are travelling Argentina seek out *Perito Moreno's Travel Journal: A Personal Reminiscence* (published by Elefante Blanco). It is a fascinating read about his travels, and his escape from capture.

Tourist information El Calafate **tourist office** ① *Rosales y Av del Libertador, T02902-491090, and at the bus station, T02902-491476, www.elcalafate.tur.ar, both daily 0800-2000,* may look disorganized, but the staff speak several languages and have a good map with accommodation shown, as well as information on estancias and tours. There's another branch at the airport. There is a **provincial tourist office**① *1 de Mayo 50, T02902-492353.*

Places in and around El Calafate
Centro de Interpretación Histórica① *Av Brown y Bonarelli, US$8,* has a very informative anthropological and historical exhibition about the region, with pictures and bilingual texts; there's also a very relaxing café/library. A recommended 15-minute walk is from the **Intendencia del Parque**, following Calle Bustillo towards the lake through a quiet residential area to **Laguna Nímez** ① *high season daily 0900-2000, low season daily 1000-1700, US$6,* a bird reserve (fenced in), with flamingos, ducks, black-necked swans and abundant birdlife; a 2.5-km self-guided trail leads through the reserve. At Punta Gualicho (or Walichu) on the shores of Lago Argentino 7 km east of town, there are cave paintings (badly deteriorated); it's a six-hour horse ride to get there (US$40 per person). Just west of the town centre is **Bahía Redonda**, a shallow part of Lago Argentino that is good for birdwatching in the evenings. It freezes in winter, when ice-skating and skiing are possible. Hike to the top of the **Cerro Calafate**, behind the town (2½ to three hours), for views of the silhouette of the southern end of the Andes, Bahía Redonda and Isla Solitaria on Lago Argentino. There is also scope for good hill-walking to the south of the town, while **Cerro Elefante**, to the west, on the road to the Perito Moreno glacier, is good for rock climbing.

A free bus runs from the provincial tourist office to the **Glaciarium** ① *6 km west of town on Ruta 11, http://glaciarium.com, daily 0900-2000, US$18, US410 (6-12s).* This is a modern museum dedicated to Patagonian ice and glaciers, with an ice-bar (daily 1100-2000, US$15 including drink), café and shop.

There are several estancias within reach, offering a day on a working farm, *asado al palo*, horse riding and accommodation. Try **Estancia Alice** (El Galpón del Glaciar) ① T02902-497503, T011-5217 6719 *(in Buenos Aires)* www.elgalpondelglaciar.com.ar. See also Helsingfors and Estancia Nibepo Aike, in Where to stay, below.

Lago Roca, 40 km southwest of El Calafate, is set in beautiful open landscape, with hills above offering panoramic views. The lake is perfect for lots of activities, including trout and salmon fishing, climbing and walking.

Lago Argentino and the glaciers → For listings, see pages 441-448.

Perito Moreno glacier

At the western end of Lago Argentino (80 km from El Calafate) the major attraction is the Glaciar Perito Moreno, one of the few glaciers in the world that is both moving and maintaining its size, despite climate change. It descends to the surface of the water over a 5-km frontage at a height of about 70 m. Several times in the past, it has advanced across the lake, cutting the Brazo Rico off from the Canal de los Témpanos; the channel is only reopened when the pressure of water in the Brazo Rico breaks through the ice. This spectacular rupture last occurred in January 2013. The glacier can be seen close up from a series of walkways descending from the car park. The vivid blue hues of the ice floes, with the dull roar as pieces break off and float away as icebergs from the snout, are spectacular, especially at sunset. The weather, however, may be rough. A 45-minute catamaran trip departs from near the walkways and gets closer to the glacier's face, US$18; this can be arranged independently through **Fernández Campbell** (see What to do, below) or is offered with the regular excursions. Another boat trip with a mini-trek on the glacier is organized by tour operators.

Upsala glacier

The fjords at the northwestern end of Lago Argentino are fed by four other glaciers. The largest is the Upsala glacier, named after the Swedish university that commissioned the first survey of this area in 1908. It's a stunning expanse of untouched beauty, covering three times the area of the Perito Moreno glacier, and is the longest glacier flowing off the Southern Patagonian ice fields. Unusually it ends in two separate frontages, each about 4 km wide and 60 m high, although only the western frontage can be seen from the lake excursion. The glacier itself, unlike its cousin Perito Moreno, is suffering badly from the changing climate. When large parts break from the main mass of ice, access by lake may be blocked.

The glacier can be reached by motor-boat from Punta Bandera, 50 km west of El Calafate, on a trip that also goes to Lago Onelli and Spegazzini glaciers. However, the best way to see the glacier is to stay at Estancia Cristina (see box, page 442) and take the trip up to the viewpoint, where vermillion rocks have been polished smooth by the glacier's approach.

Further south, the **Spegazzini** glacier has a frontage 1.5 km wide and 130 m high. In between are **Agassiz** and **Onelli**, both of which feed into **Lago Onelli**, a quiet and very beautiful lake, full of icebergs of every shape and size, surrounded by beech forests on one side and ice-covered mountains on the other.

The soaring granite of **Cerro Fitz Roy** (3405 m) rises up from the smooth baize of the steppe, more like a ziggurat than a mountain, surrounded by a consort of jagged snow-clad spires, with a stack of spun-cotton cloud hanging constantly above them. It is one of the most magnificent mountains in the world and it towers above the nearby peaks: **Torre** (3128 m), **Poincenot** (3076 m) and **Saint-Exupery** (2600 m). Its Tehuelche name

The Fitz Roy area

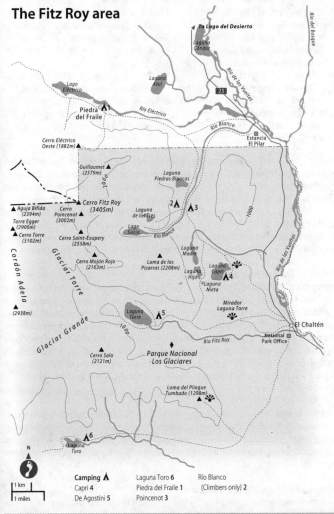

Camping **Λ**
Capri **4**
De Agostini **5**

Laguna Toro **6**
Piedra del Fraile **1**
Poincenot **3**

Río Blanco
(Climbers only) **2**

Hiking around Cerro Fitz Roy

Equipment A map is essential, even on short walks. Take plenty of warm clothes and a four-season sleeping bag, if you're camping. A gas or alcohol stove is essential, as fires are prohibited. It is possible to rent equipment in El Chaltén; ask at the park office or Rancho Grande.

Information The park's *Intendencia* provides a good map, showing walks and campsites. *Guardaparques* can advise on walks and the state of the paths. Some speak English.

Paths These are well marked. Stick to the centre of the path so as not to make it any bigger and walk in single file (this may mean that you're walking in a rut).

Rubbish Take all rubbish back down the mountain with you.

Water All river water in the national park is drinkable. Don't bathe in rivers and lakes; do not wash or bury waste within 70 m of a water source. Never go to the toilet near water sources.

Weather The weather changes hourly, so be prepared for a sudden deterioration in conditions. Always wear sunscreen (SPF 30 at least).

Wildlife As you leave El Chaltén, don't let the dogs follow you, as they frighten the huemules (a rare and endangered species of deer). For more information, see www.elchalten.com.

was El Chaltén ('smoking mountain' or 'volcano'), perhaps because at sunrise the pink towers are occasionally lit up bright red for a few seconds in a phenomenon known as the *amanecer de fuego* ('sunrise of fire'). Perito Moreno named the peak after the captain of the *Beagle*, who saw it from afar in 1833, and it was first climbed by a French expedition in 1952. It stands on the northern edge of Parque Nacional Los Glaciares at the western end of Lago Viedma, 230 km north of El Calafate, in an area of lakes and glaciers that makes marvellous trekking country. The base for walking and climbing around Fitz Roy is the modern town of El Chaltén, which has been built right next to the mountains.

Arriving in the Fitz Roy area

Getting there and around The quickest way to reach El Chaltén is on one of the frequent buses from El Calafate (about four hours). There are also daily buses to El Chaltén from Los Antiguos along Ruta 40, useful if you've crossed into Argentina from Chile Chico (see box, page 388). El Chaltén can also be reached from Villa O'Higgins on the Carretera Austral in Chile (see box, page 393). Access to the park here is free and it is not necessary to register before you set out. Most paths are very clear and well-worn but a map is essential, even on short walks; the park information centre has photocopied maps of treks but the best is one published by **Zagier and Urruty**, and is available in shops in El Calafate and El Chaltén.

Best time to visit Walking here is only really viable mid-October to April, with the best months usually March to April when the weather is generally stable and not very cold, and the autumn colours of the beech forest are stunning. Mid-summer (December and January) and spring (September to October) are generally very windy. In December and January the campsites can be full to bursting, with many walkers on the paths.

Tourist information The **Intendencia del Parque** ① *T02962-493004*, is in El Chaltén, across the bridge at the entrance to the town. It hands out helpful trekking maps of the

El Chaltén

Where to stay
Ahonikenk Chaltén 2
Albergue
Patagonia 1
Albergue Rancho
Grande 15
Camping
del Lago 11
Cóndor de
los Andes 3
El Pilar 13
Estancia La Quinta 12
Hospedaje
La Base 16
Hostería El Puma 5
Hostería Posada
Lunajuim 7
Los Cerros 10
Nothofagus 9
Senderos 17

Restaurants
Domo Blanco 2
Estepa 9
Fuegia 6
Josh Aike 1
Las Lengas 11
Pangea 4
Patagonicus 5
Ruca Mahuida 12
Zaffarancho 13

area, with paths and campsites marked, giving distances and walking times. El Chaltén's **tourist office** ⓘ *Güemes 21, T02962-493011, www.elchalten.com, Mon-Fri 0900-2000, Sat and Sun 1300-2000*, has an excellent website, with accommodation lists. Most services in El Chaltén and some hotels close out of season.

El Chaltén → *For listings, see pages 441-448. Colour map 6, A2.*

The small modern town of El Chaltén is set in a wonderful position at the foot of Cerro Fitz Roy and at the mouth of the valley of the Río de las Vueltas. Having been founded in 1985 in order to pre-empt Chilean territorial claims, it has grown with little thought for aesthetics. Now hugely popular as a centre for trekking and climbing in summer, and for cross-country skiing in winter, it's an expensive place and can be unattractive, especially when the harsh wind blows. But the steady stream of visitors creates a cheerful atmosphere and, from the town, you can walk directly into breathtaking landscapes. Accommodation ranges from camping and hostels to not-quite-luxurious *hosterías*. Food can be expensive, though there is increasingly plenty of choice. Credit cards are only accepted in larger establishments. El Chaltén is also the base for two unique expeditions onto the Southern Ice Field; consult the guides at Fitz Roy Expediciones. ⇒ *See What to do, page 447.*

Hiking around Cerro Fitz Roy → *These are the most popular walks from El Chaltén.*

Laguna Torre (short: two hours each way) Walk west to Mirador Laguna Torre (1½ hours) for views of Cerro Torre then continue to busy **Camping De Agostini** (30 minutes) on the lake shore, where there are fantastic views of the dramatic peaks of Cordón Torre.

Laguna de Los Tres (four hours each way) Walk up to Laguna Capri (two hours), with great views of Fitz Roy, then continue to **Camping Poincenot** (one hour) and **Camping Río Blanco** (only for climbers, by prior arrangement). From Río Blanco you can head southwest to Laguna de los Tres, where you'll get a spectacular view on a fine day (one hour) but in bad weather, you're better off walking to Piedras Blancas.

Laguna Torre (long: seven hours each way) A marvellous walk with views of both mountain groups. Climb past Laguna Capri and take the signed path to your left, passing two lakes (Madre and then Hija), to reach the path that leads to Laguna Torre.

Loma del Pliegue Tumbado (four hours each way) A marked path from the *guardería* (park ranger's office) leads southwest to this viewpoint where you can see both condors and Lago Viedma. This is a good day walk, best in clear weather. More experienced trekkers can continue to the glacial Laguna Toro (six hours from El Chaltén).

Río Blanco to Piedra del Fraile (seven hours each way) This beautiful walk starts at **Camping Río Blanco** and runs north along the Río Blanco and then west along the Río Eléctrico to **Camping Piedra del Fraile** (four hours), just outside the national park. From here a path leads south, up Cerro Eléctrico Oeste (1882 m) towards the north face of Fitz Roy (two hours); it's tough going but with spectacular views. You should take a guide for the last bit. Ask at **Hostería El Pilar** and outdoor centre, www.hosteriaelpilar.com.ar.

Climbing → *Colour map 2, C2.*

Base camp for ascents of Fitz Roy is **Camping Río Blanco**. Other peaks include Cerro Torre, Torre Egger (2900 m), Cerro Solo (2121 m), Poincenot, Guillaumet (2579 m), Saint-Exupery, Aguja Bífida (2394 m) and Cordón Adela (2938 m): all of these are for very experienced climbers only. However, most climbers can try ice climbing at the foot of Cerro Torre; contact **Fitz Roy Expediciones**, page 447. The best time to climb is mid-February to the end of March; November and December are very windy and May to July are extremely cold. Permits for climbing are available at the national park information office and guides are available in El Chaltén.

Around El Chaltén

The main attraction here is the trekking around Fitz Roy, but there is also stunning virgin landscape to explore outside the park, around **Lago del Desierto**, 37 km north. The long skinny lake is fjord-like and surrounded by forests. It's reached by unpaved Route 23, passing **Hostería El Pilar** (www.hosteriaelpilar.com.ar) in a stunning position with views of Fitz Roy. Accommodation is available here but you can also visit for tea or use it as an excellent base for trekking up **Río Blanco** or **Río Eléctrico**. Route 23 continues along the Río de las Vueltas via **Laguna Cóndor**, where flamingos can be seen. A mirador at the end of the road gives fine views over Lago del Desierto and a path runs along the east side of the lake to its northern tip, from where a trail leads west along the valley of the Río Diablo to **Laguna Diablo**, and north to Lago O'Higgins in Chile, see page 394. At the lake is the secluded **Aguas Arriba Lodge** ① *T011-4152 5697, www.aguasarribalodge.com*, reached only by boat, or by a two- to three-hour walk (luggage goes by boat).

 Lago Viedma to the south of El Chaltén can also be explored by boat. The trips usually pass Glaciar Viedma, with the possibility of ice trekking on some excursions. ⏵⏵ *See What to do, page 446.*

For hotel and restaurant price codes and other relevant information, see pages 14-21.

⊜ Where to stay

Río Turbio *p433*

$$ Nazó, Gob Moyano 464, T02962-421800. Modern building, rooms for 2-4, laundry service, restaurant and bar.

$ Hostería Capipe, Paraje Julia Dufour, 9 km from town, T02962-482935. Simple, with restaurant.

El Calafate and around *p433, map p434*
Prepare to pay more for accommodation here than elsewhere in Argentina. El Calafate is very popular in Jan-Feb, so book all transport and accommodation in advance. Best months to visit are Oct, Nov and Mar, Apr when it is less crowded and cheaper. Many hotels are open only Sep/Oct-Apr/May.

$$$$ El Quijote, Gob Gregores 1191, T02902-491017, www.quijotehotel.com.ar. A very good hotel, spacious, well-designed with traditional touches, tasteful rooms with TV, restaurant Sancho, stylish lobby bar, English and Italian spoken.

$$$$ Kosten Aike, Gob Moyano 1243, T02902-492424, www.kostenaike.com.ar. Relaxed yet stylish, elegant spacious rooms (some superior), jacuzzi, gym, excellent restaurant, Ariskaiken (open to non-residents), cosy bar, garden, English spoken. Open year-round. Recommended.

$$$$ Los Alamos, Gob Moyano y Bustillo, T02902-491144, www.posadalosalamos. com. Cheaper in low season. Very comfortable, charming rooms, good service, lovely gardens, good bar and without doubt the best restaurant in town, **La Posta**.

$$$ Alto Verde, Zupic 138, T02902-491326, www.welcomeargentina.com/altoverde. Top quality, **$$** in low season, spotless, spacious, helpful, also with apartments for 4.

$$$ Cabañas Nevis, Av del Libertador 1696, T02902-493180, www.cabanasnevis. com.ar. Owner Mr Patterson offers very nice cabins for 5 and 8 (price quoted is for 5), some with lake view, great value.

$$$ Casa de Grillos B&B, Los Cóndores 1215, T02902-491160, www.casadegrillos. com.ar. Welcoming B&B in the calm green area, next to Nímez nature reserve. It has all the comfort and charm of a family house, **$$** low season.

$$$ Michelangelo, Espora y Gob Moyano, T02902-491045, www.michelangelohotel. com.ar. Lovely, quiet, welcoming, restaurant. Recommended.

$$$ Patagonia Rebelde, José Haro 442, T02902-494495 (in Buenos Aires T015-5890 1276), www.patagoniarebelde. com. Charming new building in traditional Patagonian style, like an old inn with rustic decor, good comfort with well-heated bedrooms and comfy sitting-rooms.

$$$ Vientos del Sur, up the hill at Río Santa Cruz 2317, T02902-493563, www.vientosdelsur.com. Very hospitable, calm, comfortable, good views, kind family attention.

$$$-$$ Ariel, Av Libertador 1693, T02902-493131, www.hotelariel.com.ar. Modern, functional, well maintained. Breakfast included.

$$ Hostel Buenos Aires, Buenos Aires 296, 200 m from terminal, T02902-491147, www. glaciarescalafate.com. Quiet, kind owner, helpful, comfortable with doubles, cheaper without bath, good hot showers, laundry service, luggage store, bikes for hire.

$$ Sir Thomas, Espora 257, T02902-492220, www.sirthomas.com.ar. Modern, comfortable wood-lined rooms, breakfast included.

$$-$ pp Albergue y Hostal Lago Argentino, Campaña del Desierto 1050-61 (near bus terminal), T02902-491423, www. hostallagoargentino.com.ar. **$** pp shared dorms, too few showers when full, nice

Estancia Cristina

For many visitors, a visit to historical Estancia Cristina is the highlight of their trip. A boat leaves Puerto Bandera early in the morning and travels for two hours to the northernmost reaches of Lago Argentina, strewn with mighty icebergs, to see the Upsala glacier from the water. Then, having taken in the sheer size and unspoilt beauty, the boat continues to the remote estancia situated in isolation on the shores of the lake under a crown of mountains. Visit for the day to enjoy a real Patagonian *asado*, or better still, stay overnight in comfortable rooms with superb views.

An overnight stay allows for a wonderful horse-riding trip, or an excursion by 4WD to a viewpoint high above the Upsala glacier, with the still milky Prussian blue lake below and fire-coloured rocks all around. From here hike down the staggering Canyon de los Fósiles, with your own private guide: mind-blowingly beautiful. Day trips cost between US$100 and US$180, all inclusive. Add in one night's accommodation (all inclusive) and the price is US$620 for a double room. For more information contact **Estancia Cristina**, T02902-491133, www.estanciacristina.com.

atmosphere, good flats, *cabañas* and **$$** doubles on a neat garden and also in building on opposite side of road.

$$-$ pp **Marcopolo Inn Calafate**, Calle 405, T493899, www.marcopoloinncalafate. com. Part of Hostelling International. **$** pp in dorms. Laundry facilities, various activities and tours on offer.

$ pp **América del Sur**, Puerto Deseado 153, T493525, www.americahostel.com.ar. Panoramic views from this comfortable, relaxed hostel, welcoming, well-heated rooms (dorms for 4, **$$** doubles with views, 1 room adapted for wheelchair users), chill-out area, fireplace. Warmly recommended, but can be noisy.

$$-$ pp **Calafate Hostel & Hostería**, Gob Moyano 1226, T02902-492450, www. calafatehostels.com. A huge log cabin with good rooms: dorms with or without bath, breakfast extra, **$$** doubles with bath and breakfast. Book a month ahead for Jan-Feb, HI discounts, travel agency, Always Glacier and restaurant Isabel on premises.

$ pp **Hostel del Glaciar 'Libertador'**, Av del Libertador 587 (next to the bridge), T02902-492492, www.glaciar.com. HI discounts, open Sep-May. Smaller and pricier than 'Pioneros', rooms are good

and well-heated, all with own bath (US$20 pp dorms for 4 and **$$$-$$** doubles), breakfast included. Free transfer from bus terminal, laundry service. Owners run Patagonia Backpackers (see below under What to do). Recommended.

$** pp **Hostel del Glaciar 'Pioneros'**, Los Pioneros 255, T02902-491243, www.glaciar. com. Discount for HI members, open mid-Sep to mid-Mar. Accommodation for all budgets: standard **$$** doubles (also for 3 and 4) with bath, superior **$$$ doubles with bath, shared dorms up to 4 beds, US$16.50 pp. Many languages spoken, lots of bathrooms, no breakfast in dorms, only private rooms, free shuttle from bus terminal, laundry service, Wi-Fi, movie rental. Very popular, so book well in advance and double-check.

$ pp **i Keu Ken Hostel**, F M Pontoriero 171, T02902-495175, www.patagoniaikeuken. com.ar. On a hill, very helpful, friendly staff, hot water, heating, luggage store, good.

Estancias

$$$$ Estancia Cristina, see box, above.
$$$$ Estancia Nibepo Aike, in the far south of the park on the shores of Brazo Sur of Lago Argentino, T02902-492797,

www.nibepoaike.com.ar, www.lagosan martin.com. Oct-Apr. A spectacular setting inside the national park, near the shores of the lake, the house has just 15 simple rooms, decorated with lovely old furniture, and there's a cosy sitting room. Lots of activities are possible in the park, or the surrounding 12800 ha. Premises are open for day visits too.

$$$$ Hostería Alta Vista, 35 km west of El Calafate (on Ruta 15 to Lago Roca), T02902-491247, www.hosteriaaltavista.com.ar. Set within the land of Estancia Anita, the largest estancia in the area (a staggering 74,000 ha) Alta Vista is a famous spot with all facilities you could possibly need, and only 15 guests. Favoured by celebrities and politicians, the lovely house was built in the 1930s and mostly retains its original style. Full-board is possible with excellent cuisine and wines included. There are attractive walks and a great range of excursions within the vast expanse of the ranch. Recommended.

$$$$ Kau Yatún, Estancia 25 de Mayo (10 blocks from centre, east of arroyo Calafate), T02902-491059, www.kauyatun. com. Renovated main house of a former estancia, well-kept grounds, 2 excellent restaurants, only half board or all inclusive packages that include excursions in the national park.

$$$$ Los Notros, 70 km west of Calafate opposite the Moreno glacier, T02902-499510, T011-4813 7285 (Buenos Aires), www.losnotros.com. An exclusive retreat by the lake with luxurious accommodation in spacious, well-designed rooms. This is the only option if you want to wake up to views of the Perito Moreno glacier. You can walk, hike, trek and ride horses. Expensive, but there are all-inclusive packages with free transfers to the glacier *pasarelas* included.

Camping

AMSA, Olavarría 65 (50 m off the main road, turning south at the fire station), T02902-492247. Hot water, open in summer, US$6.50 pp.

Bahía Escondida, 7 km east of the glacier. Facilities include fireplaces, hot showers and a shop. Crowded in summer.
Correntoso, 10 km east of the glacier. An unmarked site with no facilities but a great location. No fires.
El Huala, 42 km from El Calafate, on the road to Lago Roca. Open all year round. Free with basic facilities.
Ferretería Chuar, 1 block from bus terminal. Sells camping gas.
Lago Roca, 50 km from El Calafate, T02901-43313, www. losglaciares.com/ campinglagoroca. Oct-Apr. Beautifully situated, US$6pp, bike hire, fishing licences, restaurant/*confitería*.

Fitz Roy area *p437, map p437*
There are campsites in the park at **Poincenot**, **Capri**, De Agostini (Laguna Torre) and **Laguna Toro**. **Río Blanco** is only for climbers with prior permission. Campsites have no services but all have latrines, apart from Toro. See box, page 438, for advice on camping equipment and behaviour in the national park.
Camping Los Troncos/Piedra del Fraile, on Río Eléctrico, just north of the park boundary, is a privately owned campsite with *cabañas* and hot showers (**$** per person).

El Chaltén *p439, map p439*
In high season places are full; you must book ahead. Most places close in low season.
$$$$ Hostería El Puma, Lionel Terray 212, T02962-493095, www.hosteriaelpuma. com.ar. A little apart, splendid views, lounge with log fire, tasteful stylish furnishings, comfortable, transfers and big American breakfast included. Recommended.
$$$$ Los Cerros, Av San Martín 260, T02962-493182, www.loscerrosdelchalten. com. Stylish and sophisticated, in a stunning setting with mountain views, sauna, whirlpool and massage. Half-board and all-inclusive packages with excursions available.

$$$$ Senderos, Perito Moreno 35, T02962-493336, www.senderoshosteria.com.ar. 4 types of room and suite in a new, wood-framed structure, comfortable, warm, can arrange excellent restaurant.

$$$ Lunajuim, Trevisán 45, T02962-493047, www.lunajuim.com. Stylish yet relaxed, comfortable (duvets on the beds), lounge with wood fire. Recommended.

$$$ Nothofagus, Hensen cnr with Riquelme, T02962-493087, www.nothofagusbb.com.ar. Cosy bed and breakfast, simple rooms, cheaper without bath and in low season, Oct and Apr (**$$**), good value. Recommended.

$$ Hospedaje La Base, Av Lago del Desierto 97, T02962-493031. Good rooms for 2, 3 and 4, tiny kitchen, self-service breakfast, great video lounge. Recommended.

$$-$ Ahonikenk Chaltén, Av Martín M de Güemes 23, T02962-493070. Nice simple rooms, some dorms, restaurant/pizzería attached, good pastas.

$ pp Albergue Patagonia, Av San Martín 493, T02962-493019, www.patagoniahostel.com.ar. HI-affiliated, cheaper for members, small and cosy with rooms for 2 with own bath (**$$**) or for 2 (**$$**), 4, 5 or 6 with shared bath, also has cabins, video room, bike hire, laundry, luggage store and lockers, restaurant, very welcoming. Helpful information on Chaltén, also run excursions to Lago del Desierto. Closed Jun-Sep.

$ pp Albergue Rancho Grande, San Martín 724, T02962-493005, www.ranchograndehostel.com. HI-affiliated, in a great position at the end of town with good open views and attractive restaurant and lounge, rooms for 4, with shared bath, breakfast extra. Also **$$** doubles, breakfast extra. Helpful, English spoken. Recommended. Reservations in El Calafate at Hostel/Chaltén Travel, Calafate.

$ pp Cóndor de los Andes, Av Río de las Vueltas y Halvorsen, T02962-493101, www.condordelosandes.com. Nice little rooms for up to 6 with bath, sheets included, breakfast extra, also doubles with bath (**$$$-$$**), laundry service, library, quiet, HI affiliated.

Around El Chaltén *p440, map p439*
There is a campsite at the southern end of Lago del Desierto and *refugios* at its northern end and at Laguna Diablo.

$$$$ Estancia Helsingfors, 73 km northwest of La Leona, on Lago Viedma, T011-5277 0195, reservations T02966-675753, www.helsingfors.com.ar. Nov-Apr. Fabulous place in splendid position on Lago Viedma, stylish rooms, welcoming lounge, delicious food (full board), and excursions directly to glaciers and to Laguna Azul, by horse or trekking, plus boat trips.

$$$$ Estancia La Quinta, on Ruta 23, 2 km south of El Chaltén, T02962-493012, www.estancialaquinta.com.ar. Oct-Apr. A spacious pioneer house with renovated rooms and beautiful gardens. A superb breakfast is included and the restaurant is open for lunch and dinner. Free transfer to/from El Chaltén bus terminal.

$$$ El Pilar, Ruta 23, Km 17, T02962-493002, www.hosteriaelpilar.com.ar. Country house in a spectacular setting at the meeting of Ríos Blanco and de las Vueltas, with clear views of Fitz Roy. A chance to sample the simple life with access to less-visited northern part of the park. Comfortable rooms, great food, breakfast and return transfers included.

$$$ Estancia Lago del Desierto, Punto Sur, southern tip of Lago del Desierto, T02962-493010. Basic place with *cabañas* for 5, camping US$5 per person, hot showers, kitchen. Recommended.

❼ Restaurants

El Calafate *p433, map p434*
$$ La Lechuza, Av del Libertador 1301, www.lalechuzapizzas.com.ar. Good quality pizzas, pasta, salad and meat dishes. Excellent wine list. Has another branch up the road at no.935.

$$ La Tablita, Cnel Rosales 28 (near the bridge). Typical *parrilla*, generous portions and quality beef. Recommended.

$$ La Vaca Atada, Av del Libertador 1176. Good home-made pastas and more elaborate and expensive dishes based on salmon and king crab.

$$ Mi Viejo, Av del Libertador 1111. Closed Tue. Popular *parrilla*.

$$ Pura Vida, Av Libertador 1876, near C 17. Thu-Tue 1930-2330 only. Comfortable sofas, home-made Argentine food, vegetarian options, lovely atmosphere, lake view (reserve table). Recommended.

$$ Rick's Restaurante, Av del Libertador 1091. Lively *parrilla* with good atmosphere.

$$ Viva la Pepa, Emilio Amado 833. Mon-Sat 1100-2300. A mainly vegetarian café with great sandwiches and crêpes filled with special toppings. Wi-Fi, craft beers. Child-friendly.

Cafés

Borges y Alvarez, Av del Libertador 1015 (Galería de los Gnomos), T02902-491464. Cosy wooden bar with huge windows over the shopping street below. Affordable, and delicious lunch and dinner, as well as live music and books for sale. A lively, friendly place open daily till 0400. Excellent place to hang out. Recommended.

Casablanca, 25 de Mayo y Av del Libertador. Jolly place for omelettes, hamburgers, vegetarian, 30 varieties of pizza.

Heladería Aquarela, Av del Libertador 1197. The best ice cream – try the calafate. Also home-made chocolates and local produce.

El Chaltén *p439, map p439*

$$ Estepa, Cerro Solo y Antonio Rojo. Small, intimate place with good, varied meals, friendly staff.

$$ Fuegia, San Martín 342. Dinner only. Pastas, trout, meat and vegetarian dishes. Recommended.

$$ Josh Aike, Lago de Desierto 105. Excellent *confitería*, home-made food, beautiful building. Recommended.

$$ Pangea, Lago del Desierto 330 y San Martín. Open for lunch and dinner, drinks and coffee, calm, good music, varied menu. Recommended.

$$ Patagonicus, Güemes y Madsen. Midday to midnight. Lovely warm place with salads, pastas caseras and fabulous pizzas for 2, US$3-8. Recommended.

$$ Ruca Mahuida, Lionel Terray 55, T02962-493018. Widely regarded as the best restaurant with imaginative and well-prepared food.

$$ Zaffarancho (behind **Rancho Grande**), music bar-restaurant, good range and reasonably priced. Film nights three times a week.

$ Domo Blanco, San Martín 164. Delicious ice cream.

$ Las Lengas, Viedma 95, opposite tourist office, T02962-493023, laslengaselchalten@ yahoo.com.ar. Cheaper than most. Plentiful meals, basic pastas and meat dishes. US$3 for meal of the day. Lots of information. See Transport, below, for owner's minibus services.

⬤ Bars and clubs

El Calafate *p433, map p434*

Elba'r, 9 de Julio 57. Just off the main street, this café/bar serves hard to find waffles, plus juices, home-made beer and sandwiches.

Shackleton Lounge, Av del Libertador 3287, T02902-493516. On the outskirts of town. A great place to relax, lovely views of the lake, old photos of Shackleton, great atmosphere, good music. Highly recommended for a late drink or some good regional dishes. Afternoon tea served.

El Chaltén *p439, map p439*

Cervecería Bodegón, El Chaltén, San Martín 564, T02962-493109. Brews its own excellent beer, also local dishes and pizzas, coffee and cakes, English spoken. Recommended.

✹ Festivals

El Calafate *p433, map p434*
14 Feb People flock to the rural show on **Lago Argentino Day**, www.fiestadellagoargentino.com, and camp out with live music, dancing and *asados*.
10 Nov Displays of horsemanship and *asados* on **Día de la Tradición**.

○ Shopping

El Calafate *p433, map p434*
Plenty of touristy shops in main street Av del Libertador. Recommended for home-made local produce, especially Patagonian fruit teas, sweets and liqueurs, is **Estancia El Tranquilo**, Av del Libertador 935, www.eltranquilo.com.ar.

El Chaltén *p439, map p439*
Several outdoor shops. Also supermarkets, all expensive, and with little fresh food available: **El Gringuito**, Av Antonio Rojo, has the best choice. Fuel is available next to the bridge.

◐ What to do

El Calafate *p433, map p434*
Most agencies charge the same rates and run similar excursions, including minibus tours to the Perito Moreno glacier, US$36 (park entry not included), and minitrekking tours (transport plus a 2½-hr walk on the glacier), US$128. Note that out of season trips to the glacier may be difficult to arrange and boat trips can be cancelled by bad weather.
Calafate Mountain Park, Av del Libertador 1037, T02902-491446, www.calafatemountainpark.com. Excursions in 4WD to panoramic views, 3-6 hrs. Summer and winter experiences including kayaking, quad biking, skiing and more.
Chaltén Travel, Av del Libertador 1174, T02902-492212, www.chaltentravel.com. Huge range of tours (has a monopoly

on some): glaciers, estancias, trekking, and bus to El Chaltén. Sells tickets along the Ruta 40 to Perito Moreno, Los Antiguos and Bariloche, departures 0800 on odd-numbered days (0900 from El Chaltén) mid-Nov-Apr, overnight in Perito Moreno (cheaper to book your own accommodation), 36 hrs, English spoken.
Hielo y Aventura, Av del Libertador 935, T02902-492205, www.hieloyaventura.com. *Minitrekking* includes walk through forests and 2½-hr trek on Moreno glacier (crampons included); Big Ice full-day tour includes a 4-hr trek on the glacier. Also half-day boat excursion to Brazo Sur for a view of stunning glaciers, including Moreno. Recommended.
Lago San Martín, Av del Libertador 1215, p 1, T02902-492858, www.lagosanmartin.com. Operates with Estancias Turísticas de Santa Cruz, specializing in arranging estancia visits, helpful.
Mar Patag, 9 de Julio 57, of 4, T02902-492118, www.crucerosmarpatag.com. Exclusive 2-day boat excursion to Upsala, Spegazzini and Moreno glaciers, with full board. Also does a shorter full-day cruise with gourmet lunch included.
Mundo Austral, 9 de Julio 2427, T02902-492365, www.mundoaustral.com.ar. For all bus travel and cheaper trips to the glaciers, helpful bilingual guides.
Patagonia Backpackers, at Hosteles del Glaciar, T02902-491792, www.patagonia-backpackers.com. Alternative Glacier tour, entertaining, informative, includes walking, US$45. Recommended constantly.
Solo Patagonia, Av del Libertador 867, T02902-491155, www.solopatagonia.com. This company runs two 7-hr boat trips taking in Upsala, Onelli and Spegazzini glaciers, US$92.

El Chaltén *p439, map p439*
Casa De Guías, Av San Martín s/n, T02902-493118, www.casadeguias.com.ar. Experienced climbers who lead groups to nearby peaks, to the Campo de Hielo Continental and easier treks.

Chaltén Travel, Av Güemes 7, T02962-493092, www.chaltentravel.com. See El Calafate Tour operators, above.
El Relincho, T02962-493007, www.elrelinchopatagonia.com.ar. For trekking on horseback with guides. Also trekking, accommodation and rural activities.
Fitz Roy Expediciones, San Martín 56, T02962-436424, www.fitzroyexpediciones.com.ar. Organizes trekking and adventure trips including on the Campo de Hielo Continental, ice climbing schools, and fabulous longer trips. Climbers must be fit, but no technical experience required; equipment provided. Email with lots of notice to reserve. Ecocamp with 8 wilderness cabins recently opened. Highly recommended.
Las Lengas (see Restaurants, above), www.transportelaslengas.com, runs a regular minibus to Lago del Desierto in summer passing Hostería El Pilar and some starting points for treks.
Patagonia Aventura, T02962-493110, www.patagonia-aventura.com. Has various ice trekking and other tours to Lago and Glaciar Viedma, also to Lago del Desierto.

⊖ Transport

Río Turbio *p433*
Bus
To **Puerto Natales**, 2 hrs, US$8, hourly with **Cootra** (Tte del Castillo 01, T02902-421448), and other companies. To **El Calafate**, **Cootra**, 4 hrs, US$20. To **Río Gallegos**, 5 hrs, US$28 (Taqsa/Marga, T02902-421422).

El Calafate *p433, map p434*
Air
Daily flights to/from **Buenos Aires**. Many more flights in summer to **Bariloche**, **Ushuaia** and **Trelew**. LADE flies to **Ushuaia**, **Comodoro Rivadavia**, **Río Gallegos**, **Esquel** and other Patagonian airports (office at J Mermoz 160, T02902-491262). Note that a boarding fee of US$21, not included in the airline ticket price, has to be paid at El Calafate.

Bus
Terminal on Roca 1004, 1 block up stairs from Av del Libertador. A terminal fee US$0.65, always included in bus ticket price. Some bus companies will store luggage for a fee. Take passport when booking bus tickets to Chile.

To **Perito Moreno glacier**, with Taqsa, **Interlagos**, US$25 return; also guided excursions and minibus tours (see What to do, above). To **Río Gallegos**, daily, 4-5 hrs, US$19-25, with **Sportman** (T02966-15 464841) and **Taqsa** (T02902-491843). To **El Chaltén**, 3 hrs, many daily: Taqsa, US$26; **Chaltén Travel** (T02902-492212) at 0800, 1300, 1830; **Los Glaciares**, **Cal-Tur** (T02902-491368, www.caltur.com.ar, who run many other services and tours), US$30. To **Bariloche**, with **Chaltén Travel** via Los Antiguos and Perito Moreno (see above), also **Cal-Tur**; **Taqsa** runs a bus to **Bariloche** via Los Antiguos, 36 hrs, US$108 (frequency depends on demand). To **Ushuaia**, take a bus to Río Gallegos for connections.

To Chile (direct) To **Puerto Natales**, via Río Turbio, daily in summer with **Cootra** (T02902-491444), 7 hrs, with **Pacheco**, Mon, Wed, Fri 1100, or with **Turismo Zaahj** (T02902-491631), 3-9 a week depending on season, 5 hrs, US$25 (advance booking recommended, tedious customs check at border). **Note** Argentine pesos cannot be exchanged in Torres del Paine.

Car hire
Average price under US$100 per day for small car with insurance but usually only 200 free km. **Localiza**, Av del Libertador 687, T02902-491398, localiza calafate@ hotmail.com. **Nunatak**, Gob Gregores 1075, T02902-491987, www.nunatakrentacar.com.ar. **ON Rent a Car**, Av del Libertador 1831, T02902-493788 or T02966-156 29985, onrentacar@cotecal.com.ar. All vehicles have a permit for crossing to Chile, included in the fee, but cars are poor. Bikes for hire, US$17 per day.

Taxi
Taxis charge about US$75 for 4 passengers round trip to the Moreno glacier including a wait of 3-4 hrs. A reliable driver is **Ruben**, T02902-498707. There is small taxi stand outside the bus terminal.

El Chaltén *p439, map p439*
Bus
Tax of US$1.15 is charged at the terminal. In summer, buses fill quickly: book ahead. Fewer services off season. Daily buses to **El Calafate**, 4-5 hrs (see above); most also stop at El Calafate airport. **Las Lengas** (www.transportelaslengas.com.ar) also run to **El Calafate airport** 3 times a day, 3 hrs, US$28; reserve in advance. To **Los Antiguos** and **Bariloche**, with **Chaltén Travel** (see above). **Las Lengas** have a daily service to **Piedrabuena** on Ruta 3, for connections to **Los Antiguos**, **Puerto Madryn**, etc, 6 hrs, US$37.

Taxi
Servicio de Remís El Chaltén, Av San Martín 430, T02962-493042, reliable.

ⓘ Directory

El Calafate *p433, map p434*
Banks Best to take cash as high commission is charged on exchange, but there are ATMs at airport and banks. Thaler, Av del Libertador 963, loc 2, changes money and TCs. **Post office** Av del Libertador 1133.

El Chaltén *p439, map p439*
Banks 24-hr ATM next to the gas station at the entrance to town. Credit cards are accepted in all major hotels and restaurants.

Contents

Footprint features

Border crossings

At a glance

⊖ **Getting around** Local buses
will take you to the local attractions
but not much further afield.
Some short-distance flights.
↻ **Time required** 3-4 days
will allow you to visit Ushuaia
and the surrounding area.
❀ **Weather** Mar-Nov brings harsh
winds and cold temperatures,
with snow in Jun and Jul.
✖ **When not to go** The
height of winter (May-Jul)
can be unpleasantly cold,
unless you want to ski.

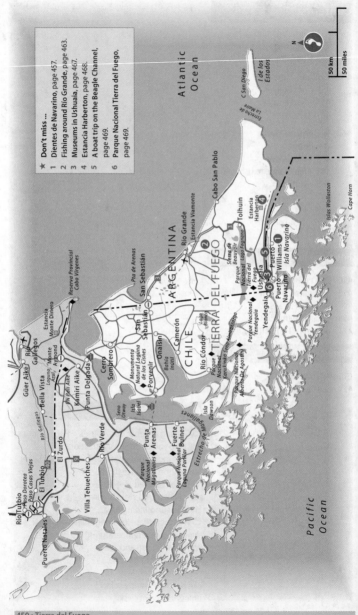

★ Don't miss ...

1 Dientes de Navarino, page 457.
2 Fishing around Río Grande, page 463.
3 Museums in Ushuaia, page 467.
4 Estancia Harberton, page 466.
5 A boat trip on the Beagle Channel,
   page 469.
6 Parque Nacional Tierra del Fuego,
   page 469.

Atlantic
Ocean

I de los
Estados

C San Diego

N

50 km
50 miles

Cabo San Pablo

ARGENTINA

Río Grande

Estancia Viamonte

Estancia
Harberton 4

Tolhuin

Sierra de
Beauvoir

Reserva Provincial
Cabo Vírgenes

Estancia
Monte Dinero

Güer Aike

Bella Vista

Río
Gallegos

Laguna
Azul

Monte
Aymond

Río Gallegos

Pali Aike

El Zurdo

Kamiri Aike

Punta Delgada

Cerro
Sombrero

Villa Tehuelches

Monumento
Natural Laguna
de los Cisnes

Parque Nacional
Pali Aike

Onaisín

Parque
Nacional
Karukinka

Bahía
Inútil

Parque Nacional
Lago Fagnano

Parque
Nacional
Yendegaia

San
Sebastián

Camerón

Pta de Arenas

San Sebastián

Punta Arenas

Isla
Isabel

Seno
Otway

Río Verde

Fuerte
Bulnes

Parque Nacional
Magallanes

Parque Nacional
Laguna Parrillar

Estrecho de Magallanes

Porvenir

Isla
Dawson

Bahía
Blanca

Parque Nacional
Alberto de Agostini

CHILE

TIERRA DEL FUEGO

Río Cóndor

Ushuaia

Puerto
Williams

Isla Navarino 1

Yendegaia

5

6 3

Parque
Nacional
Tierra del
Fuego

Puerto
Navarino

Pacific
Ocean

Estrecho de
La Maire

Islas Wollaston

Cape Horn

Puerto Natales

Paso Casas Viejas

Dorotea

Río Turbio

El Turbio

The island of Tierra del Fuego is the most mysterious and captivating part of all Patagonia. At the very foot of the South American continent and separated from the mainland by the intricate waterways of the Straits of Magellan, this is America's last remaining wilderness and an indispensable part of any trip to the south. The island is divided between Argentina and Chile by a north–south line that grants Argentina the Atlantic and southern coasts and gives Chile an expanse of wilderness to the west, where the tail of the Andes sweeps east in the form of the mighty Darwin range.

The Chilean side is largely inaccessible, apart from the small town of Porvenir, though expeditions can be organized from Punta Arenas to take you hiking and trout fishing. On the Argentine side, glaciers and jagged peaks give a dramatic backdrop to the city of Ushuaia, the island's main centre, set in a serene natural harbour on the Beagle Channel, with views of the Dientes de Navarino mountains on the Chilean island of Navarino opposite. Sail from Ushuaia along the channel to the pioneer home of Harberton; to Cape Horn; or even to Antarctica. Head into the small but picturesque Parque Nacional Tierra del Fuego for strolls around Bahía Lapataia and for steep climbs with magnificent views out along the channel. The mountain slopes are covered in lenga forest, and if you visit in autumn you might think the name 'Land of Fire' derives from the blaze of scarlet and orange leaves. Elsewhere on the island, lakes and valleys can be explored on foot or on horseback, and in winter the valleys are perfect for cross-country skiing, while the slopes at Cerro Castor offer good powder snow and skiing with spectacular views of the end of the world.

Arriving in Tierra del Fuego

Getting there

Note that accommodation is sparse, and planes and buses fill up quickly from November to March. It's essential to book ahead.

Air **Argentine Tierra del Fuego** is easy to reach with several flights daily from Buenos Aires to Río Grande and Ushuaia, and less frequent flights from El Calafate, and some other towns in Patagonia. Flights are heavily booked in advance throughout the summer months (December to February). **Chilean Tierra del Fuego** is only reached by plane from Punta Arenas to Porvenir, daily, and to Puerto Williams on Isla Navarino, Monday to Saturday (but always check for seasonal variations).

Ferry and bus There are no road or ferry crossings between the Argentine mainland and Argentine Tierra del Fuego. You have to go through Chilean territory.

From Río Gallegos, Route 3 reaches the Integración Austral border at Monte Aymond, after 67 km, passing Laguna Azul (see box, page 407). The road continues beyond the border as Chilean Route 255, reaching Kamiri Aike after 30 km. Take Route 257 for 16 km east of here to reach the dock at Punta Delgada for the 20-minute Straits of Magellan ferry crossing over the Primera Angostura (First Narrows) to Bahía Azul in Chilean Tierra del Fuego. At Punta Delgada is the **Hostería El Faro** where you can get food and drink. There are three boats working continuously, each with a café, lounge and toilets on board. Buses can wait up to 90 minutes to board and the boats run every 40 minutes from 0830 to 0100, US$25 per vehicle, foot passengers US$3. See www.tabsa.cl for more information. From Bahía Azul, the road is paved to Cerro Sombrero, from where *ripio* roads run southeast to Chilean San Sebastián (130-140 km from ferry, depending on the route taken). It's 15 km east, across the border (see box, opposite), to Argentine San Sebastián. From here the road is paved to Río Grande (see below) and Ushuaia.

The second main ferry crossing is Punta Arenas to Porvenir. The ferry dock is 5 km north of Punta Arenas centre, at Tres Puentes. The ferry crosses to Bahía Chilota, 5 km west of Porvenir, Tuesday to Sunday taking two hours 20 minutes, US$67 per vehicle, motorcycles US$19, foot passengers US$10. **Transportadora Austral Broom** ① *www. tabsa.cl*, publishes a timetable a month in advance but this is dependent on tides and subject to change, so check in advance. Reservations are essential, especially in summer. From Porvenir a 234-km *ripio* road runs east to Río Grande (six hours, no public transport) via San Sebastián. Note that fruit and meat may not be taken onto the island, nor between Argentina and Chile.

There is also a weekly ferry service on the **Yaghan** (also www.tabsa.cl) from Punta Arenas to Puerto Williams on Isla Navarino. It takes 24 passengers, US$165 for chair, US$230 for Pullman, a 30- to 34-hour trip through beautiful channels. It will not take passengers if it is carrying petrol, so ask in advance.

Getting around

There are good bus links from Punta Arenas to Río Grande in Argentina, with an option of going via Porvenir, along the decent loop of road on the Chilean side. From Porvenir your options are limited to a *ripio* road around Bahía Inútil to near Lago Blanco, though there's no public transport here. Argentine Tierra del Fuego is much easier to get around, via Route 3 between Río Grande and Ushuaia with several buses a day. A fan of roads

Border crossing: Chile–Argentina

San Sebastián

This is the border between the Chilean and Argentine sides of Tierra del Fuego and is open daily 0900 to 2300. Chilean San Sebastián is located 130 km southeast of the ferry dock at Bahía Azul, via Cerro Sombrero. It consists of just a few houses with Hostería La Frontera 500 m from the border. Argentine San Sebastián is 15 km further east, across the border. It has a seven-room ACA hostería (T02961-15-405834) and a service station, open 0700-2300. For further details, see www.gendarmeria.gov.ar/pasos/chile/fichssebas.html.

spreads out south and west from Río Grande to the estancias on the Argentine side, but these are unpaved and best attempted in a 4WD vehicle. A good *ripio* road leads east of Ushuaia along the south coast, and another goes part of the way along the north coast to Estancia San Pablo; there is no public transport here either.

Background

Tierra del Fuego's narrated history began with the early 16th-century explorers, but the island had been inhabited by indigenous groups for some 10,000 years. The most populous of these groups, the Onas (also known as the Selk'nam), were hunter-gatherers in the north, living mainly on guanaco which they shot with bow and arrow. The south eastern corner of the island was inhabited by the Haus or Hausch, also hunter-gatherers. The Yaganes or Yámana lived along the Beagle Channel and on the islands further south and were seafaring people who survived mainly on seafood, fish and birds. They were physically smaller than the Onas but with a strongly developed upper body for rowing long distances. The fourth group, the Alacalufe, lived in the west of Tierra del Fuego as well as on the Chonos Archipelago, surviving by fishing and hunting seals.

The first Europeans to visit the island came with the Portuguese navigator Fernão Magalhães (Magellan), who, in 1520, sailed through the channel that now bears his name. It was Magellan who named the island 'Land of Fire' when he saw the smoke from many fires lit along the shoreline by local inhabitants. As a result of numerous maritime disasters and the failure of Sarmiento de Gamboa's attempt to colonize the Straits in 1584, the indigenous population were left undisturbed for three centuries.

Fitzroy and Darwin's scientific visits in 1832 and 1833 recorded some fascinating interaction with the indigenous peoples, four of whom Fitzroy had earlier brought to London to see if they could be 'civilized'; he now returned the surviving three to the island. Fitzroy and Darwin's visits were a precursor to attempts to convert the indigenous groups to Christianity so that the island could be used by white settlers without fear of attack. Several disastrous missions followed, encountering stiff resistance from the inhabitants. In 1884, Reverend Thomas Bridges founded a mission at Ushuaia. He was the first European to learn the Yámana language, and he compiled a Yámana-English dictionary. He soon realized that his original task was a destructive one. The purpose of the missionary work had been to facilitate lucrative sheep farming on the island, but the Ona were attracted to the 'white guanacos' on their land and took to hunting sheep, which proved far easier than catching the fast-footed guanaco. In response, the colonists offered two sheep for each Ona that was killed (proof was provided by a pair of Ona ears). The indigenous groups were further ravaged by epidemics of European diseases. In a desperate attempt to save the Ona, Salesian missionaries founded three missions in the Straits of Magellan in the early 20th century, but, stripped of their land, the Ona lost the will to live, and the last Ona died in 1999. The Hausch also died out. The last of the Yámana, a woman called Cristina Calderón, presently survives near Puerto Williams. She is 86 years old.

Imprecision in the original colonial land division and the greed of the rush southwards led to border disputes between Argentina and Chile, which still rumble on today. The initial settlement of the dispute in 1883 was followed by a desire by both governments to populate the area by allocating large expanses of land for sheep farming. The main beneficiaries of this policy on Tierra del Fuego were the Menéndez and Braun families, already established in Punta Arenas.

For many years, the main economic activity of the northern part of the island was sheep farming, but Argentine government tax incentives to companies in the 1970s led to the establishment of new industries in Río Grande and Ushuaia and a rapid growth in the population of both cities; the subsequent withdrawal of incentives has produced increasing unemployment and migration. Tourism is increasingly important in Ushuaia.

For a detailed narrative account of Tierra del Fuego, the best book is still the classic by Lucas Bridges, *Uttermost Part of the Earth*, out of print but easily obtained second-hand on www.abebooks.co.uk. Also fascinating is *Patagonia, Natural history, prehistory and ethnography at the uttermost part of the earth* (British Museum press). *Savage – The Life and Times of Jemmy Button* by Nick Hazelwood (Hodder & Stoughton) is also recommended.

Chilean Tierra del Fuego

The Chilean half of Tierra del Fuego is in two sections: the western half of Isla Grande (the main island) and the whole of Isla Navarino, to the south of the main island. Much less developed than the Argentine side of Tierra del Fuego, it has just two small towns where Chile's Fuegians are mostly concentrated: Porvenir on Isla Grande, easily reached by ferry from Punta Arenas; and Puerto Williams on Isla Navarino, which can be reached by a flight from Punta Arenas, a weekly ferry also from Punta Arenas and by boat from Ushuaia. The northern part of Isla Grande is flat steppe, but the south is dominated by the Darwin range of mountains, which provide a dramatic visual backdrop, even if you can't easily get to them. Tourism on Chilean territory is limited, but it's possible to organize trekking tours from Punta Arenas, and there are fishing lodges offering magnificent trout fishing, particularly on the Río Grande.

Isla Grande → *For listings, see pages 459-461.*

Puerto Porvenir → *Colour map 6, C3. Phone code: +56 (0)61. Population: 5100.*

Chilean Tierra del Fuego has a population of 7000, most of whom live in the small town of Porvenir – the only town on the Chilean half of the main island. Founded in 1894 during the gold boom, when many people came seeking fortunes from Croatia and Chiloe, Porvenir is a quiet place with a wide open pioneer feel, streets of neat, brightly painted houses of corrugated zinc and quaint tall domed trees lining the main avenue. There is a small museum, the **Museo Fernando Cordero Rusque** ⓘ *Zavattaro 402, on the plaza, T061-581800, www.museoporvenir.cl, Mon-Thu 0900-1700, Fri 0900-1600, Sat-Sun 1030-1330, 1500-1700, US$0.85*, with archaeological and photographic displays on the Onas, and good displays on natural history and the early gold diggers and sheep farmers. There's little else to do here, but you could stroll around the plaza, with its **Iglesia San Francisco de Sales**, and down to the shoreside promenade, where there's a strange collection of 19th-century farm machinery and a striking wooden monument to the Selk'nam.

Tourist information is available at the museum (the best option), on notice boards outside the Municipalidad, on the seafront and elsewhere, and from a handicrafts stall in a kiosk on the seafront (opposite Comercial Tuto, No 588). See also www.patagonia-chile.com.

Beyond Porvenir

Beyond Porvenir there is wonderfully wild virgin territory to explore. However, if you want an adventure, your best bet is to arrange a trip through tour operators in Punta Arenas, since there's still very little infrastructure on the Chilean side of the island.

Shipwrecked in the Magellan Straits

The Estrecho de Magallanes, 534 km long, is a treacherous sea passage linking the Atlantic and the Pacific oceans. The eastern entrance to the straits is between Punta Dúngeness on the Argentine mainland and Cabo del Espíritu Santo on Tierra del Fuego. From here the route heads west and then south, past Punta Arenas and Fuerte Bulnes, before negotiating the channels and islands of southern Chile. The straits have a long history of claiming victims, and the hostile conditions are eloquently conveyed in the words of Sir John Narborough: "horrible like the ruins of a world destroyed by terrific earthquakes".

From the Atlantic, the first navigational problem facing sailors is simply the difficulty of entering the straits against the fierce westerly gales that prevail. Once in the straits the dangers are far from over: many ships have fallen victim to the notorious *Williwaws*, winds with the ferocity of tornados that spring up from nowhere; no less vicious are the *Pamperos*, which blow off the land with enough force to capsize a vessel.

Although in 1520 Magellan succeeded in passing through the straits that bear his name, few others managed to do so in the years that followed; of the 17 ships that attempted the passage in the early 16th century, only one, the *Victoria*, succeeded in reaching the Pacific and returning to Europe. Twelve were lost near the eastern entrance and four returned in failure. The reason these early navigators chose to attempt the dangerous voyage was the lure of a short route between Europe and the spices of the East. Even when it became clear that there was no such short route, the straits still provided a useful means for Europeans to reach the rich Pacific ports of Peru and Chile without disembarking to cross Mexico or Panama overland.

Even with the development of advanced navigation techniques in the 19th century, losses continued: in 1869, the *Santiago*, an iron paddle-steamer built in Glasgow and owned by the Pacific Mail line, went down off Isla Desolación at the western end of the straits with a cargo of gold and silver. While the Panama Canal now provides a shorter route between the Atlantic and Pacific Oceans, the size of modern ships means that the straits are still a busy shipping route. The most common cargo is now oil; casualties still occur but now, of course, with the added risk of environmental disaster from oil spillage.

All roads are good *ripio* except a paved section from Bahía Chilota to Porvenir and in Porvenir itself.➤➤ *For tour operators, see pages 410 and 460.*

North of Porvenir, 6 km, is the **Monumento Natural Laguna de los Cisnes**. Access is across private land; the owner will give permission. Another place to see wildfowl, including black-necked swans from December is **Laguna Santa María**, not far from Porvenir on the road to **Bahía Inútil**, a wonderful windswept bay. Cabo Boquerón, the headland at the start of Bahía Inútil, has great views on a clear day, as far as Cabo Froward, Isla Dawson and the distant Cordillera Darwin's snow peaks. Driving east along the bay you pass Los Canelos, with trees, a rare sight, and then the junction for the Cordón Baquedano, on the **Circuito de Oro**. This is a recommended tour, on which you can see gold panning using the same techniques that have been employed since mining began in 1881; it's a four-hour, 115-km round trip. Miner Sr Jorge Gesell Díaz is happy to show tourists his workings (very enthusiastic), in summer only; write in his visitors' book and leave a tip.

Camerón and further south

About 90 km east of Porvenir, roads head east to San Sebastián and south to Camerón via Onaisin (99 km from Porvenir). Camerón is a large farm settlement and the only other community of any size on the Chilean part of the island. It is 149 km from Porvenir on the opposite shore of Bahía Inútil. This wonderful windswept bay, with views of distant hills and the snow-capped Darwin range all along the southern horizon, was named 'useless' by British engineers making a hydrographic survey here in 1827 because it has no useful port. Nevertheless, as you near Camerón, the road passes secluded canyons and bays, interspersed with a few farms, and the whole feel is dramatic, isolated and somehow rather magical.

Other options are sailing from Porvenir to **Río Cóndor** across Bahía Inútil, south of Camerón, and trekking or riding from Camerón to **Seno Almirantazgo**, a beautiful, wild and treeless place, where mountains sink into blue fjords with icebergs.

A large part of the peninsula between Bahía Inútil and Seno Almirantazgo is covered by the **Karukinka** nature reserve (www.karukinkanatural.cl). From Camerón a road runs southeast past an airfield and into the hills, through woods where guanacos hoot and run off into glades, and the banks are covered with red and purple moss. The north shores of **Lago Blanco** can be reached by cutting east through the woods from Sección Río Grande, with superb views of the mountains surrounding the lake and the snows in the south.

Meanwhile, the rough road continues as far south as Estancia Lago Fagnano on Lago Fagnano, four hours from Onaisin. The government is hoping to complete the road to **Yendegaia** on the Beagle Channel with a view to having a summer route, including ferry, to Puerto Navarino. This would traverse the new **Parque Nacional Yendegaia**, which was created in December 2013 (www.theconservationlandtrust.org) and which adjoins the Parque Nacional Tierra del Fuego in Argentina. It's essential to organize any trip to this area through a reliable tour operator with solid infrastructure.

Isla Navarino → For listings, see pages 459-461.

Situated on the southern shore of the Beagle Channel, Isla Navarino is totally unspoilt and beautiful, offering great geographical diversity, thanks to the **Dientes de Navarino** range of mountains, with peaks over 1000 m, covered with southern beech forest up to 500 m, and south of that, great plains covered with peat bogs, with many lagoons abundant in flora. The island was the centre of the indigenous Yaganes (Yámana) culture, and there are 500 archaeological sites, the oldest dated as 3000 years old. Guanacos and condors can be seen inland, as well as large numbers of beavers, which were introduced to the island and have done considerable damage. The flight from Punta Arenas is beautiful, with superb views of Tierra del Fuego, the Cordillera Darwin, the Beagle Channel and the islands stretching south to Cape Horn.

Arriving on Isla Navarino

Ushuaia Boating (www.ushuaiaboating.com.ar) travel from Ushuaia to Puerto Williams, US$120 each way, which includes a 40-minute crossing in a semi-rigid boat to Puerto Navarino. Despite Ushuaia Boating dealing with documents when you buy the ticket, there is a lot of hanging around at Puerto Navarino, but the setting is nice and they sometimes offer coffee and pastries for impatient passengers. Then it's a one-hour ride in a combi on a lovely *ripio* road to Williams; make sure you are clear about transport arrangements for your return. **Fernández Campbell** has a 1½-hour crossing from

Ushuaia, on Friday, Saturday and Sunday at 1000, returning at 1500. Tickets (US$125 for foreigners) are sold at **Naviera RFC** in Puerto Williams and **Zenit Explorer**, Juana Fadul 126, in Ushuaia, T02901-433232.

Puerto Williams → *Colour map 7, C2. Phone code: 061. Population: 2500.*

The only settlement of any size on the island is Puerto Williams, a Chilean naval base situated about 50 km east of Ushuaia on Argentine seas across the Beagle Channel. Puerto Williams is the southernmost permanently inhabited town in the world; 50 km east-southeast is **Puerto Toro**, the southernmost permanently inhabited settlement on earth. Some maps mistakenly mark a road from Puerto Williams to Puerto Toro, but it doesn't exist; access is only by sea. Due to the long-running border dispute with Argentina here, Puerto Williams is controlled by the Chilean navy. Outside the naval headquarters, you can see the bow section of the *Yelcho*, the tug chartered by Shackleton to rescue men stranded on Elephant Island.

Your main purpose for visiting the island is likely to be the trekking on the Dientes de Navarino, but you should take time to explore the indigenous heritage here too. It's beautifully documented in the **Museo Martín Gusinde** ① *www.museoantropologico martingusinde.cl, Nov-Mar Tue-Fri 0930-1300, 1500-1800, Sat-Sun 1430-1830; Apr-Oct Tue-Fri 0930-1330, 1430-1730, Sat 1430-1830, US$1*, known as the Museo del Fin del Mundo (End of the World Museum), which is full of information about vanished indigenous tribes, local wildlife and the famous voyages by Charles Darwin and Fitzroy of the *Beagle*. A visit is highly recommended. One kilometre west of the town is the yacht club (one of Puerto Williams' two nightspots), whose wharf is made from a sunken 1930s Chilean warship. The town has a **tourist information office** ① *Municipalidad de Cabos de Hornos, O'Higgins 293, T061-262 1011, www.ptowilliams.cl/turismo.html, closed in winter*, where you can ask for maps and details on hiking; there's also a bank, supermarkets and a hospital.

Exploring the island

For superb views, climb **Cerro Bandera**, which is reached by a path from the dam 4 km west of the town (it's a steep, three- to four-hour round trip, take warm clothes). There is excellent trekking around the **Dientes de Navarino** range, the southernmost trail in the world, through impressive mountain landscape, frozen lagoons and snowy peaks, giving superb views over the Beagle Channel. It's a challenging hike, over a distance of 53 km in five days, possible only from December to March, and a good level of fitness is needed. There is no equipment rental on the island. Ask for information in the tourist office at Puerto Williams, but it's best to go with an organized expedition from Punta Arenas.

Beyond Cerro Bandera, a road leads 56 km west of Puerto Williams to **Puerto Navarino**, where there is a jetty, the Alcaldía del Mar and four more houses, plus a few horses and cows. There is little or no traffic on this route and it is very beautiful, with forests of lengas stretching right down to the water's edge. You can also visit **Villa Ukika**, 2 km east of town, the place where the last descendants of the Yámana people live, relocated from their original homes at Caleta Mejillones, which was the last indigenous reservation in the province, inhabited by hundreds of Yámana descendants. At **Mejillones**, 32 km from Puerto Williams, is a graveyard and memorial to the Yámana people. Just before Estancia Santa Rosa (10 km further on), a path is said to cross the forest, lakes and beaver dams to Wulaia (four to six hours), where the *Beagle* anchored in 1833; however, even the farmer at Wulaia gets lost following this track.

Cape Horn

It is possible to catch a boat south from Isla Navarino to Cape Horn (the most southerly piece of land on earth apart from Antarctica). There is one pebbly beach on the north side of the island; boats anchor in the bay and passengers are taken ashore by motorized dinghy. A stairway climbs the cliff above the beach, up to the building which houses the naval post. A path leads from here to the impressive monument of an albatross overlooking the wild, churning waters of the Drake Passage below. See also A cruise to the end of the world, page 412.

◉ Chilean Tierra del Fuego listings

For hotel and restaurant price codes and other relevant information, see pages 14-21.

● Where to stay

Puerto Porvenir *p455*
$$$ Hostería Yendegaia, Croacia 702, T061-258 1919, www.hosteriayendegaia. com. Comfortable, family-run inn with good facilities and helpful staff. English-speaking owner runs birdwatching tours and to the king penguins.
$$ Central, Phillipi 298, T061-258 0077, opposite **Rosas**. All rooms with bath.
$$ España, Croacia 698, T061-258 0540, www.hotelespana.cl. Comfortable, well equipped, light and spacious rooms, helpful and friendly. Good restaurant with food all day.
$$ Rosas, Phillippi 296, T061-258 0088, hotelrosas@chile.com. Heating, restaurant and bar.
$ pp Hostal Kawi, Pedro Silva 144, T061-258 1638, hostalkawi@yahoo.com. Comfortable, rooms for 3, meals available, offers fly-fishing trips.

Beyond Porvenir *p455*
If you get stuck in the wilds, note that it is almost always possible to camp or bed down in a barn at an estancia.
$$$-$$ Hostería Tunkelen, Arturo Prat Chacón 101, Cerro Sombrero, T061-221 2757, www.hosteriatunkelen.cl. 3 buildings with rooms of different standards: with private bathrooms, shared bathrooms or backpacker dorms. Restaurant. Good for groups.

$$-$ Hostería de la Frontera, San Sebastián, T061-269 6004, frontera@ entelchile.net. Where some buses stop for meals and cakes, cosy, with bath (the annex is much more basic), good food.

Puerto Williams *p458*
$$$$ Lakutaia, 2 km west of town, T061-8429 6630 (Santiago: T02-946 2703), www. lakutaia.cl. A 'base camp' for a range of activities and packages (riding, trekking, birdwatching, sailing, flights), 24 double rooms in simple but attractive style, lovely views from spacious public areas, bikes for hire, 3 golf 'holes' – most southerly in world!
$$$-$$ Hostal Bella Vista B&B, bookings through Victory Adventures, T061-222 7089, www.victory-cruises.com. Rooms and suites sleep 1-4, internet services and a minimarket.
$$ Forjadores de Cabo de Hornos, Uspashun 58, Plaza B O'Higgins, T061-262 1140, www.hostalforjadoresdelcabode hornos.cl. Simple place to stay, meals, agency for tours and transport, welcoming.
$$ Hostal Akainij, Austral 22, T061-262 1173, www.turismoakainij.cl. Comfortable rooms, very helpful, excellent, filling meals, basic English spoken, adventure tours and transfers.
$$ Hostal Coirón, Ricardo Maragaño 168, T061-262 1227, or through **Ushaia Boating** or **Sim Ltda** (see What to do). Double rooms or dorms, shared bath, helpful, good food, relaxed, quite basic, but OK.
$$ Hostal Pusaki, Piloto Pardo 222, T061-262 1116. Double room or dorms,

good meals available, owner Patty is helpful and fun.

$$ Hostal Yagan, Piloto Pardo 260, T061-262 1118, hostalyagan@hotmail.com. Comfortable, some rooms with bath, meals available, run by Daniel Yevenes, who offers tours and transport to Ushuaia.

$$ Refugio El Padrino, Costanera 276, T061-262 1136/8438 0843, ceciliamancillao@yahoo.com.ar. The vivacious Cecilia Mancilla is great fun, good food.

❼ Restaurants

Puerto Porvenir *p455*
There are many lobster fishing camps nearby, where fishermen prepare lobster on the spot.

$$ Club Croata, Señoret entre Phillippi y Muñoz Gamero, next to the bus stop on the waterfront. A lively place with good food.

$$-$ El Chispa, Señoret 202, T061-258 0054. Good restaurant for seafood and other Chilean dishes.

$$-$ La Picá de Pechuga, Bahía Chilote s/n, by ferry dock. Good fresh seafood and fish. Owner Juan Bahamonde runs **Cordillero de Darwin** tours (see below):
$ Panadería El Paine, Sampaio 368. Shop and tea room, very friendly.

Puerto Williams *p458*
There are several grocery stores; prices are very high because of the remoteness. **Simón & Simón** and **Temuco** are opposite each other on Piloto Pardo, junction Condell. The former seems to be centre of reference in town. Most hotels and hostels will offer food.

$$-$ Café Angelus, Centro Comercial Norte 151, T061-262 1080. Also travel agent and transport. Run by Loreto Camino, friendly cheerful atmosphere, small, good simple cooking, coffee (including Irish), beer.
$ Los Dientes de Navarino, Centro Comercial Sur. Popular with locals, limited fare.

ⓞ What to do

Puerto Porvenir *p455*
For adventure tourism and trekking activities contact tour operators in Punta Arenas (see What to do, page 410).
Turismo Cordillera de Darwin, run by Juan 'Pechuga' Bahamonde, T09-9888 6380, or T061-258 0167, gerencia@cordilleradarwin.com or jebr_darwin@hotmail.com (cordilleradarwin on Facebook). Runs land, fishing and boating tours. Oro circuit, 4 hrs without lunch, or 0800-1700 with lunch, including Laguna Santa María. Costs of tours to far south vary according to circumstances. Boat and fishing trips, 6 days allowing a day for unforeseen delays.

Puerto Williams *p458*
Boat trips
Australis Expedition Cruises, Av El Bosque Norte 0440, p 11, Las Condes, Santiago, T02-2442 3115, www.australis.com (see box, page 412), call at Wulaia Bay on the west side of Isla Navarino after visiting Cape Horn; you can disembark to visit the museum and take a short trek.
Victory Adventures, Tte Muñoz 118, Casilla 70, T061-222 7089, www.victory-cruises.com. Captain Ben Garrett and his family run this online travel agency for many tours and expeditions around Tierra del Fuego, Patagonia and the southern oceans to Antarctica.

Trekking
You must register first with *carabineros* on C Piloto Pardo, near Brito. Tell them when you get back, too. Sometimes they will not allow lone trekking.

Tour operators
Akainij, see Where to stay.
Sea, Ice and Mountains, Ricardo Maragaño 168, T061-262 1150, www.simltd.com. Sailing trips, trekking tours and many other adventure activities, including kayaking and wildlife spotting.

Shila, O'Higgins 322 (a hut at entrance to Centro Comercial), T061-7897 2005, www.turismoshila.cl. Luis Tiznado Gonzales is an adventure guide offering trekking and fishing, plus equipment hire (bikes, tents, sleeping bags, stoves, and more). Lots of trekking information, sells photocopied maps.

⊖ Transport

For details of how to get to Tierra del Fuego, see Arriving in Tierra del Fuego, above.

Puerto Porvenir *p455*
Air
To **Punta Arenas** (weather and bookings permitting), with **Aerovías DAP**, Señoret s/n, T061-258 0089, www.aeroviasdap.cl. Heavily booked so make sure you have your return reservation confirmed.

Bus
The only public transport on Chilean Tierra del Fuego is Jorge Bastian's minibus Porvenir–**Cerro Sombrero**, T061-234 5406/8503-3662, jorgebastian@hotmail. com, or axelvig20@hotmail.com, which leaves Sombrero 0700 on Mon, 0830 on Wed and Fri; returns from Porvenir Municipalidad, 2 hrs, US$4.50.

Puerto Williams *p458*
Air
To **Punta Arenas** with **DAP** (details under Punta Arenas). Book well in advance; long waiting lists (be persistent). The flight is beautiful (sit on right from Punta Arenas) with superb views of Tierra del Fuego, the Cordillera Darwin, the Beagle Channel, and the islands stretching south to Cape Horn. Also army flights available (they are cheaper), but the ticket has to be bought through DAP. Airport is in town.

Boat
See Arriving in Tierra del Fuego, above, for details of the **Yaghan** ferry of Broom, www. tabsa.cl. For boats services between Puerto Navarino and Ushuaia, see Arriving on Isla Navarino, above.

⊕ Directory

Puerto Porvenir *p455*
Banks There is a bank with an ATM on the plaza (not all cards accepted, best to take cash from the mainland).

Argentine Tierra del Fuego

The Argentine half of Tierra del Fuego is much easier to visit than the Chilean half and more rewarding. The northern half of the island is windswept steppe, and its only town, Río Grande, once rich in oil, is now very faded. But pause before you head straight for Ushuaia to visit two splendid estancias. Viamonte (www.estanciaviamonte.com) was built by Lucas Bridges to protect the indigenous Ona people and is an evocative place to stay, while Estancia María Behety (see www.maribety.com.ar) is world famous for its brown trout fishing. The landscape turns to hills as you head south, and there's a lovely silent lake, Lago Fagnano, ideal for a picnic.

Ushuaia is the island's centre, beautifully set on the Beagle Channel, with a backdrop of steep mountains. With a picturesque national park on its doorstep, boat trips up the Beagle Channel to the Bridges' other superb estancia, Harberton, and a ski centre at Cerro Castor, there's plenty to keep you here. Huskies will draw your sledge in winter, and in summer you can walk around Bahía Lapataia and contemplate the serenity of the end of the world.

Río Grande → *For listings, see pages 471-480. Colour map 6, C4. Phone code: 02964.*
Population: 67,000.

Río Grande is a sprawling modern coastal town, the centre for a rural sheep-farming community that grew rapidly in the 1970s, with government tax incentives. The new population was stranded when incentives were withdrawn, but revival came with expansion into mobile phone and white goods assembly. This in turn declined when Argentina relaxed import restrictions and currently the town is benefitting from the exploitation of oil and gas in the vicinity. It's a friendly place which you are most likely to visit in order to change buses. There are a couple of good places to stay, however, and a small museum worth seeing.

Arriving in Río Grande
There is an **airport** ① *T02964-420600*, 4 km west of town. A taxi to the centre costs US$3. The **tourist office** ① *Rosales 350, T02964-431324, www.tierradelfuego.org.ar, Mon-Fri 0900-1700,* in the blue-roofed hut on the plaza is small but helpful. There's also a **provincial office**① *Av Belgrano 319, T02964-422887, infuerg1@tierradelfuego.org.ar.*

Places in Río Grande
The city's architecture is a chaotic mix of smart nouveau-riche houses and humble wooden and tin constructions. It was founded by Fagnano's Salesian mission in 1893, and you can visit the original building, **La Candelaria** ① *11 km north, T02964-421642, Mon-Sat 1000-1230, 1500-1900, US$2, afternoon tea US$3, getting there: taxi US$8 with wait,* whose museum has displays of natural history and indigenous artefacts, with strawberry plantations, piglets and an aviary. The **Museo Virginia Choquintel** ① *Alberdi 555, T02964-430647, Mon-Fri 0900-1700, Sat 1500-1900,* is recommended for its history of the Selk'nam, the pioneers, missions and oil. Next door is a handicraft shop called **Kren** ('sun' in Selk'nam), which sells good local products.

Around Río Grande
The **fly fishing** in this area is becoming world-renowned and it's now possible to stay in several comfortable lodges in Río Grande and at Lago Escondido. This area is rich in brown trout, sea run brook trout and steelheads, weighing 2-14 kg; you could expect to catch an average of eight trout a day in season. Contact specialist fly-fishing tour operators. The season runs from 15 October to 14 April, with the best fishing from January to April.

Estancia María Behety, 15 km from town, built by the millionaire José Menéndez, has a vast sheep-shearing shed and is heaven for brown trout fishing. **Estancia Viamonte**, on the coast, 40 km south of town, is a working sheep farm with a fascinating history. Here, Lucas Bridges, son of Tierra del Fuego's first settler, built a home to protect the large tribe of indigenous Onas, who were fast dying out. The estancia is still inhabited by his descendants, who will take you riding and show you life on the farm. There is also a house to rent and superb accommodation, highly recommended.

Río Grande to Ushuaia → *For listings, see pages 471-480.*

From Río Grande, several roads fan out southwest to the heart of the island, though this area is little inhabited. The paved road south, Route 3, continues across wonderfully open land, more forested than the expanses of Patagonian steppe further north and increasingly hilly as you near Ushuaia. After around 160 km, you could turn left along a track to the coast to Cabo San Pablo. There is an estancia here, in a beautiful position with native woodland, although in 2014 indications were that it was not open to the public. There are also other trips to places of interest within reach. Route 3 then climbs up above Lago Fagnano and Tolhuin.

Tolhuin and around → *Phone code: 02964.*

This is a friendly, small settlement close to the shore of Lago Fagnano, a large expanse of water, right at the heart of Tierra del Fuego. The village has a stretch of beach nearby and is a favourite Sunday afternoon destination for day-trippers from Ushuaia. There's a YPF service station just off the main road, but it's worth driving into the village itself for the famous bakery **La Unión** (see Restaurants, page 474), where you can buy delicious bread, *empanadas* and fresh *facturas* (pastries). It's also a good source of information. There's a tiny, friendly **tourist office** ① *Av de los Shelknam 80, T02901-492125, tolhuinturismo@ tierradelfuego.org.ar, daily 0900-1500,* with very helpful staff. Handicrafts, including fine leather goods, are available at El Encuentro half a block from the tourist information office. From the village a road leads down to the tranquil lake shore, where there are a couple of good places to stay.

Further along Route 3, 50 km from Ushuaia, a road to the right swoops down to **Lago Escondido**, a fjord-like lake with steep, deep-green mountains descending into the water. After Lago Escondido, the road crosses the cordillera at Paso Garibaldi. It then

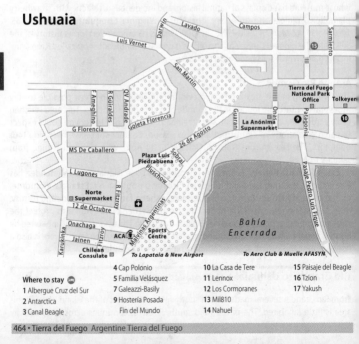

Ushuaia

	Where to stay ○	4 Cap Polonio	10 La Casa de Tere	15 Paisaje del Beagle
	1 Albergue Cruz del Sur	5 Familia Velásquez	11 Lennox	16 Tzion
	2 Antarctica	7 Galeazzi-Basily	12 Los Cormoranes	17 Yakush
	3 Canal Beagle	9 Hostería Posada	13 Mil810	
		Fin del Mundo	14 Nahuel	

descends to the Cerro Castor winter-sports complex and the Tierra Mayor Recreation area (see What to do, page 478). There is a police control just as you enter Ushuaia city limits; passports may be checked.

Ushuaia → *For listings, see pages 471–480. Colour map 6, C4. Phone code: 02901. Population: 57,000.*

The most southerly town in the world, Ushuaia's setting is spectacular. Its brightly coloured houses look like toys against the dramatic backdrop of vast jagged mountains. Opposite are the forbidding peaks of Isla Navarino, and between flows the serene green Beagle Channel. Sailing those waters you can just imagine how it was for Darwin, arriving here in 1832, and for those early settlers, the Bridges, in 1871. Though the town has expanded in recent years, sprawling untidily along the coast, Ushuaia still retains the feel of a pioneer town, isolated and expectant. There are lots of places to stay, which fill up entirely in January, a fine museum and some great fish restaurants. There is spectacular landscape to be explored in all directions, with good treks in the accessible **Parque Nacional Tierra del Fuego** ① *www.tierradelfuego. org.ar*, just to the west of the city, and more adventurous expeditions offered into the wild heart of the island, trekking, climbing or riding. There's splendid cross-country skiing and downhill skiing nearby at **Cerro Castor** ① *www. cerrocastor.com*. And to the east, along a beautiful stretch of coastline is the historic estancia of Harberton, which you can reach by a boat trip along the Beagle Channel. Ushuaia is also the starting point for expeditions to Antarctica; for more information, see www.dna.gov.ar. For more about Ushuaia, see www.e-ushuaia.com.

Restaurants 🍴			
37 Pizzas & Pastas	6 Chicho's	12 Laguna Negra	18 Sandwichería Kami
Bodegón Fueguino	8 El Bambú	13 Martinica	7 Tante Sara
Café Bar Banana	9 El Turco	14 Moustacchio	19 Tía Elvira
Café Tante Sara	10 Gadget Café	16 Parrilla La Rueda	20 Volver
	11 Kaupé	17 Ramos Generales	

Arriving in Ushuaia

Getting there The airport, **Aeropuerto Internacional Malvinas Argentinas** ① *T02901-461232 for information*, is 4 km from town on a peninsula in the Beagle Channel. A taxi to or from the airport costs US$5-7 (there is no bus). There are daily flights from Buenos Aires and Río Gallegos, and frequent flights from El Calafate and Punta Arenas, as well as weekly flights from other Patagonian towns. Schedules tend to change from season to season. Buses and minibuses from Río Grande arrive at their respective offices around town. ▶▶ *See Transport, page 479.*

Getting around It's easy to walk around the town in a morning, since all its sights are close together. You'll find banks, restaurants, hotels and shops along San Martín, which runs parallel to the shore, a block north of the coast road, Avenida Maipú. Ushuaia is very well organized for tourism, and there are good local buses to the national park and other sights, as well as many boat trips. Urban buses run from west to east across town; most stop along Maipú, US$0.50. The tourist office provides a list of minibus companies that run daily to nearby attractions; most of these use the bus stop at the junction of Maipú and Fadul (see map). Boat trips leave from the Muelle Turístico (tourist pier) by a small plaza, 25 de Mayo on the seafront.

Best time to visit Ushuaia is at its most beautiful in autumn (March to May), when the dense forests all around are turned a rich red and yellow, and there are many bright clear days. Summer (December to February) is best for trekking, when maximum temperatures are around 15°C, but try to avoid January, when the city is swamped with tourists. Late February is much better. The ski season is mid-June to October, when temperatures are around zero, but the wind drops.

Tourist information The **tourist information office** ① *San Martín 674, corner with Fadul, T02901-424550, www.turismoushuaia.com, Oct-Mar daily 1700-2100, Apr-Sep daily 0900-2000*, is one of the best in Argentina. The helpful staff speak several languages. They have a map and a series of leaflets about all the things to see and do, and can provide bus and boat times. Next door is the **Oficina Antártica** ① *at entrance to the port, T02901-430015, antartida@tierradelfuego.org.ar, Mon-Fri 0900-1700*, which has information on Antarctica and a small library with navigational charts. Other branches of the tourist office can be found at the **Pier (Muelle Turístico)** ① *T02901-437666, Oct-Mar daily, closed Apr-Sep, which has free Wi-Fi and toilets*, and at the **Airport** ① *T02901-423970, open only at flight times*. There is also a **Provincial tourist office** ① *Maipú 505, T02901-423423, info@tierradelfuego.org.ar*, and an office for the **Tierra del Fuego National Park** ① *San Martín 1395, T02901-421315*, which has a basic map of the park.

Background

Founded in 1884 after missionary Thomas Bridges had established his mission in these inhospitable lands, Ushuaia attracted many pioneers in search of gold. Keen to populate its new territory, the government set up a penal colony on nearby Staten Island, which moved to the town in 1902, and the town developed rapidly. Immigration was largely Croatian and Spanish, together with those shipwrecked on the shores, but the town remained isolated until planes arrived in 1935. As the prison closed, a naval base opened and in the 1970s there was a further influx, attracted by job opportunities in assemblage plants of electronic equipment that flourished thanks to reduced taxes. Now the city is capital of Argentina's most southerly province, and though fishing is still a traditional economic activity, Ushuaia has become an important tourist centre, particularly as the departure point for voyages to Antarctica.

Places in Ushuaia

There are several museums worth visiting if bad weather forces you indoors, and the most fascinating is **Museo del Fin del Mundo** ① *along the seafront at Maipú y Rivadavia, T02901-421863, Mon-Fri 1000-1900, Sat, Sun and bank holidays 1400-2000, US$9, guided tours 1100, 1400, 1700, fewer in winter.* Located in the 1912 bank building, it tells the history of the town through a small collection of carefully chosen exhibits on the indigenous groups, missionaries, pioneers and shipwrecks, together with nearly all the birds of Tierra del Fuego (stuffed), and you can get an 'end of the world museum' stamp in your passport. There are helpful and informed staff, and also an extensive reference library. Recommended. Further east, the old prison, Presidio, at the back of the naval base, houses the **Museo Marítimo** ① *Yaganes y Gobernador Paz, www.museomaritimo.com, daily 0900-2000, US$14, ticket valid 24 hrs,* with models and artefacts from seafaring days. The cells of most of the five wings of the huge building also house the **Museo Penitenciario**, which details the history of the prison. Excellent guided visits (1130, 1630, 1730 in Spanish; 1400 in English) also include a tour of the lighthouse (a life-size replica of the original) that inspired Jules Verne's novel, *Around the World in Eighty Days.* Recommended. Much smaller but also interesting is **Museo Yámana** ① *Rivadavia 56, T02901-422874, www.tierradelfuego.org.ar/mundoyamana, daily 0900-2000, US$7.50,* which has interesting scale models showing scenes of everyday life of Yámana people and the geological evolution of the island.

The most recently opened museum is the **Galería Temática** ① *San Martín 152, PB, 1er y 2do pisos, T02901-422245, www.historiafueguina.com, Mon-Sat 1100-2100, Sun 1700-2100, US$10,* where numerous life-sized displays take you through an informative history of Tierra del Fuego with a useful audioguide in different languages. There is also a themed garden at the back, reached through a huge souvenir shop with good knitwear and other goods.

Around Ushuaia → For listings, see pages 471-480.

Whatever you do, unless it's absolutely pouring with rain, take the chairlift (*aerosilla*) up to **Cerro Martial** ① *7 km from town, daily 1000-1730 (last ascent 1615), US$10,* for exhilarating views along the Beagle Channel and to Isla Navarino opposite. To reach the chairlift, follow Magallanes out of town; allow 1½ hours. Several companies run frequent minibus services in summer from the corner of Maipú and Fadul, US$4. Taxis charge US$7.50-9 to the base, from where you can walk all the way back. There are several marked trails, ranging from 600 m to 1 km (a leaflet is given out at the lower platform), including to a viewpoint and to Glaciar Martial itself. There is a splendid tea shop at the Cumbres de Martial *cabañas* at the base, and a basic *refugio* with no electricity up at the *cerro.* Also by the lower platform is the **Canopy** ① *T02901-15-510307, www.canopyushuaia.com.ar, US$35, US$25 for a shorter run, US$28 and US$20 under 12s,* a series of zip-lines and bridges in the trees. All visitors are accompanied by staff; it's safe and good fun. The café at the entrance, Refugio de Montaña, serves hot chocolate, coffee, cakes, pizzas and has a warm stove.

Parque Nacional Tierra del Fuego (see below), just outside Ushuaia, is easily accessible by bus and offers superb walks for all levels of fitness. Another way to get to the park

Estancia Harberton

In a land of extremes and superlatives, Harberton stands out as special. The oldest estancia in Tierra del Fuego, it was built in 1886 on a narrow peninsula overlooking the Beagle Channel. Its founder, the missionary Thomas Bridges (see box, page 471, for information on his life), was granted land by President Roca for his work amongst the indigenous people and for his help in rescuing victims of numerous shipwrecks in the channels. Harberton is named after the Devonshire village where his wife Mary was born, and the farmhouse was prefabricated by her carpenter father and assembled on a spot chosen by the Yámana people as the most sheltered. The English connection is evident in the neat lawns, shrubs and trees between the jetty and the farmhouse. Behind the buildings is a large vegetable garden, a real rarity on the island, and there's noticeably more wildlife here than in the Tierra del Fuego National Park, probably owing to its remoteness.

Still operating as a working farm, mainly with cattle and sheep, Harberton is run by Thomas Goodall, great-grandson of the founder, whose wife Natalie has created an impressive museum of the area's rich marine life with a thriving research centre. Visitors receive a guided tour of the museum, or of farm buildings and grounds with reconstructions of the Yámana dwellings. Tea or lunch (if you reserve ahead) are served in the tea room overlooking the bay, and you may well be tempted to rent one of the two simple cottages on the shore. There are wonderful walks along the coast, and nowhere in Argentina has quite the feeling of peace you'll find here. For more information, see www.estanciaharberton. com (in Spanish and English).

is on the **Tren del Fin del Mundo** ① *T02901-431600, www.trendelfindelmundo.com.ar, 4-5 departures daily, US$36.50 tourist, US$60 1st class return, US$82 premium and US$126 special (cheaper in winter), plus US$17.20 park entrance*. This is the world's southernmost steam train, running new locomotives and carriages on track first laid by prisoners to carry wood to Ushuaia. It's a totally touristy experience with commentary in English and Spanish. Sit on the left side on the outbound journey to get the views. See Transport, below, for buses to the train station.

The **Estancia Harberton** ① *T02901-422742, www.estanciaharberton.com, 15 Oct-15 Apr daily 1000-1900, except 25 Dec, 1 Jan and Easter, US$7.50 (see box, above)*, 85 km from Ushuaia, is the oldest estancia on the island and is still run by descendants of the British missionary Thomas Bridges, whose family protected the indigenous peoples here. It's a beautiful place, with the attractive wood-framed house that Thomas built sitting in quiet contemplation on a tranquil bay. You'll get an excellent guided walk (bilingual guides) around the estancia, through protected forest, and delicious teas or lunches are served in the Manacatush tea room overlooking the water. Highly recommended. The impressive **Museo Akatushún** ① *phone as above, www.acatushun.org, 15 Oct to 15 Apr daily 1000-1900, except 25 Dec, 1 Jan and Easter, US$2.25*, has skeletons of South American sea mammals, the result of 25 years' scientific investigation in Tierra del Fuego, with excellent tours in English. You can camp for free with permission from the owners, or stay in cottages. Access is along a good unpaved road (Route 33, ex 'J') that branches off Route 3, 40 km east of Ushuaia and runs 25 km through forest and then through the open country around Harberton with marvellous views; it takes about two hours, and there's no petrol outside Ushuaia and Tolhuin. See What to do and Transport, below, for trips to Harberton with Pira-Tur and bus services (irregular). For boat trips to Harberton, see below.

Excursions can be made to Lagos Fagnano and Escondido: agencies run seven-hour tours for US$70 per person without lunch; or check the list of cheaper but rather unreliable minibuses that go there, which is available at the tourist office. Tour agencies offer many good packages, which include trekking, canoeing, birdwatching and horse riding in landscape accessible only by 4WDs. See the tourist office's list of excursions, indicating which companies go where.

Boat trips
All these trips are highly recommended, but note that the Beagle Channel can be very rough. Food and drink on all boats is pricey. Excursions can be booked through most agencies, or at the Muelle Turístico where boat companies have their ticket offices; most boats leave from the Muelle Turístico, with a few excursions leaving from Muelle AFASYN (next to the old airport). All passengers must pay US$1.25 port tax; this is not included in tickets.

Most popular excursions visit the small islands southeast of Ushuaia in 2½ to three hours, all year round, passing next to the sea lion colony at Isla de los Lobos, Isla de los Pájaros and Les Eclaireurs lighthouse. Alternatively, they add an hour or so for a landing on Bridges Island. Prices vary depending on whether trips are made on big catamarans or on more exclusive sailing boats. A few pricier services include lunch onboard; otherwise a light snack or a coffee is served. Summer options add more to the itinerary, with some trips going further east past the Isla Martillo penguin colony and on to Estancia Harberton. Note that Harberton is included only on a few trips, and you should check that your tour actually visits the estancia and not just the bay, as some do. A few excursions also go west to the national park in about 5½ hours. See What to do, page 476, for companies and prices.

Parque Nacional Tierra del Fuego → *For listings, see pages 471-480.*

Covering 63,000 ha of mountains, lakes, rivers and deep valleys, this small but beautiful park stretches west to the Chilean border and north to **Lago Fagnano**, though large areas have been closed to tourists to protect the environment. All walks are best attempted in the early morning or afternoon to avoid the tour buses. You'll see lots of geese, the beautiful torrent duck, Magellanic woodpeckers and austral parakeets.

Arriving in Parque Nacional Tierra del Fuego
Access and information The park entrance is 12 km west of Ushuaia, on the main road west signposted from the town centre, where you'll be given a basic map with marked walks. Entry is US$17.20. The **park administration** ① *San Martín 1395, T02901-421315, tierradelfuego@apn.gov.ar, Mon-Fri 0900-1600*, is in Ushuaia. Ask at the tourist office for bus details (see also Transport, below) and a map of the park, with walks. There are no legal crossing points from the park to Chile. Wear warm, waterproof clothing: in winter the temperature drops to as low as -12°C, and although it can reach 25°C in summer, evenings can be chilly. There's a helpful *guardaparque* (ranger) at Lago Acigami (formerly known as Roca) and good camping here too in a picturesque spot, with a *confitería*.

For a really rich experience, go with guides who know the territory well and can tell you about the wildlife. Inexpensive trips for all levels are available with the highly recommended **Compañía de Guías de Patagonia** ① *www.companiadeguias.com.ar.*

Walks

The leaflets provided at the entrance show various walks, but these are recommended:

Senda Costera ⓘ *8 km, 3 hrs each way* This lovely easy walk along the shore gives you the essence of the park, its rocky coastline, edged with a rich forest of beech trees and glorious views of the low islands with a backdrop of steep mountains. Start at Bahía Ensenada (where boat trips can be taken around the bay, and where the bus can drop you off). Walk along a well-marked path along the shoreline, and then rejoin the road briefly to cross Río Lapataia (ignoring signs to Lago Acigami to your right). After crossing the broad green river and a second stretch of water (where there's a small camping spot and the *gendarmería*), it's a pleasant stroll inland to the beautifully tranquil **Bahía Lapataia**, an idyllic spot, with views across the sound.

Senda Hito XXIV ⓘ *Along Lago Acigami (Roca), 3.5 km, 90 mins one way.* Another easy walk beside this peaceful lake, with lovely pebble beaches, and through dense forest at times, with lots of birdlife. This is especially recommended in the evening, when most visitors have left. Get off the bus at the junction for Lago Acigami, turn right along the road to the car park (passing the *guardaparque's* house) and follow the lake side.

Cerro Guanaco ⓘ *4 km, 4 hrs one way.* A challenging hike up through the very steep forest to a mirador at the top of a hill (970 m) with splendid views over Lago Acigami, the Beagle Channel and far-off mountains. The ground is slippery after rain: take care and don't rush. Allow plenty of time to return while it's light, especially in winter. The path branches off Senda Hito XXIV (see above) after crossing Arroyo Guanaco.

Parque Nacional Tierra del Fuego

Uttermost Part of the Earth

If you read one book about Patagonia, make it *Uttermost Part of the Earth*. The story of the first successful missionary to Tierra del Fuego, Thomas Bridges, and his son Lucas, is one of the most stirring in the whole history of pioneers in Argentina. An orphan from Bristol, Thomas Bridges was so called because he was found as a child under a bridge with a letter T on his clothing. Adopted by Rev Despard, he was taken as a young man to start a Christian mission in wild, uncharted Tierra del Fuego where no white man had survived. He brought his young wife and daughter after Despard had left following the massacre of the last lot of Christians by the indigenous inhabitants. Until his death in 1898, Bridges lived near the shores of the Beagle Channel, first creating the new settlement of Ushuaia and then at Harberton. He devoted his life to his work with the Yámanas (Yaghanes)

and soon gave up converting them, in favour of compiling a dictionary of their language, and – ultimately – protecting them from persecution. His son Lucas (1874-1949), one of six children, spent his early life among the Yámanas and Onas, living and hunting as one of them, learning their languages, and even, almost fatally, becoming involved in their blood feuds and magic rituals. Lucas became both defender and protector of the indigenous people whose culture he loved and was fascinated by, creating a haven for them at Harberton and Estancia Viamonte when most sheep farmers were more interested in having them shot. Lucas's memoirs, *Uttermost Part of the Earth* (1947), trace the tragic fate of the native population with whom he grew up. A compelling account of 20th-century man colliding with an ancient culture (out of print, but easily obtained from www.abebooks.co.uk).

◉ Argentine Tierra del Fuego listings

For hotel and restaurant price codes and other relevant information, see pages 14-21.

◉ Where to stay

Río Grande *p463*

Book ahead, as there are few decent choices. Several estancias offer full board and some, mainly on the northern rivers, have expensive fishing lodges; others offer horse riding.

$$$ Posada de los Sauces, Elcano 839, T02964-430868, www.laposadadelos sauces.com.ar. Best by far, with breakfast, beautifully decorated, comfortable, good restaurant (trout recommended), cosy bar, very helpful staff.

$$$ Villa, Av San Martín 281, T02964-424998, hotelvilla@live.com. Central,

modern, restaurant/*confitería*, parking, discount given for cash.

Estancias

$$$$ Estancia María Behety, 15 km from Río Grande, reservations at **The Fly Shop**, www.maribety.com.ar. Established in 1897 on a 40-km stretch of the river that has become legendary for brown trout fishing, this estancia has accommodation for 18 anglers, and good food. It is one of the country's priciest fishing lodges, deservedly so. Guides and equipment included.

$$$$ pp Estancia Viamonte, 40 km southeast on the coast, T02964-430861, www.estanciaviamonte.com. For an authentic experience of Tierra del Fuego, built in 1902 by pioneer Lucas Bridges, writer of *Uttermost Part of the Earth*, to protect the Selk'nam/Ona people, this working estancia has simple and beautifully furnished rooms in a spacious cottage. Price is for full board and all activities: riding and trekking; cheaper for dinner, bed and breakfast only. Delicious meals. Book a week ahead.

Camping
Club Naútico loshlelk-Oten, Montilla 1047, T02964-420536, www.nautico-rg.blogspot. com. Situated 2 km from town on the river. Clean, cooking facilities, heated building available in cold weather. YPF petrol station has hot showers.

Tolhuin and around p464
$$$ Cabañas Khami, on Lago Fagnano, 8 km from Tolhuin, T02964-15-611243, www. cabaniaskhami.com.ar. Well-equipped, rustic cabins, good value with linen. Price given for 6 people, 3-night weekend rates available.
$$ Terrazas del Lago, R3, Km 2938, T02964-432300, www.lasterrazasdellago. com.ar. A little way from the shore, smart wooden *cabañas*, well decorated, and also a *confitería* and *parrilla*.
$ pp **Refugio Solar del Bosque**, Lago Escondido, R3, Km 3020, 19 km from Ushuaia, T02901-444743. Basic hostel for walkers, with shared bathrooms, dorms for 4. Breakfast.

Camping
Camping Hain del Lago, T02964-1560 3606, robertoberbel@hotmail.com. Lovely views, fireplaces, hot showers, and a *quincho* for when it rains.
Camping La Correntina, T02964-492 137, 17 km from Tolhuin. In woodland, with bathrooms, and horses for hire.

Ushuaia p465, map p464
The tourist office has a comprehensive list of all officially registered accommodation and will help with rooms in private homes, campsites, etc. An excellent choice is to stay with Ushuaia families on a B&B basis. The

range of lodging is growing at all budget levels, from the very chic, to *cabañas*, to basic B&Bs in the centre and the suburbs. There are too many to list here. You must book in advance in high season.
$$$$ Canal Beagle, Maipú y 25 de Mayo, T02901-432303, www.hotelcanalbeagle. com.ar. ACA hotel (discounts for members), **$$$** Apr-Oct, comfortable and well-attended, with a small pool, gym, spa, business centre, some rooms with channel views (others overlook the container dock), good restaurant.
$$$$ Cap Polonio, San Martín 746, T02901-422140, www.hotelcappolonio.com. ar. Smart, central, modern, comfortable, popular restaurant/café **Marcopolo**.
$$$$ Lennox, San Martín 776, T02901-436430, www.lennoxhotels.com. Boutique hotel on the main street, with breakfast, services include hydromassage, minibar, restaurant and *confitería* on 4th floor. Laundry service.
$$$$ Mil810, 25 de Mayo 245, T02901-437714, www.hotel1810.com. City hotel with 30 standard rooms, one with disabled access, no restaurant but breakfast and *confitería*, all rooms with minibar, safe, quite small but cosy, calm colours, good views, business centre and multiple use room where you can hang out while waiting for flight.
$$$ Galeazzi-Basily, G Gob Valdez 323, T02901-423213, www.avesdelsur.com.ar. Among the best, beautiful family home, incredible welcome, in pleasant area 5 blocks from centre, 4 rooms with shared bath. Also excellent *cabañas* (**$$$**) in the garden. Highly recommended.
$$$ Hostería Posada Fin del Mundo, Rivadavia 610, T02901-437345, www. posadafindelmundo.com.ar. Family atmosphere, comfortable rooms, good value, has character.
$$$ Paisaje del Beagle, Gob Paz 1347, T421214, www.paisajedelbeagle.com.ar. Family-run, quiet, with a cosy dining area for good breakfast, laundry service. Recommended.

$$ pp La Casa de Tere, Rivadavia 620,
T02901-422312, www.lacasadetere.com.ar.
Shared or private bath, use of kitchen
facilities, freshly baked bread, open fire,
singles, doubles and triples, hot water,
helpful owner.

$$ Nahuel, 25 de Mayo 440, T02901-
423068, www.bybnahuel.com.ar.
Charming Sra Navarrete has a
comfortable B&B with channel
views from the upper rooms and the
terrace, good value, but noisy street.

$$$ Tzion, Gob Valdez 468, T02901-
432290, tzion_byb@hotmail.com. B&B
with 3 rooms, 1 with bath, high above
town, 10 mins' walk from centre, nice family
atmosphere, cheaper low season, laundry
service, English and French spoken, great
views. Highly recommended.

$$-$ Familia Velásquez, Juana Fadul 361,
T02901-421719, losnokis_figueroa@hotmail.
com. Cosy, welcoming house of a pioneer,
with basic rooms, breakfast, cooking and
laundry facilities, good.

$ pp Albergue Cruz del Sur, Deloqui 242,
T02901-434099, xdelsur@yahoo.com. Cosy,
free tea, coffee and *mate*, book in advance.

$ pp Antárctica, Antártida Argentina 270,
T02901-435774, www.antarctica hostel.
com. Central, welcoming, spacious chill-out
room, excellent 24-hr bar, dorms for 6 and
large doubles, breakfast included, game
night Thu with good prizes. Recommended.

$ pp Los Cormoranes, Kamshén 788 y
Alem, T02901-423459, www.loscormoranes.
com. Large hostel, with good views,
cosy rooms with lockers, OK bathrooms.
Doubles (**$$**) available. They can book
tours. HI member discount.

$ pp Yakush, Piedrabuena 118 y San
Martín, T02901-435807, www.hostelyakush.
com.ar. Very well run, central with spacious
dorms, also doubles (**$$**, cheaper without
bath), book exchange and library, dining
room, steep garden with views. In-house
tour operator organizes excursions.
Recommended.

Camping

La Pista del Andino, Leandro N Alem
2873, T02901-435890. Set in the Club
Andino ski premises in a woodland area,
it has wonderful views over the channel.
Electricity, hot showers, tea room and
grocery store, very helpful. Recommended.

Around Ushuaia *p467*

$$$$ Cabañas del Beagle, Las Aljabas
375, T02901-432785, www.cabanasdel
beagle.com. 3 rustic-style cabins 1.3 km
above the city, fully equipped with kitchen,
hydromassage, fireplace, heating, phone,
self-service breakfast, very comfortable,
personal attention.

$$$$ Cumbres del Martial, Luis F Martial
3560, 7 km from town, T02901-424779,
www.cumbresdelmartial.com.ar. At the foot
of the *aerosilla* to Glaciar Martial, 4 *cabañas*
and 6 rooms, beautifully set in the woods,
charming, very comfortable, cabins have
whirlpool baths. Small spa (massage extra)
with saunas and gym. The tearoom, with
disabled access, is open all year, restaurant
with traditional fondues.

$$$$ Finisterris Lodge Relax, Monte
Susana, Ladera Este, 7 km from city, T02901-
15-612121, www.finisterrislodge.com.
In 17 ha of forest, 5-star luxury in individual
cabins, with top-of-the-range fittings,
hydromassage and private spa (massage
arranged, extra), rustic style but spacious,
'home-from-home' atmosphere, 24-hr
attention from owner, given mobile
phone on arrival. Meals can be ordered
in, or private chef and sommelier can be
booked for you.

$$$$ Las Hayas, Luis Martial 1650 (road
to Glaciar Martial), T02901-430710, www.
lashayashotel.com. 4 standards of room,
all very good with TV, safe, 3 types of view,
channel, mountains or forest. 2 restaurants:
Martial for lunch and dinner, **Drake** for
breakfast. Everything is included in room
price except massages and hairdresser.
A fine hotel. Just beyond and run by the
same family company is:

$$$$ Los Acebos, Luis F Martial 1911, T02901-442200, www.losacebos.com.ar. All rooms with channel view, safe, games room, **Rêve d'Orange** restaurant independent of hotel. Golf days organized. Very comfy, as expected, but less characterful than **Las Hayas**.

$$$$ Los Cauquenes, at Bahía Cauquen, De La Ermita 3462, T02901-441300, www. loscauquenes.com. High quality 5-star hotel overlooking Beagle Channel, price varies according to size and view, spa, very tastefully decorated, prize-winning restaurant, regional food on dinner menu, wine bar with over 100 Argentine wines.

$$$$ Los Yámanas, Costa de los Yámanas 2850, western suburbs, T02901-446809, www.hotelyamanas.com.ar. In the same group as Canoero tour operator, all rooms with Channel view, spacious, well-decorated, hydromassage, fitness centre, spa and conference centre outside in wooded grounds, shuttle to town. Very pleasant.

$$$$ Tierra de Leyendas, Tierra de Vientos 2448, T02901-446565, www. tierradeleyendas.com.ar. In the western suburbs. 5 very comfortable rooms with views of the Beagle Channel, or the mountains at the back, 1 room with jacuzzi, all others with shower, excellent restaurant serving regional specialties, open only for guests for breakfast and dinner. No cable TV, but DVDs, living room with games, library, deck overlooking Río Pipo's outflow. Only for non-smokers. Recommended and award-winning.

$$$ pp Estancia Harberton, T02901-422742, www.estanciaharberton.com. Mid-Oct to mid-Apr. 2 restored buildings on the estancia (see above), very simple rooms, wonderful views, heating. Price includes walking tour and entry to museum; 2 rooms with bath, 1 room with 2 beds, shared bath, 1 room with bunks, shared bath. Kitchenette for tea and coffee. Lunch and dinner extra. No credit cards.

Parque Nacional Tierra del Fuego *p469*, *map p470*
Camping
Camping Lago Roca, T02901-433313, 21 km from Ushuaia, by forested shore of Lago Acigami (Roca), a beautiful site with good facilities, reached by bus Jan-Feb. It has a backpackers' *refugio*, toilets, showers, restaurant and *confitería*, expensive small shop; camping equipment for hire with deposit.

There are also campsites with facilities at **Río Pipo**, 16 km from Ushuaia, and at **Laguna Verde**, 20 km, near Lapataia, and at **Bahía Ensenada**, with no facilities.

❼ Restaurants

Río Grande *p463*
$$ El Rincón de Julio, next to **Posada de los Sauces**, Elcano 800 block. For excellent *parrilla*.
$$ La Nueva Colonial, Av Belgrano 489. Delicious pasta, warm family atmosphere.

Cafés
El Roca (sic), Espora 643, ½ block from Plaza. *Confitería* and bar in historic premises (the original cinema), good and popular.
Tío Willy, Alberdi 279. Serves *cerveza artesanal* (micro brewery).

Tolhuin and around *p464*
La Posada de los Ramírez, Av de los Shelknam 411. A cosy restaurant and *rotisería*, open weekends only, lunch and dinner.
La Unión bakery, Jeujepen 450, www. panaderialaunion.com. Daily 24 hrs, except Mon 2400-Tue 0600. Deservedly famous.

Ushuaia *p465*, *map p464*
Lots of restaurants along San Martín and Maipú. Most are open 1200-1500 and again from 1900 at the earliest. Several cafés are open all the time. Ask around for currently available seafood, especially *centolla* (king

crab) and *cholga* (giant mussels). Much cheaper if you prepare your own meal. But note, *centolla* may not be fished Nov-Dec. Beer drinkers should try the handcrafted brews of the **Cape Horn** brewery: Pilsen, Pale Ale and Stout.

$$$ Bodegón Fueguino, San Martín 859. Tue-Sun 1230-1500, 2000-2400. Snacks, home-made pastas and good roast lamb with varied sauces in a renovated 1896 *casa de pioneros*.

$$$ Tía Elvira, Maipú 349. Mon-Sat 1200-1500, 1900-2300. Excellent seafood.

$$$ Volver, Maipú 37. Delicious seafood and fish in atmospheric 1896 house, with ancient newspaper all over the walls. Recommended.

$$$-$$ Moustacchio, San Martín 298. Long established, good for seafood and meat, all-you-can-eat brunch US$13.

$$$-$$ Parrilla La Rueda, San Martín y Rivadavia. Good *tenedor libre* (US$24 with dessert) for beef, lamb and great salads. Recommended for freshness.

$$ 137 Pizzas and Pastas, San Martín 137. Tasty filling versions of exactly what the name says, plus excellent *empanadas*, elegant decor.

$$ Chicho's, Rivadavia 72, T02901-423469. Bright, cheerful place just off the main street, friendly staff, kitchen open to view. Fish, meat and chicken dishes, pastas, wide range of *entradas*.

$$ El Turco, San Martín 1410. A very popular place, serving generous *milanesas*, pastas, pizzas, seafood and meat. Very tasty *empanadas*.

$$-$ Martinica, San Martín entre Antártida Argentina y Yaganes. Cheap, small, busy, sit at the bar facing the *parrilla* and point to your favourite beef cut. Takeaway (T02901-432134) and good meals of the day, also pizzas and *empanadas*.

Cafés

El Bambú, Piedrabuena 276. Daily 1100-1700. One of few purely vegetarian places

in town, take-away only, home-made food, delicious and good value.

Café Bar Banana, San Martín 273, T02901-424021. Quite small, always busy, pool table, offers good fast food, such as burgers, small pizzas, puddings, breakfasts and an all-day menu for US$7.50.

Café Tante Sara, San Martín 701, opposite the tourist office. Very good, smart, good coffee, tasty sandwiches, always busy. Also has restaurant and *panadería* at San Martín 175, selling breads, sandwiches, chocolates, *empanadas* and snacks, coffee, lots of choice.

Gadget Café, Av San Martín 1256, www.gadgettugelateria.com.ar. The best ice cream parlour in town, multiple flavours, friendly, recommended.

Laguna Negra, San Martín 513. Mainly a shop selling chocolate and other fine produce, catering to the cruise ship passengers, but has a good little café at the back for hot chocolate and coffee. Also has a bigger branch at Libertador 1250, El Calafate. Sells postcards and stamps, too.

Ramos Generales, Maipú 749, T02901-424317. Daily 0900-2400 in high season. An old warehouse with wooden floors and a collection of historic objects. Sells breads, pastries, wines and drinks, also cold cuts, sandwiches, salads, ice cream, Argentine *mate* and coffee. Not cheap but atmospheric. Recommended.

Sandwichería Kami, San Martín 54. Daily 0800-2100. Friendly, simple sandwich shop, selling rolls, baguettes and *pan de miga*.

🎵 Bars and clubs

Ushuaia *p465, map p464*
Dublin Bar Irlandés, 9 de Julio 168. A favourite with locals and tourists.
Küar, Av Perito Moreno 2232, east of town, T02901-437396. Daily from 1800. Great setting by the sea, restaurant, bar and brewery.
Lennon Pub, Maipú 263. Friendly atmosphere and live music.

⊛ Festivals

Río Grande *p463*
Jan Sheep Shearing Festival. Definitely worth seeing if you're in the area.
Feb Rural Exhibition. Exhibition with handicrafts in 2nd week.
Mar Shepherd's Day. An impressive sheep-dog display during the 1st week.
21-22 Jun Winter solstice. The longest night. Fireworks and ice-skating contests; this is a very inhospitable time of year.

Ushuaia *p465, map p464*
Apr Classical Music Festival,
www.festivaldeushuaia.com.
21-22 Jun Winter solstice. The longest night. Torch-lit procession and fireworks.
Aug Dog Sled Race. Held annually.
Aug Marcha Blanca. A ski trek from Lago Escondido to Tierra Mayor valley.

○ Shopping

Ushuaia *p465, map p464*
Ushuaia's tax-free status doesn't produce as many bargains as you might hope. Lots of souvenir shops on San Martín offer good-quality leather and silver ware. The **Pasaje de Artesanías**, by the Muelle Turístico, sells local arts and crafts.
Atlántico Sur, San Martín 627. The (not especially cheap) duty free shop.
Boutique del Libro, San Martín 1120, T02901-424750, www.boutiquedellibro. com.ar. Mon-Sat 1000-1300 and 1530-2030. An excellent selection of books, including several in English and other languages on Tierra del Fuego. CDs and DVDs upstairs.

◑ What to do

Tolhuin and around *p464*
Sendero del Indio, T02901-1547 6803, http://senderoindio.com.ar. For horse riding.

Ushuaia *p465, map p464*
Boat trips and sea cruises
Sightseeing trips All short boat trips leave from the Muelle Turístico. Take your time to choose the size and style of boat you want. Representatives from the offices are polite and helpful. All have a morning and afternoon sailing and include **Isla de los Lobos, Isla de los Pájaros** and **Les Eclaireurs lighthouse**, with guides and some form of refreshment. Note that weather conditions may affect sailings, prices can change and that port tax is not included. See also **Rumbo Sur** and **Tolkeyen** under Tour operators, below.
Canoero, T02901-433893, www. catamaranescanoero.com.ar. Catamarans for 130 passengers (Ushuaia's biggest fleet), 2½ to 3-hr trips to the 3 main sites and Isla Bridges, US$54. They also have a 4½-hr trip almost daily to the Pingüinera on Isla Martillo near Estancia Harberton (Oct-Mar only), boats stay for 1 hr, but you cannot land on Martillo, US$80 (US$90 including Harberton – entry extra). Also longer tours to Estancia Harberton and Lapataia Bay.
Patagonia Adventure Explorer, T02901-15-465842, www.patagoniaadvent. com.ar. Has a sailing boat (US$60) and motor boats for the standard trip, plus Isla Bridges. Good guides.
Pira-Tour, T02901-435557, www.piratour. com.ar and www.piratour.net. Runs 2-3 buses a day to Harberton, from where a boat goes to the Pingüinera on Isla Martillo: 15 people allowed to land (maximum 45 per day – the only company licensed to do this). US$110 including entrance to Harberton.
Tres Marías, T02901-436416, www.tres mariasweb.com. The only company licensed to visit Isla H, which has archaeological sites, cormorants, other birds and plants. 2 departures 1000 and 1500, 4 hrs. Also has sailing boat for no more than 10 passengers; specialist guide, café on board. Trip costs US$60 on *Tres Marías*, US$80 on sailing boat. Highly recommended.

To Antarctica From Oct to Mar, Ushuaia is the starting point, or the last stop en route, for cruises to Antarctica. These usually sail for 9 to 21 days along the western shores of the Antarctic peninsula and the South Shetland Islands. Other trips include stops at Falkland/Malvinas archipelago and at South Georgia. Go to the **Oficina Antártica** for advice (see page 466). Agencies sell 'last-minute tickets', but the price is entirely dependent on demand. Coordinator for trips is **Turismo Ushuaia**, Gob Paz 865, T02901-436003, www.ushuaiaturismoevt.com.ar, which operates with IAATO members only. See the website for prices for the upcoming season. Port tax is US$15 per passenger and an exit tax of US$10 is also charged.

Freestyle Adventure Travel, Gob Paz 866, T02901-15-609792, www.freestyleadventure travel.com. Organizes 7- to 22-day cruises to Antarctica, particularly good for last-minute deals. Wide variety of itineraries. Cape Horn expeditions also available.

Polar Latitudes, sales@polar-latitudes. com, www.polar-latitudes.com. Antarctic cruises aboard small expedition vessels, some itineraries take in the Falklands/ Malvinas and South Georgia. All-suite accommodation onboard.

To Chile You can ask at **Muelle AFASYN**, near the old airport, T02901-435805, about possible crossings with a club member to Puerto Williams, about 4 hrs; from Puerto Williams a ferry goes once a week to Punta Arenas. There may also be foreign sailing boats going to Cabo de Hornos or Antarctica.

Australis Expedition Cruises, www. australis.com, operates 2 luxury cruise ships between Ushuaia and **Punta Arenas**, with a visit to Cape Horn, highly recommended. Full details are given in the box, page 412. Check-in at **Comapa** (see below).

Fernández Campbell has a 1½-hr crossing to **Puerto Williams**, Fri-Sun 1000, return 1500, US$125 for foreigners, tickets sold at **Zenit Explorer**, Juana Fadul 126, Ushuaia,

T02901-433232, and **Naviera RFC** in Puerto Williams.

Ushuaia Boating, Gob Paz 233, T02901-436193 (or at the Muelle Turístico), www. ushuaiaboating.com.ar. Operates a channel crossing to Puerto Navarino (Isla Navarino) all year round, 30-90 mins depending on weather, and then bus to Puerto Williams, 1 hr, US$120 one way, not including taxes.

Fishing
Trout season is Nov to mid-Apr, licences US$21 per day (an extra fee is charged for some rivers and lakes).
Asociación de Caza y Pesca, Maipú 822, T02901-423168, cazaypescaushuaia@ speedy.com.ar. Mon-Fri 1600-2000. Sells licences and has a list on the door of other places that sell them.

Hiking and climbing
The winter sports resorts along Ruta 3 (see below) are an excellent base for summer trekking and many arrange excursions.
Club Andino, Fadul 50, T02901-422335, Mon-Fri 0930-1230, 1600-2000. Sells maps and trekking guidebooks; free guided walks once a month in summer; also offers classes in yoga, dancing, karate-do and has exercise bikes.
Nunatak, 25 de Mayo 296, T02901-430329, www.antartur.com.ar. Organizes treks, canoeing, mountain biking and 4WD trips to Lagos Escondido and Fagnano. Good winter excursions.

Horse riding
Centro Hípico, Ruta 3, Km 3021, T02901-15-569099, www.horseridingtierradel fuego. com. Rides through woods, on Monte Susana, along coast and through river, 2 hrs, US$40; 4-hr ride with light lunch, US$80; 7-hr ride with *asado*, US$105. Gentle horses, well-cared for, all guides have first-aid training. Very friendly and helpful. All rides include transfer from town and insurance. Hats provided for children; works with disabled children. They can arrange

long-distance rides of several days, eg on Península Mitre.

Winter sports

Ushuaia is becoming popular as a winter resort with 11 centres for skiing, snowboarding and husky sledging. Cerro Castor is the only centre for Alpine skiing, but the other centres along Ruta 3, 18-36 km east of Ushuaia, offer excellent cross-country skiing and alternative activities in summer.

Cerro Castor, Ruta 3, Km 26, T02901-499301, www.cerrocastor.com. 24 km of pistes, a vertical drop of 800 m and powder snow. It's an attractive centre with complete equipment rental, also for snowboarding and snowshoeing.

Kawi Shiken, Las Cotorras, Ruta 3, Km 26, T02901-444152, T02901-15-519497, www.tierradelfuego.org.ar/hugoflores. Specializes in sled dogs, with 100 Alaskan and Siberian huskies, with winter rides on snow and summer rides in a dog cart.

Tierra Mayor, 20 km from town, T02901-437454. The largest and most recommended. Lies in a beautiful wide valley between steep-sided mountains. It offers half and full day excursions on sledges with huskies, as well as cross country skiing and snowshoeing. Equipment hire and restaurant.

Tour operators

Lots of companies offer imaginative adventure tourism expeditions. All agencies charge the same fees for excursions; ask tourist office for a complete list: Tierra del Fuego National Park, 4 hrs, US$50 (entry fee US$14 extra, valid for 48 hrs); Lagos Escondido and Fagnano, 7 hrs, US$70 without lunch. With 3 or 4 people it might be worth hiring a *remise* taxi.

All Patagonia, Juana Fadul 58, T02901-433622, www.allpatagonia.com. Trekking, ice climbing, and tours; trips to Cabo de Hornos and Antarctica.

Canal, Roca 136, T02901-435777, www.canalfun.com. Huge range of activities,

trekking, canoeing, riding, 4WD excursions. Recommended.

Comapa, San Martín 409, T02901-430727, www.comapa.tur.ar. Conventional tours and adventure tourism, bus tickets to Punta Arenas and Puerto Natales, trips to Antarctica, agents for Australis Expedition Cruises. Recommended.

Compañía de Guías de Patagonia, San Martín 628, T02901-437753, www.companiadeguias.ar. The best agency for walking guides, expeditions for all levels, rock and ice climbing (training provided), also diving, sailing, riding, 7-day crossing of Tierra del Fuego on foot and conventional tours. Recommended.

Rumbo Sur, San Martín 350, T02901-421139, www.rumbosur.com.ar. Flights, buses, conventional tours on land and sea, including to Harberton, plus Antarctic expeditions, mid-Nov to mid-Mar, English spoken.

Tolkar, Roca 157, T02901-431412, www.tolkarturismo.com.ar. Flights, bus tickets to Argentina and Punta Arenas/Puerto Natales, conventional and adventure tourism, canoeing and mountain biking to Lago Fagnano.

Tolkeyen, San Martín 1267, T02901-437073, www.tolkeyenpatagonia.com. Bus and flight tickets, catamaran trips (50-300 passengers), including to Harberton (Tue, Thu, Sat-Sun, US$94) and Parque Nacional, large company.

Travel Lab, San Martín 1444, T02901-436555, www.travellab.com.ar. Conventional and unconventional tours, mountain biking, trekking etc, English and French spoken, helpful.

⊙ Transport

Río Grande p463

Book ahead in summer as buses and planes fill up fast. Take passport when buying ticket.

Air

To **Buenos Aires**, daily, 3½ hrs direct. **LADE** flies to **Río Gallegos**.

Bus

To **Punta Arenas**, Chile, via Punta Delgada, 7-9 hrs, with **Pacheco** (Finocchio 1194, T02964-425611, Mon-Sat) and **Tecni Austral** (Moyano 516, T02964-430610), US$42. To **Río Gallegos**, with **Tecni Austral**, Mon-Sat, 8 hrs; with **Marga/Taqsa** (Mackinley 545, T02964-434316), daily 0815, US$55, connection to El Calafate and Comodoro Rivadavia. To **Ushuaia**, 3½-4 hrs, with **Montiel** (25 de Mayo 712, T02964-420997) and **Líder** (Perito Moreno 635, T02964-420003, www.lidertdf.com.ar), US$25; both use small buses and have frequent departures; they stop en route at **Tolhuin**, US$15; also with **Tecni Austral**, about 1600 (bus has come from Punta Arenas) **Marga** and **Pacheco**, US$18-20.

Ushuaia *p465, map p464*
Air

Book ahead in summer; flights fill up fast. In winter flights are often delayed.

To **Buenos Aires** (Aeroparque or Ezeiza), 3½ hrs. To **El Calafate**, 1 hr, and **Río Gallegos**, 1 hr; also to **Río Grande**, 1 hr, several a week (but check with agents). In summer **LAN** flies to **Punta Arenas** twice a week. The **Aeroclub de Ushuaia** flies to **Puerto Williams** and organizes flight tours of Tierra del Fuego from the downtown airport, www.aeroclubushuaia.com.

Boat
See What to do, above.

Bus
Local To **Parque Nacional Tierra del Fuego,** in summer buses and minibuses leave hourly from 0900 from the bus stop on Maipú at the bottom of Fadul, including **Transporte Lautaro** and **Transporte Santa Lucía**, 3 a day each, last return 1900, US$12.50 single, US$19 return. From same bus stop, many *colectivos* go to the **Tren del Fin del Mundo** (0900 and 1400, return 1200, 1700 and 1745), **Lago Escondido**, **Lago Fagnano** (1000 and 1100, return

1400 and 2200) and **Glaciar Martial** (1000 and 1200, return 1400 and 1600). For **Harberton**, check the notice boards at Maipú y Fadul. The only regular bus is run by **Pira-Tur**, see What to do, above.

Long distance Passport needed when booking international bus tickets. Buses always booked up Nov-Mar; buy your ticket to leave as soon as you arrive. To **Río Grande**, 3½-4 hrs, combis run by **Líder** (Gob Paz 921, T02901-436421), and **Montiel** (Gob Paz 605, T02901-421366), US$25, also buses en route to Río Gallegos and Punta Arenas. To **Río Gallegos**, with **Tecni Austral**, 0500, 13 hrs, US$72 (book through Tolkar; see Tour operators), and **Marga/Taqsa** (Gob Godoy 41), daily 0500. To **Punta Arenas**, US$68-81, with **Tecni Austral**, Mon, Wed, Fri, 0500, 11-12 hrs (book through Tolkar); with **Pacheco**, 0700 Mon, Wed, Fri, 12-13 hrs (book through Tolkeyen, see above), with **Bus Sur** (at Comapa) Tue, Thu, Sat, Sun 0800; Bus Sur also goes to **Puerto Natales**, US$70, Tue, Sat 0800.

Car hire
Most companies charge minimum US$60-70 per day, including insurance and 200 km per day, special promotions available. **Localiza**, Sarmiento 81, T02901-437780, www.localizadietrich.com. Cars can be hired in Ushuaia to be driven through Chile and then left in any Localiza office in Argentina, but you must buy a one-off customs document for US$50 to use as many times as you like to cross borders. Must reserve well in advance and pay a drop-off fee. **Budget**, Godoy 49, T02901-437373.

Taxi
Cheaper than *remises*, T02901-422007, T02901-422400. Taxi stand by the Muelle Turístico.
Remises Carlitos y Bahía Hermosa, San Martín y Rosas, T02901-422222.

● Directory

Río Grande *p463*
Banks ATMs at several banks on San Martín by junction with Av 9 de Julio. **Link** ATM at YPF station at river end of Belgrano. **Thaler** *cambio*, Espora 631, Mon-Fri 1000-1500. **Consulates** Chile, Belgrano 369, T02964-430523, Mon-Fri 0830-1330.

Ushuaia *p465, map p464*
Banks Open 1000-1500 in summer. ATMs are plentiful all along San Martín, using credit cards is easiest (but machines can be empty on Sat, Sun and holidays). **Agencia de Cambio Thaler**, San Martín 209, T02901-421911, www.cambio-thaler.com, Mon-Fri 1000-1500 (extended hours in high season). **Consulates** Chile, Jainén 50, T02901-430909, Mon-Fri 0900-1300. **Useful addresses** Dirección Nacional de Migraciones, Fuegia Basket 187, T02901-422334. **Biblioteca Popular Sarmiento**, San Martín 1589, T02901-423103. Mon-Fri 1000-2000, library with a good range of books about the area.

Contents

Chilean Pacific Islands

At a glance

⊕ **Getting around** Walking and
by boat on Juan Fernández; walking
or hiring a car on Easter Island.
⊙ **Time required** 3 days to
a week for each island.
❀ **Weather** Warm and humid
with occasional rain all year round.
⊗ **When not to go** Juan
Fernández can be pretty
wet in winter (Jun-Aug).

Far out in the Pacific are two Chilean island possessions: the Juan Fernández Islands, famed for Alexander Selkirk's enforced stay in the 17th century (the inspiration for Defoe's *Robinson Crusoe*), and the Polynesian island of Rapa Nui, better known as Easter Island, the most isolated inhabited spot on earth. Both possess dramatic views of the Pacific. Juan Fernández is famous for the huge cliffs that rise sheer from the ocean, while Easter Island is home to hundreds of mysterious and imposing *mo'ai*. Although the cost of getting to these islands is prohibitive for many visitors, both can be reached relatively easily by air from Santiago.

Islas Juan Fernández

Situated 667 km west of Valparaíso, this group of small volcanic islands is a national park administered by CONAF and was declared a UN World Biosphere Reserve in 1977. There are three islands: Isla Alejandro Selkirk (4952 ha), the largest; Isla Robinson Crusoe (4794 ha); and Isla Santa Clara (221 ha), the smallest. The islands enjoy a mild climate and the vegetation is rich and varied: the Juan Fernández palm, previously used widely for handicrafts, is now a protected species, but the *sandalo* (sandalwood tree), once the most common tree on the islands, is now extinct owing to its overuse for perfumes. Fauna includes wild goats, hummingbirds and seals. The islands are famous for langosta de Juan Fernández (a pincerless lobster) that is prized on the mainland. Infrequent boats go between Robinson Crusoe and Alejandro Selkirk if the *langosta* catch warrants it, so you can visit either for a few hours or a whole month.

Background

The islands are named after João Fernández, a Portuguese explorer in the service of Spain, who was the first European to visit them (in 1574). For the next 150 years, they were frequented by pirates and *corsairs* resting up before attacking Spanish America. In 1704, Alexander Selkirk, a Scottish sailor, quarrelled with his captain and was put ashore from HMS *Cinque Ports* on what is now Isla Robinson Crusoe, where he stayed alone until 1709, when he was picked up by the *Duke*; his experience inspired *Robinson Crusoe*.

Isla Robinson Crusoe

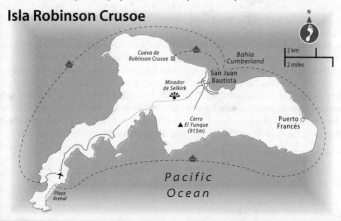

Cueva de Robinson Crusoe
Bahía Cumberland
San Juan Bautista
Mirador de Selkirk
Cerro El Yunque (915m)
Puerto Francés
Playa Arenal
Pacific Ocean
2 km
2 miles
N

From 1750 the Spanish took steps to defend the archipelago, founding San Juan Bautista and building seven fortresses. During the Wars of Independence the islands were used as a penal colony for Chilean independence leaders captured after the Battle of Rancagua. In 1915, two British destroyers, HMS *Kent* and *Glasgow* cornered the German cruiser, *Dresden*, in Bahía Cumberland. The German vessel was scuttled and still lies on the bottom; a monument on shore commemorates the event and, nearby, unexploded shells are embedded in the cliffs. Some of the German crew are buried in the cemetery.

Legends of buried pirate treasure have abounded over the years and several attempts have been made to find it. In recent years a team using a Chilean-built robot with a penetrative sensor claimed to have discovered signs of the treasure, leading to massive media interest, but so far have failed to unearth anything of interest.

Arriving in Islas Juan Fernández → *Phone code: 032. Colour map 3, B2. Population: 500.*
Getting there and around The best time for a visit is between October and March. Air taxis from Santiago land on an airstrip in the west of the island, from where passengers are taken by boat to San Juan Bautista. (The boat transfer should be included in the price of the air ticket.) There are also boats to the islands from Valparaíso. Isla Robinson Crusoe is small enough to explore on foot. You will need a boat on the other islands.

Tourist information The **CONAF office** ① *Vicente González 130, San Juan Bautista, T032-268 0381, parquenjfernandez@yahoo.com, Mon-Fri 0800-1250, 1400-1800,* can give information on flora, fauna and services. Park entry is US$5.50, children US$1.50. The best time to visit is October-March; take insect repellent.

Places in Islas Juan Fernández
The only settlement in the archipelago is **San Juan Bautista**, a fishing village of simple houses. Many facilities close to the shore were destroyed by the February 2010 tsunami, but are slowly recovering. Located on Bahía Cumberland on the north coast of Isla Robinson Crusoe, it has a church, schools, post office, police station and radio station. San Juan Bautista is overlooked by the remains of the **Fuerte Santa Bárbara**, the largest of the Spanish fortresses, while in the village itself is a **Casa de la Cultura** with exhibition rooms. Nearby are the **Cuevas de los Patriotas**, home to the deported Chilean independence leaders. The island's other famous cave, where Alexander Selkirk spent his years of isolation, is 4 km northwest of the village and can be visited by boat.

South of the village is the **Mirador de Selkirk**, the hill where Selkirk lit his signal fires. A plaque was set in the rock at the lookout point by British naval officers from HMS *Topaze* in 1868; nearby is a more recent plaque placed by Selkirk's descendants. The mirador is the only easy pass between the north and south sides of the island. A footpath leads further south to the anvil-shaped **El Yunque**, 915 m, the highest peak on the island, where Hugo Weber, a survivor from the *Dresden*, lived as a hermit for 12 years: some remains of his dwelling can be seen. The only sandy beach on Robinson Crusoe is **Playa Arenal**, in the extreme southwest corner, two hours by boat from San Juan Bautista.

⊚ Islas Juan Fernández listings

For hotel and restaurant price codes and other relevant information, see pages 14-21.

⊜ Where to stay

See www.comunajuanfernandez.cl, www.sernatur.cl and www.turismo robinsoncrusoe.com for other accommodation options.
$$$$ Crusoe Island Lodge, T02-2946 1636, T09-9078 1301, www.crusoeisland lodge.com. An ecolodge which offers many packages and activities, as well as therapies in its spa. It also has a gourmet restaurant.
$$$$ Más a Tierra Ecolodge, Subida el Castillo 128, T09-5379 1915, www. masatierraecolodge.com. Bed-and-breakfast or half-board available, 4 rooms with bath and terrace, price includes welcome drink, internet, use of kayaks, tours arranged.

⊛ Festivals

Feb A yachting regatta visits the islands. It sets out from Algarrobo (see page 102) to Isla Robinson Crusoe and thence to Talcahuano and Valparaíso. At this time, Bahía Cumberland is full of colourful and impressive craft, and prices in restaurants and shops double.

⊘ What to do

The following tour operators offer all-inclusive packages, some including flights:
Endémica Expeditions, Sector del Muelle s/n, T032-275 1227, www.endemica.com.
Inside Nature Expeditions, lactorisfernandeziana@hotmail.com, offers guided day hikes. English spoken.
Refugio Náutico, see Where to stay.

⊜ Transport

Air
Aerolíneas ATA, Av Diego Barros Ortiz 2012B, Aeropuerto Arturo Merino Benítez, Santiago, T02-2611 3670 (on Robinson Crusoe T09-7389 1826), www.aerolineasata.cl, and **LASSA**, Av Larraín 7941, Tobalaba, Santiago, T02-2734 3353, lassa@tie.cl, fly the year round (subject to demand) between **Santiago** and the islands, 2½ hrs (US$975 round trip). Planes leave from **Tobalaba Aerodrome** in La Reina (eastern outskirts of city) and land on an airstrip in the west of the island; passengers are taken by boat to San Juan Bautista (1½ hrs, US$2 one way). For cargo by sea, see **http://navieraiorana.cl**.

⊙ Directory

There are no exchange facilities. Only pesos and US dollars cash are accepted; no credit cards and no traveller's cheques.

Rapa Nui (Easter Island)

Isla de Pascua, or Rapa Nui, lies in the Pacific Ocean just south
of the Tropic of Capricorn and 3790 km west of Chile; its nearest
neighbour is Pitcairn Island. The island is triangular in shape, with
an extinct volcano at each corner. The original inhabitants called
the island *Te Pito o te Henua*, 'the navel of the world'. The unique
features of the island are the many *ahu* (ceremonial altars) on top
of some of which stand 600 (or so) *mo'ai*, huge stone figures up to
10 m in height, representing the deified ancestors of the Rapa Nui
people. The islanders have preserved their indigenous songs and
dances and are extremely hospitable.

Background
By the beginning of the 21st century, Thor Heyerdahl's theories basing the colonization
of Easter Island on South American influence, as expressed in *Aku-Aku, The Art of Easter
Island* (1975), had become less widely accepted and the theory of Polynesian origin
had gained ascendency. According to the latter theory, colonizers came from possibly
the Marquesas Islands or Mangareva, between about AD 400-600 and by AD 1000 the
island's society was established.

Rapa Nui - Easter Island

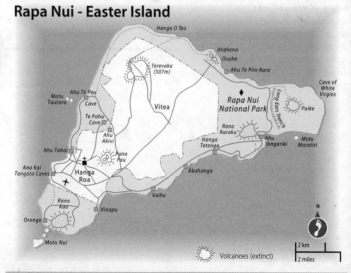

Easter Island geology and the making of the *mo'ai*

In geological terms Easter Island is a youthful 2.5 million years old. It is located above a tectonic 'hot spot', an active upwelling of magma emerging from beneath the crust of the earth and solidifying. Enough molten rock has poured out to form a mountain nearly 3000 m high, the altitude of Easter Island if measured from the sea bed. There are, however, no records of volcanic activity since humans arrived. The three high peaks are all volcanic in origin and are mostly basalt. In the cliffs of Rano Kau, different layers of basalt can be identified, indicating the existence of distinct lava flows. Caves have been formed where the lava has solidified on the outside but continued to flow downhill on the inside. On Terevaka, where the roofs of some of these caves have collapsed, long caverns up to 10 m high can be seen.

The volcanic nature of the island contributed to the carving of the *mo'ai*. Extremely hard basalt from Terevaka was used to make the tools for carving, and sharp-edged implements were fashioned using obsidian, volcanic glass formed by lava cooling very rapidly. The *mo'ai* were carved from tuff, a porous rock much softer than basalt but also volcanic. Tuff can be found at Rano Raruka, a secondary cone on the side of Terevaka.

The very precise stone fitting of some of the ahu and the tall gaunt mo'ai with elongated faces and ears, for which Easter Island is best known, came quite late in the development of island culture. The *mo'ai* were sculpted at the Rano Raraku quarry and transported on wooden rollers over more or less flat paths to their final locations; their red topknots were sculpted at and brought from the inland quarry of Puna Pau; and the rounded pebbles laid out checkerboard fashion at the *ahu* all came from the same beach at Vinapu.

The theory held that with the growth in sophistication of Easter Island society, almost all the island's trees were felled. The wood was used for building fishing vessels and most probably for transporting and supporting statues. Deforestation led to soil erosion, the extinction of up to half the native plants, loss of nesting sites for birds and no means of making fishing boats. Rapa Nui, according to Jared Diamond in *Collapse: How Societies Choose to Fail or Succeed* (2005), was "the clearest example of a society that destroyed itself by overexploiting its own resources". What followed were brutal wars between the clans that erupted by the end of 17th century.

After the islanders had lost their clan territoriality and were concentrated at Hanga Roa, inter-clan rivalry was stimulated by the birdman cult at Orongo. The central feature was an annual ceremony in which the heads of the lineages, or their representatives, raced to the islets of Motu Nui, Motu Iti and Motu Kao to obtain the first egg of the sooty tern (known as the Manatara). The winning chief was named Bird Man, Tangata Manu, for the following year. It appears that the egg represented fertility to the cult, although it is less clear what the status of the Tangata Manu actually was.

The "ecocide" theory and almost everything to do with it was questioned by Carl Lipo and Terry Hunt in *The Statues that Walked* (2011). They claim that Polynesians arrived in about AD 1200 and that the rats that arrived with them caused far greater destruction of the palm forests, by eating the tree roots, than the humans. They also suggest that the statues were "walked", not rolled to their ceremonial sites (much as Heyerdahl demonstrated) and that the population, after rapid growth, was stable until the arrival of Europeans. The environment was damaged, but as other research has proposed, the people learnt how to prevent soil erosion by "sowing" stones on their fields and supplemented their diet with rat meat. Serious decline was precipitated by the arrival of European diseases, not before.

European contact with the island began with the visit of the Dutch admiral, Jacob Roggeven, on Easter Sunday 1722, who was followed by the British navigator James Cook in 1774 and the French sailor Le Perouse in 1786. The population of the island remained stable at around 4000 until the 1850s, when Peruvian slavers, smallpox and emigration to Tahiti (encouraged by plantation owners) reduced the numbers. Between 1859 and 1862, over 1000 islanders were transported as slaves to work in the Peruvian guano trade. The island was annexed by Chile in 1888 and from 1895 to 1952 most of it was leased to a private company that bred sheep on its grasslands: a wall was built around the Hanga Roa area, which islanders were forbidden to cross.

Now, about half the island is used for grazing and agriculture, while the other half constitutes a national park. Tourism has grown rapidly since the air service began in 1967 and the island is now also regularly visited by cruise ships. Many of the *mo'ai* have now been restored to their original positions. According to the 2012 census, the islands has about 5800 residents, of whom about 60% are descendants of the aboriginal Rapa Nui.

Modern Easter Island Although part of Chile, Easter Island is run (at least in theory) by an independent Council of Chiefs and elected local officials. Chile provides good education and health care for all and the local diet is much healthier than on many Pacific islands. The range of services includes a modern mobile phone network, reliable internet, a television station, stadium, gymnasiums, a modern bank and excellent running water and electricity. Foreigners and Chileans from the mainland cannot own land on Easter Island, even if they live and work there, or are married to a local. Nevertheless, islanders own very little land outside Hanga Roa; the national park covers more than a third of the island. Easter Islanders do not pay taxes and they refuse entry to insurance companies, junk food outlets, public buses and other concepts they find hostile to their traditional culture. In 2007, a constitutional reform gave Easter Island and Juan Fernández the status of special territories. Administratively, Easter Island belongs to the Valparaíso Region (V) and is the only commune of the Provincia de Isla de Pascua. The flag of Easter Island is white charged with a red reimiro, a wooden pectoral ornament once worn by the women of the island. It was adopted on 9 May 2006.

Climate and landscape Unlike most Polynesian islands, Easter Island has no coral reef as winter temperatures are too cold for coral to survive. As a result, the coastline has been eroded in parts to form steep cliffs, around Poike, Rano Kao and on the northern side of Terevaka. There is no high central plateau and consequently little gully erosion, which would normally lead to the development of streams and rivers. Moreover, much of the island's rainfall drains away underground into the huge caverns formed by the collapse of basalt caves. As a result, although annual rainfall is usually above 1000 mm, there is always a severe shortage of water and in many years several months of drought. Humidity is usually high and the rainy season is March to October, with the wettest weather in May. Average monthly temperatures range from 15-17°C in August, up to 24°C in February, the hottest month.

Arriving on Rapa Nui → *Phone code: 032. Population 3800.*

Getting there and around The high tourist season is September to April, although there are tourists year-round. The only ways to reach the island are by **LAN** plane from Santiago, or on a cruise ship. Easter Island's airport is just south of Hanga Roa. The airport runway has been improved to provide emergency landing for US space shuttles! The terminal is tiny but it has several reasonably priced souvenir shops and a café. There's no internet, but the mobile phone signal is good. For those in transit, the garden at the departure lounge has one lonely mo'ai. A taxi to the town centre costs US$4.

There are numerous taxis available on the island and an unreliable summer bus service. Horses, bicycles, motorbikes and cars can all be hired. If you're driving yourself, visit the sites from south to north since travel agencies tend to start their tours in the north. A basic loop around the island is 50 to 80 km, depending whether you go off road or not.

Tourist information For general information, contact **Sernatur** ① *C Policarpo Toro s/n, T032-210 0255, ipascua@sernatur.cl, Mon-Fri 0900-1800, Sat 0900-1400.* Over a third of the island constitutes a national park (entry US$60, children US$10 – Chileans pay less), payable at the airport when flights arrive, or at the **CONAF office** ① *Mataveri Otai s/n, T032-210 0236, hotu.pate@conaf.cl, winter daily 0900-1800, summer daily 0900-1900.* CONAF can give good advice on special interests (biology, archaeology, handicrafts, etc). Useful websites include **http://islandheritage.org** (Easter Island Foundation, in English) and **www.rapanui.co.cl**, the Easter Island newspaper. The English-language book, *A Companion to Easter Island*, by James Grant Peterkin, the **British Consul** ① *c/o Easter Island Spirit, Tu'u Koihu s/n, T032-210 0024, james@easterislandspirit.com,* is on sale on the island and in Santiago airport.

Hanga Roa and around

There is one village on the island, Hanga Roa, where most of the population live. In front of the football field is **Ahu Tautira**. Next to it is a swimming area marked out with concrete walls and a breakwater (cold water). There is a cultural centre next to the football field, with an exhibition hall and souvenir stall. To the east is an interesting modern church with locally stylized religious art and carvings, mixing Catholic themes with elements of the cult of the Bird Man. Services are held on Sundays with hymns sung in Rapa Nui.

The **Museo Antropológico Sebastián Englert** ① *2 km north of town, very near Ahu Tahai, T032-255 1020, www.museorapanui.cl, Tue-Fri 0930-1730, Sat and Sun 0930-1230, closed for some public hols, US$2,* has good descriptions of island life, although most of the objects are reproductions since the originals were removed from the island. Free guided visits are available with advance notice. In the same complex is the excellent **William Molloy Library** ① *Tue-Fri 0930-1230,* where only locals are allowed to borrow books.

A 15-minute walk from town is **Ahu Tahai** (a *mo'ai* with eyes and topknot, plus a cave house). It's a great place for watching the sunset and is the start of a six-hour walk along the west coast. Two caves can be reached north from here: the one inland appears to be a ceremonial centre, while the other (nearer the sea) has two 'windows' (take a strong flashlight and be careful). Further north is **Ahu Te Peu**, with a broken *mo'ai* and ruined houses. Beyond here you can join the path to Hanga o Teo (see below), or turn right, inland to **Te Pahu** cave and the seven *mo'ai* at **Akivi**. Either return to Hanga Roa or continue to the **Puna Pau** crater (two hours), where the *mo'ai*'s distinctive red topknots were carved.

South of Hanga Roa is **Rano Kau**, the extinct volcano where the curious Orongo ruins can be seen. The road south from Hanga Roa passes the two caves of **Ana Kai Tangata**,

Tapati, or Semana Rapa Nui

Held each year in late January/early February, Tapati is organized as a huge competition between groups, many of them families, each of which elects a beauty queen. It begins slowly butbuild momentum as the fortnight goes on. Families score points by participating in a wide variety of competitions, including gastronomy, necklace-making, sculpting mo'ai, body painting, dancing, singing, horse racing, swimming and a modified decathlon. In the most spectacular event, men, dressed only in the traditional thong and with their bodies painted, compete to slide down the side of a volcano, sitting on a kind of sledge made from the trunks of two banana plants.

one of which has paintings, and continues southeast. If, however, you're on foot, take the path just past the CONAF sign for a much shorter route to the impressive Rano Kau crater. A lake with many reed islands lies 200 m below the rim of the crater. Locals occasionally scramble down to collect medicinal herbs. On the seaward side of the volcano is **Orongo** ① *entrance fee included with national park ticket*, one of the most important sites on the island with many ruined buildings and petroglyphs, where the bird man cult flourished. Out to sea are the 'bird islets', Motu Nui, Motu Iti and Motu Kao. It is very windy at the summit, with good views at sunset or under a full moon. It is easy to follow the road back to Hanga Roa in the dark.

Rest of the island

A tour of the main part of the island can be done on foot, but this would need at least two days, returning to Hanga Roa on the first day and setting out again the next day. For more extensive exploration you could hire either a bicycle, horse or a car. A high-clearance vehicle is better suited to the smaller roads than a normal car. From Hanga Roa, take the road going southeast past the airport; at the oil tanks turn right to **Vinapu**, where there are two *ahu* and a wall whose stones are joined with Inca-like precision. Head back northeast along the south coast to reach first **Vaihu** (an *ahu* with eight broken *mo'ai* and a small harbor), then **Akahanga** (an *ahu* with toppled *mo'ai*) and **Hanga Tetenga** (a toppled *mo'ai* and an *ahu*, with bones visible inside). Beyond is **Ahu Tongariki**, the largest platform on the island with a row of 15 *mo'ai*, which was damaged by a tidal wave in 1960 and later restored with Japanese aid. Turn left here to **Rano Raraku** (2 km), the volcano where the *mo'ai* were originally carved and where many statues can still be seen, some of them buried to the neck, a breathtaking sight. In the crater is a small lake surrounded by reeds; swimming is possible beyond the reeds.

The road heads north past 'the trench of the long ears'; an excursion can be made from here east to **Poike** headland to see the open-mouthed statue that is particularly popular with local carvers. Ask the farmer for permission to cross his land. At the northeast end of the headland is the cave where a virgin was kept before marriage to the victor of ceremonies during the time of the bird man cult; ask someone for directions.

The road along the north coast passes **Ahu Te Pito Kura**, where the 10-m-tall *mo'ai* is one of the largest ever brought to a platform. The road continues to **Ovahe** where there is a very attractive beach with pink sand and some rather recently carved faces and a cave.

From Ovahe, you can return direct to Hanga Roa or continue to the palm-fringed, white-sand beach at **Anakena**, the site of the village of the island's first king, Hotu Matua, and the spot where Thor Heyerdahl landed in 1955; his visit is commemorated with a plaque. The *mo'ai* here has been restored to its probable original state. There is a picnic area and stalls selling meat and tuna empanadas (US$4.50). From Anakena a coastal path of variable quality runs west, passing beautiful cliff scenery and interesting remains. The path skirts the island's highest point, the extinct volcano of Terevaka (507 m), to which you can trek for a view of the ocean on all sides. At **Hanga o Teo**, there appears to be a large village complex, with several round houses, while further on is a burial place, built like a long ramp with several ditches containing bones. From Hanga o Teo the path goes west then south, inland from the coast, to meet the road north of Hanga Roa.

⦿ Rapa Nui listings

For hotel and restaurant price codes and other relevant information, see pages 14-21.

⦿ Where to stay

Hanga Roa and around *p489*
Unless it is a particularly busy season, there is no need to book in advance; mainland agencies make exorbitant booking charges. The airport information desk has an accommodation list. Flights are met by large numbers of hotel and *residencial* representatives with whom you can negotiate. Alternatively, take a taxi to the centre of Hanga Roa, drop your things in a café and look around. Many places offer accommodation and tours (rates ranging from US$25 to US$150 pp, includes meals). Rates, especially in *residenciales*, can be cheaper out of season and if you do not take full board.

$$$$ Explora En Rapa Nui, reserve in Santiago T02-2395 2800, in US T1-866 750 6699, or through www.explora.com. All-inclusive hotel, easily one of the poshest in the South Pacific. Intentionally hard to find (take Cross Island road, turn right about 6 km from town on the wider unpaved road), transport provided for guests, as are all food, drinks and tours. Views of the ocean are tremendous and each room has a jacuzzi.
$$$$ Gomero, Av Tu'u'Koihu, T032-210 0313, www.hotelgomero.com. Comfortable place near the beach, spotless, cosy rooms. Restaurant, pool.

$$$$ Hanga Roa, Av Pont, T02-2957 0300, www.hotelhangaroa.cl. The largest hotel in town, within walking distance of centre. Full board, excellent ocean views, spa and pool.
$$$$ Iorana, Ana Magara s/n, outside Hanga Roa, opposite airport, 30 mins' walk from town, T032-210 0608 (Santiago T02-2695 2058), www.ioranahotel.cl. 3-star, hot water morning and evening, comfortable, small pool, good views.
$$$$ O'Tai, Te Pilo Te Henua s/n, T032-210 0250, www.hotelotai.com. Great location, pool, lovely gardens, restaurants, best rooms with terrace, family-run.
$$$$ Taha Tai, Api Na Nui s/n, T032-255 1192, www.hoteltahatai.cl. Well-kept bright hotel with rooms or cabins, sea view, small swimming pool, tours organized.
$$$$-$$$ Chez Cecilia, Policarpo Toro y Atamu Tekema, near Tahai Moai, T210 0499, www.rapanuichezcecilia.com. Packages with tours offered, excellent food, Rooms, *cabañas* or camping, quiet, free airport transfer.
$$$$-$$$ Taura'a, C Principal s/n, T032-210 0463, www.tauraahotel.cl. Upmarket B&B, very comfy, good beds, spacious bathrooms, nice garden, good service. **Taura'a Tours** is also good.
$$$ Cabañas Mahevi, Kaituoe s/n, T032-8742 3987, maheva_hiturangi@hotmail.com. Cabins for 3-4 people, furnished with kitchen or microwave, breakfast available, near airport, views of Ranu Kau volcano. Packages up to 5 nights available, also car hire, island tours.

$$$ Cabañas Sunset, near Ahu Tahai site and old cemetery, T032-255 2171. Spotless *cabañas* overlooking the sea, discounts for Handbook users, ask for the owner, Ms 'China' Pakarati. She also arranges full day tours for groups of 1-4.

$$$ HI Kona Tau, Avareipua, T032-210 0321. HI hostel, **$** pp in dorms, all rooms with bath.

$$$ Inaki Uhi, Atamu Tekena s/n, T032-255 1160, www.inakiuhi.com. Clean hostel and a central, good option. 15 rooms (triples available). Also arranges a wide range of tours.

$$$ Mana Nui Inn, Tahai s/n, opp cemetery, T032-210 0811, www.mananui.cl. Pleasant cabins and rooms on north edge of town, airport transfers, tours run.

$$$ Martín and Anita's hotel, Simón Paoa s/n, opposite hospital in Hanga Roa, T032-210 0593, www.hostal.co.cl. Full board and multi-day packages available, good food. Can arrange car, bike and horse hire, guides and tours.

$$$ Orongo, Atamu Tekena s/n, T032-210 0572, www.hotelorongo.com. Half-board available (excellent restaurant), good service, nice garden.

$$$ Residencial Tadeo y Lili, Apina Ichi s/n, T032-210 0422, tadeolili@entelchile.net. Simple but clean, French-Rapa Nui run, all rooms with sea view and terrace, tours.

$$$-$$ Ana Rapu, Av Apina, T032-210 0540, www.anarapu.cl. Camping US$15. Legendary budget lodging with great range of accommodation, rooms or cabins sleep 1-4, all spotless. Bike and car hire, boat trips, horse riding and other excursions.

$$ Mihinoa, Av Pont s/n, T032-255 1593, www.camping-mihinoa.com. Campsite, which hires out camping equipment, with a few rooms and cabin. Huge kitchen for campers, airport transfers, welcoming, exceptional value.

Camping

Camping is not allowed anywhere in the national park. Many people offer campsites

in their gardens, check availability of water first. Some families can also provide food.

❼ Restaurants

Hanga Roa and around *p489*
Some *residenciales* offer full board. Vegetarians will have no problems on the island; locally produced fruit and vegetables are plentiful and cheaper than meat and other foodstuffs, which are imported from mainland. Locally caught fish is also good value. Wine and beer are expensive by Chilean standards because of freight charges.

$$$ La Kaleta, Hanga Roa, T032-255 2244. Superb ocean views and great seafood. Try the tuna steak or ceviche, arguably the best on the island. Tucked away behind the diving schools.

$$$ Te Moana, Hanga Roa. Lovely outdoors terrace with ocean views, good steaks, fresh seafood, creative cuisine. Live music at weekends.

$$ Haka Honu, Av Policarpo Toro s/n . Popular seafood restaurant, excellent tuna carpaccio, great (and huge) salads. Also good for a cocktail in the evening. Friendly staff, sea views.

$$ Tataku Vave, Caleta Hanga Piko s/n. T032-255 1544. Worth the detour, this ocean front restaurant offers great pastas and salads, as well as seafood dishes. One-way taxi fare to the restaurant included if you book in advance.

$ Ariki o Te Pana (also known as **Tía Berta**), Av Atamu Tekena s/n, T032-210 0171. Mon-Sat lunch and dinner. Aunt Berta makes delicioos empanadas, filled with tuna, cheese, meat, veggies etc. Great value at US$6 per huge empanada.

$ Carrito Hitu, Tuu Maheke s/n (near corner of Apina), Hanga Roa. Try tuna *empanadas* and delicious fruit juices; also has a good *menú del día*.

$ Donde el Gordo, Av Te Pito o te Henua, near Av Atamu Teken. The best place for complete, plus wraps, huge

empanadas, fruit juices etc, at very
affordable prices.

$ Los Carritos, Hanga Roa. A local favourite
among a group of cheap eateries near the
football field.

$ Mi Kafé Gelatería, Caleta Hanga Roa
near Mike Rapu Diving Center. For real
coffee and good ice cream.

$ Toromiro Café, Av Atamu Tekena s/n,
Excellent Jamaican coffee and great value
for money breakfast and lunch.

🍸 Bars and clubs

Hanga Roa and around *p489*
Action begins after 0100. Drinks are
expensive. Try **Piriti**, near airport, Thu-Sat;
Toroko, Caleta Hanga Roa, near harbour,
which has a slightly "rougher" ambience;
and **Topa Tangi**, Atamu Tekena, Thu and
Sat 2300-0300, a popular pub with free
dance shows on Thu.

🎭 Entertainment

Hanga Roa and around *p489*
Several places in town offer traditional
music and entertainment; one of the best is
Kari Kari at **Hotel Hanga Roa** (see Where to
stay), T032-210 0595. 3 times a week, US$20,
very elaborate show.
Music at the **church**, Av Te Pito Ote Henua,
for the 0900 Sun mass has been described
as "enchanting".

🎉 Festivals

Rapa Nui *p486, map p486*
Jan-Feb Tapati, or **Semana Rapa Nui**
from the end of Jan for 2 weeks, see box,
page 490.

🛍 Shopping

Hanga Roa and around *p489*
All shops and rental offices close 1400-1700.
On Av Atamu Tekena, the main street, there
are lots of small shops and market stalls

(which may close during rain) and a couple
of supermarkets; the cheapest are **Kai Nene**
or **Tumukai** (good panadería inside).

Handicrafts

Wood carvings and stone *mo'ais* are
available throughout Hanga Roa. The
expensive **Mercado Artesanal**, left of
church, will give you a good view of what
is available – authentic, no compunction
to buy. Good pieces cost from US$50 to
US$200. Souvenirs at dozens of decent
places on Atamu Tekena.

⚙ What to do

Rapa Nui *p486, map p486*
Diving
Mike Rapu, Caleta Hanga Roa Otai s/n,
T032-255 1055, www.mike rapu.cl.
Diving courses, expeditions, fishing
trips and kayaks.
Orca, Caleta Hanga Roa, T032-255 0877,
www.seemorca.cl. Run by Michel and Henri
García, very experienced (Henri is a member
of the Cousteau Society), PADI courses, with
dive shop and surf equipment rental.
Both have similar prices: introductory dive
US$70; single dive for experienced diver
US$53-62; also night dives and boat trips
with snorkeling (from US$26). Both at the
harbour, all equipment provided.

Hiking
To walk around the island in 1 or 2 days
you would need to be in great shape. Once
you leave Hanga Roa services (including
lodging and food) are scarce, so take
plenty of food and water and inform
your hotel or park rangers of your exact
route. Good free bilingual tourist maps are
available at Sernatur information office,
hotels and tour agencies. More detailed
maps (recommended for hiking, driving
or bicycling) are sold on Av Policarpo Toro
for US$15-18, or at the ranger station at
Orongo for US$10. Sample trekking (and
cycling) distances and times: Hanga Roa

to Anakena Beach, 17 km, 4½ hrs (1¾ hrs by bike); Hanga Roa to Jau-Orongo, 4 km, 1 hr (30 mins); Hanga Roa to Rano Raraku, 25 km, 6½ hrs (3 hrs).

Horse riding

This is the best way to see the island, provided you are fit: horses, US$65 for a day, including guide. **Cabañas Pikera Uri**, T032-210 0577, www.pantupikerauri.cl, offer several riding tours, as well as *cabañas* for overnight stays.

Tour operators

Many agencies, *residenciales* and locals arrange excursions around the island. The English of other tour guides is improving. Half- and full-day tours of the island by minibus cost US$60-100 pp, including guide, without lunch. For the best light go early or late in the day.

Aku-Aku Tours, Tu'u Koihu s/n, T032-210 0770, www.akuakuturismo.cl. Wide range of tours.

Hanga Roa Travel, T032-210 0158, hfritsch@entelchile.net. English, German, Italian and Spanish spoken, offers good-value all-inclusive tours.

Haumaka Archeological Guide Services, Av Atamu Tekena y Hotu Matua, T032-210 0274. English spoken.

Rapa Nui Travel, Tu'u Koihu s/n, T032-210 0548, www.rapanuitravel.com. Recommended agency with years of experience. Ask for Terangi Pakarati, a well-informed and super friendly local guide, who speaks English, Spanish and Rapa Nui.

● Transport

Rapa Nui *p486, map p486*
Air

LAN fly daily in high season, less often in low season to/from **Santiago**, 3½-4 hrs going west, 5-5½ hrs going east. Most westbound flights continue to Papeete, Tahiti. However, if you fly between Papeete and Santiago or vice versa, you will be

considered in transit and will not be allowed to exit the airport at Rapa Nui, unless you have checked this in advance. **LAN** office on Av Atamu Tekena s/n, near Av Pont, Mon-Fri 0900-1630, Sat 0900-1230, T032-210 0279/210 0920. The cheapest return fare from **Santiago**, booked well in advance, is about US$550, with occasional special deals available through travel agents. Under 24s and over 65s are often eligible for a 28% discount on some fares.

Car hire

Many vehicle hire agencies on the main street. US$80-100 per day for a small 4WD with manual transmission (usually). In theory, a Chilean or international driving licence is necessary, but your national licence will usually do. If a rental company makes a fuss, go next door. There is no insurance available, drive at your own risk; be careful at night, since deep potholes and wild horses are not uncommon. Speeding, drunk driving and poor driving skills are also a problem on the island. If you are hit, demand that the person who dented your car and the rental car agency settles the bill. If you hit something or someone, you will be expected to pay, cash only. The speed limit in Hanga Roa is under 30 kph. Check oil and water before setting out. There is only one petrol station, near the airport. **Moira Souvenir Rent a Car**, Te Pito o te Henua s/n, T032-210 0718. About US$60 a day for small, beat-up but functional 4WD, no papers asked for, just a reasonable deposit. **Motorbike hire**: about US$60 a day including gasoline (*Suzuki* or *Honda 250* recommended because of rough roads). You can also rent scooters (US$50 for 24 hrs), bicycles (from US$12 from your *residencial*) and quadbikes.

Taxi

Taxis cost a flat US$4 within Hanga Roa. Longer trips can be negotiated, with the cost depending mainly on the time. For example, a round-trip to the beach at

Anakena costs US$30 (per taxi); be sure to arrange for the taxi driver to pick you up at a predetermined time. **Radiotaxi Vai Reva**, Sergio Cortés, Petero Atamu s/n, T032-210 0399, 24 hrs, reliable. For touring the island, it is cheaper to hire a car or take a tour if there are more than 3 people sharing.

❶ Directory

Hanga Roa and around *p489*
Banks US dollars may be accepted, at poor rates. Banco del Estado, Av Pont, T032-210 0221, Mon-Fri 0800-1300, with an ATM, accepts MasterCard and Cirrus, cash advances on Visa, reasonable rates for dollars or euros. **Banco Santander**, on Policarpo Toro on the waterfront, T032-251 8007, has an ATM that accepts Visa and MasterCard, Mon-Fri 0800-1300. It also has an ATM at the airport (departure area). There is another reliable ATM at the gas station shop on Av Hotu Matua. ATMs can dispense 10,000 pesos per transaction. Cash can be exchanged in shops, hotels, etc, at about 5% less than Santiago. Credit cards are widely accepted for purchases, but some places add a surcharge. **Internet and telephones** Omotohi Cybercafé, Av Te Pito o te Henua, offers fast and reliable internet at US$3 per hr, daily 0900-2200. Phone calls are expensive; the cheapest way to call home or mainland Chile is via the internet.
Medical facilities Small but well-equipped **Hospital Hanga Roa**, Av Simón Paoa, near the church, T032-210 0215.
Pharmacy Cruz Verde, Av Atamu Tekena. T032-255 1540. **Post office** Half a long block up from Caleta Hanga Roa on Av Te Pito o te Henua, sells Easter Island stamps, post cards and will put a souvenir stamp in your passport on request, Mon-Fri 0900-1300, 1430-1800, Sat. 0900-1200.

Contents

Footprint features

Background

History

Origins

It used to be generally accepted that the earliest settlers in South America were related to people who had crossed the Bering Straits from Asia and drifted through the Americas from about 13,000 years ago (the Clovis model). In recent years, however, a growing number of discoveries from earlier dates in North and South America have raised doubts about this. In South America these include a coastal site in southern Chile called Monte Verde from 14,800 years ago, stone tools from the Serra da Capivara in northeastern Brazil from some 22,000 years ago and paleontological evidence from Uruguay from earlier still. If nothing else, these finds question the theory of a single migration into South America from the north. Other early evidence of human presence has been found at various sites: in the Central Andes (with a radiocarbon date between 12,000 and 9000 BC), northern Venezuela (11,000 BC), southeast Brazil, south-central Chile and Argentine Patagonia (from at least 10,000 BC). After the Pleistocene Ice Age, 8000-7000 BC, rising sea levels and climatic changes introduced new conditions as many mammal species became extinct and coastlands were drowned. A wide range of crops was brought into cultivation and camelids and guinea pigs were domesticated. It seems that people lived nomadically in small groups, mainly hunting and gathering but also cultivating some plants seasonally, until villages with effective agriculture began to appear, it was originally thought, between 2500-1500 BC. The earliest ceramic-making in the western hemisphere was thought to have come from what is now Colombia and Ecuador, around 4000 BC, but fragments of painted pottery were found near Santarém, Brazil, in 1991 with dates of 6000-5000 BC.

The beginnings of agriculture

Gradually, the settled life of agricultural subsistence took over from the more nomadic hunting lifestyle. Remains of slingshot stones and what seem to be *bolas* (weights attached to cords used to bring down prey by entangling their legs) have been found alongside bones of mastodons in Monte Verde, near Puerto Montt. Other remains found nearby included agricultural tools and medicinal plants, hearths and house foundations, all indications that the site was inhabited for some time by one community. Crop seeds have also been found, including those of potatoes, evidence of very early contact with cultures from as far afield as the Central Andes. Some of these remains were found in a remarkable condition, owing to being buried in a peat bog; mastodon bones even had traces of meat on them. It is widely agreed that the site was settled 10,000 years ago, although lower levels have been controversially dated from as early as 34,000 years ago.

As sources of game in forested valleys dried up, some groups settled along the coasts, particularly drawn by the abundance of marine life provided by the cold Humboldt current in the Pacific. Some of the earliest evidence of humans in Chile has been found in the north, both on the coast and in the parched Atacama Desert. The coastal people lived on shellfish gathered by the shore and on fish and sea-lions speared from inflated seal-skin rafts.

One such group, the Las Conchas people, migrated from the inland valleys to the coast near Antofagasta around 7500 BC. They were one of the first peoples in South America to take hallucinogenic drugs. Many graves excavated in this region contain mortars, which may have been used to grind up seeds also found nearby. These seeds contained an alkaloid similar to that found in the ayahuasca plant, which is still used for its hallucinogenic effects by the Shuar in Peru – indeed, the Shuar are believed by some to be descendants of these Atacameño peoples, having migrated to the Amazon in order to hide from the Spanish. Some specialists believe that the many geoglyphs of the Atacama Desert (see box, page 202) – the most famous ones being the Nazca Lines in Peru – were maps for shamans undergoing the hallucinatory experience of flight after taking drugs such as ayahuasca.

By about 2500 BC, agriculture was practised throughout much of Chile, as it was across the rest of the continent. Maize, beans and squash have been found in northern Chile from as early as 5000 BC. However, people in the south only turned definitively to agriculture at a much later date. In Araucanía, horticulture was not practised until around AD 500. These people also had unusual burial practices, placing the body in an urn inside a funerary canoe, perhaps reflecting the local dependence on fishing for their livelihood. Elaborate artefacts found in some graves, such as stone and copper jewellery and ceramic offerings, suggest a stratified society of both rich and poor.

Northern influences
In the north, the extremely dry climate is a great preservative, allowing archaeologists to build up a detailed picture of early life. The people in the Atacama lived in solidly built adobe houses, arranged in complexes around inner courtyards and corridors, such as can be seen in the village of Tulor near San Pedro de Atacama.

These northern peoples had contact with neighbouring highland communities, shown by the presence there of plants and other goods found only in the adjacent regions. The important Altiplano culture of **Tiahuanaco** in present-day Bolivia is thought to have had particularly close links with northern Chile, helping to stimulate the growth of settlements such as that at San Pedro de Atacama. Trade with Tiahuanaco, through llama caravans bringing highland goods and produce, boosted the wealth and cultural development of the desert people. Some very fine textiles were found in this area, showing distinct design similarities with those of Tiahuanaco. The textiles were hand-spun and coloured with vegetable and cochineal dyes. Clothing and jewellery adornments containing feathers suggested contact even with tropical regions, although these may have been obtained through their Altiplano intermediaries. Local ceramics were mostly plain and highly polished, but some items decorated with elaborate dragon-like figures had probably been traded with Tiahuanaco.

Mummification was practised from as early as 2500 BC by the Chinchorro people. They buried their dead stretched out straight, in contrast to the foetal position used by other Chilean and Peruvian cultures. Internal organs and the brain were removed and the body was stuffed with a variety of materials to preserve it. Sticks were attached to the limbs to keep them straight. A mask was placed over the face and a wig of real human hair was attached to the head. The body was then coated in a layer of clay and wrapped in animal skins or mats. According to the person's status, they were often buried with their personal possessions: clothing, jewellery, musical instruments and copper items.

In the period AD 500-900 the association between San Pedro de Atacama and Tiahuanaco had become even stronger. In return for trading their agricultural produce and other goods, it is thought that the Tiahuanaco people sought copper, semi-precious stones and the use of grazing lands in northern Chile. As with the Araucanía in the south, some graves from this period contained bodies with more elaborate clothing, jewellery, imported ceramics and other valuables, suggesting the existence of a wealthy elite, which was also common in central Andean cultures.

Following the demise of Tiahuanaco in about AD 1100, a number of cultures arose in the adjacent area bordering southern Bolivia, northern Chile and Argentina, practising derivative agriculture, with terraces and irrigation, and producing ceramics in similar styles. In the Quebrada de Humahuaca in present-day Argentina, several small defensive towns were built with fortified walls and stone houses. Grave remains have revealed that metallurgy was well developed here; some bodies were adorned with pectorals, bracelets, masks and bells, made of copper, silver and gold. Shells from the Pacific and ceramics from present-day Bolivian cultures, such as the Huruquilla, show the existence of widespread trade links.

Inca expansion

The next major empire to touch northern Chile was that of the Incas, which, at the peak of its growth in the late 15th and early 16th centuries, stretched as far south as the Aconcagua Valley near modern-day Santiago. The advancing armies of Inca Topa Yupanqui suppressed resistance in the valleys of the central region and replaced local structures with their own military administration. They were finally stopped by hostile forest tribes at the Río Maule near present-day Talca. This was the southernmost limit of the Inca Empire, some 3840 km south of the equator and the deepest that any imperial movement had penetrated into the southern hemisphere.

One major group that survived the Inca incursion and resisted conquest by the Europeans right up until the 19th century was the **Mapuche** (see box, page 267). They were concentrated in the central valley south and east of the Cordillera de Nahuelbuta. The Mapuche were primarily farmers but also hunted and fished, both inland and along the coasts and lake shores. Their large cemeteries contained a variety of burial sites, some in canoes or stone chambers and some in simple earthen graves. Grave goods were plentiful, with elaborate ceramics, wooden and stone artefacts and jewellery made of copper and semi-precious stones.

The Far South

Despite the apparently inhospitable conditions, these regions were home to a sizeable population of hunting, fishing and gathering peoples from very early times continuously up to the 19th century AD. Bones of horses and extinct giant sloths, dating from approximately 8000 BC, have been found near to stone arrowheads in sites such as Fells's Cave and Pali Aike Cave on the Magellan Straits – evidence of the earliest hunters.

Four distinct cultures developed here: the Haush or Haus, Ona (also known as the Selk'nam), Yámana (or Yaganes) and Alacalufe. The oldest of these was the **Haush**, nomadic hunters of the guanaco mainly confined to the farthest southeastern tip of Tierra del Fuego, in present-day Argentina. The Haush hunted with bows and arrows, using guanaco skins for clothing and sometimes for covering their stick-framed houses. They also gathered shellfish and caught fish by the shore, using spears and harpoons.

The **Ona** people also hunted guanaco, ranging on foot across most of the Isla Grande of Tierra del Fuego in family groups. They were strong runners and tall people, some of them 6 ft tall; in fact, all these hunters and gatherers are thought to have been the tallest of the first South American peoples. They wore guanaco skin robes, fur side out, and also guanaco fur moccasins, known as *jamni*. They made open-topped shelters out of guanaco skins, which were weatherproofed with a coating of mud and saliva, and sometimes painted red. The Ona did not use harpoons or spears and only collected shellfish from beaches at low tide.

The **Yámana** were nomadic coastal hunters, travelling in canoes up and down the coasts of the Beagle Channel and around the islands southwards to Cape Horn. They caught otters, fish and seals, using spears and harpoons, and used slings and snares to catch birds. The Yámana houses were simple, made of sticks and grass, and they wore little clothing, perhaps a small seal skin and skin moccasins in winter.

Like the Yámana, the **Alacalufes** were also nomadic coastal peoples, roaming from Puerto Edén in the Chilean channels, to Yendegaia in the Beagle Channel. There was some contact with the Yámana, with whom they would sometimes exchange goods and inter-marry. The Alacalufes had similar lifestyles to the Yámana but developed various additions, such as raising a sail on their canoes and using a bow and arrow in addition to the sling when hunting birds or guanaco.

Spanish conquest and early settlement

The first Spanish expeditions to Chile were led by **Diego de Almagro** and **Pedro de Valdivia**, both of whom followed the Inca road from Peru to Salta and then west across the Andes. Almagro's expedition of 1535-1537, which included 100 Spaniards, African slaves, crypto-Jews and some thousands of indigenous Americans – many of whom perished – reached the heartland but, bitterly disappointed at not finding gold, returned to Peru almost immediately. Valdivia's expedition then carried out what initially appeared to be a swift and successful conquest, founding Santiago in February 1541 and a series of other settlements in the following years. But, in the 1550s, these Spanish settlements were shaken by a Mapuche rebellion, which led to the death of Valdivia.

The two major indigenous figures in this early resistance to the Spaniards were the *caciques* Lautaro and Caupolicán. Lautaro was an interesting case: initially an adjutant of Pedro de Valdivia (known by the conquistador as Felipe), he turned against Validivia and led the expedition that captured him in 1553. Lautaro went on to lead several successful campaigns, before being killed by the Spaniards in the Mataquito Valley in 1557. Caupolicán fought alongside Lautaro, but was eventually captured in the *cordillera* in 1558 and impaled on a stake by the Spaniards. Nevertheless, the two Mapuche heroes had successfully undermined the Spanish colony and their struggles set the tone for the colonial period in Chile. Lacking precious minerals, threatened by the warlike Mapuche and never less than four months' journey from Europe, the colony was of relatively little importance to Spain, except as a frontier zone.

The motivation of these early expeditions – as in Mexico and Peru – was greed. The Spanish crown did nothing to finance the ventures, so all the risk was shouldered by those who participated, who therefore had a pressing need to find silver and gold to recompense themselves. Nevertheless, a fifth of all gold and silver that was found in the New World went into the royal coffers; an influx of precious metal that was urgently needed to prop up the falling value of coinage in Europe at this time.

The greedy motivations of the early arrivals made control in distant Chile difficult for the Castillian crown to exercise. Chile was effectively run by men such as **Francisco de Aguirre**, a conquistador who had accompanied Pedro de Valdivia's initial expedition. As one of the first Spaniards on the scene, Aguirre was made Governor of Tucumán – just across the Andes in modern-day Argentina – and later founded La Serena. He was, however, deeply anti-clerical and proclaimed himself "Pope and King" in Chile, saying that he would rather have a farrier than a priest. The Inquisition eventually caught up with Aguirre in the Río de la Plata in the 1570s and he died poor, bitter and disgraced in La Serena.

Town planning in the 16th century

Perhaps the most obvious influence of Spanish colonial settlement for a visitor is the characteristic street plan of towns and cities. Colonial cities were founded by means of an official ceremony, which involved tracing the central square and holding a mass. A series of Royal Ordinances issued in Madrid in 1573 laid down the rules of town planning: the four corners of the main plaza had to face the four points of the compass; the plaza and the main streets had arcades and, away from the plaza, the streets were traced out with a cord and ruler in the now-familiar grid-pattern. Once this was done, building lots near the plaza were distributed, allocated by lottery to those settlers who had rights to be there.

The Ordinances specified the principles underlying the distribution of the major public buildings. Churches were to be distant from the plaza and built on high ground, so that they were easy to see and people had to climb up to them on steps, thereby forcing a greater reverence. The *cabildo* and the customs house were to be built nearby, while the hospital of the poor and those sick with non-contagious diseases was to be north-facing, planned so that the inmates could enjoy southern exposure.

The Ordinances also advised settlers on how to deal with local suspicion and hostility: "While the new town is being built the settlers ... shall try to avoid communication and intercourse with the Indians. Nor are the Indians to enter the circuit of the settlement until the latter is complete and in condition for defence and the houses built, so that when the Indians see them they will be filled with wonder and will realize that the Spaniards are settling there permanently and not temporarily."

'Royal Ordinances Governing the Laying Out of New Towns' by Zelia Nuttall, *Hispanic American Historical Review*, May 1922.

In addition to trying to exert effective control over the Spaniards in their territory, one of the main concerns of Chile's Spanish governors after Valdivia was the war against the Mapuche successors to Lautaro and Caupolicán. Known by the Spanish as Araucanos, the Mapuche were fearsome opponents. In 1598, they began a general offensive that destroyed all of the Spanish settlements south of the Río Biobío, revealing the weakness of a colony whose Spanish population was under 8000. Pushed back into the northern part of the Central Valley, the Spanish were forced to build a string of forts along the Río Biobío, guarded by a frontier army of 2000 men, the only force of its type in Spanish America, financed by a special subsidy from the viceregal capital of Lima. However, Chile was not important enough to warrant a full-scale Spanish assault on the Mapuche and, for the rest of the colonial period, the Spanish presence south of the river would be limited to the island of Chiloé and to the coastal city of Valdivia.

The Chilean colony

As in the other colonies in the Americas, Chilean society under Spanish rule was not the two-sided world of Spanish settlers and Amerindian peoples that official histories would have us believe. From very early on, two other groups became increasingly important: *marranos* – or forced converts from Judaism to Christianity, who had fled Inquisitiorial persecution in Spain and Portugal – and slaves from West Africa. The *marranos* controlled large parts of the trade in South America and suffered bouts of persecution from the Inquisitional office in Lima, while the Africans did much of the manual labour in the colony. Although both groups eventually became absorbed into Chile, the legacy of their presence can perhaps be felt today in the widespread stereotyping of Africans and Jews in mainstream Chilean society.

African slaves started arriving from very early on in the colonial period, principally because the Spanish found that the indigenous people were not hardy enough to do the work required of them. By the end of the 16th century, Africans in Chile were working as cattle ranchers and as *stevedores*, and as blacksmiths, tailors, carpenters and servants in every city. They were mostly sold as contraband, brought over from Buenos Aires instead of through the 'official' port of entry at Cartagena, Colombia, and originated from all parts of the West African coast, from Senegambia to Angola.

By the turn of the 17th century, much of the trade of the fledgling colony was in the hands of the *marranos*, who were prohibited from holding positions of authority. Their main port of entry was Buenos Aires, from where they travelled overland to Potosí and Lima by way of Tucumán.

In the following years, colonial Chile achieved a degree of stability and developed as a compact society; most of its population inhabited the Central Valley and most trade was through Valparaíso. By the end of the 17th century, there were few people of pure indigenous blood, most having died, inter-married or escaped south of the Río Biobío. The majority of the population was *mestizo* (mixed race), though the society was dominated by a small white elite. Chile was, however, highly isolated, being cut off from the rest of the continent in winter. People dared not use the lower passes to the south for fear of the Mapuche, and the high passes near Mendoza and Santiago were blocked by snow for months at a time.

During the colonial period, the *hacienda*, or landed estate, was the most important feature of rural society in the Central Valley. In the 17th century, Chilean agriculture expanded to meet demands for wheat, tallow, salted beef and cattle hides from Peru; hides were also sent to Potosí and mules to the great fair in Salta. These exports and the need to feed the frontier army led to the development of large-scale agriculture. As the *haciendas* grew, small farmers and tenants were gradually forced to become *inquilinos*, a class of peasants tied to the land. The *inquilino* is regarded as the ancestor of the *huaso*, the Chilean cowboy, a figure seen as resourceful, astute, cunning and archetypally Chilean.

Although *haciendas* grew in response to food shortages, they were very self contained, with their own supplies of food and clothing, their own vineyards, forges and workshops. Ownership of a *hacienda* was one of the clearest marks of upper-class status, although many were the property of religious orders. The *hacienda* remained at the centre of rural life in the Central Valley and social relations between landowners and *inquilinos* changed little until the Agrarian Reforms of the 1960s. Although no colonial *haciendas* remain, a few dating from the 19th century can be visited, notably Villa Huilquilemu, near Talca (see page 241).

Chile was governed as part of the Viceroyalty of Peru, with its capital in Lima; until the 18th century, all trade with Spain had to pass via Lima and trade with other countries was forbidden. This led to uncontrolled smuggling and, by 1715, there were 40 French vessels trading illegally along the Chilean coast. In 1740, direct trade with Spain was permitted for the first time and, in 1750, Chile was allowed to mint her own currency.

The War of Independence

Independence came to Spanish America as a direct result of Napoleon's invasion of Spain. As Spanish guerrilla forces fought to drive the French out, these events led the colonial elites to debate where their loyalties lay: to Napoleon's brother Joseph, now

War of the Pacific, 1879-1883

One of the few major international wars in Latin America after Independence, the War of the Pacific had its roots in a dispute between Chile and Bolivia over national boundaries in the Atacama Desert. There had already been one military conflict in 1836-1839, when Chile defeated Peru and Bolivia, but relations were further complicated by the discovery of nitrates in the Atacama in the 1860s, particularly in the then-Bolivian province of Antofagasta.

The war also has to be put into the wider international context of the late 1870s. The years 1873-1875 saw a serious recession, with plunging commodity prices around the world. This was followed in 1876 by one of the most severe El Niño weather patterns the world has ever seen, leading to the deaths of tens of millions of people from famine. Santiago had its lowest ever barometric reading in 1877, Peru suffered widespread floods and there were devastating droughts in the Bolivian Altiplano.

The Bolivian government was forced to impose port taxes to support its weak economy and, in 1878, attempted to tax the Chilean-owned Antofagasta Railroad and Nitrate Company. When the company refused to pay, its assets were seized, sparking claims of foul play by the Chilean government. Peru announced that it would honour a secret alliance with Bolivia, so the Chilean president, Aníbal Pinto, declared war on both states.

None of these three countries was prepared for military conflict; they lacked skilled officers and adequate weapons. Control of the sea was vital: when the Chileans blockaded the Peruvian nitrate port of Iquique with two wooden ships, the *Esmeralda* and the *Covadonga*,

Peru retaliatied with her two best iron-clad ships, the *Huáscar* and the *Independencia*. In the Battle of Iquique, 21 May 1879, the *Esmeralda* was sunk, but the *Independencia* ran aground and was captured, thus altering the balance of power between the two navies. Later in October 1879, the two Chilean iron-clads, *Blanco Encalada* and *Cochrane*, captured the *Huáscar* off Angamos, near Antofagasta. (The ship can now be visited in the harbour at Talcahuano.)

Rather than attack the Peruvian heartland, the Chileans invaded the southern Peruvian province of Tarapacá and then took the town of Tacna, in May 1880, before capturing Arica, further south. In January 1881, fresh Chilean armies seized control of Lima. Bolivia signed a ceasefire, giving up her coastal province, and eventually, under the 1883 peace settlement, Peru gave up Tarapacá to Chile. The provinces of Tacna and Arica were occupied by Chile for 10 years, and it was not until 1929 that an agreement was reached under which Tacna was returned to Peru.

The war gave Chile a monopoly over the world's supply of nitrates and enabled her to dominate the southern Pacific coast. Some idea of its importance in official Chilean history can be gained by the number of streets and squares named after the war heroes, especially Arturo Prat and Aníbal Pinto, and after the two Chilean vessels *Esmeralda* and *Blanco Encalada*. Chile's relations with her northern neighbours, however, remain sour. There is widespread racism in Chile towards the indigenous peoples in Peru and Bolivia, while signs in Bolivia proclaim that the Pacific coastline is still Bolivian.

officially King? Or to the overthrown king, Ferdinand VII, now in a French prison? Or to the Spanish resistance parliament in Cádiz?

In 1810, a group of leading Santiago citizens appointed a Junta to govern until Ferdinand returned to the throne. Although they protested loyalty to Ferdinand, their move was seen as a challenge to the crown by the viceregal government in Lima, which sent an army to Concepción. War broke out between the Chilean Patriots and the Royalist troops supporting Lima. The defeat of the Patriot army led by **Bernardo O'Higgins** at Rancagua in October 1814 led to a restoration of colonial rule, but O'Higgins was able to escape across the Andes to join forces with Buenos Aires' liberation hero, José de San Martín. The turning point came in 1817, with the invasion of Chile from Mendoza by San Martín's Army of the Andes, a force of 4000 men, which defeated the Royalists at Chacabuco on 12 February 1817. A Royalist counter-attack was defeated at Maipó, just south of Santiago, on 5 May 1818, putting an end to Royalist power in the Central Valley. The victory of the small Patriot navy led by **Lord Cochrane** at Valdivia in January 1820 helped clear the Pacific coast of Royalist vessels and paved the way for San Martín to launch his seaborne invasion of Peru.

Nineteenth-century expansion

In most of former Spanish America, Independence was followed by a period of political turmoil, marked by civil wars and dictatorship, which in some cases lasted until the 1860s. Many Independence heroes had tragic ends: disgusted at the chaos, San Martín retired to France; Simon Bolívar died penniless and in hiding in a boarding house in Santa Marta, Colombia; and O'Higgins was quickly overthrown. O'Higgins' demise was followed by a brief period of instability in Chile but, in 1830, conservative forces led by Diego Portales restored order and introduced the Constitution of 1833, which created a strong government under a powerful president. Portales, a Valparaíso merchant, who never became president, explained his actions thus: "If one day I took up a stick and gave tranquillity to the country it was only so that the bastards and whores of Santiago would let me get on with my work in peace."

Chile became famous throughout Latin America as the great example of political stability: the army was reduced to 3000 men and kept out of politics; after 1831, four successive presidents served the two five-year terms permitted under the constitution. However, this stability had another side: civil liberties were frequently suspended, elections rigged, opponents exiled and power lay in the hands of a small landowning elite. Neither was the stability perfect: there were short civil wars in 1851, 1859 and 1891.

The latter half of the 19th century saw Chile's great period of expansion. In 1881, when victory over Peru in the War of the Pacific was assured (see box, opposite), the much-enlarged army was sent to put an end to Mapuche independence and thus secure continuous Chilean control over the entire Pacific coastline south of Arica. In the few short years between 1879 and 1883, Chilean territory had expanded both northwards and southwards. However, some Chileans still argue that the victory over Peru and Bolivia came at the price of losing both the region around Mendoza and most of Patagonia to Argentina; according to some, this should, by dint of colonial land divisions under the Viceroyalty, be Chilean territory. It is certainly true that maps from the early 19th century show Chilean territory crossing the Andes and advancing halfway to the Atlantic Ocean, while early colonial documents speak of "the city of Mendoza in Chile".

From the 1860s onwards, conflict between President and Congress became a constant feature of political life. The War of the Pacific brought the Chilean government a new source of income through the tax levied on nitrate exports coming from the new territories of the Atacama (see box, opposite) but it also increased rivalry for control of this income. When, in 1890, Congress rejected the budget, President Balmaceda announced he would use the 1890 budget for 1891. Congressional leaders denounced this as illegal and fled to Iquique, where they recruited an army, which defeated Balmaceda's forces and seized the capital. Balmaceda took refuge in the Argentine embassy, where he committed suicide. His defeat was important: between 1891 and 1924 Chilean presidents were weak figures and real power lay with Congress, ruled by the elite.

Twentieth-century politics

In the years before the First World War, the income from nitrates helped build a large railway network, roads and ports and the best education system on the continent. However, the collapse of the industry during the First World War led to worker and student unrest, which brought down the constitutional system in 1924 when the military intervened. A new constitution restored the strong presidency, which had apparently served Chile so well in the 19th century, but the Great Depression brought further economic stress, which resulted in a series of short-lived governments, including a military-led 100-day Socialist Republic in 1932.

As economic conditions recovered in the 1930s, Chile once again became a model of political stability. Between 1932 and 1970, Chile developed a complex multiparty system: two left-wing parties, the Socialists and Communists, representing the urban workers and miners; the Conservative and Liberal parties, dating from the 19th century, representing the landowners; and the Radicals, a centre party representing the middle classes. The Radicals became the key to power, winning the presidency in 1938, 1942 and 1946. However, one major group remained excluded from political life: the peasants, whose votes, controlled by their landlords, gave the Liberals and Conservatives their representation in Congress and enabled the landlords to block rural reform.

In the 1958 election, the Socialist **Salvador Allende** (see box, opposite) only narrowly failed to defeat the Conservative Jorge Alessandri. This shook both the right-wing parties and (in the aftermath of the Cuban Revolution), the US government. In 1964, the US and the Chilean right-wing threw their weight behind **Eduardo Frei Montalva**, a Christian Democrat who promised a 'revolution in freedom'. Frei Montalva's achievements in office were impressive: state ownership of 51% of the copper industry; minimum wage and unionization rights for agricultural workers; and the 1967 agrarian reform, which began replacing the *haciendas* with family farms. However, these measures raised hopes that could not be satisfied, especially in the countryside where workers now enjoyed rights and pushed for faster land reform. Hostility from the landowners was reflected in Congress where the National Party, formed in 1966 by the merger of the Conservatives and Liberals, denounced the government. The President's Christian Democrat Party was divided between supporters and opponents of reform. Nevertheless, Frei Montalva has been an enduringly popular President – his memory was widely seen as a key factor in the landslide victory of his son, Eduardo Frei Ruiz-Tagle, in the 1993 presidential elections.

The 1970 election was narrowly won by Salvador Allende, polling just over 36.3% of the vote, with the electorate split in three. Allende headed a left-wing alliance called Unidad Popular, which launched an ambitious programme of reforms: banking, insurance, communications, textiles and other industries were taken over in the first year and the nationalization of copper was completed (this last even with the support of the right-wing parties). After that, the government ran into major problems: the nationalizations had depleted Chile's currency reserves, while hostility by domestic business groups and the US caused capital flight and a US-led boycott on international credit. In Congress, an alliance between the Christian Democrats and National Party impeached several

Salvador Allende Gossens

Born in 1908 into an upper-middle-class Valparaíso family, Salvador Allende's childhood ambition was to be a doctor, like his grandfather Ramón Allende Padín, a respected Radical politician who became Serene Grand Master of the Chilean freemasons. While studying medicine, Salvador discovered first-hand the appalling living conditions of the poor and the links between poverty and disease. Even before he qualified as a doctor, he became active in politics and was briefly imprisoned during the Ibáñez dictatorship. He was a founder member of the Chilean Socialist party in 1933; at about the same time he also became active in the Freemasons.

Elected to Congress for Valparaíso at the age of 29, he served as Minister of Health in Aguirre Cerda's Popular Front government of 1939-1942 and was elected to the Senate in 1945, becoming Senate president in 1965. Allende was a candidate in four presidential elections. In 1952, he gained only 5.45% of the votes but, in 1958, as candidate of the Front for Popular Action, an alliance between the Socialists and Communists, he lost narrowly to the right-wing candidate, Jorge Alessandri. Easily defeated in 1964 by the Christian Democrat, Eduardo Frei, he finally won the presidency in 1970. However, without a majority in Congress, heading a broad but divided coalition of eight parties, and facing the hostility of much of the Chilean population and of Washington, Allende found himself with increasingly little room for political manoeuvre.

When news of the military revolt came through in the early hours of 11 September 1973, Allende went to the Moneda Palace and spoke twice on the radio before communications were cut. Although he was offered a flight out of the country in return for his resignation, Allende refused, and the palace was bombed by three Hawker Hunter jets. Most accounts now accept that Allende committed suicide. He was buried in an unmarked grave in Viña del Mar. In September 1990, following the return to civilian rule, his body was exhumed and transported to Santiago for a state funeral, thousands of people lining the route from the coast.

ministers. At grassroots level, a series of anti-government strikes by truck drivers and professional groups brought the country to a halt in October 1972 and again in August 1973, while the supplies in shops were unable to keep pace with the wider purchasing power of many social classes, leading to long queues for foodstuffs and a rise in annual inflation to over 300% in 1973.

Despite these negative effects, Allende's Socialist experiment did have a measure of success: agricultural production increased and, by 1972, there were 27% more foodstuffs available in Chile than there had been in 1970. However, even this increase in supply was outstripped by the demand caused by a real rise in wages among the poor. This was a sign that Allende's goal of eradicating poverty was bearing some fruit, with per capita consumption rising for all foodstuffs except red meat. The upper and middle classes who bemoaned the queues in the shops were, in fact, venting frustration that their customary position at the head of affairs was finally being usurped.

The Pinochet era

Allende's popularity in some quarters was demonstrated by the March 1973 Parliamentary elections, at which the Unidad Popular polled 43.4% of the vote, 7% more than in 1970.

Nevertheless, the coup of 11 September 1973, led by **General Augusto Pinochet** (born 1915), was widely expected, the armed forces having received open encouragement from Allende's opponents in Congress, including the Christian Democrats, and from opposition groups on the streets; it later became clear that the CIA had had a major role in fomenting the unrest that led to the pre-coup stand-off.

The brutality of the coup shocked people who were accustomed to Chile's peaceful traditions. Left-wing activists and people mistakenly identified as leftists were arrested, thousands were executed, torture was widespread, with at least 7000 people held in the national football stadium, and, by 1978, there were 30,000 Chilean exiles in Western Europe alone. With political parties and labour unions banned, the government adopted neo-liberal economic policies under the influence of the 'Chicago Boys' – local economists who had been trained at the University of Chicago under the tutelage of Milton Friedman.

Pinochet installed himself as the undisputed head of a military junta. Those who did not approve of his methods often met grisly ends, including the former head of the Army, Carlos Prats, who was assassinated by a car bomb in Buenos Aires in 1974. Pinochet increased his hold on power by his control over the regime's notorious secret police, the DINA, which was headed by a close colleague, General Manuel Contreras, while silencing exiles and international critics through Operation Condor, an international anti-leftist terrorist movement. Under a new constitution, adopted in 1980, Chile became a 'protected democracy' based on the exclusion of political parties and the 'guardianship' of the armed forces, who put forward a single candidate for an eight-year presidential term in 1981. To no one's surprise that candidate was Pinochet, who, during his second term (1981-1989) became the longest-serving Chilean president. With his stern features enhanced by dark glasses, Pinochet became the stereotype of the South American dictator. Often seen as a bluff, no-nonsense character, he was also noted for his astuteness, his suspicious mind, his ruthlessness, his hatred of communism and distrust of democracy.

It would be wrong to see his dominance as merely the result of repression and fear. For many Chileans, who had hated Allende and feared his liberal policies, the human rights abuses and destruction of democracy were seen as a price worth paying. In spite of his widespread vilification in much of the Western press, Pinochet retained popularity among many Chileans, polling 44% of the vote in a plebiscite in 1988. This bid for a further eight-year term was unsuccessful but, when the first results came in, the military government initially tried to maintain that the 'si' vote (yes to Pinochet) had triumphed. Even when this position became untenable, the constitution of 1980 ensured that Pinochet still had 18 months before he had to relinquish power.

Eventually, presidential and congressional elections were held in 1989. A veteran Christian Democrat politician, **Patricio Aylwin Azócar**, the candidate of the Coalition of Parties for Democracy (CPD, or Concertación), was elected President and took office in March 1990 in a peaceful transfer of power. General Pinochet remained as Army Commander, although other armed forces chiefs were replaced. The new Congress set about revising many of the military's laws on civil liberties and the economy, but in December 1990, questions in Congress and in the press about financial scandals involving army officers and Pinochet's own son-in-law led the Army Commander to order all troops to report to barracks. In May 1993, Pinochet surrounded the Ministry of Defence with soldiers and ordered generals to wear battle dress to work for a day.

In 1991, the National Commission for Truth and Reconciliation (the RETTIG Commission) published a report detailing those who had been killed under the military regime. The

RETTIG commission established that 3197 people had died as the result of the violation of human rights, but opposition by the armed forces and an amnesty law protecting members of the military prevented mass human rights trials. At this time, prosecution of those guilty of human rights abuses in Chile was widely seen as impossible.

Presidential elections in December 1993 resulted in victory for the Christian Democrat, Eduardo Frei Ruiz-Tagle, candidate of the Concertación coalition but, in congressional elections held at the same time, the Concertación failed to achieve the two-thirds majority required to reform the constitution, replace the heads of the armed forces and end the system of designated senators whose votes enabled the right-wing parties and the military to block reform. As a result Frei's presidency became an exercise in balancing the demands of the parties of the Concertación against the entrenched power of the military and the right-wing. Although the Concertación won a comfortable victory in congressional elections in December 1997, it still failed to achieve the majority necessary to break the deadlock; the position of the military was strengthened in March 1998 when General Pinochet retired as Army Commander-in-Chief and, as a former president who had held office for six years, took up his lifetime seat in the Senate.

In October 1998, General Pinochet was arrested in London at a private clinic, while recovering from a back operation. The arrest warrant had been issued by a Spanish judge, Baltasar Garzón, for murder and torture of Spanish citizens under the military regime. Pinochet's arrest put the Frei government under great pressure: Pinochet's supporters demanded action, while some of the government's supporters, especially those in the Socialist party, were privately delighted. Meanwhile, the families of those who had disappeared during Pinochet's regime continued to demand news of the whereabouts of the victims' corpses, and the prosecution of those responsible. Combined with the worsening economic situation and the choice of the first Socialist to head the Concertación into presidential elections, these dramatic events made the December 1999 poll unexpectedly close. The Concertación candidate, Ricardo Lagos, eventually won with a tiny majority in a second-round ballot against the populist Mayor of Las Condes, Joaquín Lavín (one of the bright young 'Chicago boys' of the 1970s), although Lavín had won more votes in the first round of polling.

The ructions caused by the Pinochet affair were significant. Having allowed the extradition process to continue, Jack Straw, the British Home Secretary, permitted Pinochet to return to Chile on grounds of ill health in March 2000. However, a legal case started by Judge Juan Guzmán Tapia in the Chilean courts in January 1998 meant that Pinochet still faced a legal challenge. In July 1999, the Supreme Court ruled that, in cases where the fact of death could not be certified, amnesty did not apply, thereby laying Pinochet and the military open to charges regarding the 'disappeared'. This was followed in June 2000 by an Appeal Court ruling that stripped Pinochet of his immunity from trial. The decision was confirmed by the Supreme Court in August, and Pinochet was finally indicted by Judge Guzmán on 29 January 2001. The charges of kidnapping and murder related to the infamous 'caravan of death' in 1973, when many political detainees 'disappeared' in the north of the country. However, in July 2001, the court ruled narrowly that Pinochet's worsening health meant that he was not capable of mounting a proper defence and that the case could not be continued. Judge Guzmán was soon forced to take sick leave as a result of stress induced by the case. Although appeals were mounted by the families of victims of the military government, Pinochet eventually won the right not to stand trial under a Supreme Court Ruling in July 2002, although he resigned his position as senator for life.

Recent history

It appeared that the July 2002 ruling would finally allow some distance to be put between Chile and its troublesome former President. However over the next two years a series of human rights abuse charges were made against Pinochet. Each followed the same course as the last; first Pinochet had to be stripped of immunity for a particular charge, then he was indicted and placed under house arrest before being ruled too infirm to stand trial. For some time Chileans had been cynical about the prospects of 'Pinocchio' ever being brought to justice and the ruling simply seemed to confirm most people's suspicions. Indeed, 'the old man' still retained sizeable support amongst large sectors of the population who maintained that his acts were justified in as much as they were borne of patriotic ideals and served to save Chile from communism and transform it into the modern country of today. However all this changed in 2004 when it was discovered that Pinochet had stashed away US$27 million in secret foreign bank accounts. He was charged along with his wife and four of his children (one of whom laughably tried to claim political asylum in the US) for tax evasion and holding false passports. Now, suddenly, the same people who had defended Pinochet's murders were aghast at the idea that he may have been stealing money from them. To add further fuel to the fire, in July 2006, Manuel Contreras, the former head of the DINA, claimed that Pinochet made this money by the large-scale production and sale of cocaine to Europe and North America. This new case was never resolved, Pinochet dying under house arrest on 10 December 2006 to a bizarre mixture of raucous celebration and quasi-religious grief, never having been brought to justice but equally failing to end his life with the respect and authority he had tried to develop. Denied the state burial he craved, he was nevertheless buried with full military honours.

Back to 2002 and President Lagos urgently needed to concentrate on important national economic issues: in particular, the impact of the economic meltdown in neighbouring Argentina – Chile's main trading partner and the source of the majority of its overseas visitors. As political uncertainty increased across the continent – with coups and counter-coups in Venezuela, the collapse of Argentina and the victory of the left in presidential elections in Brazil – 2002 was a difficult year to be steering the Chilean ship. The government's decision in August 2002 to freeze the minimum wage in an effort to reduce unemployment caused widespread protests, largely because most people's experience of economic realities did not match the government's subsequent statements as to the "improving situation".

The early months of 2003, however, saw Lagos able to reassert his statesmanship through his renewed importance on the global stage: Chile now occupied one of the 15 seats on the UN Security Council. As the international crisis over Iraq reached a head, Lagos did not desert his old support base, with Chile proving to be one of the most intractable of the "six undecided council members", and putting forward a strong case against pre-emptive military invasion. This resistance to pressure from the 'yanquis' and the Brits reflected the mood in the country and enhanced Lagos's popularity. But opposition to war in Iraq did not come without a price; the Americans subsequently postponed signing a free trade agreement with Chile.

In his last two years of office, president Lagos concentrated on important social and democratic themes. The Plan Auge aimed to create a more European-style healthcare system heavily subsidizing treatment for an increasing number of illnesses to low-income families and in some cases allowing them access to private clinics, while the justice system was shaken up in an effort to speed up processes that had often seen prisoners on remand for longer than they were finally sentenced for. Agreement was finally reached to phase out the system of appointed senators, paving the way for a return to true democracy, while in 2005 the president was at last given the authority to dismiss leaders of the armed forces, once again making the military subordinate to democratic institutions. When President Lagos finally stepped down, he enjoyed the highest popularity rating of any Chilean leader.

Elections at the end of 2005 threw up a three-way contest. The Concertación put forward the Socialist Michelle Bachelet, while the right put up two candidates, Joaquín Lavín for the UDI and Sebastián Piñera for the RN. After Lavín was knocked out in the first round, the final result seemed too close to call. Over a series of television debates, Piñera, owner of Chile's national airline and a major television channel, came across as a slightly false patronizing and domineering figure, and in the end Bachelet won by a comfortable 7%.

In many ways Bachelet broke the mould in Chilean politics. A woman president in a still very much male-dominated country, Bachelet was not a career politician. Tortured alongside her father, Alberto (a military man who had remained loyal to Allende), she worked for many years as a paediatrician before being made Health and then Defence Minister under Lagos. Although she had a quiet start to her presidency she continued the progressive reforms of her predecessor.

Concertación's supremacy could not prevent an upsurge in unrest, starting in 2006 with strikes by secondary school students, copper workers and, in 2008, government workers demanding better pay, and demonstrations against potentially environmentally damaging mining and energy projects. Bachelet's response to these disturbances and the chaotic introduction of the new Transantiago transport system did not initially restore confidence and her popularity ratings fell. In early 2009 ex-president Eduardo Frei was chosen as Concertación's candidate for the December 2009 elections, but Sebastián Piñera, his main opponent, ended the coalition's hold on power. Piñera's first challenges were to deal with reconstruction after the massive earthquake of February 2010 and the rescue of 33 miners trapped underground near Copiapó for 69 days later in the year. The success of the former aided a spurt in economic growth and job creation, while the latter captivated the world's media.

Throughout Piñera's presidency, the economy remained strong. Demonstrations by various groups recurred, however, including miners seeking better pay and conditions and supporters of indigenous rights and gender equality. Environmentalists protested against a number of hydroelectric schemes, most notably a project in Aysén which would flood 6000 ha on the Ríos Baker and Pascua. The scheme was approved in April 2012, only to be abandoned in 2014. Student protests over unequal opportunities in education for those from poorer backgrounds began in 2011 and continued into 2013. With presidential elections due on 17 November 2013, ex-president Bachelet included in her campaign for re-election policies to confront social inequality and provide free university education by raising taxes. The ruling Conservative Alliance eventually settled on Labour Minister Evelyn Matthei as Bachelet's main rival, two earlier candidates having resigned: Laurence Golborne, after a financial scandal, and Pablo Longueira because of ill health. Like Bachelet, Matthei's father had been a general when Salvador Allende was deposed, but General Fernando Matthei was in favour of the coup. Over two rounds, Bachelet secured a return to the presidency with a large majority (62% against Matthei's 38%). Many regard as ambitious her manifesto pledge to earmark US$15 bn for educational reform, income redistribution, improvements in health care and the reform of political and economic structures that have remained in place since the Pinochet era.

Modern Chile

An overview

The Pinochet affair forced Chileans to confront their recent past. Although old wounds reopened, the increasing political apathy of the young, which was apparent in the early 1990s, was nipped in the bud. While the presidencies of the Concertación continued the Pinochetista neo-liberal policies that made Chile such a banker's favourite in the 1980s, these have been accompanied by a genuine attempt at more inclusive government, including significant increases in the national minimum wage, at rates well above that of inflation. With a pension system on which countries such as Britain have modelled their own 'stakeholder' schemes, urban Chile is now, for the most part, modern and dynamic.

There are, however, several problems that the government needs to address. While there has been a limited rise in living standards among the inhabitants of Santiago's *callampas* (shanty towns), urban poverty remains widespread. Over a third of the population lives in the capital or the surrounding Región Metropolitana, and Chile's unusual geography means that Santiago is a natural focal point, on which the rest of the country is all too dependent.

Chile managed to weather the short *'crisis económica'* in the first decade of the 21st century. The government did extremely well to stave off inflationary pressures, and, buoyed by the rise in copper, the steady growth and prosperity that characterized the 1990s in some senses returned. Although this might be the case on a macro level and although Chile's economy remains the most stable in South America, the economic situation of the lower and middle classes remains tough. There is an all-too-apparent wealth gap, while the working week is a hefty 45 hours (reduced from 48 by Lagos). In order to avoid having to make redundancy payments, jobs are often offered on short-term contracts, and it is not surprising that people talk about the difficulty of finding – and keeping – work.

Chile's income tax system is symptomatic of the country's traditional conservatism. Direct income tax is exceptionally low and business tax is almost non-existent. While Chile's lower and middle classes can clearly not afford to pay more income tax, this is far from true of the country's upper classes. The inability of recent governments to tackle this subject is evidence both of the oligarchic stranglehold that the Chilean aristocracy retains on the state and of the taboo status of even the slightest economic redistribution – thanks to the 'anti-Communist wars' waged by the military government in the 1970s and 1980s and to the psychological scars caused by the Allende government's economic policies and their consequences.

Perhaps the most fundamental long-term problem, however, is that Chile's wealth depends in part on the ongoing exploitation of its extensive natural resources, often by multinational companies; industries such as logging and intensive fishing, while successful at present, have the potential to ruin Chile's future. According to one estimate, Chile lost 80% of its marine life in the 1980s and its native forests continue to disappear at alarming rates. Environmentalists have joined forces with farmers to highlight the environmental damage caused by introduced species such as the eucalyptus, which extracts most of the goodness from the soil, and by plantations of pine, which acidify the soil. Chile's Free Trade Agreements with Europe, North America and China are not seen as beneficial in all quarters.

However, these moves are symbolic of Chile's increasingly outward-looking mentality. After four centuries characterized by isolation and insularity, the ramifications of Chile's recent history have put the country onto the international map in an unprecedented manner. Whereas, until recently, Chileans compared themselves to Europeans, they now take increasing national pride in their own achievements. Even though Pinochet was not put on trial in Chile, the case and its consequences mean that the country is at the vanguard of one of the most significant human rights movement in history; one that, in a short space of time, has already had repercussions for repressive former heads of state elsewhere.

Constitution and government

Chile is governed under the 1980 Constitution, introduced by the military government of General Pinochet and approved in a plebiscite on 11 September 1980. Important amendments were made during the transition to civilian rule in 1989-1990 and other amendments have been made subsequently. The constitution provided for an eight-year non-renewable term for the President of the Republic, a bicameral legislature with a Congress and a Senate and an independent judiciary and central bank, although it was only after the rejection of Pinochet in the 1988 vote that most of the provisions of the constitution come into operation. A two-thirds majority in both houses of legislature is required to reform the constitution. In February 1994, the legislature cut the presidential term of office from eight years to six, and in 2006 it was further reduced to four years. Presidents are prohibited from holding two consecutive terms of office. The legislature is composed of a 120-seat Chamber of Deputies and a 38-seat Senate.

The dominant political party in Chile is the Christian Democrats, a centre party that grew rapidly after its foundation in 1957. The Christian Democrats welcomed the overthrow of Allende but later became the focus of opposition to the dictatorship. Not strong enough to rule on its own, since 1990 the party has contested elections in an alliance known as the **Concertación**. The other members are the Socialists, a centre-left party traditionally split between the Radicals and the Partido por la Democracía, a centre-left grouping led by ex-Socialists. The main opposition to the Concertación comes from the right wing, of which the two main parties, Renovación Nacional and Unión Democrática Independiente, have formed the **Alianza para Chile** (Alliance, or Coalition for Change). Chile is divided into 15 regions, usually referred to by Roman numerals (although they also have names). The government of each region is headed by an *intendente*, who is appointed by the president.

Economy

Chile's economy is dependent on the mining sector. Mineral ores account for half of total export revenue. Copper is the most important mineral, with Chile being the world's largest producer. It provides 19% of government revenue. Although the Pinochet government of 1973-1990 sold off most state-run industries to the private sector, CODELCO (the state copper mining company) was not touched. La Escondida, where production began in 1990, with an output of almost 1.5 million tonnes a year, is the world's leading mine (see page 184), while Chuquicamata is the biggest open-cast mine in the world. Other mineral resources in Chile include around 70% of the world's lithium reserves and about 12% of the world's known molybdenum ore reserves. Fluctuations in world prices for minerals can have a great impact on the country's balance of payments.

The country's diverse environment means that agriculture is also of great importance. Traditional crops, such as cereals, pulses and potatoes, and industrial crops, such as sugar beet, sunflower seed and rape seed, account for about a third of the value of agriculture, while vegetables account for a quarter. Fruit growing has expanded rapidly, while timber and wood products make up the fourth place in exports. Chile is the most important fishing nation in Latin America and the largest producer of fishmeal in the world; it is also one of the world's leading salmon farmers.

Chile is fortunate in possessing reserves of oil, natural gas and coal, and abundant hydroelectricity potential. Almost all the country's hydrocarbon reserves are in the extreme south, on Tierra del Fuego, in the Strait of Magellan. Manufacturing activity is mostly food processing, metalworking, textiles, footwear and fish processing.

The government follows anti-inflationary policies, accompanied by structural adjustment and reform. Privatization has been widespread, although certain key companies, such as CODELCO, remain in state hands. Rising investor confidence has brought reasonably stable economic growth since the late 1980s and the Chilean model has been held up as an example for other debtor countries.

Culture

Chilean culture is rooted in the nation's hybrid soul. European guitars blend with panpipes and *queñas*; religious art flourishes alongside traditional crafts; literature scales the heights of modernism, while never losing track of the natural beauty from which it is born.

Society

Chile is a deeply conservative country: it was the first newly independent state in Latin America fully to embrace the Catholic church and has the most stable 'democratic' (or, until the 1950s, oligarchic) tradition in the region.

There is less racial diversity in Chile than in most Latin American countries. About 90% of the population of 17.3 million is *mestizo* (mixed race). There are hardly any people of African origin – in sharp contrast to, say, Brazil or Colombia – and there has been much less immigration from Europe than in Argentina and Brazil. The German, French, Italian and Swiss immigrants came mostly after 1846 as small farmers in the forest zone south of the Biobío. Between 1880 and 1900, gold-seeking Serbs and Croats settled in the far south and the British took up sheep farming and commerce in the same region.

There is disagreement over the number of indigenous people in Chile. Survival International estimates the **Mapuche** population to be one million, but other statistics – including the official ones – put it at much less. There are also 45,000-50,000 **Aymara** in the northern Chilean Andes and 4500 **Rapa Nui** on Easter Island. A political party, the Party for Land and Identity, unites many indigenous groupings, and legislation is proposed to restore indigenous people's rights.

The population is far from evenly distributed: Middle Chile, from La Serena to Concepción, consisting of 20% of the country's area, is home to over 77% of the population, with the Metropolitan Region of Santiago containing, on its own, about 35% of the total. Population density in 2014 was estimated at an average of 23 people per sq km, but in the Metropolitan Region it was 8470 per sq km. Since the 1960s, heavy migration from the countryside has led to rapid urbanization. By 2012, 89.2% of the population lived in urban areas.

According to a 2013 poll conducted by Pontifical Catholic University of Chile, 61% of citizens identify as Catholic while 17% identify as Protestant. Membership of Evangelical Protestant churches has grown rapidly in recent years. There are also small Jewish communities in Santiago and Temuco especially.

Chilean literacy rates are higher than those of most other South American states; according to the 2002 census over 95% of the population above the age of 10 is literate (other statistics put the rate at 98.6% in 2009). Census returns also indicated that, among the over-25s, 16% had completed higher education, 52% had completed secondary education and 41% had only completed primary education. Higher education provision doubled in the 1980s through the creation of private universities.

In November 2004, and to the consternation of the Catholic church and most conservative politicians, Chile became one of the last countries in the world to legalize divorce. Until then, couples that wanted to separate had to go through the farcical process of getting a notary to swear that they were married in an inappropriate municipality and that their marriage certificate is therefore invalid. Even now the process is not cheap, as it almost always requires a lawyer. The upshot for impoverished rural populations is that divorce – and remarriage – is still, in effect, impossible.

Traditional arts and crafts

Chile's traditional crafts are often specific to particular places and all have a long history. Present-day handicrafts represent either the transformation of utilitarian objects into works of art, or the continued manufacture of pieces that retain symbolic value. A number of factors threaten these traditions: the loss of types of wood and plant fibres through the destruction of forests; the mechanization of farm labour, reducing the use of the horse; other agricultural changes, which have, among other things, led to reductions in sheep farming and wheat growing; and migration from the countryside to the city. On the other hand, city dwellers and tourists have created a demand for 'traditional' crafts so their future is to some degree assured.

Basketry Mapuche basketry is made for domestic, agricultural and fishing uses in Lago Lanalhue and the Cautín region. Apart from the Mapuche areas, one of the great centres of basket-making is Chimbarongo, just south of San Fernando in the Central Valley. Here, weaving is done in almost every household, usually by the men. One of the main materials used is willow, which is collected in June when it is still green and then soaked in water for four months, at the end of which the bark peels off. The lengths of willow are split into four and finished with a knife. Baskets, chairs and lamps are the most common objects made. Willow is not the only fibre used. Many items are made from different types of straw, including little boxes made of wheat; although the latter are produced throughout the country, the most famous are from La Manga, Melipilla. Note also the yawl made for fishing, typical of Chiloé. Other important centres of basket-making are Ninhue-Hualte in Ñuble (Región VIII), Hualqui, 24 km south of Concepción, and San Juan de la Costa, near the coast of Osorno, Región X.

Carving and woodwork The people of the Atacama region edge trays with cactus wood and make little churches – traditionally the doors of the old churches were made of cactus – and they also use cactus for drums, while bamboo is used for flutes of various sizes. Different types of wood are used in the construction of guitars, *guitarrones*, harps and *rabeles* (fiddles), mainly in the Metropolitan Region. Villarrica (see page 279) is a major producer of wooden items: plates, kitchen utensils, but especially decorative objects like animals and birds, jointed snakes and *picarones* (small figures, which, when picked up, reveal their genitals). Wooden ships in bottles are made in Coronel, while in Loncoche, south of Temuco, a workshop specializes in fine carvings, in native wood, of country and Mapuche scenes. Another craft from the Mapuche region is the carving of horn or antler (*asta*) in Temuco, to make animals, birds, cups, spoons, etc.

Ceramics The two most famous places for ceramics are Quinchamalí near Chillán, where the traditional blackware is incised with patterns in white, and Pomaire, west of Santiago (see page 67), which is renowned for heavy terracotta household items that are used in many Chilean homes. Less well known is the pottery of the Atacama zone, the clay figures of Pañul and Lihueimo (Región VI), the household items, clay figurines and model buildings of Pilén de Cauquenes-Maule (Región VII) and the scented pottery of the nuns of the Comunidad de Santa Clara (Convento de Monjas Claras in Santiago and Los Angeles). These highly decorated pieces have been made since colonial times, when they achieved great fame.

Cowboy equipment and clothing Items can be found in any part of the country where there are *huasos*: Rancagua, San Fernando, Chillán, Curicó, Colchagua, Doñihue and also in Santiago. Saddles of leather, wood and iron, carved wooden stirrups in the old style, leather reins, spurs (some of them huge and very elaborate – *huasos* are always proud of their spurs) and hats of straw or other materials are the types of equipment you will see. The clothing comprises ponchos (long, simple in colour and design, often with one or two coloured stripes), *mantas* (shorter, divided into four with a great variety of colour), *chamantos* (luxurious *mantas*, double-sided, decorated with fine patterns of vines, leaves, flowers, small birds etc) and sashes/*fajas* (either single or tri-coloured, made to combine with *mantas* or *chamantos*).

Knitwear and textiles Chiloé is famous for its woollen goods, hand-knitted and coloured with natural dyes. With the atrocious weather, clothing (such as sweaters, knitted caps, *mantas*, socks) is very popular; this and rugs, blankets and patch dolls are all sold locally and in Puerto Montt. The main knitting centres are Quinchao, Chonchi and Quellón. Other crafts of Chiloé are model-boat building and basketware from Quinchao and Quellón, where mats and figurines such as birds and fish are also made.

The Mapuche are also weavers of sheep's wool, making ponchos, *mantas*, sashes (*fajas*), reversible rugs (*lamas*) with geometric designs and bedspreads (*pontros*). The colours come from natural dyes. The main producing areas are around Lago Lanalhue, Chol Chol, Nueva Imperial and other small settlements in the Mapuche heartland between Temuco and the coast.

Silverware Although silverware is one of the traditional crafts of the Mapuche, its production is in decline owing to the cost of the metal. Traditional women's jewellery includes earrings, headbands, necklaces, brooches and *tupus* (pins for fastening the *manta* or shawl). Nowadays, the most common items to be found for sale are *chawai* (earrings), but these are smaller and in simpler shapes than those traditionally worn by

Mapuche women. It is a matter of debate whether Mapuche silversmiths had perfected their skills before the arrival of the Spaniards; certainly the circulation of silver coins in the 18th century gave great impetus to this form of metalwork. The Universidad Católica in Temuco is in charge of a project to ensure the continuance of the art.

Specialist crafts The Mapuche make musical instruments: the *trutruca*, a horn 1.5 to 4 m long; *pifilka* (or *pifüllka*), a wooden whistle; the *kultrún* drum; *cascahuilla*, a string of bells; and *trompe*, similar to a Jew's harp. The village of Rari, near the Termas de Panimávida, some 25 km northeast of Linares (Región VII), specializes in beautiful, delicate items made from dyed horsehair: bangles and brooches in the shape of butterflies, little hats, flowers, etc.

Mined in the Cordillera de Ovalle, lapis lazuli is a blue stone, only found otherwise in Afghanistan. It is set in silver to make earrings, necklaces and bracelets. Many shops in Santiago sell the semi-precious stone and objects that incorporate it. Of growing popularity in recent years, combarbalita is a smooth, marble-like stone found only around the remote town of Combarbalá in Región IV. A very beautiful stone that comes in a variety of hues, it is used to make everything from jewellery and cutlery holders to bedside tables and can be very good value.

Fine art and sculpture

The colonial period

There was little home-grown art during the colonial period in Chile but trade with other regions was extensive and Santiago in particular has good collections of non-Chilean art. The Catholic church inevitably dominated fine art and sculpture; the new religious foundations needed images of Christ and the saints to reassure Christian settlers and also to instruct new converts. The importation of works from Spain was very costly, so most patrons relied instead on the major colonial artistic centres of Cuzco, Potosí and Quito.

The churches and monasteries of Santiago give a vivid sense of the thriving art market in colonial Spanish America: sculptures were shipped down the coast from Lima and from Quito via Guayaquil; canvasses were carried across the Andes on mule trains from Cuzco and Potosí; and occasionally an itinerant Spanish-trained artist would pass through in search of lucrative commissions. Extensive cycles of the lives of Christ, the Virgin and selected saints were popular: a cycle of 40 or 50 large canvasses representing the exploits of, say, St Francis, provided instant cover for large expanses of bare plaster, a good clear narrative and an exemplary life to follow.

San Francisco in Santiago (see page 47) has a cycle of 53 paintings of the life of St Francis painted in Cuzco in the late 17th century. These are based on a similar cycle in the Franciscan monastery in Cuzco by the indigenous artist Basilio de Santa Cruz Pumacallao, which is in turn derived from a series of European engravings. One of the Santiago paintings, the Funeral of St Francis of 1684, is signed by **Juan Zapaca Inca**, an indigenous artist and follower of Santa Cruz, who probably oversaw production of the whole series. Wherever possible the artist has introduced bright-coloured tapestries and rich fabrics embellished with lace and gold embroidery, a mark of the continuing importance of textiles in Andean culture. This is a typical pattern for colonial art: a set of European engravings forms the basis for a large painted cycle which in turn becomes the source for further copies and derivatives. The narrative content and general composition remain constant, while the setting, attendant figures, costume and decorative detail are often translated into an Andean idiom.

There are, of course, many different categories of colonial art. The big painted cycles were produced more for the educated inhabitants of the monastic establishments than for a lay audience, and were intended for edification rather than devotion. Popular devotion tends to create increasingly decorated and hieratic images. A good example is that of the so-called Cristo de Mayo. Early in the 17th century Pedro de Figueroa, a friar of the Augustinian monastery in Santiago, carved a figure of the crucified Christ, which still hangs in the church of **San Agustín** (Estado 170, not far from Cerro Santa Lucía). This passionate, unusually defiant image was credited with miraculous powers after it survived a serious earthquake in Santiago in May 1647 (hence the popular name *de Mayo*). The only damage was that the crown of thorns slipped from Christ's head and lodged around his neck. A cult quickly grew up around the image, creating a demand for painted copies, which are identifiable by the upward gaze, the distinctive necklace of thorns and the evenly distributed lash marks across the body. The Carmelite convent of San José has a locally produced 18th-century example of the Cristo de Mayo that includes attendant saints and garlands of bright flowers, the latter like pious offerings. The Jesuits established a school of sculpture on Chiloé, where, up until the late 19th century, native craftsmen continued to produce boldly expressive Christian images.

After Independence

In the 19th century, Chile's distance from the old colonial centre of viceregal power worked to its advantage in the field of art. The Lima-born artist **José Gil de Castro** (died 1841), known as El Mulato Gil, accompanied Bernardo O'Higgins on the campaign for Chilean Independence from 1814, working both as engineer and map-maker and as a portrait painter. His portrait of O'Higgins of 1820 in the **Museo Histórico Nacional** in Santiago represents the hero as a towering giant of a man, immovable as the rocky mountains behind him. Another 1818 painting in the **Municipalidad of La Serena** shows San Martín standing beside a writing desk, his hand inside his jacket in a distinctively Napoleonic pose.

The 19th century also brought European traveller-artists to Chile, who helped to confirm the Chilean landscape, peoples and customs as legitimate subjects for paintings, including the German Johann Moritz Rugendas, who lived in Chile from 1833 to 1845, and the Englishman Charles Wood (in Chile from 1819 to 1852). Examples of both artists' work can be seen in the **Museo Nacional de Bellas Artes** (see page 45). The Frenchman Raymond Monvoisin also spent many years in Chile, from 1843 to 1857. His perceptive portraits of members of the government and the literary elite are interesting for the way in which they link the Chilean tradition of Gil de Castro with European sources. After his return to France he produced the first major painting dedicated to an event from colonial history, the Mapuche hero Caupolicán taken prisoner by the Spaniards (1859). Caupolicán was celebrated in Chile 10 years later in a bronze statue by Nicanor Plaza (1844-1914) erected on the Cerro Santa Lucía in Santiago, and although it originated as an entry for a competition organized by the US government for a statue to commemorate the Last of the Mohicans, it represents the incorporation of indigenous people into the national mythology.

The **Chilean Academy of Painting** was founded in 1849 and, although its first presidents were mediocre European artists, they too helped to make Chilean subject matter respectable. The Academy also acted as a focus for aspiring young artists.

Antonio Smith (1832-1877) rebelled against the rigidity of the academic system, working as a political cartoonist as well as a painter, but his dramatic landscapes grew out of the gradual awakening of interest in Chilean scenery. He transformed the picturesque view into a heroic vision of mountains and valleys, full of air and space and potential. Cosme San Martín (1850-1906), Pedro León Carmona (1853-1899), Pedro Lira (1845-1912), Alfredo Valenzuela Puelma (1856-1909) and English-born Thomas Somerscales (1842-1927) extended the range of possible national subjects in the fields of landscape, portraiture, history and genre. The late 19th century saw a number of important commissions for nationalistic public statuary including the peasant soldier *El Roto Chileno* in Santiago's Plaza Yungay by Nicanor Plaza's pupil Virginio Arias (1855-1941), and several monumental works by Rebecca Matte (1875-1929).

The 20th century
From the later 19th century until well into the 20th century, Chilean painting was dominated by refracted versions of Impressionism. Artists such as **Juan Francisco González** (1853-1933) and **Alfredo Helsby** (1862-1933) introduced a looser technique and more luminous palette to create landscapes full of strong contrasts of sunlight and shadows, a tradition continued by, for example, **Pablo Burchard** (1873-1964), **Agustín Abarca** (1882-1953), **Arturo Gordon** (1883-1944) and **Camilo Mori** (1896-1973).

The Chilean avant garde has been dominated by artists who have lived and worked for long periods abroad, many as political exiles. After studying with Le Corbusier in Switzerland and encountering the Surrealists in Paris, **Roberto Matta** (1911-2002) moved to New York in 1939 and began painting uniquely unsettling space-age monsters and machines that circulate in a multi-dimensional chaos; he is perhaps the most famous artist to have come from Chile. **Nemesio Antúnez** (1918-1993) developed more earth-bound abstractions of reality: volcanic landscapes viewed through flames and falling rocks, or milling crowds, faceless and powerless.

Eugenio Dittborn (born 1943) sends 'Airmail Paintings' around the world in an exploration of ideas of transition and dislocation and, because many contain photographs of victims of political violence, of anonymity and loss. **Alfredo Jaar** (born 1956) creates installations using maps and photographs to document the destructive exploitation of the world's resources, both human and natural, including the aftermath of the Rwandan genocide.

Art today
In recent years many exiles have returned home and Santiago is now a cultural centre of growing importance, with women particularly well represented (for example **Carmen Valbuena** (born 1955), and **Bernarda Zegers** (born 1951). Chile is the home of an interesting ongoing project called '**Cuerpos Pintados**' (Painted Bodies), whereby artists from Chile and other Latin American countries are invited to Santiago to paint nude models in the colours and designs of their choice. It is worth watching out for exhibitions of the stunning photographs that are the project's permanent outcome; and also for one-off exhibitions up and down the country of the many very talented local artists (especially in cultural centres such as Valparaíso and Concepción).

Literature

From colonial times to Independence

The long struggle of the Spaniards to conquer the lands south of their Peruvian stronghold inspired one of the great epics of early Spanish American literature, *La Araucana* by **Alonso de Ercilla y Zúñiga** (1533-1594). Published in three parts (1569, 1578 and 1589), the poem tells of the victories and defeats of the Spaniards. Nothing like an apologia, the work endures because it recognizes the brutal actions of the Spaniards. Like a subsequent work, *Arauco domado* (1596), by the *criollo* **Pedro de Oña** (1570-1643), the point of view is that of the conquering invader, not a celebration of Chilean, or American identity, although Ercilla does show that the people who resisted the Spaniards were noble and courageous. After Ercilla, literature written in what was to become Chile concentrated on chronicling either the physical or the spiritual conquest of the local inhabitants.

Writers in the 18th and early 19th centuries tended to mirror the colonial desire to consolidate the territory that was in Spanish, rather than Mapuche hands. Post-Independence, the move was towards the establishment of the new republic. To this end, the Venezuelan **Andrés Bello** (1781-1865) was invited to Santiago from London in 1829 to oversee the education of the new elite. Already famous for his literary journals and strong views on Romantic poetry, Bello made major contributions to Chilean scholarship and law. His main work was *Gramática de la lengua castellana destinada al uso de los americanos* (1847). As Jean Franco says, "He was one of the first of many writers to see that a general literary Spanish could act as an important cohesive factor, a spiritual tie of the Hispanic peoples".

A cultural haven

Chile's relative political stability in the 19th century helped Santiago to become a cultural centre that attracted many foreign intellectuals, such as the Argentine Diego Sarmiento and the Nicaraguan Rubén Darío. At this time, Chilean writers were establishing a national literary framework to replace the texts of the colonial era. This involved the spreading of *buenas costumbres*, a movement to shift literary subject matter onto Chilean territory, a republican education for the middle classes and the founding of a national identity. Realist fiction captured the public interest. **José Victorino Lastarria** (1817-1888) wrote *costumbrista* stories, portraying national scenes and characters, while **Alberto Blest Gana** (1829-1904) enjoyed two periods of success as a novelist, heavily influenced by Balzac. His most popular novel was *Martín Rivas* (1862), the love story of a young man who wins a wife of a higher class. For some, Blest Gana's presentation of Santiago and its class structure is a worthy imitator of the French *comédie humaine*; for others, his realism fails either to unite his themes to his sketches of Chilean life or to rise above a pedestrian style.

Twentieth-century prose writing

Realism remained the dominant mode of fiction until well into the 20th century, but it appeared in several guises. **Baldomero Lillo** (1867-1923) wrote socialist realist stories about the coal miners of Lebu: *Sub terra* (1904) and *Sub sole* (1907). Lillo and other regionalist writers shifted the emphasis away from the city to the countryside and the miserable conditions endured by many Chileans. Other novelists, including **Luis Orrego Luco** (1866-1948) and **Joaquín Edwards Bello** (1887-1968), concentrated on the crisis of aristocratic values and the gulf between the wealthy and the deprived.

Another strand was *criollismo*, a movement seeking to portray Chile and the tribulations of Chileans without romanticism, championed especially by short story writers like **Mariano Latorre** (1886-1955). His main interest was the Chilean landscape, which he described almost to the point of overwhelming his characters. A different emphasis was given to regionalism and *criollismo* by **Augusto d'Halmar** (Augusto Goeminne Thomson, 1882-1950), whose stories in *La lámpara en el molino* (1914) were given exotic settings and were labelled *imaginismo*. D'Halmar's followers, the Grupo Letras (1920s and 1930s), became openly antagonistic towards the disciples of Latorre: **Luis Durand** wrote books in the 1920s and 1940s that described *campesino* life in detail. Another branch of realism was the exploration of character through psychology in the books of **Eduardo Barrios** (1884-1963), such as *El niño que enloqueció de amor* (1915), *El hermano asno* (1922) and *Los hombres del hombre* (1950).

The anti-fascist views of a group of writers known as the Generation of 1938 (**Nicomedes Guzmán**, 1914-1965, **Juan Godoy**, **Carlos Droguett**, born 1915, and others) added a politically committed dimension, which coincided with the rise to power of the Frente Popular, a Socialist movement. At the same time, *Mandrágora*, a journal principally dedicated to poetry, introduced many European literary ideas, notably those of the surrealists. Its influence, combined with a global decline in Marxist writing after the Second World War and the defeat of the Frente Popular, contributed to the rise of a new generation of writers in the 1950s, whose main motivation was the rejection of all the *'ismos'* that had preceded it. These novelists, short story writers and dramatists were characterized by existential individualism and political and social scepticism. Many writers started publishing in the 1950s; among them was **Volodia Teitelboim** (1916-2008), a communist exiled to the USSR after 1973, whose novels *Hijo del salitre* (1952) and *La semilla en la arena* (1957) were portrayals of the struggles of the Chilean masses. In 1979 he published *La guerra interna*, which combined real and imaginary characters in a vision of post-coup Chile.

From the 1920s on, a significant development away from *criollismo* was the rise of the female voice. The first such novelist to achieve major recognition was **Marta Brunet** (1901-1967), who brought a unique perspective to the rural themes she handled (including the need to value women), but who has also been described as a writer of the senses (by Nicomedes Guzmán). Her books include *Montaña adentro* (1923), *Aguas abajo* (1943), *Humo hacia el sur* (1946) and *María Nadie* (1957). Of the same generation, **María Flora Yáñez** (1898-1982) wrote about the alienation of women with great emphasis on the imagination as an escape for her female protagonists from their routine, unfulfilled lives (*El abrazo de la tierra*, 1934; *Espejo sin imágen*, 1936; *Las cenizas*, 1942). **María Luisa Bombal** (1910-1980) took the theme of alienated women even further (*La última niebla*, 1935; *La amortajada*, 1938, and various short stories): her narrative and her characters' worlds spring from the subconscious realm of female experience and are expressed through dreams, fantasies and journeys loaded with symbolic meaning.

Manuel Rojas (1896-1972) was brought up in Argentina, but his family moved to Chile in 1923. His first short stories, such as *Hombres del sur* (1926), *Travesía* (1934) and the novel *Lanchas en la bahía* (1932) were undoubtedly *criollista* in outlook, but he devoted a greater importance to human concerns than his *criollista* contemporaries. By 1951, Rojas' style had changed dramatically, without deserting realism. *Hijo de ladrón* (1951) was perhaps the most influential 20th-century Chilean novel up to that time. It describes the adventures of Aniceto Hevía, the son of a Buenos Aires jewel thief, who crosses the Andes to Valparaíso, ending up as a beachcomber. Nothing in his life is planned or motivated by anything other than the basic necessities. Happiness and intimacy are only brief moments in an unharmonious, disordered life. Aniceto's adventures are continued in *Mejor que el vino* (1958), *Sombras contra el muro* (1963) and *La obscura vida radiante* (1971). To describe the essential isolation of man from the inside, Rojas relaxes the temporal structure of the novel, bringing in memory, interior monologue and techniques to multiply the levels of reality (to use Fernando Alegría's phrase).

The demise of *criollismo* coincided with the influence of the US Beat Generation and the culture epitomized by James Dean, followed in the 1960s by the protest movements in favour of peace, and black and women's rights. The Cuban Revolution inspired Latin American intellectuals of the left and the novel-writing 'boom' gained momentum. At the same time, the national political process that led ultimately to Salvador Allende's victory in 1970 was bolstered by writers, folk singers and painters who questioned everything to do with the Chilean bourgeoisie.

José Donoso (1924-1996) began publishing stories in 1955 (*Veraneo y otros cuentos*), followed two years later by his first novel, *Coronación*. This book describes the chaos caused by the arrival of a new maid into an aristocratic Santiago household and introduces many of Donoso's recurring themes: the closed worlds of old age and childhood, madness, multiple levels of reality, the inauthenticity of the upper classes and the subversion of patriarchal society. The stories in *Charleston* (1960), *El lugar sin límites* (1966), about a transvestite and his daughter who live in a brothel near Talca, and *Este domingo* (1966) mark the progression from *Coronación* to *El obsceno pájaro de la noche* (1970), a labyrinthine novel (Donoso's own term) narrated by a schizophrenic, throwing together reality, dreams and fantasy, darkness and light. Donoso achieved the same status as Gabriel García Márquez, Julio Cortázar and Mario Vargas Llosa with this, his most experimental novel. Between 1967 and 1981 he lived in Spain; in the 1970s he published several novels, including *Casa de campo* (1978), which relates the disintegration of a family estate when the children try to take it over. Back in Chile, he published, among others, *El jardín de al lado* (1981), which chronicles the decline of a middle-aged couple in exile in Spain, *Cuatro para Delfina* (1982), *La desesperanza* (1986) about the return of a left-wing singer from Paris to the daily horrors of Pinochet's regime.

Another writer who describes the bad faith of the aristocracy is **Jorge Edwards** (born 1931). His books include *El patio* (1952), *Los convidados de piedra* (1978), *El museo de cera* (1980), *La mujer imaginaria* (1985) and *Fantasmas de carne y hueso* (1993). His book *Persona non grata* (1973) describes his experiences as a diplomat, including his expulsion from Cuba. His most recent novels include El inútil de la familia (2004) and La casa de Dostoievski (2008).

Fernando Alegría (1918-2005) spanned all the movements since 1938, with a variety of work including essays, highly respected literary criticism, poetry and novels. He was closely associated with Salvador Allende and was his cultural attaché in Washington 1970-1973. *Recabarren* was published in 1938, after which followed many books, among them *Lautaro, joven libertador del Arauco* (1943), *Caballo de copas* (1957), *Mañana los guerreros* (1964), *El paso de los gansos* (1975), about a young photographer's experiences in the 1973 coup, *Coral de guerra* (1979), also about brutality under military dictatorship, *Una especie de memoria* (1983), Alegría's own memoir of 1938 to 1973, and *Allende: A Novel* (1992). Having been so close to Allende, Alegría could not write a biography, he had to fictionalize it, he said. But the rise and fall of Allende becomes a realization that history and fiction are intimately related, particularly in that Chilean epoch.

Ariel Dorfman

As expressed in the subtitle of his memoir, *Heading South, Looking North* (1998), the literary and political career of Ariel Dorfman has taken the form of a 'bilingual journey', between the United States and South America, between English and Spanish. Born in Buenos Aires in 1942, as the son of Russian Jewish immigrants, Dorfman and his family were expelled from Argentina in the mid-1940s due to his father's political activism. They took up residence in New York, until McCarthyism sent the Dorfmans once more south in 1954, this time to Chile. Here, the monolingual, English-speaking adolescent gradually focused his attention on the Spanish language and on Chilean politics and culture, until the military coup of 1973 drove Dorfman once again into exile, where he became one of the most articulate, bilingual voices against the military regime.

Since the return to civilian government in 1990, Dorfman has divided his time between Santiago and a professional post at Duke University, writing and broadcasting in both Spanish and English. Dorfman's work, as a poet, novelist, short story writer, essayist, playwright and more recently scriptwriter, is concerned, in his words, with, "on the one hand, the glorious potential and need of human beings to tell stories and, on the other, the brutal fact that in today's world, most of the lives that should be telling those stories are generally ignored, ravaged and silenced". He is perhaps best known for his early critique of US cultural imperialism, *How to Read Donald Duck* (1971) and for *Death and the Maiden* (1990), later filmed by Roman Polanski, which deals with torture and resistance.

He often adapts his own work to different genres: *Widows* started as a poem, became a novel and later a play. Much of the work focuses on torture, disappearance, censorship and the exile condition, but also demonstrates staunch rebellion and resistance and optimism for our future. For further details, see page 542.

Writers in exile

The death of Salvador Allende in 1973, and with it the collapse of the left's struggle to gain power by democratic means, was a traumatic event for Chilean writers. Those who had built their careers in the 1960s and early 1970s were for the most part exiled, forcibly or voluntarily, and thus were condemned to face the left's own responsibility in Allende's failure. René Jara says that before 1970 writers had not managed to achieve mass communication for their ideas and 1970-1973 was too short a time to correct that. Once Pinochet was in power, the task became how to find a language capable of expressing the usurping of democracy without simplifying reality. Those in exile still felt part of Chile, a country temporarily wiped from the map, where their thought was prohibited.

There are many contemporary novelists who deserve mention: **Antonio Skármeta** (born 1940) was exiled in Germany until 1980, writing short stories and novels and directing theatre and film. His short-story collections include *El entusiasmo* (1967), *Desnudo en el tejado* (1969), *Tiro libre* (1973) and his novels *Soñé que la nieve ardía* (975), *No pasó nada* (1980), *Ardiente paciencia* (1985) and *Match-ball* (1989). *Ardiente paciencia*, retitled *El cartero de Neruda* after its successful filming as *Il postino*, is a good example of Skármeta's concern for the enthusiasms and emotions of ordinary people, skilfully weaving the love life of a postman and a bar owner's daughter into the much bigger picture of the death of Pablo Neruda and the fall of Allende.

A different take entirely on the legacy of Neruda and Chilean letters in general is provided by **Roberto Bolaño** (1950-2003) – also an exile – whose satirical novel *Nocturno de Chile* (2000 – English translation, *By Night in Chile*) provides both an understanding of the fate of the Chilean literary world under Pinochet and of the nature of that world itself. Bolaño's family moved to Mexico when he was 15, but he returned to Chile briefly at the time of the Pinochet coup. He escaped back to Mexico and then spent the later part of his life in Europe. Besides Nocturno de Chile, he is best known for Los Detectives Salvajes (The Savage Detectives, 1998), and the posthumous 2666 (2004).

Another famous Chilean exile is **Ariel Dorfman** (1942-), who divides his time between Chile and the USA and whose work exemplifies the struggle of the exile to find a bridge between his social reality overseas and his Chilean identity. His prolific output includes the novels *Moros en la costa*, 1973 (Hard Rain), *La última canción de Manuel Sendero*, 1982 (The Last Song of Manuel Sendero), *Mascara*, 1988, *Viudas*, 1981 (Widows), *Konfidenz*, 1995, La nana y el iceberg (*The Nanny and the Iceberg*), 1999; the plays *Death and the Maiden, Reader* (1995), *Widows* (1997); two further dramas co-written with his son Rodrigo; a number of works with another son, Joaquín; several volumes of essays and memoirs and many poems (some collected in English as *Last Waltz in Santiago and other poems of Exile and Disappearance* (1988). He has also written extensively about Pinochet. Most of Dorfman's work is currently in print in English.

One of the most successful Chilean novelists today is **Isabel Allende** (born 1942). Her book *La casa de los espíritus* (1982) was a phenomenally successful novel worldwide. Allende, a niece of Salvador Allende, was born in Peru and went into exile in Venezuela after the 1973 coup. *The House of the Spirits*, with its tale of the dynasty of Esteban Trueba interwoven with Chilean history throughout much of the 20th century, ends with a thinly disguised description of 1973. It was followed in 1984 by *De amor y de sombra*, a disturbing tale set during the Pinochet regime. The main motivation behind these novels is the necessity to preserve historical reality (see the brief prologue to *Of Love and Shadows*, "Here, write it, or it will be erased by the wind"). The same thing applies in *Paula* (1994), Allende's letter to her daughter in a coma, where possible salvation from the devastation of not being able to contact Paula comes through the "meticulous exercise of writing". She has also written *Eva Luna* (1987) and *Los cuentos de Eva Luna* (1990), about a fictional Venezuelan storyteller and her stories, *El plan infinito* (1991), *Daughter of Fortune* (1998), *Portrait in Sepia* (2002), and *Mi país inventado* (2002), a look at Chile and her people. Her memoir, *La suma de los días* (*The Sum of Our Days*) was published in 2008, followed by three more novels: *La isla bajo el mar* (*The Island beneath the Sea*, 2010), *El cuaderno de Maya* (*Maya's Notebook*, 2011) and *El juego de Ripper* (*Ripper*, 2014).

Like her predecessors, Allende employs the marvellous and the imaginary to propose alternatives to the masculine view of social and sexual relations. The same is true of **Lucía Guerra** (born 1942), who published *Más allá de las máscaras* in exile in 1984. Another example might be **Daniela Eltit** (born 1949), who did not leave Chile after 1973 and was actively involved in resistance movements. Her provocative, intense fiction confronts issues of exploitation, violence, the oppression of women and volatile mental states. In *Vaca sagrada* (1991) at least, the protagonist's vulnerability is expressed through her body, by her blood, her two lovers' effects upon it, the brutality inflicted upon it and her obsession with her heartbeat. The main characters live out their obsessions and fears in a city in which there are no jobs and no warmth. All her novels, from *Lumpérica* (1983) to Fuerzas especiales (2013) maintain the same experimental, challenging approach to contemporary Chilean society and reflect her work as a performance artist and her political engagement.

Pablo Neruda

Pablo Neruda was born in Parral on 12 June 1904 as Ricardo Neftalí Reyes. Two months later, his mother died and his father and stepmother subsequently moved the family to Temuco. Neruda's childhood memories were dominated by nature and, above all, rain, "my only unforgettable companion", as he described it in *Confieso que he vivido*. Among his teachers in Temuco was Gabriela Mistral. In 1921, he went to study in Santiago, but he had already decided on a literary career. His first book of poems *Crepusculario* (1923), was published under the pseudonym Neruda, borrowed from a Czech writer; it was postmodernist in style but did not yet reveal the poet's own voice. His next volume, *Veinte poemas de amor y una canción desesperada* (1924) catapulted him into the forefront of Latin American poetry. The freedom of the style and the natural, elemental imagery invoking the poet's two love affairs, made the collection an immediate success. Three books followed in 1926 before Neruda was sent to Rangoon as Chilean consul in 1927. His experiences in the Orient, including his first marriage, inspired one of his finest collections, *Residencia en la tierra*, in which the inherent sadness of the *Veinte poemas* becomes despair at the passing of time and human frailty. Reinforcing this theme is a kaleidoscope of images, seemingly jumbled together, yet deliberately placed to show the chaos and fragmentary nature of life.

In the 1930s, Neruda moved to Spain, where he met many poets. The Civil War, especially the death of Federico García Lorca, affected him deeply and his poetic vision became more direct, with a strong political orientation. 'Explico algunas cosas' in *Tercera residencia* (1947) explains the move towards militancy.

Between 1938 and the election of Videla to the Chilean presidency, Neruda worked with the Frente Popular and was consul general in Mexico. He also composed his epic poem of Latin American and Chilean history, from a Marxist stance, *Canto general* (1950). Its 15 cantos chronicle the natural and human life of the Americas, from the conquered pre-Columbian inhabitants to the 20th-century labourers. One of its most famous sections is 'Alturas de Machu Picchu', which mirrors the poet's own development: from the universal to 'minuscule life' from introspection to a new-found role as the voice of the oppressed. Canto general defined Neruda's subsequent enormous output.

The political commitment remained but did not submerge his respect for and evocation of nature in *Odas elementales* (1954), *Nuevas odas elementales* (1957) and *Tercer libro de odas* (1959), which begins with 'El hombre invisible'. He also never tired of writing lyric verse, such as *Los versos del capitán* (1950), *Cien sonetos de amor* (1959), and wrote memoirs such as *Memorial de Isla Negra* (1964) and *Confieso que he vivido* (1974). *Extravagaria* (1958), whose title suggests extravagance, wandering and variety, is full of memory, acceptance and a world-weary joy.

Neruda was awarded the Nobel Prize in 1971 but died of cancer two years' later. His death was hastened by the coup and the military's heartless removal of him from Isla Negra to Santiago. The poet's three houses were either ransacked or shut up by the dictatorship, but many of the Chileans for whom the poet spoke visited Isla Negra to leave messages of respect, love and hope until democracy returned. See Ariel Dorfman's 'Afterword' in *The House in the Sand*, translated by Dennis Maloney and Clark Zlotchew, 1990, Milkweed).

Other popular writers include **Robert Ampuero** (1953-), several of whose books concern the detective Cayetano Brulé. During the 1970s and '80s he was exiled in Cuba, East and West Germany and, after a time in Chile, now lives in Sweden. *Los amantes de Estocolmo* (*The Swedish Lovers*, 2003), achieved great success. Another popular novelist and poet is **Hernán Rivera Letelier** (1950-) from Antofagasta. His prize-winning novel *El arte de la resurrección* (*The Art of Resurrection*, 2010) is set in the nitrate-mining zone of the northern desert in the 1940s.

Poetry from 1900 to today

In many ways, poetry is the lifeblood of Chilean culture; the country's poetic output is prodigious, with poetry circles thriving even in remote rural areas. In the first half of the 20th century, four figures dominated Chilean poetry, Gabriela Mistral, Vicente Huidobro, Pablo Neruda and Pablo de Rokha. The three men were all socialists, but their politics and means of expression followed different trajectories. Neruda overshadows all other Chilean poets on an international level, and for this reason he is discussed separately, see box, page 525.

Gabriela Mistral (1889-1957) wrote poetry that rejected elaboration in favour of a simple style using traditional metre and verse forms. Her poetry derives from a limited number of personal roots: she fell in love with Romelio Ureta who blew his brains out in 1909. This inspired the *Sonetos de la muerte* (1914), which were not published at the time. She never lost the grief of this tragic love, which was coupled with her love of God and her "immense martyrdom at not being a mother". Frustrated motherhood did not deprive her of tenderness, nor of a deep love for children. The other main theme was her appreciation of nature and landscape, not just in Chile, but also in North and South America and Europe, which she visited as a diplomat. Her three principal collections are *Desolación* (1923, but re-edited and amplified frequently), *Tala* (1938) and *Lagar* (1954). She also wrote many poems for children.

If Gabriela Mistral relied on tradition and verse to present her unique view of a lone woman trying to find a place in a male-oriented world, **Vicente Huidobro** (1893-1948) wanted to break with all certainties. He made grand claims for the poet's role as nothing short of a quest for the infinite and for the language to liberate it. From Santiago he moved to Buenos Aires, then Paris, where he joined the Cubists, collaborated with Apollinaire and others, began to write in French and got involved in radical politics. Between the 1920s and 1940s he moved from Europe to the USA to Chile, back to Spain during the Civil War, before retiring to Llolleo to confront time and death in his last poems, *Ultimos poemas*, 1948. Huidobro considered himself at the forefront of the avant garde, formulating *creacionismo*, a theory that the poet is not bound by the real world, but is free to create and invent new worlds through the complete freedom of the word. Nevertheless, all the experimentation and imagery which "unglued the moon", was insufficient to achieve the language of revelation. So in 1931 he composed *Altazor*, a seven-canto poem that describes simultaneously the poet's route to creation and the ultimate frustration imposed by time and the human condition.

Pablo de Rokha (Carlos Díaz Loyola, 1894-1968) was deeply concerned for the destiny of the Chilean people and the advance of international socialism. His output was an uncompromising epic search for Chilean identity and through his work, for all its political commitment, there runs a deep sense of tragedy and inner solitude (especially true in *Fuego negro*, 1951, written after the death of his wife). *Los gemidos* was his first major book (1922); others included *Escritura de Raimundo Contreras* (1929), a song of the Chilean peasant, *Jesucristo* (1933) and *La morfología del espanto* (1942).

Violeta Parra

Violeta Parra was brought up in Chillán as one of 11 children. Her father, Nicanor, was a music teacher, while her mother, Clarisa, was a seamstress who played the guitar and sang. Violeta sang with her sister Hilda in Santiago bars for several years. She also worked in the circus. Another child, Nicanor, became a professor of maths and physics, and a poet (see below).

Violeta travelled the length of Chile and abroad with the Chilean poet Pablo de Rokha (see page 526), collecting material and promoting their idea of Chilean-ness. While de Rokha expressed himself in the lyrical epic, Violeta sang, wrote songs, made tapestries, ceramics, paintings and sculpture. All her work was based on a philosophy of helping those in need. In France she was recognized as a great artist and her works were exhibited in the Louvre in 1964, but at home recognition was only grudgingly given.

In the 1960s Violeta set up La Carpa de la Reina as a centre for popular art in the capital. It was here, in February 1967, that she committed suicide, her head resting on her guitar. The national grief at her funeral far outweighed the acclaim given her during her life. Neruda called her 'Santa Violeta'; the Peruvian novelist Jose María Arguedas described her as 'the most Chilean of all Chileans I could possibly know, but at the same time the most universal of all Chile'.

For Violeta, folklore was a form of class struggle. Her influence on a whole generation of Latin American folk singers was enormous and long-lasting. Without her, Salvador Allende would not have had the folkloric backing of Víctor Jara, Inti-Illimani, Los Quilapayún and the Parras themselves. After Violeta's death, her brother Nicanor published *Décimas*, a sort of autobiography in verse, full of simple humanity.

Although these poets, and Neruda especially, furthered the Chilean poetic tradition, those who came after were not necessarily keen to emulate his style or his politics. From the 1950s, poets were still critical of society but, taking their cue from **Nicanor Parra** (born 1914), they did not elevate the writer's role in denouncing inhumanity, alienation and the depersonalization of modern life. Instead writer and reader are placed on the same level; rhetoric and exuberant language are replaced by a conversational, ironic tone. **Parra** (see also box, above), a scientist and teacher, called this attempt to overcome the influence of Neruda *antipoesía* (anti-poetry). In the poem '*Advertencia al lector*' in *Poemas y antipoemas* (1954), he writes:

According to the doctors of the law this book should not be published:
The word rainbow does not appear in it,
Let alone the word grief,
Chairs and tables, yes, there are aplenty,
Coffins! Writing utensils!
Which fills me with pride
Because, as I see it, the sky is falling to bits.

Obra gruesa anthologizes his work to 1969, followed by *Emergency Poems* (1972, bilingual edition, New York), which contain a darker humour and satire, but remain compassionate and socially committed, *Artefactos* (1972) and *Artefactos II* (1982), *Sermones y prédicas del Cristo de Elqui* (1979) and *Poesía política* (1983).

The adherents of *antipoesía* continually sought new means of expression, so that the genre never became institutionalized. There are too many poets to list here, but **Gonzalo Rojas** (1917-2011), **Enrique Lihn** (1929-1988), **Armando Uribe** (born 1933) and **Miguel Arteche** (born 1926) are perhaps the best known.

Another poetic development of the 1950s onwards was *poesía lárica*, or *de lares*, poetry of one's place of origin (literally, of the gods of the hearth). Its founder and promoter was **Jorge Teillier** (1935-1996), whose poems describe a precarious rural existence, wooden houses, fencing, orchards, distant fires, beneath changing skies and rain. The city dweller is an exile in space and time who returns every so often to the place of origin. See especially *'Notas sobre el último viaje del autor a su pueblo natal'*, which evokes the lost frontier of his youth, the changed countryside and his city life. As for the future, "if only it could be as beautiful as my mother spreading the sheets on my bed", but it is only an unpaid bill; "I wish the UFOs would arrive." In his later poems, the violence of the city and the dictatorship invade the *lares*. Among Teillier's books are *Para angeles y gorriones* (1956), *Para un pueblo fantasma* (1978), *Cartas para reinas de otras primaveras* (1985) and *Los dominios perdidos* (1992). A variation on this type of poetry comes from **Clemente Riedemann** (born 1953), whose *Karra Maw'n* deals with the Mapuche lands and German immigration in the area.

Many poets left Chile after 1973 but others stayed to attack the dictatorship from within through provocative, experimental works. In a country with such a strong poetic tradition and such a serious political situation, poets understood that their verses had to mutate in order to reflect and comment on their contemporary realities. A more experimental and opaque poetry developed as a result, dealing with themes such as the reaffirmation of colloquialism, the city (developed through the slang of *antipoesía*), and poetry itself, unravelling contexts and bridging the past and the present. Several writers were members of the Grupo Experimental de Artaud, including Daniela Eltit (see above), Eugenia Brito, Rodrigo Cánovas and **Raúl Zurita**, perhaps the most celebrated poet in Chile today: his verse is a complex and at times difficult union of mathematics and poetry, logical, structured and psychological. *Purgatorio* (1979) had an immediate impact and was followed by *Anteparaíso* (1982), *El paraíso está vacío* (1984), *Canto a su amor desaparecido* (1986) and *El amor de Chile* (1987). 'Pastoral de Chile' in *Anteparaíso* reveals most of Zurita's obsessions: Chilean landscapes, love, Chile's distress, sin and religious terminology.

Other significant poetic works of the 1980s include *La Tirana* (1985) by **Diego Maquieira**, a complex, multireferential work, dealing with a Mapuche virgin, surrounded by a culture that oppresses her and with which she disguises herself. It is irreverent; a 'black mass', threatening to the régime. Carmen Berenguer's *Bobby Sands desfallece en el muro* (1983) is a homage to the IRA prisoner and thus to all political prisoners. She also wrote *Huellas del siglo* (1986) and *A media asta* (1988). Carla Grandi published *Contraproyecto* in 1985, an example of feminine resistance to the coup.

Poetry continues to be significant in Chile. There are numerous workshops and organizations for young poets; the *Taller de Poesía de la Fundación Pablo Neruda* (www.fundacionneruda.org) is particularly influential. There are also important underground literary movements. Interesting contemporary poets include **Carolina Cerlis** and **Javier del Cerro**, both maintaining the experimental and free verse tradition of Zurita and others.

Not many months after the first screening organized by the Lumière brothers in Paris in December 1895, moving pictures were exhibited in Chile on 25 August 1896. Initially all the films were imported, but from 1902 local artists and entrepreneurs began to produce short documentaries. The first narrative movie, *Manuel Rodríguez*, was screened in September 1910. From about 1915, with European production semi-paralyzed by war, the pre-eminence of Hollywood cinema was established. The modern dreams of Hollywood were often more complex, technologically superior and more entertaining than the products of rudimentary national cinemas. The historian of Chilean silent films, Eliana Jara Donoso, quotes a publicity handout for a local movie that read, "it's so good that it doesn't seem Chilean".

But despite the overwhelming presence of Hollywood, local film-makers in the silent era could still establish a small presence in the market. In the main they made documentaries, for this was a niche free of international competition: regional topics, football competitions, civic ceremonies, military parades. Almost 100 feature films were also made, but these are the domain of the film historian, since only one such movie has survived (carefully restored by the University of Chile in the early 1960s): *El húsar de la muerte* (The Hussar of Death), directed by Pedro Sienna in 1925. It was, like many movies in Latin America at the time, a historical melodrama, exploring the fight for Chilean independence from Spanish rule in the 1810s through the heroic exploits of the legendary Manuel Rodríguez. It achieved great box office success in a year when 16 Chilean films were screened. Never again would so many national movies be produced annually.

The coming of synchronized sound created a new situation in Latin America. In those countries with a large domestic market – in particular Mexico, Argentina and Brazil – investment was made in expensive machinery, installations and rudimentary studios. Elsewhere, and Chile is a telling example, sound devastated local production due to its cost and complexity. Local entrepreneurs were usually unwilling to make the risky capital investment, and the history of Chilean cinema thereafter is littered with tales of self-sacrifice on the part of cast and crew. The first non-silent film made in Chile was *Norte y Sur*, directed by **Jorge Délano** in 1934, telling the story of a love triangle where a woman is the object of the attentions of a Chilean and an American engineer. It was a rare example of sophisticated cinema at a time when Chilean film output was reverting to often formulaic stories of young men seducing innocent ladies, or the naïve idealization of rural landscapes. Délano stood out in this age – another film of his, *Escándalo* (1940) dealt with the lives of the middle class, rather than those of the aristocracy or the peasantry. Nevertheless, Tobías Barros, an important director of the time, summed up the mood when he sarcastically described his *Río Abajo* as a film "where there are neither illegitimate nor lost children".

An attempt was made in the 1940s to stimulate cinema through state investment. The state agency CORFO saw cinema as an important growth industry and in 1942 gave 50% finance to set up **Chile Films**. Costly studios were erected, but the plan proved over-ambitious and Argentine film-makers ended up using most of the facilities; by 1947 Chile Films had collapsed. In 1959, however, the Universidad de Chile set up a Centre for Experimental Cinema under the direction of a documentary film-maker Sergio Bravo, which trained aspirant directors from Chile and elsewhere in Latin America (notably the Bolivian Jorge Sanjinés).

Cinema became intricately involved in the wider political discussions of the 1960s. The years 1968-1969 saw the maturity of Chilean cinema. Five features came out: **Raúl Ruiz**'s

Tres tristes tigres (Three Sad Tigers); Helvio Soto's *Caliche sangriento* (Bloody Nitrate); Aldo Francia's *Valparaíso mi amor* (Valparaíso My Love); Miguel Littín's *El chacal de Nahueltoro* (The Jackal of Nahueltoro) and Carlos Elsesser's *Los testigos* (The Witnesses). These film-makers came from different ideological and aesthetic tendencies, from the inventive maverick Raúl Ruiz to the sombre neo-realism of Francia, but they can be seen as a group, working with very scarce resources: the films by Ruiz, Elsesser, Francia and Littín were made, consecutively, with the same camera; furthermore, many of the directors sought to break down the traditionally melodramatic themes of Chilean cinema, employing more realistic language and situations more reflective of everyday social problems. Aldo Francia, a doctor by profession, also organized a famous 'Meeting of Latin American Film-makers' at the Viña del Mar film festival in 1967. This would be one of the key events to cause growing awareness of cineastes across the continent that they were working with similar ideas and methods, producing 'new cinemas'.

The narrow victory of the Popular Unity parties in the election of 1970 was greeted by film-makers with an enthusiastic manifesto penned by **Miguel Littín**; Littín himself was put in charge of the revived state institution Chile Films. He lasted for only 10 months, tiring of bureaucratic opposition and inter-party feuding, as the different members of Popular Unity all demanded a share of very limited resources. Few films were made between 1970 and 1973; Raúl Ruiz was the most productive film-maker of the period, with a number of films in different styles. Littín was working on an historical feature *La tierra prometida* (The Promised Land) when the 1973 coup occurred and post-production took place in Paris.

The most ambitious film to trace the radicalization of Chile in 1972 and 1973 was Patricio Guzmán's three-part documentary *La batalla de Chile* (The Battle of Chile), which was edited in exile in Cuba. In the first years of exile, this film became Chile's most evocative testimony abroad and received worldwide distribution. Paradoxically, Chilean cinema, which had little time to grow under Popular Unity, strengthened in exile.

Policies following the coup practically destroyed internal film production for several years. Film personnel were arrested, tortured and imprisoned and many escaped into exile. Severe censorship was established: even *Fiddler on the Roof* was banned for displaying Marxist tendencies. It is from the exiled directors that the continuity of film culture can be seen. Littín took up residence in Mexico, supported by Mexican President, Echeverría, and became an explicit spokesman for political Latin American cinema, making the epic *Actas de Marusia* (Letters from Marusia) in 1975 and several other features in Mexico and later in Nicaragua. In the mid-1980s he returned clandestinely to Chile with several foreign film crews to make the documentary *Acta General de Chile* in 1986, a perilous mission documented by Gabriel García Márquez in his reportage *Clandestine in Chile* (1986). Raúl Ruiz took a less visible political role, but since his exile to France, he has produced a body of work that has earned him a reputation as one of the most innovative directors in Europe, the subject of a special issue in 1983 of France's distinguished journal *Cahiers du Cinéma*. He makes movies with great technical virtuosity and often great speed: on a visit to Santiago to celebrate the return to civilian rule in 1990, he shot a film, entitled *La telenovela errante* (The Wandering Soap Opera), in less than a week for US$30,000. Other exile directors to make their mark include Ruiz's wife Valeria Sarmiento, Gastón Ancelovici and Carmen Castillo, all based in France, Patricio Guzmán in Spain, Marilú Mallet in Canada, Angelina Vásquez in Scandinavia, Sebastián Alarcón in the Soviet Union and Antonio Skármeta in Germany.

Inside Chile, the output under censorship varied from maritime adventures such as *El Ultimo grumete* to Silvio Caiozzi's *Julio comienza en julio* (Julio begins in July, 1979), one of the first films made in the period, set carefully in a turn-of-the-century historical location and self-financed through Caiozzi's work in commercials. It would take him a further 10 years to produce a second feature, *La luna en el espejo* (The Moon in the Mirror), evocatively set in Valparaíso, which was screened in 1990. An example of increased critical debate within Chile in the last years of the Pinochet régime can be found in Pablo Perelman's *Imagen latente* (Latent Image, 1987) which tells of a photographer's search for a missing brother who disappeared after the coup; although the film was not released in Chile until 1990, it was possible to make the film in the country in the mid-1980s. Another case is that of *Hijos de la Guerra Fría* by Gonzalo Justiniano (1985), which is replete with metaphors of a society asphyxiated by a repressive system.

The return to civilian rule had some benefits for film-makers, most notably the easing of censorship. The Viña del Mar Film Festival was symbolically reinstated after 20 years and saw the emotional return of many exiled directors, but that, in itself, could not solve the problems of an intellectual community dispersed around the world and the chronic underfunding and under-representation of Chilean films in the home market. New names have emerged and some internationally successful films have been made, most notably Ricardo Larraín's *La Frontera* (The Frontier, 1991), one of the best Chilean films ever made, which tells of a school teacher's internal exile in the spectacular scenery of southern Chile in the late 1980s, which as Gustavo Graef-Marino's *Johnny Cien Pesos* (1993), which deals with violence in Chilean society. The latter was produced by Chile Films, a short-lived production company made up of film directors and producers financed by a State Bank credit loan. The loan was withdrawn, however, when other productions failed at the box office.

The last few years have seen the screening of one or two Chilean features a year, the best received being the political thriller *Amnesia* (1994), directed by Gonzalo Justiniano, Andrés Wood's vogue-ish *Historias de Futbol* (1997) and Sergio Castillo's 1997 *Gringuito*, which focuses on the problems of children brought up in exile, returning as foreigners to Chile. This gentle comedy of reintegration has been made to seem somewhat tame by the demonstrations in Chile surrounding the Pinochet extradition process. Larraín's latest feature *El entusiasmo* (Enthusiasms, 1999) did not live up to its title among local audiences but it garnered international recognition, as did Andrés Wood's new films, *Loco Fever,* an engaging comedy about two conmen's frenzied search for as many 'locos' – the shellfish, not the crazies – as possible; *Machuca,* a socio-political drama centred around the friendship of two boys, one rich and one poor, during the final doomed days of Allende's regime; and *Violeta se fue a los cielos*, a biopic about popular singer Violeta Parra, which won the World Cinema Jury Prize at the 2012 Sundance Film Festival. While there are many talented young film-makers, such as Nicolás Lopez and Alicia Scherson, and although government art grants are becoming more available, the increasing globalization of the culture industry, however, means that the pattern of scarce local production is likely to continue.

Music and dance

Traditional forms

As far as **traditional dance** goes, at the very heart of Chilean music is the *cueca*, a courting dance for couples, both of whom make great play with a handkerchief waved aloft in the right hand. The man's knees are slightly bent and his body arches back; in rural areas, he stamps his spurs together for effect. Guitar and harp are the accompanying instruments, while handclapping and shouts of encouragement add to the atmosphere. The dance has a common origin with the Argentine *zamba* and Peruvian *marinera* via the early 19th-century *zamacueca*, in turn descended from the Spanish *fandango*. The most traditional form of song is the *tonada*, with its variants the *glosa*, *parabienes*, *romance*, *villancico* (Christmas carol) and *esquinazo* (serenade), in common with the *custon* in Argentina, this may be heard in the form of a *contrapunto* or *controversia*, a musical duel. Among the most celebrated groups are **Los Huasos Quincheros**, Silvia Infante with **Los Condores** and the **Conjunto Millaray**, all of which are popular at rural dances, with their poignant combination of formal singing and rousing accordian music. Famous folk singers in this genre are the **Parra family** from Chillán (see box, page 527), **Hector Pávez** and **Margot Loyola**.

In the north of the country the music is Amerindian and closely related to that of Bolivia. Groups called 'Bailes' dance the *huayño*, *taquirari*, *cachimbo* or *rueda* at carnival and other festivities as well as pre-Columbian rites like the *cauzulor* and *talatur*. Instruments are largely wind and percussion, including *zampoñas* (pan pipes), *lichiguayos*, *pututos* (conch shells), *queñas* (flutes) and *clarines*. There are some notable religious festivals that attract large crowds of pilgrims and include numerous groups of costumed dancers. The most outstanding of these festivals are those of the **Virgen de La Tirana** near Iquique (see box, page 201), the **Virgen de la Candelaria** of Copiapó (see page 146) and the **Virgen de Andacollo** (see page 120).

In the south the Mapuche nation have their own songs, dance-songs and magic and collective dances, accompanied by wind instruments like the great long *trutruca* horn, the shorter *pifilka* and the *kultrún* drum. Further south still, Chiloé has its own unique musical expression: wakes and other religious social occasions include collective singing, while the recreational dances, all of Spanish origin – such as the *vals*, *pavo*, *pericona* and *nave* – have a heavier and less syncopated beat than in central Chile. Accompanying instruments here are the *rabel* (fiddle), guitar and accordion.

Nueva canción

The most famous Chilean movement on the international stage was that of the *nueva canción*, or new song, which arose in the late 1960s and early 1970s under such luminaries as **Violeta Parra** (see box, page 527) and **Víctor Jara**. This movement, which scorned commercialism and sought to give a political meaning to its songs – whether overt or suggested – gave a whole new dimension to the Chilean musical scene, and was part of a wider movement across the continent, involving people such as Mercedes Sosa in Argentina and Sílvio Rodríguez in Cuba.

Beginning as an underground movement, far away from the usual round of publicity and radio stations, the *Nueva Canción* protagonists rose to prominence during the 1970 election campaign, which resulted in the victory of Salvador Allende. Although related to folk rhythms, the movement sought to be dynamic and not confined to any particular style. Violeta Parra's suicide and the subsequent coup of 1973 forced its protagonists into exile – Inti Illimanni to Italy, Illapu to France. But Víctor Jara was imprisoned in the National Stadium after the coup and was hauled to his death, singing Violeta Parra's famous song, 'Gracias a la vida' (I give thanks to life).

Land and environment

Chile is smaller than all other South American republics except Ecuador, Paraguay, Uruguay and the Guianas. It is 4329 km long and, on average, no more than 180 km wide. In the north Chile has a short (150 km) east-west border with Peru. In the far north its eastern frontier is with Bolivia – 750 km long – but from San Pedro de Atacama south to Tierra del Fuego it shares over 3500 km of border with Argentina. In the main this frontier follows the water margin of the Andes but, in the far south, where the Andes are lower, or where icefields cover the border area, there have been frequent frontier disputes with Argentina; these still rumble on. Chilean sovereignty over the islands south of Tierra del Fuego gives it control over Isla Navarino, on which Puerto Williams is the most southerly permanent settlement in the world (apart from scientific bases in Antarctica). Various island archipelagos in the Pacific, including Easter Island/Rapa Nui and the Juan Fernández group, are under Chilean jurisdiction.

Geology

The Quaternary Period, 1.6 million years ago, was marked by the advance and retreat of the Antarctic Ice Sheet which, at its maximum extent, covered all of the Chilean Andes and the entire coastline south of Puerto Montt. However, although there are surface remnants of older rock formations, most have disappeared with the dramatic creation of the Andes, which started around 80 million years ago and continues to this day. The South American Plate, moving westwards, meets the Nazca and Antarctic plates, which are moving eastwards and sinking below the continent. These two plates run more or less parallel between 26°S and 33°S and the friction between them creates a geologically unstable zone, marked by frequent earthquakes and volcanic activity. The area of Concepción has been particularly susceptible to both land and undersea quakes and the city was twice destroyed by tidal waves in the 18th century before being moved to its present site.

All of the Chilean Pacific islands were formed by underwater volcanoes associated with fracture zones between the Nazca and Antarctic Plates. Easter Island gained its characteristic triangular shape from the joining together of three lava flows.

Northern desert

Northern Chile has a similar form to Peru immediately to the north: the coastal range rises to 1000-1500 m; inland are basins known as *bolsones*, east of which lie the Andes. The Atacama Desert is, by most measures, the driest area on earth, and some meteorological stations near the coast have never reported precipitation. Water is therefore at a premium as far south as Copiapó; it is piped in from the east and, in the Andean foothills, streams flow into alluvial fans in the inland basins, which can act as reservoirs and may be tapped by drilling wells. One river, the Río Loa, flows circuitously from the Andes to Calama and then through the coastal range to the coast; however, for most of its length it is deeply entrenched and unsuitable for agriculture. East of Calama and high in the Andes are the geysers of El Tatio, more evidence of volcanic activity, which are fed by the summer rains that fall in this part of the Andes.

In the past, notably as the ice sheets retreated, there were many lakes in the depressions between the Coastal Range and the Andes. These dried out, leaving one of the greatest concentrations of salts in the world, rich in nitrates: there has been extensive mining activity here since the late 19th century.

Glacial landscapes

Southern Chile provides some of the best examples of glacial landscapes on earth. One common sign of the region's glacial past is the U-shaped valleys. Good examples can be seen throughout the south, but perhaps one of the best is the Río Simpson between Coyhaique and Puerto Aysén. High above these valleys, sharp mountain ridges can often be seen, which have been caused by the eroding action of the ice on two or more sides. In some places, the resulting debris or 'moraine' formed a dam, blocking the valley and creating a lake, as in he Lake District at Lagos Calafquén, Panguipulli and Riñihue.

The drowned coastline south of Puerto Montt also owes its origin to glaciation. The ice that once covered the southern Andes was so heavy that it depressed the relatively narrow tip of South America. When the ice melted and the sea level rose, water broke through, leaving the western Andes as islands and creating the Chilean fjords, glaciated valleys carved out by the ice and now drowned.

Central Chile

South of Copiapó the transition begins between the Atacama and the zone of heavy rainfall in the south. At first, the desert turns to scrub and some seasonal surface water appears. The Huasco and Elqui rivers follow deep trenches to reach the sea, allowing valley bottoms inland to be irrigated for agriculture. Further south, near Santiago, the Central Valley between the Coastal Range and the Andes reappears, the rivers flowing westwards across it to reach the Pacific. Further south is the Lake District, with its many lakes formed by glaciation and volcanic activity, its attractive mountain scenery, its rich volcanic soils and fertile agricultural land.

Southern Chile

South of Valdivia, the Coastal Range becomes more broken until near Puerto Montt it becomes a line of islands as part of a 'drowned coastline' that extends all the way south to Cape Horn. The effects of glaciation can be seen in the U-shaped valleys and the long deep fjords stretching inland. This is a land of dense forests with luxuriant undergrowth that is virtually impenetrable and difficult to clear owing to the high water content. Further south in Chilean Patagonia, coniferous forests are limited in expanse because glaciers have stripped the upper slopes of soil. Some of the remaining glaciers reach sea level, notably the San Rafael, which breaks off the giant icefields of the *Campo de Hielo Norte*.

The Andes

The whole of Chile is dominated by this massive mountain range, which reaches its highest elevations in the border region between Chile and Argentina. In the north, near the Peruvian border, the ranges that make up the Andes are 500 km wide, but the western ranges, which mark the Chilean border, are the highest. Sajama, the highest peak in Bolivia, lies only 20 km east of the border, along which are strung volcanoes including Parinacota (6330 m). Further south, to the southeast of San Pedro de Atacama, lies the highest section of the Andes, which includes the peaks of Llullaillaco (6739 m) and Ojos del Salado (altitude 6864 m or 6893 m depending on your source). Still further south, to the northeast of Santiago and just inside Argentina, lies Aconcagua (6960 m).

South of Santiago, the Andes begin to lose altitude. In the Lake District, the mountain passes are low enough in places for crossing into Argentina. South of Puerto Montt, the

Endurance in the Antarctic

Ernest Shackleton's 1914-1916 Antarctic expedition is one of the epics of polar exploration. Shackleton's vessel, *Endurance*, which left England in August 1914 with 28 men aboard, became trapped in pack-ice in January 1915. After drifting northwards with the ice for eight months, the ship was crushed by the floes and sank. With three boats, supplies and the dogs, the group camped on an ice floe which continued to drift north for a further eight months. In April 1916, after surviving on a diet largely of seals and penguins, the party took to the boats as the ice broke up. After seven days at sea they reached Elephant Island. From there, Shackleton and five other men sailed 1300 km to South Georgia, where there were whaling stations. At first Shackleton, from whom nothing had been heard for 18 months, was not recognized.

The British government sent a rescue vessel to Elephant Island. After ice had prevented three rescue attempts Shackleton persuaded the Chilean authorities to permit a fourth attempt using the tug *Yelcho*. Leaving Punta Arenas on 25 August 1916, the small vessel encountered thick fog but, unusually for the time of year, little ice and it quickly reached Elephant Island where the men, who had endured an Antarctic winter under upturned boats, were down to four days of supplies.

Although the expedition failed to cross Antarctica, Shackleton's achievement was outstanding: the party had survived two Antarctic winters without loss of life. Shackleton himself returned to the region in 1921 to lead another expedition but, in January 1922, aged only 47, he suffered a fatal heart attack in South Georgia.

Andes become more inhospitable, however, as lower temperatures bring the permanent snowline down from 1500 m at Volcán Osorno near Puerto Montt to 700 m on Tierra del Fuego. Towards the southern end of the Andes stand Mount Fitz Roy (3406 m) – in Argentina – and the remarkable peaks of the Paine massif in Chilean territory.

Climate

It is only to be expected that a country that stretches over 4000 km from north to south will provide a wide variety of climatic conditions. Annual rainfall varies from zero in northern Chile to over 4000 mm on the offshore islands south of Puerto Montt. Rainfall is heavier in the winter months (May to August) throughout the country, except for in the northern Altiplano where January and February are the wettest months.

Variations in the Chilean climate are concentrated by two significant factors: altitude and the cold waters of the Humboldt Current. The Andes, with their peaks of over 6000 m, are rarely more than 160 km from the coastline. On average, temperatures drop by 1°C for every 150 m you climb. The Humboldt Current has perhaps even more impact. The current flows in a northeasterly direction from Antarctic waters until it meets the southern coast of Chile, from where it follows the coastline northwards. Cold polar air accompanies the current on its journey, eventually colliding with warmer air moving in from the southwest. The lighter warm air is forced to rise over the dense cold air, bringing rainfall all year round to the area south of the Río Biobío and rain in winter further north in the Central Valley.

Paradoxically, the ocean also has a moderating effect on temperatures, which are not generally extreme and decrease less than might be expected from north to south.

As a result of the Humboldt Current, temperatures in northern Chile are much lower than they are for places at corresponding latitudes, such as Mexico. In the far south, the oceans have the opposite effect and temperatures rarely fall below -6°C despite the high latitude. Detailed temperature and rainfall patterns are given in the text.

Flora

The diversity of Chilean flora reflects the geographic length and climatic variety of the country. Although the Andes constitute a great natural barrier, there are connections between the flora of Chile and that of the eastern side of the mountain range, most notably in the far north with the Bolivian Altiplano and in the south with the temperate forests of Argentina.

Far North

The arid central plain of northern Chile forms one of the driest areas on earth. Vegetation is limited to cacti, among them the *cardon* (*Echinopsis atacamensis*) and, in the Pampa de Tamarugal around Iquique, the *tamarugo* (*Proposis tamarugo*), a tree specially adapted to arid climates. On the western slopes of the Andes, ravines carry water, which has permitted the establishment of small settlements and the planting of crops. The only native tree of this area, *queñoa* (*Polylepis tomentella*) – heavily over-exploited in the past – grows in sheltered areas, mainly near streams, at altitudes between 2000 and 3500 m. Among cacti are the *candelabros* (genus *Browningia*) and, at higher altitudes (between 3000 and 4000 m) the *ayrampu* (genus *Opuntia*).

The northern Altiplano supports only sparse vegetation. Many plants found in this area, such as the *llareta* (genus *Laretia*) and the *tola* (genus *Baccharis*) have deep root systems and small leaves. Near streams, there are areas of spongy, wet salty grass, known as *bofedales*.

To the west of the central plain, the Pacific coastal area is almost complete desert, although in places the influence of the Humboldt Current is offset by the *camanchaca*, an early morning coastal fog that comes off the sea and persists at low altitudes, permitting the growth of vegetation, notably in the Parque Nacional Pan de Azúcar, north of Chañaral, and around Poposo, south of Antofagasta, where about 170 flowering plants, including shrubs, bromeliaceae and cacti can be found.

Norte Chico

Lying between the northern deserts and the matorral of central Chile, the Norte Chico is a transition zone: here annual rainfall averages from 30 to 100 mm, increasing southwards. In the main dry areas native flora, such as *pingo-pingo* (*Ephedra andina*), *jarilla* (*Larrea nitida*) and *brea* (*Tessaria absinthoides*) can be found. On the rare occasions when there is spring rainfall, the desert comes to life in a phenomenon known as the 'flowering of the desert' (see box, page 143). The central plain is crossed by rivers; in the valleys irrigation permits the cultivation of fruit, such as chirimoya, papaya and grapes.

On the coast near Ovalle, sea mists support a forest of evergreen species, including the *olivillo* (*Aextoxicon punctatum*), *canelo* or winter's bark (*Drimys winteri*) and *arrayán* (*Luma chequen* or *Myrtus chequen*) in the Parque Nacional Fray Jorge.

Central Chile

The Central Valley, with its dry and warm summers and mild winters, is home to the *matorral*, a deciduous scrubland ecologically comparable to the chaparral in California and consisting of slow-growing drought-resistant species with deep roots and small spiny sclerophyllous leaves. The original plant cover has been modified by human impact, particularly in the form of livestock agriculture, charcoal-burning and irrigation. In many areas, from the Río Limari in the north to the Río Laja in the south, the result is *espinal* (*Acacia cavan*), usually considered to be a degraded form of the original matoral and characterized by open savannah scattered with *algarrobo* trees (*Prosopis chilensis*). Along ravines and on western facing slopes, there are areas of evergreen sclerophyllous trees, including the *peumo* (*Cryptocarpa alba*), *litre* (*Lithrea caustica*) and *boldo* (*Peumos boldos*) and, along the banks of the great rivers, the *maiten* (*Maytenus boaria* or *Maytenus chilensis*) and a local species of willow can be found.

Towards the coast more hygrophilous species grow on hills receiving coastal fogs: among these are *avellano*, *lingue* (*Persea lingue*), *belloto* or northern acorn (*Beilschmiedia miersii*) and *canelo* as well as bromeliads and epiphytic lichens and mosses. Species of southern beech (*Nothofagus*) and the formerly endemic Chilean or ocoa palm (*Jubea chilensis*), grow under protection in the Parque Nacional La Campana between Santiago and Valparaíso.

Subantarctic temperate forests

As a result of the fragmentation of the great landmass of Gondwana some 120 million years ago, some of the species in these forests (*Araucaria araucana*, *Nothofagus* and *Podocarpus salingus*) share affinities with flora found in Australia and New Zealand as well as with fossils uncovered in Antarctica. Similar affinities of some insect groups have also been established. However the isolation of these subantarctic forests, with the nearest neighbouring forests 1300 km away in northwestern Argentina, has led to the evolution of many unique endemic species, with volcanic activity also having had an important influence.

Nowadays these forests are mainly of broad-leafed evergreen species; in contrast to temperate forests in the northern hemisphere there are few species of conifers. The dominant genus is the Nothofagus or southern beech, of which eight species are found in Chile. In the Maule area *roble* (*Nothofagus obliqua*) and *hualo* (*Nothofagus glauca*) can be found, while further south there is a gradual transitional change via the Valdivian rainforest (see below), to the southern deciduous Nothofagus forests. The latter, which can also be found at higher altitudes along the Andes, include the Patagonian and Magellanic forests. From the Valdivian forest south to the Magellanic forests all species of Nothofagus attract fungis from the genus Cyttaria and, especially in the south, the *misodendron* or South American mistletoe.

Around the Río Biobío, the Valdivian rainforest predominates. This is a complex and diverse environment, which includes ferns, bromeliads, lichens including old man's beard, and mosses, as well as a variety of climbing plants including the *copihue* or Chilean bell flower (*Lapageria rosea*), the national flower of Chile. Colourful flowering plants that can easily be identified include the firebush or *ciruelillo* (*Embothrium coccineum*), several species of alstroemeria and berberis and the fuschia. Near the Andes, for example in the Parque Nacional Puyehue, the forests are dominated by two species of Nothofagus, the evergreen *coihue* or *coigüe* (*Nothofagus dombeyi*) and the deciduous *lenga* (*Nothfagus pumilio*) as well as by the Podocarpus (*Podocarpus salingus*) and, near water, myrtle trees like the *arrayán*. The under-storey is dominated by tall *chusquea* bamboos. However many of these endemic species of flora are currently under threat from the proposed damming of the Río Biobío by Endesa, the Chilean electricity company, in violation of a law of 1993 which safeguards people from signing away their lands if they do not want to.

In the northern parts of the Valdivian forest, at altitudes mainly between 900 m and 1400 m, there are forests of monkey puzzle trees (*Araucaria araucana*), Chile's national tree. The most important of these forests are in the Parque Nacional Nahuelbuta in the coastal *cordillera* and in the Parque Nacional Huerquehue in the Andean foothills (see also box, page 272).

Other species include the giant larch (*Fitzroya cupressoides*), known as the *alerce* or *lahuén*, which has some of the oldest individual specimens on earth (3600 years). Athough this conifer grew extensively as far south as the 43° 30' south, excessive logging has destroyed most of the original larch forest. Some of the best examples of *alerce*, which is now a protected species, can be seen in the Parque Nacional Andino Alerce and in the Parque Pumalín.

The Patagonian and Magellanic forests are less diverse than their Valdivian counterpart, mainly due to lower temperatures. The Magellanic forest, considered the southernmost forest type in the world, includes the evergreen Nothofagus betuloides, the deciduous *lenga* (*Nothofagus pumilio*) and Nothofagus antarctica, and the *canelo*. Firebush and berberis can also be found, as well as several species of orchids and beautiful native species of Calceolaria or slipper plants. Shrubland in the south is mainly characterized by mounded shrubs, usually found in rocky areas. Common species include *mata barrosa* (*Mullinum spinosum*), a yellow-flowered shrub, and *mata guanaco* (*Anartrophyllum desideratum*), a red-flowered shrub of the legume family.

Pacific Islands

In the Juan Fernández Islands and Easter Island there are endemic species. In the forests of the Juan Fernández Archipelago, at altitudes above 1400 m, important species of fern can be found, as well as tree species such as *luma*, *mayu-monte*, giant *naranjillo* and the *yonta* or Juan Fernández palm, which, along with the ocoa palm, is one of only two palms native to Chile. The native forests of Easter Island were destroyed, first by volcanic activity and later by human impact, leaving land covered partially with pasture. Although native species, such as the *toromiro*, can be found, introduced species such as the eucalyptus are more common.

Fauna

Chile is an ecological island. Fauna that is commonplace in neighbouring countries has not been able to migrate here because of the Andes, the desert, the ice and the sea. This explains why there are no land tortoises, squirrels, jaguars or poisonous snakes in the country. Surrounded by natural barriers on all sides, its isolation has contributed to a range of endemic wildlife – something that Darwin glimpsed in microcosm on Chiloé in 1835, when he observed a fox unique to that island.

The one geographical constant from top to bottom of the country is the **Pacific Ocean**, the world's richest ocean for marine species. Coldwater species live near Chile's mainland, feeding off the rich nutrients in the Humboldt Current, while subtropical species inhabit the warmer waters around the Juan Fernández archipelago, and tropical species can be found in the waters around Easter Island. This explains the diversity of Chilean marine life, from hake, swordfish, bream and bass to countless shellfish, such as abalones, mussels, sea urchins, lobsters and a variety of crabs. Nine of the world's 18 species of **penguins** also live in Chile. The Humboldt penguins can be found between Arica and Chiloé, while the King, Adelia and Emperor penguins live solely in Antarctica. There are numerous colonies of sea-lions up and down the coast; dolphins are often seen off the shore of Chiloé and even killer whales abound.

Inland, there are some 680 species of mammal, amphibian, reptile and bird. In the north, the **camelids** predominate among mammals: the alpacas, guanacos, llamas and vicuñas, with the guanaco also being found as far south as Tierra del Fuego. These South American camels are adapted for the mountainous terrain by having narrower feet than the desert forms of the species. All four species can be seen in Chile, although three are found only in the north. Like horses and donkeys, all the camelids can breed with one another, arising to some confusion as to their origins. There is a long-held view that both the llama and the alpaca are descended from wild guanaco.

Guanaco, coffee coloured with a dark head and tail and weighing up to 55 kg, were once found throughout Chile except in rainforest areas. Both grazers and browsers, they live in deserts, shrub land, savannah and occasionally on forest fringes. In many areas hunted to extinction, an estimated 20,000 now survive in the far north, especially in the Parque Nacional Lauca, in coastal and mountain areas between Antofagasta and Lago Rapel and in parts of the far south, such as the Parque Nacional Torres del Paine.

Vicuña, weighing up to 20 kg, are like half-sized guanaco, although with a much finer yellower coat and coffee-coloured head and tail. Hunted almost to extinction, there were only around 400 in Chile in 1970. Protection has increased their numbers to around 12,000, mainly in the far north at altitudes of 3700-4800 m.

Alpaca are domesticated animals, weighing 20-30 kg, but seeming to be much larger because of their wool. Colours vary between black, coffee coloured, mahogany, grey and white. An estimated 20,000 can be found in drier parts of the northern Altiplano.

Llama are also domesticated and are usually found with alpacas. Larger than alpacas and weighing up to 55 kg, their wool varies in colour but is shorter than that of alpacas. They are found only in the area of their domestication, which first occurred around Lake Titicaca some 4000-5000 years ago. Used as pack animals, males can carry loads of up to 40 kg. There are some 40,000 in the Tarapacá and Antofagasta regions of Chile.

Perhaps surprisingly, the north is also one of the avian capitals of Chile, with three of the world's six species of **flamingo** – the James, Chilean and Andean – all to be found around the saltpans of the Atacama. The **Parque Nacional Lauca** is also exceptional for birdlife, with over 120 species of either resident or migrant birds (see box, page 219).

As the land becomes more humid, south of the desert, there are naturally many changes in wildlife. One of the few constants is the famous **puma**, which is found in the *cordillera* all the way from Arica to the Straits of Magellan, albeit in increasingly small numbers; the puma is understandably shy of humans, and is rarely spotted. There are several species of fox, particularly in the mountains, and the Central Valley is also a haven for spiders, including dangerous **arañas de rincón** and tarantulas.

Further south, in the lush forests of the Lake District and down towards the Carreterra Austral, two of the most interesting creatures are the **huemul** and the **pudú**. Both are species of deer. The huemul's northernmost group is found around Chillán; it is a medium-sized creature, well adapted for life in the mountains. The pudú is an extraordinary creature, a deer just 40 cm high, very shy and extremely difficult to spot, although it can sometimes be seen in the more remote parts of Chiloé and the Carreterra Austral.

The **Parque Nacional Torres del Paine** is a haven for wildlife, sheltering guanacos, condors, pumas and foxes. On Isla Magdalena and Seno Otway, both near Punta Arenas, there are famous Magellanic penguin colonies, while Isla Navarino has a colony of beavers (unintentionally introduced from Canada), as well as some fantastic birdlife including petrels and even – on a good day – albatrosses.

Wine → See also pages 18-20.

Chile is a major producer and exporter of fine wines. The fine wine-producing area stretches from the valley of the Río Aconcagua in the north to the Maule Valley in the south. Grapes are also produced outside this area, notably around Ovalle and in the Elqui Valley near La Serena, which is the main production centre for *pisco*, a clear distilled spirit commonly drunk with lemon as pisco sour, although the distillery that many hold to be the best is Alto del Carmén, in the upper reaches of the Huasco Valley.

The great majority of Chilean wines come from the Central Valley. The hot, dry summers guarantee exceptionally healthy fruit. Chilean wine is famous for being free from diseases such as downy mildew and phylloxera. As a result, growers are spared the costs of spraying and of grafting young vines onto phylloxera-resistant rootstocks.

There are eight denominated wine-growing regions, based around the valleys of the Ríos Limarí, Aconcagua, Casablanca, Maipo, Cachapoal, Colchagua, Curicó, Maule and Biobío. The heartland of Chilean red wine production is the Maipo Valley, just south of Santiago, which is home to many of the most prestigious names in Chilean wine. Although the Maipo produces far less wine than the regions to the south, it is considered by many experts to produce the best wines in Chile as a result of the lime content of its soils. For visits to vineyards in this area, see page 68. In recent years the Casablanca Valley has emerged as a fine producer of Chardonnay and crisp Sauvignon blancs, while the recent rediscovery of the lost Carmenere grape is helping to give Chilean wine its own identity.

The main harvest period begins at the end of February, for early maturing varieties such as Chardonnay, and runs through to the end of April for Cabernet Sauvignon, although there are regional variations. Harvest celebrations are often accompanied by two drinks: *chicha*, a partly fermented grape juice, and *vino pipeño*, an unfiltered young wine which contains residue from the grapes and dried yeast.

Although the vine was introduced to Chile in the mid-16th century by the Spanish, the greatest influence on Chilean vineyards and wine making has been exerted by the French. In the 1830s, one prominent Frenchman, Claudio Gay, persuaded the Chilean government to establish the Quinta Normal in Santiago as a nursery for exotic botanical specimens including vines. In the 1970s domestic consumption of wine dropped and wine prices fell, leading to the destruction of many vineyards. In the last two decades, however, large-scale investment, much of it from the United States and Europe has led to increases in wine production, increasingly of quality wines destined for export. Chilean wines are now widely available around the world; they are also very popular within Latin America.

Chileans are justly proud and are increasingly becoming connoisseurs of their wines. More and more top-end wines are sold on the domestic market each year. However, there remains a marked distinction between these fine wines and wines sold in tetrapacks and grown exclusively for mass domestic consumption. The most commonly planted grape variety is still the dark-skinned *Pais*, found only in Chile, and thought to be a direct descendant of cuttings imported by Spanish colonists. Although Chilean wines, especially those produced for export, are typically very clean and fruity, they have only recently developed a full-bodied structure. Most export wines are red Cabernet Sauvignon, Merlot and Carmenere and white Chardonnay and Sauvignon Blanc.

Four large companies now account for 80% of all the wine sold inside Chile: Concha y Toro, Santa Rita, San Pedro and Santa Carolina. There are perhaps a hundred other smaller producers, many of which concentrate on the export market.

Books

Travelogues

Chatwin, Bruce, *In Patagonia* (1977), Pan. A modern classic for those visiting the far south, although it concentrates mainly on Argentina.

Chouinard, Yvon; Johnson, Jeff; Malloy, Chris, *180° South: Conquerers of the Useless* (2010), Patagonia Books. Account of a group of young adventurers retracing Yvon Chouinard's 1968 piligrimage to Chilean Patagonia. Stunning photographs.

Cooper, Marc, *Pinochet and Me* (2001), Verso. Fascinating account of the 1973 coup by Salvador Allende's English translator, intermingled with his account of modern Chile and the coup's legacy.

Darwin, Charles, *The Voyage of the Beagle* (1989), Penguin. Still fascinating reading of the great naturalist's voyage and adventures from Cape Horn to Copiapó in the 1830s.

Giménez Hutton, Adrian, *La Patagonia de Chatwin* (1999), Editorial Sudamericana. Interesting Argentine perspective on Chatwin and Patagonia (both Argentine and Chilean).

Green, Toby, *Saddled with Darwin* (2000), Phoenix House. A former author of this book retraces Darwin's route in South America on horseback.

Keenan, Brian and McCarthy, John, *Between Extremes* (2000), Black Swan. The 2 friends from Lebanon travel together again, this time through Chile.

Lucas Bridges, E, *Uttermost Part of the Earth* (1948), Hodder & Stoughton. Brilliant and beautiful account of his adventurous life in Tierra del Fuego with the Yámana and Ona peoples; the classic text on Tierra del Fuego.

Pilkington, John, *An Englishman In Patagonia* (1991), Century. Heavily critical of Chatwin.

Reding, Nick, *The last cowboys at the end of the world* (2001), Random House. Quirky yet evocative and highly readable account of the lives of the dying breed of gauchos in central Patagonia.

Souhami, Diana, *Selkirk's Island* (2001), Weidenfeld & Nicolson. The extraordinary story of Alexander Selkirk and his island, inspirations for Robinson Crusoe and for the community of San Juan Bautista on modern-day Isla Robinson Crusoe. A prize-winning account.

Swale, Rosie, *Back to Cape Horn* (1988), Fontana. Swale tells of her epic journey from Antofagasta to Cape Horn on horseback.

Wheeler, Sara, *Travels in a Thin Country* (1994), Little, Brown & Co. Popular account of the author's 6-month stay in Chile.

Fiction and poetry

Allende, Isabel, the doyenne of modern Chilean letters. Her books include: *The House of the Spirits* (1994), Black Swan. Brilliant, evocative, allegorical magical-realist account taking the reader through 20th-century Chilean history. *Of Love and Shadows* (1988), Black Swan. Painful story about a journalist uncovering evidence of military atrocities under the military regime. *Paula* (1996), Flamingo. A beautiful 'letter' written from Allende to her daughter, who is stuck in a coma after a car accident, taking in the modern history of Chile and Allende's emotional roots. More recent books include *Daughter of Fortune* (2000), Flamingo, and *Portrait in Sepia* (2002), Flamingo, both of which are lyrical prequels to the story that made Allende's name: *The House of the Spirits*.

Bolaño, Roberto, *By Night in Chile* (2003), Harvill. A caustic, brilliant novel, as an ageing Chilean priest lives through the last night of his life, and recalls teaching Marxism to General Pinochet and various surreal encounters with the Chilean literary establishment – thereby exposing the complicity of so many in the 'normality' that accompanied the military government.

Donoso, José, *The Garden Next Door* (1994), Grove Press. Evocative novel that deals with the ageing process of a couple in Spain. *The Obscene Bird of the Night* (1995), Grove Press. Donoso's most famous, experimental novel, which gained him international acclaim across Latin America.

Dorfman, Ariel, *Death and the Maiden* (1996), Nick Hern Books (also in the collected volume *The Resistance Trilogy*; 1998). Subtle, moving tale of torture and resistance, an allegory for the state of Chile. *The Nanny and the Iceberg* (1999), Sceptre. Cross-cultural story of Chile and North America told with Dorfman's usual eloquence.

Neruda, Pablo, *Selected Poems* (trans/ed Ben Bellit (1961), New York Grove Press. Bilingual anthology of the master's work.

Richards, Ben, *The Mermaid and the Drunks* (2003), Weidenfeld & Nicolson. An English novel set in Chile, which gives an entertaining picture of modern Chile from the perspective of a longtime friend of the country.

Skármeta, Antonio, *Il Postino* ('The Postman', 1996), Bloomsbury. Beautiful novel about the relationship between Neruda and his postman while the poet is in exile in Italy, made into a famous film. *Watch Where the Wolf is Going* (1991), Readers' International. Another novel in Skármeta's trademark style of eloquence and emotional honesty.

Adventure sports

Biggar, John, *The High Andes* (1996), Castle Douglas, Kirkudbrightshire. Andes contains 3 chapters with information on Chilean peaks.

CONAF, *Guía de Parques Nacionales y Otras Areas Silvestres Protegidas de Chile*, US$12, a very useful guide to the main parks, with information on access, campsites, flora

and fauna. It also publishes *Chile Forestal*, a monthly magazine with articles on the parks and ecological issues.

Fagerstrom, René Peri, *Cuentos de la Carretera Austral*, on the Camino Austral. *Regata*, a monthly sailing magazine. Climbers will also find *Cumbres de Chile* of interest: 2 books with accompanying tapes, each covering 20 peaks.

Mantellero, Alberto, *Una Aventura Navegando Los Canales del Sur de Chile*, a guide to sailing the southern coast, with maps.

Reference and background

Almarza V, Claudio, *Patagonia* (Punta Arenas: GeoPatagonia). A book of photographs, with text, on the region.

Araya, B and Millie, G, *Guía de Campo de Las Aves de Chile*. Bird-lovers will appreciate this guide to Chile's feathered population.

Bahn, Paul and Flenley, John, *Easter Island, Earth Island* (1992), Thames and Hudson. A comprehensive appraisal of Easter Island's archaeology.

Cárdenas Saldivia, Umiliana, *Casos de Brujos de Chiloé* (1989), Editorial Universitaria. Fascinating tales of witchcraft on Chiloé.

Castillo, Juan Carlos (ed) *Islas Oceánicas Chilenas* (1987), Ediciones Universidad Católica de Chile. Much information on the natural history and geography of Juan Fernández and Easter Islands.

Clissold, Stephen, *Chilean Scrapbook* (1952), The Cresset Press. Gives an evocative historical picture of Chile, region by region.

Collier, S and Sater, WF, *A History of Chile 1808-2002* (2004), Cambridge University Press. The definitive single-volume history of Chile in English.

Coña, Pascal, *Memorias de un Cacique Mapuche* (1930), publisher unmarked. An account of Mapuche traditions and history by a Mapuche chief in his 70s.

Constable, Pamela and Valenzuela, Arturo, *Chile: A Nation of Enemies* (1991), Norton. Excellent and readable take on the Pinochet years.

Crow, Joanna, *The Mapuche in Modern Chile: A Cultural History* (2013), University Press of Florida. In-depth chronicling of the history of Chile's indigenous peoples.

Dinges, John, *The Condor Years* (2004), The New Press. Thorough examination of the Condor anti-leftist terrorist operation set up by South American dictators, including Pinochet.

Dorfman, Ariel, *Unending Terror: The Incredible Unending Trial of General Augusto Pinochet* (2003), Pluto Press. A gripping account of the Pinochet affair from one of the most perceptive living writers on Chile. His memoir *Heading North, Looking South* (1998) is also essential reading.

Elsey, Brenda, *Citizens & Sportsmen* (2011), University of Texas press. A look at how Chile's futbol clubs connected working-class men with politics.

Goni, Uki, *The Real Odessa: How Perón Brought the Nazi War Criminals to Argentina* (2002), Granta. Although based on the Argentine hiding of Nazi war criminals, this book has a continent-wide significance, as it reveals how this movement shaped the fascist attitudes of military governments of the 1970s.

Haslam, Jonathan, *The Nixon Administration and the Death of Allende's Chile* (2005), Verso. This book examines the involvement of Nixon and the CIA in the 1973 coup.

Hazlewood, Nick, *Savage: The Life and Times of Jemmy Button* (2001), Sceptre. Interesting if hyperbolic history of Jemmy's tale.

Heyerdahl, Thor, *Aku-Aku, The Art of Easter Island* (1975), New York: Doubleday.

Hutchison, Elizabeth Quay; Klubock, Thomas Miller; Milanch, Nara B, *The Chile Reader: History, Culture, Politics* (2013), Duke University Press. Comprehensive tome covering every corner of Chilean life and history, from the country's origins all the way up to 2013.

Kornbluh, Peter, *The Pinochet File* (2003), The New Press. Declassified CIA documents together with editorial explanations relating to US government involvement and collusion in the 1973 coup.

Lagos, Ricardo, *The Southern Tiger: Chile's Fight for a Democratic and Prosperous Future* (2012), Palgrave Macmillan. A former political prisoner under the Pinochet regime chronicles his country's ascent from darkness to become one of the most prosperous nations in Latin America.

Montecino, Sonia, *Historias de Vida de Mujeres Mapuches* (1985), Centro de Estudios de la Mujer. Interviews with Mapuche women giving a real insight into their lives.

O'Shaughnessy, Hugh, *Pinochet: The Politics of Torture* (2000), Latin American Bureau. Informed and up-to-date analysis of the whole Pinochet affair.

Porteous, J Douglas, *The Modernization of Easter Island* (1981), Department of Geography, University of Victoria, BC, Canada. A very thorough illustrated book.

Read, Jan, *The Wines of Chile* (1994), Mitchell Beazley. A gazetteer of the vineyards and wineries of Chile, ideal for the specialist.

Rector, John, *The History of Chile* (2005), Palgrave MacMillan. A readable general history of Chile.

South American Explorers Club, *The South American Explorer* (126 Indian Creek Road, Ithaca, New York 14850, USA). This journal regularly publishes articles on Chile including Easter Island.

Spooner, MH, *Soldiers In A Narrow Land* (1994), University of California Press. A readable account of the Pinochet dictatorship by a North American journalist resident in the country at the time.

Wearne, Philip, *Return of the Indian: Conquest and Revival in the Americas* (1996), Cassell/Latin America Bureau. Information on the Mapuche within the entire Amerindian context.

Maps and guidebooks

Chiletur, published by **Copec**, www. copec.cl, is very useful for roads and town plans, but not all distances are exact. It is published annually in 3 parts; Norte, Centro, and Sur (in Spanish only), alongside a separate volume dedicated to national parks. It contains a wealth of maps covering the whole country and neighbouring tourist centres in Argentina, and is well worth getting, particularly for those with their own transport. Each volume costs around US$10, but buying the whole set is better value. Available from larger Copec service stations.

Sernatur publishes a free *Guía Turística/Tourist Guide* in Spanish and English, with good maps, useful text, while **CONAF** publishes a series of illustrated booklets in Spanish/English on Chilean trees, shrubs and flowers, as well as *Juventud, Turismo y Naturaleza*, which lists national parks, their facilities and the flora and fauna of each.

A recommended series of general maps are published by **International Travel Maps** (**ITM**), 345 West Broadway, Vancouver, V5Y 1P8, Canada, T604-8793 621, compiled with historical notes, by Kevin Healey

Contents

Footnotes

Basic Spanish for travellers

Learning Spanish is a useful part of the preparation for a trip to Latin America and no volumes of dictionaries, phrase books or word lists will provide the same enjoyment as being able to communicate directly with the people of the country you are visiting. It is a good idea to make an effort to grasp the basics before you go. As you travel you will pick up more of the language and the more you know, the more you will benefit from your stay.

General pronunciation

Whether you have been taught the 'Castilian' pronounciation (z and c followed by i or e are pronounced as the th in think) or the 'American' pronounciation (they are pronounced as s), you will encounter little difficulty in understanding either. Regional accents and usages vary, but the basic language is essentially the same everywhere. In Argentina, the accent is distinctly different to the rest of Latin America in one crucial area. The letters ll in all other Spanish-speaking countries are pronounced like the y in yellow, in Argentina they are pronounced similar to the sh in she. The letter y in Argentina is also pronounced like the sh in she, instead of the ee in feet. Another change is that Argentines tend to use vos instead of tú.

Vowels
a   as in English cat
e   as in English best
i   as the ee in English feet
o   as in English shop
u   as the oo in English food
ai   as the i in English ride
ei   as ey in English they
oi   as oy in English toy

Consonants
Most consonants can be pronounced more or less as they are in English. The exceptions are:
g   before e or i is the same as j
h   is always silent (except in ch as in chair)
j   as the ch in Scottish loch
ll   as the y in yellow
ñ   as the ni in English onion
rr   trilled much more than in English
x   depending on its location, pronounced x, s, sh or j

Spanish words and phrases

Greetings, courtesies
hello hola
good morning buenos días
good afternoon/evening/night
  buenas tardes/noches
goodbye adiós/chao
pleased to meet you mucho gusto
see you later hasta luego
how are you? ¿cómo está?/¿cómo estás?
I'm fine, thanks estoy muy bien, gracias
I'm called... me llamo...
what is your name? ¿cómo se llama?/
  ¿cómo te llamas?

yes/no sí/no
please por favor
thank you (very much) (muchas) gracias
I speak Spanish hablo español
I don't speak Spanish no hablo español
do you speak English? ¿habla inglés?
I don't understand no entiendo/
  no comprendo
please speak slowly hable despacio por favor
I am very sorry lo siento mucho/disculpe
what do you want? ¿qué quiere?/
  ¿qué quieres?

I want *quiero*
I don't want it *no lo quiero*

leave me alone *déjeme en paz/no me moleste*
good/bad *bueno/malo*

Questions and requests

Have you got a room for two people?
  ¿Tiene una habitación para dos personas?
How do I get to_? *¿Cómo llego a_?*
How much does it cost?
  ¿Cuánto cuesta? ¿cuánto es?
I'd like to make a long-distance phone call
  Quisiera hacer una llamada de larga distancia
Is service included? *¿Está incluido el servicio?*
Is tax included? *¿Están incluidos los impuestos?*

When does the bus leave (arrive)?
  ¿A qué hora sale (llega) el autobús?
When? *¿cuándo?*
Where is_? *¿dónde está_?*
Where can I buy tickets?
  ¿Dónde puedo comprar boletos?
Where is the nearest petrol station?
  ¿Dónde está la gasolinera más cercana?
Why? *¿por qué?*

Basics

bank *el banco*
bathroom/toilet *el baño*
bill *la factura/la cuenta*
cash *el efectivo*
cheap *barato/a*
credit card *la tarjeta de crédito*
exchange house *la casa de cambio*
exchange rate *el tipo de cambio*

expensive *caro/a*
market *el mercado*
note/coin *le billete/la moneda*
police (policeman) *la policía (el policía)*
post office *el correo*
public telephone *el teléfono público*
supermarket *el supermercado*
ticket office *la taquilla*

Getting around

aeroplane *el avión*
airport *el aeropuerto*
arrival/departure *la llegada/salida*
avenue *la avenida*
block *la cuadra*
border *la frontera*
bus station *la terminal de autobuses/
  camiones*
bus *el bus/el autobús/el camión*
collective/fixed-route taxi *el colectivo*
corner *la esquina*
customs *la aduana*
first/second class *primera/segunda clase*
left/right *izquierda/derecha*
ticket *el boleto*
empty/full *vacío/lleno*
highway, main road *la carretera*
immigration *la inmigración*
insurance *el seguro*

insured person *el/la asegurado/a*
to insure yourself against *asegurarse contra*
luggage *el equipaje*
motorway, freeway *el autopista/la carretera*
north, south, east, west *norte, sur, este
  (oriente), oeste (occidente)*
oil *el aceite*
to park *estacionarse*
passport *el pasaporte*
petrol/gasoline *la gasolina*
puncture *el pinchazo/la ponchadura*
street *la calle*
that way *por allí/por allá*
this way *por aquí/por acá*
tourist card/visa *la tarjeta de turista*
tyre *la llanta*
unleaded *sin plomo*
to walk *caminar/andar*

Accommodation

air conditioning *el aire acondicionado*
all-inclusive *todo incluido*
bathroom, private *el baño privado*
bed, double/single *la cama matrimonial/ sencilla*
blankets *las cobijas/mantas*
to clean *limpiar*
dining room *el comedor*
guesthouse *la casa de huéspedes*
hotel *el hotel*
noisy *ruidoso*

pillows *las almohadas*
power cut *el apagón/corte*
restaurant *el restaurante*
room/bedroom *el cuarto/la habitación*
sheets *las sábanas*
shower *la ducha/regadera*
soap *el jabón*
toilet *el sanitario/excusado*
toilet paper *el papel higiénico*
towels, clean/dirty *las toallas limpias/sucias*
water, hot/cold *el agua caliente/fría*

Health

aspirin *la aspirina*
blood *la sangre*
chemist *la farmacia*
condoms *los preservativos, los condones*
contact lenses *los lentes de contacto*
contraceptives *los anticonceptivos*
contraceptive pill *la píldora anti-conceptiva*
diarrhoea *la diarrea*

doctor *el médico*
fever/sweat *la fiebre/el sudor*
pain *el dolor*
head *la cabeza*
period/sanitary towels *la regla/las toallas femeninas*
stomach *el estómago*
altitude sickness *el soroche*

Family

family *la familia*
friend *el amigo/la amiga*
brother/sister *el hermano/la hermana*
daughter/son *la hija/el hijo*
father/mother *el padre/la madre*

husband/wife *el esposo (marido)/la esposa*
boyfriend/girlfriend *el novio/la novia*
married *casado/a*
single/unmarried *soltero/a*

Months, days and time

January *enero*
February *febrero*
March *marzo*
April *abril*
May *mayo*
June *junio*
July *julio*
August *agosto*
September *septiembre*
October *octubre*
November *noviembre*
December *diciembre*

Monday *lunes*
Tuesday *martes*
Wednesday *miércoles*

Thursday *jueves*
Friday *viernes*
Saturday *sábado*
Sunday *domingo*

at one o'clock *a la una*
at half past two *a las dos y media*
at a quarter to three *a cuarto para las tres/ a las tres menos quince*
it's one o'clock *es la una*
it's seven o'clock *son las siete*
it's six twenty *son las seis y veinte*
it's five to nine *son las nueve menos cinco*
in ten minutes *en diez minutos*
five hours *cinco horas*
does it take long? *¿tarda mucho?*

Numbers

one	uno/una	sixteen	dieciséis
two	dos	seventeen	diecisiete
three	tres	eighteen	dieciocho
four	cuatro	nineteen	diecinueve
five	cinco	twenty	veinte
six	seis	twenty-one	veintiuno
seven	siete	thirty	treinta
eight	ocho	forty	cuarenta
nine	nueve	fifty	cincuenta
ten	diez	sixty	sesenta
eleven	once	seventy	setenta
twelve	doce	eighty	ochenta
thirteen	trece	ninety	noventa
fourteen	catorce	hundred	cien/ciento
fifteen	quince	thousand	mil

Food

avocado	la palta	hot, spicy	picante
baked	al horno	ice cream	el helado
bakery	la panadería	jam	la mermelada
banana	la banana	knife	el cuchillo
beans	los frijoles/las habichuelas	lemon	el limón
beef	la carne de res	lobster	la langosta
beef steak	el lomo	lunch	el almuerzo/la comida
boiled rice	el arroz blanco	meal	la comida
bread	el pan	meat	la carne
breakfast	el desayuno	minced meat	la carne picada
butter	la manteca	onion	la cebolla
cake	la torta	orange	la naranja
chewing gum	el chicle	pepper	el pimiento
chicken	el pollo	pasty, turnover	la empanada/el pastelito
chilli or green pepper	el ají/pimiento	pork	el cerdo
clear soup, stock	el caldo	potato	la papa
cooked	cocido	prawns	los camarones
dining room	el comedor	raw	crudo
egg	el huevo	restaurant	el restaurante
fish	el pescado	salad	la ensalada
fork	el tenedor	salt	la sal
fried	frito	sandwich	el bocadillo
garlic	el ajo	sauce	la salsa
goat	el chivo	sausage	la longaniza/el chorizo
grapefruit	la toronja/el pomelo	scrambled eggs	los huevos revueltos
grill	la parrilla	seafood	los mariscos
grilled/griddled	a la plancha	soup	la sopa
guava	la guayaba	spoon	la cuchara
ham	el jamón	squash	la calabaza
hamburger	la hamburguesa	squid	los calamares

supper	la cena	turkey	el pavo
sweet	dulce	vegetables	los legumbres/vegetales
to eat	comer	without meat	sin carne
toasted	tostado	yam	el camote

Drink

beer	la cerveza	ice/without ice	el hielo/sin hielo
boiled	hervido/a	juice	el jugo
bottled	en botella	lemonade	la limonada
camomile tea	la manzanilla	milk	la leche
canned	en lata	mint	la menta
coffee	el café	rum	el ron
coffee, white	el café con leche	soft drink	el refresco
cold	frío	sugar	el azúcar
cup	la taza	tea	el té
drink	la bebida	to drink	beber/tomar
drunk	borracho/a	water	el agua
firewater	el aguardiente	water, carbonated	el agua mineral con gas
fruit milkshake	el batido/licuado	water, still mineral	el agua mineral sin gas
glass	el vaso	wine, red	el vino tinto
hot	caliente	wine, white	el vino blanco

Key verbs

to go	**ir**
I go	voy
you go (familiar)	vas
he, she, it goes,	
you (formal) go	va
we go	vamos
they, you (plural) go	van

to be	**ser** (permanent state) **estar**
(positional or temporary state)		

I am	soy	estoy
you are	eres	estás
he, she, it is,		
you (formal) are	es	está
we are	somos	estamos
they, you (plural) are	son	están

to have (possess)	**tener**
I have	tengo
you (familiar) have	tienes
he, she, it,	
you (formal) have	tiene
we have	tenemos
they, you (plural) have	tienen
there is/are	hay
there isn't/aren't	no hay

This section has been assembled on the basis of glossaries compiled by André de Mendonça and David Gilmour of South American Experience, London, and the Latin American Travel Advisor, No 9, March 1996.

Index → Entries in bold refer to maps.

Advertisers' index

Acknowledgements

This Handbook is based on the earlier work of **Janak Jani**, owner of **Luna Sonrisa** in Valparaíso, who wrote several editions of the *Chile Handbook*. The following have worked on sections of the book: **Anna Maria Espsäter** updated Patagonia. Anna Maria would like to thank **Australis Expedition Cruises**, with special thanks to Leandro S Bruno and Marcelo Gallo; Gareth Lyons and Simon Heyes of Senderos, and the staff at **Tierra Patagonia**. **Chris Wallace** updated the northern Lake District and the area around San Pedro de Atacama. **Christian Martínez** updated the Easter Island section. **Ben Box** updated Santiago, Valparaíso and Chiloé. In Santiago de Chile, Ben would like to thank Marilú Cerda of **Marilú's B&B**; in Valparaíso, Janak Jani.

About the authors

Ben Box

One of the first assignments Ben Box took as a freelance writer in 1980 was subediting work on the *South American Handbook*. The plan then was to write about contemporary Iberian and Latin American affairs, but in no time at all the lands south of the Rio Grande took over, inspiring journeys to all corners of the subcontinent. Ben has contributed to newspapers, magazines and learned tomes, usually on the subject of travel, and became editor of the *South American Handbook* in 1989. He has also been involved in Footprint's Handbooks on *Central America & Mexico, Caribbean Islands, Brazil, Peru, Peru, Bolivia & Ecuador* and *Cuzco & the Inca Heartland*. Having a doctorate in Spanish and Portuguese studies from London University, Ben maintains a strong interest in Latin American literature. In the British summer he plays cricket for his local village side and year round he attempts to achieve some level of self-sufficiency in fruit and veg in a rather unruly country garden in Suffolk.

Anna Maria Espsäter

Originally from Sweden, Anna Maria Espsäter first started discovering Latin America at 20, when she moved to Mexico to teach and work in an orphanage. Based in London for many years, she works as a freelance travel and food writer, specializing in Latin America and Scandinavia. Despite having visiting 90 countries to date, Latin America remains one of her favourite places to roam and write. She hopes to return to Patagonia before long. www.annamariaespsater.co.uk.

Chris Wallace

Chris Wallace has been travelling through, and writing about, Central and South America since 2004. He has lived in Colombia, Argentina, Chile, Brazil and Peru. He has tailored travel and tourism content for entrepreneurs and publishers alike, and, more than 10 years in, he feels he's barely scratched the surface of what the South American continent has to offer.

Credits

Footprint credits

Editor: Sophie Blacksell Jones
Production and layout: Emma Bryers
Maps: Kevin Feeney

Publisher: Patrick Dawson
Managing Editor: Felicity Laughton
Advertising: Elizabeth Taylor
Sales and marketing: Kirsty Holmes

Photography credits

Front cover: Superstock/Stefan Schurr
Back cover: Superstock/Angelo Cavalli

Colour section

Page i: dreamstime: Dmitry Pichugin/
Dreamstime.com
Page ii: Superstock: Robert Harding Picture
Library/Robert Harding Picture Library
Page iii: dreamstime: Tero Hakala/
Dreamstime.com
Page vi: dreamstime: Soren Egeberg/
Dreamstime.com
Page vii: Superstock: Radius/Radius;
dreamstime: Jeremy Richards/
Dreamstime.com
Page viii: dreamstime: Andria Hautamaki/
Dreamstime.com
Page ix: Superstock: Robert Harding Picture
Library/Robert Harding Picture Library
Page x: Superstock: Robert Harding Picture
Library, age fotostock/age fotostock,
Prisma/Prisma

Printed in India by Thomson Press Ltd,
Faridabad, Haryana

Publishing information

Footprint Chile
7th edition
© Footprint Handbooks Ltd
February 2015

ISBN: 978 1 910120 064
CIP DATA: A catalogue record for this book
is available from the British Library

® Footprint Handbooks and the Footprint
mark are a registered trademark of
Footprint Handbooks Ltd

Published by Footprint
6 Riverside Court
Lower Bristol Road
Bath BA2 3DZ, UK
T +44 (0)1225 469141
F +44 (0)1225 469461
footprinttravelguides.com

Distributed in the USA by
National Book Network, Inc.

Footprint
Mini Atlas
Chile

PERU

BOLIVIA

Arica
Iquique

San Pedro
de Atacama

Antofagasta

Copiapó

*Pacific
Ocean*

La Serena

*Islas Juan
Fernández*

Valparaíso

To Rapa Nui ←

SANTIAGO □

Rancagua

Talca

ARGENTINA

Concepción

Temuco
Pucón
Valdivia
Osorno
Puerto Montt
Castro
Chiloé

Coyhaique

*Atlantic
Ocean*

	National highway
	Major road
	Unpaved or ripio road
	Railway
	Ferry between Puerto Montt & Puerto Natales (Puerto Edén)
	Ferry between Puerto Montt & Puerto Chacabuco/ Laguna San Rafael
	Ferry between Quellón & Chaitén
	Salt flats

Altitude in metres
4000
3000
2000
1000
500
200
0

Neighbouring
country

200 km
200 miles

N

Puerto
Natales

Punta
Arenas

*Tierra del
Fuego*

Map 1

Map 3

REGION IV

La Paloma · Chilecito
Punitaqui
Ligua Bajo
Combarbalá

Canela
Baja
Illapel
Reserva Nacional Las Chinchillas

Los Vilos
Vizcachas (1969m)
Loma Blanca (1861m)
Salamanca · Limpo
Caimanes
Morado (4114m)
Jorquera (3743m)

Río Quilimarí
Pichidangui
Petorca
Los Molles

La Ligua · Cabildo

REGION V
Papudo
Zapallar
Cachagua
Maitencillo
Horcón
Quintero
La Calera
Putaendo · Termas de Jahuel
San Felipe
Los Andes · Redentor Tu
Portillo · Caracoles

Quillota
Concón
La Campana
Viña del Mar
Parque Nacional La Campana
Valparaíso
Limache
Tunnel Chacabuco

Reserva Nacional Peñuelas
Termas de Colina
Casablanca · Lampa
Colina
Las Condes
La Parva
Santuario de la Naturaleza Yerba Loca

El Quisco
Algarrobo
Curacaví
Isla Negra
Cartagena
San Antonio
Peñaflor
Rocas de Santo Domingo
Pomaire
SANTIAGO
Puente Alto
Lagunillas
Farellones
El Colorado
Tupungato (6570m)
San José de Maipo
Melocotón

Melipilla
Buin
Parque Nacional Río Clarillo
Baños Morales
Parque Nacio El Morado
Paine
El Volcán
Lo Valdés

San Francisco de Mostazal
Chapa Verde
Machalí
Sewell

Rapel
Navidad
Villa Alhué
Doñihue
Rancagua

Lago Rapel
Litueche
Pichilemu
Marchihue
Peumo
Rengo
Peleguén
El Portillo (4986m)

Peralillo
San Vicente de Tagua Tagua
Santa Cruz
Los Lingues
San Fernando
Sierra Belle Vista
Tinguiririca (4280m)

Bucalemu
Chimbarongo
REGION VI
Llico
Lolol
Lago Vichuquén
Vichuquén
Rauco
Romeral
Termas del Flaco

Iloca
Licantén
Huala né
Curicó
Molina

Pudú
Cumpeo
REGION VII
Paso Vergara del Planchón

Constitución
Pelarco
Area Protección Radal Siete Tazas
Vol. Descabezado (3850m)

Río Maule
Talca
Aurora
Reserva Nacional Altos del Lircay

Maule
San Clemente
El Colorado
Vilches

Villa Alegre
San Javier
Colbún
Lago Colbún
Armerillo

Reserva Nacional Federico Albert
Chanco
Putagán
Termas de Panimávida

Reserva Nacional Los Ruiles
Curanipe
Villa Seca

El Boldo
Longaví
Linares
Miraflores

Cauquenes
Hualve
Copihue

Quelli
Retiro
Aduana Pejerrey
Laguna de Maule

Cobquecura
Porquilauquén
Parral

Quirihue
Niquén
San Gregorio
Termas de Catillo

Coelemu
Magdalena
San Carlos
Paso Pehuenche

Dichato
Quinchamalí
San Fabián de Alico

Tomé
Ricapequén
Chillán
Coihueco

Talcahuano
Penco
Bulnes
Pinto
Esperanza
Recinto

Lama
Lirquén
Río Itata
Termas de Chillán

Colorado
Concepción
Pemuco
Las Trancas

Coronel
REGION VIII
Monte Aguila

Lota
Yumbel
Campanario

Pacific Ocean

Islas Juan Fernández

N
30 km
30 miles

Map 4

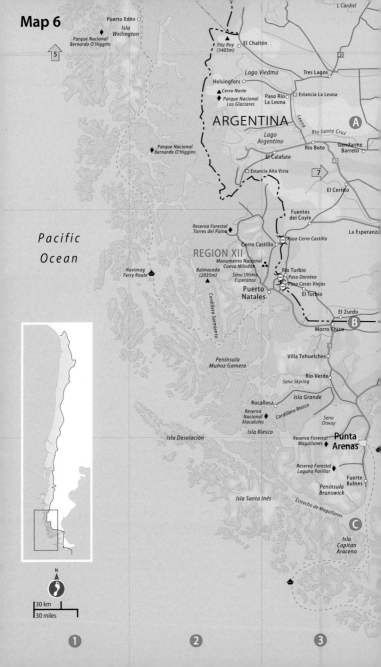

Map 6

Puerto Edén
Isla Wellington
Parque Nacional Bernardo O'Higgins

5

L Cardiel

Fitz Roy (3405m)
El Chaltén

Lago Viedma
Tres Lagos

Helsingfors
Cerro Norte
Parque Nacional Los Glaciares

Estancia La Leona

ARGENTINA

Paso Río La Leona

Lago Argentino

Parque Nacional Bernardo O'Higgins

Río Bote

Río Santa Cruz

Leona

A

Gendarme Barreto

El Calafate

Estancia Alta Vista

7

El Cerrito

Pacific Ocean

Fuentes del Coyle

Reserva Forestal Torres del Paine

La Esperanza

Cerro Castillo

Paso Cerro Castillo

REGION XII

Navimag Ferry Route

Monumento Nacional Cueva Milodón

Balmaceda (2035m)

Río Turbio
Paso Dorotea
Paso Casas Viejas
El Turbio

Seno Última Esperanza

Puerto Natales

El Zurdo

B

Cordillera Sarmiento

Morro Chico

Villa Tehuelches

Península Muñoz Gamero

Río Verde
Seno Skyring

Rocallosa
Isla Grande

Reserva Nacional Alacalufes
Cordillera Riesco

Seno Otway

Isla Riesco

Isla Desolación

Reserva Forestal Magallanes

Punta Arenas

Reserva Forestal Laguna Parillar

Fuerte Bulnes

Península Brunswick

Isla Santa Inés

Estrecho de Magallanes

C

Isla Capitan Aracena

N

30 km
30 miles

1   **2**   **3**

Map 7

ARGENTINA

Piedrabuena
Santa Cruz
Rincón Grande
Río Santa Cruz
endarme Barreto
Cañadón de las Vacas

Atlantic Ocean

La Esperanza
A
Bahía Grande
Puerto Coig

Río Coig
6
5
Río Gallegos
Güer Aike
Río Gallegos

Zurdo
Bella Vista
Laguna Azul
Parque Nacional Pali Aike
Punta Delgada
Cabo Vírgenes
Punta Espora
Estrecho de Magallanes
Cabo Espíritu Santo

Monumento Natural Los Pingüinos
Isla Magdalena
B
Isla Isabel
Cerro Sombrero
Primavera
Cullén
Península El Páramo
Bahía San Sebastián

Punta Arenas
Porvenir
Onaisín
San Sebastián
San Sebastián
Fuerte Bulnes
nsula swick
Bahía Inútil
Camerón
Río Grande

Isla Dawson
CHILE
Lago Lynch
Lago Chico
Lago Blanco
Estrecho de Magallanes
Canal Whiteside
Puerto Arturo

Isla Capitán Aracena

Tierra del Fuego

Península Brecknock
Cordillera Darwin
Lago Fagnano
Cabo San Diego
Lago Escondido
Ushuaia
ARGENTINA
C
Estrecho de Lo Ma
Beagle Channel
Estancia Harberton
Sierra Lucía Lopez
Puerto Navarino
Wulara
Puerto Williams
Puerto Toro
Península Cloué
Isla Hoste
Isla Navarino
Isla Picton
Península Rous
Isla Lennox
Isla Nueva
Península Hardy
Isla Wollaston
Cape Horn

30 km
30 miles
N

1
2
3

Index

Distance chart

	Antofagasta	Arica	Castro	Concepción	Copiapó	Coyhaique*	Iquique	La Serena	Osorno	Pucón	Puerto Montt	Puerto Natales*	Punta Arenas*	San Pedro de Atacama	Santiago	Talca	Temuco	Valdivia
Arica	701																	
Castro	2552	3253																
Concepción	1880	258	801															
Copiapó	566	1261	1992	1320														
Coyhaique*	3011	3712	414†	1260	2451													
Iquique	492	316	3044	2372	1058	3503												
La Serena	887	1588	1665	993	333	2124	1377											
Osorno	2274	2975	284	523	1708	743	2766	1387										
Pucón	2150	2851	515	399	1584	974	2641	1263	227									
Puerto Montt	2377	3078	175	626	1811	634	2869	1490	109	340								
Puerto Natales*	4464	5165	2472‡	2707	3904	1593	4956	3577	2190	2639	2299							
Punta Arenas*	4451	5152	2461†	2700	3890	1580	4943	3564	2177	2404	2286	254						
San Pedro de Atacama	320	719	2870	2198	876	3329	515	1209	2592	2470	2605	4784	4769					
Santiago	1361	2062	1191	519	801	1649	1853	474	913	789	1016	3103	3090	1679				
Talca	1618	2319	934	262	1052	1393	2110	731	656	532	759	2844	2833	1936	257			
Temuco	2038	2738	514	287	1472	973	2530	1151	236	112	339	2424	2413	2356	677	420		
Valdivia	2202	2903	391	452	1640	850	2694	1313	107	145	210	2295	2177	2520	839	584	162	
Valparaíso	1319	2020	1312	639	759	1769	1811	432	1033	909	1136	3223	3210	1637	120	377	797	961

* via Carretera Austral
† via Ferry Quellón-Chaitén
‡ via Puerto Montt

Distances in kilometres   1 kilometre = 0.62 miles

Map symbols

□ Capital city	Ⓜ Metro station	Ⓟ Police
○ Other city, town	- - - - Cable car	Ⓢ Bank
International border	+++++ Funicular	@ Internet
Regional border	Ferry	♪ Telephone
Customs	Pedestrianized street	Market
Contours (approx)	)(Tunnel	Medical services
▲ Mountain, volcano	→ One way-street	Ⓟ Parking
Mountain pass	Steps	Petrol
Escarpment	Bridge	Golf
Glacier	Fortified wall	Archaeological site
Salt flat	Park, garden, stadium	National park, wildlife reserve
Rocks	Where to stay	Viewing point
Seasonal marshland	Restaurants	Campsite
Beach, sandbank	Bars & clubs	Refuge, lodge
Waterfall	Building	Castle, fort
Reef	Sight	Diving
Motorway	Cathedral, church	Deciduous, coniferous, palm trees
Main road	Chinese temple	Mangrove
Unpaved or ripio (gravel) road	Hindu temple	Hide
Track	Meru	Vineyard, winery
Footpath	Mosque	Distillery
Railway	Stupa	Shipwreck
Railway with station	Synagogue	Historic battlefield
Airport	Tourist office	Related map
Bus station	Museum	
	Post office	